New Dynamics in Old Age
Individual, Environmental, and Societal Perspectives

Edited by

Hans-Werner Wahl
Institute of Psychology
University of Heidelberg

Clemens Tesch-Römer
German Centre of Gerontology, Berlin

Andreas Hoff
Oxford Institute of Ageing
University of Oxford

Society and Aging Series
Jon Hendricks, *Series Editor*

Routledge
Taylor & Francis Group
LONDON AND NEW YORK

First published 2007 Baywood Publishing Company, Inc.

Published 2017 by Routledge
2 Park Square, Milton Park, Abingdon, Oxfordshire OX14 4RN
711 Third Avenue, New York, NY 10017, USA

First issued in paperback 2016

Routledge is an imprint of the Taylor & Francis Group, an informa business

Library of Congress Catalog Number: 2006042782
ISBN: 0-89503-322-4 (cloth)

Library of Congress Cataloging-in-Publication Data

New dynamics in old age : individual, environmental, and societal perspectives / edited by Hans-Werner Wahl, Clemens Tesch-Römer, and Andreas Hoff.
p. cm. -- (Society and aging series)
Includes bibliographical references and index.
ISBN 0-89503-322-4 (cloth)
1. Aging--Social aspects. 2. Gerontology. I. Wahl, Hans-Werner, 1954- II. Tesch-Römer, Clemens. III. Hoff, Andreas. IV. Series.

HQ1061.N665 2006
305.26--dc22 2006042782

ISBN 13: 978-0-415-78462-7 (pbk)
ISBN 13: 978-0-89503-322-2 (hbk)

Table of Contents

PART VII: NEW CHALLENGES

PREFACE

On New Person-Environment Dynamics in Old Age: Opportunities and Constraints

Not only does gerontology come in many disciplinary stripes, it comes in multiple nationalities as well. Each has a unique contribution to make, and each helps the field move ever closer to adequately grasping what it means to grow old. The study of aging is itself dynamic, continually on the move—addressing enduring questions and mounting a search for elusive solutions.

As this volume makes clear, the big picture sometimes gets lost in the quest for day-to-day answers. As Immanuel Kant put it, there is nothing quite so useful as good theory, and the reader will be convinced of that assertion after reading the material included in *New Dynamics in Old Age: Individual, Environmental, and Societal Perspectives.* Wahl, Tesch-Römer, and Hoff have assembled a world-class cadre of insightful scholars from both sides of the Atlantic, and they represent some of the best thinking available on the interlocking and overlapping levels of analysis of the aging experience.

Trajectories of individual aging cannot help but reflect societal transformations: demographic, economic, and in terms of policies and practices. In fact, global changes are felt at the local level and by individuals growing old, whether they are cognizant of that fact or not. As worldwide economic integration occurs, local policies are not insulated from what is going on halfway around the world. A single example should suffice: local retirement policies may affect a corporation's decision to stay put or to move off-shore, and that decision will in turn affect how individuals in a given locale experience their own aging. The same is true of medical discoveries that know no international boundaries and are able to reach out and affect the meaning of one condition or another, which is likely to be part of the lives of individuals who may not even be aware of where the discoveries are made.

Given the dynamic nature of aging, the past may not be prologue to the future insofar as the aged of tomorrow are not likely to replicate the patterns demonstrated by past cohorts. That fact is liberating and serves to complicate the task facing gerontologists who attempt to gaze into crystal balls and prognosticate what the future holds. Within the discussions by Fry, Manton, and Gu, and the editors themselves in the opening section of this volume are clues as to why that will be the case and options for making sense of what is about to happen or what will be the case as members of the baby boom generation arrive at the doorstep of old age. What their presentations establish is that consideration of structure along with people is crucial to interpreting the daily activities through which old age is created. By examining those activities, the processual nature of age-related experiences can be placed in context as part of a broader ranging current of change. Individuals bring to their lives a panoply of personal resources composed of individual characteristics and opportunities organized by their structural surround. As one or another dimension of those personal resources undergoes transformation, a rebalancing is necessary to maintain personal well being.

Running throughout this volume is a recognition that the first order of theorizing occurs in the constructs individuals develop to explain their own lives. What we as gerontologists do is weave those first-order constructions into inclusive conceptualizations that we label as theories of social gerontology. The editors and authors of this volume contribute to the latter by reviewing the former and the ways in which one or another type of environmental conditions become a context for aging.

Surely part of the gerontological imagination referred to in subsequent chapters is an appreciation that the meaning of aging is being recast in a global light. Yet, these influences play out in the daily lives of aging individuals and can be seen as an influence there given thoughtful scrutiny. As the contributors to this volume make readily apparent, the social, immediate home, and extended larger environments are in constant flux, and that fact alone is enough to ensure that aging will also demonstrate dynamic changes. Factor in the rapidity of technological innovations as contextual elements impinging on every aspect of the process of aging, and the concatenated nature of the experience grows awesomely complicated. Indeed, the name of the aging game can be none other than continuous change.

Jon Hendricks
Oregon State University
Corvallis, OR USA

PART I. Introduction

CHAPTER 1

Searching for the New Dynamics in Old Age—A Book Opener

Hans-Werner Wahl, Clemens Tesch-Römer, and Andreas Hoff

It has been said that old age is young. What Paul Baltes (e.g., 2001), the originator of this paradoxical statement, was referring to, is the emergence of "old age" as an issue for many current societies. In addition, it is fascinating to see that old age—which has never been of central interest to our science, culture, and society—has assumed a position of preeminence in all of these spheres around the globe. The "aging revolution" which silently began in the first half of the twentieth century as part of a much broader "demographic revolution," has recently become a "loud" and obtrusive societal trend. In fact, this development has culminated at the turn of the millennia with age-related economic, societal, and political discussions topping the agenda not only of many welfare states but other political systems as well. In parallel, professional gerontologists, frequently seen as practicing an "esoteric" branch of science not long ago, are gaining increasing recognition as those operating in the eye of the hurricane, that is known as the aging revolution.

However, as is well known, the gerontology enterprise is a broad and diverse scientific field cutting across many scientific disciplines and addressing aging from a huge variety of perspectives. Gerontology seeks to understand the aging revolution, be it on the microlevel, such as exploring the cognitive plasticity of old age, or on the macrolevel, such as researching age-related care needs and their economic impact. In the turmoil of doing the day-to-day business of gerontology, one often overlooks the big picture. We tend to lose sight of previous and ongoing trends and dynamics, the old and the new, of the aging revolution. Such reflection is important because of its potential to provide basic insights into what's going on in the aging population over time and in societies at large; it is also important to review our "state of knowledge" of aging research, because change in that regard may lead to the reframing of scientific questions, research strategies, and what is sometimes regarded as time- and context-invariant "laws of aging." What you have in hand is an attempt to find the bigger picture of the new dynamics (and thus also of the old dynamics) of aging and to identify their implications from a variety of points of view.

OLD AGE UNDER TRANSFORMATION

It is well known that old age has undergone pronounced transformation since the end of the 19th century. A variety of influences, operating at different levels, from the micro to the macro, from individual to societal and political, have brought about this transformation. Empirical aging research conducted since the 1950s has demonstrated how cohort effects have shaped both intellectual functioning and general health. As has repeatedly been confirmed, both intellectual performance and health have significantly improved among older adults over the last four to five decades, which is particularly true for those frequently labeled as the "young-old"; that is, those roughly between 65 and 80 years of age (e.g., Manton, Corder, & Stallard, 1993; Schaie, 1996; see also Manton & Gu, this volume). In addition, substantial change in lifestyle (a term used here for introductory purposes, but obviously in need of clarification; see Kolland, this volume) in late adulthood seems to have occurred over the last 20 years. It is a truism that today's older adults are more mobile (e.g., they travel around the world, make seasonal migrations to the Iowa-Arizona sun belt) and flexible (e.g., they may relocate after 70 years of age to a newly built home in a new neighborhood). Older individuals are more culturally and socially active than ever; they possess a growing self-awareness of being important as consumers and influential as members of the political system (see chapters of Walker and Naegele, Gerling, & Scharfenorth in this volume). Both scientists and lay persons extrapolate characteristics about the baby boomer generation into forthcoming cohorts of older people—high education and substantial economic wealth, ongoing growth of awareness of one's power as a consumer and political actor, and a positive outlook on one's aging process in general terms—provide the most recent expression of such ongoing change dynamics (e.g., Silverstone, 1996).

On the macrolevel, the demographic revolution has catapulted older societal members into the center of social policy considerations. By comparison, the stagnation or decrease in birthrates has almost become a minor issue. The exploding number of older individuals has produced pronounced ambivalence in terms of the mix of expected potential and economic cost (see chapters of Philippson and Walker in this volume). All this has to be seen in the light of the continuing growth of life expectancy that seems to show no sign of deceleration (e.g., Oeppen & Vaupel, 2002). The ambivalence particularly applies to the "old-old" individuals whose number is quite dramatically increasing in many Western societies. The very old have been diagnosed as the prototypes of the incompleteness of the human architecture (Baltes & Smith, 1999) and the "Mängelwesen Mensch," as German anthropologist Arnold Gehlen (1956) has coined the fundamental existential incompleteness of the human being.

Taking this macrolevel of analysis further, it might be argued that the first decades of the 20th century bore witness to the formation of adolescence as an autonomous period of the lifespan. This development was echoed in the foundation of many youth-related associations and other forms of institutionalization in many countries around the world. It is highly likely that the closing decades of the twentieth century and the beginning decades of the twenty-first century will be acknowledged by future historians as the period in which old age made its breakthrough as a phase of the human lifespan standing on its own. This event has been heralded by the growing power of organizations such as the American Association of Retired Persons with its now over 35 million members over the age of 50 (AARP; http//www.aarp.org/) or the "Bundesarbeitsgemeinschaft der Senioren-Organisationen" in Germany (BAGSO; (http://www.bagso.de/bagso.html), representing more than 10 million of Germany's older adults.

LACK OF CONSIDERATION OF THE "OLD" AND "NEW" DYNAMICS OF OLD AGE

This book makes the following argument: although the very concept of aging has taken on a completely new form over the last decade, scientific research has not reflected much upon this transformation in a systematic and comprehensive manner. Our understanding of "new aging" is fragmented at best: the debate on what frequently is called the "new agers" is based on all kinds of selective observations and evaluations, but a well-coordinated, multidisciplinary exploration of the phenomenon of new aging has not yet been undertaken.

To put it in the form of a question: Does the average individual today, living in normal circumstances, have any semblance to his or her counterpart from yesterday, say, those elders from the '60s or '70s? Are there continuities on the individual and societal level that accompany aging? Or rather, are there discontinuities that make growing old today a completely different enterprise than growing old a couple of decades ago? And what can we expect in the future? How will the dynamics of aging societies impact on our lives beyond the mere economic and fiscal concerns that are dominating the discussion in most "graying" countries?

The answers to such questions have many important implications. First, gerontology and life-course research may need to acknowledge discontinuity and change across historical time in their object of study, i.e., aging people (see also Hendricks, 1992). This requires systematic synthesis, differentiation, and interpretation of the body of knowledge available in this regard. Second, well-developed knowledge on the ongoing dynamics in old age enables us to reflect upon the roles played by aging men and women within our societies, forecast societal trends, and thus plan and implement appropriate social policy measures. Such knowledge also improves our understanding of the emerging culture of aging and promotes professional education and intervention planning. Third, developed and proven knowledge on the dynamics of old age across time may also become important for aging individuals and their respective associations and organizations, which seem at present to oscillate between traditional, "modern," and "postmodern" images of aging. Classic examples of this are the efforts among elders and their organizations to become part of the information society by, for instance, seeking access to the Internet. At the same time, there is much concern that this powerful communication technology may lead to social deprivation and contribute to the erosion of traditional family interaction patterns in the long run (see chapters of Czaja and Melenhorst, Rogers, & Fisk, in this volume).

In order to understand the flux of ongoing dynamics in old age, what can be achieved and expected, it is essential to narrow our historical time frame. There are at least four reasons why the time period since the end of World War II is a promising reference for considering the flux of old and new dynamics in old age from today's perspective: (1) Since the end of World War II there has been a sustainable increase in life expectation, most notably in Western industrialized countries. This has made old age an expected and normative part of the life span. The "new" dynamics of aging, however, are due to the changing societal experiences that accompanied the shift in life expectancy and not due merely to the objective increase in life expectancy that has been observed around the globe since the middle of the 19th century (Oeppen & Vaupel, 2002). (2) Related to the first argument is the fact that both societal and individual awareness of age as a social category emerged after the war. The needs of the elderly and the societal investment in caring for the elderly, such as pensions, healthcare, have never been so large as post World War II. (3) Around the middle of the 20th century, gerontology emerged as an academic field in many countries around the world (Achenbaum, 1995). Its goal was to explain the biological, psychological, and social processes of aging. The major theories of aging, data-collection endeavors— including landmark cross-sectional and longitudinal studies—and methodological breakthrough all appeared after World War II, although influential precedents of these developments should not be discarded (Cowdry, 1939). (4) The period since the end of World War II, lasting now for more than half a century, is probably long enough to observe the flux of old and new dynamics of old age and aging over time. This applies to societal and cultural changes, with implications for aging as well as the impact of measurable cohort change that is evident over decades and not from year to year (Mannheim, 1964/1928; Schaie, 1965). The chapters directly addressing such historical change operate mainly within the timeframe we have adopted.

But what has really changed regarding the many facets of old age and aging at both individual and societal levels over the second half of the twentieth century? What are the underlying mechanisms that have shaped, for example, new lifestyles for elders and aging welfare states? And to what extent has social and behavioral gerontology addressed this process of transformation? The present volume addresses these core questions from diverse scientific perspectives. We explore the dimensions of the new dynamics of old age, and how theoretical and empirical arguments can describe their qualities. Of course, addressing the new dynamics of aging must also consider aspects of aging that may not have changed at all during recent time, indicating certain persistent, perhaps even universal characteristics of aging. Hence both change and continuity of aging as an individual and social process deserves attention.

In the next section of this introduction, we will provide more in-depth interpretation of such fundamental age dynamics since World War II. In conclusion, we introduce the concept of the book and provide a brief overview of its chapters.

ON THE DYNAMICS OF OLD AND NEW AGING: ATTEMPT TO DEFINE A FUZZY CONCEPT

Given the need to address the ongoing dynamics of aging across time in terms of continuity and change, the next question is how such dynamics can be conceptually defined and what kind of fundamental approach is needed to address this issue. In other words, are there theories and concepts in the current aging literature that can address and provide a better understanding of the ongoing dynamics of old age since World War II? Surprisingly or not, there has been little theory on the matter. A good starting point may be the identification of major developmental issues that afford insights into the old and new dynamics of aging. In the following, we provide three examples.

The Emergence of the Fourth Age

One line of work that might help understand continuity and discontinuity in the dynamics of old age over time is represented by historical sociology. In particular, the emergence of what has been referred to by Peter Laslett (1989) and later on by P. B. Baltes and others (e.g., Baltes & Smith, 1999) as the Fourth Age—the age beyond 80 to 85 years—addresses a major change in old age that evolved over the last half of the century or so. In contrast to the "success story" (M. Baltes, 1999) of the Third Age, the Fourth Age constitutes a new and still hard to estimate challenge to societies as well as to aging individuals in quantitative and qualitative terms. Never were so many very old individuals in societies, and never was the quantitative burden of pension, health, and care costs so high. Moreover, aging has become qualitatively different: the individual must cope with frailty and chronic disease after a long and active life and "third" aging; and society must come to grips with its basic insecurity with assigning societal roles for so many very old people. These quantitative and qualitative changes illustrate a major shift in aging across time. However, this shift always must be seen as operating in context with the other old and new ages of man. Part of the change dynamic also is the emergence of a new Third Age that has more and more become an extension of the Second Age or, more specifically, what is frequently called the period of middle adulthood of the human life span (Lachman, 2004). In addition, this development has implications for the First Age as well. Ongoing age dynamics also impact on questions related to investments in one's youth and balancing societal investment between generations.

The Scientific Management and Biomedicalization of Old Age

The ongoing dynamics of old age across recent decades are also addressed in concepts of changing welfare states, historically and politically oriented analyses of old age, and society-related health management systems. Thomas Cole's (1988) historical analyses of how societies deal with the changing roles of the aged and how they attempt to cope with health and disease issues that stem from the surge in older demographic categories are especially informative in this regard. Drawing upon Cole's distinction between the "practical" and "existential" changes concomitant to the emergence of old age in many societies (p. 47), it seems that the practical side, i.e., the "scientific management of aging" (p. 47) has been emphasized since World War II. Conversely, the existential challenges of longevity and an elaboration of old age as a more and more normative phase of the human life span has largely been ignored. According to Cole, the complex interaction between the scientific evolution of gerontology, societal developments, and individual aspirations comes with certain risks: "I believe that much of the pathos of aging today derives from the one-sidedness of the scientific management of aging, which essentially represses the existential dimension of aging and undermines earlier religious and philosophical traditions that addressed it. The demise of these traditions leaves contemporary culture with an impoverished sense of the meanings and possibilities of growing old" (Cole, 1988, p. 48). Estes, Binney, and Culbertson (1992) have used the term "biomedicalization" not only to address the change in individual expectations about aging, but also to the change in research funding policy (specifically in the United States). Since the 1980s, research funding has been consistently put toward "putting out fires" rather than accumulating basic scientific knowledge by means of macrolevel, structural, and nonclinical lines of investigation.

If Cole and Estes are right in their diagnosis, "Anti-Aging Medicine" may represent the culmination of the "practical" side of aging and its promises to improve the lives of older people. This new dynamic of old age has created tension between the expectations of many middle-aged and old individuals (just do a simple Internet search to see the many promises of "Anti-Aging") and scientific, evidence-based reactions to the "Anti-Aging" propaganda such as Binstock's (2003) essay on "The War on 'Anti-Aging' Medicine" and a published statement written by 52 researchers in the biology and medical field in the *Journal of Gerontology: Biological Sciences* (Olshansky, Hayflick, & Carnes, 2002).

Changing Dynamics in the Gerontological Imagination

In Estes et al. (1992), the reconstruction of major developments within what they have called the "gerontological imagination" after 1945 allows for the identification of additional elements of the dynamics of old age across this period of time. Although the concept applies well to the situation within the United States, it is also generalizable to some extent to other Western societies. With respect to the period between 1945 (also the date of the establishment of the Gerontological Society of America) and 1959, the societal category of "old age" began to take shape. Societal attention began to shift to older people due to the sharp rise in the proportion of older people (in the United States from 4.1% in 1900 to 8.5% in 1955), old age became synonymous with retirement, and the social and care-related challenges of old age stimulated a discussion on new professions needed to serve this portion of the population. Moreover, major emphasis was also put on the individual welfare of older people or, as it was labeled more frequently, successful adaptation to aging in terms of individual life satisfaction (e.g., Havighurst & Albrecht, 1953). It is no accident that the AARP was founded in 1958. The 1960s and 1970s gave birth to major societal developments such as the war against poverty, the civil rights and women's movements, Medicare and Medicaid, the Older Americans Act (1965), and the Age Discrimination in Employment Act (1967).

Institutions for the elderly were being put in place in (West) Germany around the same time. In 1962, the "Kuratorium Deutsche Altershilfe" (German Foundation for the Care of Older People) was founded as the first institute serving the aged. The KDA was created to provide care and housing support to older people and thus was the first "official" German acknowledgment of old age as a relevant societal category.

The outgrowth of pension reform dating from 1957 marked Germany's evolution to a welfare state. Since then, many older persons have enjoyed financial security in both qualitative and quantitative terms. Apart from the societal acknowledgment of old age as a period of the life span, and the recognition that elders require financial support, care, and housing, another emerging movement at this time led to the introduction of educational programs for older people. Among these educational opportunities was the founding of Universities of the Third Age; the first European program was introduced at the University of Toulouse (France) in the year 1972.

New Societal Discourses about Aging

The development of gerontological imagination during the last decades was embedded in societal discourses about aging. Up to the early 1970s, old age did not dominate societal discourse, despite the demographic developments alluded to above. However, in the late 1970s, demographic change and the "aging of societies" became hot topics in the societal and political discourses. One example is the first "International Plan of Action on Aging," the so-called Vienna Plan, passed by the UN plenary assembly in 1982 (United Nations, 1982). Two topics characterized the Vienna Plan: On the one hand, the plan made recommendations regarding the improvement of living conditions for old and very old people. On the other hand, the plan discussed the implications of demographic change for the economic development of societies. This focus on possible negative developments within "aging societies" was mirrored in societal discourse of old age as being a "burden" (Kondratowitz, 1988). Since then, the dynamics of societal discourse seemed to be divided more strongly than ever into a variety of different and sometimes even contradictory trends.

To name just some of these: Older workers—regarded as the most expensive portion of the labor force—began to leave the labor force earlier than ever in work history due to economic necessity. This trend was observed both in the United States as well as in many European welfare states (although the legislative circumstances were different). Cutting off older people from productive endeavors and extending the period thereafter, which was expected to be filled with other forms of meaningful activity, created a rather paradoxical situation. A potential answer to this was a trend toward a new understanding of old age that began in the 1980s; old age began to be characterized by attributes such as high activity, good health, ongoing education, and pronounced economic welfare.

In Germany, for instance, a congress of the German Society of Gerontology in 1989 addressed this movement (Die Neuen Alten) for the first time, although it was regarded as a minority issue within the older population as a whole (Tokarski & Karl, 1989). The societal discourse on demographic change has been characterized by the search for the potentials and promises of aging ever since. Yet another trend of old age dynamics that grew during the 1980s was the fear that the years of life expectancy gained come with the price of chronic physical and mental disease, as well as concomitant costs regarding individual quality of life and need for societal care provision. Not by accident, the classic treatise on the Compression of Morbidity Hypothesis also appeared at the beginning of the 1980s, an essay that was well-received but has remained controversial in gerontology until this very day (Fries & Crapo, 1981). Since then, the idea of preventive medicine has influenced lifestyles in Western societies and held hope for healthy aging. Over the last few years, however, dementia-related disorders have gained broad societal attention, leading to a dramatic re-orientation in research funding policy. The intrusion of dementia into the everyday world of aging, and its impact on both formal and informal caregiving, culminated during the 1990s to represent another important facet of the new dynamic of old age, one which shall certainly cross over to the new millennium.

APPROACHING THE NEW AGING: CONCEPT OF THE BOOK

On the basis of these far-reaching issues, we decided to follow a down-to-earth approach to address the new dynamics of aging. The master hypothesis upon which the present book is based maintains that the new (and old) dynamics of old age and aging can best be observed in a range of everyday life-aging contexts that echo major person/environment-interchange dynamics evolved during the second half of the 20th century. In particular, five areas will be treated in depth. New and persistent dynamics regarding (1) the social environment, (2) the home environment, (3) the outdoor environment, (4) the technology environment, and (5) the societal environment. Thus, the term environment is used as an organizing concept of the book in its broadest understanding and embraces both social and physical as well as micro- and macrolevels of analysis.

The introductory section of the book lays the foundation for discussing these five areas; the "social" and the "physical" aspects of human aging are considered to be fundamental backgrounds for a more detailed view of new aging. In her chapter, Christine L. Fry addresses what frequently is taken for granted today: that age has emerged as an ongoing story of change in terms of the social construction of age and the experience of aging. Data provided by Kenneth G. Manton and XiLiang Gu add to this "change story" on the basic level of cohort effects in the health domain, both with respect to somatic and mental functioning.

Aging and the social environment is discussed in Kristine J. Ajrouch, Hiroko Akiyama, and Toni C. Antonucci's chapter, which provides conceptual as well as empirical findings for better understanding change dynamics in social relations as people age over historical time. Andreas Hoff and Clemens Tesch-Römer address the role of aging persons within perhaps the most important social context of all, i.e., family relations; and Steven H. Zarit and Elizabeth R. Braungart search for old and new dynamics in caregiver relations with older adults.

The section targeting the home environment begins with Laura N. Gitlin's treatment of core questions and issues related to the potential of housing as people age. This chapter is followed by an exploration of what frequently is seen as a major characteristic of "new aging," namely relocation in the later years, provided by Frank Oswald and Graham D. Rowles. That housing and home are not always desirable environments for the new aged is supported in the Thomas Scharf, Chris Philippson, and Allison Smith chapter, with rare data on the effects of aging in urban environments in the United Kingdom.

In the section focusing on the outdoor environment, out-of-home mobility is first generally analyzed by Heidrun Mollenkopf, Isto Ruoppila, and Fiorella Marcellini with recent data coming from a variety of European countries. Karlene K. Ball,

Virginia G. Wadley, David E. Vance, and Jerri D. Edwards write on driving as the major mode of mobility in American elders, a trend that is sure to be observed in many European and other countries around the world. On a more general level, Franz Kolland provides a broad analysis of the new and old leisure world of aging.

The section on technology begins with Sara J. Czaja and Chin Chin Lee's research on the impact of the Internet on aging processes and outcomes, followed by a more generally framed treatment of current and future home technology written by Annie-Sophie Melenhorst, Wendy A. Rogers, and Arthur D. Fisk. In addition, William C. Mann and Sumi Helal explore how old and new assistive-devices technology is able to affect older adults' quality of life in the situation of chronic conditions.

The final section, on the new dynamics of old age in society, Chris Phillipson and Alan Walker address the scope of political spheres from the global to the local. Gerhard Naegele, Vera Gerling, and Karin Scharfenorth add to this with their reflections on the consumer potential of today's and tomorrow's older people.

In the closing part of the book, entitled "New Challenges," Svein Olav Daatland and Andreas Motel-Klingebiel describe cross-cultural challenges for aging research, placing emphasis on the methodology used to understand the new dynamics of aging. Finally, Eva-Marie Kessler and Ursula M. Staudinger give their view on linking the micro- with the macrolevel with special emphasis on two fundamentals of life-span development, i.e., individual plasticity and social contexts.

REFERENCES

Achenbaum, W. A. (1995). *Crossing frontiers: Gerontology emerges as a science.* New York: Cambridge University Press.

Baltes, M. M. (1999). Die heutigen Generationen bauen die Straßen, auf denen die nächsten fahren: Über den Lebenslauf und die Zukunft des Alters [Today's generations are building the streets on which future generations drive: About the life course and the future of age]. In J. Delius (Ed.), *In Memoriam Margret M. Baltes* (pp. 57-70). Berlin: Max-Planck-Institut für Bildungsforschung.

Baltes, P. B. (2001). Das Zeitalter des permanent unfertigen Menschen: Lebenslanges Lernen nonstop? [The age of the permanent unfinished man: Life-long learning nonstop?] *Aus Politik und Zeitgeschichte, B 36,* 24-32.

Baltes, P. B., & Smith, J. (1999). Multilevel and systemic analyses of old age. Theoretical and empirical evidence for a fourth age. In V. L. Bengtson & K. W. Schaie (Eds.), *Handbook of theories of aging* (pp. 153-173). New York: Springer.

Binstock, R. H. (2003). The war on "Anti-Aging Medicine." *The Gerontologist, 43*(1), 4-14.

Cole, T. R. (1988). Aging, history, and health: Progress and paradox. In J. J. F. Schroots, J. E. Birren, & A. Svanborg (Eds.), *Health and aging* (pp. 45-63). New York: Springer.

Cowdry, E. (Ed.). (1939). *Problems of aging. Biological and medical aspects.* Baltimore: Williams & Wilkins.

Estes, C. L., Binney, E. A., & Culbertson, R. A. (1992). The gerontological imagination: Social influences on the development of gerontology, 1945-present. *International Journal of Aging and Human Development, 35*(1), 49-65.

Fries, J. F., & Crapo, L. M. (1981). *Vitality and aging. Implications of the rectangular curve.* San Francisco: Freeman.

Gehlen, A. (1956). *Urmensch und Spätkultur* [Early man and late culture]. Bonn: Athenäum.

Hendricks, J. (1992). Generations and the generation of theory in social gerontology. *International Journal of Aging and Human Development, 35*(1), 31-47.

Havighurst, R. J., & Albrecht, R. (1953). *Older people*. New York: Longmans, Green & Co.

Lachman, M. E. (2004). Development in midlife. *Annual Review of Psychology, 55*, 305-331.

Laslett, P. (1989). *A fresh map of life: The emergence of the Third Age*. London: Weidenfeld and Nicolson.

Mannheim, K. (1964). Das problem der generationen [The problem of generations] (Erstausgabe 1928; wieder abgedruckt in K. Mannheim, Wissensoziologie). In H. Maus & F. Fürstenberg (Eds.), *Soziologische texte* [Sociological texts] (Vol. 28, pp. 509-656). Neuwied: Luchterhand.

Manton, K. G., Corder, L. S., & Stallard, E. (1993). Estimate of change in chronic disability and institutional incidence and prevalence rates in the U.S. elderly population from the 1982, 1984 and 1989 National Long Term Care Survey. *Journal of Gerontology: Social Sciences, 48*, S153-S166.

Oeppen, J., & Vaupel, J. W. (2002, May). Broken limits to life expectancy. *Science, 296*(10), 1029-1031.

Olshansky, S. J., Hayflick, L., & Carnes, B. A. (2002). Position statement on human aging. *Journal of Gerontology: Biological Sciences, 57A*(8), B292-B297.

Schaie, K. W. (1965). A general model for the study of developmental problems. *Psychological Bulletin, 64*, 91-107.

Schaie, K. W. (1996). Intellectual development in adulthood. In J. E. Birren & K. W. Schaie (Eds.), *Handbook of the psychology of aging* (4th ed., pp. 266-286). San Diego, CA: Academic Press.

Silverstone, B. (1996). Older people of tomorrow: A psychosocial profile. *The Gerontologist, 36*(1), 27-32.

Tokarski, W., & Karl, F. (1989). Die "neuen" alten. Zur einordnung eines ambivalenten begriffs [The "new" aged. Analysis of an ambivalent term]. In F. Karl & W. Tokarski (Eds.), *Die "neuen" alten. Beiträge der XVII. Jahrestagung der Deutschen Gesellschaft für Gerontologie, Kassel, 22.-24.09.1988* [The "new" aged. Contributions to the XVII. Conference of the German Society of Gerontology] (Vol. 6, Kasseler Gerontologische Schriften). Kassel: Gesamthochschulbibliothek.

United Nations. (1982). *International Plan of Action on Aging* (Resolution 37/51). New York: United Nations.

von Kondratowitz, H. J. (1988). Allen zur Last, niemandem zur Freude. Die institutionelle Prägung des Alternserlebens als historischer Prozeß [The institutional framing of the experience of old age as seen from a historical perspective]. In G. Göckenjan & H.-J. von Kondratowitz (Eds.), *Alter und alltag* [Age and everyday life] (pp. 100-136). Frankfurt/M.: Suhrkamp.

CHAPTER 2

The Social Construction of Age and the Experience of Aging in the Late Twentieth Century

Christine L. Fry

Age is a socially constructed category. Age stratification is a characteristic of all human societies. However, not all societies use chronological age in the design of their life courses. Generational life courses, age-classed life courses, and staged life courses are major variants. Chronological age is also a social construct based on a calendar, but has major implications in the way time and age are perceived and used. In this chapter, alterations in the way age is experienced in the last half of the twentieth century is seen through changes in educational achievement, marriage and the family, and in the policies of the state in the financing of retirement and healthcare. Finally, the salience of age to identity is explored.

Issues that seem simple often turn out to be complex. Complexity, on the other hand, usually reduces to simplicity. Age is one of those factors that is both simple and complex. In its simplicity, age, chronological age is very easy to figure out. All one does is take the year of one's birth and subtract it from the present year. The result is an integer representing a year that ranges from 1 to 100+. If one wants more refinement, one can calculate the number of months, days, or even fractions of days (hours, minutes, and seconds). Age is simply time that is measured, and we calculate the intervals between two points in time.

Age, in its complexity, is more than mere time (Hendricks, 2001). Age is a complex set of cultural ideas about time. In many respects, time just happens. The corner of the universe in which we live experiences intervals of duration punctuated by change. Because of celestial bodies in orbit, humans experience intervals of day and night, phases of the moon, seasonality, and can predict when specific stars and constellations will appear in the sky. Although this happens and has happened for eons before humans evolved, humans have "domesticated" time by making it a subject of cultural interpretation. Our present calendar, based on the Gregorian Reform of 1582, provides us with a time line that has the illusion of transcending culture. Culturally, the calendar permeates lives in ways ranging from schedules to fixing contracts in time to ordering lives. It is this complexity that is the subject of this chapter. Four topics structure our inquiry:

1. The invention and uses of chronological age
2. Age structures and age stratification
3. Age stratification and the experiences of growing older
4. The experience of old age

THE INVENTION AND USES OF CHRONOLOGICAL AGE

The invention of chronological age is one of the more interesting and important social constructs of all historical time. In this section we examine how humans invented a precise way of measuring age; then we turn to the question of why it is important for individuals to know their age.

Calendars, Timelines, and Chronology

The known timeline for humans, earth, and the universe extends back to the big bang some 20 billion years ago and races forward into an uncertain future. That expanse of time is pretty meaningless for most human concerns; but chronological age does place human lives into this immense timeline. Our abilities to reckon age center on the invention of a calendar that reasonably approximates the celestial events that define a year, such as the orbit of the earth around the sun. Because of seasonality (cold and warm, wet and dry) one would think that the unit of a year would not be too difficult to figure out; yet it took over 18,000 years—from the early markings on Magdalenian calendar sticks (Marshack, 1991) until in the sixteenth century the Gregorian Reform—to figure out a calendar that would come close to the true measurement of a year. Most calendars approximated a year, but over a number of centuries, these calendars gradually saw the days "creep" out of synch with the sun and the stars. The Gregorian calendar of 1582 is a remarkable invention. This reform of the Julian calendar is the culmination of several millennia of cross-cultural work that included the efforts of thinkers from most of the Classical World, including Mesopotamia, Egypt, India, Greece, Rome, Christendom, and the Arab world (Duncan, 1998).

In addition to calibrating the calendar fairly exactly to the duration of a year, the Gregorian calendar is a cultural construction that is noteworthy for three additional accomplishments. First, it removed the calculation of time from the more localized political and religious institutions. The calendar is no longer reset with the inauguration of a new king or emperor. The saints's days have pretty much vanished from most calendars, but the holy days of many world religions are noted according to the specific markets. Second, the calendar fits into a yearly count of the passage of time. This annual count has a reckoning from an absolute fixed point. Because this is based on the Christian calendar and the work of a little-known monk, Dionysius Exiguss (561 A.D.), that point is anchored at the birth of Christ. This is the year one (zero had not been invented). From this point, one counts forward to the present or backward (also in an ascending count) into the distant past. Third, the Gregorian calendar has the illusion of being extrasocietal. It is not extracultural since the actual construction of the calendar is based on a host of scientific, mathematical, and cultural conventions (Crump, 1990). The illusion is that the count of years is connected to the timeline of the universe.

The net effect of the not-so-obvious accomplishments of the calendar is that it makes chronological age extremely easy to figure out. All one needs are a little skill in rudimentary mathematics, knowledge of the year of birth, and the current year: one simply subtracts and the result is chronological age. But why would anyone want to know this? What does age mean? Why is it important?

WHY IS IT IMPORTANT TO KNOW YOUR AGE?

One could not operate very well in a contemporary urbanized, industrialized, and bureaucratized society without knowledge of his or her personal age (Chudacoff, 1989). Not only are records kept of birth and death, but certificates are also given to legally commemorate these events. People preserve these documents to be able to present legal proof or their own age or of the identity of deceased relatives. Individuals also must be able to provide information about their age when they fill out myriad documents required by various organizations and societal institutions. Most people even carry with them documents that certify their age such as driver's license or other identity papers. The reason for the ubiquitous nature of age is because the state has codified age as an important dimension to organize their citizen's lives.

All contemporary nation-states have selected age as an explicit and impartial variable to use in regulating large populations and assigning the rights of citizenship (Kohli, 1986; Kohli & Meyer, 1986; Mayer & Schopflin, 1989). Age becomes the basis for norms that are largely codified in law. These legalized age norms don't spring out of a vacuum, but are based on cultural assumptions about the life course. There are ages when one is not culturally competent, and thus there are behaviors and activities that should be restricted. On the other hand, age is associated with competence and privileges, so benefits should be granted. The resulting life course is by and large one that defines the rights and duties of citizenship. We identify this as the "tripartite" life course since it divides up citizenship into three stages (Fry, 2002). These are (1) childhood and adolescence, (2) adult citizenship, and (3) postadulthood or old age. In the larger scheme of life, there is poignant meaning for actors in each stage.

Childhood and Adolescence

Childhood is not a time of life when one is considered to be competent. Instead, a child is to master the knowledge and skills that will serve well into adulthood. Adolescence is a little more problematic since physical and social maturity is nearing. Yet adolescence is clearly a time of denial. Adult privilege and full adult status is out of reach. Just ask a 15-year-old who has bought a car but must wait for the sixteenth birthday to drive it. There are very clear laws about what adolescents can and cannot do. Smoking and drinking are risky behaviors. Young people are required to wait to purchase the offending substances until they are considered to be old enough to make informed decisions. Likewise voting, driving, marriage, and working all are activities or statuses that assume those who engage in the associated behaviors are competent to do so. The life task of an adolescent is to acquire the necessary knowledge and skills that will serve them well in adulthood. Thus, the emphasis is on education and preparation for the launch into full adult status. When adolescents violate the age norms by assuming adult privileges too early, the state intervenes rather quickly and sometimes harshly.

Adulthood and Full Citizenship

Adulthood means full citizenship. Ostensibly, competence has been achieved, and adults are ready to assume social roles with responsibility. They are also considered to be accountable for their own actions. Most of the responsible roles are centered within the contexts of family and work. Family usually involves interdependency between spouses and responsibility for the care and development of dependent children. Similarly, work careers involve responsibilities for one's tasks within the division of labor. Ages of marriage, work, and the completion of education propel one into the world of adults defined largely through work, family, and children.

Postadult or Old Age

Withdrawal from the adult status of working is perhaps the singular defining event opening the door to the third stage of the life course, old age (Henretta, 2003). Retirement ends the responsibilities within the division of labor. In addition, the responsibility for dependent children is usually ended by this time since they have matured and left the parental nest. States compensate their citizens for the loss of income and health benefits that are associated with the workplace. To activate these entitlements, explicit age requirements must be met. To be eligible for Social Security in the United States, one must be at least 62 and preferably 67. For the state subsidized health insurance program of Medicare, one must be at least 65. There are also age requirements governing other aspects of the financial life course, such as private pensions or when one can access their retirement savings without tax penalty. Just as in adolescence, if an older person violates these norms, they don't get very far. Without work, this last stage of life is reserved for domestic life and leisure.

AGE STRUCTURES AND AGE STRATIFICATION

Humans live in time, but there is more than one kind of time. Years are a unit of measure that is meaningless. It is culture and how we use years that give them meaning. An alternate temporal framework is far more integral to human lives. This is life time and generational time. Humans are mammals with fixed life spans who, in order to perpetuate the species, must reproduce. Life time is punctuated by a maturational cycle of immaturity, maturity, and senescence. A requirement of reproduction is that mature individuals give birth to the immature; thus parents are always older than children. Human societies, like most mammalian societies, consist of multiple individuals of differential maturity. Maturational differences are an integral part of the social order known in gerontology as age stratification or age structuring.

Age stratification is a cultural interpretation of maturational difference. Because each culture is unique, the variation can be quite considerable. However, culture is not totally random since it must deal with physical phenomena. Life time and generational time happen in the same time as defined by the time line calibrated by the

Gregorian calendar. The precision of the calibration and the importance of each kind of time for human lives are quite different. For age stratification, a major divide is to be found between cultures that define age as chronology in addition to life time and generational time, and those that see age only as life time and generational time.

Hierarchy is central to every social group. Animal ethnologists were impressed by the presence of dominance hierarchies in the social life of most mammals ranging from dogs to primates. Among chimpanzees, dominance is the focus of most adults (Goodall, 1986, 1988; Waal, 1998). Males compete with one another in strength, learn social skills, and form coalitions with the intent of ascending the hierarchy. The rewards are sex and food. Even females arrange themselves into a hierarchy, reinforcing the male hierarchy. Age is a part of this hierarchy in that only adults are the major players. Since physical strength and skill underwrite much of the status of males at the top of the hierarchy, age is a major component. For humans, dominance becomes far more complicated because of culture. Social stratification supplants dominance, confusing wealth and resource accumulation with social power. Age hierarchies also become more complex with cultural knowledge and accumulation of experience. In this section, we examine the age hierarchy in the simplest of human societies and then in larger scaled societies organized by capitalism. Small-scaled societies are domestically organized and egalitarian: the age hierarchy is the major hierarchy. Age is pervasive and either informally recognized or explicitly defined. First, using various indicators based on social maturation, we examine age hierarchies that are informally defined. Then we turn to age hierarchies predicated on chronological age.

AGE WITHOUT CHRONOLOGY

What would a life course look like without chronological age to map and gradate the social actors? On one hand, the absence of chronology would not significantly alter life since all humans pass through the same time regardless of how it is calibrated. On the other hand, the way time is perceived and the social construction and use of age are very different. Without the passing of numbered years, age is seen as a combination of physical maturation combined with the passage through social statuses mostly defined by kinship. These life courses fall into two broad types: the generational life course and the age-classed life course.

Generational Life Courses

Comparatively speaking, the generational life course is the least recognized but most common. The reason is that the generational life course is found in small-scaled or domestically organized societies. Unfortunately, age is not of interest to the researchers looking into these societies. Other issues, such as subsistence, politics, or conflict resolution have proven to be more interesting. Fortunately, domestic organization and kinship have been extensively studied. Kin and the social maturation involved with marriage and parenting roughly calibrate the generational life course.

Age grades are not sharply defined. Generations are defined by descent. Parents give birth to children, and children are graded by birth order; however, the boundaries between generations are often difficult to define and can actually be confusing. First, families are generally large and marked by extended periods of reproduction. Consequently, the actual age between the first and last child could be greater than the age difference between the first child and the parent. Second, when we look at an extended web of kin, it is not unusual to find further generational blurring given the length of the reproduction course. For instance, an ego's uncle (a kin type of an ascending generation) may be younger than the ego and more logically of a cousin generation.

When looking at societies that use generational age, one is struck by two issues. The first is the prevalence of the age hierarchy and how seniority structures social rank. For instance, Sharp (1977) describes the kin roles in a foraging society of Canada, the Chippewa. All kinship statuses within a hunting unit are ranked by age and generation: a son is subordinate to his parents and his elder brothers. Among the Tlingit of Southern Alaska, age is important in the relationships between brothers (Oberg, 1997). Priority in leadership, ceremonial life, and in inheritance is always given to the older brother. For the matrilineal Pawnee, age defines the relationships between the women of an earth lodge and where women resided.

> The functions of the women in the earth lodge were subdivided roughly according to age. The north and south quarters of the circumference of the house were each subdivided into three "stations." The central one of these (due north and due south) was the core position and it was occupied by the mature women of the lodge. They furnished the main provisions and directed the necessary work. At the inner or western station on each side was the place of the immature girls and newly married young women. The outer or eastern station on each side was for the old women, symbolically on the way out and physically nearest to the exit (or entryway) of the lodge. Most commonly each of these stations was occupied by several women who carried out its special functions jointly (Weltfish, 1965, p. 15).

It is relative age that is important in these societies, not absolute age expressed chronologically. The !Kung of southern Africa (Shostak, 1981) express the passage of time as "we lived and lived." If pushed for quantification, the expression is usually in terms of seasonality. For example, "We got married many rains ago." The Fulani of western Africa are noted for a system of numbered years (Stenning, 1958). Yet these do not translate into chronological age. Similarly, the Herero (Keith et. al., 1994), pastoralists of southern Africa, name their years for the most significant event of the year: "the year the chief died" or "the year of severe draught." Again in ordinary life, these translate as ways of determining if one individual is older or younger than another.

The second issue concerning generational age is rather interesting. With the absence of chronological age, ethnographers are a little uncomfortable and feel compelled to figure it out. For the Chukchi of Siberia, Sverdrup (1938) comments that, "No one could tell me how many days are between two full moons, nor in a year. They do not count. Since the Chukchi do not count the years, no one knows his own age" (pp. 75-76). From this point, he gives an elaborate account of how he figured out his informant's age. Given the chronocentrism of most ethnographers, one comes to suspect references to and statements about chronological age are more a product of the observer than the people being observed.

With no institutional basis from which to sharply calibrate age, generational distinctions are ambiguous. It is possible for people in these societies to think about age and to make distinctions based on maturity; in reality they seldom do. With a generational life course, the life plan is to mature into adulthood, have a family, work to provide for that family, and to simply live.

Age-Classed Life Courses

Ethnographers in Africa, South America, and North America encountered domestically organized societies where maturity formed the basis for explicitly organized life courses that formed corporate groups of men who were recruited on the basis of age. These "age-classed" life courses caught the attention of early gerontological researchers who formulated many of our basic concepts about age norms and grades. Although these societies are well documented, the life course has not been seen as a decidedly different one.

Age-class societies have developed a system of age stratification whereby males are organized into explicitly defined and sharply bounded age sets. From the age of initiation to the most senior set, a man will pass through life by graduating from the junior to the more senior sets. This is not an individual rite of passage, but a collective transition as an entire group of men move from one stage to the next. All groups move upward in seniority.

The literature on age-class societies is quite extensive (see Bernardi, 1985 for a review). We will briefly examine the age organization of the Piegan or Blackfoot tribe of the Great Plains of North America, which is quite different from that of the Massai of eastern Africa. According the Whissler:

> The men of the Peigan tribe were organized into a series of warrior societies in which membership was based on age. Arranged in the order of the age of their members these groups were: Doves, Flies, Braves, All Brave Dogs, Tails, Raven Bearers, Dogs, Kit-foxes, Catchers, and Bulls. As a whole they were known as All Comrades. The function of the societies was primarily to preserve order in the camp, during the march, and on the hunt, to punish offenders against the public welfare; to protect the camp by guarding against possible surprise by an enemy; to be informed at all times as to the movements of the buffalo herds and secondarily by intersociety rivalry to cultivate the military spirit, and by their feasts and dances to minister to the desire of members for social recreation. . . . The members of the younger society purchased individually, from the next older one, its rights and privileges, paying horses for them. For example, each member of the Mosquitoes would purchase from some member of the Braves his right of membership in the latter society. The man who has sold his rights is then a member of no society, and if he wishes to belong to one, must buy into the one next higher. Each of these societies kept some old men as members, and these old men acted as messengers, orators, and so on (Whissler, 1913, p. 367).

These age societies had multiple functions and gave a male a chance to achieve higher status as he aged and moved to more prestigious levels or sets. In contrast, the Massai enters into his life course through the ritual of circumcision, a rite signifying spiritual purification, and moves up through a series of sets, each with more responsibility. According to Huntingford (see also Spencer 1988):

> From birth to circumcision a male is a boy, ol-ayioni . At circumcision he enters an age-set and becomes a warrior, ol-murrani, "one who is circumcised," and may associate with unmarried girls. At the olesher ceremony he becomes an

> elder, ol-moruo. Warriors may marry when they become senior warriors. After the olesher the newly made elders attend to their family concerns, and get wives if they are not already married. They have duties also towards the uncircumcised boys as guardians and instructors, while the elders of the ol-aji senior to them are said to be responsible for the ol-aji of the warriors (Huntingford, 1953, p. 112).

For the few societies in which age is formalized into classes, it appears that kinship rather than age is the organizing principle. Age-classed life courses are a variant of the generational life course. The specifics of how the age classes are defined and function are quite diverse; however, a minimal rule governing recruitment into the classes is that a father and a son must belong to different classes. In an age-classed life course, generational differences are extended beyond kinship and cut across an entire community. Otherwise, the resultant life course is not much different than a generational life course since it is based on kinship and relative age as the medium through which time and life are calibrated.

AGE WITH CHRONOLOGY

Chronological age alters the perception of the passage of time. Instead of being relative in terms of seniority or simply being older or younger than someone else, chronology adds precision. Age is expressed as the passage of units of time. Years are most commonly used, although months and days are sometimes added to tombstones. Chronology removes age from the language of kinship and domestic organization. Age is numbers, and most notably these numbers reflect their social uses. But some ages are more important than others. Generally, these are the ages that entitle one to new statuses, privileges, and resources. These are such transitions as voting, driving, drinking, or retirement and health benefits. The net effect of chronological age is that the life course is seen as a staged affair.

Age Statuses and Staged Life Courses

The "staged" life course has become the model for the life course understood in gerontology. "Institutionalized" is another way we have come to look at the life course in urban, capitalistic societies. A basic assumption is that age grades are life stages defined by chronology and normative transitions that are meaningful as people plan their lives. The "age" in the age norms that shape the life stages are anchored in a social clock based on chronological age and the legislation of the norms for the institutions of industrial societies. The net result is a life course that divides life into three stages: the socially immature, the mature, and the postmature.

Age Stratification and the Experiences of Growing Older

The purpose of this volume is to examine any changes that have happened in aging and the diverse experiences of its effects within the past 50 years. Aging per se has probably not seen much change. Certainly the ability to figure out one's age has not changed within the past five decades. The actors who are most likely to be aware of their ages are the same. These are the adolescents who are being denied their full adult status. Older people are also likely to be aware of their age as they anticipate and make their financial plans for retirement. Once the transitions have occurred, then age will most likely fade into the background. Indeed, one of the lessons from survey research is not to ask people their age. Instead, we ask in what year they were born. This reduces the thinking and calculation on the respondent's part and increases accuracy.

Nevertheless, there are a number of interesting long-term trends that either alter the transitions to the next life stage or change the meaning and the blueprint for that life stage. The salient changes are to be found in factors that will alter the timing of transitions into adulthood or old age. Changes in the institutions through which a life unfolds are also likely to alter perceptions of age and the plans that people make as they pass through those institutions. These are to be found in education, marriage, and family life, and the state itself in terms of policies regulating the workplace as well as financial and medical benefits.

Education

Most of the transitions into adulthood are legislative age norms granting such privileges as voting, driving, or the consumption of alcohol. These are straightforward with adolescents either too young or who have attained the appropriate age. Education is a little different. Here one must participate in a series of finely age-graded classes. Although there are explicit age norms regulating participation (e.g., in the United States one must attend school around age 5 or 6 and remain there until at least age 16), the majority remain in school much longer. There have always been social class differences in education. Working-class children are more likely to exit earlier and assume adult roles. Middle-class children are more likely to complete their secondary education and go on to college. Across the second half of the twentieth century, we have seen the expansion of colleges and universities. The educational attainment of the general population is steadily rising (over 25% college education), with 60% to 70% of the recent cohorts having college degrees. Increased educational achievement is partially due to an increase in wealth, educational loans, and the desire to improve one's occupational chances in the labor market. For age awareness, increased education prolongs the transition into adulthood or blurs and extends the transition.

Marriage and Family

Kinship in the late twentieth century has been transformed by the sexual revolution of the 1960s. The introduction of effective birth control not only changed the meaning of sex but has also changed marriage and family (Strathern, 1992). The sexual revolution enabled both adults and adolescents to be sexually mature and active without the consequences of having children. Families as the arena in which aging takes place have been significantly altered.

1. Marriage is often delayed for several years. Either educational attainment or the establishment of significant long-term relationships tends to promote later births. The decision to marry is often associated with the decision to have children. By postponing marriage and children, one is also postponing one of the major sets of status associated with adulthood.

2. Reduced fertility means that many people will have no children. Either they make the decision to never marry, remain in a childless long-term relationship, or marry

and remain childless. The net effect is that these individuals are relatively "ageless." This is because they have no dependent children to "age" them. As children mature and pass through the age-graded educational system, their development reflects on the social age of their parents. It is much different being the parent of preschool children compared with being a parent of high school children. Ageless individuals begin to age again once they go through the transitions into old age.

3. The children are usually planned for and deliberately spaced. Previously, most parents hoped to reproduce in their 20s and certainly before age 35 and to have only one or two children, thus producing offspring that are between 20 and 30 years younger than the parental generation. This compares with an older pattern of large families whose reproduction is continuous until reproduction ceases. Children in the past could be anywhere between 15 to 45 years younger than the parental generation. In these families, there is no empty nest and the youngest children are still at home even in old age and after the death of one parent. With reduced and planned reproduction, parents can expect 10 to 20 years of an empty nest before they enter old age. Another consequence of reduced fertility is that genealogical generations are more distinct and more sharply defined.

4. High divorce rates not only confuse kinship, but they also alter the salience of kinship for age. Many parents, usually women, will raise their children without a spouse. Divorce often results in the establishment of new relationships and second or third marriages. With second families, not only do families and their extended kin relationships become more complicated, but also the resulting children are born at a more advanced age (usually for men) and in two sets. Age becomes blurred just as in the larger family with continuous reproduction.

5. Generational succession within families has become of less importance as the capitalist economy has shifted from manufacturing to service. Children are no longer expected to take over the parent's resources such as farms or family businesses. Instead, children are expected to find careers of their own choice as they are being launched. Consequently, the roles between parents and children change as families no longer work together in a longer-term arena.

Policies of the State

State policies are most likely to affect individuals by way of retirement and health-care benefit systems (Settersten, 2003).

1. The financing of retirement has changed significantly over the last half of the twentieth century. Pensions have shifted from the defined benefit pensions to financial plans based on deferred income and investment for the financing of retirement. As a result, two of the three components of retirement financing (individual investment, pensions, social security) are more subject to individual decision making and market forces. Thus the decision to retire is much more ambiguous in terms of age as people ascertain whether they can afford to retire or if they must continue to work or get a transitional job. Also in the late twentieth century, most states increased the age of entitlement. Social Security in the United States presently has elevated the age for full entitlement from 65 to 67, and people are encouraged to think about waiting until they are in their 70s. The age of early retirement remains at 62. However, early retirement

entails significantly reduced benefits which encourage individuals to remain in the work force longer in order to increase their income in retirement.

2. Over the twentieth century, the technology of healthcare has seen marked improvement. The net effect is that people live longer and are able to live with a number of disabilities for considerable time. On the average, old age has been extended for at least a decade if not longer (Seltzer, 1995). Thus, some people may be spending up to a quarter or a third of their lives in old age. With increased longevity, the transitions into old age have become more complicated. Withdrawal from the labor force and altered sources of income signal the beginning of this period; however, people in good health actually do not experience much of a shift into postadulthood. With the increased medicalization of old age, the real transition for many is a major illness. Physical status, combined with the status of retirement, mark passages into the "oldest old." A major transition is when disability necessitates a change in residence. If one can no longer perform the activities of daily life, then supportive care removes them from their usual environment into a quasi- or total institutional setting. This requires additional support from the state. In the United States, medical crises often involves Medicare and, if necessary, Medicaid.

THE EXPERIENCE OF OLD AGE

The Invention of Old Age

Old age as a social category is clearly an invention of the late nineteenth and early twentieth centuries. The social policies defining a threshold for benefits in old age was not a widespread experience, however, until the mid twentieth century (Haber & Gratton, 1994). Early cohorts eligible for benefits were small, but by mid century they became and have become increasingly large. Old age became a normative part of the life course with new definitions. Contrary to a life course where one worked until disability made employment difficult with a short old age, the experiences of cohorts charted new grounds. Old age is not short and is not a period of poverty for most. Instead, one can expect at least 10 years in retirement and, with adequate income, it is a period of leisure and relaxation. If there is change here, it is that old age has lost its stigma.

Time and the Ageless Self

Selves develop through time from birth to death. Selves change through time, but they retain a sense of continuity across years. In her interviews, Sharon Kauffman (1986) discovered her informants did not experience changes in self with increased age, selves appear to be ageless.

Do individuals identify with their age? The answer to this question is probably negative. The only reason people would identify with their age is if there were benefits in doing so. At the transition into full adulthood and into retirement, age awareness is likely to increase because of the rewards that come with age. Most adults carry with them documents that explicitly state their age: most likely a driver's license; yet most people do not think about their age on a daily basis. In Project AGE (Keith et al., 1994), we asked people what marked their transitions across the life course. Some pointed to the state regulated transitions of completing education for entry into adulthood and retirement for the exit from full adulthood. Interestingly, the vast majority stated, "age," "time," or "it's natural." There are things far more interesting than time to organize lives. Lives are lived in time, but it is what happens in time that makes them worth living. Family, friends, work, leisure, spirituality, and the like compose the fabric of life. Even in settings where age is relatively homogenous, such as retirement communities, senior centers, assisted living residences, nursing homes, or even school classrooms, age is not paramount. Ethnographic studies of these settings reveal that other dimensions of social life absorb people's attentions and identities. It is only gerontologists who view the world through the lens of the human passage through time and conclude that age is important.

REFERENCES

Bernardi, B. (1985). *Age class systems: Social institutions and polities based on age* (D. I. Kertzer, Trans.). Cambridge: Cambridge University Press.

Chudacoff, H. P. (1989). *How old are you? Age consciousness in American culture.* Princeton, NJ: Princeton University Press.

Crump, T. (1990). *The anthropology of numbers.* Cambridge: Cambridge University Press.

Duncan, D. E. (1998). *Calendar: Humanity's epic struggle to determine a true and accurate year.* New York: Avon.

Fry, C. L. (2002). The life course as a cultural construct. In. R. A. Settersten (Ed.), *Invitation to the life course* (pp. 269-294). Amityville, NY: Baywood.

Goodall, J. (1986). *The chimpanzees of Gombe: Patterns of behavior.* Cambridge, MA.: Belknap Press of Harvard University Press.

Goodall, J. (1988). *In the shadow of man.* Boston: Houghton Mifflin.

Haber, C., & Gratton, B. (1994). *Old age and the search for security: An American social history.* Bloomington: Indiana University Press.

Hendricks, J. (2001). Its about time. In S. H. McFadden & R. C. Atchley (Eds.), *Aging and the meaning of time* (pp. 21-50). New York: Springer.

Henretta, J. C. (2003). The life-course perspective on work and retirement. In. R. A. Settersten, Jr. (Ed.), *Invitation to the life course: Toward new understandings of later life* (pp. 85-106). Amityville, NY: Baywood.

Huntingford, G. W. (1953). *The southern Nilo-Hamites.* London: International African Institute.

Kaufmann, S. R. (1986). *The ageless self: Sources of meaning in old age.* Madison: University of Wisconsin Press.

Keith, J. K., Fry, C. L., Glascock, A. P., Ikels, C., Dickerson-Putman, J., Harpending, H. C., & Draper, P. (1994). *The aging experience: Diversity and commonality across cultures.* Thousand Oaks, CA: Sage.

Kohli. M. (1986). The world we forgot: A historical review of the life course. In V. Marshall (Ed.), *Later life* (pp. 271-292). Beverly Hills, CA: Sage.

Kohli, M., & Meyer, J. W. (1986). Social structure and the social construction of life stages. *Human Development, 29,* 145-149.

Marshack, A. (1991). *The roots of civilization: The cognitive beginnings of mans first art, symbols and notation.* Mount Kisco, NY: Moyer Bell.

Mayer, K. U., & Schopflin, U. (1989). The state and the life course. *Annual Review of Sociology, 15,* 187-209.

Oberg, K. (1997). *The social economy of the Tlingit Indians.* New Haven, CT: HRAF.

Seltzer, M. M. (1995). *The impact of increased life expectancy: Beyond the gray horizon.* New York: Springer.

Settersten, R. A., Jr. (2003). Rethinking social policy: Lessons of a life-course perspective. In. R. A. Settersten, Jr. (Ed.), *Invitation to the life course: Toward new understandings of later life* (pp, 191-224). Amityville, NY: Baywood.

Sharp, H. S. (1977). The Chipewyan hunting unit. *American Ethnology, 4,* 377-393.

Shostak, M. (1981). *Nisa: The life and words of a !Kung woman.* Cambridge, MA: Harvard University Press.

Spencer, P. (1988). *Maasai of Matapato: A study of rituals and rebellion.* Bloomington: Indiana University Press.

Stenning, D. J. (1958). Household variability among the pastoral Fulani. In. J. Goody (Ed.), *The developmental cycle in domestic groups* (pp. 92-119). Cambridge: Cambridge University Press.

Strathern, M. (1992). *After nature: English kinship in the late twentieth century.* Cambridge: Cambridge University Press.

Sverdrup, H. U. (1938). *With people of the tundra.* Oslo: Gyldendal Morsk Forlas.

Waal, F. B. M. de (1998). *Chimpanzee politics: Power and sex among apes.* Baltimore: Johns Hopkins University Press.

Weltfish, G. (1965). *The lost universe.* New York: Basic Books.

Whissler, C. (1913). *Societies and dance associations of the Blackfoot Indians.* New York: The Trustees.

CHAPTER 3

Changes in Physical and Mental Function of Older People: Looking Back and Looking Ahead

Kenneth G. Manton and XiLiang Gu

We found declines in the prevalence of chronic disability in the U.S. elderly population in analyses of the 1982 to 1999 National Long Term Care Survey (NLTCS). An important component of the disability decline was severe cognitive impairment. We found 310,000 fewer severely cognitively impaired elderly in 1999 than 1982. Age-standardized decreases were from 1.545 million (1982) to 1.024 million (1999), a decline in prevalence from 5.7% to 2.9%. These were even larger than declines in physical disability (Manton & Gu, 2001). They seem, in part, due to increases in the years of school completed by "new" elderly (65+) and oldest-old (85+) cohorts. Advances in biomedical technology and Medicare benefits appear also to play an important role.

THE NEW HEALTHY ELDERLY: ONLY GETTING BETTER

Changes in the prevalence of chronic physical and cognitive impairment in the population aged 65+ are a concern for the U.S. Medicare and Social Security systems because of population aging (Manton & Gu, 2001). This is because qualitatively poor health and functioning would multiply the increasing population burden on the Medicare and Medicaid healthcare programs, and because the health and functional status of elderly persons will determine their ability to work in the labor force—a factor that will increase in importance as the normal retirement age for U.S. Social Security benefits is gradually increased, by 2027, from age 65 to 67—with various other policy discussions of whether the age of eligibility could be further increased (e.g., to 70 or more).

Until relatively recently, epidemiological theory and some data suggested that the average health and functional status of the elderly population might continue to worsen. Omran (1971) promulgated a theory of the "epidemiological transition," which argued that social and economic conditions in modern industrialized societies will increase the risk of chronic disease for individuals, especially circulatory diseases. Kramer (1980) and Gruenberg (1977) suggested the United States was entering a period of a "pandemic" of disability and chronic diseases based largely on examples of greatly extended survival of certain relatively infrequent genetic disorders such as Down's syndrome.

Indeed, the Social Security population projections for 1977 assumed life expectancy in the United States had reached its biological limits (Myers, 1981). Part of this pessimism was based on the fact that U.S. male mortality did not significantly decline from 1954 to 1968 (though female mortality did decrease), largely due to increases in male cardiovascular risks. Starting in 1969, however, consistent declines in U.S. (1964 in Britain) male mortality started so that by 1982 it was clear that the long range fiscal planning for the U.S. Social Security Trust Fund had serious problems. In 1982-1983, the U.S. Congress took actions to increase the normal retirement age from 65 to 67 between 2000 and 2022 to account for the rapid increase in U.S. life expectancy.

This increase raised the related question of how mortality is affected while chronic disease risk is increased (as is argued by the epidemiological transition model). Fries (1989) proposed that current U.S. life expectancy was limited to an absolute biological limit of 85 years, and that chronic disease prevalence might be reduced by delaying the age at onset of chronic disease. Manton (1989) felt that it was unlikely that the age at death from chronic diseases could vary independently from the age at onset of chronic disease and argued that there was not a fixed biological limit to life expectancy that currently operated to limit mortality declines in the United States; and that age at onset and age at death from a chronic disease had to be correlated as events for the same process with the likelihood that active life expectancy should increase as life expectancy increased and that a focused National Health Policy could make active life expectancy increase relatively more rapidly than overall life expectancy. Evidence of this was found in analyses of the 1982, 1984, and 1989 NLTCS (Freedman & Soldo, 1994).

The recent data from the five National Long Term Care Surveys (NLTCS) confirm there has been a large and accelerating decline in chronic disability prevalence (inclusive of disability due to cognitive impairment) for the U.S. elderly population (Manton & Gu, 2001; Manton, Corder, & Stallard, 1997; Singer & Manton, 1998). Rates declined 1.0% per annum from 1982 to 1989, 1.6% per annum from 1989 to 1994, and 2.6% per annum from 1994 to 1999 (Manton & Gu, 2001). Declines in U.S. disability prevalence were confirmed in the National Health Interview Survey (NHIS) by Waidmann, Bound, and Schoenbaum (1995), in the Current Medicare Beneficiary Surveys (Waidman & Liu, 2000), in the NHIS and NHIS Supplement on Aging (Crimmins, Saito, & Reynolds, 1997) and the Survey of Income and Program Participation (Freedman & Martin, 1998).

In this chapter, we explore an important determinant of overall disability prevalence, severe cognitive impairment, whose prevalence is estimated from the 1982, 1984, 1989, 1994, and 1999 NLTCS. We do this to see how it relates to the rate of decline in functional impairment in the U.S. elderly population, in the size of the U.S. nursing home population, and to educational trends in the U.S. elderly and oldest-old populations. As a determinant of the ability to continue to work, it is also of importance to determine how human capital can be maintained for the U.S. economy as the population ages and younger generations entering the labor force cannot continue to grow without limit. This means fewer younger workers will be available to support a growing elderly population. Developed country economies also cannot continue to use ever-growing numbers of guest workers to sustain their national labor forces and support the growth of the elderly population.

DATA AND METHODS

The data to be analyzed comes from the 1982, 1984, 1989, 1994, and 1999 NLTCS and continuous Medicare bill record history for NLTCS respondents accumulated for twelve-month periods after the interview date of each individual in the 1994, and later in the 1999, samples. Sample design, field procedures and survey instrumentation were held constant over time to minimize bias due to changes in methodology (Manton & Gu, 2001). The NLTCS describes the level and types of chronic disability, self-reports of medical problems, and the need for medical and long-term care for persons aged 65+.

NLTCS samples were drawn from Medicare enrollment lists to ensure the entire U.S. population aged 65+ was represented. Thus, the sample, based on a list of all Medicare eligible persons, represents the combined U.S. community and institutional elderly population. All sample persons selected in each survey year were tracked through the Medicare record system so that all survey nonrespondents have healthcare use, healthcare costs (and medical diagnoses), and date of death (if applicable) recorded. Surviving disabled subjects in each NLTCS were included in subsequent surveys. Each survey, after 1982, included an "age-in" sample of 5,000 persons aged 65 to 69 at the new survey date newly drawn from Medicare lists to maintain cross-sectional representation of the entire U.S. population aged 65+ at each date. Supplementary samples of person's aged 95+ were drawn in 1994 ($N = 540$) and 1999 ($N = 600$) to increase precision of estimates for this very elderly group, with a high utilization of nursing homes and with a high prevalence of severe cognitive impairment.

The NLTCS is conducted in two stages. A screening interview detects cases of chronic disability defined as limitations in Activities of Daily Living (ADL (Katz & Akpom, 1976) or Instrumental Activities of Daily Living (IADL (Lawton & Brody, 1969) lasting, or expected to last, 90+ days. Second, persons with disability (or their proxies) were given either a detailed community or institutional interview to better describe their traits. Persons in any NLTCS receiving a detailed interview were automatically re-interviewed in all later NLTCS (until death) to measure improvements, as well as decrements, in function. In 1994, 1,762 "healthy" persons, not chronically disabled on the screener, were given a community interview to increase precision of estimates of their socioeconomic, housing, and other traits. The "healthy" oversample in 1999 was augmented to replace deaths occurring from 1994 to 1999. The detailed interview response rate is over 95% in all NLTCS (Manton & Gu, 2001). Thus, response rate changes are unlikely to affect estimates of other physical or cognitive disability trends.

Severe cognitive impairment was defined from the NLTCS by the subject not being able to answer successfully any questions in a brief cognitive screen (either the Short Portable Mental State Questionnaire (SPMSQ) 1982 to 1994 or the Mini Mental State Evaluation (MMSE) which contains the questions in the SPMSQ, in 1999); or the interviewer determining the necessity, due to severe cognitive impairment, for a proxy respondent to answer questions.

No attempt was made to diagnose incident Alzheimer's disease (AD) in the NLTCS since that requires a physician following symptoms (e.g., decline in memory) over time (e.g., six months). However, we did ask respondents or proxies to report if they had received a diagnosis of Alzheimer's disease or other dementia from a physician and we examined ICD 9 codes (and appropriate four digit codes) 290, 310, 331, and 797 in 1994 and 1999 from Medicare records where diagnoses are reported for re-imbursement of medical services. These codes were selected because they were used to compare Medicare diagnoses of dementia against a clinical standard (Taylor, Fillenbaum, & Ezell, 2002). They approximate ICD-9 codes defining AD and related dementias (ADRD) as suggested by NINDS (National Institute of Neurological Disorders and Stroke). We could only examine Medicare diagnoses for 1994 and 1999 since it was in 1990 that CMS (Center for Medicare/Medicaid Studies; formerly the Health Care Finance Administration) started recording diagnostic codes for all service encounters.

To evaluate changes in the tendency to diagnose ADRD over time, the occurrence of these codes on U.S. death certificates from 1979 to 1991 were examined (National Centers for Health Statistics, 1996). Physicians became more likely to report ADRD as a cause of death on death certificate after 1979 with a slowing of the rate of increase of such reporting by 1988.

We estimated ADRD (ICD-9 codes) prevalence over a twelve-month interval directly from Medicare records for NLTCS institutional samples in 1994 and 1999. For 1982, 1984, and 1989, prevalence was estimated by linear interpolation of the institutional prevalence of dementia reported on the 1985 and 1995 National Nursing Home Surveys (NNHS), normed to NLTCS estimates of the size of the institutional population. ADRD (or its equivalent from 1982 to 1989) prevalence in institutions was estimated to be 37.6% (1982), 36.6% (1984), 31.8% (1989), 30.2% (1994), and 29.2% (1999).

Taylor et al. (2002) examined the quality of Medicare diagnoses for AD and ADRD. Using three (of seven) types of Medicare service records for 1991 to 1995, they found a 90% correspondence of ADRD diagnoses on Medicare records and clinical diagnoses for 417 patients evaluated at memory clinics at 23 tertiary-care medical centers. Taylor et al. (2002) found dementia cases with severity scores of 2 to 5 a third more likely to be detected than mild dementia. In our analyses, we examined the prevalence of the ICD-9 codes in all seven (not just three) types of Medicare service records. This increased detection of ADRD ICD-9 diagnoses over a one-year period. Thus, we used Medicare diagnoses generated from seven types of records for a one-year window in 1994 and 1999 to compare to NLTCS interview cases of severe cognitive impairment. We found a good correspondence of severe cognitive impairment from the NLTCS screener with ADRD Medicare ICD-9 diagnoses made in the twelve-month period after the survey.

Subjects were divided into three groups. "No disability" cases were community residents with no limitations. They could, for example, eat, dress, get in and out of bed, get around inside, use the toilet, and bathe without help. "Significant disability" cases had 1 or more ADL or IADL chronic limitations. Nursing home residents were severely impaired averaging 4.8 of 6 ADLs chronically impaired.

Prevalence rates for severe cognitive impairment specific to age and gender were calculated for each NLTCS—either for overall disability or for disability groups. Prevalence rates were also calculated for 1982, 1984, 1989, and 1994 standardized to the 1999 population/age distribution.

RESULTS

Population Counts

The number of severely cognitively impaired persons age 65+ (Table 1) declined from 1.33 million in 1982 to 1.02 million in 1999—or 310,000 (a decline of 23.3%) despite 29.6% growth (+9 million persons) in the U.S. population aged 65+. There were 144,000 fewer institutional residents and 166,000 fewer disabled community residents with severe cognitive impairment. There were 649,000 severely cognitively impaired persons aged 65 to 79 in 1982 and 403,000 in 1999—a decline of 246,000. A decline of 61,000 was found for persons aged 80+.

In 1982, 5.0% of the U.S. elderly population had severe cognitive impairment, 2.9% in 1999 ($t = -10.0$, $p << 0.0001$)—a 42% relative decrease. Significant declines from 1982 to 1999 were found for disabled community (2.8% to 1.7%; *S.E.* = ±0.16, $t = -6.9$, $p << 0.0001$) and institutional (2.1% to 1.2%; $t = -6.9$, *S.E.* = ±0.13, $p << 0.0001$) residents. For those aged 65 to 79, severe cognitive impairment prevalence dropped from 3.0% in 1982 to 1.5% in 1999. Prevalence at ages 80+ declined from 12.2% to 6.9%.

Age Standardized Rates and Counts

Standardization adjusts trends in rates for changes in population structure by comparing age-specific disability rates equally weighted at each date. Declines in severe cognitive impairment are larger after standardizing. In Table 2, the 1982 (age standardized) to 1999 decline from 1.55 to 1.02 million severely cognitive impaired persons is presented.

The age standardized prevalence for persons aged 65 to 79 declined from 1982 to 1999 from 658,000 to 403,000, or from 3.3% to 1.5%; (*S.E.* = ±0.19, $t = -9.5$, $p = 0.0001$). Prevalence declined from 888,000 to 623,000 for persons age 80+. Declines for disabled community (5.2% to 3.3%; *S.E.* = ±0.38, $t = -5.0$, $p << 0.0001$) and institutional (7.6% to 3.5%; *S.E.* = ±0.44, $t = -9.3$, $p = 0.0001$) residents aged 80+ are also highly significant.

Total age-standardized prevalence declined from 5.7% in 1982 to 2.9% in 1999 (*S.E.* = ±0.21, $t = -13.3$, $p << 0.0001$) a relative decline of 49%. The age-standardized 1982 rate of 5.7% predicts 2.0 million Americans age 65+ would have been severely cognitively impaired in 1999 if 1982 age specific disability rates had not changed—only 1.03 million severe cognitively impaired persons were observed in 1999.

DISCUSSION AND CONCLUSIONS

The U.S. prevalence of severe cognitive impairment was expected to increase as the population ages because of a number of projections that showed large increases in Alzheimer's disease and other dementing illnesses believed to underlie most serious losses of cognitive function with age. Projections of these increases are quite variable but generally indicate that, without changes in age specific dementia rates, the increase would represent a major factor in the growth of U.S. health care and LTC expenditures.

Table 1. Population Counts of Severely Cognitively Impaired Persons Age 65+ in 1982, 1984, 1989, 1994, and 1999

	No-Disability (× 1,000s)			Disability (× 1,000s)			Nursing home residents (× 1,000s)			Total (× 1,000s)		
	Cases	%	*S.E.* (%)	Cases	%	*S.E.* (%)	Cases	%	*S.E.* (%)	Cases	%	*S.E.* (%)
All Subjects												
1982												
cognitively impaired	0	0.0	±0.00	758	2.8	±0.12	576	2.1	±0.10	1,334	5.0	±0.16
not impaired	21,032	78.1		3,603	13.4		956	3.6		25,591	95.0	
1984												
cognitively impaired	0	0.0	±0.00	616	2.2	±0.10	564	2.0	±0.10	1,180	4.2	±0.14
not impaired	21,951	78.2		3,950	14.1		978	3.5		26,879	95.8	
1989												
cognitively impaired	0	0.0	±0.00	576	1.9	±0.11	532	1.7	±0.10	1,108	3.8	±0.15
not impaired	24,395	79.0		2,672	13.7		1,153	3.7		28,220	96.2	
1994												
cognitively impaired	0	0.0	±0.00	445	1.4	±0.09	511	1.5	±0.09	956	2.9	±0.13
not impaired	26,489	80.0		4,498	13.6		1,183	3.6		32,170	97.1	
1999												
cognitively impaired	0	0.0	±0.00	592	1.7	±0.10	432	1.2	±0.08	1,024	2.9	±0.13
not impaired	29,038	82.4		4,128	11.7		1,049	3.0		34,215	97.1	

Age 65 to 79												
1982												
cognitively impaired	0	0.0	±0.00	474	2.3	±0.12	175	0.8	±0.07	649	3.0	±0.14
not impaired	18,010	84.6		2,276	10.7		366	1.7		20,652	97.0	
1984												
cognitively impaired	0	0.0	±0.00	347	1.5	±0.09	170	0.8	±0.07	517	2.3	±0.12
not impaired	18,823	85.1		2,410	10.9		362	1.6		21,595	97.7	
1989												
cognitively impaired	0	0.0	±0.00	323	1.4	±0.11	138	0.6	±0.07	461	1.9	±0.13
not impaired	20,504	86.1		2,444	10.3		420	1.8		23,368	98.1	
1994												
cognitively impaired	0	0.0	±0.00	197	0.8	±0.08	147	0.6	±0.07	344	1.4	±0.11
not impaired	21,890	86.7		2,580	10.2		343	1.4		24,813	98.6	
1999												
cognitively impaired	0	0.0	±0.00	289	1.2	±0.10	114	0.4	±0.06	403	1.5	±0.12
not impaired	23,313	89.2		2,152	8.2		274	1.0		25,739	98.5	

Table 1. (Cont'd.)

	No-Disability (× 1,000s)			Disability (× 1,000s)			Nursing home residents (× 1,000s)			Total (× 1,000s)		
	Cases	%	*S.E.* (%)	Cases	%	*S.E.* (%)	Cases	%	*S.E.* (%)	Cases	%	*S.E.* (%)
Age 80+												
1982												
cognitively impaired	0	0.0	±0.00	283	5.1	±0.31	401	7.1	±0.36	684	12.2	±0.48
not impaired	3,022	53.7		1,326	23.6		590	10.5		4,938	87.8	
1984												
cognitively impaired	0	0.0	±0.00	269	4.5	±0.30	394	6.6	±0.36	663	11.1	±0.46
not impaired	3,128	52.6		1,540	25.9		618	10.4		5,286	88.9	
1989												
cognitively impaired	0	0.0	±0.00	252	3.6	±0.27	394	5.6	±0.33	646	9.2	±0.43
not impaired	3.891	55.3		1,772	25.2		732	10.4		6,395	90.8	
1994												
cognitively impaired	0	0.0	±0.00	249	3.2	±0.25	364	4.6	±0.30	613	7.8	±0.39
not impaired	4,599	58.3		1,830	23.2		839	10.6		7,268	92.2	
1999												
cognitively impaired	0	0.0	±0.00	304	3.3	±0.22	319	3.5	±0.23	623	6.9	±0.32
not impaired	5,767	63.4		1,928	21.2		774	8.5		8,469	93.1	

Table 2. Number of Severely Cognitively Impaired Cases After Age Standardization

	Disability (× 1,000s)			Nursing home residents (× 1,000s)			Total (× 1,000s)		
	Cases	%	S.E. (%)	Cases	%	S.E. (%)	Cases	%	S.E. (%)
All Subjects									
1982	814	3.0	±0.12	731	2.7	±0.12	1,545	5.7	±0.17
1984	672	2.4	±0.10	678	2.4	±0.10	1,350	4.8	±0.15
1989	610	2.0	±0.11	604	2.0	±0.11	1,214	3.9	±0.16
1994	468	1.4	±0.09	545	1.6	±0.10	1,013	3.1	±0.13
1999	592	1.7	±0.10	432	1.2	±0.08	1,024	2.9	±0.13
Age 65 to 79									
1982	454	2.3	±0.12	204	1.0	±0.08	658	3.3	±0.15
1984	335	1.6	±0.10	169	0.8	±0.07	504	2.4	±0.12
1989	319	1.4	±0.11	139	0.6	±0.07	458	2.0	±0.13
1994	199	0.8	±0.08	150	0.6	±0.07	349	1.4	±0.11
1999	289	1.1	±0.10	114	0.4	±0.06	403	1.5	±0.12
Age 80+									
1982	361	5.2	±0.31	527	7.6	±0.37	888	12.8	±0.49
1984	337	4.6	±0.30	509	7.0	±0.37	846	11.7	±0.47
1989	291	3.7	±0.27	465	5.8	±0.34	756	9.5	±0.44
1994	262	3.1	±0.25	396	4.6	±0.30	658	7.7	±0.39
1999	304	3.3	±0.22	319	3.5	±0.23	623	6.8	±0.32

Such projections, however, ignore available population and epidemiologic information on possible recent declines in dementia, age-specific prevalence rates, and factors causing declines. For example, projections based on the East Boston EPESE project showed large increases in the number of cases of dementia. However, the projected increase could be halved if the projections used education-specific rates (Evans et al., 1992). In addition, projections were often made of either probable or possible diagnosis of dementia, which meant there were large uncertainties in the projections due to difficulties with disease definition and measurement. Clearly, projections limited to serious cases of dementia are likely more reliable, as confirmed by Taylor et al. (2002).

These projections also point to a serious problem in the use of health projections. Projections prepared for actuarial and fiscal purposes (e.g., to anticipate future Social Security Trust Fund liability) are often designed to have a fiscally conservative bias. A problem arises when such projections are used to predict the actual state of health or longevity of the population, which is not what they are constructed to do. Such projections tend to be statistically biased and fail to exploit all relevant population health data. Nonetheless, such projections are often modified and used to predict future health states, often to justify federal funding on specific health problems. Not only will the projection not be an adequate basis for such planning but they also tend to create both public misperception (e.g., of the "inevitable" future large burden of Alzheimer's disease) and could alter physician behavior. For example, analyses by Taylor et al. of linked Medicare records suggest that, for a patient at a specific age with myocardial infarction, there is a usual treatment response. However, for a person who has a diagnosis of Alzheimer's disease with a clinically similar myocardial infarction, there is often less rigorous treatment. Given the difficulty of making a diagnosis of Alzheimer's disease, the expectation of a high prevalence of Alzheimer's disease at ages 85+ due to such projections might have consequences for the provision of acute-care series.

We documented significant changes (declines) in the prevalence of severe cognitive impairment (Manton & Gu, 2001). In the 1982, 1984, 1989, 1994, and 1999 NLTCS, the prevalence of severe cognitive impairment declined from 1982 to 1999, i.e., in absolute terms by 310,000 cases, 976,000 after age standardization of 1982 rates. Age-standardized relative declines were 49%—from 5.7% using 1982 rates to 2.9% observed. Declines were highly significant over ages 65+, 1982 to 1999. Declines were largest in institutions at ages 80+. Prevalence declines were also found over a recent, but shorter, period in a comparison of the 1993 Asset and Health Dynamics among the Oldest Old Study, with the 1998 Health and Retirement Survey (Freedman, Aykan, & Martin, 2001) and are suggested by several other studies (e.g., Freedman et al., 2001; Freedman, Aykan, & Martin, 2002; Liao, McGee, Cao, & Cooper, 2000).

We believe our estimates of declines in severe cognitive improvement are robust and significant for health policy. Methods used to identify and describe cases in the NLTCS were constant over time. Each NLTCS used the same instruments, sample design, field methods, and sets of experienced interviewers to produce comparable responses from participants over time. Greater awareness of dementia, as indicated by cause of death studies (National Centers for Health Statistics, 1996), suggest severe cognitive impairment should be reported *more* completely in *recent* years. Thus, measurement bias in trends is likely toward the null hypothesis of no decline in prevalence *reducing,* not exaggerating, declines in the prevalence of severe cognitive impairment. Further, we were able to validate our case-by-case NLTCS screener determination of severe cognitive impairment with ICD-9 diagnosis of ADRD in linked Medicare records in 1994 and 1999.

Though mortality differs by disability level and degree of cognitive impairment, this does not bias prevalence estimates because our sampling procedure produces a representative cross section of all persons aged 65+ for each year. To generate such a representative cross section, the sample was augmented by compensating for loss of severely cognitively impaired and chronically disabled persons due to mortality. Tests conducted using mortality data and Medicare records, suggest few persons with chronic disability were missed.

The severe cognitive impairment decline over 17 years (1982 to 1999) coincides with decreases in chronic disability prevalence in the NLTCS and other U.S. longitudinal national surveys (Freedman & Martin, 1998; Freedman et al., 2001). The rate of disability decline is smaller than for severe cognitive impairment, though accelerating: 1% per year from 1982 to 1989, 1.6% per year from 1989 to 1994, and 2.6% per year from 1994 to 1999. There is a 42% relative decline (3% per annum, nonstandardized) of severe cognitive impairment from 1982 to 1999. The largest declines are for institutional residents. Thus, severe cognitive impairment declines significantly contributed to overall disability prevalence declines observed from 1982 to 1999. It is currently planned to redo the NLTCS in 2004. That will allow us to see if declines, in severe cognitive impairment, and total chronic disability, continues. The period from 1999 to 2004 will be of significant interest since the effects of improvements in education at later ages will be starting to mitigate so that biomedical innovations, such as increased prescription of statin medications, will have to play an increasing role for declines to continue.

The 1982 to 1999 NLTCS showed large absolute declines (300,000) in the institutional population aged 65+ from 1.76 million in 1994 to 1.46 million in 1999 (Manton & Gu, 2001) despite an increase of 9 million persons in the U.S. elderly population over that period. Declines in nursing home use rates, where the prevalence of severe dementia is high, were also found in the 1985 and 1995 NNHS (Bishop, 1999) and the 1987 and 1996 Medical Expenditure Surveys (Rhoades, 1998). This may partly be due to the effects of the Medicare hospice benefit. When started, only 5% of Medicare decedents, many of them cancer patients, took advantage of this program. Recently, 17% of Medicare decedents utilized hospice home care and other diagnoses, such as dementing illnesses and heart disease, were increasingly cited. This would partly explain the reduction in the nursing home populations with more demented persons being cared for at home. However, the community prevalence of severe cognitive impairment is also declining despite transfers from nursing homes.

What disease dynamics might explain the decline in severe cognitive impairment? One is that the dementing diseases causing severe cognitive impairment are prevented (i.e., cases never occur). However, it may be that a disease process is slowed so that its age at clinical manifestation is delayed past the age at which the person would die without the dementing illness. This is illustrated in Figure 1.

Curve C is the survival curve for the 1982 NLTCS population and C′ is the survival curve for the 1999 NLTCS population. Curve A is the conditional (on survival) age

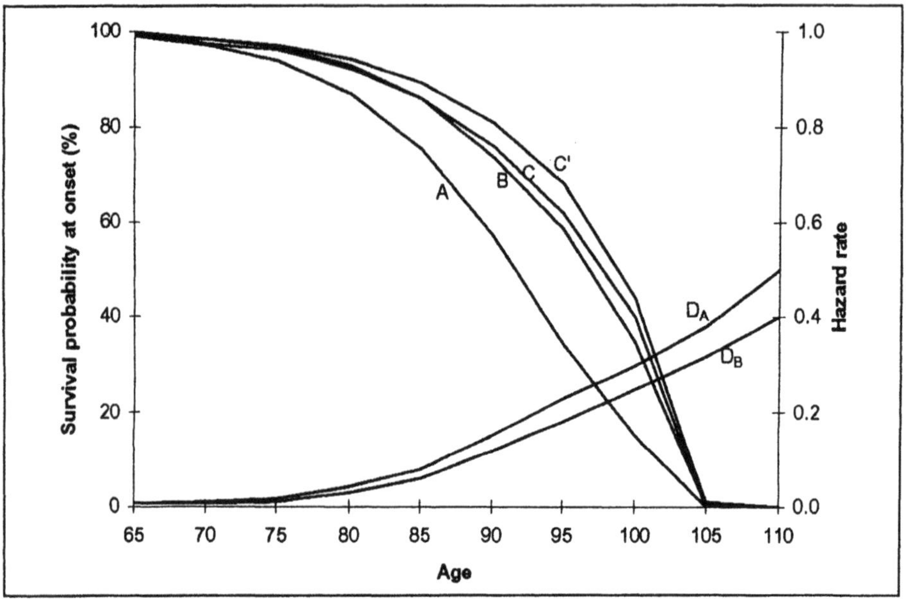

Figure 1. Age specific probability of onset for 1982 and 1999 severe cognitive impairment.

specific prevalence of severe cognitive impairment based on the 1982 NLTCS rates. Curve B is the conditional age-specific prevalence of severe cognitive impairment in 1999. The shift from curve A to B implies a shorter lifetime for persons with cognitive impairment if life expectancy after age 65 changed little from 1982 to 1999 after onset of impairment, thus reducing the prevalence of persons with cognitive impairment.

If curves A and B were described by a Gompertz hazard function, then an analysis of the doubling times of the dementia hazard after age 65 could be easily done. The hazard of impairment onset might be shifted from curves D_A to D_B (Brody, 1985). If the doubling time of dementia risk is 5 years, a delay in the age at onset of cognitive impairment of 5 years would reduce prevalence 50%—we observed an age standardized decline of 49% from 1982 to 1999. Interestingly, at late ages, these curves are not described by a Gompertz function because the age rate of increase in incidence past age 90 slows significantly.

Which scenario, prevention or delay, might be true depends on the disease mechanisms and processes leading to severe cognitive impairment and how they are modified. For example, if one views Alzheimer's disease as a vascular disease with neurodegenerative consequences, like de la Torre (2002), early interventions in circulatory diseases (e.g., increased use of statins to control cholesterol) should translate into reduced AD prevalence later; that is, declines in circulatory disease risks due to current improvements in the therapy and prevention of circulatory disease should later generate significant declines in Alzheimer's disease prevalence. This reflects another shortcoming of the Alzheimer's disease projection; they are conducted independently of data on other health trends. Since there is considerable evidence of a linkage of Alzheimer's disease to cholesterol metabolism and other circulatory disease risks, it is hard to research the improvements in circulatory disease, mortality, and morbidity with the major increases projected in Alzheimer's disease if they are dependent on many common factors and processes.

One important factor in the decline of severe cognitive impairment is improvement in the education of the U.S. elderly and oldest-old population. The education of the U.S. oldest-old, measured by years of schooling, has been increasing. In 1980, 60% of person's aged 85 to 89 had less than 8 years of education. By 2015 this decreases to only 15% (Preston, 1992). A similar trend is found in the NLTCS. Between 1982 and 1999 the percent of all persons aged 65+ (persons aged 81+ in 2015) with 8 or fewer years of school dropped from 48.0% to 18.6%. In contrast, the percentage of persons who attended college increased from 11.4% in 1982 to 33.8% in 1999. Similar education trends can be seen for the 85+ U.S. populations in the NLTCS.

The prevalence of the Medicare diagnosis of ADRD for NLTCS respondents in 1999 is shown for different education levels in Table 3.

We found lower ADRD rates for persons with higher levels of education as do several other studies (Stern, Gurland, Tatemichi, Tang, Wilder, & Mayeux, 1994). In Table 3 the Grade 13+ diagnosis rate is only about one-third of that for the Grade 0-8 group. This was found in the East Boston study (Evans et al., 1992), which showed that higher education levels could roughly halve projected future dementia rates.

Since we can only examine Medicare ADRD diagnoses for 1994 to 1999 in Table 4, for consistency we examine the prevalence of severe cognitive impairment as reported in the NLTCS for three levels of education for these age groups in 1982 and 1999.

Table 4 shows the decline in severe cognitive impairment prevalence from 1982 to 1999 is largest for the group with the highest education (i.e., for those with some college, it declines 63%; for those with 8 or fewer years of education, only 11%). Our cognitive impairment rate is higher and is thus more inclusive than the Medicare ADRD diagnosis rate. Education was less protective in 1982 (–13%) than 1999 (–62%). There is a large relative, 26% (from 10.8 to 8.1%), decline in prevalence with education for those age 85 and over in 1999 that is not evident in 1982.

Numerous explanations for the lower rate of dementia among better-educated persons have been put forth, such as better fetal nutrition, less alcohol and tobacco use, less head trauma, health benefits of affluence, long-term use of hormone replacement

Table 3. ICD-9 Dementing Diagnosis Rates (%) for Education Levels for Persons Aged 65+ in the 1999 NLTCS

	Education levels (years)		
Age	0-8	9-12	13+
Age 65-74	1.9	0.6	0.4
Age 75+	5.5	5.4	2.9
Total	4.2	2.6	1.4

Table 4. The Prevalence of Severe Cognitive Dementia Rates (%) for Different Education Levels from 1982 and 1999 NLTCS

	Education levels (years)		
Age	0-8	9-12	13+
1982			
65-84	4.4	3.3	3.8
85+	16.3	12.6	16.4
Total	6.2	4.0	5.4
1999			
65-84	4.0	2.2	1.6
85+	10.8	10.1	8.1
Total	5.5	3.0	2.1

therapy (HRT) (Zandi et al., 2002), and keeping the mind active (Snowden, Briggs, & Brooks, 1996). The last is an intriguing observation with one hypothesis being that long-term mental activity can be neuroprotective by inducing long-term cellular "potentiation," thus, changing intracellular calcium concentrations and making the cell less sensitive to oxidative and other stress (Addae, Youssef, & Stone, 2003).

All of these factors have been conduct within the context of new findings that the human brain is capable of considerable self-repair—a level of self repair that is stimulated by the stress-causing neuronal deaths (Manton & Volovyk, 2004). Twenty years ago there was little direct evidence that new neurons were generated. Now it is clear that a significant number of new neurons are generated in the olfactory bulb and in the dentate gyrus in the hippocampus (Ericksson, Perfilieva, Bjork-Ericksson, Alborn, Nordborg, & Peterson, 1998). Indeed, the methodology used to count such neuron growth may have been affected in a downward direction by biased estimates of new cells with stereotactic methods suggesting there may be little overall loss of neurons with age (Manton & Volovyk, 2004). This suggests Alzheimer's disease is clearly a pathological state, and that it is unclear whether there is necessary loss of neurons with age at all. This suggests that we can, and likely are, slowing a process of neuronal degeneration and not just the manifestation of a disease end state.

These explanations also need to be explored in the context of the interaction of education and time found in Table 4. It suggests healthcare factors may have played an important role in the decline, with education enabling care access—medical care is likely of greater benefit for various causes of dementia in 1999 than 1982. This is evident in the 1982 to 1999 trends for the 85+ population, ages where we might expect cognitive impairment to be more difficult to delay or prevent and medical factors to be more important.

This increases our interest in enabling access to resources, improved medical care, and specific treatments for the old as well as the young, and to ameliorate factors causing cognitive impairment. There may be less, and better managed, stroke and heart disease. Sight and hearing problems contributing to lack of orientation and perceived cognitive impairment may be better managed. Cataracts were far better managed (as is macular degeneration) in 1999 than in 1982. Only recently have treatments for macular degeneration been approved for Medicare reimbursement. Various common medications may significantly reduce risk of severe cognitive impairment (Jick, Zornberg, Jick, Seshardri, & Drachman, 2000; Wolozin, Kellman, Ruosseau, Celesia, & Siegel, 2000; McGeer, Schulzer, & McGeer, 1996). A meta-analysis showed long-term NSAID use associated with a 50% reduction in AD (McGeer et al., 1996). A recent study (in't Veld et al., 2001) showed AD reduction for long term NSAID use (two years prior to symptom expression) could be as high as 80%. Recent studies suggest reductions in AD risk due to ibuprofen may be both due to its anti-inflammatory properties and to interference in amyloid protein deposition (Weggen et al., 2001). Studies suggest a 60% to 73% reduction in AD for select statins (Wolozin et al., 2000). Estrogen use reduced AD's risk by 50% in observational or epidemiological studies (Tang et al., 1996). Zandi et al. (2002) found such an effect was manifest in a dose-dependent fashion (i.e., time of HRT use) fashion with HRT use >10 years reducing female risks below male risks. Testosterone may also decrease production of beta-amyloid proteins (Gouras et al., 2000). Physical activity and improved nutrition (increased antioxidant consumption (in't Veld et al., 2001; Morris et al., 2002) may reduce risk as may the use of H_2 blockers (Nelson, 2002).

A counterargument often made recently about whether the decline in disability in the elderly population will continue is that the current obesity epidemic in the United States will continue unabated leading to higher rates of adult onset diabetes and increased cardiovascular and stroke risks (Lakdawalla, Goldman, Bhattacharya, Hurd, Joyce, & Panis, 2003). Recent evidence suggesting a strong correlation of cardiovascular risks, diabetes mellitus Type II, and ADRD suggest the obesity epidemic could, in the future, increase the prevalence of dementia and related chronic functional disability.

We feel that such a pessimistic scenario is unlikely for several reasons (Manton, 2003). First, there is growing interest in physical activity, fitness, and nutrition in the U.S. elderly population. Second, there is a significant problem with malnutrition in the U.S. elderly population, with frailty often a result of loss of muscle or bone strength associated with accelerated weight loss in many very elderly persons. Third, we believe the U.S. obesity epidemic is not a simple function of the dietary behavior of the U.S. population, but one due to scientific mistakes about nutritional recommendations that were promoted by federal policy in such efforts as promoting the Department of Agriculture food pyramid, which did not accurately relate the impact of different types of food elements on lean body mass. This grew out of incomplete findings from longitudinal epidemiological studies about the different and complex roles of cholesterol components, fat, and protein consumption on heart and circulatory disease risk. Finally, the federal government, meaning the U.S. Senate and Office of Management and Budget (OMB), is now taking aggressive steps to deal directly with the current obesity epidemic, reflecting new research on nutrition and effects on body composition.

In sum, the last two decades have shown a decline in the prevalence of severe cognitive impairment that contributed significantly to the overall chronic disability decline (Manton & Gu, 2001). Though much of the decline due to improved education in the oldest-old population may be accomplished by 2010, declines may continue due to improved understanding of disease mechanisms and both serendipitous and planned use of medications with preventative benefits. The latter effects need to be better understood so such mechanisms can be systematically exploited. We do not believe the current obesity epidemic will significantly alter those trends in that action is now being taken at a national level to deal with the epidemic and its long-term consequences. We believe, however, that a coherent policy reaction is required to take full advantage of the benefits of improving health and functioning at later ages. This is, potentially, an economic, as well as a healthcare, imperative in many developed industrial countries.

REFERENCES

Addae, J. I., Youssef, F. F., & Stone, T. W. (2003). Neuroprotective role of learning in dementia: A biological explanation. *Journal of Alzheimer's Disease, 5,* 91-104.

Bishop, C. (1999). Where are missing elders? The decline in nursing home use 1985 and 1995. *Health Affairs, 18,* 146-155.

Brody, J. A. (1985). Prospects for an ageing population. *Nature, 315,* 463-466.

Crimmins, E., Saito, Y., & Reynolds, S. (1997). Further evidence on recent trends in the prevalence and incidence of disability among older Americans from two sources: The LSOA and the NHIS. *Journals of Gerontology. Series B, Psychological Sciences & Social Sciences, 52,* S59-S71.

de la Torre, J. C. (2002). Alzheimer's disease: How does it start? *Journal of Alzheimer's Disease, 4,* 497-512.

Ericksson, P., Perfilieva, E., Bjork-Ericksson, T., Alborn, A., Nordborg, C., Peterson, D., & Gage, F. (1998). Neurogenesis in the adult human hippocampus. *Nature Medicine, 4,* 1313-1317.

Evans, D., Scherr, P., Cook, N., Albert, M. S., Funkenstein, H. H., Smith, L. A., Hebert, L. E., Wette, T. T., Branch, C., Chown, M. J., Hennekens, C. H., & Taylor, J. O. (1992). The impact of Alzheimer's disease in the United States population. In R. Suzman, D. Willis, & K. Manton (Eds.), *The oldest-old.* New York: Oxford University Press.

Freedman, V., Aykan, H., & Martin, L. (2001). Aggregate changes in severe cognitive impairment among older Americans: 1993 and 1998. *Journals of Gerontology. Series B, Psychological Sciences & Social Sciences, 56,* S100-S111.

Freedman, V., Aykan, H., & Martin, L. (2002). Another look at aggregate changes in severe cognitive impairment: Further investigation into the cumulative effects of three survey design issues. *Journals of Gerontology. Series B, Psychological Sciences & Social Sciences, 57,* S126-31.

Freedman, V., & Martin, L. (1998). Understanding trends in functional limitations among older Americans. *American Journal of Public Health, 88,* 1457-1462.

Freedman, V., & Soldo, B. (1994). *Trends in disability at older ages.* Washington, DC: Committee on National Statistics.

Fries, J. (1989). The compression of morbidity: Near or far? *Milbank Quarterly, 67,* 208-232.

Gouras, G., Xu, H., Gross, R., Greenfield, J. P., Hai, B., Wang, R., & Greengard, P. (2000). Testosterone reduces neuronal secretion of Alzheimer's beta-amyloid peptides. *Proceedings of the National Academy of Sciences, 97,* 1202-1205.

Gruenberg, R. (1977). The failure of success. *Milbank Memorial Fund Quarterly, 55,* 3-24.

in't Veld, B. A., Ruitenberg, A., Hofman, A., Launer, L. J., van Duijn, C. M., Stijnen, T., Breteler, M. M. B., & Stricker, B. H. C. (2001). Nonsteroidal antiinflammatory drugs and the risk of Alzheimer's disease. *The New England Journal of Medicine, 345,* 1515-1521.

Jick, H., Zornberg, G., Jick, S., Seshadri, S., & Drachman, D. (2000). Statins and the risk of dementia. *Lancet, 356,* 1627-1631.

Katz, S., & Akpom, C. (1976). A measure of primary sociobiological functions. *International Journal of Health Services, 6,* 493-508.

Kramer, M. (1980). The rising pandemic of mental disorders and associated chronic diseases and disabilities. *Acta Psychiatrica Scandinavica, 62,* 382-397.

Lakdawalla, D., Goldman, D. P., Bhattacharya, J., Hurd, M. D., Joyce, G. F., & Panis, C. W. A. (2003). Forecasting the nursing home population. *Medical Care, 41,* 21-24.

Lawton, M., & Brody E. (1969). Assessment of older people: Self-maintaining and instrumental activities of daily living. *Gerontology, 9,* 179-186.

Liao, Y., McGee, D., Cao, G., & Cooper, R. (2000). Quality of the last year of life of older adults: 1986 vs 1993. *Journal of the American Medical Association, 283,* 512-518.

Manton, K. G. (1989). Life style risk factors. In M. Riley & J. Riley (Eds.), *The Annals of the American Academy of Political and Social Science* (Vol. 503, pp. 72-87). Newbury Park, CA: Sage.

Manton, K. G. (2003). Editorial on Lakdawalla, D., Goldman, D. P., Bhattacharya, J., Hurd, M. D., Joyce, G. F., & Panis, C. W. A. Forecasting the nursing home population. *Medical Care, 41,* 21-24.

Manton, K. G., Corder, L., & Stallard, E. (1997). Chronic disability trends in the U.S. elderly populations 1982 to 1994. *Proceedings of the National Academy of Sciences, 94,* 2593-2598.

Manton, K. G., & Gu, X. (2001). Changes in the prevalence of chronic disability in the United States black and nonblack population above age 65 from 1982 to 1999. *Proceedings of the National Academy of Sciences, U.S.A.,* 6354-6359.

Manton, K. G., & Volovyk, S. (2004). ROS effects on neurodegeneration: On environmental stresses of ionizing radiation. In preparation for *Current Alzheimer Research* (D. K. Lahiri, Ed.).

McGeer, P., Schulzer, M., & McGeer, E. (1996). Arthritis and anti-inflammatory agents as possible protective factors for Alzheimer's disease: A review of 17 epidemiologic studies. *Neurology, 47,* 425-432.

Morris, M., Evans, D., Bienias, J., Tangney, C., Bennett, D., Aggarwal, N., Wilson, R., & Scherr, P. (2002). Dietary intake of antioxidant nutrients and the risk of incident Alzheimer disease in a biracial community study. *Journal of the American Medical Association, 287,* 3230-3237.

Myers, L. (1981). Survival functions induced by stochastic covariate processes. *Journal of Applied Probability, 18,* 523-529.

National Centers for Health Statistics. (1996). *Health, United States, 1995.* Hyattsville, MD: Public Health Service.

Nelson, R. (2002). In A. M. Doherty (Ed.), *Annual Reports in Medicinal Chemistry* (pp. 197-208). New York: Academic Press.

Omran, A. (1971). The epidemiologic transition: A theory of the epidemiology of population change. *Milbank Memorial Quarterly, XLIX,* 509-538.

Preston, S. (1992). Cohort succession and the future of the Oldest Old. In R. Suzman, D. Willis, & K. Manton (Eds.), *The oldest old* (pp. 50-57). New York: Oxford University Press.

Rhoades, J. (1998). Nursing home structure and selected characteristics 1987 and 1996. *Statistics Bulletin, 79,* 2-9.

Singer, B., & Manton, K. G. (1998). The effects of health changes on projections of health service needs for the elderly population of the United States. *Proceedings of the National Academy of Science, 95,* 15618-15622.

Snowden, J., Briggs, J., & Brooks, P. (1996). Autologous blood stem cell transplantation for autoimmune diseases. *Lancet, 348,* 1112-1113.

Stern, Y., Gurland, B., Tatemichi, T., Tang, M., Wilder, D., & Mayeux, R. (1994). Influence of education and occupation on the incidence of Alzheimer's disease. *Journal of the American Medical Association, 271,* 1004-1010.

Tang, M., Jacobs, D., Stern, Y., Marder, K., Schofield, P., Gurland, B., Andrews, H., & Mayeux, R. (1996). Effect of oestrogen during menopause on risk and age at onset of Alzheimer's disease. *Lancet, 348,* 429-432.

Taylor, D., Fillenbaum, G., & Ezell, M. (2002). The accuracy of medicare claims data in identifying Alzheimer's disease. *Journal of Clinical Epidemiology, 55,* 929-937.

Waidmann, T., Bound, J., & Schoenbaum, M. (1995). The illusion of failure: Trends in the self-reported health of the U.S. elderly. *Milbank Quarterly, 73,* 253-287.

Waidmann, T., & Liu, K. (2000). Disability trends among the elderly and implications for future medicare spending. *Journals of Gerontology. Series B, Psychological Sciences & Social Sciences, 55,* S298-307.

Weggen, S., Eriksen, J., Das, P., Sagi, S., Wang, R., Pietrzik, C., Findlay, K., Smith, T., Murphy, M., Butler, T., Kang, D., Marquez Sterling, N., Golde, T., & Koo, E. (2001). A subset of NSAIDS lower amyloidogenic A 42 independently of cyclooxygenase activity. *Nature, 414,* 212-216.

Wolozin, B., Kellman, W., Ruosseau, P., Celesia, G., & Siegel, G. (2000). Decreased prevalence of Alzheimer disease associated with 3-hydroxy-3-methyglutaryl coenzyme A reductase inhibitors. *Archives of Neurology, 57,* 1439-1443.

Zandi, P. P., Carlson, M. C., Plassman, B. L., Welsh-Bohmer, K. A., Mayer, L. S., Steffens, D. C., & Breitner, J. C. S. (2002). Cache County Memory Study Investigators. Hormone replacement therapy and incidence of Alzheimer disease in older women: The Cache County Study. *Journal of the American Medical Association, 288,* 2123-2129.

PART II. New and Persistent Dynamics Regarding the Social Environment

CHAPTER 4

Cohort Differences in Social Relations among the Elderly

Kristine J. Ajrouch, Hiroko Akiyama, and Toni C. Antonucci

Social relations have consistently been identified as a critical component of the aging experience. The structure of social networks, the type of support available, and the quality of relationships with significant others have each received a great deal of attention as researchers and policy makers struggle to guarantee the quality of life of older people. Examining the nature of social relations takes on a new sense of urgency as the population of older people grows dramatically worldwide (U.S. Bureau of the Census, 1996). Social relations may be thought of as a form of social capital for elders, a key resource over the life course that provides help in times of trouble, comfort in times of pain, and information in times of need (Ajrouch, Antonucci, & Janevic, 2001). Social relations may also include negative aspects of interpersonal interactions, serving as a source of conflict and anxiety (Antonucci, Lansford, & Akiyama, 1998; Rook 1994; Thoits, 1995). The range of social relations in which elders may participate include formal (ties to government, healthcare providers, and/or other organizations) and informal (family, friends, neighbors) support. This chapter examines the role of changing demographics, economic trends, and family transformations in shaping social relations of older adults since the second half of the twentieth century. We specifically explore the degree to which things have changed and things have remained the same.

Cohort differences in social relations among elder populations may be best addressed by a discussion of the various societal trends that have emerged across the globe. Since the end of World War II, the world has undergone monumental transformations that influence the aging experience. The first area to consider involves demographic transitions related to increased life expectancy, lower birthrates, and ever-increasing geographic mobility. These trends are dramatically changing the basic structure of societies around the world and creating new and unique challenges. The result has been a tendency for societies to reflect a beanpole shape, with roughly equal numbers of old and young people, as opposed to a pyramid shape where the young far outnumber the old in society (Bengtson, Rosenthal, & Burton, 1996; Treas, 1995). The implication of this trend is that within families, there will be a higher proportion of older than younger people and therefore fewer numbers of younger people to care for greater numbers of older people in the coming years.

Economic trends over the last half century have reflected a shift in the world order and an increased globalization of markets driven by technological developments. Whereas elders living in the 1950s had experienced economic hardships in the '30s and '40s, elders living at the turn of this century experienced an economy that has become increasingly global and interdependent (Schulz, 1976; Serow, 2001). These economic trends, coupled with demographic shifts, have implications for state-sponsored support programs. Decreasing proportions of the population are contributing to social welfare in the form of taxes, but this is coupled with increasing social welfare demands as the older segments of society increase, producing a new sense of economic uncertainty. How family units and formal support alternatives respond to these economic changes makes social relations a key area of concern.

These demographic and economic trends have transformed the family, a primary source of support for elders in times of need. Indeed, the fastest growing portion of the aging population is the oldest-old, those over 85 years of age (Manton, 1990; Myers, 1990). At the same time, since increases in the proportion of two-earner families often lead to a second shift for married women who take responsibility for managing home, child, and elder care while working full time (Goldscheider, 1990; Hochschild, 1989; Moen, Robinson & Fields, 2000), women may be increasingly less available to meet these needs. However, the greater public role of middle-aged women, coupled with the improved health and increased life expectancies of their parents, suggest that grandparents can sometimes play a more active role in the lives of their grandchildren (Caldwell, Antonucci, Jackson, Wolford, & Osofsky, 1997; Pearson, Hunter, Cook, Ialong, & Kellam, 2000). Increased roles for grandparents in their grandchildren's lives may be optional in some cases, but in others they may be required, necessitated by problems of the middle generation such as AIDS, drug use, incarceration, migration, or as a result of war, revolution, and political instability. Under these circumstances, grandparents are finding themselves actually responsible for the daily care and nurturing of their grandchildren (Burton, Dilworth-Anderson, & Merriwether-de Vries, 1995) Thus, while elders are often understood to primarily receive care, they may also provide ongoing critical care to others, most often including spouse, children, and grandchildren (Rossi & Rossi, 1990).

The global trends discussed above highlight the conditions that contribute to the changing nature of social relations. While social relations have always been psychologically complex, changes have occurred so that over time close ties involve more options and a flexibility of roles that may be perceived as less binding. This development, however, is accompanied by less certainty and reduced dependability on significant network members. A result of this transformation includes network structures that are now more diffuse and less interdependent. In the following paragraphs, we describe historical changes in social relations through a discussion of past and current theoretical developments and a review of empirical studies that have addressed the nature and types of social relations over the last 50 years. We end by presenting findings from a recently completed study that analyzed cohort differences in social relations over time, followed by a summary and conclusions. Theoretical developments as well as empirical evidence suggest that whereas in the past social relations may have been perceived as both obligatory and rigid, they have transformed over time so that while social relations are still perceived as critically important, they are now likely to be thought of as both more flexible and voluntary. We turn next to a consideration of theories of social relations.

CURRENT AND PAST THEORIES OF SOCIAL RELATIONS

As Hagestad and Dannefer (2001) remind us, theories reflect their times, the social order, and history within which they are developed. This is no less true of theories of social relations. We consider six different theories and document how these theories both reflect the times and have evolved to correspond to the dynamics of historical and cultural developments as they affect aging cohorts. By some oddity, the first "modern" theory of social relations proposed a reduction in social relations with age. Disengagement theory (Cumming & Henry, 1961) reflected the societal view of old people at the time as passive, uninteresting, and uninterested in the world around them. But disengagement theory was not meant to be dismissive of older people; rather it suggested that successful adaptation to old age could best be achieved by a mutual, voluntary withdrawal of both the individual and the society each from the other. Cumming and Henry felt that with age, people were entitled, indeed, preferred to have fewer demands made upon them. They proposed that older people themselves desired less interaction with others. Old age was viewed as a rare accomplishment to be both savored and rewarded by inactivity! Not too many years later Havighurst, Neugarten, and Tobin (1968) offered an alternative view with their activity theory. In contrast to Cumming and Henry's view of old people as passive and sedentary, Havighurst et al. protested and argued that the best way to adapt to old age was to keep active. This perspective assumed that if older people engaged in numerous activities either with family or friends, or if they volunteered or engaged in other unpaid activities after retirement, there would be less chance of boredom and depression. In many ways this theory reflected the rebellious tone of the times. The late 1960s were a time of massive changes, protests for civil rights and human dignity. As oppressed peoples around the world were seeking a change in perspective to enhance their quality of life, so too were theories of social relations and aging.

Looking back, these theories may seem somewhat naïve, but they represent the basis from which many current perspectives have emerged. Each was eventually recognized to contain some element of truth. From these theories, the importance of taking a life span perspective was increasingly recognized. As people lived longer, it became apparent that activity theory turned out to best suit people who had been active throughout their lifetime, while disengagement best suited those people who tended to have consistently preferred less, rather than more, activity and engagement during their earlier years. The socioemotional selectivity theory and the convoy model are each examples of theoretical perspectives grounded in the life-span developmental perspective (see Levitt, 2000 for an overview). We, therefore, next turn to a consideration of the life-span perspective.

Although one might argue that a life-span perspective has always been implicit in psychological theories, Baltes, Reese, and Lipsitt (1980) can be credited with articulating and widely promoting this approach. The life-span perspective proposes that to understand an individual's situation or development at any point in the life span, one must take into account the past events and circumstances that he or she has experienced. Biological time, historical time, chronological time (age) and non-normative events each fundamentally influence how the individual develops. Perhaps the widespread popularity of this perspective during the latter half of the twentieth century can best be understood through a recognition of the way in which a life span could increasingly and differentially be affected by biology, history, age, and unique crises or life events. At a time when life was short (approximately 29 years at the turn of the nineteenth century), life stages were carefully proscribed (birth, childhood, marriage, childbirth, death), and what variation there was usually reflected significant illnesses or early death. One might argue that there was not much need for a life-span perspective. However, as people began to live for more years, as more children survived birth and childhood, as the period of adolescence was created and then extended, as more and more options were developed (extended schooling, later marriage, fewer children), and as the world grew smaller because of increased communication capabilities, and people were therefore increasingly affected by events, both proximal and distal, occurring in the world around them, the utility of a life-span perspective became increasingly clear.

This perspective is particularly important to the study of social relations since it is quite clear that early experiences, especially interpersonal interactions, significantly influence what one expects and how one interacts with both those same specific others as well as with people more generally. The study of close social relations usually involves the study of interactions between parent and child, husband and wife, and siblings—all relationships that are likely to exist for extended periods of time from 30 to 50 to 80 years, and which build from one period in the life cycle to the next. Understanding these relationships at any one point in time is best achieved from the long-term view of the prior experiences of the individuals. Thus, the study of a 50-year-old woman and her 70-year-old mother is best conceptualized as a social relationship that has existed for 50 years from when the 50-year-old was an infant through her early childhood, adolescence, young adulthood, and finally into the current state of middle age. Similarly, her mother was at one time a young 20-year-old mother who loved and cared for her child then and throughout the next 50 years. The resultant mother/child relationship is likely to be understood very differently depending on these lifetime-accumulated experiences and the historical context within which the relationship was experienced. For example, a specific negative experience could and would be forgiven if it followed a lifetime of positive experiences. On the other hand, a contemporary supportive interaction may be received poorly, unable to make up for a lifetime of disappointment or neglect. A small gift of food, money, or shelter might have minimal meaning in times of affluence, but may provide a crucial foundation for a significantly close relationship during times of famine, economic depression, or war. Unfortunately, all of these negative, life-threatening experiences have been plentiful around the globe in the last 50 years and must be considered when attempting to understand social relations, especially given the lifetime of experiences of those people who are now old.

Sociologists have offered intergenerational solidarity as a theoretical perspective for understanding both family and intergenerational relations (Bengtson, Rosenthal, &

Burton, 1996). In essence it adds intergenerational relations to the life-span perspective. This approach highlights the unique perceptions of each generation toward the family. The 50-year-old child and her 70-year-old mother mentioned above are examples of intrafamily intergenerational relations. Each generation views their relationship with other generations from their place in the family lineage. Intergenerational solidarity argues that older people, given their senior status in the family, their investment in the future of the family, and recognizing their own limited future are most likely to maximize the similarities across generations and their feelings of solidarity with other generational members. They are most likely to report that they provide a great deal of instrumental and affective support to their younger, junior generational family members. By contrast, younger people, while often agreeing to emotional or affective solidarity with older generations, report fewer instrumental or informational support exchanges than their senior generation relatives. Younger people are more committed to establishing themselves as independent members of the family, distinct from their elders. They often display a need to establish their own independence by distancing themselves from older generations. Bengtson et al. describe these differences as indicative of differences in developmental stake borne of different perspectives on one's place in the family and the role of the family.

Another theoretical approach to social relations is Carstensen's socioemotional selectivity theory (Carstensen, 1993; Carstensen, Isaacowitz, & Charles, 1999). Carstensen has suggested an interweaving of social relationships, emotional development, and life-span experiences. This theory builds on certain aspects of the disengagement theory and argues that at different points in the life span, people have different needs for interpersonal interaction. Carstensen suggests that at younger ages, people feel that they have a lifetime ahead of them and are motivated to expand their social network. They seek out and feel they will be advantaged by numerous exchanges and social contacts, which will provide interesting, new information. Since younger people tend to see the future as unlimited, there is little need to guard one's time or limit one's relationships. Young people look to expand their horizons and meet many and varied people. On the other hand, older people see the future as much more limited. They recognize that they have only a few years left to live and, therefore, are very selective about the people with whom they choose to spend their remaining available time. Unlike disengagement theory, which argued that all old people should withdraw from every aspect of society, socioemotional selectivity theory argues that with age, people become more motivated to attain emotion-focused goals rather than information. They are emotionally selective, choosing to socialize only with people who are close and important to them, while at the same time preferring to withdraw from relationships they do not consider close or important or that they feel are more negative than positive.

And finally, the convoy model of social relations (Antonucci, 1985; Kahn & Antonucci, 1980) offers a somewhat different, broader perspective both of causes and consequences of social relations. The convoy model is grounded within a life-span perspective recognizing that social relations are both individual and cumulative and that they reflect a lifetime of experiences and exchanges. Social relations are conceptualized as longitudinal in nature, shaped by personal (e.g., age, gender, personality) and situational (e.g., role expectations, resources, demands) characteristics, which influence both the structure of the support network and the exchange of social support. The convoy itself, including changes in the convoy over time, is hypothesized to and is empirically shown to critically affect both health and well-being. Historical change has influenced the convoy through changes in personal (e.g., higher education levels) and situational (e.g., occupying the roles of both mother and daughter) characteristics, which in turn influence the structure, function, and evaluation of social relations. Additional work in this area has extended the theory by offering a support/efficacy explanation of how social relations affect health (Antonucci & Jackson, 1987). The exchange of support is hypothesized to be effective because it communicates to the supported other that he or she is an able, worthy, capable person. This positive feedback accumulates over time and builds in the person feelings of self-worth and confidence. These positive feelings about self enable the person to face and succeed in the multiple goals and challenges of life. It should be noted that not all people receive support from those who surround them and that not all support is positive (Rook, 1992). Social exchanges can be cumulatively negative as well as cumulatively positive. Instead of being reinforced through social interactions in the belief that you are a competent, capable, and worthy person, it is possible that others may convey to you their belief that you are incompetent, incapable, and unworthy. Just as the cumulative effect of positive exchanges can have a positive affect on an individual's health and well-being, so too can the opposite have a devastating and cumulatively negative effect on health and well-being. Some support networks may produce a negative effect by supporting or encouraging behaviors detrimental to health and well-being. Drug buddies, drinking buddies, eating buddies, and buddies who discourage exercise are all examples of people who help or "support" behaviors that simply are not good for you. Historical changes have affected the support/efficacy relationship by influencing those behaviors, interactions, or goals that are valued or considered appropriate. Consider how the "appropriate" goals and characteristics for women have changed over time: nurse versus doctor, elementary school teacher versus college professor, beauty school versus graduate school, stay-at-home mom versus do-it-all super-mom. In sum, theories reflect the historical periods within which they were developed, although some appear to better explain how social relations adapt to changing times. We turn next to an empirical examination of changes in social relations over time and the degree to which these data reflect historically different theoretical perspectives.

Formal and Informal Social Relations

Life expectancy has increased over the last 50 years, simultaneously accompanied by higher proportions of women, a traditional source of informal support, working outside the home as well as increasing availability of formal care workers (Diwan & Coulton, 1994). These trends raise questions as to whether changes in both the formal and informal social relations of older people are evident within cohorts and across time periods. This information is critical for those concerned with formulating strategies to provide support for increasing numbers of elders. A significant issue with regard to aging and social relations is the changing structure of social relations as reflected in who is defined as family, patterns of friendship and organizational ties, expansion of formal support options, and living arrangements. Each of these issues will be addressed below along with a consideration of the role of age, gender, culture, and class in these relationships.

Informal Social Relations—Family

There is no doubt that families provide critical support for an aging population. Nevertheless, there is a common myth that there once existed a golden age during which older parents and their adult children mutually and willingly agreed to an arrangement that ensured the elder's material support and that this golden age has since transformed into a pervasive practice of abandonment of elders by adult children (Aboderin, 2004; Hareven, 2001). Hareven (2001) rejects this assessment and argues that changes in family roles regarding support of the elderly have more to do with redefined family functions (shifting from instrumental relationships to emotional ties) than with changes in family structure or living arrangements. While trends such as fertility and mortality rates often affect support exchanges, it may be more productive to consider and examine family composition since this accounts for the designation of who is family, as well as acknowledges the nature of these relationships and the availability of sources of informal support (Connidis, 2002).

The variation in family composition is increasingly recognized as family units cope with broad social changes. Over time and particularly evident since the 1980s, the nuclear family as the prototype of American families has become less applicable as more families break the traditional pattern through cohabitation, divorce, remarriage, and single parenthood. Families now show striking diversity with only about 6% of the population represented as two parents, one earner, two children families. Rapid change has occurred in the form of skyrocketing single-parent households and cooperative-living arrangements among nonkin adults and their families. An emphasis on the nuclear unit also ignores the increasing number of single (never married) persons and childless couples in family networks and attaches little importance to the family relationships of people who have passed the child-rearing stage—middle-aged and older adults. It also leads to the treatment of various types of family, other than nuclear family, as abnormal or less desirable (Ganong, Coleman, & Mapes, 1990). Variations in familial arrangement, however, must be more widely recognized since they reflect the diversity evident in modern society.

Family composition is also affected by demographic transitions. Greater life expectancy has had a significant impact on family structure and relations. Living longer means lengthening the amount of time spent in particular familial relationships (Farkas & Hogan, 1995; Hareven, 2001). Marriage and other intimate ties, relationships between parents and their children, between grandparents and grandchildren, and between siblings all are lasting longer. Intergenerational stake theory, combined with demographic shifts such as adult children leaving home at a later age or never leaving (Putney & Bengtson, 2001) and smaller family size (Farkas & Hogan, 1995; Hogan, Eggeboen, & Clogg, 1993), often lead to parents' greater involvement in providing financial and emotional support to their adult children. Parents' investment in children generally extends into adulthood and is strengthened with the addition of grandchildren (Farkas & Hogan, 1995). Parents can expect to know their children into their children's middle age, and an increasing number of grandparents are living to see their grandchildren reach adulthood. Now great-grandparenthood has emerged as a common life stage. Such change suggests that grandparents can sometimes play a more active role in the lives of their grandchildren (Caldwell et al., 1997).

While increased longevity also leads to an increased likelihood that multiple generations are alive at one point in time, children as main caregivers of elders continues to be the norm. The decision as to which child becomes that caregiver is often shaped by earlier experiences, gender, geographic proximity, and the "life-course continuum of reciprocal relations between the generations" (Hareven, 2001, p. 150). Family continues to serve as a major source of support for elders, however, healthcare policy in the United States has spawned a change in the mix of home care services and family support among young olds. "As people were discharged quicker and sicker, they were sent home needing more nursing care and were maintained at home under the supervision of family members, usually spouses" (Diwan & Coulton, 1994, p. 326). It still remains a fact that no real increase in home care services has occurred over the last decades, which tends to be accessed according to financial abilities as opposed to need (Diwan & Coulton, 1994). Remarriage following divorce, however, has brought new diversity within the family. "Blended families" often exhibit substantial variation in the ages of both spouses and children. Generational overlap, combined with less restrictive definitions of what constitutes family membership, makes family relations more diffuse and complex (Cherlin & Furstrenberg, 1990; Townsend, 1968; Uhlenberg, 1993). Rather than disengaging, it seems much more likely that older people are remaining active; in fact, evidence suggests that people of all ages are surrounding themselves with convoys of relationships that are flexible and changing, reflecting a more fluid and less rigid view of what a family is and what constitutes an informal social tie.

Organizational Ties and Friends

Ties with organizations and friends constitute an emerging foundation of social relations as people live longer and experience increased opportunities for diversifying social contact. Volunteer organizations are one of the major vehicles for social participation among older people. Middle-class, middle-aged women were the dominant force in the volunteer organizations in the United States during the first half of the twentieth century. Dramatic increases in labor force participation of women have made middle-aged women much less available for volunteer assignments and the young-old have become an increasingly important source of volunteers. The combination of widespread early retirement and increases in health, longevity, and affluence facilitates volunteering among older people (Bass & Caro, 2001; Caro, Morris, & Norton, 2000).

Socioeconomic status and gender seem to be those dimensions upon which cohort differences emerge with regard to social activity. For example, an examination of cohorts residing in a medium-sized city in Finland, born between 1905-1906, 1909-1910, 1917-1918, and 1921-1922 documented differences in activity levels with younger cohorts, born in 1917-1918 and 1921-1922, reporting higher interests in activities than older cohorts, born between 1905-1906 (Pohjolainen, 1991). The explanation offered relates to changes is personal characteristics, specifically higher educational and financial resources, which in turn create more opportunities. Active participation in organizations occurred more often among women in younger cohorts than women in the older cohort, although Pohjolainen (1991) reports there were no cohort differences among men regarding organizational activity, and no cohort differences for both men and women were detected regarding informal social contacts (i.e., meeting with friends).

Friendships constitute important social relations throughout adulthood. Friends provide companionship, assistance, and emotional support as they contribute to one's sense of well-being (Kastenbaum, 1993). Significant changes in people's personal environment over the past several decades have altered the importance and nature of friendship in adulthood. Particularly, with increased diversity and significantly less stability in family relations, as well as the greater autonomy that people have over the construction of their personal lives, discretional close relations, such as friendship, have become more salient in the lives of adults (Adams & Allan, 1998). Some observe increased openness and intimacy in adult friendships, particularly among women, as social values emphasized individualistic tendencies and allowed people more freedom and flexibility to construct their own personal and intimate relationships (Oliker, 1998). The degree to which these views are uniquely American is not yet completely clear, although some similarity of views has been noted by international scholars in Europe and Asia. These findings suggest little support for the disengagement theory, at least among the young old where people seem to prefer to remain actively involved in both friendship and volunteer activities. With advanced age, however, people appear to reduce the amount of informal social interactions in which they engage and appear to become more selective about their informal interactions.

Formal Support

Formal support options have steadily risen over the last half century, providing more alternatives for aid in caring for frail elders. However, the presence of this option is not necessarily accompanied by increased use (Bass & Noelker, 1987). There is little evidence to suggest that formal care services are used more frequently than informal care sources, instead findings suggest that those families possessing higher amounts of resources (i.e., income) are more apt to call upon formal home help care (Diwan & Coulton, 1994). Attitudes toward accepting formal care also differ by cohort. Those coming of age just after the Great Depression expressed more willingness to seek formal support compared to those coming of age before the Great Depression. Moreover, while objectively they fared better than the older cohort, subjectively the younger cohort was more likely to express need and deprivation than the older cohort. ". . . (as) each successive cohort of the elderly has experienced better times and a more liberal social atmosphere, they . . . feel increasingly needier and will be increasingly aggressive about getting assistance" (Moen, 1978, p. 302). Another analysis in the same period suggests that cohorts who came of age during World War II adopted more individualistic attitudes regarding family relations than those who came of age during the Great Depression and were more apt to state that government over family carry the responsibility of supporting elderly (Hareven, 2001). It is difficult to interpret these findings within the framework of existing theories of social relations. Clearly, informal ties such as family are highly valued. The value and willingness to use formal supports varies by cohort and individual resources. Intergenerational solidarity theory would argue for the continued emphasis on family support, while socioemotional selectivity most clearly suggests that with age individuals will seek less interaction with fewer people, either formal or informal ties. The convoy model, which assumes that both personal and situational characteristics will influence support exchanges, is perhaps best suited to explain the changing nature of formal relations.

Living Arrangements

One clear trend occurring over the last 50 years is the higher likelihood that elders live alone (Burnette & Mui, 1996; Diwan & Coulton, 1994; Elman, 1998). There is a reduction in the number of generations living within a household, but the essential features of kinship structure and function have remained relatively intact (Brubaker, 1990; Finch & Mason, 1990; Johnson, 1995; Wellman & Worley, 1990). Thus, although the extended family does not typically live together, multiple generations are available to one another when needed (George, 1980). Faster methods of communication (telephone, electronic mail) and travel (car, air) also became available and facilitated contact among family members who do not live in close proximity to each other. Engaging family and kin members in social exchanges were more likely to be considered voluntary and not legally binding. The term "modified extended family" was coined to describe this new type of kinship structure (Shanas, 1979).

While it is documented that greater proportions of elders live alone today than did 50 years ago, perceptions of lonely feelings do not seem to have changed. For instance, in a comparative study in Britain of cohorts aged 60 and above between 1945 and 1960 with those aged 65-74 in 1999, Victor et al. (2002) find that prevalence of loneliness is no higher or lower in 1999 than reported between 1945 and 1960. They do, however, document decreases in "never" lonely responses and slight increases in those who report that they are "sometimes" lonely. A recent study (van Tilburg, Gierveld, Lecchini, & Marsiglia, 1998) comparing older people in the Netherlands who often live alone with older people in Italy who often live with their children, found that Italians report less social integration and more loneliness than the Dutch. Thus, it may be that cultural definitions and expectations play a role (Victor et al., 2002), or it may be that simple structural aspects of relationships are not sufficiently explanatory, but instead functional or qualitative aspects of relations also critically affect an individual's health and well-being.

We turn next to a consideration of the empirical evidence available concerning cohort differences in social relations over time. We do so in an effort to better understand those factors that influence not only the social exchanges that one engages in but also how the individual interprets the social interactions that are experienced.

REVIEW OF EMPIRICAL EVIDENCE OF COHORT DIFFERENCES

Opportunities for organizational participation and various social contacts may reveal different patterns of social relations among age cohorts over time. A focused examination of social relations and how age, cohort, and time period relate to patterns of relationships, at least in the United States, was conducted in a study recently completed by the authors (Antonucci, Akiyama, & Jackson, 1998-1999). Dramatic social changes in family and work roles mark the last 50 years in the United States, and this study sought to identify the implications of these changes for both family and labor policy. As such, three core areas of social relations were examined: social contact, religious involvement, and community involvement, each carefully chosen to allow for comparability across data sets and to correspondingly tap into various dimensions of social relations.

This unique study included three nationally representative U.S. samples, which span 35 years: Americans View Their Mental Health (AVTMH), 1957 (N = 2,312); 1976 (N = 1,993); and the National Study of Families and Households (NSFH), 1992 (N = 9,946). Each study employed a national multistage-area probability sample of adults. While both AVTMH studies sampled those 21 years of age or older, and NSFH sampled those 18 years of age or older, we limit our analyses to those people age 25 and over.

Specifically, we were able to empirically examine patterns in social relations by comparing whether mean levels of social activity and contact, religious involvement, and voluntary activities varied with age and birth cohorts in the years of 1957, 1976, and 1992. A description of question format and response scales for each wave are provided below.

Social Contact

In all three waves, respondents were asked about their frequency of social contact with family and friends with the following questions: "About how often do you get together with friends or relatives—I mean things like going out together or visiting in each others' homes?" In 1957 and 1976, participants responded on a 6-point scale (1 = never; 2 = less than once a month; 3 = once a month; 4 = a few times a month; 5 = once a week; 6 = more than once a week). In 1992, participants responded on a 5-point scale (1 = never; 2 = once a year or less; 3 = once a month; 4 = once a week; 5 = more than once a week). It should be noted that in 1992, respondents were asked about contact with relatives and families separately, while in 1957 and 1976 these two categories were combined. In order to address this, we combined the 1992 questions aimed at family and friends.

Religious Involvement

Religious involvement was measured in terms of how often participants attend religious services. In 1957 and 1976, participants were asked how often they attended religious services (1 = never; 2 = a few times a year or less; 3 = once a month; 4 = two or three times a month; 5 = once a week; 6 = more than once a week). In 1992, participants indicated whether they attended services daily, weekly, monthly, or yearly. Using this information we created commensurate measures of attendance at religious services.

Community Organization Membership

In 1992, participants were asked to indicate how often they participated (the 5-point scale indicated: 0 = never; 5 = several times a week) in the following types of community organizations: (1) service clubs, fraternal groups or political groups; (2) work-related groups such as unions, farm organizations, or professional societies; (3) sports, hobby or garden organizations, or discussion groups; (4) church-affiliated groups (not including religious services). In 1957 and 1976, participants were asked the identical open-ended question: "Are you a member of any clubs or organizations—like a lodge, PTA, a community group, or any other kind of group? If yes, what are they?" The responses to the 1957 and 1976 question was coded into the four categories above, thus creating two kinds of variables: (1) whether or not respondents participate in each of the four different kinds of community groups; (2) the total number of these community groups in which they participate. These three areas, social contact, religious involvement, and community organization membership, were chosen because they seem to transcend time and historical events by remaining potentially important for all ages and cohorts, regardless of the historical point in time being considered.

Particularly unique about the approach utilized is that it allowed for the comparison of the same cohort across multiple time periods while simultaneously allowing for an examination of overall historical time effects. This cohort design is illustrated in Table 1. We first present findings related to social contact, followed by religious involvement and end with results related to community organization involvement.

Social contact, specifically the frequency with which respondents go out with or visit with friends and relatives was examined. Table 2 presents the mean response for each cohort at each time of measurement. In 1957, the effect of cohort was significant. The cohorts born between 1913 and 1932 (those between the ages of 25 and 44 in 1957) reported more personal contact than the two older cohorts, those 45 to 64 and over 65 years of age. In 1976, the pattern was similar in that the youngest cohorts (25-44) reported higher levels of contact with friends and relatives than did

Table 1. Cohort and Age Characteristics

	AVMH Time 1 (1957)	AVMH Time 2 (1976)	NSFH Time 3 (1992)
Cohort 1 (born before 1892)	65+ (*N* = 353)		
Cohort 2 (1893-1912)	45-64 (*N* = 788)	65+ (*N* = 397)	80+ (*N* = 396)
Cohort 3 (1913-1932)	25-44 (*N* = 1144)	45-64 (*N* = 674)	60-79 (*N* = 1920)
Cohort 4 (1933-1951)		25-44 (*N* = 947)	41-59 (*N* = 3358)
Cohort 5 (1952-1967)			25-40 (*N* = 4261)
Total	2285	1991	9935

Table 2. Social Contact with Friends and Relatives

	Time 1 (1957)	Time 2 (1976)	Time 3 (1992)
Cohort 1 (born before 1892)	65+ M = 1.85		
Cohort 2 (1893-1912)	45-64 M = 1.96	65+ M = 1.89	80+ M = 1.89
Cohort 3 (1913-1932)	25-44 M = 2.08	45-64 M = 1.84	60-79 M = 1.75
Cohort 4 (1933-1951)		25-44 M = 2.02	41-59 M = 1.65
Cohort 5 (1952-1967)			25-40 M = 1.81
Across Cohorts	M = 2.00	M = 1.94	M = 1.75

the older two cohorts (45-64; 65+). However, in 1992 the data revealed a somewhat different pattern of results in that the cohort born between 1933 and 1951 (41-59) reported less social contact than each of the other cohorts (25-40; 60-79; 80+).

An examination of cohorts across time revealed that while social contact with friends and relatives remained relatively constant for the cohorts born between 1893 and 1912 across all three times of measurement, for the cohorts born from 1913 to 1932 and 1933 to 1951, personal contact was lower in later time periods.

Finally, results demonstrate that social contact with friends and relatives generally was lower among those surveyed in 1992 than in 1976 and 1957. In fact, with each successive time period the mean level of personal contact decreased across all ages from an average of 2.00, to 1.94 in 1976 and 1.75 in 1992. Overall these results might best be explained by the increase in multiple roles and the amount of time people, especially middle-aged people, spent in each role. This increased time in work and family role activities must have necessarily resulted in decreased leisure time—time for organizational and volunteer activities.

Overall, contrary to popular opinion, evidence for diminished contact in old age was not found. The lowest levels of social contact with friends and relatives were found among those people who were middle aged. However, while some cohorts did not report changes in levels of personal contact over time (those born between 1893 and 1912), others did experience decreases in successive time periods (those born from 1913 to 1932 and 1933 to 1951). This finding may be attributed to age differences; that is, personal contact with friends and relatives is more likely to decrease from young age to middle age than it is to change from middle age to young old, or from young old to old old. The overall decrease in contact between 1957 and 1992 may reflect the emergence of other means of communication, including the telephone and electronic communication as well as the increased likelihood of geographic mobility due to increased education levels over time and accompanying job opportunities. In sum, the empirical evidence suggests that social relations remain strong across time periods, although type and amount of exchanges appear to vary both by age and cohort.

How do these data reflect existing theories of social relations? While there is some support for both the disengagement and activity theories considering an age-based approach, the cohort data clearly indicate that patterns of exchange have changed over time. The age pattern, indicating a decrease in social contacts as reported by young compared to older people, suggests support for the socioemotional selectivity theory. These data do not, however, permit consideration of the intergenerational solidarity theory since more or less contact does not reveal anything about the perceived solidarity experienced within those exchanges. The convoy model, on the other hand, would account for both age and cohort changes since social contact can be predicted to change with individual or personal characteristics such as age, and with situational characteristics as might be evidenced with historical change (higher likelihood of living in a multigenerational family). One historical pattern seems noteworthy, and that is the decreased social contact reported by people of all ages in 1992. Given what is known about increased hours at work, decreases in financial security, and increases in multiple roles, especially for women, these findings are alarming in that they suggest that these multiple stresses are not being offset by informal social interactions.

We turn next to a consideration of religious involvement, specifically the frequency with which people attend religious services. This form of social contact seems particularly important since it has historically often been considered an important social outlet for elders. An overview of our findings by time/year and cohort are presented in Table 3.

In 1957 there were no cohort differences in frequency of attending religious services. In 1976 individuals born between 1933 and 1951 (aged 25-44) attended religious services less frequently than those who were born between 1893 and 1932 (aged 45-64; 65+). In 1992 significant differences demonstrate a similar pattern in that the cohort born between 1913 and 1932 (aged 60-79) reported the highest average frequency of attending services.

Results that examine the cohorts aging across time illustrate a decrease in religious involvement for those born between 1893 and 1912, those 45-64 in 1957; their attendance at religious services decreased as they aged to 65+ in 1976 and 80+ in 1992. For those born between 1913 and 1932, 25-44 in 1957, the pattern is curvilinear so that the lowest frequency of religious involvement occurred in 1976, when this cohort was between the ages of 45 and 64. For both of these cohorts, religious involvement was highest in 1957. For the cohort born between 1933 and 1951, religious activity did not differ between 1976 and 1992.

Comparison of age groups over time indicates that young adults reported less religious involvement from 1957 to 1976 and 1976 to 1992. The same pattern occurred for middle-aged adults, as religious involvement was highest among middle-aged adults in 1957 and decreased across subsequent times. Among older adults, religious involvement was lowest in 1992.

Table 3. Religious Involvement

	Time 1 (1957)	Time 2 (1976)	Time 3 (1992)
Cohort 1 (born before 1892)	65+ $M = 3.72$		
Cohort 2 (1893-1912)	45-64 $M = 3.83$	65+ $M = 3.74$	80+ $M = 3.59$
Cohort 3 (1913-1932)	25-44 $M = 3.80$	45-64 $M = 3.52$	60-79 $M = 3.65$
Cohort 4 (1933-1951)		25-44 $M = 3.12$	41-59 $M = 3.20$
Cohort 5 (1952-1967)			25-40 $M = 2.97$
Across Cohorts	$M = 3.80$	$M = 3.38$	$M = 3.20$

In sum, the decrease in religious involvement suggests both life-span continuity and historical change. While it is generally true that older people are more religiously involved than younger people, it is interesting that this was not true in 1957 when people across all ages were about equally involved with religious activities and the oldest age group was least involved. Generally speaking, however, these data suggest that there is life-span continuity in that earlier age cohorts remained more religious over time than did later age cohorts—people born in 1913 were consistently more religious in 1957, 1976, and 1992, whereas people in later age cohorts were consistently less religiously involved. Finally, we present data on patterns of community organization involvement by age, time period, and cohort. Illustrative data are provided of community organization membership by time/year and cohort (see Table 4).

One might note that overall community organizational membership is relatively small across age, cohort, and time period. Nevertheless, some interesting patterns do emerge. Cohort differences within a single year are examined first. In 1957 there were cohort differences in community organization involvement. The youngest cohort (aged 25-44) in this time period, individuals born between 1913 and 1932, represented the highest proportion involved in community organizations. In 1976, however, there is no cohort effect, while in 1992 there were significant main effects of cohorts where again younger cohorts demonstrate more community involvement than did older cohorts.

Cohorts aging across time reveal a curvilinear pattern with cohorts in 1976 exhibiting the lowest levels of community involvement, and those sampled in 1992 reporting the highest levels of community organization involvement.

Comparing age groups over time illustrates significant time-period effects for middle-aged adults. Middle-aged adults (45-64) in 1992 demonstrated more community

Table 4. Community Organization Membership

	Time 1 (1957)	Time 2 (1976)	Time 3 (1992)
Cohort 1 (born before 1892)	65+ *M* = .41		
Cohort 2 (1893-1912)	45-64 *M* = .51	65+ *M* = .43	80+ *M* = .53
Cohort 3 (1913-1932)	25-44 *M* = .57	45-64 *M* = .47	60-79 *M* = .64
Cohort 4 (1933-1951)		25-44 *M* = .45	41-59 *M* = .75
Cohort 5 (1952-1967)			25-40 *M* = .73
Across Cohorts	*M* = .52	*M* = .45	*M* = .71

involvement than the other two time periods. There were also time-period effects for older adults (over 60), with the highest community involvement demonstrated in 1992. In sum, across all three time periods, the youngest cohorts report the highest levels of community activity, however, over time community involvement has varied with the most recent time period, 1992, exhibiting the highest levels of activity, significantly among both younger and older cohorts. Time period differences reveal that religious involvement decreased and community organization activity increased among older age groups, signifying that traditional roles for elders may be expanding.

General age differences in patterns of community organization membership might be interpreted as supporting the disengagement theory since people tend to report less involvement with age in all historical time periods. However, the notable increase in community organization membership suggests that both individual and situational characteristics, as noted in the convoy model, should be considered in order to fully understand community organization membership.

SUMMARY AND CONCLUSIONS

Social relations represent critical pathways to well-being over the life course. Demographic, economic, and sociopolitical changes shape the nature of social relations, creating both challenges and opportunities. Theoretical developments have moved away from considering the aging individual as living in a vacuum, as one might characterize both the disengagement and activity theories, and increasingly acknowledge the significance of historical context, personal biography, and social structural forces (Antonucci, 1985; Barresi, 1987) as indicated by the life-span developmental perspective, the socioemotional selectivity, and the convoy theories. Longer life expectancies affect the structure of family relations, but not necessarily the quality of these relationships (Connidis, 2002). Value orientations emphasizing individuality as well as longer life expectancies, decreasing birth rates, and economic growth contribute to expanding informal (i.e., friends) and formal care options, such as home help care (Adams & Allan, 1998; Diwan & Coulton, 1994; Oliker, 1998). In sum, social relations remain as critical today as they were in the past. However, the nature and structure of relations adapt to the opportunities and constraints that emerge within a given social, cultural, and historical context.

Social relations over time have incurred dynamics that speak to changing demographic realities. Historic changes include longer life expectancies coupled with familial relationships that are more fluid and less binding. As a result, network structures are more diffuse. For instance, it still remains that elders favor family to help in times of need. Spouses and children continue to be the preferred source of support (Hareven, 2001). However, blended families created by remarriage following divorce have had a significant impact on the availability of a kinship pool in late life. Any yet it is not clear whether this will emerge as a disadvantage or as an adaptive advantage. Rather than less informal support available because of less binding family relationships, it may be that more informal support will be available since the boundaries of kin networks have been widened to encompass several degrees of step-kin and in-laws, single parent families, adopted and other members (Riley & Riley, 1993). Such trends may actually widen the net of kin carers, despite the decline in fertility and weakening traditional types of family structure. Nonkin, such as professionals, friends, and neighbors have begun to play a more prominent role as sources of support and caregiving for older adults. These trends suggest that helping networks have become more diffuse, comprising others beyond family members. Obligations based on family ties no longer dictate who serves as a source of support. Instead, pragmatic realities deriving from economic and demographic shifts have increased options, while concurrently contributed to less certainty that immediate family will be available to offer support to elders. At the same time, one must recall Hareven's (2001) admonition that the golden age of family support is more myth than reality.

New patterns of social relations evident from the research reviewed and presented include living arrangements, expanding formal support options, decreased religious involvement, and increased community organization involvement. The higher tendency for elders to live alone reflects their increased economic independence, but does not inevitably signify abandonment. Contact with significant others remains and loneliness is not necessarily connected to living arrangements (van Tilburg et al., 1998; Victor et al., 2002). The life-course perspective provides a useful lens through which to understand changing trends in social relations. As the convoy model proposes, previous experiences coupled with personal biography and current opportunities contribute to support patterns. For example, the establishment of formal support options, particularly assisted living facilities and home help care agencies, reflect changing demographics; however, their use is tied to the economic status of the elder and his/her family rather than to fundamental or physical need (Bass & Noelker, 1987; Diwan & Coulton, 1994). Also, active participation in religious services and organizational ties seems to have changed over the last 50 years in the United States, particularly among elders.

Religious involvement was lowest in 1992 compared to 1957 and 1976, yet older adults (over 60) reported the highest community involvement in 1992 compared to 1957 and 1976. These trends suggest that the "modern" cohort of elders may find meaning beyond religion in old age, or perhaps reflects the varied organizational opportunities available because of changing demographic realities. As societies develop the ability to provide for basic needs, familial obligations weaken, options for other sources of support increase, and elders are, therefore, less likely to depend on traditional sources of support but also potentially more likely to increase their quality of life through the expansion of potential support sources.

Planning future programs for elders designed to improve social relations and social support must be sensitive to individuals, and yet not encourage or induce dependence (Silverstein, Chen, & Heller, 1996). Social support can be most useful when it instills in the individual a feeling of being valued and competent, of being worthy and capable. We are just beginning to understand how this might happen. Acknowledged possibilities include the exchange of support that involves both receiving and providing support, reciprocity in social relations, efficacy-enhancing exchanges, and the convergence of expectations, perceptions, and receipt of support. The next important challenge in this area is finding ways to incorporate what we know about social support specifically and social relations more generally into prevention and intervention programs that will enhance the physical and mental health of people of all ages.

On a global level, social relations among elders are inextricably tied to demographic transitions, economic development, and cultural norms. While previous theories of social relations have been useful for both guiding and explaining research, it seems clear that these patterns of social relations must reflect the intersection of historical developments and cultural norms with personal preferences and expectations. The varied ways by which elders negotiate relations with network members, both informally and formally, provide insights into pathways toward achieving an optimal quality of life and well-being both for the elderly and those who care about them.

REFERENCES

Aboderin, I. (2004). Modernization and aging theory revisited: Current explanations of recent developing world and Western historical shifts in material family support for older people. *Ageing & Society, 24,* 29-50.

Adams, R. G., & Allan, G. (1998). *Placing friendship in context.* Cambridge, MA: Cambridge University Press.

Ajrouch, K. J., Antonucci, T. C., & Janevic, M. R. (2001). Social networks among Blacks and Whites: The interaction between race and age. *Journal of Gerontology: Social Sciences, 56,* S112-S118.

Antonucci, T. C. (1985). Social support: Theoretical advances, recent findings and pressing issues. In I. G. Sarason & B. R. Sarason (Eds.), *Social support: Theory, research and applications* (pp. 21-37). The Hague: Marinus Nijhof.

Antonucci, T. C., Akiyama, H., & Jackson, J. S. (1998-1999). Aging in America: A study of three cohorts. Funded by National Institute of Health, Washington, DC.

Antonucci, T. C., & Jackson, J. S. (1987). Social support, interpersonal efficacy, and health. In L. L. Carstensen & B. A. Edelstein (Eds.), *Handbook of clinical gerontology* (pp. 291-311). New York: Pergamon Press.

Antonucci, T. C., Lansford, J. E., & Akiyama, H. (1998). Negative effects of close social relations. *Family Relations: Interdisciplinary Journal of Applied Family Studies: Special Issue: The family as a context for health and well-being, 47,* 379-384.

Baltes, P. B., Reese, H. W., & Lipsitt, L. P. (1980). Life-span developmental psychology. *Annual Review of Psychology, 31,* 65-110.

Barresi, C. M. (1987). Ethnic aging and the life course. In D. E. Gelfand & C. M. Barresi (Eds.), *Ethnic dimensions of aging* (pp. 18-34). New York: Springer.

Bass, D. M., & Noelker, L. S. (1987). The influence of family caregivers on elder's use of in-home services: An expanded conceptual framework. *Journal of Health and Social Behavior, 8,* 184-196.

Bass S. A., & Caro F. G. (2001). Productive aging: A conceptual framework. In N. Morrow-Howell, J. Hinterlong, & M. Sherraden (Eds.), *Productive aging: Concepts and challenges* (pp. 37-78). Baltimore: The Johns Hopkins University Press.

Bengtson, V. L., Rosenthal, C., & Burton, L. (1996). Paradoxes of families and aging. In R. H. Binstock & L. K. George (Eds.), *Handbook of aging and the social sciences* (pp. 253-282). San Diego, CA: Academic Press.

Brubaker, T. H. (1990). Families in later life: A burgeoning research area. *Journal of Marriage and the Family, 52,* 959-981.

Burnette, D., & Mui, A. C. (1996). Psychological well-being among three successive cohorts of older American women who live alone. *Journal of Women & Aging, 8,* 63-80.

Burton, L. M., Dilworth-Anderson, P., & Merriwether-de Vries, C. (1995). Context and surrogate parenting among contemporary grandparents. *Marriage and Family Review, 20,* 349-366.

Caldwell, C. H., Antonucci, T. C., Jackson, J. S., Wolford, M. S., & Osofsky, J. D. (1997). Perceptions of parental support and depressive symptomalogy among Black and White adolescent mothers. *Journal of Emotional & Behavioral Disorders, 5,* 173-183.

Caro, F. G., Morris, R., & Norton, J. R. (2000). *Advancing aging policy as the 21st century begins.* Binghamton, NY: Haworth Press.

Carstensen, L. L. (1993). Motivation for social contact across the life span: A theory of socio-emotional selectivity. In J. E. Jacobs (Ed.), *Nebraska symposium on motivation* (pp. 209-254). Lincoln: University of Nebraska Press.

Carstensen, L. L., Isaacowitz, D., & Charles, S. T. (1999). Taking time seriously: A theory of socioemotional selectivity. *American Psychologist, 54,* 165-181.

Cherlin A., & Furstrenberg, D. (1990). *The new American grandparent.* New York: Basic Books.

Connidis, I. A. (2002). The impact of demographic and social trends on informal support for older persons. In D. Cheal (Ed.), *Aging and demographic change in Canadian context* (pp. 105-132). Toronto: University Toronto Press.

Cumming, E., & Henry, W. H. (1961). *Growing old: The process of disengagement.* New York: Basic Books.

Diwan, S., & Coulton, C. (1994). Period effects on the mix of formal and informal in-home care used by urban elderly. *The Journal of Applied Gerontology, 13,* 316-330.

Elman, C. (1998). Intergenerational household structure and economic change at the turn of the twentieth century. *Journal of Family History, 23,* 417-440.

Farkas, J. I., & Hogan, D. P. (1995). The demography of changing intergenerational relationships. In V. L. Bengtson, K. W. Schaie, & L. Burton (Eds.), *Adult intergenerational relations: Effects of social change* (pp. 1-18). New York: Springer.

Finch, J. F., & Mason, J. (1990). Filial obligations and kin support for elderly people. *Aging & Society, 10,* 151-175.

Ganong, L. H., Coleman, M., & Mapes, D. (1990). A meta-analytic review of family structure stereotypes. *Journal of Marriage and the Family, 52,* 287-297.

George, L. (1980). *Role transition in later life.* Monterey, CA: Brooks–Cole.

Goldscheider, F. K. (1990). The aging of the gender revolution: What do we know and what do we need to know? *Research on Aging, 12,* 531-545.

Hagestad, G., & Dannefer, D. (2001). Concepts and theories of aging: Beyond microfication in social science approaches. In R. Binstock & L. George (Eds.), *Handbook of aging and the social sciences* (pp. 3-21). San Diego, CA: Academic Press.

Hareven, T. (2001). Historical perspectives on aging and family relations. In R. H. Binstock & L. K. George (Eds.), *Handbook of aging and the social sciences* (pp. 141-159). San Diego, CA: Academic Press.

Havighurst, R. J., Neugarten, B. L., & Tobin, S. S. (1968). Disengagement and patterns of aging. In B. Neugarten (Ed.), *Middle age and aging: A reader in social psychology* (pp. 161-172). Chicago, IL: University of Chicago Press.

Hochschild, A. R. (1989). *The second shift: Working parents and the revolution at home.* New York: Viking.

Hogan, D. P., Eggebeen, D. J., & Clogg, C. C. (1993). The structure of intergenerational exchanges in American families. *American Journal of Sociology, 98,* 1428-1458.

Johnson, M. (1995). Interdependency and the generational compact. *Ageing & Society, 15,* 243-265.

Kahn, R. L., & Antonucci, T. C. (1980). Convoys over the life course: Attachment, roles, and social support. In P. B. Baltes & O. Brim (Eds.), *Life span development and behavior* (Vol. 3, pp. 253-286). New York: Academic Press.

Kastenbaum, R. (1993). Disengagement theory. In R. Kastenbaum (Ed.), *Encyclopedia of adult development* (pp. 126-130). Phoenix: Oryz Press.

Levitt, M. J. (2000). Social relations across the life span: In search of unified models. *International Journal of Aging and Human Development, 51,* 71-84.

Manton, K. G. (1990). Mortality and morbidity. In R. H. Binstock & L. K. George (Eds.), *Handbook of aging and the social sciences* (pp. 64-90). San Diego, CA: Academic Press.

Moen, M. (1978). The reluctance of the elderly to accept help. *Social Problems, 25,* 293-303.

Moen, P., Robinson, J., & Fields, V. (2000). Women's work and caregiving roles: A life course approach. In E. P. Stoller & R. C. Gibson (Eds.), *Worlds of difference* (pp. 165-175). Thousand Oaks, CA: Pine Forge Press.

Myers, C. G. (1990). Demography of aging. In R. H. Binstock & L. K. George (Eds.), *Handbook of aging and the social sciences* (pp. 19-44). San Diego, CA: Academic Press.

Oliker, S. J. (1998). The modernization of friendship: Individualism, intimacy, and gender in the nineteenth century. In R. Adams & G. Allan (Eds.), *Placing friendship in context.* Cambridge, MA: Cambridge University Press.

Pearson, J. L., Hunter, A. G., Cook, J. M., Ialongo, N. S., & Kellam, S. G. (2000). Grandmother involvement in child caregiving in an urban community. In E. P. Stoller & R. C. Gibson (Eds.), *Worlds of difference* (pp. 252-259). Thousand Oaks, CA: Pine Forge Press.

Pohjolainen, P. (1991). Social participation and life-style: A longitudinal and cohort study. *Journal of Cross-Cultural Gerontology, 6,* 109-117.

Putney, N. M., & Bengtson, V. L. (2001). Families, intergenerational relationships, and kin-keeping in midlife. In M. E. Lachman (Ed.), *Handbook of midlife development* (pp. 528-570). New York: John Wiley & Sons.

Riley, M. A., & Riley, J. W. (1993). Connections: Kin and cohort. In V. L. Bengston & W. A. Achenbaum (Eds.), *The changing contract across nations* (pp. 169-189). New York: Aldine de Gruyter.

Rook, K. S. (1992). Detrimental aspects of social relationships: Taking stock of an emerging literature. In H. O. F. Veiel & U. Baumann (Eds.), *The meaning and measurement of social support* (pp. 157-169). New York: Hemisphere.

Rook, K. S. (1994). Assessing the health-related dimensions of older adults' social relationships. In M. P. Lawton & J. A. Teresi (Eds.), *Annual review of gerontology and geriatrics* (pp. 142-182). New York: Springer.

Rossi, A. S., & Rossi, P. H. (1990). *Of human bonding: Parent-child relations across the life course.* New York: Aldine de Gruyter.

Schulz, J. H. (1976). Income distribution and the aging. In R. H. Binstock, & E. Shanas (Eds.), *Handbook of aging and the social sciences* (pp. 561-591) New York: Litton Educational Publishing Co.

Serow, W. J. (2001). Economic and social implications of demographic patterns. In R. H. Binstock & L. K. George (Eds.), *Handbook of aging and the social sciences* (pp. 86-102). San Diego, CA: Academic Press.

Shanas, E. (1979). Social myth as a hypothesis: The case of the family relations of old people. *The Gerontologist, 19,* 3-9.

Silverstein, M., Chen, X., & Heller, K. (1996). Too much of a good thing? Intergenerational social support and the psychological well-being of older parents. *Journal of Marriage and the Family, 58,* 970-982.

Thoits, P. A. (1995). Stress, coping, and social support processes: Where are we? What next? *Journal of Health and Social Behavior, Extra Issue,* 53-79.

Townsend, P. (1968). The emergence of the four-generation family in industrial society. In B. L. Neugarten (Ed.), *Middle age and aging: A reader in social psychology* (pp. 255-257). Chicago: The University of Chicago Press.

Treas, J. (1995). Older Americans in the 1990's and beyond. *Population Bulletin, 50,* 2-46.

Uhlenberg, P. (1993). Demographic change and kin relationships in later life. In G. L. Maddox & M. P. Lawton (Eds.), *Annual review of gerontology and geriatrics* (pp. 219-238). New York: Springer.

U.S. Bureau of the Census. (1996). Current Population Reports. Retrieved from http://www.census.gov

van Tilburg, T., de Jong Gierveld, J., Lecchini, L., & Marsiglia, D. (1998). Social integration and loneliness: A comparative study among older adults in the Netherlands and Tuscany, Italy. *Journal of Social and Personality Relationships, 15,* 740-754.

Victor, C. R., Scambler, S. J., Shah, S., Cook, D. G., Harris, T., Rink, E., & De Wilde, S. (2002). Has loneliness amongst older people increased? An investigation into variations between cohorts. *Ageing & Society, 22,* 585-597.

Wellman, B., & Worley, S. (1990). Different strokes from different folks: Community ties and social support. *American Journal of Sociology, 96,* 558-588.

CHAPTER 5

Family Relations and Aging—Substantial Changes Since the Middle of the Last Century?

Andreas Hoff and Clemens Tesch-Römer

Families are among the oldest institutions of mankind. It is in the family context where two or more generations meet. The family is the only social institution that remains important over the entire life course, "from the cradle to the grave." Nearly every individual is born into a family. There, he or she grows up and remains embedded in family relations throughout his or her lifetime. In between are a multitude of relationships with various family members, time spent together and shared experiences, exchange of resources and mutual solidarity. According to commonly agreed-upon norms and values, families are both first and last resorts for socializing individuals and caring for them in times of need. The life experiences of any age group are closely linked to their families. Thus, examining the family ties of older individuals will result in a better understanding of what it means to be an old person (Connidis, 2001).

Families have undergone extraordinary changes at an unprecedented speed in the past century. Developments after World War II in particular have been characterized by historically rapid changes in contradictory directions. The so called golden age of marriage of the 1950s and 1960s was greatly influenced by experiences of personal hardship and misery during the 1930s (Great Depression) and the 1940s (World War II). The middle-class ideal of the "modern bourgeois family" living in economic wealth and security, with the husband earning the family's livelihood and his wife dedicating her life to family, home, and children, had long captured the imagination of the lower classes (Rosenbaum, 1978). But only the combined effects of rapidly increasing wages, universal introduction and extension of government pension schemes, and a widespread "retreat into privacy" in the 1950s enabled families from working-class backgrounds to realize that dream. The age of couples getting married fell significantly for the first time in the twentieth century, and fertility rates increased (Coontz, 2000). The married couple with children became the standard model of modern family life. A similar dominance of one family type was previously unknown and has remained so ever since.

Subsequently, family structure has moved in the opposite direction again. Married couples with children are still the most common family type; their dominance, however, has been challenged by the evolution of so-called new family forms, including single parents, cohabiting couples with children, or "patchwork families." Divorce rates have multiplied while marriage rates have decreased. At the same time, birth rates have dropped dramatically, and the number of single person households as well as the number of couples without children have significantly increased. In contrast, rising life expectancy combined with decreasing numbers of young people have resulted in an increasing weight of elders in relation to younger generations. As a consequence, we are facing a global challenge of rapidly aging societies, with the Western world and Japan being furthest down the road.

It will be a central objective of this chapter to describe consequences of demographic and family change for the family relations of today's and tomorrow's elders. We will start with some general reflections upon key concepts. Secondly, we will explore what kind of changes in the family cycle took place in the last decades and the implications of these changes on the role of older family members. We will then look at both intragenerational and intergenerational family ties of older persons and the changes that have taken place in these relations since World War II. Specifically, the relationship between aging spouses, between aging parents and adult children, and between grandparents and grandchildren will be in the focus of this section. The future of intergenerational solidarity within families as well as implications for family research and policymaking will be outlined in the concluding section. As the concepts of family cycle and life course are closely linked, we adopt a life-course perspective in the present chapter. This enables us to understand, for example, the variability in support patterns and expectations of support provision in later life (see, for example, Fry & Keith, 1982; Jackson, Antonucci, & Gibson, 1990; Kohli, 1986).

CHANGING NOTIONS ON FAMILY AND KINSHIP

Theoretical notions on family and kinship have changed in the past decades. Beginning with definitions of the concept of the family, we will discuss the broader concept of kinship and finally explore the two sides of exchanges within networks of families and kin: support and conflict.

Family

Scientific notions about the family in the middle of the last century were based on the following criteria: separation of home and workplace, relative autonomy, concentration on parent/child relationships, and a strong focus on intimate/expressive functions. Hence, a family was defined as "monogamous marriage of heterosexual adult partners" living with their legitimate biological children in "permanent kinship relation" in the same household (Peuckert, 1991). The division of labor within the family was seen as highly differentiated: whereas the male breadwinner is responsible for earning the family's livelihood in the "public" realm of society, the wife is assigned the "private" roles of being mother as well as home and care worker. Kaufmann (1990) referred to the same phenomenon as "polarization of gender roles." Another element of the modern family is its intimate/expressive function or "cultural code of romantic love" (Meyer, 1992). Compared with families in previous centuries, the evolutionary process of the separation of public and private roles was commonly seen as a constituting criterion of modern (bourgeois) society (Habermas, 1962; Geiger, 1991).

Several developments, though, challenged this view of the family. Firstly, with the increasing plurality of family forms, some of these defining criteria have become relaxed or replaced by new criteria. Marriage is no longer seen as precondition, although it has remained institutionalized in legislation (e.g., family law, constitutional protection). Similarly, the criteria of "heterosexual parenthood," "legitimacy," and "biological children" are no longer seen as essential. In this regard, legislation has started to change as well (see, for example, the legal recognition of homosexual marriages; equal treatment of legitimate and illegitimate children in inheritance law). Thus, contemporary family definitions stress as a minimal requirement the existence of "at least one parent/child relationship" (Huinink, 1995, p. 120; cf. Kaufmann, 1995, pp. 42-43).

Secondly, a life-course perspective in respect to the family cycle has been introduced into mainstream family research. Substantial parts of family research in sociology and psychology still concentrate on the reproductive stages of the family cycle, such as family formation, parenthood, and empty nest (see for instance Allan, 1999; Hill & Kopp, 2002; Schneewind, 1999). However, beginning in the late 1960s, researchers with a gerontological orientation demonstrated that there are strong family ties between aging parents and adult children (Rosenmayr & Köckeis, 1965), and that support between generations continues in aging families living apart (Bengtson & Cutler, 1976). In short, family members are a highly relevant part of the "social convoy over the life course" (Kahn & Antonucci, 1980). Hence, notions about the family have changed from household centered definitions toward the consideration of family as a network of different generations living in multiple households (Bertram, 1995).

Kinship

A concept closely related to family is kinship. The concept of kinship, however, allows a broader perspective of family relations and interactions (Allan, 1996). Kinship means relatedness based on "blood-ties." Primary kinship refers to "next of kin" or close relatives (i.e., parent/child relationships and relationships among siblings). Secondary kin includes all other "distant relatives," including aunts and uncles, nephews and nieces, cousins, etc. But there is more to kinship than relatedness through blood-ties. A higher degree of social closeness (or a lesser degree of social distance) entails different degrees of mutual obligation. Whereas relations with secondary kin tend to be "permissive" rather than "obligatory" (Firth, 1956) primary kin relations involve a high degree of mutual support obligations (Millar & Warman, 1996). A number of kinship studies undertaken between World War II and today (see, for example, Allan, 1979; Finch & Mason, 1993; Firth, Hubert, & Forge, 1970; Qureshi & Walker, 1989; Rosser & Harris, 1965; Strathern, 1981; Townsend, 1963; Young & Willmott, 1957) resulted in converging propositions. Primary kin remains important throughout a lifetime, while involvement with secondary kin is much more varied and dependent on individual circumstances. Mutual commitment decreases with genealogical distance. The nature of the relationship is determined by individual circumstances as well as by specific family network characteristics, such as the role of intermediate kin (Allan, 1996). Hence kinship (as extended family) is generally an important resource of, most notably, social support and a means of social integration that does not presuppose reciprocity. Finally, it should be emphasized that families and kin do not live in isolation, they are embedded in a broad network of social relations (for a detailed analysis of social networks of old people, see the chapter by Ajrouch, Akiyama, & Antonucci, this volume).

Support and Conflict

While the concepts of family and kinship emphasize structural aspects of social relations, the contents of social interactions should not be overlooked. "The support network is that subset of the larger social network to which a person routinely turns or could turn for assistance (or which spontaneously provides such assistance) in managing demands and achieving goals" (Vaux, 1988, p. 28). Material, practical, or emotional supports are seen as important mechanisms in maintaining individual well-being and "buffering" the individual against damaging external effects (Laireiter & Baumann, 1992). Although the positive effects of social support on individual well-being are no longer contentious, it remains unclear how exactly these effects occur. Social support was initially applied to questions of individual well-being only, but in the last 30 years or so, it has become a more abstract metaconcept that considers social aspects of providing social support as well (Veiel & Baumann, 1992). However, besides the positive aspects of social support, there has also been discussion on the possible negative aspects of social interactions and their harmful effects on well-being (Rook, 1984).

In respect to old age, it has been proposed that over the life course, people build up nonequitable relationships by providing more support in early life so that support will be available to them in later phases of the life span (Antonucci, Sherman, & Akiyama, 1996; Kahn & Antonucci, 1980). However, while the 1960s and 1970s saw emphasis on more harmonious notions of positive intergenerational exchange (most notably through the concept of "intergenerational family solidarity," Bengtson & Black, 1973; Bengtson & Cutler, 1976; Bengtson & Roberts, 1991), the last 10 years have witnessed a change toward more problematic aspects of relations in aging families. Triggered by work on the negative side of the social interaction mentioned above, theoretical conceptions of family relations in late life have undergone change. In addition to solidarity, the dimension of conflict has been added to the model of "intergenerational family relations" (Bengtson, Rosenthal, & Burton, 1990; Silverstein & Bengtson, 1997). In recent times, the concept of intergenerational ambivalence has profoundly challenged the picture of a one-dimensional, simple, and positive relationship between adult generations within a family (Connidis & McMullin, 2002; Lüscher & Pillemer, 1998). The term "intergenerational ambivalence" has been proposed to reflect the contradictions in relationships between older parents and their adult children. These contradictions might arise from the struggle between autonomy and dependency or conflicting norms regarding intergenerational relations.

In sum, theoretical notions on family and kinship have changed fundamentally in the past decades. These concepts define family relations more broadly, and reveal a rich variety of family forms and exchanges. After having discussed these changing notions on family and kinship, we will now look at changes in the family cycle from a life-course perspective.

CHANGING FAMILY CYCLE

The family cycle can be defined as a predictable sequence of family related events, which are experienced by (most) family members within his or her life course. The typical family cycle in contemporary Western societies includes events of family formation (marriage, birth of children), temporary crises (illnesses, disability), and family dissolution (divorce/separation, death).

At birth, a child automatically becomes part of an existing network of family members. Relations with siblings are characterized by a symmetry of resources and interaction. Contrarily, parent/child relations are asymmetric and hierarchic (at least) throughout childhood and adolescence—parents are in control of resources, and they exercise power in the process of socialization. During adolescence, relationships with individuals outside the family network (peer groups) are perceived as being more important than relationships with next of kin. The transitional period of children leaving their parents' home results in a fundamental change of relations between (marriage) partners. Family sociologists coined the phrase "empty nest" to describe that life phase. Parent/child relations become more balanced, though an asymmetry of resource flows may persist for some time to come until the children become financially fully independent. When children (as young adults) enter a new world of opportunities, form new social relations, find a partner, and found their own nuclear family through marriage and birth of their first child, their parents become grandparents, entering themselves into a new stage in their life course. The last stage of a partnership is the death of one partner, with women experiencing this loss more often than men. Finally, frailty may mean increased need for support from family members as the end of the life span approaches.

This short description of the family cycle is highly idealized and, if ever true for a majority, has changed fundamentally in the last decades. Although there have been several important trends, three of them are of special interest in the present context. Augmented longevity, decreasing fertility rates, and increasing plurality of family forms in particular have altered the role of old family members substantially.

Augmented Longevity

Changes in the family cycle have been caused substantially by demographic trends—notably rapidly increasing life expectancies. Average life expectancy in Germany at the end of the nineteenth century was less than 40 years (38.5 years for women, 35.6 years for men); it doubled within a century to 74.4 years for men and 80.6 years for women, respectively (Roloff & Schwarz, 2002). This was the precondition for the development of old age as a general life stage that (nearly) everybody can nowadays expect to reach. The "institutionalization of the life course" (Kohli, 1985) formalized the generalized expectations about social welfare state entitlements as well as reaching and passing through certain life phases.

Augmented longevity has important consequences for the role of the partner in aging couples. Although widowhood is still a frequent life experience in later life, typically experienced by women, the gender gap has narrowed, if not entirely closed. Increased life expectancy has led in the past decades to a higher proportion of couples living together well into old age. As a result, a reorientation in the aging couple's social relationships takes place following the empty-nest situation. Aspects of partner relations other than caring for children, such as friendship, intimacy, and companionship are revived. Friends, too, become more important again. Today, these are characteristics of an extended period of adulthood before people retire from employment and are labeled old aged or elders by society, in accordance with the "institutionalized" life stage they have now reached (see Kohli's, 1985, argument of the "institutionalization of the life course"). However, it remains true that elders have smaller social networks than younger people (Lang & Carstensen, 1998). Many older people prefer fewer contacts with a limited number of emotionally close family members or friends (Lang, 2000). The increase in life expectancy implies that aging family members will spend more joint-life time with their children and grandchildren. Hence, more grandparents today than 50 years ago may not only accompany their grandchildren into adulthood, but could also experience the birth of great-grandchildren.

Decreased Fertility Rates

Family relations have also been influenced by decreasing fertility rates. In the last five decades, fertility rates have shrunk dramatically. In West Germany,[1] for example, women had 2.1 children on average in 1950, climbing up to 2.37 in 1960. Since then, fertility rates per woman have steadily decreased to 1.38 in 2000 (Engstler & Menning, 2003). Although fertility rates started to fall from the beginning of the twentieth century, in the 1950s and 1960s fertility was well above the so-called net reproduction rate. It was in these years after World War II that the numerically large cohorts of the "baby boomers" were born. Since then, the situation has changed fundamentally: presently, the fertility rates in most Western countries are below the "net reproduction rate," although there is substantial variation between countries. This drop in fertility was fueled not only by decreasing average numbers of children per family, but also by the increasing percentages of women (and men) without children.

Declining numbers of children within families have consequences for the role of older family members. While those who became parents after World War II could expect to live in a intergenerational family network until the end of their lives, this has changed today for a large proportion of adult men and women who will grow old without the experience of parenthood (and the possible protection of family support in old age). There is a growing proportion both of singles who have been living on their own prior to growing old, as well as formerly single parents. The number and proportion of married couples who never had any children will also continue to rise. Cohabiting, not married

[1] The overall trend is the same for East Germany (though fertility rates vary slightly). The early 1990s, however, witnessed an unprecedented drop in birthrates following German unification: less than one child per woman, with the lowest fertility rate ever recorded in Germany at 0.77 in 1994. Since then, fertility rates have normalized at levels only slightly below that of West Germany (2000: 1.22 in East Germany, 1.38 in West Germany) (Engstler & Menning, 2003).

couples, however, will remain a rare exception. Family research currently sees childless people as having the highest risk of low functionality in terms of lack of family care and, hence, dependency on institutional care (Schütze, 2000).

Interestingly, grandparenthood has been influenced in a complex manner by both augmented longevity and declining fertility. On the one hand, longer life has heightened the likelihood of grandchildren having four living grandparents at birth—in 1900 this was 23.8%, in 2000 it was 67.8%. Nowadays, even a substantial proportion of adult grandchildren have living grandparents. For instance, the percentage of those having at least one grandparent when the grandchild reaches the age of 40 has increased from 1.0% in the year 1900 to 21.0% in the year 2000 (Uhlenberg & Kirby, 1998, p. 25). On the other hand, declining fertility has lead to a smaller number of grandchildren: the (estimated) number of grandchildren per woman has declined from about 12 in the year 1900 to about 6 in the year 1980, with a further declining trend (Uhlenberg & Kirby, 1998, p. 29). However, although the percentage of women without children and grandchildren is rising (around 9% and 12%, respectively in 2000), the high rates of the 1930s have not yet been reached (around 25% and 28%, Uhlenberg & Kirby, 1998, p. 28).

Plurality of Family Forms

Much has been written about so-called new family forms, including single parents, cohabiting couples with children, families living "apart-together," and so-called "patchwork families" consisting of several parent/child relations involving more than the biological parents and their kin. Demographic data in most if not all countries of the Western world provide evidence of the universal character of this development (e.g., Engstler & Menning, 2003 for Germany; Kiernan, Land & Lewis, 1998 for the United Kingdom; Teachman, Tedrow, & Crowder, 2000 for the United States). This data also shows rapidly increasing numbers of single parent families—their proportion of all families with dependent children had multiplied by the end of the 1990s, with 28% of children under the age of 18 living with a single parent in the United States (U.S. Bureau of the Census, 1998), compared to 20% in the United Kingdom (Kiernan, Land, & Lewis, 1998) and 13% in West Germany[2] (Engstler & Menning, 2003).

These trends toward plurality of family forms have influenced the relations between aging marriage partners, old parents and their adult children, and between grandparents and grandchildren. Although couples may have the chance to grow old together, there is a higher percentage of divorce at advanced age than before. Consequently, relationships with children have changed as well. Older parents may have relationships with biological and stepchildren. This has led to a larger variety of parent/child relationships, but could also imply decreased reliability of support in times of need. Finally, grandparents have become more important to grandchildren when parents separate. The rising proportion of single parent families has led to more responsibilities for grandparents in respect to financial transfers and support in (grand-)child care.

[2] The proportion of children living with a single parent in East Germany is still – 14 years after German unification – significantly higher than in West Germany.

Augmented longevity, decreased fertility, and increasing plurality in family types over the last five decades have led to changes in the life cycle. However, not only the chances of growing old together and living in an intergenerational family network have changed, but also the quality of family relationships. We will now look more specifically at the exchange and quality of three types of family relations: partners and siblings, old parents and adult children, and grandparents and grandchildren.

CHANGES IN FAMILY RELATIONS

Partners and Siblings in Old Age

The sociology of the family has mainly focused on the roles of family members in bringing up and socializing their children (Allan, 1999; Bengtson & Lowenstein, 2003). Thus, the so-called empty-nest phase marked the end of immediate parental responsibility for offspring rather than the beginning of a new stage in family life. It is the children who enter the new stage of family formation by finding a life partner, engaging in courtship, and eventually forming a new household, thereby extending the existing family network. For their parents, this period is usually described in terms of rediscovery—the middle-aged couple is pictured as being free again to reignite their partnership. In contrast, the psychological literature acknowledged the empty-nest phase as an individual developmental task of adapting to a new life situation.

Older couples tend to be more satisfied with their marriage, to have fewer conflicts, and to enjoy more intimacy and joint activities in their marriages or partnerships (Levenson, Carstensen, & Gottman, 1994). In very old age, the number of close relationships diminishes with every death of a family member; network sizes become even smaller. Due to their higher life expectancy, it is mainly women who have to cope with this loss (and the resulting lack of social contacts). In contrast, most men in the oldest age groups continue to enjoy their partners' presence throughout their late life (Wagner, Schütze, & Lang, 1999).

Social relations with brothers and sisters are special, and they become even more so in old age (Connidis, 2001), in particular, in old age when parents have become frail or died. Once our parents are dead, siblings are often the only living persons who have known us as children. We share with our siblings unique biographical and historical experiences. Thus, they become important sources of identity in old age. As with parent/child relations, frequency of contact and of mutual support is dependent on geographical proximity (Lang, 2000). Well-being derived from social relations with our brothers and sisters, however, is primarily dependent on emotional closeness and the quality of our previous relationship with our siblings (Antonucci & Akiyama, 1995; Lang & Carstensen 1998).

Old Parents and Adult Children

Historically, intergenerational solidarity is a somewhat new phenomenon. In contrast to romantic idealizations of family life in past centuries, elders in traditional, premodern societies had to earn their livelihood themselves unless they had savings that they could utilize for that purpose, which only very few had (Borscheid, 1992). Otherwise, they had to rely on what their local communities were prepared to give them, often enough not very much. This did not change until the beginning of modern society when parents' relationships with their children were emotionalized and vice versa. Only then did the expectation that adult children would look after their frail and needy parents in old age emerge and become a normative guiding principle in parent/child relations (Schütze, 2000).

The reliability of intergenerational relations has proved to be highly dependable and stable in the last decades. Parent/child relations are characterized by a high degree of mutual exchange, including financial, instrumental, and emotional support. Kohli, Künemund, Motel, and Szydlik (2000a, 2000b) found—based on data from the first wave of the German Ageing Survey (1996), a nationally representative, longitudinal study of the German community dwelling population aged 40 to 85—that old parents support their adult children primarily through financial transfers, while the younger generation predominantly reciprocates by instrumental support. These results were confirmed in the second wave of the German Ageing Survey in 2002 (Hoff, 2006a). The provision of instrumental social support is primarily dependent on geographical proximity, whereas emotional support provision depends on relationship quality (Schütze & Wagner, 1995). Hence, contrary to widespread assumptions, intergenerational relations between parents and their adult children are the most reliable relationship for people in old age.

Close relationships with their adult children remain important until the end of their lives, though for most of that time, parents do not live at the same place as their children. Rosenmayr and Köckeis (1965) coined the phrase "intimacy at a distance" to describe such parent/child relations in old age. Nevertheless, as empirical research has proven many times since, the vast majority of parents and children report "very close" or "close" mutual relationships. It is noteworthy, however, that parents perceive their relationships with their children as being even closer than the latter see their relationships with their parents[3] (Bengtson & Kuypers, 1971; Giarrusso, Stallings, & Bengtson, 1995; Kohli, Künemund, Motel, & Szydlik, 2000a).

A crucial quality of social support is its "buffering effect," the potential to mitigate harmful or negative effects (Caplan, 1974; Cassel, 1974; Cobb, 1976; Laireiter & Baumann, 1992). Trust in the accessibility of social support in times of need significantly increases a person's well-being, as the authors in Cohen and Syme (1985) demonstrated for older people. Nevertheless, most elders insist on mutuality—not being able to reciprocate reduces that positive effect considerably. But it is more than obedience to the reciprocity norm[4] that is important in this context: older people gain a lot of self-esteem when feeling needed and trusted by others (Thomae, 1994).

In contrast, severe illness and/or need of care may result in a new quality of (mainly intergenerational) family relations, especially when elders move into an adult child's household when no longer able to care for themselves. Care of dependents has always remained a core activity of contemporary families. Thus, the family is still the main

[3] Data of the German Ageing Survey provide evidence that more than three-quarters of interviewed adult children regard their relationship with their parents as close or very close, while 92.3 % of interviewed parents report such relationships with their adult children (Kohli, Künemund, Motel, & Szydlik, 2000a).

[4] For a detailed elaboration of the reciprocity norm, see Gouldner (1960).

source of long-term care. Contrary to common belief, however, care for elderly family members is a relatively recent phenomenon: first of all, not many lived long enough in previous decades, let alone centuries, to receive long-term care. Second, only recent technological improvements in medical care have enabled families to cope with the challenge of long-term care in their homes (Coontz, 2000). A strong gender bias prevails in this—it is almost exclusively women who care for family members in need. Caring has traditionally been assigned to women (the home and care workers of the "modern bourgeois family"). Some see the female role as family carer as biologically determined, citing the examples of chimpanzees and other primates, our closest relatives in the fauna. Another argument that defends this division of labor within the family as "a fact of nature" points to women's higher life expectancy compared to men. This difference is often aggravated by the tradition that men marry relatively younger women (Lang, 2000). Thus, it is mainly women who care for their frail husbands and not vice versa. When women are in need of care, it is usually other female family members, most likely their daughters (Lewis & Meredith, 1988) or daughters-in-law who will care for them. As recent research has shown, though, this may be beginning to change.

But the OASIS study, a very recent cross-nationally comparative study of intergenerational relationships in the context of five distinct European welfare-state regimes (see also the chapter by Daatland & Motel-Klingebiel in this book), provides evidence of cross-national variations in this regard. While the family-care norm was dominant in more conservative, family-oriented societies (Germany, Spain), state institutions were expected to deliver these services in Norway (Motel-Klingebiel, Tesch-Römer, & von Kondratowitz, 2003; Tesch-Römer, Motel-Klingebiel & von Kondratowitz, 2002). But even in family-oriented societies, adherence to this norm seems to vary. Thus, Schütze and Wagner (1995) found the family-care norm more prevalent among children whose parents enjoyed good health, while children caring for an elderly parent stressed the importance of institutional care.

Grandparents and Grandchildren

The most widely acknowledged family function of elders in contemporary societies is grandparenting. Contrary to widespread belief, relationships across three generations in the past were very rare and lasted only a short time (Hareven, 1994, 2001; Lauterbach, 1995). But even today, intergenerational relationships involving more than three generations are rare exceptions (Rossi & Rossi, 1990). Most members of the parent generation become grandparents at some stage nowadays thanks to extended life expectancies and improved health in old age, though fewer might get a chance to experience grandparenthood in the future as a consequence of decreasing fertility. Findings of the German Ageing Survey show that almost half of those aged 55 to 69 lived within a family network consisting of at least three generations (Kohli, Künemund, Motel, & Szydlik, 2000a).

Grandparenthood symbolizes the continuation of the family cycle and has been widely associated with intergenerational family harmony; the roles of grandparents have always been complex, heterogeneous, and dynamic (Szinovacz, 1998). Much of today's assignment of family roles to elder family members is based on the assumption and expectation that grandparents will be available and in good health to carry out these tasks, which is taken for granted nowadays and may seem self-evident, but is a relatively recent development. Many grandparents report new role identities very much different from those when they were parents with young children. In the absence of the main responsibility for the child's socialization, the grandparent/grandchild relationship is freed for other occupations, such as joint activities. Grandparents generally enjoy this role and associate it with very positive feelings and high social satisfaction (Lang, 2000). Nevertheless, grandparents continue to play a role in socializing their grandchildren. Intergenerational relationships can become important social capital that will possibly be beneficial to the cognitive and/or social development of a child (Coleman, 1990). These social resources can become a comparative advantage for children in the development of their human capital (Bourdieu, 1982; Flap & de Graaf, 1986). Lüscher and Liegle (2003) used the term "Generationenlernen" (generation learning) to describe how members of the older generations transmitted their knowledge and experiences to younger generations, including their grandchildren. They explicitly stressed the mutual character of this specific intergenerational relationship, which is that grandparents also learn from their grandchildren (for example, how to use computers).

Elders play a vital role in providing childcare for their grandchildren, thereby enabling their adult children (mainly daughters) to find employment. The availability of grandparents to care for their grandchildren has become a precondition for female employment in the absence of other alternatives. This is particularly the case in countries with lack of affordable and good-quality public childcare provision, and affects certain family forms more than others, e.g., single parents (Hoff, 2006b).

THE FUTURE OF FAMILY LIFE IN OLD AGE

Summarizing, it can be stated that there has been both change and stability in the family relations of old people within the last five decades. The family cycle has changed profoundly: the sequence of family-related events has lost its normative and predictive power. However, the exchange between family members and quality of family relationships has remained amazingly stable. In this concluding outlook into the future, a vision of future family life for elders will be developed. Short-term demographic trends (for the next 10-20 years) have to be distinguished from long-term demographic changes and their consequences for aging families. These predicted changes will be discussed with respect to the relations between the welfare state and the family. Finally, perspectives for future research will be outlined.

Short-Term Demographic Change and the Family

At the time of publication of this book, the age cohorts born during or shortly after World War II (i.e., the beginning of the observational period of this book), who married during the years of the "golden age of marriage," will approach retirement age. In other words, we do not expect to see much change in the prevalent patterns of their family relations in old age in the near future. Thanks to further increasing life expectancy, many more people will be in the position to enjoy a prolonged period of reasonably good health throughout their 60s and 70s, which will provide them with opportunities to be more actively involved in shaping family relations up to higher ages than ever before.

Facing an increasingly insecure employment situation, many young parents could be happy to take advantage of the (grand)parents' readiness to spend time with their grandchildren as well as to accept other forms of social support provided by their aging parents, not the least of which is financial and material support.[5] Hence, one can assume that the importance of family for older people will remain a stable and reliable source for the next few decades.

Long-Term Demographic Change: New Family Forms and Childlessness

However, in the long run, fundamental demographic changes could challenge the central role of the family for older people. Fewer and fewer elders will be in the position to enjoy grandparenthood due to decreasing and stagnating birth rates. By extrapolating contemporary demographic trends based on today's distribution of family forms, it is safe to assume that the proportion of singles among elders will continue to rise. Moreover, people who have lived in diverse "new" family forms will be approaching retirement age in the years to come: not much is known about what that will mean for tomorrow's elders. It has been a major concern of policymakers and family researchers alike that these new families may be incapable or less capable of fulfilling traditional family functions for their older members, especially within the context of rapidly aging societies. So far, indications of future development are rare and often contradictory.

Individuals who spent part of their life in so-called new family forms will not approach retirement age (provided it remains at the same age as it is now) until the next 10-20 years. Single parenthood and other nontraditional family forms have become a life-cycle stage through which a significant proportion of the population passes (Ford & Millar, 1998). According to estimates based on British Household Panel Study data, as many as 40% of all British mothers will have had sole responsibility for raising their children at some point in their lives (Ermisch & Francesconi, 2000). Thus, it is very likely that we will witness increasing variability and complexity as well as diminishing predictability of family relations in the decades to come; but there is no indication that the basic principles of mutual support within the family network will be undermined.

It is a different story with childless individuals: they are much more likely to be deprived of family relations in old age and of social support in case of need, particularly in very old age. Those more affluent among them may be able to compensate for lack of social support by purchasing services instead. Data from the second wave of the German Ageing Survey already provide evidence of first tendencies pointing in this direction (Hoff, 2003). In any event, childless people will need additional savings to compensate for lack of family support in old age. Otherwise, they will be entirely dependent on public service provision in this regard. It will be even more difficult to compensate for lack of family relations as a resource of joint activities. Friendship as much as partnership relations are usually maintained with members of the same generation, with the resulting dilemma that they may need support at the same time.

[5] This may change in the more distant future should current changes to public pensions systems in Europe revive the specter of old age poverty once again.

It remains to be seen if new forms of intergenerational relationships that are not based on kinship will develop.

Family and the Welfare State

The introduction of comprehensive welfare-state systems, most notably in Europe, has contributed to the decline of the family's public role during the twentieth century. On the one hand, public pension and healthcare systems relieved the family of a significant burden, permitting the majority of the population in the industrialized world to take advantage of technological progress in human medicine. Modern welfare states guarantee security in case of retirement, old-age care, sickness, invalidity, and unemployment independent of families. On the other hand, demographic aging of societies endangers the very foundations of these public achievements.

The relative importance of family relations and family support in contemporary Western societies may have diminished, but as empirical findings of many studies into the object have shown, family relations have remained a reliable and stable source of social support, despite publicly provided support alternatives. For instance, the results of the German Ageing Survey demonstrate that, despite the existence of comprehensive welfare state systems, the older generations have retained a crucial role in distributing financial and material resources within the family (Kohli, Künemund, Motel, & Szydlik, 2000a; Motel-Klingebiel, 2000), thus improving or sustaining their adult children's living standard. The flow direction of intrafamilial transfers is opposite to that of social insurance systems, in particular public pension schemes (Kohli, Künemund, Motel, & Szydlik, 2000a). This outcome confirms earlier German findings based on Family Survey data (Marbach, 1994) and findings from France (Attias-Donfut, 1995) and can be interpreted as an indicator of the persistence of a cascade model of social support.

As outlined above, older, childless individuals without significant financial means are likely to become dependent on public-service provision and may become a new target category of social-policies for the aged. Current social-policy reform in Europe is almost entirely focused on cost containment. The most obvious examples are public pensions and healthcare systems. Political and mass media rhetoric paints an image of intergenerational conflict. What has been missing so far are cross-sectional, integrated concepts of generation policies, as suggested by Lüscher and Liegle (2003). The argument is that the challenges of an aging society can only be met by a joint effort of all generations that requires concerted public policies crosscutting the policy domains of family policy, aging policy, educational policy, and policy on children. We feel inclined to add the remaining fields of social-policy action, since these are based on intergenerational support (albeit as a societal category) too.

IMPLICATIONS FOR FUTURE RESEARCH, THEORY FORMATION, AND POLICY RECOMMENDATIONS

Resulting implications for future research and theory formation need to be suggested. The future distribution of labor between private and public responsibilities will be among the main challenges. It is an open question as to whether the resulting conflict of private versus public interests will be driven by pragmatic considerations, such as lack of public funding, or whether we will see a revival of a moral rhetoric to justify a retreat of the state at the expense of the family (which translates, in fact, at the expense of women). However, given the combined effects of radical-norm changes as to the role of women in the family and society plus the prospect of a dwindling workforce in coming years (due to low birthrates in most European countries in recent decades), a return to the traditional division of labor in the family, with women devoting their lives to the housewife role, is neither conceivable nor desirable.

Yet the challenge of aging societies could result in a revival of functionalist approaches in family and aging research. Although family change is irreversible, we assume that academics and policymakers alike may return to more functional perceptions of scientific thought than in the past two decades. Future family research as well as gerontological research will have to focus a good deal of attention on the consequences of family change, notably the so-called new family forms and childless people, for family relations in old age. Henceforth, it will be advisable to use the potential of longitudinal research designs in order to describe, understand, and explain the development of family relations across the life course. Currently, much effort has been focused on specific life stages only, which is illustrated by the labels attached to these surveys (e.g. Family Survey, Aging Survey, Youth Survey). Instead, we recommend designing long-term longitudinal studies to explore the development of intergenerational relationships across the life course.

A subsequent challenge will be comparing the outcomes of these national surveys cross-nationally or cross-culturally, and designing cross-national surveys for studying the development of intergenerational relations (see, for example, the European study OASIS that is described in more detail in the chapter by Daatland & Motel-Klingebiel in this volume). The need for cross-cultural research on intergenerational relations and resulting policy implications is aggravated by the prospect of aging societies as a global phenomenon, with the developing countries expected to catch up with these demographic trends at an even more rapid pace than in the industrialized world in the past decades. Thus, by 2030 about three-quarters of older people worldwide will be living in developing countries (Pohlmann, 2002). Keeping in mind the absence of social-welfare-state systems in these countries, which even today find it extremely difficult to meet the basic needs of their populations, it is hard to imagine how intergenerational relations and family networks will cope with an increasingly aging population proportion under these circumstances. Global aging is likely to become the main challenge of the twenty-first century—cross-cultural family research may contribute to mastering that challenge.

REFERENCES

Allan, G. (1979). *A sociology of friendship and kinship.* London: Allen and Unwin.

Allan, G. (1996). *Kinship and friendship in modern Britain.* Oxford: Oxford University Press.

Allan, G. (Ed.). (1999). *The sociology of the family.* Oxford: Blackwell.

Antonucci, T. C., & Akiyama, H. (1995). Convoys of social relations: Family and friendships within the life span context. In R. Blieszner & V. H. Bedford (Eds.), *Handbook of aging and the family* (pp. 355-371). Westport, CT: Greenwood Press.

Antonucci, T. C., Sherman, A. M., & Akiyama, H. (1996). Social networks, support, and integration. In J. E. Birren (Ed.), *Encyclopedia of gerontology* (Vol. 2, pp. 505-515). San Diego, CA: Academic Press.

Attias-Donfut, C. (1995). *Les solidarités entre générations: Vieillesse familles, État* [Solidarity between generations: Aging families]. Paris: Nathan.

Bengtson, V. L., & Black, K. D. (1973). Intergenerational relations and continuities in socialization. In P. B. Baltes & K. W. Schaie (Eds.), *Life-span developmental psychology: Personality and socialization* (pp. 207-234). New York: Academic Press.

Bengtson, V. L., & Cutler, N. E. (1976). Generations and intergenerational relations: Perspectives on age groups and social change. In R. H. Binstock & E. Shanas (Eds.), *Handbook of aging and the social sciences* (pp. 130-159). New York: Van Nostrand Reinhold Company.

Bengtson, V. L., & Kuypers, J. A. (1971). Generational difference and the developmental stake. *Aging and Human Development, 2,* 249-260.

Bengtson, V. L., & Lowenstein, A. (Eds.). (2003). *Global aging and challenges to families.* Hawthorne, NY: Aldine de Gruyter.

Bengtson, V. L., & Roberts, R. E. L. (1991). Intergenerational solidarity in aging families: An example of formal theory construction. *Journal of Marriage and the Family, 53,* 856–870.

Bengtson, V. L., Rosenthal, C., & Burton, L. (1990). Families and aging: Diversity and heterogeneity. In R. H. Binstock & L. K. George (Eds.), *Handbook on aging and the social sciences* (3rd ed., pp. 263-287). San Diego: Academic Press.

Bertram, H. (1995). Individuen in einer individualisierten Gesellschaft [Individuals in an individualized society]. In H. Bertram (Ed.), *Das Individuum und seine Familie* [The individual and his family] (pp. 9-34). Opladen: Leske + Budrich.

Borscheid, P. (1992). Der alte Mensch in der Vergangenheit [The old person in the past]. In P. B. Baltes & J. Mittelstraß (Eds.), *Zukunft des Alterns und gesellschaftliche Entwicklung* [The future of aging and societal development] (pp. 35-61). Berlin: de Gruyter.

Bourdieu, P. (1982). *Die feinen Unterschiede. Kritik der gesellschaftlichen urteilskraft* [Distinction: A social critique of the judgment of taste]. Frankfurt/Main: Suhrkamp.

Caplan, G. (1974). *Support systems and community mental health: Lectures on concept of development.* New York: Behavioral Publications.

Cassel, J. (1974). An epidemological perspective of psychological factors in disease etiology. *American Journal of Public Health, 64,* 1040-1043.

Cobb, S. (1976). Social support as moderator of life stress. *Psychosomatic Medicine, 38*(5), 300-314.

Cohen, S., & Syme, S. L. (Eds.). (1985). *Social support and health.* New York: Academic Press.

Coleman, J. S. (1990). Foundations of social theory. Cambridge/MA: Belknap.

Connidis, I. (2001). *Family ties and aging.* Thousand Oaks: Sage.

Connidis, I. A., & McMullin, J. A. (2002). Sociological ambivalence and family ties: A critical perspective. *Journal of Marriage and the Family, 64,* 558-567.

Coontz, S. (2000). Historical perspectives on family studies. *Journal of Marriage and the Family, 62,* 283-297.

Engstler, H., & Menning, S. (2003). *Die Familie im Spiegel der amtlichen Statistik* [The family in national statistics] (Extended new ed.). Bonn: Bundesministerium für Familie, Senioren, Frauen und Jugend (BMFSFJ).

Ermisch, J. F., & Francesconi, M. (2000). The increasing complexity of family relationships: Lifetime experience of single motherhood and stepfamilies in Great Britain. *European Journal of Population, 16,* 235-249.

Finch, J., & Mason, J. (1993). *Negotiating family responsibilities.* London: Routledge.

Firth, R. (1956). *Two studies of kinship in London.* London: Athlone.

Firth, R., Hubert, J., & Forge, A. (1970). *Families and their relatives.* London: Routledge and Kegan Paul.

Flap, H. D., & de Graaf, N. D. (1986). Social capital and attained occupational status. *The Netherlands' Journal of Sociology, 22,* 145-161.

Ford, R., & Millar, J. (1998). Lone parenthood in the UK: Policy dilemmas and solutions. In R. Ford & J. Millar (Eds.), *Private lives and public responses. Lone parenthood and future responses in the UK* (pp. 1-21). London: Policy Studies Institute.

Fry, C. L., & Keith, J. (1982). The life course as a cultural unit. In M. W. Riley, R. P. Abeles, & M. S. Teitelbaum (Eds.), *Ageing from birth to death* (pp. 51-70). Boulder: Westview Press.

Geiger, T. (1991). *Demokratie ohne Dogma* [Democracy without dogma] (4th ed.). Berlin: Duncker & Humblot.

Giarrusso, R., Stallings, M., & Bengtson, V. L. (1995). The "intergenerational stake" hypothesis revisited: Parent-child differences in perceptions of relationships 20 years later. In V. L. Bengtson, K. W. Schaie, & L. M. Burton (Eds.), *Adult intergenerational relations: Effects of societal change* (pp. 227-263). New York: Springer.

Gouldner, A. W. (1960). The norm of reciprocity: A preliminary statement. *American Sociological Review, 25,* 161-179.

Habermas, J. (1962). *Strukturwandel der Öffentlichkeit—Untersuchungen zu einer Kategorie der bürgerlichen Gesellschaft* [The structural transformation of the public sphere]. Darmstadt: Neuwied.

Hareven, T. K. (1994). Aging and generational relations: A historical and life course perspective. *Annual Review of Sociology, 20,* 437-461.

Hareven, T. K. (2001). Historical perspectives on aging and family relations. In R. H. Binstock & L. K. George (Eds.), *Handbook of aging and the social sciences* (5th ed., pp. 141-159). San Diego: Academic Press.

Hill, P. B., & Kopp, J. (2002). *Familiensoziologie* [Sociology of the family] (2nd ed.). Opladen: Westdeutscher Verlag.

Hoff, A. (2003). *Family change and intergenerational support—Source of new ine-quality in old age?* Conference Proceedings of the 6th Conference of the European Sociological Association (ESA), "Ageing Societies, New Sociology," September 23-26, 2003, Murcia, Spain.

Hoff, A. (2006a). Intergenerationale Familienbeziehungen im Wandel [Changing intergenerational family relations]. In C. Tesch-Römer, H. Engstler, & S. Wurm (Eds.), *Altwerden in Deutschland. Sozialer Wandel und individuelle Entwicklung in der zweiten Lebenshälfte* [Getting old in Germany. Social change and individual development in the second half of life] (pp. 231-287). Wiesbaden: Verlag für Sozialwissenschaften.

Hoff, A. (2006b). *Lone mothers between the welfare state and informal support.* Lewiston: The Edwin Mellen Press.

Huinink, J. (1995). *Warum noch Familie? Zur Attraktivität von Partnerschaft und Elternschaft in unserer Gesellschaft* [Why still having a family? About the attractiveness of partnership and parenthood in our society]. Frankfurt/Main: Campus.

Jackson, J. S., Antonucci, T. C., & Gibson, R. C. (1990). Cultural, racial and ethnic influences on aging. In J. Birren & K. W. Schaie (Eds.), *Handbook of psychology of aging* (pp. 103-123). San Diego: Academic Press.

Kahn, R. L., & Antonucci, T. C. (1980). Convoys over the life course: Attachment, roles, and social support. *Life Span Development, 3,* 253-286.

Kaufmann, F. X. (1990). *Zukunft der Familie. Stabilität, Stabilitätsrisiken und Wandel der familialen Lebensformen sowie ihrer gesellschaftlichen und politischen Bedingungen* [The future of the family. Stability, stability risks, and change of familial life forms as well as their societal and political conditions]. München: Beck.

Kaufmann, F. X. (1995). *Zukunft der Familie im vereinten Deutschland. Gesellschaftliche und politische Bedingungen* [The future of the family in the united Germany. Societal and political conditions]. München: Beck.

Kiernan, K., Land, H., & Lewis, J. (1998). *Lone motherhood in twentieth-century Britain. From footnote to front page.* Oxford: Clarendon.

Kohli, M. (1985). Die Institutionalisierung des Lebenslaufs. Historische Befunde und theoretische Argumente [The institutionalization of the life course. Historical findings and theoretical arguments]. *Kölner Zeitschrift für Soziologie und Sozialpsychologie, 37,* 1-29.

Kohli, M. (1986). Social organization and subjective construction of the life course. In A. B. Sorenson, F. E. Weinert, & L. R. Sherrod (Eds.), *Human development and the life course: Multidisciplinary perspectives* (pp. 271-292). Hillsdale: Lawrence Erlbaum.

Kohli, M., Künemund, H., Motel, A., & Szydlik, M. (2000a). Generationenbeziehungen [Intergenerational relations]. In M. Kohli & H. Künemund (Eds.), *Die zweite Lebenshälfte. Gesellschaftliche Lage und Partizipation im Spiegel des Alters-Survey* [The second half of life. Societal circumstances and participation in the German Ageing Survey] (pp. 176-211). Opladen: Leske + Budrich.

Kohli, M., Künemund, H., Motel, A., & Szydlik, M. (2000b). Families apart? Intergenerational transfers in East and West Germany. In S. Arber & C. Attias-Donfut (Eds.), *The myth of generational conflict. The family and state in ageing societies* (pp. 88-99). London: Routledge.

Laireiter, A., & Baumann, U. (1992). Network structures and support functions—Theoretical and empirical analyses. In H. O. F. Veiel & U. Baumann (Eds.), *The meaning and measurement of social support* (pp. 33-55). New York: Hemisphere.

Lang, F. R. (2000). Soziale Beziehungen im Alter: Ergebnisse der empirischen Forschung [Social relations in old age: Results of empirical research]. In H.-W. Wahl & C. Tesch-Römer (Eds.), *Angewandte gerontologie in schlüsselbegriffen* [Applied gerontology in keywords] (pp. 142-147). Stuttgart: Kohlhammer.

Lang, F. R., & Carstensen, L. L. (1998). Social relationships and adaptation in late life. In B. Edelstein (Ed.), *Comprehensive clinical psychology. Vol. 7: Geropsychology* (pp. 55-72). Oxford: Elsevier Science.

Lauterbach, W. (1995). Die gemeinsame Lebenszeit von Familiengenerationen [The joint life time of family generations]. *Zeitschrift für Soziologie, 24,* 22-41.

Levenson, R. W., Carstensen, L. L., & Gottman, J. M. (1994). The influence of age and gender on affect, physiology, and their interrelations: A study of long-term marriages. *Journal of Personality and Social Psychology, 67,* 56-68.

Lewis, J., & Meredith, B. (1988). *Daughters who care. Daughters caring for mothers at home.* London: Routledge.

Lüscher, K., & Liegle, L. (2003). *Generationenbeziehungen in Familie und Gesellschaft* [Intergenerational relations in family and society]. Konstanz: UVK.

Lüscher, K., & Pillemer, K. (1998). Intergenerational ambivalence: A new approach to the study of parent-child relations in later life. *Journal of Marriage and the Family, 60,* 413-425.

Marbach, J. H. (1994). Tauschbeziehungen zwischen Generationen: Kommunikation, Dienstleistungen und finanzielle Unterstützung in Dreigenerationenfamilien [Exchange relations between generations: Communication, services, and financial support in three-generation-families]. In W. Bien (Ed.), *Eigeninteresse oder Solidarität. Beziehungen in modernen Mehrgenerationenfamilien* [Self-interest or solidarity. Relationships in contemporary multi-generational families] (pp. 163-196). Opladen: Leske + Budrich.

Meyer, T. (1992). *Modernisierung der Privatheit. Differenzierungs- und Individualisierungsprozesse des familialen Zusammenlebens* [The modernization of privacy. Differentiation and individualization processes in families]. Opladen: Westdeutscher Verlag.

Millar, J., & Warman, A. (1996). *Family obligations in Europe.* London: Family Policy Studies Centre.

Motel-Klingebiel, A. (2000). *Alter und Generationenvertrag im Wandel des Sozialstaats. Alterssicherung und private Generationenbeziehungen in der zweiten Lebenshälfte* [Old age and intergenerational contract in the context of a changing welfare state. Social security in old age and private intergenerational relationships]. Berlin: Weißensee Verlag.

Motel-Klingebiel, A., Tesch-Römer, C., & von Kondratowitz, H. J. (2003). The role of family for quality of life in old age—A comparative perspective. In V. L. Bengtson & A. Lowenstein (Eds.), *Global aging and challenges to families* (pp. 327-354). Hawthorne, NY: Aldine de Gruyter.

Peuckert, R. (1991). *Familienformen im sozialen Wandel* [Family forms and social change]. Opladen: Leske + Budrich.

Pohlmann, S. (2002). Ageing as a global phenomenon. In S. Pohlmann (Ed.), *Facing an ageing world—Recommendations and perspectives* (pp. 1-12). Regensburg: Transfer Verlag.

Qureshi, H., & Walker, A. (1989). *The caring relationship.* London: Macmillan.

Roloff, J., & Schwarz, K. (2002). Bericht 2001 über die demographische Lage in Deutschland mit dem Teil B "Sozioökonomische Strukturen der ausländischen Bevölkerung" [Report 2001 about the demographic situation in Germany. Part B "Socio-economic structures of the foreign population"]. *Zeitschrift für Bevölkerungswissenschaft, 27,* 3-68.

Rook, K. S. (1984). The negative side of social interaction: Impact on psychological well-being. *Journal of Personality and Social Psychology, 46,* 1097-1108.

Rosenbaum, H. (1978). *Familie als Gegenstruktur zur Gesellschaft. Kritik grundlegender theoretischer Ansätze der westdeutschen Familiensoziologie* [The family as a counter-structure of the society. Critique of fundamental theoretical approaches of the West German sociology of the family]. Stuttgart: Enke.

Rosenmayr, L., & Köckeis, E. (1965). *Umwelt und Familie alter Menschen* [Environment and family of old people]. Neuwied: Luchterhand.

Rosser, C., & Harris, C. (1965). *The family and social change.* London: Routledge and Kegan Paul.

Rossi, A. S., & Rossi, P. H. (1990). *On human bonding: Parent-child relationships across the life-course.* Hawthorne, NY: Aldine de Gruyter.

Schneewind, K. (1999). *Familienpsychologie* [Psychology of the family] (2nd ed.). Stuttgart: Kohlhammer.

Schütze, Y. (2000). Generationenbeziehungen [Intergenerational relations]. In H.-W. Wahl & C. Tesch-Römer (Eds.), *Angewandte Gerontologie in Schlüsselbegriffen* [Applied gerontology in keywords] (pp. 148-152). Stuttgart: Kohlhammer.

Schütze, Y., & Wagner, M. (1995). Familiale solidarität in den späten phasen des familienverlaufs [Family solidarity in the later phases of family life]. In B. Nauck & C. Onnen-Isemann (Eds.), *Familie im Brennpunkt von Wissenschaft und Forschung* [The family in the focus of science and research] (pp. 307-327). Neuwied: Luchterhand.

Silverstein, M., & Bengtson, V. L. (1997). Intergenerational solidarity and the structure of adult child-parent relationships in American families. *American Journal of Sociology, 103*(2), 429-460.

Strathern, M. (1981). *Kinship at the core.* Cambridge: Cambridge University Press.

Szinovacz, M. E. (1998). Research on grandparenting: Need refinements in concepts, theories, and methods. In M. E. Szinovacz (Ed.), *Handbook on grandparenthood* (pp. 257-288). Westport, CT: Greenwood.

Teachman, J. D., Tedrow, C. L. M., & Crowder, K. D. (2000). The changing demography of America's families. *Journal of Marriage and the Family, 26,* 1234-1246.

Tesch-Römer, C., Motel-Klingebiel, A., & von Kondratowitz, H.-J.(2002). Die Bedeutung der Familie für die Lebensqualität alter Menschen im Gesellschafts- und Kulturvergleich [The importance of the family for the quality of life of older people in cross-national and cross-cultural comparisons]. *Zeitschrift für Gerontologie und Geriatrie, 35,* 335-342.

Thomae, H. (1994). Trust, social support, and relying on others. *Zeitschrift für Gerontologie, 27,* 103-109.

Townsend, P. (1963). *The family life of old people.* Harmondsworth: Penguin.

Uhlenberg, P., & Kirby, J. B. (1998). Grandparenthood over time: Historical and demographic trends. In M. E. Szinovacz (Ed.), *Handbook on grandparenthood* (pp. 23-39). Westport, CT: Greenwood.

U.S. Bureau of the Census. (1998). Statistical Abstract of the United States: 1998 (11th ed.). Washington, DC: U.S. Government Printing Office.

Vaux, A. (1988). *Social support. Theory, research, and intervention.* New York: Praeger.

Veiel, H. O. F., & Baumann, U. (1992). The many meanings of social support. In H. O. F. Veiel & U. Baumann (Eds.), *The meaning and measurement of social support* (pp. 1-12). New York: Hemisphere.

Wagner, M., Schütze, Y., & Lang, F. R. (1999). Social relationships in old age. In P. B. Baltes & K. U. Mayer (Eds.), *The Berlin Aging Study: Aging from 70 to 100* (pp. 282-301). Cambridge: Cambridge University Press.

Young, M., & Willmott, P. (1957). *Family and kinship in East London.* London: Routledge and Kegan Paul.

CHAPTER 6

Elders as Care Receivers: Autonomy in the Context of Frailty

Steven H. Zarit and Elizabeth R. Braungart

For the past 25 years, family caregiving has been a prominent focus of gerontological research and practice. This emphasis has led to many important findings about the role of families and the burdens they experience; but this emphasis has caused us at times to lose sight of the person receiving care. From both legal issues and ethical perspective, older people themselves should be at the heart of decision making about their care, but their status as dependent often results in the presumption that they are no longer capable of making decisions for themselves. As a result, their preferences about the kind of care they would like to receive and their opinions about the care they are receiving have frequently been overlooked in the literature and in everyday practice. In this chapter, we propose that older people need to be included in the decision-making process about care, both for ethical and practical reasons; and that programs and services need to incorporate their perspective, even in situations when they can no longer articulate their needs. We look first at the theoretical and legal basis for autonomy. We then discuss the involvement of people who are cognitively intact in determining care preferences. The final section addresses issues of incorporating the perspective of people with dementia in planning their own care, including approaches for determining their preferences and examples of innovative programs that support their autonomy.

GIVING PEOPLE A VOICE IN THEIR OWN CARE: THEORETICAL AND LEGAL ORIGINS

There are many good reasons for why the values and beliefs of people receiving care should be reflected in the kind of assistance they receive. For practical reasons, people will be more amenable to and cooperative with care that shows respect for their individuality. A strong rationale for including the perspective of care receivers draws upon work in two separate domains: the social psychology of aging, which has stressed that autonomy and control are basic components of well-being, and legal developments concerning the rights of people to be involved in decisions about their own care.

Personal Control and Well-Being

Personal control has been defined and measured in numerous, and sometimes overlapping ways: locus of control, mastery, primary and secondary control, and self-efficacy to name a few (see Skinner, 1995). The various definitions include beliefs about control as well as actions to assert control over a situation. Whatever the particular construct, there is a consensus, backed by empirical evidence, that people who believe that they have more control function better in most, but not all, circumstances. Schulz, Wrosch, and Heckhausen (2003) have even argued that seeking control represents a fundamental evolutionary trend. As evidence of the widespread acceptance of the idea that control is linked to adaptation, control beliefs have been incorporated into multidimensional frameworks for characterizing well-being (e.g., Ryff, 1995).

It is generally assumed that feelings of personal control decline with aging, or at least with some of the events associated with aging. It can be hypothesized, for example, that loss of control results from a decline in an older person's resources and influence, or because of illness and disability that restricts the person's ability to assert control in some situations (Krause, 2003). The empirical evidence about decline in control appears mixed, and may depend on the particular control construct and measure. Global measures of control such as feelings of mastery often remain stable over time, while perceptions of control in specific domains may decline (e.g., Aneshensel, Pearlin, Mullan, Zarit, & Whitlach, 1995; Femia, Zarit, & Johansson, 1997; Johnson & Barer, 1997; Schulz et al., 2003). Schulz and colleagues (2003), for example, posit that older people are less likely to use strategies to maintain active control strategies, or what they call primary control, and are more likely to increase their use of secondary control, for example, redefining goals in a situation.

Some early gerontological theories suggested that giving up control and accepting dependency was developmentally appropriate (e.g., Goldfarb, 1969; Jung, 1933). From this perspective, older people should learn to let others help them in a graceful way. Giving up control was an implicit part of disengagement theory (Cumming & Henry, 1961), and in Erikson's (1963) characterization of the psychosocial challenge of aging as "integrity versus despair." These theories, however, were not without criticisms. Disengagement theory in particular led to a strong counterattack that emphasized the role of activity and staying involved as adaptive in later life (Havighurst, 1968).

Over time, the debate between disengagement and activity theory gradually lost its force. P. Baltes (1987) reformulated these issues in his developmental model of selective optimization with compensation (SOC). Acknowledging that there are losses associated with aging, P. Baltes suggested that people may maintain valued activities by developing compensatory strategies and by conserving energy and resources for those activities by discarding less-important involvements. Selective optimization is an active process in which people make choices about their preferences. Löckenhoff and Carstensen (2003) apply the theory of selective optimization with compensation to control, arguing that people may maintain primary control over valued roles and activities, but give up control in other areas.

A compelling observational study of the oldest old (85+) conducted by Johnson and Barer (1997) illustrates the relation of personal control and SOC. In that study, older people living at home often experienced multiple illnesses and growing levels of disability that greatly restricted their mobility. To compensate, they conserved energy by rarely venturing out and by maintaining a strict basic routine that allowed them to exercise control over the tasks that were necessary to support their independence. In other words, they exercised control in an area that was important and valued (maintaining their household), doing so by cutting back on other activities. In another study of the oldest old, Femia et al. (1997) found that people with higher feelings of global mastery were less likely to decline over time in their performance of everyday activities.

The link between control and adaptation may be strongest in institutional settings. Despite speculation that people who were more dependent or accepting of their situation would do better (Felton & Kahana, 1974), studies of adaptation to institutionalization have suggested that loss of control has a variety of deleterious effects, including increased mortality (Schulz & Brenner, 1977).

Institutional settings have long been characterized as taking control away from their "inmates" (Goffman, 1962). In his critique of nursing homes, Kahn (1975; Kahn & Zarit, 1974) posited that institutional settings take away independent activities and decision making. This increased dependency leads to the loss of ability to perform activities, or what Kahn called "excess disabilities." According to Parmalee and Lawton (1990), interactions in institutional settings are influenced by the autonomy-security dialectic. From this perspective, autonomy and security are basic human needs. Although institutions usually try to support individual differences in values and lifestyle, they are faced with myriad regulations that tip the balance toward an emphasis on security over autonomy. The risks associated with actions that might result in harm or injury far outweigh the positive good that might result from allowing people the opportunity to exercise greater control over behavior. Consider the person who walks with an unstable gait. The positive consequences of allowing that person autonomy is that he or she will be able to maintain functioning longer and will be able to move around the facility independently. Should that person fall, however, he or she could break a bone, and the institution might receive a fine from the authorities and be sued by the family. An individual living independently can willingly assume that risk, but the consequences of an adverse event in an institution are too severe to tolerate potentially dangerous behavior. As a result, institutions end up making a variety of large and small decisions over how the person lives and spends his or her time. The rules and routines give little opportunity for expression of individual autonomy in areas as diverse as when one wakes or goes to bed, what one eats, or even who one socializes with. Consistent with the notion of person-environment fit (Lawton & Nahemow, 1973), the impact of institutional control will be greater on people who value autonomy more and who retain a greater ability to exercise individual decisions.

This cycle of dependence and decline in institutional settings was depicted in a series of groundbreaking studies by Margret Baltes and her colleagues (M. Baltes & Horgas, 1997; M. Baltes, Kindermann, Reisenzein, & Schmid, 1987; M. Baltes & Reisenzein, 1986; M. Baltes & Wahl, 1992). Drawing upon structured observations of interactions in nursing homes, M. Baltes and colleagues described staff as following "dependency-support scripts," that is, giving residents support and attention when they acted in a dependent way and when they allowed staff to help them in their self-care behaviors. Conversely, staff often ignored or punished residents who tried to perform their own care. Residents themselves reported being acquiescent when staff tried to help, and not performing activities even when they were still able to do so (Wahl, 1991). Family caregivers also sometimes follow these dependency scripts (M. Baltes & Horgas, 1997).

Although the links among control, adaptation and well-being need further examination in both community and institutional settings, the available findings indicate that opportunities to exercise control over preferred activities is adaptive and linked to improved functioning and well-being. This relation appears to hold both among healthy older people, as well as those with mental and physical dependencies. A major challenge for care is to identify how people who have lost control in basic abilities can still exercise some control in their daily lives. As we shall see, most care remains mired in a dependency framework, but a few new models of care create opportunities for personal control.

Autonomy and the Legal Status of Care Receivers

The role of personal control in the lives of older people has a parallel in the emphasis on personal autonomy in the legal system. Principles of autonomy, which have a long tradition in Western law, have recently been extended to encompass older people. Autonomy can be contrasted with the principle of beneficence, which was applied implicitly or explicitly when decisions had to be made about an older person. Beneficence assumed that certain classes of people (mentally ill, elderly) could not make informed decisions about their medical care or how they were leading their life, and so it was necessary for an unbiased person to make judgments that reflected the best interests of the other individual. Autonomy, by contrast, emphasizes reliance on an individual's own judgment whenever possible or on what that person previously indicated as his or her preferences in the event of no longer being competent to make decisions.

Autonomy depends on competence to make informed decisions. Changes in our concept of competence have given more people a potential voice in decisions over how they live. In the past, legal definitions of competence were broad, and in some jurisdictions "old age" was a sufficient criterion for being declared incompetent (Willis, 1996). Likewise, the procedures for determining if someone was incompetent were vague, often requiring only presentation of a medical opinion. In the United States, new laws at the state level have made the definition and procedures for determining competence more specific. These laws make a number of important distinctions (see Sabatino, 1996, for a review). First, a basic principle is that a person is considered to be competent, unless court proceedings decide otherwise. From a legal standpoint, another person, even a family member, cannot take over decision making for finances, healthcare or where the person should live without a determination of competency. People who are competent, however, can grant power-of-attorney to another individual to make those kinds of decisions in the event they become unable to do so. Second, competence is viewed as multidimensional, rather than all-or-none. A person may be found not to be competent to manage his or her money, but may be able to make other decisions. Third, a medical diagnosis such as Alzheimer's disease is not sufficient evidence by itself to declare someone incompetent. There must instead be objective findings that the person is impaired in specific abilities. Finally, there is recognition that a person may be only temporarily incapacitated and may recover the ability to make decisions for him/herself.

Autonomy in Everyday Decisions

It is hard to know how much this new legal emphasis has changed everyday decisions. It was fairly common in the past for family or medical personnel to make the decision to place a person in an institution, even when that individual was not mentally incapacitated, and this situation probably continues today. In many instances, families try to take the person's preferences and values into account. People without family or other advocates, however, are particularly vulnerable to receiving care they have not chosen.

There are at least three factors that limit autonomy among older people. The first is the laziness and lack of imagination of some providers of care to older people. It is often easier, for example, to place a person in an institution than to arrange for community services to keep someone at home, where he or she prefers to live. Care managers and other providers may take this route because they do not have the time or patience to arrange for home services. The piecemeal system of services and funding for care in the United States adds a layer of difficulty in arranging care at home that is not found in countries that have universal access and affordability of services (Shea et al., 2003). Consistent with the autonomy-security dialectic, some providers may be afraid of the liability involved if they do not place a frail person in a setting that provides around-the-clock supervision and care.

A second challenge is the belief among physicians and other healthcare professionals that they know what is best for the patient. This type of paternalism is gradually fading away, but may still be fairly common. Giving people autonomy in their decision making can, of course, lead to some complex dilemmas, for example, when a person willingly and competently chooses a course of action that increases the risk of harm or even death. Many healthcare professionals would have difficulty with this kind of situation, even when they otherwise value personal autonomy.

The third challenge is that supporting the patient's preferences may undermine the well-being of family caregivers. Doctors and other health professionals frequently tell families to institutionalize an older relative out of concern for the caregiver's well-being. There are compelling findings that caregivers can suffer adverse emotional and health effects because of the strain caused by caregiving, including increased risk of mortality (Schulz & Beach, 1999). Aneshensel and colleagues (1995) found that the interests of people with dementia and their family caregivers were in conflict around the question of institutionalization. For patients, remaining at home was associated with lower mortality, while for caregivers, keeping the patient at home longer led to an erosion of well-being. Although we stress autonomy of care receivers in the following sections, it is important to keep in mind the potential risks to caregivers. Supporting autonomy without also addressing the concerns of families and, in some cases, staff in institutional settings, would be irresponsible. One of the most compelling questions in the field is the extent to which supportive services can effectively reduce strain on caregivers while maintaining well-being of care receivers.

CARE OF ELDERS: DECISION MAKING AND AUTONOMY

We view personal control and autonomy as basic principles for evaluating the care that people receive. Certainly, many other dimensions could be considered, such as the quality of interactions between helpers and care receivers as well as the features and resources within an institutional setting. We believe, however, that personal control provides an overarching framework within which these other qualities can be evaluated; that is, that caregivers and programs that assist dependent elders can be judged by the extent to which they support the autonomy and respect the preferences and individuality of the person receiving care.

We begin our discussion of personal control in decision making by examining its most basic component: the extent to which care receivers' views have been elicited and taken into account in providing care. It is clear that the ability to express such preferences is highly dependent on the care receiver's capacity to communicate effectively. The great dividing line in communication in old age care is between people with and without cognitive impairment. Although nonimpaired older adults may have some difficulty in communicating their preferences, people with dementia pose a more daunting, though not insurmountable challenge. As noted, competence is not an all-or-nothing distinction, and dividing people into categories of impaired versus nonimpaired oversimplifies the situation. However, we argue that in discussing care preferences, the distinction is a valuable one due to the fact that impaired adults encounter unique challenges in expressing their preferences. For that reason, we have divided the rest of the chapter into two sections. In the first section, we will review what is known about eliciting the preferences of cognitively intact people in planning their own care and how they can be empowered to exercise more control over their care. In the second section, we will look at people with dementia in terms of their ability to convey their own preferences about care; and then will view how programs for them can support autonomy.

CARE OF COGNITIVELY INTACT ELDERS: RESPECTING PERSONAL PREFERENCES

The literature on care preferences of cognitively-intact older adults can be organized into two major topics: preferences for end-of-life decisions, such as use of life-sustaining medical treatments; and preferences for formal and informal care services during a period of dependency. A brief review of empirical findings related to these issues is provided.

End-of-Life Decisions

The majority of studies of care preferences focus on end-of-life decisions. Some research, for example, focuses on predictors of specific end-of-life choices. Bookwala and colleagues (2001) found gender differences regarding values about death and use of technology to sustain life. In general, men supported life-sustaining treatments more so than women and were also more likely to endorse specific types of treatment, such as CPR (cardiopulmonary resuscitation), surgery, and artificial feeding. Hamel and colleagues (Hamel et al., 2000) posited that age is a predictor of preferences for life-sustaining measures. In a large sample of seriously ill patients, older individuals preferred less-aggressive methods of sustaining life than their younger counterparts. Nonetheless, families underestimated the levels of aggressive care that they thought their older family member desired. Studies such as these indicate that preferences for end-of-life care may not be invariable and may not always be accurately assessed by younger family members. This has important implications for cases where substituted judgments are needed for end-of-life decisions of an incapacitated person. Current research is attempting to better understand the relationships involved in these issues in hopes of being able to represent more accurately care receivers' preferences.

One of the most promising tools for determining preferences for end of life care is the advance directive. The advance directive is a signed and witnessed legal document in which a person outlines his or her preferences for care and designates a proxy who would be able to make decisions about care and treatment should the person become unable to do so. This document came into widespread use in the United States in the 1990s following a highly publicized court case where the family of a young woman in a persistent vegetative state argued that she had previously expressed preferences not to have her life extended by artificial means. The court decision in that case (Cruzan vs. Director, Missouri Dept. of Health) affirmed that people had the right to determine their preferences about medical care, even if they subsequently became incompetent (Brechling & Schneider, 1993). Thus, the advantage of the advance directive is that it allows the person's choices to be taken into consideration in his or her own treatment, and family members and doctors are not left to guess what the person would have wanted. In addition, as a legal document, it can be used in court, should a dispute over a person's medical care arise. Because this form needs to be filled out while the person is cognitively able to do so, it involves early planning, but when done correctly it may be the best way to represent the wishes of a person, even if that individual has subsequently become incapacitated.

In the United States, the Patient Self-Determination Act of 1990 required all Medicare/Medicaid providers to advise patients of their right to use advance directives in making healthcare decisions. All 50 states have enacted legislation supporting advance directives, however, there are no definitions or legislation at a national level that would allow for the creation of a standardized form that would be valid throughout the country (Gunter-Hunt, Mahoney, & Sieger, 2002). Despite the fact that different states use different definitions and different formats in their creation of advance directives, the various approaches can be grouped into three general categories: the living will, the Durable Power of Attorney for Health Care (DPAHC), and the advance health care directive. A living will is a signed, dated, and witnessed document in which a person answers questions regarding his or her wishes on particular end-of-life medical treatments. The Durable Power of Attorney for Health Care allows a person to formally designate a surrogate decision maker who will act on behalf of this person should he or she become unable to do so alone. This tool is slightly broader than a living will, allowing for the surrogate to make decisions about treatment and care, as well as decisions on end-of-life issues (Brechling & Schneider, 1993). The advance healthcare directive includes a combination of the previous forms; it designates a surrogate and also outlines specific instructions for end-of-life medical treatments (Gunter-Hunt et al., 2002).

Despite the support that advance directives have received from researchers and advocates, only a minority of the population in the United States (5%-25%) has utilized these documents (Bravo, Dubois, & Paquet, 2003; Douglas & Brown, 2002; Fazel, Hope, & Jacoby, 1999; Hahn, 2003). Some of the reasons why people report not using them include: (1) lack of understanding of what they are, (2) lack of information about them, (3) lack of access to the forms, (4) lack of understanding of how to complete the forms, (5) lack of discussion with a physician, and (6) lack of family agreement on the end-of-life treatment preferences (Douglas & Brown, 2002). There are some discrepancies in the literature, however, research shows that people who are more likely to have advance directives are older (Bravo et al., 2003; Brechling & Schneider, 1993; Douglas & Brown, 2002), women (Bravo et al., 2003; Douglas & Brown, 2002), Caucasians (Douglas & Brown, 2002), in poorer health (Douglas & Brown, 2002) and/or know someone with dementia (Bravo et al., 2003). Education has been linked to the use of advance directives, for example, Brechling and Schneider (1993) found that higher education was a significant predictor of the use of advance directives. Moody, Small, and Jones (2002) found that of their participants who had advance directives, those with higher education were more likely to support living wills, DNR (do not resuscitate) orders, no hospitalization orders, and no medication and treatment orders.

Advance directives are not without problems. In a study of healthcare professionals, Thompson, Barbour, and Schwartz (2003) found evidence that despite the labeling of specific medical treatments in the forms, the advance directives were still open to interpretation either because they were worded too ambiguously or because healthcare professionals drew different conclusions about the "right thing to do." Surrogates may also not be able to interpret accurately the preferences the patient has listed in his or her advance directives (Ditto et al., 2001). Because it may be difficult to apply the scenarios listed on the forms when the actual clinical circumstances involved are different, some researchers have tried using values-based directives instead of scenario-based directives. Approaches such as Pearlman's values history (PVH) (Pearlman, Starks, Cain, Rosengren, & Patrick, 1998) allow people to describe their values and goals in terms of end-of-life scenarios, which in turn can be applied by the surrogate in a broader range of situations. Research in which older adults were randomly assigned to fill out either the PVH or Emanuel's Medical Directive (EMD; a scenario-based advance directive) found that both groups had positive reactions to the forms, but more people in the EMD group felt the form gave them control over a physician's treatment at the end of life. On the other hand, more people in the EMD group worried that if they changed their minds later it would be harder to change their choices, and fewer people in the EMD group actually named a surrogate. In other words, there were pros and cons to both of these approaches.

Preference for Care

As stated previously, in addition to end-of-life issues, the other main area of research for care preferences in cognitively intact elders focuses on preferences for personal care during periods of dependency. Types of care generally fall into two categories: informal and formal assistance. Informal assistance includes help from spouses or other family members, friends, and neighbors, while formal assistance includes help from paid in-home services, assisted-living facilities, and nursing homes.

While some researchers have argued that older people nearly uniformly prefer informal family assistance over formal care (Cantor, 1979), a study by Pinquart and Sörensen (2002) found that only a minority of their sample of U.S. and German elderly favored informal help alone, and half of the sample preferred a combination of formal and informal services. Men, people with more children, and those who had a higher frequency of contact with their relatives were more likely to favor informal assistance. In addition, preferences for care were associated with the length of care needed. Informal and mixed assistance was preferred for shorter-term-care needs, but formal assistance was favored for long-term-care needs. This study, like others, also found national and ethnic trends in preferences for care. West Germans' responses were similar to those of the U.S. participants, however, people from the former East Germany had a greater preference for informal assistance and had less preference for mixed assistance. A nationwide study of Swedish individuals over the age of 65 found that participants strongly preferred informal services, and most support with activities of daily living that they received was, indeed, from informal sources (Johansson & Thorslund, 1992). Formal services were preferred only for people who needed the most care.

While many studies have found that people often prefer informal over formal services, Roberto, Allen, and Bleiszner (2001) caution that this is not always the case. They found that having a conflictive family relationship was related to making future care plans that did not include family assistance. Other authors posit that even in supportive family relationships, many older adults do not want to burden their children and therefore prefer to utilize formal services (McCullogh, Wilson, Teasdale, Kolpakchi, & Skelly, 1993).

Based on these findings, it becomes clear that there is variability in preferences for care during times of needed assistance, as well as variability in preferences for how to handle life-sustaining treatment. Research has shown that some of this variability can be accounted for by factors such as age, gender, ethnicity, family context, severity of deficits, and nationality. While studies such as these help uncover the predictors of care preferences for most of the population, determining the preferences of people with dementia offers unique challenges.

CARE OF PEOPLE WITH DEMENTIA

The difficulty in determining care preferences for people with dementia is how to best incorporate individual preferences and values when people cannot indicate their preferences clearly. The problem varies, of course, depending on the severity of cognitive impairment. In early stages of dementia, it may still be possible to elicit people's preferences and to engage them in meaningful ways in planning for their later care. As the disease progresses, however, these opportunities are lost, and there may be little direct communication on which to base decisions about care. We begin the section by discussing how to determine preference in early-stage and then in later-stage dementia. We then look at programs and services that allow people with pronounced cognitive difficulties to exercise autonomy and personal control.

Communication of Preferences in Early-Stage Dementia

Increasingly, diagnosis of Alzheimer's and other dementias is taking place earlier in the course of the disease. When people are identified in the early stages of dementia, there is an opportunity for engaging them in decisions about their care (Cotrell & Schulz, 1993; Feinberg & Whitlatch, 2002). Even in middle stages, many people with dementia are able to verbally reflect upon their care experiences (Simmons et al., 1997).

Case studies have found that people who are mildly to moderately impaired are able to discuss their feelings and opinions, and make self-assessments about their quality of life and status of their health (Parmelee, Lawton, & Katz, 1989). Even when people make errors in identifying time and place, they still may be able to make decisions about many aspects of their own healthcare. The problem, though, is that it is sometimes difficult to tell who is and who is not capable of competent decisions. Complicating the situation is the fact that the people with dementia can fluctuate in cognitive clarity from day to day or even within the day (Brechling & Schneider, 1993). There are no good standardized methods of determining decision-making capacities in people with dementia (Gerety, Chiodo, Kanten, Tuley, & Cornell, 1993). Widely used global measures of cognitive impairment, such as the Mini Mental State Examination (MMSE) (Folstein, Folstein, & McHugh, 1975), are particularly ineffective in predicting who has the ability to make preferences and choices (Ashford et al., 1992).

The lack of viable measurement tools, however, does not negate the ability to elicit care preferences. Cheston, Bender, and Byatt (2000) reviewed the methodologies used in assessing care satisfaction and found that structured or semistructured interviews are generally preferred over written forms or questionnaires that may seem confusing to the patient. In a study that included both persons with dementia and their caregivers, Feinberg and Whitlatch (2001) found that interviewing people with mild dementia can generate reliable information about preferences.

Despite the fact that it is possible to measure care preferences, very few studies have done so. In one innovative project, Feinberg and Whitlatch (2002) asked people with dementia and their caregivers (independently) about the patient's preferred sources of care within multiple categories of needs. The results indicated that for all categories of activities of daily living, people with dementia preferred informal assistance over formal services, and 73% of them said it was very important not to live in a nursing home. Ninety percent were able to identify someone as a surrogate decision maker and, of those capable of doing so, 93% named a family member as this surrogate. In addition, caregivers' and care receivers' responses about care preferences were highly congruent. The success of this study in identifying care preferences necessitates a more careful look at when and to what extent people with dementia can competently direct their own future care. This study also identifies the burden placed on informal caregivers who face the prospect of providing most of the care to their relative if they are to support his or her preferences.

Advance Directives and Dementia

Despite the sometimes mixed findings about having people with dementia complete advance directives, researchers have suggested that it may not be "too late" for some cognitively impaired people to put a directive in place. A potential barrier is the attitudes of physicians who believe that a diagnosis of dementia automatically determines a person to be too incompetent to fill out an advance directive (Markson, Kern, Annas, & Glantz, 1994). Nonetheless, as indicated, many early-stage and at least some mid-stage patients may be able to indicate their end-of-life preferences. In a sample that included early- and middle-stage patients, Fazel et al. (1999) found that 20% were capable of completing an advanced directive with assistance from a surrogate, especially those people with a higher premorbid intelligence. It should be noted, however, that this study did not provide details on the exact procedures used for involving impaired patients, nor how evaluations were made to determine a person's capability of completing an advanced directive. Clearly, additional information is needed to better understand the circumstances under which people with dementia can express their preferences. Eliciting preferences as early as possible in the disease process would be the most ideal situation, although there may be options for people who have waited "too long."

The idea of providing directives for other kinds of care is also emerging. Brechling and Schneider (1993) propose that advance directives should cover plans for housing needs, preferences for participating in research, the decision to use or not use long-term-care insurance, decisions about the management of personal property, and decisions about driving ability, in addition to end-of-life medical choices. The legal standing of these broad directives remains to be established; and there are potential problems, such as the possibility that a person will insist on remaining at home, no matter what, despite the limited physical and financial resources of family caregivers. But some form of advance planning, whether prior to the onset of dementia or in its early stages, can be very useful in helping families and other caregivers provide assistance that it consistent with the person's own preferences and values.

Mid- to Late-Stage Dementia

As dementia progresses, people's ability to communicate preferences and make competent judgments declines. As a result, it is not uncommon for other people, whether family caregivers or paid helpers, to take over for patients, sometimes with little regard to their preferences or values. Care situations can become dehumanized, with family or staff expressing little recognition of the person's identity or needs.

Responding to the lackluster and dehumanizing care that people with dementia often receive, Kitwood (1997) argued in his influential book, *Dementia Reconsidered,* that at least part of their behavioral and emotional problems were the result of the pathological interactions they had with other people. As a way of countering these negative influences, he proposed a person-centered approach to the care. Person-centered care is built around recognition of the basic humanity of the patient (Woods, 1999a, 1999b). It gives them a voice in their care by taking into account their past preferences as well as their personal and cultural identity. It also stresses learning how to recognize that they communicate through their emotions rather than cognition. By developing person-centered programs and care settings, it is possible to emphasize quality of life as they might define it themselves.

Kitwood and his colleagues (e.g., Kitwood & Bredin, 1994) developed an assessment tool, Dementia Care Mapping (DCM), that evaluates the quality of interactions in settings that serve people with dementia in ways that are consistent with a person-centered approach. DCM is designed to be used by a trained observer. The observer follows the activities, behaviors, and responses of the patient, as well as the care that he or she is receiving during the time of observation. By taking note of the actions and reactions of both the patient and the institution's staff, this method provides an opportunity to assess the quality of care, and also gives feedback to the staff about the satisfaction of care. The method is designed to give the person a "voice" in his or her care experiences. While some authors caution that the observed assessment is not necessarily identical to the experience (Barnett, 1997), the tool has still been viewed as a successful way to use person-centered care in determining unmet needs (Cheston, Bender, & Byatt, 2000).

Other methods have been developed for eliciting patient preferences. Family Stories Workshops and other similar programs have been successful in providing staff with information about past preferences and by emphasizing the self of the patient (Clarke, Hanson, & Ross, 2003; Hepburn et al., 1997). The workshops are opportunities for the person with dementia, his or her family, and the staff within the nursing home to listen to biographical narratives, delivered by friends and family members about that person. Photographs of the person throughout his or her life may also be brought in, and stories about the person, as well as his or her personal preferences, are discussed as a group. Results from studies such as these conclude that both staff and families find these sessions helpful in drawing attention to the identity of the patient. Although more empirical testing of these programs is needed, initial results indicate that staff find these sessions help them deliver more individualized care, and understand and deal with the idiosyncrasies of their patients (Clarke et al., 2003; Hepburn et al., 1997).

The biographical narrative and dementia-care mapping tools are both examples of person-centered programs in institutional settings that are designed to individualize the person with dementia. These programs remind us that institutions can focus on both medical and emotional needs and are able to gather information about past or present preferences and reactions of patients, despite the fact that they may be unable to communicate verbally.

AUTONOMY IN PROGRAMS AND SERVICES FOR PEOPLE WITH DEMENTIA

Other types of programs have attempted to support autonomy and quality of life for people with dementia in institutional settings. In a necessarily brief and selective review, we describe programs that elicit the views of these patients and that encourage autonomy. As before, we begin with early-stage programs, and then discuss care in later stages of the disease.

Early-Stage Programs

The type of help most likely to be available for early stage patients is support groups (e.g., Goldsilver & Gruneir, 2001; Yale, 1989; 1999). Early-stage support groups allow patients and caregivers the opportunity to share their feelings and learn from one another (Yale, 1999). Participants learn about resources and form bonds with others with the same condition. Clare (2002) has observed that two pivotal issues in early-stage groups are how much to focus on seeking a cure and how much to emphasize coming to terms with the disease and its consequences.

Little evaluation has been done to date on early-stage programs. Moniz-Cook and her colleagues (Moniz-Cook, Agar, Gibson, Win, & Wang, 1998) used a highly individualized treatment program for early-stage people that provided, in varying degrees, information about the disease, strategies for coping, memory improvement strategies, and linking to community services. The results indicated better outcomes for both patients and caregivers, compared to a no-service control group.

Another approach, called Memory Club, is a structured, time-limited group that involves both people with early stage dementia and their family caregivers in a series of discussions around key issues in dementia, including information about the disease, planning for the future, and finding ways to strengthen the dyad's relationship in the face of the changes that are taking place (Zarit, Femia, Watson, Rice-Oeschger, & Kakos, 2004). In each of the 10 sessions, people with dementia and their "care partners" meet together for part of the time and separately for part of the time. Some of the issues raised in the separate sessions are brought back for joint discussion at the end, but participants may decide that other issues are too sensitive, at least for the time being, for discussions with their relative. An evaluation of Memory Club included the perspective of both caregivers and their patients (Zarit et al., 2004). Caregivers reported that they valued the information and support they received from the leaders. They also rated highly having the opportunity to get together with and learn from other people in their circumstances. People with dementia also rated their experience in the group highly, valuing the information they received and the support from leaders. Interestingly, they were less positive than the caregivers about being with people in a similar situation to them. There are two implications of these findings. First, people with early-stage dementia can participate in the evaluation in a meaningful way, and second, it remains to be determined whether a group intervention is the best approach for them.

Middle- and Late-Stage Programs

In middle- and late-stage programs, the challenge of finding ways to support people's individuality and autonomy is considerably greater. Few studies have incorporated the perspective of care receivers in the evaluation of programs and services (Zarit, Gaugler, & Jarrott, 1999), and so data are lacking on many important points of care. Despite this limitation, some useful concepts for guiding care have emerged from the literature. One principle is the importance of keeping people engaged in usual activities. Activity may help maintain self-esteem, reduce boredom, and delay functional decline. It may even head off problems such as restlessness and difficulty falling asleep at night. We can also assume that we are supporting individual preferences; that is, that people will enjoy the activities that they liked in the past.

In a similar way, maintaining people in familiar settings may be useful. People with dementia may be able to preserve habits in their usual setting, since familiar stimuli may trigger those behaviors. Of course, as any caregiver knows, there can be difficulties, such as when patients no longer recognize their home. Nonetheless, there is probably a better likelihood that a home-like environment will elicit appropriate behavior as well as feelings of comfort as opposed to an institutional setting.

An interesting adaptation of the principle of familiarity is home day care, a program developed in Scotland in which private persons operate small-scale programs in their own homes for people with dementia (Mitchell, 1999). The activities in these programs are built around normal social routines, for example, serving tea and lunch, conversation, as well as games and outings. A definitive evaluation remains to be done, but preliminary reports suggest that the program can be implemented and sustained effectively.

One of the most promising approaches for supporting both patients and families is adult day services (ADS). By providing care on a regular basis, ADS programs reduce family caregivers' exposure to care-related stressors and allow them uninterrupted time to take care of other needs. Although the results of evaluations of the impact of ADS have been mixed, caregivers who use this service on a regular basis experience decreases in primary subjective stress associated with care and also lower feelings of depression and anger (Zarit, Stephens, Townsend, & Greene, 1998). Care receivers may also benefit (Jarrott, Zarit, Stephens, Townsend, & Greene, 1999; Zank & Schacke, 2002). Jarrott and colleagues found that caregivers reported improvements in patients' behavior as a result of their use of ADS. Patients were evaluated as more alert, having fewer behavior problems and sleeping better following use of ADS. Caregivers also reported that their relative had few adjustment problems associated with going to or coming home from ADS, such as refusing to go in the morning or getting upset with the caregiver after attending the program. There remains a need for a more systematic study of the effects of ADS on the mood and behavior of clients, as well as an examination of how particular programs and activities might affect clients.

A pioneering strategy for supporting family caregivers is "holiday relief" or overnight respite, as it is more commonly called. These programs provide short-term placement for people with dementia and other serious disabilities, allowing caregivers to get a sustained break. There is ongoing interest in this type of arrangement, and the program can be found on a small scale in some European countries and in North America. This type of program, though, may pose a considerable challenge to patients who have difficulty adjusting to change. In one of the few evaluations of overnight respite, Burdz, Eaton, and Bond (1988) found that clients, most of whom had dementia, had fewer behavior problems and better physical functioning after two weeks of institutional care. The source of the reports, however, was caregivers, so it is possible that the perceived improvements were the result of the relief they experienced, rather than objective changes in the care recipient.

As this example illustrates, our reliance on caregivers as the main source of information about the value of any particular service or program can be problematic. They are neither unbiased in their assessments, nor are they trained to make systematic observations. Staff ratings can also be valuable but are subject to the same limitations. As people with dementia lose the ability to report on their own well-being, other strategies need to be employed to assess the impact of various programs and services. Observational approaches such as Dementia Care Mapping have the potential to overcome communication difficulties. Using this approach, Jarrott and Bruno (2003) evaluated the effects of patient participation in an innovative program of intergenerational activities. During interactions with children, these patients had a more positive affect than when engaging in activities with their age peers. More of the intergenerational activities led to person-centered interactions as well. These results demonstrate how a promising assessment strategy can be used to evaluate programs.

One of the greatest challenges is improving care in institutional settings. Given their difficulties communicating and the prevailing therapeutic nihilism that has not changed much since Goffman's (1962) classic formulation of the total institution, these patients often experience uninspired, demoralizing, and sometimes degrading care. New types of programs have been developed, however, that support autonomy and provide more personalized care (Cohen & Day, 1994; Cohen & Weissman, 1991; Lidz & Arnold, 1990; Regnier & Scott, 2001). These programs include special care units in nursing homes, as well as assisted living and similar facilities that emphasize a social, rather than medical model of care. They typically use environmental designs that encourage social participation while minimizing typical dementia-related problems, such as trying to leave. There is also an emphasis on familiar activities to help residents remain active and retain their functional competencies as long as possible (Malmberg, 1999; Malmberg & Zarit, 1993). Of course, not all "special" dementia programs incorporate therapeutic design or programming, and many offer little more than a marketing brochure and locked door (Regnier & Scott, 2001). Nonetheless, there are now notable models that demonstrate the possibility of providing residences that emphasize quality of life.

Many promising programs have been developed in Britain, the Scandinavian countries, and the Netherlands (Regnier, 1994, 2002; Regnier & Scott, 2001). In Sweden, small group homes for dementia patients were developed nationwide (Malmberg, 1999; Malmberg & Zarit, 1993). Group homes are small, with five to seven residents living in two linked units; the design of facilities and programming emphasizes autonomy. Residents have their own apartments and, indeed, sign a lease for it. They have keys to their apartments and can go inside when they want and lock the door. The apartments typically open out into a common area that includes a kitchen, dining room, laundry facilities, and recreational areas. The exit is secured so that residents cannot go outside without supervision. Thus, autonomy is created within a limited domain—residents are free to roam within the facility or to have privacy within their own apartments, but their access to the wider world is limited. Residents' autonomy is supported in other ways: they furnish and decorate apartments with their own belongings. Staff encourages them to perform familiar activities, such as setting a table or loading a dishwasher. The small scale of the facilities and high staff to resident ratio (3 staff for every 10 residents during the daytime, 2 during the evening, and 1 at night) assures that personal relationships develop.

The particular settings for group homes vary. Some have been developed within traditional institutions, and others are located in apartment complexes or even homes that have been reconfigured to provide a secure entrance and exit. A definitive evaluation of group homes has not been made, but observations of programs suggest that residents are able to function well in this setting, with few behavioral disturbances (Malmberg & Zarit, 1993). Despite the apparent success of group homes, however, there is now a trend to integrate people with dementia back into mixed-care units.

Programs such as group homes for dementia patients raise a number of intriguing hypotheses about how environmental design and programming may affect behavior and quality of life. A central question is whether the autonomy offered within those types of programs, as well as the homelike surroundings, provide more comfort and security to residents than an institutional setting. A related issue is the value of the homelike setting and routines built around a typical person's day in eliciting established habits and socially appropriate behavior. As an example, group homes maintain the strong Swedish tradition of coffee breaks, which give a structure and familiarity to the day. Contrast coffee breaks to the typical nursing home regimen where residents have little social interaction with one another, and routines are set according to staff needs. The goal of engaging in familiar activities, whether coffee breaks, or setting or clearing the table, is to help residents remain independent for a longer period of time; but whether that happens remains to be determined.

Although there are now very intriguing models for residential care, and more than two decades experience with these types of settings, there has been surprisingly little evaluation of how specific design and program features are associated with resident outcomes. The results of the available literature are mixed, sometimes supporting innovative models and sometimes not finding clear differences. In one sobering example, Kuhn and his colleagues (Kuhn, Kasayka, & Lechner, 2002) found little difference in activities or quality of life between residents with dementia in small, dementia-specific assisted living facilities and those living in larger sites that were not dementia-specific. Staff in both types of setting spent most of their time attending to basic needs and had little time left for more individualized social and leisure activities. Clearly, the claims of proponents of these programs must be evaluated carefully.

CONCLUSIONS

Despite the extensive focus on disability in later life, we understand relatively little about the experiences of people who receive care. We have posited that personal control and autonomy play a critical role in adaptation, not only for healthy, older people, but also for the disabled. Control may become focused on fewer activities, and the person may conserve resources to be able to participate in more highly valued tasks. One way of approaching the question of control is by understanding ways that people can express their preferences about care. This can be done both for cognitively intact people as well as those suffering from dementia, although the task becomes increasingly difficult as cognitive functioning worsens. Autonomy can also be incorporated into the design of programs, so that people can exercise control in many everyday matters.

As the older population grows and the need for a variety of services increases, there will be pressure to provide care in the most cost-efficient manner. Standardization of care to increase efficiencies and decrease staff costs will, in all likelihood, undercut support for individual differences and preferences. The challenge ahead is to base care on sound principles and not just cost. These principles should place the needs and preferences of care recipients at the heart of our care system. We need to find ways to support autonomy and personhood even in the face of serious disability, and to evaluate and disseminate the imaginative models of care that successfully implement these concepts.

REFERENCES

Aneshensel, C., Pearlin, L. I., Mullan, J. T., Zarit, S. H., & Whitlatch, C. J. (1995). *Profiles in caregiving: The unexpected career.* New York: Academic Press.

Ashford, J. W., Kumar, U., Barringer, M., Becker, M., Bice, J., Ryan, N., & Vicari, S. (1992). Assessing Alzheimer's severity with a global clinical scale. *International Psychogeriatrics, 4,* 55-74.

Baltes, M. M., & Horgas, A. L. (1997). Long-term care institutions and the maintenance of competence: A dialectic between compensation and overcompensation. In S. L. Willis, K. W. Schaie, & M. Hayward (Eds.), *Societal mechanisms for maintaining competence in old age* (pp. 142-164). New York: Springer.

Baltes, M. M., & Reisenzein, R. (1986). The social world in long-term care institutions: Psychosocial control toward dependency? In M. M. Baltes & P. B. Baltes (Eds.), *The psychology of control and aging* (pp. 315-343). Hillsdale, NJ: Erlbaum.

Baltes, M. M., & Wahl, H. W. (1992). The dependency-support script in institutions: Generalization to community settings. *Psychology and Aging, 7*(3), 409-418.

Baltes, M. M., Kindermann, T., Reisenzein, R., & Schmid, U. (1987). Further observational data on the behavioral and social world of institutions for the aged. *Psychology and Aging, 2,* 390-403.

Baltes, P. B. (1987). Theoretical propositions of life-span developmental psychology: On the dynamics between growth and decline. *Developmental Psychology, 23,* 611-626.

Barnett, E. (1997). Listening to people with dementia and their carers. In M. Marshall (Ed.), *State of the art in dementia care.* London: Centre for Policy on Ageing.

Bookwala, J., Coppola, K. M., Fagerlin, A., Ditto, P. H., Danks, J. H., & Smucker, W. D. (2001). Gender differences in older adults' preferences for life-sustaining medical treatments and end-of-life values. *Death Studies, 25*(2), 127-149.

Bravo, G., Dubois, M. F., & Paquet, M. (2003). Advance directives for health care and research: Prevalence and correlates. *Alzheimer's Disease and Associated Disorders, 17*(4), 215-222.

Brechling, B. G. & Schneider, C. A. (1993). Preserving autonomy in early state dementia. *Journal of Gerontological Social Work, 20*(1/2), 17-33.

Burdz, M. P., Eaton, W. O., & Bond, J. B., Jr. (1988). Effect of respite care on dementia and nondementia patients: Boundary ambiguity and mastery. *Family Process, 29,* 1-10.

Cantor, M. H. (1979). Neighbors and friends: An overlooked resource in the informal support system. *Research on Aging, 1,* 434-463.

Cheston, R., Bender, M., & Byatt, S. (2000). Involving people who have dementia in the evaluation of services: A review. *Journal of Mental Health, 9*(5), 471-479.

Clare, L. (2002). We'll fight it as long as we can: Coping with the onset of Alzheimer's disease. *Aging and Mental Health, 6,* 139-148.

Clarke, A., Hanson, E. J., & Ross, H. (2003). Seeing the person behind the patient: Enhancing the care of older people using a biographical approach. *Journal of Clinical Nursing, 12*(5), 697-706.

Cohen, U., & Day, K. (1994). Emerging trends in environments for people with dementia. *The American Journal of Alzheimer's Care and Related Disorders and Research, 9*(1), 3-11.

Cohen, U., & Weissman, J. (1991). *Holding on to home: Designing environments for people with dementia.* Baltimore: Johns Hopkins University Press.

Cotrell, V., & Schulz, R. (1993). The perspective of the patient with Alzheimer's disease: A neglected dimension of dementia research. *The Gerontologist, 33*(2), 205-211.

Cumming, E., & Henry, W. R. (1961). *Growing old: The process of disengagement.* New York: Basic Books.

Ditto, P. H., Danks, J. H., Smucker, W. D., Bookwala, J., Coppola, K. M., Dresser, R., Fagerlin, A., Gready, R. M., Houts, R. M., Lockhart, L. K., & Zyzanski S. (2001). Advance directives as acts of communication: A randomized controlled trial. *Archives of Internal Medicine, 161*(3), 421-430.

Douglas, R., & Brown, H. N. (2002). Patient's attitudes toward advanced directives. *Journal of Nursing Scholarship, 34*(1), 61-65.

Erikson, E. H. (1963). *Childhood and society* (2nd ed.). New York: Norton.

Fazel, S., Hope, T., & Jacoby, R. (1999). Dementia, intelligence, and the competence to complete advanced directives. *The Lancet, 354*(9172), 48.

Feinberg, L. F., & Whitlatch, C. J. (2001). Are persons with cognitive impairment able to state consistent choices? *The Gerontologist, 41*(3), 374-382.

Feinberg, L. F., & Whitlatch, C. J. (2002). Decision-making for persons with cognitive impairment and their family caregivers. *American Journal of Alzheimer's Disease and Other Dementias, 17*(4), 237-244.

Felton, B., & Kahana, E. (1974). Adjustment and situationally-bound locus of control among institutionalized aged. *Journal of Gerontology, 29*(3), 295-301.

Femia, E. E., Zarit, S. H., & Johansson, B. (1997). Predicting change in activities of daily living: A longitudinal study of the oldest old. *Journal of Gerontology: Psychological Sciences, 52B,* P292-P304.

Folstein, M. F., Folstein, S., & McHugh, P. R. (1975). Mini-mental state: A practical method for grading the cognitive state of patients for the clinician. *Journal of Psychiatric Research, 12,* 189-198.

Gerety, M. B., Chiodo, L. K., Kanten, D. N., Tuley, M. R., & Cornell, J. E. (1993). Medical treatment preferences of nursing home residents: relationship to function and concordance with surrogate decision makers. *Journal of the American Geriatrics Society, 41,* 953-960.

Goffman, E. (1962). *Asylums.* Garden City, NY: Doubleday.

Goldfarb, A. I. (1969). The psychodynamics of dependency and the search for aid. In R. Kalish (Ed.), *The dependencies of old people.* Ann Arbor, MI: Institute of Gerontology.

Goldsilver, P. M., & Gruneir, M. R. (2001). Early stage dementia group: An innovative model of support for individuals in the early stages of dementia. *American Journal of Alzheimer's Disease, 16,* 109-114.

Gunter-Hunt, G., Mahoney, J. E., & Sieger, C. E. (2002). A comparison of state directive documents. *The Gerontologist, 42*(1), 51-61.

Hahn, M. E. (2003). Advance directives and patient-physician communication. *Journal of the American Medical Association, 289*(1), 96.

Hamel, M., Lynne, J., Teno, J. M., Covinsky, K. E., Wu, A. W., Galanos, A., Desbiens, N. A., & Phillips, R. S. (2000). Age-related differences in care preferences, treatment decisions, and clinical outcomes of seriously ill hospitalized adults: Lessons from SUPPORT. *Journal of the American Geriatrics Society, 48*(5), S176-S182.

Havighurst, R. (1968). Personality and patterns of aging. *The Gerontologist, 38,* 20-23.

Hepburn, K. W., Caron, W., Luptak, M., Ostwald, S., Grant, L., & Keenan, J. M. (1997). The family stories workshop: Stories for those who can't remember. *The Gerontologist, 37*(6), 827-832.

Jarrott, S. E., & Bruno, K. (2003). Intergenerational activities involving persons with dementia: An observational assessment. *American Journal of Alzheimer's Disease and Other Dementias, 18*(1), 31-37.

Jarrott, S. E., Zarit, S. H., Stephens, M. A. P., Townsend, A., & Greene, R. (1999). Caregiver satisfaction with adult day service programs. *American Journal of Alzheimer's Disease, 14,* 233-244.

Johansson, L., & Thorslund, M. (1992). Care needs and sources of support in a nationwide sample of elderly in Sweden. *Zeitschrift fuer Gerontologie, 25*(1), 57-62.

Johnson, C. L., & Barer, B. M. (1997). *Life beyond 85 years: The aura of survivorship.* New York: Springer.

Jung, C. G. (1933). *Modern man in search of a soul.* New York: Harcourt Brace Jovanovich.

Kahn, R. L. (1975). The mental health system and the future aged. *Gerontologist, 15,* 24-31.

Kahn, R. L., & Zarit, S. H. (1974). The evaluation of mental health programs for the aged. In P. O. Davidson, F. W. Clark, & L. A. Hamerlynck (Eds.), *Evaluation of behavioral programs*. Champaign, IL: The Research Press.

Kitwood, T. (1997). *Dementia reconsidered: The person comes first*. Bristol, PA: Open University Press.

Kitwood, T., & Bredin, K. (1994). *Evaluating dementia care: The Care Mapping Method* (6th ed.). Bradford: Bradford University Dementia Group.

Krause, N. (2003). The social foundations of personal control in late life. In S. H. Zarit, L. I. Pearlin, & K. W. Schaie (Eds.), *Personal control in social and life course contexts* (pp. 45-70). New York: Springer.

Kuhn, D., Kasayka, R. E., & Lechner, C. (2002). Behavioral observations and quality of life among persons with dementia in 10 assisted living facilities. *American Journal of Alzheimer's and Other Dementias, 17*(5), 291-298.

Lawton, M. P., & Nahemow, L. (1973). Ecology of the aging process. In C. Eisdorfer & M. P. Lawton (Eds.), *The psychology of adult development and aging* (pp. 619-674). Washington, DC: American Psychology Association.

Lidz, C. W., & Arnold, R. M. (1990). Institutional constraints on autonomy. *Generations, 14* (Suppl), 65-68.

Löckenhoff, C. E., & Carstensen, L. L. (2003). Is the life span theory of control a theory of development or a theory of coping? In S. H. Zarit, L. I. Pearlin, & K. W. Schaie (Eds.), *Personal control in social and life course contexts* (pp. 263-280). New York: Springer.

Malmberg, B. (1999). Swedish group homes for people with dementia. *Generations, 23*(3), 82-84.

Malmberg, B., & Zarit, S. H. (1993). Group homes for people with dementia: A Swedish example. *The Gerontologist, 33*(5), 682-686.

Markson, L. J., Kern, D. C., Annas, G. J., & Glantz, L. H. (1994). Physician assessment of patient competence. *Journal of the American Geriatric Society, 42*, 1074-1080.

Mitchell, R. (1999). Home from home: A model of daycare for people with dementia. *Generations, 23*(3), 78-81.

McCullogh, L. B., Wilson, N., Teasdale, T. A., Kolpakchi, A. L., & Skelly, J. R. (1993). Mapping personal, familial, and professional values in long-term care decisions. *The Gerontologist, 33*, 324-332.

Moniz-Cook, E., Agar, S., Gibson, G., Win, T., & Wang, M. (1998). A preliminary study of the effects of early intervention with people with dementia and their families in a memory clinic. *Aging and Mental Health, 2*, 199-211.

Moody, L. E., Small, B. J, & Jones, C. B. (2002). Advance directives preferences of functionally and cognitively impaired nursing home residents in the United States. *Journal of Applied Gerontology, 21*(1), 103-118.

Parmelee, P., Lawton, M. P., & Katz, I. R. (1989). Psychometric properties of the Geriatric Depression Scale among the institutionalized aged. *Psychological Assessment, 1*, 331-338.

Parmelee, P. A., & Lawton, M. P. (1990). The design of special environments for the aged. In J. E. Birren & K. W. Schaie (Eds.), *Handbook of the psychology of aging* (3rd ed., pp. 464-488). San Diego, CA: Academic Press.

Pearlman, R., Starks, H., Cain, K., Rosengren, D., & Patrick, D. (1998). *Your life, your choices—Planning for future medical decisions: How to prepare a personalized living will.* Springfield, VA: U.S. Department of Commerce; National Technical Information Service PB#98159437.

Pinquart, M., & Sörensen, S. (2002) Older adults' preferences for informal, formal, and mixed support for future care needs: A comparison of Germany and the United States. *International Journal of Aging and Human Development, 54*(4), 291-314.

Regnier, V. (1994). *Assisted living housing for the elderly: Design innovations from the United States and Europe*. New York: Van Nostrand Reinhold.

Regnier, V. (2002). *Design for assisted living: Guidelines for housing the physically and mentally frail.* New York: Wiley.

Regnier, V., & Scott, A. C. (2001). Creating a therapeutic environment: Lessons from Northern European models. In S. Zimmerman, P. D. Sloane, & M. G. Ory (Eds.), *Assisted living: Needs, practices and policies in residential care for the elderly* (pp. 53-77). Baltimore: Johns Hopkins University Press.

Roberto, K. A., Allen, K. R., & Bleiszner, R. (2001). Older adults' preferences for future care: Formal plans and familial support. *Applied Developmental Science, 5*(2), 112-120.

Ryff, C. D. (1995). Psychological well-being in adult life. *Current Directions in Psychological Science, 4,* 99-104.

Sabatino, C. P. (1996). Competency: Refining our legal fictions. In M. Smyer, K. W. Schaie, & M. B. Kapp (Eds.), *Older adults' decision-making and the law* (pp. 1-28). New York: Springer.

Simmons, S. F., Schnelle, J. F., Uman, G. C., Kulvicki, A. D., Lee, K. O. H., & Ouslander, J. G. (1997). Selecting nursing home residents for satisfaction surveys. *Gerontologist, 37*(4), 543-550.

Schulz, R., & Brenner, G. (1977). Relocation of the aged: A review and theoretical analysis. *Journal of Gerontology, 32,* 323-332.

Schulz, R., & Beach, S. R. (1999). Caregiving as a risk factor for mortality: The caregiver health effects study. *Journal of the American Medical Association, 282,* 2215-2219.

Schulz, R., Wrosch, C., & Heckhausen, J. (2003). The life span theory of control: Issues and evidence. In S. H. Zarit, L. I. Pearlin, & K. W. Schaie (Eds.), *Personal control in social and life course contexts* (pp. 233-262). New York: Springer.

Shea, D. G., Davey, A., Femia, E. E., Zarit, S. H., Sundstrom, G., Berg, S., & Smyer, M. A. (2003). Exploring assistance in Sweden and the United States. *Gerontologist, 43,* 712-721.

Skinner, E. A. (1995). *Perceived control, motivation, & coping.* Thousand Oaks: Sage.

Thompson, T., Barbour, R., & Schwartz, L. (2003). Adherence to advance directives in critical care decision making vignette study. *British Medical Journal, 327*(7422), 1011.

Wahl, H. W. (1991). Dependence in the elderly from an interactional point of view: Verbal and observational data. *Psychology and Aging, 6*(2), 238-246.

Willis, S. L. (1996). Assessing everyday competence in the cognitively challenged elderly. In M. Smyer, K. W. Schaie, & M. B. Kapp (Eds.), *Older adults' decision-making and the law.* New York: Springer.

Woods, B. (1999a). The person in dementia care. *Generations, 23*(3), 35-39.

Woods, B. (1999b). Promoting well-being and independence for people with dementia. *International Journal of Geriatric Psychiatry, 14*(2), 97-105.

Yale, R. (1989). Support groups for newly-diagnosed Alzheimer's clients. *Clinical Gerontologist, 8,* 86-89.

Yale, R. (1999). Support groups and other services for individuals with early-stage Alzheimer's disease. *Generations, 23*(Fall), 57-61.

Zank, S., & Schacke, C. (2002). Evaluation of geriatric day care units: Effects on patients and caregivers. *Journal of Gerontology: Psychological Sciences, 57B,* P348-P357.

Zarit, S. H., Femia, E. E., Watson, J., Rice-Oeschger, L., & Kakos, B. (2004). Memory Club: A group intervention for people with early-stage dementia and their care partners. *Gerontologist, 44,* 262-269.

Zarit, S. H., Gaugler, J. E., & Jarrott, S. E. (1999). Useful services for families: Research findings and directions. *International Journal of Geriatric Psychiatry, 14,* 165-177.

Zarit, S. H., Stephens, M. A. P., Townsend, A., & Greene, R. (1998). Stress reduction for family caregivers: Effects of day care use. *Journal of Gerontology: Social Sciences, 53B,* S267-S277.

PART III. New and Persistent Dynamics Regarding the Home Environment

CHAPTER 7

The Impact of Housing on Quality of Life: Does the Home Environment Matter Now and into the Future?

Laura N. Gitlin

Along the continuum of living arrangements available in the United States, the home, a long-term private residence that is owned or rented, remains the primary context in which people choose to grow old, even for individuals with significantly compromised health (American Association of Retired Persons (AARP), 1990, 2003; Golant & LaGreca, 1994). As such, with age, the home takes on increasing importance as the principal context for socialization, leisure participation, as well as health care delivery (Binstock, & Cluff, 2000). The home as epicenter, particularly in very old age, is a persistent trend that is expected to increase now and into the future (Wahl & Gitlin, 2003).

The purpose of this chapter is to explore the present status and future role of one dimension of home life—its physicality—and the specific contributions of strategies that modify this aspect for life quality and continuance at home. A discussion of the physical aspect of home and its relationship to life quality now and into the future must necessarily consider a broad range of relevant factors at both the individual (micro) and societal (macro) level. Specifically, central to an understanding of persons and homes is the consideration of current and future projections of the number of elderly and their health status, current and projected housing conditions, health and housing policy, and the evidence regarding the role of home modifications for helping people continue to live there.

Much has been written previously about the home environment and its impact on daily life starting with the early ground-breaking research on housing satisfaction by Lawton (Lawton & Simon, 1968) and Carp (1966), leading to the study of time use and psycho-social processes (Moss & Lawton, 1982; Rubinstein, 1989), relocation decision making and housing adaptations (Reschovsky & Newman, 1990; Struyk & Katsura, 1988), residential satisfaction and housing policies (Golant, 2003a); and more recently, as part of an ongoing larger discussion of environmental design and aging processes (see Golant, 2003b; Wahl & Weisman, 2003). Likewise, previous research assuming a more microscopic perspective has extensively examined the presence and use of, and the need for home modification and assistive devices (see Charness & Schaie, 2003; Gitlin, 1998; Pynoos, Cohen, Davis, & Bernhardt, 1987), with recent research evaluating longitudinal trends in the balance of home modification and personal assistance use using large population-based surveys (Manton, Corder, & Stallard, 1997). Building then on these previous efforts, the purpose of this chapter is twofold: to identify key points of knowledge from diverse but related streams of research from which to characterize the current status of home environments and the intersection with quality of life; and to offer a prognosis of the future of aging in place at home in the United States.

Based on a review of this extensive research, three themes emerge: first, although previous and current research demonstrates the inextricable links between housing and health, particularly for frail elders, the lack of integration of housing with healthcare delivery, supportive services, and policy decisions persists and continues to serve as a barrier to enabling older people to age in place now and into the future.

Second, it is evident that the complexity and individuation of aging processes and life choices coupled with social-structure factors (e.g., housing- and home-modification policies, socioeconomic status) precludes a singular housing solution that fits all aging persons and their needs. A significant development is that, despite our knowledge of demographic projections and consequences for unmet health and housing needs, a "quiet crisis" looms, indicating a substantially inadequate supply of affordable housing that will be unable to meet the imminent demands imposed by the unprecedented changes in the age structure of the United States (Commission on Affordable Housing and Health Facility Needs for Seniors in the 21st Century, 2002).

A third emergent point is that the essential questions posed over the past 40 years by environmental psychologists and gerontologists remain unresolved and are still pertinent to present day and future considerations pertaining to the role of physical environments in helping people age at home. The basic questions that are relevant today are: "What aspects of community context are likely to help the older person maintain residence in the community and avoid institutionalization?" (Lawton, 1981, p. 102); How to anchor household behavior conceptually (Lawton, 1990); What is the role of the home in long-term care? ". . . how can the expected rise in the demand for long-term care be accommodated?" (Newman, 1985, p. 35).

This chapter begins by articulating theoretical considerations and the links between home, health, and life quality. The three themes stated above will become evident by examining key demographic and disability trends, housing and home modification needs, and the evidence for the supportive role of the physical home environment.

THEORETICAL NOTE AND BASIC ASSUMPTIONS

Although the purpose of this chapter is not theoretical advancement per se, it is important to denote the theoretical basis for a discussion of the physical home environment in relation to life quality and how such a discussion fits into broader conceptual understandings. On a theoretical level, a discussion of home and life quality is inevitably embedded in the larger foundations and concerns of environmental gerontology and, at its broadest base, models of quality of life. As such, the central tenets of ecology of aging perspectives and multidimensional quality of life models can be applied to this particular context: the home. At the conceptual level, of particular significance is Lewin's (1951) notion of "life space," which implicitly sets household behaviors (e.g., decision to remain at home, adaptation of specific coping strategies) within a transactional perspective. Such a perspective assumes the inextricable connections between physical and social, person and environment, objective and subjective, and context as both resource and constraint.

Nevertheless, the particular focus and discussion of this chapter on one dimension of life space, the physical environment, at the exclusion of the sphere as a whole assumes that specific characteristics of persons and environments are independent and predictive of the other. This more interactional perspective assumed here seems appropriate for our purposes with the caveat that by so doing we run the risk of compartmentalizing and losing links with other determinants of household behaviors such as the personal (e.g., presence of others), and suprapersonal environment (e.g., geographic proximity to transportation, neighbors, shopping) that may influence aging at home (Lawton, 1999; Wahl, 2001; Wahl & Lang, 2004). These aspects of life space are addressed in other book chapters in hope of allowing for such connections to be eventually forged. The spotlight on the physicality of home environments here allows greater particularization of one component of person-environment dynamics from which to explicate the specific challenges of aging in place at least from the vantage point of physical considerations.

Even within this one realm of the life space, the physical, we have the dilemma of definition and taxonomy with little consistency and agreement found in the literature. Adding complexity is the conceptualization and measurement of the physical environment in terms of its duality: objective conditions and how they are subjectively experienced. The objective physical environment has been simply defined by Lawton as "all that lies outside the skin of the participant, is animate, and may be specified by counting or by measuring in centimeters, grams or seconds" (Lawton, 1999, p. 106); whereas the subjective refers to the cognitive and affective "personal meanings or functional significance for the individual" (Lawton, 1999, p. 106). When applied to home life, both objective and subjective aspects of housing must be considered since they both contribute to behavioral outcomes such as home modification use and relocation decisions.

Within the home as life space, it is also important to theoretically anchor the person. Verbrugge and Jette's (1994) disablement model suggests two related notions of competency that are relevant to our discussion here: an individual's ability regardless of context, which is referred to as intrinsic ability; and an individual's ability as supported or constrained by the person's physical and social environment, referred to as actual disability. Here the implication is that the interaction between a person's intrinsic abilities and the built environment, including both its physical and social characteristics, yields actual disability. Thus, one conclusion is that disability is an outcome of potentially modifiable factors and can therefore be minimized. Although Verbrugge and

Jette's model does not articulate the specific pathways between human behavior and the physical environment, it provides a framework for such links to be examined and underscores that objective conditions (e.g., presence of external supports, home modification) may offset further disablement independently of and/or in conjunction with personal appraisals and social resources.

THE INTERSECTION OF HOME, HEALTH, AND LIFE QUALITY

As the centerpiece in which aging unfolds, the home affords certain advantages in health and well-being that have been characterized by Lawton (1989) as maintenance, stimulation, and support. Maintenance refers to the constancy and predictability of an environment. As such, the home provides a minimally restrictive and familiar context offering predictability and continuance of established and valued daily patterns, as well as personal meaning and autonomy (Parmelee & Lawton, 1990; Rubinstein, 1989). Related to maintenance is the role of stimulation, which refers to the affordance of novelty and appropriate levels of arousal. Since older people and, in particular, the oldest old spend most time at home, the stimulating role of this context becomes increasingly important (Baltes, Maas, Wilms, Borchelt, & Little, 1999). Finally, in its supportive capacity, the home environment may help compensate for lost or reduced capabilities. Home modifications can enhance accessibility and minimize barriers imposed by standard housing, particularly for persons with mobility disorders and other impairments for which ambulation at home may be problematic (Schaie, Wahl, Mollenkopf, & Oswald, 2003).

Newman (2003) suggests three specific pathways in which ordinary housing may affect health outcomes in older adults. First, the housing and neighborhood environment may affect the feasibility of delivering quality home care services (Mann, 1997). Newman and colleagues have shown how objective conditions such as the physical features of a dwelling—lack of space for a modification (e.g., ramp, stair lift)—or that of the community (e.g., safety, access) can increase the cost of service, preclude their actual delivery, or serve as a barrier to quality care (Newman, Struyk, Wright, & Rice, 1990). Although little is still understood as to the effect of specific environmental features on obtaining services and their outcome, there is strong evidence that objective environmental features of any job can affect the quality of care provided (Newman, 1995).

A second way in which ordinary housing may affect health is that objective physical conditions of a home may place an occupant at risk. This is particularly the case for vulnerable elders who may not have the physical and/or cognitive capacity to address basic home maintenance or repair needs nor obtain needed home modification, and this, in turn, may contribute to or exacerbate the disablement process.

Yet a third link between home, health, and life quality concerns the characteristics of the immediate neighborhood, including rate of crime, convenience of stores and transportation, and access to social opportunities. Here the notion of "social capital" and its intersection with the physical home environment is important to consider (Cannuscio, Block, & Kawachi, 2003). Social capital, defined as the resources available to an individual through social connections in their communities, has important health benefits. Nevertheless, access to traditional forms of social capital (e.g., engagement with neighbors, civic involvement), is on the decline in the United States. Cannuscio and colleagues (2003) argue for the infusion of social capital in the design of new housing communities and naturally occurring retirement communities. Also, proximity of key services and venues become increasingly important to the physical housing situation, particularly if driving and use of public transportation become problematic with older age.

CURRENT DEMOGRAPHIC TRENDS AND IMPLICATIONS FOR HOME ENVIRONMENTS

Several key trends have particular import to considerations of home and life quality and are now well-established demographic facts in the United States. The most compelling trend of course is the shear numbers of people who are entering old age. In just 16 years, one out of every 6 persons, or 20% of the population (about 60 million), in the United States will be 65 years of age or older. Of equal significance is that the fastest growing segment of the older population continues to be the 85+ group, with the number of centenarians increasing more rapidly than initially projected. Concomitantly, the number of persons who care for a family member either at home or by long distance is increasing. Currently, one out of every three persons is or will be a caregiver of a family member or loved one. Close to half of persons 50+ years of age is a caregiver and of this group, 10% report substantial burdens (AARP, 2004). These changes in the age structure of the United States, due to numerous converging factors, including the aging of the Baby Boom generation and advances in medical science, is unprecedented and promises to transform housing and healthcare delivery systems.

The implications of these basic demographic facts for housing, life quality, and aging in place are manifold and serve as the backdrop for future projections. First, the oldest old are at greatest risk of requiring personal assistance, living alone, having lower income, being socially isolated, and living in homes that are also aging, in need of repair, and/or pose accessibility issues. The link between home and health is therefore particularly powerful for the oldest old who are at greater risk for chronic diseases and functional vulnerabilities that impact on everyday living at home (Pynoos & Liebig, 1995). The everyday difficulties imposed by age-related diseases, chronic conditions, and physical frailty, significantly affects the dynamics of persons and environments, tipping the delicate balance between functional capacity and home environments as people age.

On a historic note, whereas the private home environment has always been an object of study in gerontology with interest increasing by the late nineties (Wahl & Weisman, 2003), demographic and disability trends favor even more focused research and attention to this aspect of life quality (Gitlin, 2003). Unfortunately, with few exceptions both in the past (Lawton's "good life," 1991) and present, (REACH stress-related health model, Schulz, Gallagher-Thompson, Haley, & Czaja, 1999), the physical home environment has not been systematically conceptualized as part of models concerning quality of life, and health or risk indicators.

AGING AND INDIVIDUAL DECLINE

The majority of older people in the United States today is living longer and better than previous cohorts and rates their health as good or excellent. A recent report by the American Association of Retired Persons (AARP, 2004), based on five different government surveys and one initiated by AARP itself, found that 47% of persons 50+ years of age reported their health as excellent or very good. This represents an increase of 2 percentage points from 10 years ago. Nevertheless, whereas 46% of those between 50 and 64 report their health as less than good, this increases to 62% for those 65+.

A related point is that the fastest growing segments of the aging population are minority groups, including African Americans, Hispanics, and Asians, who experience a range of health disparities. Most notably is a significant disability gap between White and African Americans in the United States, with African Americans having much poorer physical functioning and higher risk for a wide range of disabling health conditions that persist into old age (Kelley-Moore & Ferraro, 2004). This group, in particular, confront multiple social structure jeopardies, including low income, lower home ownership rates, higher unmet needs in rental accommodations, and higher rates of disability and health problems, which potentially confound an individual's choice to age in place.

A substantial body of research has shown a strong relationship between health problems and activity limitations (Fukukawa et al., 2004). Activity limitations represent a major adverse outcome of the types of health problems that typically confront people as they age, such as physical frailty, stroke, arthritis, diabetes, osteoporosis, memory impairment, depressive symptoms, or heart disease. They represent a diminished capacity to perform self-care and instrumental tasks that further compromise the ability to stay at home with life quality (Fried & Guralnik, 1997). Thus, limitations in daily activities imposed by health problems of a chronic nature are the primary threat to quality of life and aging in place at home.

Although the prevalence of disability among the older population has declined, the absolute size of the physically disabled older population is increasing (Manton et al., 1997). As such, the number of elderly at risk of disability is expected to increase as a function of the aging population, with an anticipated number of older persons with a disability exceeding 12 million by 2030 (Congressional Budget Office, 1999).

The proportion of older adults with one or more limitations increases with age. An estimated 35% of adults age 65+ years and 62% of those 85+ living at home report difficulty with one or more activities of daily living. Additionally, these difficulties are more prevalent among older people who are low-income and minority group members (Diehl, 1998). Those most vulnerable to functional difficulties are the oldest old, women, minority group members and low-income elders for whom housing choices and access to supportive services may be limited.

Activity limitations or having functional difficulties are associated with the need for increased personal assistance. This need (presence and intersection of the social with the physical sphere) is one of the chief factors contributing to relocating to either the home of a family member or residential facility. The need for personal assistance with everyday activities increases with age such that 50% of persons 85+ in the United

States are estimated to require help with basic self-care activities, including bathing, getting around inside the home, preparing meals, and shopping (Federal Interagency Forum on Aging Related Statistics, 2000). Thus, although many people live alone in good health, as a group, they face increasing dependency, declining health, and social isolation. This is particularly the case for the fastest growing segment of the elderly population, the oldest old (85+).

Nevertheless, new research confirms that disablement is not an inevitable outcome of aging. Although with aging, there are small declines in physical functioning; older adults who do not have health problems can expect to live relatively free of disability (Fukukawa et al., 2004). Moreover, a growing body of research suggests that disability is not static, but rather a dynamic process resulting in improvement, worsening, or stabilization over time (Freedman, Aykan, Wolf, & Marcotte, 2004; Freedman, Martin, & Schoeni, 2002). Thus, of increasing importance is the potential of the role of the physical home environment in supporting persons with different and highly individualized aging and disability trajectories, as will be discussed below.

With regard to cognitive impairment, it is estimated that approximately 6 million persons in the United States have memory problems, with close to 4.5 million diagnosed with dementia. This number is expected to increase by 300% within the next 20 years (Herbert, Scherr, Bienias, Bennett, & Evans, 2003). Currently, close to 80% of persons with dementia are living at home either alone or with a family member. The role of the home environment in supporting persons with different cognitive and memory impairments is a recent area of investigation.

In summation, exciting new research is changing our basic understanding of disablement and its underlying causes. This research suggests that disability is not a necessary outcome of aging; frailty is a complex syndrome with identifiable contributing factors that may be modifiable (Fried et al., 2001). Thus, based on such emerging understandings, aging in place is a reasonable assumption for the vast majority of older adults. Nevertheless, despite reason for optimism, health disparities continue to persist, with gaps found particularly between White and African American older adults, and for persons with low income and few social supports. Such disparities, coupled with social-structure factors (e.g., shortage of affordable housing), place specific groups of older adults at greater risk than others of not being able to age in their long-term residence.

HOUSING AND HOME MODIFICATION NEEDS

The vast majority of older people in the United States currently own their own home, with ownership rates much higher for White than Hispanic and African American elders. Homeownership has continued to increase each decade such that from 1980 to 1987, rates increased from 77% to 81% for people aged 65 to 74, and by 1% for those over 75. This is in contrast to a very small number of people 65+ who live in nursing homes. Over the past 20 years, the United States federal government has followed a policy of de-institutionalizing the elderly, resulting in significant declines in nursing home residents even among the 85+ or oldest old group (Cannuscio et al., 2003; Lawton, 1995). Reductions in Medicare and Medicaid funding for institutional care, previous moratoria in nursing home construction, and increases in expenditures for home care through Medicare and Medicaid, have resulted in presently only approximately 1.47 million or 4.3% of the United States population 60+ (National Center for Health Statistics, 2000) living in a nursing home setting. Assisted-living facilities, a relatively new housing alternative primarily for middle- and upper-income older adults, currently have 600,000 to 1 million residents (Cannuscio et al., 2003).

Much of what is currently known about the conditions of homes as well as the presence, use, and need of home modifications by older people in the United States, is based on 10 population-based national surveys and their supplements (see Table 1).

Complementing these well-designed population-based surveys are regional surveys by builders and housing researchers that provide insight into current preferences and market trends among aging boomers in geographically targeted areas. While these surveys represent a rich source of data, a continuing difficulty with both regional and national probability surveys is the lack of agreed-upon and uniform terminology and set of questions that are consistently used across studies to obtain information on housing conditions, and home modification use (Cornman, Freedman, & Agree, 2004). Each survey evaluates different person and environmental attributes and uses distinct terminology making it difficult to compare findings across surveys. Thus, the scope of inquiry and our understanding of levels and types of disability, housing conditions, and modification need and use are restricted by this significant methodological limitation.

Nevertheless, important findings have been derived about housing and home modification needs. Foremost, it can be said that housing conditions over time have generally improved for the vast majority of adults in the United States. However, key findings from the report "A Quiet Crisis" by the Commission on Affordable Housing and Health Facility (2002) are truly alarming. Based on 1999 data, the Commission projects that by 2020 the number of older households living in unaffordable or poor-quality units will reach 11.3 million; the waiting lists for subsidized housing are too long; and about 324,000 federal Section 8 rent-assisted units are at risk of being converted to private-market development or being demolished. Also, the Commission found that investment in affordable housing has declined over the past three decades, with resource allocation to home and community-based services still far less than those committed to nursing facilities. This situation is compounded by declines in income, assets and pension coverage, and limited economic progress for over a decade among Americans 50+ (AARP, 2004).

To age in place also implies the aging of the residential setting itself. Here the question is whether older households are more likely to have deficient accommodations that could compromise even further the ability to age in place (Golant & LaGreca, 1994). That is, are older residents able to maintain the physical upkeep of their homes or apartments? While length of residency is not necessarily predictive of home maintenance difficulties, Golant and LaGreca (1994) did find this relationship to be the case for certain subgroups such as renters, the very poor, African Americans, and men living alone who are less able to maintain their homes. Thus, previous research on this critical question suggests that part of an aging-in-place social policy should include home repair, particularly for vulnerable elders (Struyk & Soldo, 1980).

With regard to home modification use, the evidence from population-based surveys has been consistent in showing that older adults with low income and who are frail are at greatest risk of having unmet modification and housing needs. Newman (2003),

Table 1. Summary of Key Population-Based Data Sets for Information on Housing and Home Modifications

Survey	Sampling frame	Environmental content
American Housing Survey (AHS)	Department of Housing and Urban Development and produced by Bureau of the Census	Householders of all ages (43,436 household units)
Survey of Housing Adjustments (supplement to Annual Housing Survey)	Houston, Texas, Standard Metropolitan Statistical Area, head or spouse of household 55+ years	• Housing and neighborhood characteristics • Housing adjustments: room use alteration, special features, residential moves.
Housing Modification Supplement to Annual Housing Survey	70,000 dwelling units	• Mobility limitations in rooms of home • Dwelling modifications
National Health Interview Survey (1994-1995 NHIS-D-Disability Supplement)	Assistive Devices Supplement sample of 117,042 adults	• Use of specific devices or equipment (ramps, extra-wide doors, stair lifts, elevators, grab bars, raised toilets, levers, push bars, special knobs, lowered counters, slide-resistant floors, other.
National Health and Nutrition Examination Survey (NHANES I) Epidemiologic Follow-Up Study	National multi-stage probability sample of noninstitutional U.S. population of 35-74 years	• Use of a mechanical aid or device if difficulty doing 28 everyday tasks.
National Long-Term Care Surveys	U.S. elderly Medicare-enrolled population, 65+ chronically disabled community residents	• Use of 7 types of physical aids (wheelchair, railing, walker, cane, crutches, bed lift, other) • Use of home modification
National Survey of Self-Care and Aging	Community-dwelling Medicare beneficiaries, 65+ years	• Use of equipment (cane, adapted telephone, clothing, other devices) • Behavior changes (avoiding stairs. going outside) • Home modifications (rearrangement of items)
Longitudinal Study on Aging (LSOA)	Began in 1984 with 3 follow-ups over 6 years. Initial sample = 7,527	Functional characteristics and features of housing
Survey of Asset and Health Dynamics of the Oldest Old (AHEAD)	Began in 1994. Sample = 7,447 over 70 years. Interviews at 2-year intervals	Functional characteristics and features of housing
National Medical Expenditure Survey	Noninstitutionalized sample of 14,000 households, about 5,750 were aged 65+	Use devices such as mobility aids

using data from the 1995 National American Housing Survey, found that 14% of older people had a housing-related disability, 49% had at least one home modification, and 23% had an unmet need for modifications. Half of those with a modification also reported unmet need, this being greater among the poor. LaPlante, Hendershot, and Moss (1992) similarly found that although people with low income reported use of devices, they also had more unmet needs with financial considerations being the primary barrier reported. Reschovsky and Newman (1990), using the Survey of Housing Adjustments (a supplement from the Annual Housing Survey), found that frail households are more likely to report that they have unmet needs for carrying out household tasks with about 40% of persons with a mobility limitation reporting an unmet need such as a handrail or ramp. Due in part to the lack of consistency among survey instruments, estimates of the presence of at least one home modification in the homes of frail elders vary widely from 10% (Struyk & Katsura, 1998) to 33% (Soldo & Longino, 1988).

Supportive Role of Home Environments

Unmet home modification needs are particularly distressing in view of the growing body of research showing that environmental features can decrease the need for personal assistance enabling people to stay at home. Recent documented declines in disability-prevalence trends (what Verbrugee & Jette, 1994, would refer to as actual disability) have been attributed in large part to the role of the physical home environment. For example, using data from four waves of the National Long Term Care Survey (NLTCS) representing three five-year periods between 1984 and 1999, Spillman (2003) concluded that declines in disability rates may reflect improvements in the use of the external environment including home modifications and assistive devices that make it easier to stay at home. Manton, Corder, and Stallard (1997) similarly found a trend toward increased assistive-device and home modification use and a subsequent decline in reliance on personal assistance among functionally impaired older adults. An AARP survey (2003) also found that the number of disabled persons 65+ living in the community and using assistive devices has increased since the mid-1980s.

Knowledge concerning the specific environmental attributes that support autonomy at home is also emerging, although information about housing features remains insufficient. Using data from a supplement to the 1994 and 1995 National Health Interview Survey (NHIS-D), Allen, Foster, and Berg (2001) found that cane and crutch use reduced both formal and informal hours of care received weekly, whereas the use of walkers and wheelchairs did not. Other research has shown that the decline in disability among those with less severe levels of impairment can be attributed to the use of assistive devices and environmental supports such as ramps, grab bars, and stair lifts (AARP, 2003). Statistically significant decline in reliance on personal assistance and a concomitant increase in independence for bathing was found for a sample of older African American women living alone in rental units who received equipment such as grab bars, tub benches, and hand-held showers (Gitlin, Swenson-Miller, & Boyce, 1999).

Use of assistive devices in the home appears to vary by level of disability and type of activity. Findings from the National Survey of Self-Care and Aging showed that people with severe disability used assistive devices to supplement personal assistance

(Norburn et al., 1995). Aids for self-care and mobility tend to be used more frequently than for instrumental activities of daily living. Research also consistently shows that older adults living alone are more likely to use home modification than persons who live with others.

It is important to recognize that the home environment is equally as salient for older adults who report no difficulties and independence in performing everyday activities of living. Fried, Young, Rubin, and colleagues (2001) have shown that older people who report no activity limitations still indicate the use of a wide range of adaptive strategies, including assistive devices, performing tasks less frequently, or modifying the way the task is performed (e.g., sit instead of stand). The use of compensatory strategies has also been reported for older people with difficulties in everyday activities and a range of physical and sensory impairments (Gignac, Cott, & Badley, 2000; Wahl, Oswald, & Zimprich, 1999). Moreover, recent research shows that frail older adults may perform daily living activities at close to maximum capacity such that even a small change in their environment or health status may lead to greater disablement (Hortobagyi, Mizelle, Beam, & DeVita, 2003). These findings would suggest that attention to the physical environment, in part, may help maintain and support older people with physical decline.

The use of strategies such as assistive devices and home modifications has been found to have positive benefits for psychological well-being as well. Research shows that persons who use only assistive devices have greater sense of self-efficacy when compared to those who depend on personal assistance (Verbrugge, Rennert, & Madans, 1997). Furthermore, use of environmental strategies can safeguard against depressive symptoms associated with increasing functional difficulties (Gitlin, Dennis, Hauck, Winter, & Schinfeld, 2003).

There is also evidence to suggest that home modification can make everyday caregiving easier. Previous research has shown that families implement a wide range of physical adaptations to the home to accommodate caregiving needs, and that use of environmental strategies can reduce upset and caregiver burden (Gitlin, Winter, et al., 2003; Newman et al, 1990; Olsen, Ehrenkrantz, & Hutchings, 1993; Pynoos & Ohta, 1991). Although there is no evidence to suggest that the presence or absence of home attributes directly affect decisions to institutionalize, it may have an indirect impact by strengthening the ability to provide adequate care to a person at home (Newman, 1995).

Finally, there appears to be a hierarchy in strategy use with older adults initially modifying behaviors in the home (e.g., changing frequency of engaging in an activity, taking more time), then augmenting this strategy with assistive device use, and lastly, using a combination of behavioral and environmental modification and device use with informal and formal assistance when necessary (Norburn et al., 1995). Thus, home modifications and assistive devices become key features in the trajectory of health decline and in turn, have the potential of enhancing self-management of the consequences of chronic conditions.

Continuum of Home Modification Options

The use of home modifications as a recognized strategy for older people represents a relatively new paradigm reflecting emergent concerns with such concepts as self-management and habilitation. It provides an approach to supporting everyday living with existing abilities in the least restrictive environment in order to help people retain the greatest autonomy. The past 15 years of research on home modifications can be categorized as occurring at four interrelated levels as shown in Figure 1.

It is the contention here that the future of aging in place is dependent upon the continuation and growth of these streams of research: identifying and testing new products, describing acceptability and utility, evaluating environmental strategies and their specific mediation role between intrinsic and actual disability, and the quality of life effects of home modification interventions.

Although these areas of research are interrelated, they have not been addressed as such in the literature. Traditionally, environmental psychology and gerontology has

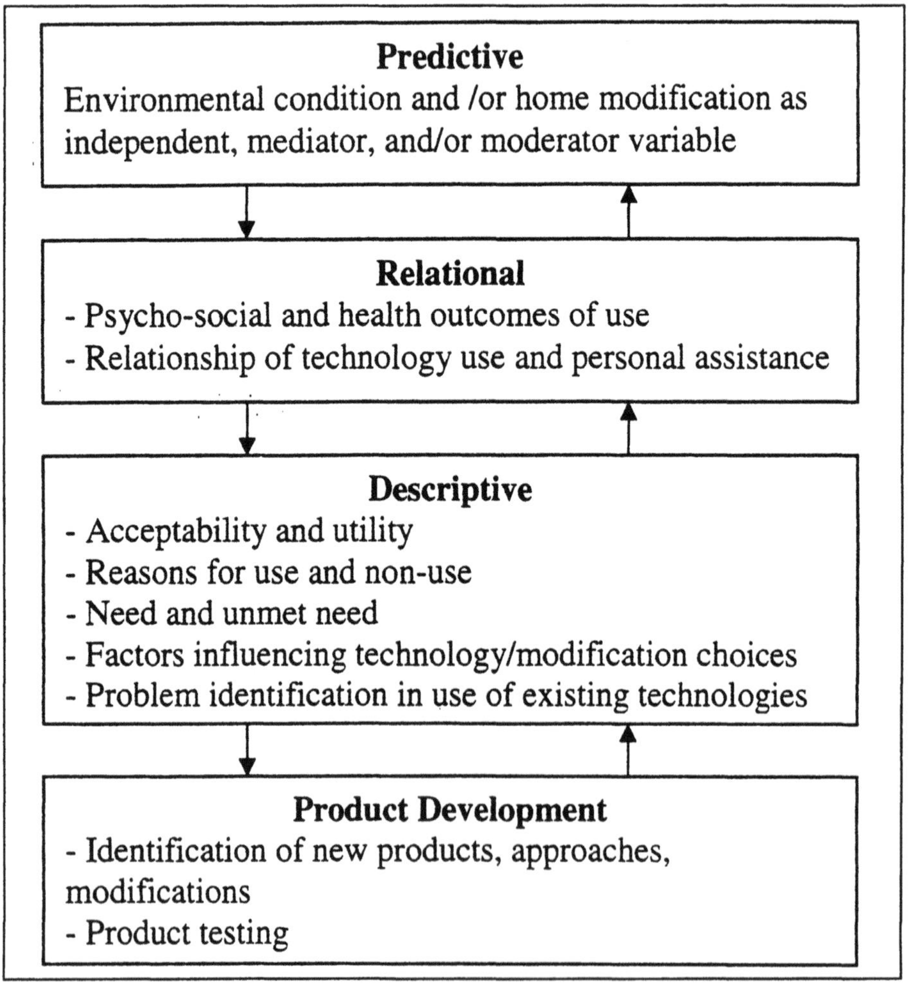

Figure 1. Integrated and ongoing streams of research on home modification.

tended to dismiss product development as not within its scope or vision, a stance that perhaps should be reconsidered. Product-development research is critical to providing options in the built environment; in turn, this basic level of research development would benefit from more sophisticated and theory-driven understandings of human-factor considerations related to aging and subjective processes that influence product acceptability and use. Home-care medical devices have been one of the fastest growing segments of the medical-device industry throughout the 1990s. New advancements, such as electronic communication and information technology systems, interactive video monitoring systems, tele-health technologies, and smart house technologies provide real opportunities for extending the potential of aging in place. Systematic study and knowledge of older people's perceived and actual utility, acceptability and integration into daily life are critical in order to advance these technologies.

Home modification can be thought of as occurring along a continuum. As shown in Figure 2, the most fundamental approach involves retrofitting or introducing modifications in regular homes and developing new products and strategies that fit preexisting specifications. Here the issue is access to and resources to purchase and install existing products and approaches to modifying the home.

A second-level approach involves integrating universal design features and planning homes with an "aging perspective" in new home construction such as new housing that offers "mother-in-law" suites or first floor living. With regard to new construction,

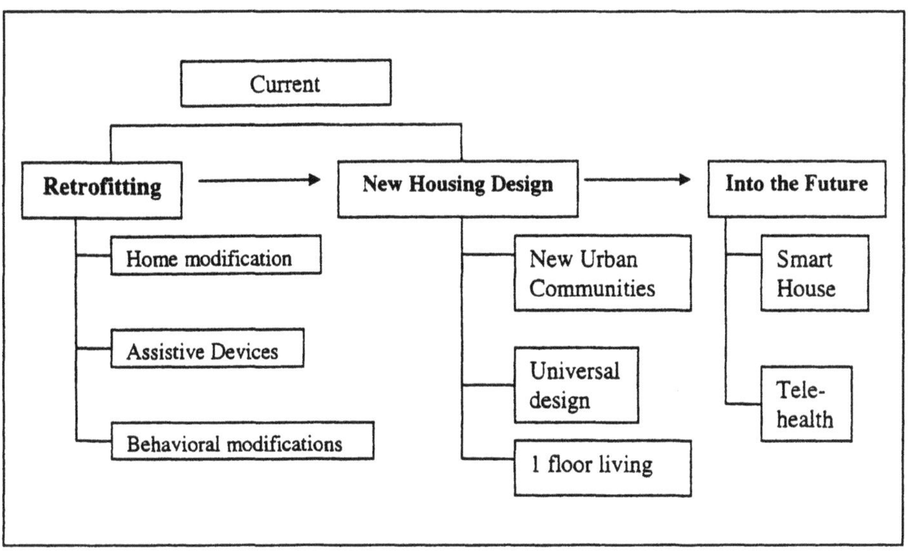

Figure 2. Continuum of housing modification options.

planned gated communities (e.g., restricted environments) are rapidly increasing, with almost 9 million residents reported living in this type of new home and community in 1997 (Cannuscio et al., 2003). This approach, having initially begun in Florida and California, will increase with about 50% of all new homes in major metropolitan areas expected to be within private community associations that provide added security with gates and guards, a neighborhood store (e.g., a place to purchase small items), social networking opportunities, and basic services such as home repair and gardening. It is unclear as to the success of this approach, and some have argued whether it has an integrative or segregationist effect.

Another housing phenomenon is the rise of naturally occurring retirement communities (NORCs), which are also rapidly increasing in major cities throughout the United States. NORC refers to ordinary apartment buildings that become populated primarily by older people who in turn may need supportive services to remain in the community. NORCs provide a natural setting for integrating supportive housing services.

The third level of home modification refers to future potentials and involves testing innovative ideas for housing including the smart house concept, homes outfitted for tele-health capacity, use of robotics, and other types of computer-driven prompters for persons with cognitive impairments.

The Future of Aging At Home

Despite the emergent research documenting the critical role of home environments in supporting everyday quality of life, the future of aging at home is at best mixed for many older people, particularly those aging with low incomes, multiple disabling conditions, and poor social supports. While there are positive trends (e.g., decline of disablement) and conditions (e.g., new technologies such as tele-healthcare) that make aging at home even in remote rural areas a strong possibility, there are also critical social-structure factors that jeopardize this life choice now and into the future.

First, the good news is that people are living free of disability longer. Nevertheless, there is recent evidence indicating that the vast majority of vulnerable older people do not receive appropriate, evidence-based, and effective healthcare, particularly for chronic conditions (Wenger et al., 2003). Also, there continues to be a lack of integration of housing considerations in addressing the medical aspects of chronic illness. The home environment is ignored or, at best, treated as a postscript in national discussions of public health concerns, health promotion and prevention initiatives, and the "hot" geriatric topics of aging (Morley, 2004). Although there is increased awareness of the importance of early detection of various diseases and impairments, there is no such recognition of the preventive and restorative role of the physical home; it is the older people, health professionals, and health and housing policymakers who must proactively consider ways to systematically improve maintenance and the supportive role of the home at the time of a diagnosis and/or during the course of managing chronic illness in the community.

There are perhaps several reasons for this: one is the continued medicalization of many aging-related concerns at the exclusion of the consideration of functional-related consequences of disease and chronic illness; another reason remains the fragmentation of long-term care policies and programs as well as multiple funding streams that present barriers to integrated service delivery (see Pynoos & Liebig, 1995, for a historical perspective); still another is the lack of an integrated and interdisciplinary-driven healthcare system to address chronicity and disease management, the primary issues of old age. These of course are well-recognized characteristics of our aging society that have negative consequences, particularly for the oldest old, who are approaching a stage in life in which some level of assistance will most likely be required. The needs of this group alone challenge us to elevate the physical home environment as a critical public health consideration.

A second factor explaining why the future of aging at home may be in jeopardy for many older people is the "quiet crisis" mentioned in the availability of affordable housing earlier. According to the Commission on Affordable Housing (2002), there are currently an insufficient number of affordable housing stocks and by the year 2020, nearly three-fourths of senior homeowners will have significant unmet housing needs. The crisis is particularly acute for low-income older tenants in government-subsidized rental housing who are often women with multiple cognitive or physical impairments who need help with home upkeep, self-care, and obtaining other supportive services (Golant, 2003a). As Golant (2002, 2003a) cogently argues, despite the fact that we have full recognition and understanding of the scope of the problem, as well as knowledge of effective solutions, unmet housing needs for this group persist due primarily to political and organizational barriers. As such, these persistent issues threaten the viability of aging in place for those most vulnerable.

The future viability of aging in place will also be contingent upon focused research to address critical gaps in knowledge. Little is still known about the intersection of housing and life quality with regard to specific health conditions and outcomes (Newman, 2003). Moreover, we do not yet have a comprehensive understanding of the trajectory of disability and individual decline. The newest research, as discussed earlier, suggests that, although disability is associated with aging, it is not a necessary outcome of aging processes (Fukukawa et al., 2004), nor is disability static (Freedman et al., 2004). Emerging understandings of frailty as a geriatric syndrome (Fried et al., 2001) promise to yield new and effective clinical strategies for its prevention and/or management, thus changing not only current models of disability, but also the landscape of who becomes frail and the population-based estimates of persons in need. Thus, currently, it is difficult to project the type and number of home-based services and the right mix of environmental, social, and community support necessary at each critical juncture along the aging trajectory that may enable people to successfully stay placed. Other questions as well persist that require systematic inquiry, such as: Is aging in one's long-term residence a realistic goal for all older people, and if not, what are the risk factors for relocation? Still, there is a neglected but nagging question regarding the potential for unforeseen or hidden negative consequences of aging at home such as increased social isolation; and for whom and how can this be addressed?

Moving forward, there are several interrelated approaches to supporting aging at home from a physical environmental perspective. At the individual level, there is the need for improving coordination and content of home-modification services to address mismatches between person capabilities and the physical home. Improvements include developing more systematic and tested assessment approaches to match person capabilities with home-modification solutions; systems for reaching urban elders with limited resources as well as elders in remote and rural areas who may not have access to home modification experts; better integration of new product developments and/or refinements into everyday service delivery; and use of best practices in determining effective modification solutions. At the societal level, there is the need for policy changes to provide more affordable and supportive housing opportunities that are inextricably linked to supportive services. Currently, public policy and healthcare practices place a significant constraint on the integration of environmental strategies in the home as a basic component of long-term healthcare for older people.

CONCLUSION

There is every indication, based on demographic, housing, and health trends, that the private residence will continue to serve as the principal context for aging into the future (Gitlin, 2003; Wahl & Gitlin, 2003). This chapter has discussed the role of private home residences in promoting quality of life now and into the future in relation to changing demographic trends, housing, and home modification use. It is suggested that while previous and current research supports the inextricable link of home and life quality, this relationship still remains poorly understood, particularly as it manifests across the trajectory of individual decline (both physical and cognitive). Moreover, the home environment, identified over 40 years ago by gerontologists and environmental psychologists as critical to the well-being of older persons, is still not well-integrated into healthcare delivery or national policies related to housing, health, and the aging network of services. Whereas research on physical home environments has persisted for over five decades, its recognition as part of a broader set of issues related to self-management of chronic disease and health promoting behaviors is relatively new. Thus, while there is a historic interest and precedence in recognizing the importance of staying in one's private residence, it is of heightened significance now.

The private residence, owned or rented, is a complex setting; a reflection of the macro and micro—the highly personal and individualized expressions of adaptation, aging, and particular life circumstances as well as national healthcare delivery structures and housing and health policies (e.g., access to government-assisted rental housing and home subsidies, affordable housing, home-modification and home repair services). Perhaps in no other aspect of life is the intersection of the individual and societal/political-level factors apparent as in the private home. The home represents the interface of private-life choices, public-housing options, and resources afforded by social structure placement. Here, within the life space of people's homes, the dialectic of the particular, personal appraisals and life style choices, individual biography and meanings, and general sociopolitical forces play out.

Given the complexity and individuation of personal needs and preferences as people age, one must conclude that in the United States there is no single or simple housing solution that best fits all aging persons. Thus, in the future, a wide range of housing options to fulfill diverse desires, healthcare needs, and resources must be made available. Even though aging at home continues to be the expressed goal of older people and their families, this may not be a feasible, appropriate or life enhancing choice for all people, particularly among the oldest old. Thus, other "home-like" alternatives, such as experimentation with community-like residential settings and specialized assisted-living facilities that emanate the meaning and significance of home may also need to be advanced.

We know that older adults who fit a particular profile, individuals who are of low income, socially isolated, and physically frail, have greater housing disability and are at higher risk of relocating to a nursing home facility. Research is necessary to identify the particular factors that may enable even the frailest to remain at home and how the physical environment interdigitates with other factors such as the availability of social capital to influence home-modification access and use.

Successful aging, a controversial term, has been defined, in part, as the ability to maintain control over life choices. As such, deciding and being able to remain autonomous at home with age is one aspect of that definition. However, the ability to successfully age in place now and into the future will depend on new approaches to home modifications and retrofitting, as well as new housing solutions (e.g., construction involving universal design; affordable housing choices), the integration of an environmental perspective within healthcare delivery as well as national housing and long-term care policies, with special attention to the particular needs of frail elders who are at most risk of having unmet housing and health needs. The situation portrayed here is not unique to the United States, but resonates in other countries throughout the world who are confronted with a similar dramatic restructuring of the demographic landscape.

Finally, given the weight of evidence regarding the role of physical environments in promoting life quality, it is disconcerting that housing still remains an "orphan issue" (Newman, 2003). Thus, we are left with several critical/strategic questions that need to inform next steps in research, health advocacy, and policy formulation: How can we assure the integration of the home environment into standard healthcare practices for older people? How can we elevate the status of the home environment to the equivalence of other recognized "lifestyle" risk factors, such as nutrition, diet, weight, and exercise? How can we bring the home environment to the forefront of public health concern?

ACKNOWLEDGMENT

The preparation of this chapter was supported in part by funds from the National Institute on Aging (Grants # R01 AG13687 and K07 AG00998).

REFERENCES

Allen, S. M, Foster, A., & Berg, K. (2001). Receiving help at home: The interplay of human and technological assistance. *Journal of Gerontology: Social Sciences, 56B,* S374-S382.

American Association of Retired Persons (AARP). (2004, February). The state of 50+ America. http://research.aarp.org/general/fifty_plus_2004.html.

American Association of Retired Persons (AARP). (2003, February). *A report to the nation on independent living and disability.* Washington, DC: AARP.

American Association of Retired Persons (AARP). (1990). *Demographics.* Washington, DC: AARP.

Baltes, M. M., Maas, I., Wilms, H.-U., Borchelt, M., & Little, T. (1999). Everyday competence in old and very old age: Theoretical considerations and empirical findings. In P. B. Baltes & K. U. Mayer (Eds.), *The Berlin Aging Study* (pp. 384-402). Cambridge, UK: Cambridge University Press.

Binstock, R. H., & Cluff, L. E. (2000). *Home care advances: Essential research and policy issues.* New York: Springer Publishing Co.

Cannuscio, C., Block, J., & Kawachi, I. (2003). Social capital and successful aging: The role of senior housing. *Annals of Internal Medicine, 139*(5), 395-400.

Carp, F. M. (1966). *A future for the aged.* Austin: University of Texas Press.

Charness, N., & Schaie K. W. (Eds.). (2003). *Impact of technology on successful aging.* New York: Springer Publications.

Commission on Affordable Housing and Health Facility Needs for Seniors in the 21st Century. (2002). *A quiet crisis in America: A report to Congress by the Commission on Affordable Housing and Health Facility Needs for Seniors in the 21st Century.* U.S. Government Printing Office (stock number 052-003-01492-1; www.seniorscommission.gov).

Congressional Budget Office. (1999). *Projections for long-term care services for the elderly.* www.cbo.gov.

Cornman, J., Freedman, V. A., & Agree, E. (2004, April). *The effect of assistive technology measurement on late life disability rates.* Paper presented at the annual meeting of the Population Association of America, Boston, MA.

Diehl, M. (1998). Everyday competence in later life: Current status and future directions. *The Gerontologist, 38,* 422-433.

Federal Interagency Forum on Aging-Related Statistics. (2000). *Older Americans 2000: Key indicators of well-being.* Federal Interagency Forum on Aging-Related Statistics, Washington, DC: U.S. Government Printing Office.

Freedman, V. A., Aykan, H., Wolf, D. A., & Marcotte, J. E. (2004). Disability and home care dynamics among older unmarried Americans. *Journal of Gerontology: Social Sciences, 59B,* S25-S33.

Freedman, V. A., Martin, L. G., & Schoeni, R. (2002). Recent trends in disability and functioning among older adults in the United States: A systematic review. *Journal of American Medical Association, 288,* 3137-3146.

Fried, L. P., & Guralnik, J. M. (1997). Disability in older adults: Evidence regarding significance, etiology, and risk. *Journal of the American Geriatrics Society, 45*(1), 92-100.

Fried, L. P., Young, Y., Rubin, G., Bandeen-Roche, K., & WHAS II Collaborative Research Group. (2001). Self-reported preclinical disability identifies older women with early declines in performance and early disease. *Journal of Clinical Epidemiology. 54*(9):889-901.

Fried, L. P., Tangen, C. M., Walston, J., Newman, A. B., Hirsch, C., Gottdiener, J., Seeman, T., Tracy, R., Kop, W. J., Burke, G., McBurnie, M. A., & Cardiovascular Health Study Collaborative Research Group. (2001). Frailty in older adults: Evidence for a phenotype. *Journals of Gerontology Series A-Biological Sciences & Medical Sciences, 56(*3): M146-156.

Fukukawa, U., Nakashima, C., Tsuboi, S., Naoakira, N., Ando, F., Kosugi, S., & Shimokata, H. (2004). The impact of health problems on depression and activities in middle-aged and older adults: Age and social interactions as moderators. *Journal of Gerontology: Psychological Sciences, 59B,* P19-P26.

Gignac, M. A. M., Cott, C., & Badley, E. M. (2000). Adaptation to chronic illness and disability and its relationship to perceptions of independence and dependence. *Journal of Gerontology: Psychological Sciences, 55B,* P362-P372.

Gitlin, L. N. (2003). Conducting research on home environments: Lessons learned and new directions. *The Gerontologist, 43*(5), 628-637.

Gitlin, L. N. (1998). Testing home modification interventions: Issues of theory, measurement, design, and implementation. In R. Schulz, G. Maddox, & M. P. Lawton (Eds.), *Annual review of gerontology and geriatrics. Focus on interventions research with older adults* (Vol. 18, pp. 190-246). New York: Springer.

Gitlin, L. N., Swenson-Miller, K., & Boyce, A. (1999). Bathroom modifications for frail elderly renters: Outcomes of a community-based program. *Technology and Disability, 10,* 141-149.

Gitlin, L. N., Winter, L., Corcoran, M., Dennis, M., Schinfeld, S., & Hauck, W. (2003). Effects of the home environmental skill-building program on the caregiver-care recipient dyad: Six-month outcomes from the Philadelphia REACH Initiative. *The Gerontologist, 43*(4), 532-546.

Gitlin, L. N., Dennis, M., Hauck, W., Winter, L., & Schinfeld, S. (2003, November). *Relationship of functional difficulty levels to adaptive strategy use and psychological well-being among frail elders.* Paper presented as part of the F. Oswald, H. Wahl Symposium, Psychological Dimensions of Aging in Place: Processes and Outcomes, to the Gerontological Society of America Annual Meeting, San Diego, CA.

Golant, S. M. (2003a). Political and organizational barriers to satisfying low-income U.S. seniors' need for affordable rental housing with supportive services. *Journal of Aging & Social Policy, 15*(4), 21-48.

Golant, S. M. (2003b). Conceptualizing time and behavior: Promising pathways in environmental gerontology. *The Gerontologist, 43*(5), 638-648.

Golant, S. M. (2002). Geographic inequalities in the availability of government-subsidized rental housing for low-income older person in Florida. *The Gerontologist, 42*(1), 100-108.

Golant, S. M., & LaGreca, A. J. (1994). Housing quality of U.S. elderly households: Does aging in place matter? *The Gerontologist, 34*(6), 803-814.

Herbert, L. E., Scherr, P. A., Bienias, J. L., Bennett, D. A., & Evans, D. A. (2003). Alzheimer disease in the US population; Prevalence estimates using the 2000 Census. *Archives of Neurology, 60,* 1119-1122.

Hortobagyi, T., Mizelle, C., Beam, S., & DeVita, P. (2003). Old adults perform activities of daily living near their maximal capabilities. *Journal of Gerontology Medical Science, 58A,* 453-460.

Kelley-Moore, J. A., & Ferraro, K. F. (2004). The black/white disability gap: Persistent inequality in later life? *Journal of Gerontology: Social Sciences, 59B,* S34-S43.

LaPlante, M., Hendershot, G., & Moss, A. (1992). Assistive technology, devices and home accessibility features: Prevalence, payment, need, and trends. *Advance Data, 217,* 1-11.

Lawton, M. P. (1981). Community supports for the aged. *Journal of Social Sciences, 37*(3), 102-115.

Lawton, M. P. (1990). Aging and performance of home tasks. *Factors, 32*(5), 527-536.

Lawton, M. P. (1995). Forward. In J. Pynoos & P. S. Liebig (Eds.), *Housing frail elders: International policies, perspectives, and prospects* (p. ix-xi). Baltimore: The Johns Hopkins University Press.

Lawton, M. P. (1989). Three functions of the residential environment. *Journal of Housing for the Elderly, 5,* 35-50.

Lawton, M.P. (1991). A multidimensional view of quality of life in frail elders. In J. E. Birren, J. E. Lubben, J. C. Rowe, & D. E. Deutchman (Eds.), The concept and measurement of quality of life in the frail elderly (pp. 3-27). San Diego: Academic Press, Inc.

Lawton, M. P. (1999). Environmental taxonomy: Generalizations from research with older adults. In S. Friedman & T. Wachs (Eds.), *Measuring environment across the life span: Emerging methods and concepts* (pp. 91-124). Washington, DC: American Psychological Association.

Lawton, M. P., & Simon, B. B. (1968). The ecology of social relationships in housing for the elderly. *The Gerontologist, 8,* 108-115.

Lewin, K. (1951). *Field theory in social science.* New York: Harper.

Mann, K. J. (1997). The home as a framework for health care. *Disability and Rehabilitation, 19,* 128-129.

Manton, K., Corder, L., & Stallard, E. (1997). Chronic disability trends in elderly United States populations: 1982-1994. *Proceedings of the National Academy of Sciences, 94,* 2593-2598.

Morley, J. E. (2004). The top 10 hot topics in aging. *Journal of Gerontology: Medical Sciences, 59A,* 24-33.

Moss, M., & Lawton, M. P. (1982). Time budgets of older people: A window in four life styles. *Journal of Gerontology, 37,* 115-123.

National Center for Health Statistics. (2000, March 1). An overview of nursing home facilities: Data from the 1997 National Nursing Home Survey. Advance Data No. 311.

Newman, S. J. (1995). Housing policy and home-based care. *The Milbank Quarterly, 73*(3), 407-441.

Newman, S. J. (1985). Housing and long-term care: The suitability of the elderly's housing to the provision of in-home services. *The Gerontologist, 25*(1), 35-40.

Newman, S. J. (2003). The living conditions of elderly Americans. *The Gerontologist, 43,* 99-109.

Newman, S., Struyk, R., Wright, P., & Rice, M. (1990). Overwhelming odds: Caregiving and the risk of institutionalization. *Journal of Gerontology, 45*(5): S173-S183.

Norburn, J. E. K., Bernard, S. L., Konrad, T. R., Woomert, A., DeFriese, G. H., Kalsbeek, W. D., Koch, G. G., & Ory, M. G. (1995). Self-care and assistance from others in coping with functional status limitations among a national sample of older adults. *Journal of Gerontology Social Sciences, 50B,* S101-S109.

Olsen, R. V., Ehrenkrantz, E., & Hutchings, B. (1993). Creating supporting environments for people with dementia and their caregivers through home modifications. *Technology and Disability, 2,* 47-57.

Parmelee, P., & Lawton, M. P. (1990). The design of special environments for the aged. In J. E., Birren & K. W. Schaie (Eds.), *Handbook of the psychology of aging* (3rd ed., pp. 465-489). New York: Academic Press.

Pynoos, J., Cohen, E., Davis, L., & Bernhardt, S. (1987). Home modifications. Improvements that extend independence. In V. Regnier & J. Pynoos (Eds.), *Housing the aged. Design directives, policy considerations* (pp. 277-304). New York: Elsevier Science Publication Co. Inc.

Pynoos, J., & Liebig, P. S. (Eds.). (1995). H*ousing frail elders: International policies, perspectives, and prospects.* Baltimore: The Johns Hopkins University.

Pynoos, J., & Ohta, R. J. (1991). In-home interventions for person with Alzheimer's disease and their caregivers. *Occupational Therapy and Physical Therapy in Geriatrics, 9,* 83-92.

Reschovsky, J. D., & Newman, S. J. (1990). Adaptations for independent living by older frail households. *The Gerontologist, 30*(4), 543-552.

Rubinstein, R. L. (1989). The home environments of older people: A description of the psychosocial processes linking person to place. *Journal of Gerontology, 44,* S45-S53.

Schaie, K. W., Wahl, H.-W., Mollenkopf, H., & Oswald, F. (Eds.). (2003). *Aging independently: Living arrangements and mobility.* New York: Springer Publications.

Schulz, R., Gallagher-Thompson, D., Haley, W., & Czaja, S. (1999). Understanding the intervention process: A theoretical/conceptual framework for intervention approaches to caregiving. In R. Schulz (Ed.), *Handbook on dementia caregiving: Evidence-based interventions for family caregivers* (pp. 33-60). New York: Springer Publishing Company.

Soldo, B., & Longino, C. (1988). Social and physical environments for the vulnerable aged. In Institute of Medicine and National Research Council (Ed.), *American's aging: The social and built environment in an older society* (pp. 103-1333). Washington, DC: National Academy Press.

Spillman, B. C. (2003). *Changes in elderly disability rates and the implications for health care utilization and cost.* Report prepared under contract #HHS-100-97-0010 between the U.S. Department of Health and Human Services, Office of the Assistant Secretary for Planning and Evaluation, Office of Disability.

Struyk, R. J., & Katsura, H. M. (1998). *Aging at home: How the elderly adjust their housing without moving.* New York: Haworth Press.

Struyk, R. J., & Soldo, B. J. (1980). *Improving the elderly's housing: A key to preserving the nation's housing stock and neighborhoods.* New York: Ballinger Publishing Company.

Verbrugge, L. M., & Jette, A. (1994). The disablement process. *Social Science and Medicine, 38*(1), 1-14.

Verbrugge, L. M., Rennert, C., & Madans, J. H. (1997). The great efficacy of personal and equipment assistance in reducing disability. *American Journal of Public Health, 87,* 384-392.

Wahl, H.-W. (2001). Environmental influences on aging and behavior. In J. E. Birren & K. W. Schaie (Eds.), *Handbook of the psychology of aging* (5th ed., pp. 215-237). San Diego, CA: Academic Press.

Wahl, H.-W., & Gitlin, L. N. (2003). Future developments in living environments for older people in the U.S. and Germany: Potential and constraints. In K. W. Schaie, H.-W. Wahl, H. Mollenkopf, & F. Oswald (Eds.), *Aging in the community: Living arrangements and mobility* (pp. 281-301). New York: Springer Publications.

Wahl, H.-W., & Lang, F. R. (2004). Aging in context across the adult life course: Integrating physical and social environmental research perspectives. In H.-W. Wahl, R. Scheidt, & P. Windley (Eds.), *Annual review of gerontology and geriatrics, 23 (Aging in context: Socio-physical environments* (pp. 1-33). New York: Springer Publications.

Wahl, H.-W., Oswald, F., & Zimprich, D. (1999). Everyday competence in visually impaired older adults: A case for person-environment perspectives. *The Gerontologist, 39,* 140-149.

Wahl, H.-W., & Weisman, G. (2003). Environmental gerontology at the beginning of the new millennium: Reflections on its historical, empirical, and theoretical development. *The Gerontologist, 43*(5), 616-627.

Wenger, N. S., Solomon, D. H., Roth, C. P., MacLean, C. H., Saliba, D., Kamberg, C. J., Rubenstein, L. Z., Young, R. T., Sloss, E. M., Louie, R., Adams, J., Chang, J. T., Venus, P. J., Schnelle, J. F., & Shekelle, P. G. (2003). The quality of medical care provided to vulnerable community-dwelling older patients. *Annals of Internal Medicine, 139,* 740-759.

CHAPTER 8

Beyond the Relocation Trauma in Old Age: New Trends in Elders' Residential Decisions

Frank Oswald and Graham D. Rowles

SETTING THE STAGE

Development in later life involves a dynamic of person-environmental exchanges over time. One of the most important developmental events in this regard is relocation. Although most elders want to remain in their homes, ". . . to move or not to move is really part of the aging in place debate" (Pastalan, 1995, p. 1). Consider two archetypical scenarios. First, there is the voluntary decision to move after a long period of residential stability, often early in retirement. This decision to relocate from one residence to another may be made after months or even years of evaluating positive and negative aspects of a long distance migration. It may involve discussions with friends and relatives, comparing costs of living and climates, reflection on vacation experiences and a final decision to move with a spouse to a more attractive setting with better amenities. In studying such moves, one might focus on demographic and geographical patterns, on personal and environmental predictors, on motivations, on the subjective experience of the event itself, or on the process of settling in and accommodation to the new environment. Under a second scenario, one may think of relocation as the result of a sudden health-related crisis in very old age. After an extended period of frailty and a short-term stay in a hospital, there may be a reluctant relocation into a long-term care facility. Again we may focus on demographics, on risk factors, on the relocation itself and on emotionally laden and often traumatic consequences of having to give up one's home—a process that may lead to further health decline and even death.

It is important at the outset to clarify our use of the words migration, relocation, and movement. In this chapter the notion of moving refers to all changes in location. By migration we are referring primarily to long-distance moves. Use of the word relocation refers primarily to short-distance moves. Clearly there is considerable overlap among these three concepts.

In recent decades, the contrast between our two scenarios has come into sharper focus with increasing differentiation between elders in their "Third Age" and those in their "Fourth Age" (Baltes & Smith, 1999). Whereas long-planned decisions to migrate from one home to another are often made by relatively healthy and affluent elders, the sudden and unexpected loss of home tends to occur more frequently among very old and frail individuals. Indeed, the growing number and proportion of very old people in the population can be anticipated to lead to an absolute increase in the number of relocations in very old age. Migration from one community to another is increasingly popular: it is a relatively common, anticipated, and generally positively evaluated event. In contrast, relocation into a long-term care facility is a clearly nonnormative experience with arguably adverse effects on health and well-being (Ryff, Singer, & Seltzer, 2002; see also Gitlin in this volume).

The diversity of housing arrangements for elders has increased during recent decades, affecting residential needs and decisions as well as subsequent outcomes for both those who move and those who remain in place (Krout & Wethington, 2003). Moves now take place not only from one community residence to another or from a traditional family home to an institution. Today, the phenomenon also embraces moves to an array of different kinds of purpose-built dwellings, often providing supportive services and characterized by the umbrella term "assisted living." Continuing care retirement communities (CCRCs), independent and assisted living facilities (in the United States), co-housing and assisted housing (in Europe) as well as an increasing number of facilities specially designed for demented elders are now important options within the relocation landscape. In addition, this landscape now encompasses naturally occurring retirement communities (NORCs), which result from increasing concentrations of elders left behind as younger persons move out of an area or increasing numbers of elder "snowbirds" or "sunbirds" who engage annually in seasonal migration, temporarily moving to environmentally attractive, amenity-rich locations. Even for those who choose to remain in place, there are now many alternatives as a result of environmental adaptations and technical aids that allow the individual to remain in a familiar dwelling, even when suffering from significant loss of environmental competence.

As understanding of diverse types of relocation increases, growing sophistication is reflected in distinctions between voluntary and involuntary moves. Voluntary moves generally involve a combination of personal and environmental factors. The main reasons for involuntary moves continue to be declining physical health and, to an increasing degree, progressive cognitive impairment. In most cases, relocation involves a mixture of voluntary and involuntary factors, especially in very old age. Increasing sophistication is also apparent in considering the dichotomy of "push" (away from the old location) versus "pull" (toward the new location) motivations (e.g., Haas & Serow, 1993), and "basic" versus "higher-order" needs in accounting for migration (Carp & Carp, 1984). Finally, there is increasing recognition of the need to regard relocation from experiential and life-course perspectives and to place emphasis on understanding the processes involved in successfully re-establishing a sense of place attachment after losing a home through relocation (Rowles & Watkins, 2003).

As we focus on experiential aspects of relocation, the contrast of our two scenarios becomes ever more blurred. In this chapter, our goal is to clarify the current status of knowledge by reviewing aspects of relocation and residential decision making and by identifying recent trends likely to have significant impact on the relocation patterns and processes of future cohorts of elders. We begin by discussing options that often precede or provide an alternative to relocation, emphasizing the increased role of housing modification as an adaptive strategy. Against this baseline, the core of the chapter considers theoretical perspectives and presents empirical data from four different paradigms of relocation in old age in order to give a comprehensive picture of the complex societal and individual phenomenon of relocation. Employing a *demographic* perspective, we focus first on the prevalence of relocation as a changing societal phenomenon reflected in trends such as increasing numbers of moves into purpose-built homes and the emergence of seasonal migration as a significant phenomenon. Next, adding a process-oriented *decision-making* perspective, individual motivations for relocation are considered, moving beyond a simple push versus pull dichotomy. Differences in motivations between relocationing from home to home into purpose-built homes versus into institutions are explored. A third paradigm enriches our understanding by adding an *outcomes* perspective that weighs both positive and negative consequences of relocation. Although we consider relocation to be basically a stressful event, we also emphasize positive aspects of a change of residence (Golant, 1998). Finally, adopting an *experiential life-course* perspective that further broadens and deepens the realm of discourse, we focus on relocation and the transformation of place in old age, considered from both short-term and long-term temporal perspectives. Together, the decision-making perspective, outcome perspective, and experiential life-course perspective provide a comprehensive window on the developmental impact of relocation in later life. In a concluding section, the four paradigms are melded within some integrative and future-oriented remarks.

STAYING PUT: THE BASELINE

Although the likelihood of living in a nursing facility increases with age and the number of alternative purpose-built homes is increasing in modern Western societies, elders have a high degree of residential stability; most want to avoid relocation, and the majority wish to live independently for as long as possible. This preference has resulted in growing emphasis on aging-in-place as a policy priority (BMFSFJ, 2001; Rowles, 1993; U.S. Bureau of the Census, 1996). This has been accompanied by a recent increase of scientific interest in the phenomenon (e.g., Gitlin, 2003; Wahl & Weisman, 2003).

As people age-in-place, decrease of functional capacity often leads to increased environmental press and a person-environment misfit (Kahana, 1982; Lawton & Nahemow, 1973). Recent decades have witnessed an increasing propensity for retro-fitting housing with environmental aids and other forms of home modification and adaptation (Gitlin, 1998; Lanspery & Hyde, 1997; Pynoos, 2000; Regnier, 2003). Although systematic analysis of home modification for older adults has revealed somewhat mixed results (Gitlin, 1998), there is evidence of positive outcomes with respect to maintaining daily activities (Harper & Bayer, 2000). Finally, the emergence of universal design and growing recognition of the value of "smart home" technologies is transforming the potential for elders to remain in and function effectively in familiar settings (Mann, 2001; Mollenkopf & Fozard, 2003). For some elders, extensive modifications may facilitate remaining in the familiar space of home for an extended period. For others, this solution may not be viable, particularly if the home cannot be easily adapted to cope with changing circumstances. To conclude, changes in relocation patterns cannot be regarded independently from increasing numbers of moving alternatives for today's elders to facilitate remaining in place, as "staying put" remains an important potential outcome of the residential decision-making process in old age.

PARADIGMS OF RELOCATION IN OLD AGE

A Demographic Perspective on Relocation

Relocation as a societal phenomenon has often been addressed from a demographic perspective (Carlson, Junk, Fox, Rudzitis, & Cann, 1998; Golant, 1998; Longino, 2004; Pastalan, 1995; Serow, 2001). Transitions in older adults' living arrangements are relatively rare events in Western societies (Brown et al., 2002; Speare, Avery, & Lawton, 1991; U.S. Bureau of the Census, 1996). "In any recent five-year period, people of retirement age are only about half as likely to make long-distance moves as is the U.S. population as a whole. So most people tend to stay put when they retire" (Longino, Perzynski, & Stoller, 2002, p. 45; for further information see Longino, 2004). However, extrapolations based on a German survey revealed that an increasing number of elders in their Third Age expect to move at least once before they reach their Fourth Age (Socio-Economic Panel, SOEP; Heinze, Eichener, Naegele, Bucksteeg & Schauerte, 1997). Many existing studies are based on theoretical frameworks identifying moving types. Litwak and Longino (1987), for example, divided relocations in late life into first, second, and third moves. First moves often take place close to retirement during the Third Age and are usually prompted by amenities associated with a desired place of residence. Second moves tend to be characterized by moves back to a place of origin. Third moves often are disability-related relocations of frail elders to institutions during their Fourth Age (Hazelrigg & Hardy, 1995; Litwak & Longino, 1987). Although this typology provides a useful global perspective on migration and relocation patterns in old age, it understates the broad range of conceivable environmental changes and alternative-housing opportunities confronting elders.

Moving from Home to Home

Relocation behavior among relatively healthy and affluent elders in their Third Age has changed over time. Paradoxically, older adults today are both increasingly attached to their familiar residence *and,* at the same time, increasingly mobile (Clark & Davies, 1990).

Relocations within community boundaries, often the same county, are the most frequent in old age (e.g., Krout, Moen, Holmes, Oggins, & Bowen, 2002; Oswald, Schilling, Wahl, & Gäng, 2002). As the spatial range of activities decreases, the proximate living environment, including the home, the area immediately outside—the "surveillance zone" (Rowles, 1981)—and the neighborhood, become more important, especially in very old age. Two-thirds of 217 involuntary movers in a German study have moved within the same town, half of them within the same district (Oswald et al., 2002). In a recent European study on housing and health with 1314 elders (65 years and older), 46% would chose to relocate within the same neighborhood, if necessary (World Health Organization (WHO), 2004). Moving within a neighborhood facilitates achieving the benefits of a supportive home without losing social contacts, outdoor routines, and emotional bonding to a familiar place.

At the same time, the number of elders undertaking long-distance migration is increasing (Longino, 2004). Research on older international migrants within Europe has focused on flows of British, German, and Norwegian retirees to southern Europe, with the majority of studies concentrating on older migrants on the coasts of Spain (King, Warnes, & Williams, 2000; Wolthuis, 1997). Little is known about the long-term consequences of such migration. Supplementing permanent migration, there is a growing trend, especially within the United States, toward seasonal migration (McHugh & Mings, 1996; Scheidt & Windley, 1998). Although permanent migration has been well-documented, this is not the case with seasonal migration (Hogan & Steinnes, 1998). Increasing numbers of elders now have different homes for different seasons, sometimes maintaining dual residences over decades. Living in such a "circle of migration" (McHugh & Mings, 1996) is a relatively new phenomenon that affects the structure and temporal dynamics of person-environment transactions in terms of everyday behavior, environmental preferences, and place attachment. Thus, basically, the number of elders who relocate in the near future (baby boomers) will increase and the pattern of migration will change in terms of a greater variety of destinations and in terms of more cyclic patterns of seasonal migration (Longino, 2004).

Moving into Purpose-Built Homes

Increasing numbers of older adults are moving into purpose-built dwellings or assisted-living facilities designed to address specific support needs. In the United States, about 2.4% of those 65 and older reside "in congregate facilities or assisted and/or board and care homes" (Administration on Aging, 1996, cited in Krout et al., 2002, p. 237). In Germany, the corresponding figure is about 2.6% (Großjohann, 2003). The number and proportion of elders living in purpose-built homes is increasing. Some authors suggest that proportions up to about 10% of those 65 years and older are living in an array of purpose-built alternatives, including retirement communities and subdivisions, senior apartments, congregate housing, assisted living, continuing-care retirement communities (CCRCs), and skilled nursing facilities (Regnier, 2003). In Europe, co-housing (Palsig, 2000) and "assisted housing" options (Großjohann, 2003; Saup, 2001) have proliferated during the last decade. Assisted living provides an alternative for those who want to combine the amenities of modern community residence with a guarantee of easy access to basic social support or healthcare services in the future.

Moving into an Institution

Relocation to a nursing home has long been a major topic of research and application (e.g., Aldrich & Menkoff, 1963; Bourestom & Tars, 1974; Green & Ondrich, 1990; Schulz & Brenner, 1977; Tobin, 1989). Although a small number of people 65 years and older are residing in institutions at any particular time, the lifetime risk of relocation to a care facility is much higher. Kemper and Murtaugh (1991) projected that, in the United States, 43% of the population turning 65 years of age in 1990 would be admitted to a nursing facility at some time during their life. Due to different life expectancies, the risk is twice as high for women compared to men. In Germany, about 20% of men and 40% of women will be admitted to a nursing facility during their lifetime (BMFSFJ, 2001).

Large-scale hospital-like nursing homes of the past are being replaced by small-scale, skilled nursing-care facilities, especially for the very frail, the demented, and the oldest old (persons 85 years of age and older). Numerous purpose-specific, creatively designed nursing homes and small-scale dementia-care settings have been established (e.g., Weisman, 2003; Weisman, Chaudhury, & Moore, 2000). As a result of rapidly increasing prevalence rates of dementia, relocations due to cognitive deficits, especially dementia, have and are likely to continue to increase. Relocation into an institution often occurs due to a combination of the increased caregiving burden on a spouse at home and/or the potential for obtaining more specifically targeted skilled nursing care in an institutional setting. As a result, nursing homes are dealing with increasing numbers and proportions of demented residents—often about 50%. Recent studies suggest that interventions, involving combinations of environmental adaptation and training, enable some elders who are not living alone to remain at home (Gitlin, Corcoran, Winter, Boyce, & Hauck, 2001).

Facing increasing numbers of very old elders who will need to move to a dementia care-setting, recent model facilities have focused on innovations based on a more sophisticated understanding of dementia. There is increased emphasis on building into design not only recognition of specific cognitive and physical impairments but also the creation of home-like places that recognize the social and emotional needs of the most vulnerable cognitively impaired elders in "special care units," although in the future, positive results are likely to extend beyond these model facilities (Day, Carreon, & Stump, 2000; Weisman, 2003).

A DECISION-MAKING PROCESS PERSPECTIVE ON RELOCATION

Moving beyond the demographic perspective, we turn to a focus on the individual. "The essential problem of studying the migration decision is that it is a process" (Longino et al., 2002, p. 33). We consider the process of relocation decision making, risk factors for relocation, and subjective motivations for moving—juxtaposing consideration of relocation from home to home with moves into purpose-built residences and into institutions. The decision-making process that leads to relocation in old age can take many years to crystallize and is triggered and shaped by several moderating factors (Johnson-Carroll, Brandt, & McFadden, 1995; Ryff & Essex, 1992; Smider, Essex, & Ryff, 1996).

One of the most often cited theoretical perspectives on relocation is the "retirement-migration model" (Wiseman, 1980) a two-stage model of migration decision making—showing that the decision to move and the decision of where to move are influenced by different factors. This model has been extended to a heuristic framework based on key events in the migration process (Haas & Serow, 1993), on reasons for choosing a destination (Cuba, 1991), and other considerations affecting the relocation process (Carlson et al., 1998).

Empirical evidence from a subjective motivational perspective often differentiates between push and pull factors in the relocation process. Factors that pull or attract an elder to a new destination seem to be more important than those that push older adults away from a current location (Carlson et al., 1998; De Jong, Wilmoth, Angel, & Cornwell, 1995; Haas & Serow, 1993). The push-pull dichotomy is useful, and its value is enhanced by examining the motivations (e.g., personal considerations versus environmental forces) that lead to relocation. A similar motivation (e.g., having extensive living space) can, in one case, be a push factor and, in another case, a pull factor influencing an elder's decision-making process (Oswald et al., 2002).

Finally, an important differentiation can be made on the basis of the "complementary-congruence model" of person-environment fit (Carp & Carp, 1984). It is plausible to assume that a hierarchy of intrinsic environmental needs permeates the relocation process. Carp and Carp's model differentiates between "basic environmental needs" and "higher-order needs." Basic needs are oriented toward maintaining personal autonomy with respect to necessary activities of daily living and competencies in everyday life. Higher-order needs reflect more subjective development-oriented domains, including privacy, comfort, familiarity, stimulation, or favored personal activities. Research on relocation motivation would benefit from this more differentiated categorization of reasons for moving with respect to both the content and level of intrinsic need (Carp & Carp, 1984).

Moving from Home to Home

Previous empirical research, primarily addressing processes of voluntary relocation, has uncovered a great deal about the differential importance of personal and environmental factors in the decision-making process. Such factors include age, health and well-being (e.g., Choi, 1996; Nelson, 1997; Ryff & Essex, 1992), proximity to kin, socioeconomic and demographic considerations (e.g., Hazelrigg & Hardy, 1995), environmental bonding, neighborhood ties, and the chance to form attachments with new places (e.g., Carlson et al., 1998; Rowles & Ravdal, 2001; Rowles & Watkins, 2003). In a comparative study on relocation in the United States and Germany, Friedrich (1995) identified three typical moving incentives: to have an "attractive home" (especially in the Third Age); to be "closer to the family" (especially in the Fourth Age); and to "overcome bad housing conditions" (see also Serow, Friedrich, & Haas, 1996).

The bulk of the evidence suggests that good health is a major predictor of migration to amenity-rich destinations (first moves at around the time of retirement; Litwak & Longino, 1987); whereas poor health is a major contributing factor to relocation to medically and socially supportive settings and to healthcare facilities (second and third moves) (e.g., Silverstein & Zablotzky, 1996). Findings from a recent nine-year longitudinal study reinforce the conclusion that poor physical and mental health conditions trigger transitions in living arrangements (Brown et al., 2002). In contrast, a recent investigation of the actual health status of community-dwelling elders found that health status did not predict future housing expectations (Robinson & Moen, 2000).

Beyond physical and mental health, psychological resources, such as environmental mastery, purpose in life, or positive relations with others, have been hypothesized as factors influencing the process of relocation decision making (Ryff et al., 2002; Ryff & Essex, 1992; Smider et al., 1996). For example, Rutman and Freedman (1988) reported increases in environmental satisfaction following relocation that were related to perceived control beliefs. Participants in their study reported dealing with stress by exercising personal control over their environment. Nearly all the respondents wanted to view the relocation process as one over which they had choice and control. An ability to transfer treasured possessions and to re-create interior environments providing a semblance of the abandoned setting through, for example, a similar spatial arrangement of furniture and artifacts, may significantly reduce the stress of relocation through its ability to sustain elements of the individual's sense of control (Rowles & Ravdal, 2001; Rowles & Watkins, 2003).

To learn about relocation decision making, it is important to compare elders who make a move with older adults who decide to remain in place and to explore the processes of their decision making or avoidance of decision making (residential inertia) in temporal context (Krout, Holmes, Erickson, & Wolle, 2003). In a recent study of retirement migration decision-making among 848 older persons from the United States, Longino and colleagues empirically demonstrated that not only the relocation decision itself but also features of the potential future destination, the pre-retirement location, pre-retirement familiarity with potential destinations, and lifetime migration experiences constituted key elements of a life-course perspective on relocation (Longino et al., 2002). Comparing those who moved with those who remained in place, Longino and colleagues revealed that the most important factors influencing relocation decisions included climate (cold: push, warm: pull), personal ties (proximity to family/friends as a factor in residential inertia), community characteristics (high costs of living: push, natural beauty: pull), lifetime migration experiences and past vacation experiences.

Another study providing empirical evidence on motivations for moving involved a group of 217 older adults in Germany who moved from one home to another within the three-year period, immediately prior to being interviewed. Using a combined qualitative and quantitative methodology, data on reasons for moving were obtained by assessing responses to open-ended questions supplemented by more in-depth probing of each of the motivating factors identified by the participants. The study differentiated between content (e.g., person, physical environment, social environment) and level of need-related motivations (basic needs, higher-order needs) (Oswald et al., 2002). It emerged that the subjects of this study had multiple reasons for moving, with many of these involving the satisfaction of higher-order needs (see Figure 1).

Participants mentioned an average of four different reasons for moving. These reasons reflected different combinations of the levels and categories shown in Figure 1. With respect to the content level of motives, physical-environment-related motivations were the most prevalent. These included basic housing needs ("I found the apartment was too large to do my daily work") as well as higher-order needs ("We wanted to have a balcony and a view"). In the domain of motives pertaining to the social environment, the differentiation between basic ("My daughter can do the shopping for me now, because she lives just around the corner") and higher-order needs ("I wanted to spend more time with my grandchildren") can also be shown. We conclude that there is rarely one single reason for moving, but rather a set of needs that, in conjunction, lead to relocation. Although the participants in this study varied in health status and basic needs, most reported that higher-order needs became increasingly significant elements of relocation decision making in old age (Oswald et al., 2002). In sum, results on voluntary moving

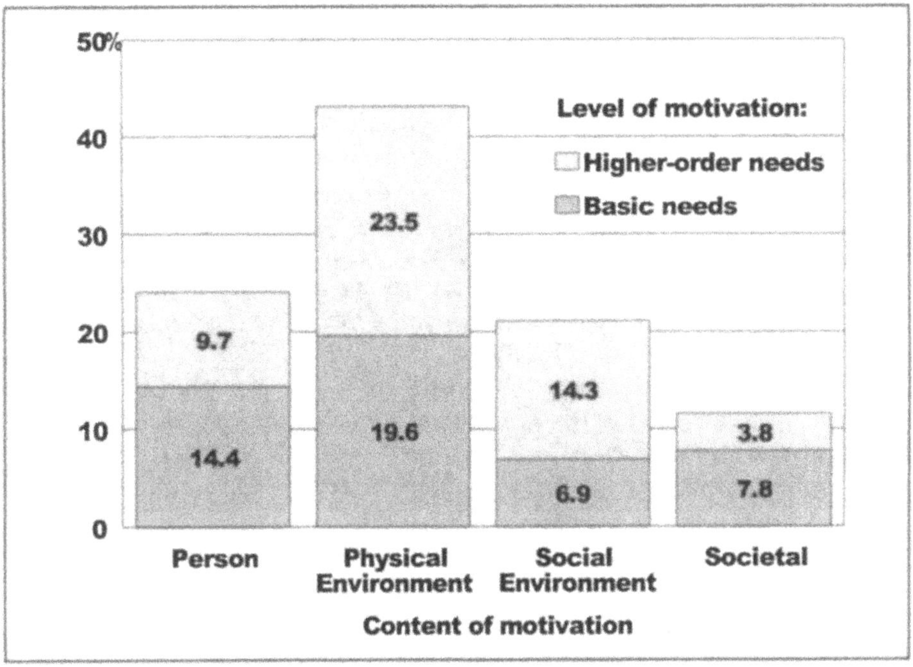

Figure 1. Reasons for moving cross classified by level and content of motivation.
Note: The relative frequency of varying move motives are shown above.
A total of 961 reasons for the move were coded from $N = 217$ participants,
which represents a mean of 4.4 reasons for moving per person.
Source: Reproduced from Oswald, F. (2003). Linking subjective housing needs
to objective living conditions among older adults in Germany.
In K. W. Schaie, H.-W. Wahl, H. Mollenkopf, & F. Oswald (Eds.),
Aging independently: Living arrangements and mobility (p. 141).
Used with permission from Springer Publishing Company, Inc., New York 10012.

from home to home consistently show that the complexity of the residential decision process necessitates more sophisticated methodologies.

Moving into Purpose-Built Homes

There is accumulating empirical evidence on the decision-making processes involved in relocation to purpose-built senior housing and assisted-living residences. In a sample of 868 elders (60 years and older) living in different housing arrangements (Krout & Wethington, 2003), the "Pathways" study revealed in great detail the process of residential decision making over time by comparing elders who moved to senior housing facilities or other dwellings within the community with those who remained in place.

Moving into the typical CCRC "guarantees lifetime access to housing and health care in return for an up-front 'buy-in' cost and fixed monthly fees" (Krout et al., 2002, p. 237). The amount of guaranteed support in comparable European "assisted-housing" facilities is generally more limited; it involves the provision of barrier-free apartments, medical-emergency call systems, and an in-house warden who can facilitate access to medical care and provide healthcare information and counseling.

As a pilot study of the Pathways survey, an assessment of 91 older adults who subsequently moved to a new CCRC facility revealed that primary motivations for their relocation involved the anticipation of future needs (Krout et al., 2002, 2003). There was a desire to remain independent, a desire for continuing care, for freedom from the upkeep and maintenance required in the participants' current residence, and the desire to avoid dependency or becoming a burden to anyone. The location and reputation of the facility were also mentioned as important motivating factors. As Krout and his colleagues note, "Relocation to a CCRC can be seen as an anticipatory move taken by people who are relatively healthy and wealthy and who want to combine amenities with the guarantee of further health care in a community that may be near to family" (Krout et al., 2002, p. 241).

Comparable conclusions are reached in a study of 173 older adults residing in seven assisted-housing facilities in Germany (Saup, 2001). The longitudinal component of this study revealed, however, that the participants held unrealistic expectations and were poorly informed about housing alternatives. Assessments conducted both before and after relocation indicated that participants had moved in order to circumvent or anticipate certain risks they perceived would occur in their old age, though many of them were already suffering from loss of competence when they moved in. The majority expected that they would be able to remain in their new home until death, even if intensive care was required or if they were to exhibit mental deterioration. These were unrealistic expectations given the mandate of the assisted housing to provide only non-intensive support within home-like housing with barrier-free environments and some basic instrumental and social support (Saup, 2001). The increasing numbers who relocate to special purpose-built housing clearly demonstrate that the current generation of elders considers both amenities and anticipated future needs for support when they select their future home. Unfortunately, in most areas there is a discontinuity between elders' preferences and available options (Golant, 1992). The potential for combining an attractive home in a pleasant location with good supportive care that is less expensive than skilled nursing home care is limited. This is especially the case with respect to purpose-specific care units for persons with dementia (Regnier, 2003).

Moving into an Institution

A basic underlying motivation of most elders is to avoid moving to an institution. Indeed, relocation into an institution presents a paradigm of involuntary transition in residence. Often there is limited personal involvement in the decision-making process. Consequently, relocation into institutions has been viewed primarily from a loss perspective, emphasizing the risks and consequences of stress and trauma. Many of these risks and consequences stem from the poor health status and functional-cognitive impairment of persons making this move (e.g., Coffman, 1981; Green & Ondrich, 1990; Schulz & Brenner, 1977). Low socioeconomic status and ethnicity may also be contributing factors. Other risk factors directly or indirectly relate to social context, for example, living alone or having no children living nearby (e.g., Silverstein & Zablotzky,

1996). High levels of loneliness increase the likelihood of and accelerate nursing home admissions, even after controlling for other variables (Russel, Cutrona, de la Mora, & Wallace, 1997). Beyond the negative outcomes of involuntary relocation (trauma, accelerated health decline and death), the impact of limited personal (especially psychological) resources to cope with the new situation, the process of relocation itself, and the impact of the institutional environment in determining well-being have each been analyzed. Lack of control before and after the move, as well as difficulties in making necessary adjustments to different levels of care, are responsible for high levels of relocation stress and trauma (Coffman, 1981; Langer & Rodin, 1976; Rodin & Langer, 1977; Schulz & Brenner, 1977). There is accumulating empirical evidence that those elders who can anticipate and who have enough time to prepare for their move can adjust more easily to the new environment (Coffman, 1981; Kruse & Wahl, 1994; Thorson & Davies, 2000). Building on this insight, Lee, Woo, and Mackenzie's (2002) qualitative research revealed that newly admitted elders in institutions "adjusted through the stages of orienting, normalizing, rationalizing, and stabilizing as they struggled to regain normality with a life that was as close to that lived before admission as possible" (Lee, Woo, & Mackenzie, 2002, p. 667).

Not only purpose-built homes but also institutions are increasingly designed to address the specific needs of demented, very old, and frail elders (e.g., Day et al., 2000). Relocation into a skilled nursing facility in the case of dementia cannot easily be discussed from the perspective of decision making, as the elder may only be marginally involved in the relocation decision, especially when relocation occurs late in the progress of the dementia.

AN OUTCOMES PERSPECTIVE ON RELOCATION

Moving to a third paradigm, we consider positive and negative outcomes of relocation in old age. Relocation in old age is a stressful event per se (e.g., Ryff et al., 2002) and there is evidence of negative consequences, especially with respect to involuntary relocation into institutional settings. Although evidence is sparse, we want also to emphasize some positive outcomes, both for voluntary and involuntary relocation. Within this rubric, a wide range of theoretical perspectives on healthy aging, well-being, stress, and morbidity derived from disciplines ranging from health psychology to gerontology can be interrelated. From the perspective of theory in environmental gerontology (e.g. Kahana, 1982; Lawton & Nahemow, 1973), we can focus on the increase of person-environment fit or decrease of person-environment misfit through environmental adaptation following relocation.

Within the "environmental proactivity" model (Lawton, 1985), the individual's active shaping of his or her environment becomes very important, especially when interpreting the outcome of moving in response to a perceived misfit between the person and the environment (Kahana, 1982; Lawton, 1985, 1998; Parmelee & Lawton, 1990, p. 470). Accordingly, the outcomes of environmental changes due to relocation can be examined to determine the degree to which they represent truly goal-directed efforts to optimize an environmental context or merely happenstance events unrelated to the quest for improved person-environment congruence. Some recent models explain outcomes of environmental change by recourse to consideration of temporal context—in terms of the individual's life course, past levels of experienced person-environment fit, and other individually defined subjective reference points for the assessment of current outcomes (Golant, 1998; Wheeler, 1995). Although identification of moderating aspects of time on individual relocation decisions is integral to such research, the more interesting question is how subjective motivations and subsequent environmental changes are linked to outcomes with respect to well-being throughout the life course.

Moving from Home to Home and into Purpose-Built Homes

In order to describe positive and negative outcomes of relocation from home to home, one might ask if subsequent environmental conditions have changed for better or for worse. It is also important to know the manner in which environmental changes are related to pre-relocation expectations and motives. In one study of relocation motivation, objective changes in the environment due to relocation were examined through a list of detailed questions on "household amenities," "stimulation characteristics of the setting," "availability of resources," and the "social network" of the person (Oswald et al., 2002). Most participants reported high levels of stability with an optimization of relationship with the new environment more prevalent than deterioration of the relationship with the old one. Participants optimized their homes in all domains as a result of their relocation—even with respect to visual stimulation (e.g., scenic view). Beyond the environmental outcomes of the relocation itself, the relationship between objective change and subjective motivation was analyzed. Links were found between basic housing needs and physical barrier reduction, as well as between social motives and the proximity of family after the relocation (Oswald et al., 2002). Thus, elders who are able to exercise choice do not necessarily report negative outcomes of changes in their home environment when moves are voluntary. Rutman and Freedman (1988) have reported increases in environmental satisfaction following relocation. Based on a register of 22,579 older persons, Danermark and colleagues analyzed the effects of residential relocation among elders. They found "that residential relocation among elderly people does not have any significant effect on mortality or consumption of health services" (Danermark, Ekstrom, & Bodin, 1996, p. 212). However, it should be noted that for the subgroup of elders who moved permanently and, presumably, reluctantly as a result of urban renewal, the mortality rate was higher than among nonmovers and those who moved for other reasons.

The Pathways study recently explored how housing types and residential decisions affect different aspects of health, well-being, and life quality. As far as the impact of relocation on social integration is concerned, differences between long-term and new CCRC residents are reported. Whereas long-term residents in CCRCs with high attachment to their facilities perceived an increase in role participation, recent movers reported fewer social roles after the move (Moen, Dempster-McClain, Erickson, & Boyce, 2003).

Moving into an Institution

Involuntary environmental changes such as forced relocation to a nursing facility, can result in increased mortality rates, seriously compromise functional health, reduce life satisfaction, and undermine the psychological well-being of elders, especially if they are already vulnerable in terms of declining health or financial status (Danermark et al., 1996; Pruchno & Resch, 1988). Early studies on relocation to institutions emphasized "relocation trauma" or "transfer trauma," phrases used to describe harm that may occur when an older person is moved. An involuntary relocation may lead to physical or psychological decline and even death. Indeed, a series of studies conducted in the 1960s and 1970s documented significantly increased mortality rates as a result of relocation (Bourestom & Tars, 1974; Killian, 1970). In Bourstom and Tars' study, almost twice as many persons died in the year after the relocation in a "radical environmental change" group in comparison with a matched control group that did not relocate. Those who did not die as a result of the relocation frequently became depressed and disoriented and reduced their level of activity (Bourestom & Tars, 1974). Psychological deterioration and serious physical illness were also reported to be more pronounced as a result of relocation (Miller & Lieberman, 1965).

Declines in health status after relocation can be attributed to a combination of effects, including characteristics of the person, the nature of the transfer, and the environment itself. Personal effects included selectively more illness in those who moved than in those who did not, controlling for health status prior to the move, and an increase in mortality and morbidity rates after unexpected relocation into institutions. Characteristics of the new environment (e.g., lack of amenities, limited recreation facilities, high population density, and lack of personal space) can have a negative impact on the individual, leading to a decrease in health status (Bourestom & Tars, 1974; Kruse & Wahl, 1994; McKinney & Melby, 2002). Finally, the "social dislocation" of relocation to an institutional setting is disorienting for a frail older person and may itself cause a "cultural shock" leading to negative outcomes (Tobin,1989).

Although consequences of relocation of elders with dementia are not easily documented, recent data show negative outcomes. Using data on 272 persons with Alzheimer's disease who were admitted to a nursing facility, Aneshensel and colleagues found that, on the one hand "relocation is associated with a two-fold increase in mortality risk net of health status" (Aneshensel, Pearlin, Levy-Storms, & Schuler, 2000, p. S152). As one might assume, these researchers found selection effects for postadmission mortality due to poor health, advanced age, being male, and being White. On the other hand, none of the specific indicators of stressful admission or unsatisfactory nursing home conditions were significantly related to mortality for this group of demented elders, although the authors emphasize a couple of methodological caveats.

Studies in this area, and especially those which suggest moderate or even low mortality and morbidity rates after relocation to nursing facilities (e.g., Borup, 1983), have repeatedly been criticized for methodological flaws. Such shortcomings include selectivity problems which lead, for instance, to the exclusion of noninterviewable elders (Horowitz & Schulz, 1983). In one study of 269 elders moving into a new nursing home, no increase in mortality was found (Thorson & Davies, 2000). However, there was an increase in mortality in the one-year preparation phase prior to this relocation. The authors argue that this outcome may have resulted from unintentionally creating great stress among those to be moved during the anticipatory period prior to the actual move (see also Tobin & Lieberman, 1976).

There are somewhat mixed results on the outcomes of the relocation of persons with dementia into special care units (Borup, 1983; Day et al., 2000). Some elders suffer from high rates of depression and mortality following relocation. However, moving from a nonsupportive setting to a new and more pleasant environment can reduce negative impacts for some residents (e.g., McAuslane & Sperlinger, 1994). Increasing knowledge and expertise with respect to the design of specialized units for persons with dementia (Day et al., 2000) will likely lead to improved outcomes and enhancement of resident well-being.

AN EXPERIENTIAL LIFE-COURSE PERSPECTIVE ON RELOCATION

In recent years, studies of relocation in old age have increasingly adopted a phenomenological life-course perspective (McHugh & Mings, 1996; Rowles, 1983; Rowles & Ravdal, 2001; Wheeler, 1995). From a long-term temporal perspective, relocation can be understood as a dynamic ecological transition: a developmental process in which each change of residence is experientially linked to the move that preceded it and to future moves that are anticipated to follow as a normative component of the individual's life course (Bronfenbrenner, 1999). Within this rubric, life events such as widowhood and severe disability trigger relocations to more supportive settings—purpose-built special housing, assisted-living facilities, or even skilled-care nursing homes (e.g., Walters, 2002). From an experiential life-course perspective, each move is not an independent event but rather an integral part of a life trajectory—the elder's story. Each move along a life-course trajectory involves the transference and re-creation of a sense of place as the individual adapts to changing circumstances and engages in processes of place modification to facilitate or preserve a sense of being in place.

Individual relocation histories manifest a wide array of mobility scenarios ranging from, at one extreme, the residential inertia of lifetime residence in a single dwelling to a history of frequent relocation. Wherever along this life-course-mobility continuum an individual's experience may lie, it provides the template for relocation decisions in old age. The individual's personal history of moving also determines his or her patterns or styles of adaptation to each new environment (Longino et al., 2002; Rowles & Ravdal, 2001; Rowles & Watkins, 2003). Persons who relocate relatively frequently develop learned processes of "place making" that involve the transference of elements of previous experience. Adapting to a new environment involves processes of creating or, more accurately, re-creating a sense of comfort, of "being in place" or "at home." The underlying motivation in most cases is to develop a relationship with each new setting that is both consonant with changed circumstances and consistent with the individual's evolving personal history and identity (Oswald & Wahl, 2005; Rowles & Watkins, 2003; Wheeler, 1995).

Place making and developing a sense of being in place has a number of components. It involves reconciling elements of previously established patterns of habitation of familiar spaces (the places of our past) with the constraints and opportunities provided by the size, architecture, spatial configuration, and social context of each new residence (the place of our present). Typically, this process involves the transference of selected possessions such as furniture, photographs, and other treasured artifacts (Belk, 1992). If the move is to a smaller space, for example from a family home to an apartment, there may be some anguish in this process as the elder is obliged to divest him or herself of treasured possessions accumulated over a lifetime—possessions that may have become not only cues to the resurrection of fond memories but also important symbols of continuing identity. There is a need for much more research on this process of divestiture of possessions as a component of relocation in old age (Ekerdt, Sergeant, Dingel, & Bowen, 2004). With respect to the transference of possessions, accommodating to a new space following relocation may be eased by a conscious attempt to arrange furniture in a configuration similar to that which existed within the former environment (Hartwigsen, 1987). Over a succession of moves, there is a tendency to establish a distinctive style of place making as each new environment is transformed from a space to a place and endowed with meanings that blend the old and familiar with the new and novel (Reed, Cook, Sullivan, & Burridge, 2003; Rowles & Watkins, 2003; Wheeler, 1995).

For elders with a history of frequent relocations, re-creating a sense of familiarity and being in place in a new environment may be relatively easy: emotional bonding is achieved rapidly. For others, especially those who have relocated on only a few previous occasions or perhaps never at all, the process of establishing a sense of identification and belonging within a new space may take much longer and be highly stressful. Some elders experience great difficulty adapting to a new setting even after a lengthy period of residence. For a small but regionally significant number of snowbird elders both in the United States and Europe, the process of place making following relocation involves an annual ritual of establishing seasonal place attachments to two or more residences as, over the years, they migrate between winter and summer residences (McHugh & Mings, 1996). Such individuals tend to develop a distinctive style of being in place within each residence and to decorate each interior space accordingly (McHugh & Mings, 1996).

Placing these themes within a life-course-developmental perspective, Rowles and Watkins (2003) recently proposed a conceptual model of accumulating relocation experience that blends the trajectory of relocations over the life course with subjective attendants and sequelae (Figure 2). Building on the transactional person/environment framework employed by most environmental gerontology theories (e.g., Kahana, 1982; Lawton and Nahemow, 1973; Rowles, 1978; Scheidt & Windley, 1998), this model is a modification of the transactional "attunement" model of Kindermann and Skinner (1992). The focus is on the process whereby an individual involved in relocation attunes him or herself to new circumstances as, over time, he or she accommodates to a new setting.

The x-axis of Figure 2 represents age/time. Each paired individual (open circle) and environment (shaded circle) represents a five-year period extending from the age of 5 to 90. Influence/exchange magnitude (the y-axis) refers to the lagged arrows representing an evolving individual/environment relationship, with longer arrows representing greater magnitude of influence. As the individual's capabilities change, he or she may modify the context. This may involve modification of the existing setting to make it more consonant with personal capabilities. Alternatively, it may involve relocation; perhaps a move to an assisted-living facility. Three event scenarios, each tracing potentially disruptive relocations, are depicted in Figure 2. Event A represents a midlife employment-related move, event B represents Litwak and Longino's

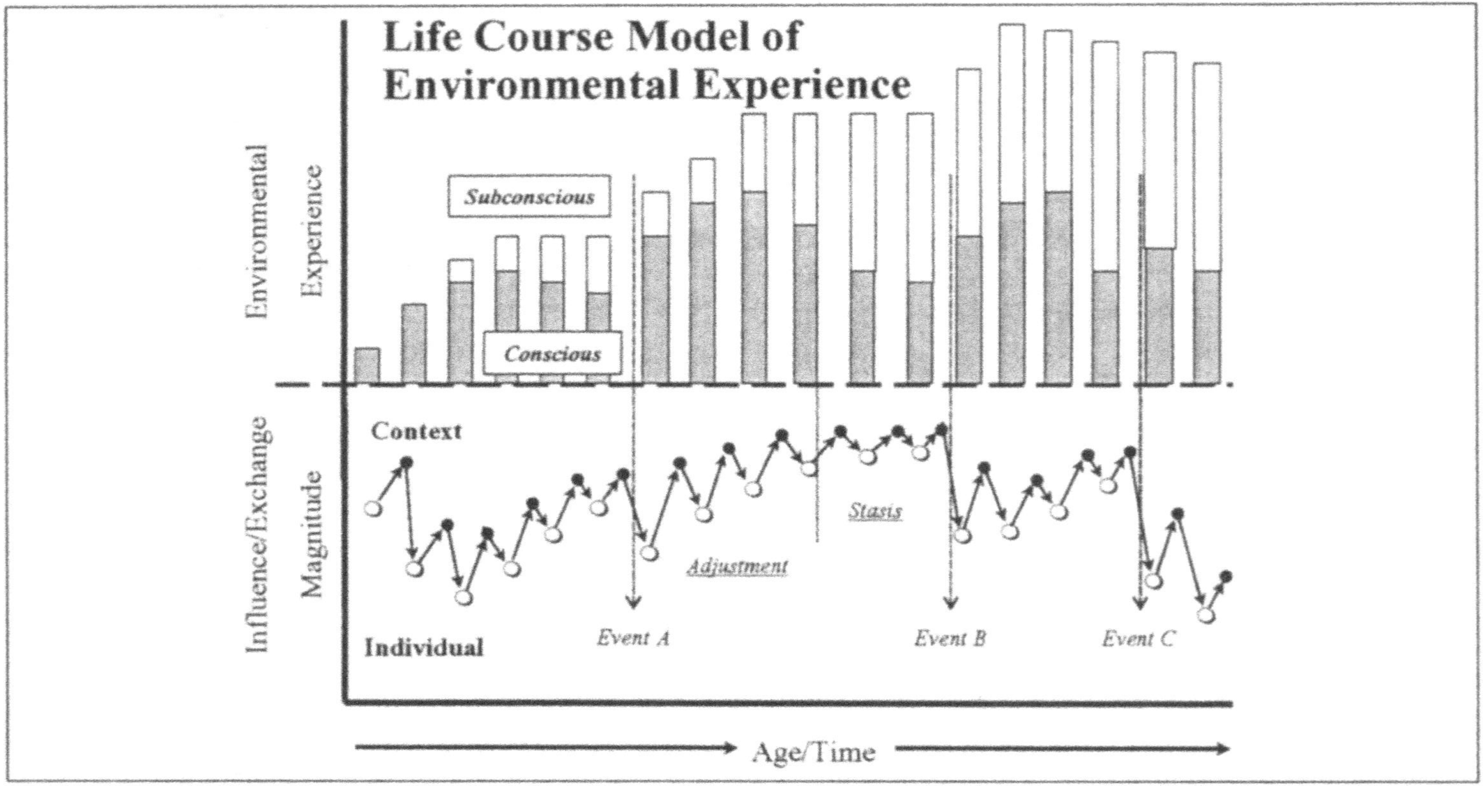

Figure 2. Life-course model of environmental experience.
Reproduced from Rowles, G. D., & Watkins, J. F. (2003).
Used with permission from Springer Publishing Company, Inc., New York 10012.

retirement-related "first move," and event C represents a long-term care relocation for assistance—Litwak and Longino's "second or third move" (Litwak & Longino, 1987). In each case, the model hypothesizes an initial lack of congruence between the individual and the environmental context. Over time, as the individual accommodates to the new setting and transforms it from a space into a place, there is a progression toward stasis and a new level of person-environment congruence.

Paralleling this process, the model suggests a transition in the reservoir of place images that constitute the totality of the individual's environmental experience (represented in the model by each column). Environmental experiences available to immediate consciousness are represented by the shaded area, while those that remain latent or relegated to the subconscious are represented by the open area. The model hypothesizes that relocation results in heightened environmental awareness and increased utilization of the individual's reservoir of environmental experiences, including latent experiences raised to consciousness by the event. Thus, from a life-course-experiential perspective, relocation involves a synthesis of new experience, the sloughing off of redundant elements of an abandoned space, and selective resurrection and transference of prior environmental experience during the process of transforming a new environment from a space into a place. With progression toward person-environment stasis, an increasing proportion of the individual's reservoir of environmental experiences lapses into the subconscious. Over time, a process of habituation to the new space once again results in a taken-for-granted affinity associated with an increasing sense of being in place. Clearly, the nature of the environment and the degree to which it facilitates the individual's accommodation to new circumstances is a strong determinant of the rate at which this process can occur. While it suggests interesting new directions for research, this model has still to be empirically tested.

PATHWAYS TO THE FUTURE: TOWARD AN INTEGRATIVE PERSPECTIVE

Although they provide different theoretical and empirical lenses on relocation in old age, the perspectives presented in the previous pages are very much intertwined. From a demographic perspective, migration trends, relocation alternatives and accommodation options for an increasingly diverse group of elders in their Third and especially Fourth Age have been presented. Processes of individual decision making shaped by personal, biographical, and environmental influences have been explored. A broad range of both positive and negative outcomes of relocation—from enhanced autonomy and well-being to stress, morbidity and mortality—have been discussed. Finally, an experiential perspective on relocation has been presented. This perspective has considered relocation, an emotionally meaningful event at any time in the life course but particularly so in old age, as involving the re-creation of place in a manner that is embedded within autobiography.

Both theory and empirical evidence in each of these domains are currently somewhat fragmentary. There is evidence on relocation motivations and the process of decision making for relocation from home to home and into special purpose-built residences. We know most about risk factors and outcomes when we consider relocation into institutional settings. The evidence clearly indicates that different motivations underlie different types of relocation in old age. Functional environmental characteristics (e.g., cost of living, environmental barriers, amenities, distance to services), community attributes (natural beauty of the physical environment, climate), personal ties (proximity to family and friends), and lifetime migration and vacation experiences may all be considered when moving from home to home. A combination of search for a simplified lifestyle (e.g., freedom from upkeep and maintenance of a current residence) and anticipation of future needs (e.g., opportunity for access to support, potential for continuing care, desire to avoid dependency or becoming a burden to anyone) appear to be prominent considerations when relocating into purpose-built special-housing alternatives. Prominent risk factors in relocation to a nursing facility include poor health, functional-cognitive impairment, low socioeconomic status, living alone, having no children living nearby, and experiencing loneliness. Relocation to a care facility is eased by a sense of perceived control, low levels of stress, and successful adjustment to different levels of care both prior to and after the move. For elders with dementia, relocation to dementia-care facilities may have a positive effect on maintaining a sense of partial autonomy and well-being (at least temporarily) as a result of features of the designed environment and the presence of specially trained and skilled staff, although outcome effects are difficult to measure.

EMERGENT TRENDS

To integrate the different perspectives, we conclude by projecting some trends, based on the evidence presented, that indicate possible cohort changes in relocation patterns and motivations among older adults that go "beyond the relocation trauma."

Relocation in old age is becoming increasingly prevalent, perhaps reflecting the growing mobility of Western societies. Although most elders want to remain in familiar settings and consider home adaptations and refitting measures as well as new technologies to avoid involuntary relocation, voluntary relocation, including seasonal migration and relocation to forms of assisted living (e.g., CCRCs), is becoming an increasingly common event and is likely to become even more so among future cohorts of elders.

We detect a trend toward increasing variability in the relocation process on several levels. With regard to the relationship between the selection of housing alternatives and personal circumstances, the simple elegance of past perspectives—for example, Litwak and Longino's three-fold typology of late life relocation decisions (1987)—is giving way to an increasingly variegated array of strategies and options. Conceptual boundaries among housing alternatives are becoming increasingly blurred. Most relocations from home to home still take place among the relatively healthy and wealthy young old. Relocation to long-term care facilities most often involves frail elders in their Fourth Age, many of whom are suffering from dementia. Data on relocation decision-making processes reveal more complex combinations of motives (e.g., Krout et al., 2002; Krout & Wethington, 2003; Oswald et al., 2002). Generally, there is no single motive for relocation. Rather, a combination of motivations are brought into play, reflecting a meshing of basic and higher-order needs (Carp & Carp, 1984) during both the Third and Fourth age.

The proliferation of new types of assisted-living facilities (including CCRCs) seems to address these mixtures of future-oriented basic and higher-order needs among both young-old and old-old elders (Krout et al., 2003). From a demographic view, there is evidence of an increasing number of short-distance relocations within the same district or county, and an increase of mobility, shown, for instance, in the increasing numbers of temporary or seasonal long-distance migrations (Hogan, & Steinnes, 1998). The range and variety of housing options for elders along the continuum that has replaced a historical dichotomy of private homes and institutions has already tremendously increased (Großjohann, 2003; Regnier, 2003). But there is still a lot to be done in terms of clarifying and assessing the advantages and disadvantages of different types of facilities and related services.

We detect significant trends in the emergence of residential settings designed for demented elders. While the emphasis of research on risk factors for morbidity and mortality continues, new data reveal more highly differentiated explanations for negative outcomes and suggest the importance of intrapersonal resources such as anticipation, control, and monitoring in coping with the stressful relocation event. The focus has changed, in part, because relocation into institutions is increasingly a phenomenon experienced by elders with dementia and those who are very frail. Comparing the sociophysical setting and care of persons living at home with their situation following a move to a modern, skilled nursing facility, one may argue for positive effects of relocation as a result of the creation of especially supportive environments and services (Day et al., 2000; Weisman, 2003).

There is an emerging emphasis on preparation for relocation as an element of elders planning for their future. Reducing the potential for relocation trauma in old age is one outcome of the anticipation of different relocation possibilities earlier in life (e.g., during the Third Age). Engaging in informed discussions with friends and relatives, making anticipatory arrangements with a partner and, perhaps most important, visiting alternative community- and institutional-care settings can be helpful in enhancing the psychological permeability of residential alternatives (Rowles, Concotelli, & High, 1993). Such strategies are important in terms of information gathering, the exchange of opinions, and most significantly, as a component of the development of a life-course perspective on the process of relocation. Such a perspective, we suggest, is enriched by the accumulating reservoir of relocation experience that results from each residential change. Such an information- and experience-based perspective may be helpful in reducing feelings of anxiety when relocation is necessitated by changing personal capabilities or environmental circumstances—it may facilitate our moving beyond the relocation trauma. Finally, increasing focus on anticipatory awareness of the process of environmental change over the life course may provide an important stimulus to movement from a diffuse, often inchoate, understanding of future residential possibilities toward more concrete and deliberate planning for a personal future. Anticipatory planning for diverse possible exigencies of the Fourth Age may translate directly into actions ranging from a postretirement relocation into a CCRC or assisted-living facility to the decision to prepare for staying put and aging in place in a residence that is adapted according to principles of universal design and the use of "smart home" technology.

Finally, we perceive increasing emphasis on developing deeper understanding of the experiential processes involved in transforming spaces into places that may be a critical element of relocation adjustment. Progress in this domain offers considerable potential for developing interventions to minimize the trauma of relocation and promote effective adjustment to new spaces through assistance with the process of regaining a sense of normalcy following relocation. Such interventions (e.g., offers of relocation assistance as part of housing counseling for elders and their partners or relatives, or as part of the geriatric assessment in hospitals) may be especially important for frail and/or demented individuals in facilitating their adjustment to institutional living. The key here lies in evolving person-focused interventions that are consistent with the elder's life experience and sociocultural values. Progress in these directions will enable us to move beyond the relocation trauma in innovative ways that enable us to enrich the lives of even the most vulnerable of our elders.

ENRICHING METHODOLOGIES IN RELOCATION RESEARCH

In providing deeper insight into these emerging trends, it will be important to engage in research that is especially attuned to the identification and interpretation of the subtleties and complexities of contemporary relocation transitions. In order to accomplish this, it is necessary to confront some methodological constraints that have limited the conclusions that we have been able to draw from previous studies. Consequently, we conclude this chapter with considerations of two methodological issues.

There is a need for more detailed and discriminating analyses of specific predictors and outcomes of relocation. Much of the established evidence on push versus pull influences on community migration (e.g., socioeconomic status, climate, costs of living, available amenities) and stressful consequences of relocation into institutions (e.g., functional limitations, compromised cognitive and physical health) can still be regarded as valid. However, there is a need for more refined predictors (e.g., in the relation between health and relocation). While some data support the suggestion that good health tends to trigger amenity-seeking relocations and poor health serves as a predictor of relocation to supportive settings (e.g., Silverstein & Zablotzky, 1996), other community relocation studies conclude that health status does not predict future housing expectations (e.g., Robinson, & Moen, 2000), and findings on actual relocation into CCRCs suggest that high levels of perceived health are associated with positive outcomes (Krout et al., 2002, 2003). In sum, more discriminating and sensitive predicting indices of relocation and its outcomes are needed to disentangle the diverse elements that contribute to contemporary trends.

Studies of relocation and residential decision making need to utilize more sophisticated methodologies to reveal subtle dimensions of the relocation process. This is true for both qualitative and quantitative research. Studies of the process and consequences of relocation decision making are compromised by methodological shortcomings. In some studies, the relocation process is only addressed from the perspective of a limited population of already relocated persons who can only view their experience from the potentially distorting perspective of hindsight; such an approach increases the risk of selective recall in the sample and the retrospective adjustment of both perceived needs and wishes (e.g., Oswald et al., 2002). Sometimes resource limitations dictate a focus solely on the *post hoc* recollections of a sample of relocated individuals. There is a need to complement such work with data collection at different phases of the relocation process, that is, prior to and following the relocation (e.g., Krout & Wethington, 2003; Saup, 2001). Unfortunately, most studies do not have the resources to follow relocation trajectories as they evolve longitudinally over many years and in parallel with the process of aging and an individual's passage through multiple residential transitions (Brown et al., 2002). Other forms of research-design-related selectivity, for example the selective effects of increased stress-related mortality during the pre-relocation phase, should also be avoided (Thorson & Davies, 2000). Finally, to develop a fully comprehensive perspective on the relocation decision, it will be necessary to compare the deliberative processes of people who decide to relocate with those whose resolution is not to move but rather to remain aging in place in a familiar although perhaps unsuitable environment. To date, few research endeavors have had the capacity to consider both populations. The development of such studies would facilitate the comparison of risk factors, the development of insights into the resources used in making decisions, and more in-depth understanding of the decision-making process (e.g., Krout & Wethington, 2003; Longino et al., 2002).

REFERENCES

Aldrich, C., & Menkoff, E. (1963). Relocation of the aged and disabled, a mortality study. *Journal of American Geriatrics Society, 11,* 185-194.

Aneshensel, C. S., Pearlin, L. I., Levy-Storms, L., & Schuler, R. H. (2000). The transition from home to nursing home: Mortality among people with dementia. *Journal of Gerontology: Social Sciences, 55B*(3), S152-162.

Baltes, P. B., & Smith, J. (1999). Multilevel and systemic analyses of old age: Theoretical and empirical evidence for a Fourth Age. In V. L. Bentson & K. W. Schaie (Eds.), *Handbook of theories of aging* (pp. 153-173). New York: Springer.

Belk, R. W. (1992). Attachment to possessions. In I. Altman & S. M. Low (Eds.), *Human behavior and environment, Vol. 12: Place attachment* (pp. 37-62). New York: Plenum.

Borup, J. H. (1983). Relocation mortality research: Assessment, reply, and the need for refocus on the issues. *The Gerontologist, 14,* 506-510.

Bourestom, N., & Tars, S. (1974). Alterations in life patterns following nursing home relocation. *The Gerontologist, 14,* 506-510.

Bronfenbrenner, U. (1999). Environments in developmental perspective: Theoretical and operational models. In S. L. Friedman & T. D. Wachs (Eds.), *Measuring environment across the life span* (pp. 3-28). Washington, DC: American Psychological Association.

Brown, J. W., Liang, J., Krause, N., Akiyama, H., Sugisawa, H., & Fukaya, T. (2002). Transitions to living arrangements among elders in Japan: Does health make a difference? *Journal of Gerontology: Social Sciences, 57B*(4), S209-S220.

Bundesministerium für Familie, Senioren, Frauen und Jugend (BMFSFJ) [Federal Ministry for Family Affairs, Senior Citizens, Women and Youth]. (Ed.). (2001). *Dritter Altenbericht der Bundesregierung. Alter und Gesellschaft* [Third report on the situation of older people. Ageing and society]. Bonn: Eigenverlag.

Carlson, J. E., Junk, V. W., Fox, L. K., Rudzitis, G., & Cann, S. E. (1998). Factors affecting retirement migration to Idaho: An adaption of the amenity retirement migration model. *The Gerontologist, 28*(1), 18-24.

Carp, F. M., & Carp, A. (1984). A complementary/congruence model of well-being or mental health for the community elderly. In I. Altman, M. P. Lawton, & J. F. Wohlwill (Eds.),

Human behavior and environment, Vol. 7: Elderly people and the environment (pp. 279-336). New York/London: Plenum Press.

Choi, N. G. (1996). Older persons who move: Reasons and health consequences. *Journal of Applied Gerontology, 15*(3), 325-344.

Clark, W. A., & Davies, S. (1990). Elderly mobility and mobility outcomes: Households in the later stages of the life course. *Research on Aging, 12*(4), 430-462.

Coffman, T. (1981). Relocation and survival of institutionalized aged: A re-examination of the evidence. *The Gerontologist, 21*(5), 483-500.

Cuba, L. (1991). Models of migration decision making reexamined: The destination search of older migrants to Cape Cod. *The Gerontologist, 31*(2), 204-209.

Danermark, B. D., Ekstrom, M. E., & Bodin, L. L. (1996). Effects of residential relocation on mortality and morbidity among elderly people. *European Journal of Public Health, 6*(3), 212-217.

Day, K., Carreon, D., & Stump, C. (2000). The therapeutic design of environments for people with dementia: A review of the empirical research. *The Gerontologist, 40,* 397-416.

De Jong, G. F., Wilmoth, J. M., Angel, J. L., & Cornwell, G. T. (1995). Motives and the geographic mobility of very old Americans. *Journal of Gerontology: Social Sciences, 50B*(6), S395-S404.

Ekerdt, D. J., Sergeant, J. F., Dingel, M., & Bowen, M. E. (2004). Household disbandment in later life. *Journal of Gerontology: Social Sciences, 59B*(5), S265-S273.

Friedrich, K. (1995). *Altern in räumlicher Umwelt. Sozialräumliche Interaktionsmuster in Deutschland und in den USA* [Aging in the spatial context. Social-environmental patterns of interaction in Germany and the U.S.A.] Darmstadt: Steinkopff.

Gitlin, L. N. (1998). Testing home modification interventions: Issues of theory, measurement, design, and implementation. In R. Schulz, G. Maddox, & M. P. Lawton (Eds.), *Annual review of gerontology and geriatrics. Interventions research with older adults* (pp. 190-246). New York: Springer.

Gitlin, L. N. (2003). Conducting research on home environments: Lessons learned and new directions. *The Gerontologist, 43*(5), 628-637.

Gitlin, L. N., Corcoran, M., Winter, L., Boyce, A., & Hauck, W. W. (2001). A randomized controlled trial of a home environmental intervention: Effect on efficacy and upset in caregivers and on daily function of persons with dementia. *The Gerontologist, 41*(1), 4-22.

Golant, S. M. (1992). *Housing America's elderly: Many possibilities, few choices.* Thousand Oaks, CA: Sage Publications.

Golant, S. M. (1998). Changing an older person's shelter and care setting: A model to explain personal and environmental outcomes. In R. J. Scheidt & P. G. Windley (Eds.), *Environment and aging theory. A focus on housing* (pp. 33-60). Westport, CT: Greenwood Press.

Green, V. L., & Ondrich, J. I. (1990). Risk factors for nursing home admissions and exits: A discrete time hazard function approach. *Journal of Gerontology: Social Scienes, 45,* S250-S258.

Großjohann, K. (2003). Purpose-built housing for older adults: The German perspective. In K. W. Schaie, H.-W. Wahl, H. Mollenkopf, & F. Oswald (Eds.), *Aging independently. Living arrangements and mobility* (pp. 118-129). New York: Springer.

Haas, W. H., & Serow, W. J. (1993). Amenity retirement migration process: A model and preliminary evidence. *The Gerontologist, 33*(2), 212-220.

Harper, L., & Bayer, A.-H. (2000). *Fixing to stay. A national survey of housing and home modification issues.* Washington, DC: AARP Independent Living Program.

Hartwigsen, G. (1987). Older widows and the transference of home. *International Journal of Aging and Human Development, 25*(3), 195-207.

Hazelrigg, L. E., & Hardy, M. A. (1995). Older adult migration to the sunbelt. *Research on Aging, 17*(2), 209-234.

Heinze, R. G., Eichener, V., Naegele, G., Bucksteeg, M., & Schauerte, M. (1997). *Neue wohnung auch im alter* [New homes for the aged]. Darmstadt: Schader-Stiftung.

Hogan, T. D., & Steinnes, D. N. (1998). A logistic model of the seasonal migration decision for elderly households in Arizona and Minnesota. *The Gerontologist, 38*(2), 152-158.

Horowitz, M. J., & Schulz, R. (1983). The relocation controversy: Criticism and commentary on five recent studies. *The Gerontologist, 23,* 229-234.

Johnson-Carroll, K. J. A., Brandt, J. A., & McFadden, J. R. (1995). Factors that influence pre-retirees' propensity to move at retirement. In L. A. Pastalan (Ed.), *Housing decisions for the elderly: To move or not to move* (pp. 85-105). New York/London: Haworth Press.

Kahana, E. (1982). A congruence model of person-environment interaction. In M. P. Lawton, P. G. Windley, & T. O. Byerts (Eds.), *Aging and the environment. Theoretical approaches* (pp. 97-121). New York: Springer.

Kemper, P., & Murtaugh, C. M. (1991). Lifetime use of nursing home care. *New England Journal of Medicine, 324,* 595.

Killian, E. C. (1970). Effect of geriatric transfer on mortality rates. *Social Work, 15*(1), 19-26.

Kindermann, T. A., & Skinner, E. A. (1992). Modeling environmental development: Individual and contextual strategies. In A. B. Asendorpf & J. Valsiner (Eds.), *Stability and change in development: A study of methodological reasoning* (pp. 155-190). Newbury Park, CA: Sage.

King, R., Warnes, A. M., & Williams, A. M. (2000). *Sunset lives: British retirement to the Mediterranean.* Oxford: Berg.

Krout, J. A., Holmes, H., Erickson, M. A., & Wolle, S. (2003). Residential relocation. In J. A. Krout & E. Wethington (Eds.), *Residential choices and experiences of older adults. Pathways to life quality* (pp. 27-48). New York: Springer.

Krout, J. A., Moen, P., Holmes, H. H., Oggins, J., & Bowen, N. (2002). Reasons for relocation to a continuing care retirement community. *Journal of Applied Gerontology, 21*(2), 236-256.

Krout, J. A., & Wethington, E. (Eds.). (2003). *Residential choices and experiences of older adults. Pathways to life quality.* New York: Springer.

Kruse, A., & Wahl, H.-W. (Eds.). (1994). *Altern und Wohnen im Heim. Endstation oder Lebensort?* [Aging and housing in institutions. A place to die or a place to live?]. Bern: Huber.

Langer, E. J., & Rodin, J. (1976). The effects of choice and enhanced personal responsibility for the aged: A field experiment in an institutional setting. *Journal of Personality and Social Psychology, 34*(2), 191-198.

Lanspery, S., & Hyde, J. (Eds.). (1997). *Staying put. Adapting the places instead of the people.* Amityville, NY: Baywood.

Lawton, M. P. (1985). The elderly in context. Perspectives from environmental psychology and gerontology. *Environment and Behavior, 17*(4), 501-519.

Lawton, M. P. (1998). Environment and aging: Theory revisited. In R. J. Scheidt & P. G. Windley (Eds.), *Environment and aging theory. A focus on housing* (pp. 1-31). Westport, CT: Greenwood Press.

Lawton, M. P., & Nahemow, L. (1973). Ecology and the aging process. In C. Eisdorfer & M. P. Lawton (Eds.), *The psychology of adult development and aging* (pp. 619-674). Washington, DC: American Psychological Association.

Lee, D. T. F., Woo, J., & Mackenzie, A. E. (2002). Cultural context of adjusting to nursing home life: Chinese elders' perspectives. *The Gerontologist, 42*(5), 667-675.

Litwak, E., & Longino, C. F., Jr. (1987). Migration patterns among the elderly: A developmental perspective. *The Gerontologist, 27,* 266-272.

Longino, C. F., Jr. (2004). Socio-physical environments at the macro level: The impact of population migration. In H.-W. Wahl, R. Scheidt, & P. G. Windley (Eds.), *Aging in context: Socio-physical environments* (Annual Review of Gerontology and Geriatrics, 2003) (pp. 110-129). New York: Springer.

Longino, C. F., Perzynski, A. T., & Stoller, E. P. (2002). Pandora's briefcase: Unpacking the retirement migration decision. *Research on Aging, 24*(1), 29-49.

Mann, W. C. (2001). Potential of technology to ease the care provider's burden. *Generations, 25*(1), 44-48.

McAuslane, L., & Sperlinger, D. (1994). The effects of relocation on elderly people with dementia and their nursing staff. *International Journal of Geriatric Psychiatry, 9,* 981-984.

McHugh, K. E., & Mings, R. C. (1996). The circle of migration: Attachment to place in aging. *Annals of the Association of American Geographers, 86*(3), 530-550.

McKinney, A. A., & Melby, V. (2002). Relocation stress in critical care: A review of the literature. *Journal of Clinical Nursing, 11*(2), 149-157.

Miller, D., & Lieberman, M. A. (1965). The relationship of affect state and adaptive capacity to reactions to stress. *Journal of Gerontology, 20*(1-4), 492-494.

Moen, P., Dempster-McClain, D., Erickson, M. A., & Boyce, A. (2003). Roles, identities, and residence: Continuity and changes in later adulthood. In J. A. Krout & E. Wethington (Eds.), *Residential choices and experiences of older adults. Pathways to life quality* (pp. 71-91). New York: Springer.

Mollenkopf, H., & Fozard, J. L. (2003). Technology and the good life: Challenges for current and future generations of aging people. In H.-W. Wahl, R. Scheidt, & P. G. Windley (Eds.), *Aging in context: Socio-physical environments (Annual Review of Gerontology and Geriatrics, 2003)* (pp. 250-279). New York: Springer.

Nelson, H. C. (1997). To move or not to move: The role of health and well-being. *Health Care in Later Life, 2,* 143-154.

Oswald, F. (2003). Linking subjective housing needs to objective living conditions among older adults in Germany. In K. W. Schaie, H.-W. Wahl, H. Mollenkopf, & F. Oswald (Eds.), *Aging independently: Living arrangements and mobility* (pp. 130-147). New York: Springer.

Oswald, F., Schilling, O., Wahl, H.-W., & Gäng, K. (2002). Trouble in paradise? Reasons to relocate and objective environmental changes among well-off older adults. *Journal of Environmental Psychology, 22*(3), 273-288.

Oswald, F., & Wahl, H.-W. (2005). Dimensions of the meaning of home. In G. D. Rowles & H. Chaudhury (Eds.), *Home identity in late life: International perspectives* (pp. 21-45). New York: Springer.

Palsig, S. (2000). *Co-housing in Denmark.* Copenhagen, Denmark: Danish Center for Gerontology.

Parmelee, P. A., & Lawton, M. P. (1990). The design of special environments for the aged. In J. E. Birren & K. W. Schaie (Eds.), *Handbook of the psychology of aging* (3rd ed., pp. 464-488). New York: Academic Press.

Pastalan, L. A. (Ed.). (1995). *Housing decisions for the elderly: To move or not to move.* New York/London: Haworth Press.

Pruchno, R. A., & Resch, N. L. (1988). Intrainstitutional relocation: Mortality effects. *The Gerontologist, 28,* 311-317.

Pynoos, J. (2000). *Home modifications.* Los Angeles: Andrus Gerontology Center.

Reed, J., Cook, G., Sullivan, A., & Burridge, C. (2003). Making a move: Care-home residents' experiences of relocation. *Ageing & Society, 23,* 225-241.

Regnier, V. (2003). Purpose-built housing and home adaptations for older adults: The American perspective. In K. W. Schaie, H.-W. Wahl, H. Mollenkopf, & F. Oswald (Eds.), *Aging independently: Living arrangements and mobility* (pp. 99-117). New York: Springer.

Robison, J. T., & Moen, P. (2000). A life-course perspective on housing expectations and shifts in late midlife. *Research on Aging, 22*(5), 499-532.

Rodin, J., & Langer, E. J. (1977). Long-term effects of a control-relevant intervention with the institutionalized aged. *Journal of Personality and Social Psychology, 35,* 897-902.

Rowles, G. D. (1978). *Prisoners of space?* Boulder, CO: Westview Press.

Rowles, G. D. (1981). The surveillance zone as meaningful space for the aged. *The Gerontologist, 21*(3), 304-311.

Rowles, G. D. (1983). Geographical dimensions of social support in rural Appalachia. In G. D. Rowles & R. J. Ohta (Eds.), *Aging and milieu. Environmental perspectives on growing old* (pp. 111-129). New York: Academic Press.

Rowles, G. D. (1993). Evolving images of place in aging and "aging in place." In D. Shenk & W. A. Achenbaum (Eds.), *Changing perceptions of aging and the aged* (pp. 115-125). New York: Springer.

Rowles, G. D., Concotelli, J., & High, D. M. (1993). Community integration of a rural nursing home. *Journal of Applied Gerontology 15*(2), 188-201.

Rowles, G. D., & Ravdal, H. (2001). Aging, place, and meaning in the face of changing circumstances. In R. Weiss & S. Bass (Eds.), *Challenges of the Third Age: Meaning and purpose in later life* (pp. 81-114). New York: Oxford University Press.

Rowles, G. D., & Watkins, J. F. (2003). History, habit, heart and hearth: On making spaces into places. In K. W. Schaie, H.-W. Wahl, H. Mollenkopf, & F. Oswald (Eds.), *Aging independently: Living arrangements and mobility* (pp. 77-96). New York: Springer.

Russel, D. W., Cutrona, C. E., de la Mora, A., & Wallace, R. B. (1997). Loneliness and nursing home admission among rural older adults. *Psychology and Aging, 12*(4), 574-589.

Rutman, D. L., & Freedman, J. L. (1988). Anticipating relocation: Coping strategies and the meaning of home for older people. *Canadian Journal on Aging, 7*(1), 17-31.

Ryff, C. D., & Essex, M. J. (1992). The interpretation of life experience and well-being: The sample case of relocation. *Psychology and Aging, 7,* 507-517.

Ryff, C. D., Singer, B. H., & Seltzer, M. M. (2002). Pathways through challenge: Implications for well-being and health. In L. Pulkkinen & A. Caspi (Eds.), *Paths to successful development: Personality in lifecourse* (pp. 302-328). Cambridge: Cambridge University Press.

Saup, W. (2001). Ältere Menschen im Betreuten Wohnen. Ergebnisse der Augsburger Längsschnittstudie (Band 1) [Older persons in assisted living facilities. Results from the Augsburg longitudinal study (Vol. 1)]. Augsburg: Verlag für Gerontologie.

Scheidt, R. J., & Windley, P. G. (Eds.). (1998). *Environment and aging theory. A focus on housing.* Westport, CT: Greenwood Press.

Schulz, R., & Brenner, G. (1977). Relocation of the aged: A review and theoretical analysis. *Journal of Gerontology, 32*(3), 323-333.

Serow, W. J. (2001). Retirement migration counties in the Southeastern United States: Geographic, demographic, and economic correlates. *The Gerontologist, 41,* 220-227.

Serow, W. J., Friedrich, F., & Haas, W. H. (1996). Residential relocation and regional redistribution of the elderly in the USA and Germany. *Journal of Cross-Cultural Gerontology, 11,* 293-306.

Silverstein, M., & Zablotzky, D. L. (1996). Health and social precursors of later life retirement-community migration. *Journal of Gerontology, 51B*(3), S150-S156.

Smider, N. A., Essex, M. J., & Ryff, C. D. (1996). Adaptation to community relocation: The interactive influence of psychological resources and contextual factors. *Psychology and Aging, 11,* 362-372.

Speare, A., Jr., Avery, R., & Lawton, M. P. (1991). Disability, residential mobility, and changes in living arrangements. *Journal of Gerontology: Social Sciences, 46,* S133-S142.

Thorson, J. A., & Davies, R. E. (2000). Relocation of the institutionalized aged. *Journal of Clinical Psychology, 56*(1), 131-138.

Tobin, S. S. (1989). The effects of institutionalization. In K. S. Markides, & C. L. Cooper (Eds.), *Aging, stress, and health* (pp. 139-163). New York: John Wiley & Sons Ltd.

Tobin, S. S., & Lieberman, M. A. (1976). *Last home for the aged: Institutionalization effects and their cause.* San Francisco: Jossey-Bass.

U.S. Bureau of the Census (1996). *Current population reports, special studies, P23-10, 65+ in the United States.* Washington, DC: U.S. Government Printing Office.

Wahl, H.-W., & Weisman, J. (2003). Environmental gerontology at the beginning of the new millennium: Reflections on its historical, empirical, and theoretical development. *The Gerontologist, 43*(5), 616-627.

Walters, W. H. (2002). Place characteristics and later-life migration. *Research on Aging, 24*(2), 243-277.

Weisman, G. D., Chaudhury, H., & Moore, K. D. (2000). Theory and practice of place: Toward an integrative model. In R. Rubinstein, M. Moss, & M. H. Kleban (Eds.), *The many dimensions of aging: Essays in honor of M. P. Lawton* (pp. 3-21). New York: Springer.

Weisman, G. D. (2003). Creating places for people with dementia: An action research perspective. In K. W. Schaie, H.-W. Wahl, H. Mollenkopf, & F. Oswald (Eds.), *Aging independently: Living arrangements and mobility* (pp. 162-173). New York: Springer.

Wheeler, W. M. (1995). *Elderly residential experience: The evolution of places as residence.* New York: Garland.

Wiseman, R. F. (1980). Why older people move. Theoretical issues. *Research on Aging, 2,* 141-154.

Wolthuis, A. (1997). Nederlanders verblijven in Spanse verpleeghuizen [Dutch residents in Spanish nursing homes]. *Zorginstellingen,* 14-17.

World Health Organization (WHO). (2004). *LARES* (Large analysis and review of European housing and health status). Unpublished working document. WHO Office, Bonn, Germany.

CHAPTER 9

Aging in a Difficult Place: Assessing the Impact of Urban Deprivation on Older People

Thomas Scharf, Chris Phillipson, and Allison Smith

This chapter examines some of the key impacts upon older people associated with residence in what might be regarded as "difficult settings"—socially deprived neighborhoods of the inner city. The chapter is divided into three parts. First, it explores a number of key changes that have occurred in urban areas over recent decades. Here, emphasis is placed upon the degree to which growing older in changing urban environments may be associated with a range of risks that can potentially limit the quality of older people's daily lives. Amongst such risks are those posed to individuals' sense of self-identity as reflected in the degree to which they express attachment to their residential neighborhood and their feelings of security within and beyond the home. Second, the chapter presents findings from an empirical study of older people living in deprived urban areas of England. Data analysis assesses the extent to which a differentiated older population experiences forms of risk, and highlights some of the coping strategies used by older people to manage the challenges of everyday life. Third, in summarizing the empirical data, the chapter seeks to provide evidence of the adaptability of older people to a changing urban environment, and concludes with a discussion of the implications of these findings for future research on aging.

OLDER PEOPLE IN A CHANGING URBAN ENVIRONMENT

The context for this analysis is the need for critical perspectives in gerontology to devote greater attention to issues concerning place and location in later life. While critical gerontology has succeeded in highlighting some of the structural sources of inequality and disadvantage in old age (Minkler & Estes, 1998; Phillipson, 1998; Townsend, 1981), it has tended to overlook the relevance of environmental characteristics in relation to the experience of aging. The chapter seeks to build upon the recent resurgence of interest in environmental issues and aging (Kendig, 2003; Wahl

& Lang, 2003; Wahl, Scheidt, & Windley, 2004; Wahl & Weisman, 2003), and extend the scope of such research. While providing important insights into the experience of everyday life in old age, environmental gerontology has often failed to connect its work to wider theoretical perspectives, including those relating to the impacts of changing urban settings. In this respect, the Chicago school of urban sociology continues to exercise considerable influence, while more recent research focusing on globalization and urbanization (Sassen, 2001), the impact of social exclusion (Madanipour, Cars, & Allen, 1998), and postmodern perspectives on the city (Soja, 1989) are given limited acknowledgment.

In relation to aging, the emphasis on the urban reflects the interaction between the trend toward the spatial concentration of populations (with 60% of the world's population living in cities by 2030) and the impact upon cities of demographic aging (Rodway & Gusmano, 2002; Thorns, 2002). A reliance on traditional approaches to understanding urban environments tends to draw attention away from the structural processes that have led to a transformation in the cities of advanced industrial nations in recent decades. Over the past 50 years, cities have undergone radical change, notably through the process of globalization, which has promoted accelerated growth in some urban centers while contributing to economic and social decline for others (Sassen, 2000a, 2001). Increasing spatial polarization in countries such as England, especially in the final decades of the twentieth century, has led to a much greater concentration of poor people in particular urban communities, often located only a short distance from relatively affluent areas (Social Exclusion Unit, 1998). In relation to aging, the growing polarization within and between cities gives rise to a need to examine the differential impact upon older people associated with residence in cities with a variety of characteristics. It should also be acknowledged that globalization increasingly highlights the major contradictions faced by cities in the twenty-first century: for example, between the demands of a "hypermobile" minority on the one side and the needs of a majority including older people, women living alone with children, disabled people and other groups, on the other side. Moreover, the relatively close proximity of neighborhoods that differ significantly in terms of the socioeconomic status of their residents serves to sharpen the focus on the unequal life chances facing those who live in poor urban communities and those living in mainstream society (Glennerster, Lupton, Noden, & Power, 1999; Lupton, 2001; Social Exclusion Unit, 2001).

Urban sociology has also developed new approaches to understanding issues such as the dynamics of urban poverty, social relations within neighborhoods, and changing relations between different class, gender, ethnic, and age-based groups (Sassen, 2000b; Savage & Warde, 2003). Indeed, when describing the city, urban sociologists point to Aristotle's view that "A city is composed of different kinds of men (sic); similar people cannot bring a city into existence" (cited in Sennett, 1994). While relatively stable informal social relationships may have represented the norm for urban older people at the time of pioneering studies by Young and Willmott (1957) and Townsend (1957), the conditions underpinning such stability have altered dramatically. The desire for "sameness"—often expressed by older people who wish to be surrounded by those similar to themselves (Cattell & Evans, 1999)—has become increasingly difficult to realize. This applies in particular to "zones of transition," which have traditionally thrived on a rapid turnover of population. It is also difficult to maintain sameness in housing areas described by Power (2000, p. 12) as "nonviable"—those unpopular urban neighborhoods characterized by low housing demand and subsequent abandonment of housing by all but the very poorest or least mobile residents.

The impact of changes in urban areas has given rise to a number of recent studies highlighting a range of potential risks for older people associated with the phenomenon of "aging in place" within cities. Some of these risks have been the traditional concern of gerontological research. For example, Townsend's (1957) study of the family life of older people in the East End of London highlighted the intensity of poverty faced by this population group, while Sheldon's (1948) investigations provided an illustration of the degree to which older people in Wolverhampton were prone to social isolation and loneliness. However, the increasing polarization between and within cities has generated research into different types of risk faced by older people in particular types of urban setting, including deprived inner cities (Hannan Foundation, 2001; Newman, 2003; Phillipson, Bernard, Phillips, & Ogg, 2001; Scharf, Phillipson, Smith, & Kingston, 2002). Such risks are closely related to changes in the physical fabric of cities, high rates of population turnover, and a broad array of social problems. In the context of this chapter, four categories of risk have gained prominence in relation to the situation of older people in deprived neighborhoods: a risk to self-identity, a risk that limits the maintenance of a "normal" everyday life, a risk associated with limited access to key services, and a risk arising from a loosening of social ties.

While some risks apply to residents of urban areas regardless of their age, one can argue that they may exercise a disproportionate impact on older people. This is the case in the first risk category, which emphasizes the challenge to older people's sense of identity posed by residence in a perpetually changing inner city neighborhood. The neighborhood contributes greatly to shaping the identities of all those who reside in them (Marcuse, 1996). However, for two reasons the immediate residential environment may represent a more important element of older people's sense of identity than would be the case for younger people. On the one hand, many older people will have spent a substantial period of their lives in a particular neighborhood, deriving a strong sense of emotional investment both in their home and in the surrounding community (Phillipson et al., 2001; Young & Willmott, 1957). On the other, the aging process is associated with what Rowles (1978, p. 200) refers to as a "selective intensification of feelings about spaces," with the increasing relevance of space and place allowing older people to maintain a sense of identity within a changing environmental context. One significant result of the rapid change experienced in some urban neighborhoods (Power, 2000) might therefore be an undermining of older people's sense of identification with the local community. It is also evident that older people can be highly selective in how they view the consequences of urban change, and that this may ultimately be reflected in dissatisfaction with the neighborhood (Burrows & Rhodes, 1998).

A second type of risk is specific to neighborhoods characterized by poverty and intense levels of social deprivation. In such areas, disproportionately high rates of both personal and property crime and the fear of becoming a victim of crime may limit the ability of residents to maintain a normal daily life (Scharf, Phillipson, Kingston, & Smith, 2001). As a result, older people may be less likely to leave their homes after dark (Phillipson et al., 2001; Raphael, Steinmetz, & Renwick, 1999), or may even feel insecure when in their homes. As a result, residents of neighborhoods threatened by depopulation and urban decay may experience a significant reduction in their subjective well-being (Rogers & Power, 2001).

A third category of risk associated with residence in some urban neighborhoods arises from what Gans (1972) refers to as "institutional isolation." Research suggests that the situation of people living in deprived areas has significantly worsened in recent decades and is likely to continue to deteriorate further, as their communities are deserted by a range of institutional capacities and resources (Lash & Urry, 1994). Reflecting the limited power of local residents within an increasingly global marketplace (Bowring, 2000, p. 312f), nonprofitable neighborhoods and their residents have been prone to the steady withdrawal of both private and public sector institutions. Residents of deprived areas may consequently find it difficult to access such basic services as energy, food retailing, telephones, and banking (Kempson & Whyley, 1999; Speak & Graham, 2000). For older people with limited incomes or restricted mobility, the loss or absence of local services, including post offices or affordable local shops, can be especially problematic, necessitating dependence upon others or the use of more costly means of transport. Inaccessibility of services may even serve to reinforce an inhibition among some older people to use services in the first place (Kempson & Whyley, 1999).

Finally, there may also be risks associated with a loosening of social ties, which under extreme circumstances can pose acute difficulties for some groups of older people. The clearest recent illustration of this arises from Klinenburg's (2002) study of the 1995 Chicago heat wave, in which he explores the circumstances leading to the deaths in one month of around 600 people, three-quarters of whom were aged 65 and over. Many older people died alone and seemingly unnoticed by family and neighbors. Arguing that such deaths did not simply represent a function of age or biology under extreme weather conditions, Klinenburg interprets the deaths as "biological reflections of social fault lines." In particular, many older people inadvertently placed themselves at risk by their fear of crime—not wishing to leave their overheated homes or by not opening doors and windows lest someone enter. Klinenburg's (2002) study displays striking parallels with what proved to be a much deadlier heat wave in France in the summer of 2003, where official estimates suggested 14,800 excess deaths (Bosch, 2003, p. 1208). Of these deaths, 82% occurred among people aged 75 and over, most of whom lived in densely populated metropolitan areas (Grynszpan, 2003, p. 1169).

RELEVANCE OF THE TOPIC

Against a background of profound urban change, research in social and environmental gerontology increasingly needs to generate a clearer understanding of the nature of the risks faced by older people who live in diverse urban areas. In this context, the experiences of older people living in deprived inner city areas can be regarded as being symptomatic of the ways in which older people both perceive and respond to urban change. It is beyond the scope of this chapter to focus on all aspects of older people's experience of aging in "difficult places"; for that reason, subsequent analysis limits itself to two aspects of the risk highlighted above. First, in relation to a potential risk to self-identity, it explores the degree to which older people in deprived areas express attachment to their communities. Second, it addresses the issue of older people's vulnerability to crime, a key dimension of the risk faced by those wishing to lead a normal life. Where appropriate, comparisons are made between the situation of older people living in deprived areas and the general population of older people. Given the potential that such environmental risks are distributed unevenly across the older population, particular attention is focused on our analysis of the dimensions of age, gender, and length of residence in the neighborhood.

METHODOLOGY

Design

In order to address these issues, this chapter draws upon original empirical data from a study conducted in socially deprived neighborhoods of three English cities. Using an official government measure (DETR, 1998), Liverpool, Manchester, and the London Borough of Newham were identified as the three most deprived local authorities in England. To account for variation in the spread and intensity of deprivation across what are very different cities in terms of their socioeconomic profile and historical development, the three most deprived electoral wards in each city—all ranked among England's 50 most deprived wards in 1998—were selected as the locations for a program of investigation.

For the purposes of this chapter, primary data collection consisted of a survey of 600 people aged 60 and over. Recruitment to the study occurred in two ways. An initial group of participants was randomly selected from local electoral registers using a coding classification based on individuals' first names. In this way 2,302 individuals were selected, of whom 1,116 were subsequently deemed ineligible on the grounds that they had moved, were the wrong age, were too ill to participate, or had died. Of the 1,186 potentially eligible respondents, 360 refused to participate and 325 could not be contacted. In all, 501 interviews were completed, giving a response rate of 42%. One limitation of using a sampling method based on respondents' first names is that the approach is unable to identify people of the appropriate age who belong to some minority ethnic groups. To overcome this difficulty and to generate sufficiently large samples from particular groups to facilitate statistical analysis, an additional sample of people belonging to the largest minority ethnic groups in each electoral ward was recruited to the study. This group was accessed through a range of community organizations and previously established contacts within the study localities. Ninety-nine older people belonging to four different minority groups were recruited by this method.

Participant Characteristics

A description of the study population provides some initial indicators of the unique characteristics of the population of older people living in deprived urban areas of England. For ease of comparison with nationally representative population samples, Table 1 presents a description of research participants' characteristics broken down according to different age groups. While the gender distribution of the deprived-areas sample broadly reflects the national pattern, it differs significantly in relation to other sociodemographic factors. Compared with national data, fewer older people in deprived

Table 1. Sample Characteristics:
Older People in Deprived Areas and Great Britain (in %)

	General Household Survey 2000/2001		Deprived Areas Survey 2000/2001	
	65-74 years	75 and over	65-74 years	75 and over
Sex				
Male	47	38	43	37
Female	53	62	57	63
Marital status				
Single	6	7	9	8
Married/living as a couple	66	41	46	27
Widowed	21	49	33	60
Separated/divorced	7	4	12	6
Household composition				
% living alone	29	50	37	60
Health				
% reporting longstanding illness	57	64	66	68
% reporting limiting longstanding illness	37	47	47	60
Base	(*n* = 4719)	(*n* = 3888)	(*n* = 251)	(*n* = 205)
	60-69 years	70 and over	60-69 years	70 and over
Years resident in neighborhood[a]				
0-4 years	9	8	6	3
5-19 years	23	20	21	11
20 or more years	68	72	73	87
Base	(*n* = 1124)	(*n* = 1404)	(*n* = 266)	(*n* = 319)
Housing tenure[b]				
Owner occupier	76	65	52	37
Social renter	20	29	39	54
Private renter	4	6	10	9
Base	(*n* = 3195)	(*n* = 4559)	(*n* = 266)	(*n* = 319)

[a]Coulthard, Walker, and Morgan (2002).
[b]General Household Survey 2002 data.
Sources: General Household Survey 2000/01 and Deprived Areas Survey 2000/01.

areas were married or living as a couple, and there were higher proportions who were widowed, divorced or separated, or who had never married (see Arber & Ginn, 2004, p. 4). The proportion of those who live alone was higher in the deprived areas sample, and their health, as reflected in the reporting of chronic illness, was generally worse. The sample was also more diverse than the general older population with regard to respondents' ethnic origin. While 92% of people aged 65 and over in Great Britain describe themselves as White (Office for National Statistics, 2004, p. 18), the equivalent proportion in deprived areas was 74%. Thirteen percent of respondents described themselves as Black Caribbean, 6% as Somali, 3% as Pakistani, and 4% as of Indian origin. In terms of housing tenure, which in the British context provides an indirect measure of social class, the proportion of respondents who owned their own homes was significantly lower than the national average, especially amongst those aged 70 and over. Conversely, older people in deprived areas were much more likely to rent their homes from social landlords than those in Britain as a whole. This highlights the concentration of survey respondents within lower socioeconomic groups, a feature borne out by the degree to which older people in deprived areas are subject to poverty. Using equivalent measures, a recent national survey classified 21% of people aged 60 and over as poor (Patsios, 2001). The corresponding proportion in the deprived areas study was 45% (Scharf et al., 2002). Finally, for the purposes of this analysis, it is also important to note that the study population shows signs of a remarkable residential stability. Of those aged 70 and over, just 14% had lived in their present community for fewer than 20 years. In the general population, the equivalent proportion was 28%. This aging in place is also evident within the 60-69 age group, around three-quarters of whom are long-term residents of their neighborhood.

The description of the deprived areas sample of older people illustrates some of the key ways in which this group differs from the older population of Great Britain in general. While this confirms the need to explore aspects of the experience of aging in different environmental settings, it also emphasizes the limits to which it is possible to generalize findings from this study to the older population as a whole. Moreover, while the achieved response rate of 42% represents a good outcome in geographic areas sometimes neglected by social researchers on the grounds of concern about high population turnover and interviewer safety, it is not possible to comment on the characteristics of the 58% of non-respondents. These points should be borne in mind when interpreting the research findings.

FINDINGS

Attitudes to the Neighborhood

Within the context of a relatively stable residential population, the first substantive issue to be addressed concerns older people's attitudes toward their neighborhood. Here, the focus is placed on the degree to which older residents of deprived urban areas display signs of attachment to their communities. As suggested above, those who are dissatisfied with their residential environment may experience difficulty in maintaining a sense of self-identity within a changing urban setting. An initial question sought to assess the degree to which older people in deprived areas were satisfied with their neighborhoods. Overall, 68% of respondents were either very or fairly satisfied with their neighborhood as a place to live. A much smaller proportion, just under one-fifth (19%), was either slightly dissatisfied or very dissatisfied. These proportions varied little according to individuals' characteristics, such as gender, age, or length of residence in the neighborhood.

At first glance, these findings suggest that older people in deprived areas generally display a high degree of satisfaction with their residential neighborhood; however, comparison with data arising from national surveys portrays a rather different picture (Table 2). In general population surveys, older people tend to express much higher levels of neighborhood satisfaction than younger age-groups, in part reflecting a longer period of residence in the community, but also the necessity of psychological adaptation to one's place of residence in order to maintain a sense of self. Thus, while 49% of people interviewed in the nationally representative Survey of English Housing 2000/2001 were very satisfied with their neighborhood, this proportion rose to 55% of those aged 65-74 years and 61% of people aged 75 and over. The proportion of people expressing some degree of dissatisfaction with their neighborhood was broadly similar across age groups, representing less than 10% of the population. While community dissatisfaction tends to be more pronounced in England's most deprived areas, even there more people are satisfied than dissatisfied.

Comparison of findings from the deprived areas study with those from the national survey indicates that older people in disadvantaged urban neighborhoods are actually considerably less satisfied with their place of residence than one might initially think. Indeed the proportion of respondents in our survey who were very satisfied with their neighborhood was less than half the national figure, and also lower than the equivalent

Table 2. Satisfaction with Neighborhood, Deprived Areas and England (in %)

	Survey of English Housing 2000/2001			All ages—10% most deprived areas	Deprived Areas Survey 2000/2001	
	65-74 years	75 and over	All ages		65-74 years	75 and over
Very satisfied	55	61	49	29	23	24
Fairly satisfied	33	29	37	43	48	43
Neither satisfied nor dissatisfied	3	3	5	8	15	13
Slightly dissatisfied	5	5	6	12	7	9
Very dissatisfied	4	3	3	8	8	12
Total	100	100	100	100	100	100
(Base)	(2509)	(2378)	(20225)	(3319)	(251)	(205)

Sources: Survey of English Housing 2000/01 and Deprived Areas Survey 2000/01.

proportion in the 10% most deprived areas of England. Conversely, the share of older people in deprived areas who were dissatisfied with their neighborhood at ages 65 and above was more than double the national rate.

These findings raise questions about the characteristics of deprived urban environments that older people both like and dislike. This issue was addressed by inviting survey respondents to identify both positive and negative features of their neighborhood. The degree to which older people relate to their residential environment is reflected in the fact that just 7% of those questioned were unable to highlight at least one positive or negative feature of their neighborhood. In this study, therefore, only a small minority of respondents appeared indifferent to their neighborhoods. Taking the positive features of the neighborhood first, three-quarters of older people in deprived areas could identify something that they liked about their neighborhood (Table 3). While this proportion appears high, in an equivalent representative study in Scotland 96% of people aged 65 and over identified at least one aspect of their neighborhood that they

Table 3. Older People's Perceptions of the Neighborhood, Deprived Areas

Thinking about this neighborhood, is there anything you particularly like/dislike about living here?

	% Identifying something they like	% Identifying something they dislike
Sex		
Male	72	58
Female	77	58
Age groups		
60-74 years	77	56
75 years and above	70	61
Ethnic background		
White	73	62
Black Caribbean	83	46
Indian	72	24
Pakistani	69	24
Somali	87	82
Years resident in neighborhood		
0-4 years	68	52
5-19 years	73	51
20 or more years	76	61
All (Base)	75 (*n* = 450)	58 (*n* = 345)

liked (Scottish Executive Central Research Unit, 2001, p. 23). In the deprived areas survey, the proportion of respondents identifying positive features of an area hardly varied according to characteristics such as age, gender, or individuals' length of residence in the community. Moreover, the features of the neighborhood regarded favorably by residents were broadly similar across the study areas. In response to an open-ended question inviting respondents to specify what it was they liked about their neighborhood, more than half of those who could identify something that they liked (53%) commented on the presence of good neighbors, friends, and family. The local availability and ease of access to shops and amenities was ranked second, with 42% of people identifying this as a positive feature of their neighborhood. Also significant for almost one-quarter of respondents (24%) were positive descriptions of their local area. Such descriptions become even more important when viewed within the context of widely held negative attitudes toward disadvantaged neighborhoods. In this respect, respondents commented favorably on such features as local parks, buildings that had been improved by public investment, and a range of efforts to clean up the community. A number of older people suggested that they liked their neighborhood simply because it was peaceful or quiet (Scharf, Phillipson, & Smith, 2003).

These findings broadly match those reported in a range of similar studies. For example, the People's Panel survey of people aged 50 and over identified friendly people and neighbors, a peaceful and quiet neighborhood, and the appearance and look of buildings as being good features of the residential environment (Cabinet Office, 1999, p. 48). Similarly, the Scottish Household Survey 2001 showed that people aged 65 and over particularly liked the peace and quiet of their neighborhoods, the presence of good neighbors and friendly people, as well as convenient shops and amenities (Scottish Executive Central Research Unit, 2001, p. 23).

Turning to less favorable aspects of the neighborhood, 58% of older people in deprived areas could identify at least one feature of the local community that they disliked (Table 3). This is somewhat lower than the proportion of those identifying aspects that they liked and is substantially higher than the 19% of people aged 65 and over identifying area dislikes in the Scottish Household Survey (Scottish Executive Central Research Unit, 2001, p. 23). Long-term residents of the community and those aged 75 and over were slightly more likely to identify something that they disliked than those who had not lived in the neighborhood as long or who were younger.

The aspects of the neighborhood that older people disliked could be grouped under three broad headings. Ranked first were negative descriptions of the local area and references to the way in which the neighborhood had seemingly deteriorated in recent years. These were mentioned by 42% of those identifying dislikes. This category encompasses concerns about the general dilapidation of the area, the apparent lack of maintenance of buildings and public spaces, and environmental problems such as traffic noise. Second, a slightly smaller proportion (39%) identified other local people as being in some way problematic. The characteristics of the groups viewed negatively tended to vary from locality to locality. In some areas, neighbors appeared to represent a problem; in others it was people belonging to other ethnic groups, young people, or drug addicts. A third category of older people's dislikes, also identified by 39% of those questioned, encompassed a range of perceived social problems in the neighborhood. In particular, frequent references were made to the incidence of various types of crimes and to other forms of antisocial behavior. National surveys of older people highlight similar concerns, albeit with a lower degree of intensity. In the previously mentioned survey of older people in Scotland, young people hanging about and vandalism were the two neighborhood characteristics most frequently mentioned as aspects that were disliked (Scottish Executive Central Research Unit, 2001, p. 24). In the People's Panel survey of people aged 50 and over, local traffic problems represented the issue of greatest concern (Cabinet Office, 1999, p. 49).

Understanding the nature of individuals' neighborhood dislikes provides some important clues to older people's ability to cope with broader processes of urban change. Many of those who expressed negative views about their neighborhood drew unfavorable comparisons between the current state of their community and an earlier time. Within the context of national studies that universally report higher degrees of neighborhood satisfaction and fewer area dislikes, it is evident that some older people living in deprived areas experience difficulty in coping with the consequences of a changing environment. This is especially evident in relation to population turnover. For example, some long-term residents, especially in the Newham neighborhoods in the East End of London, expressed concern about living side by side with people from a variety of ethnic backgrounds. More generally, negative perceptions of the neighborhood were associated by some older people with the loss of particular neighbors and friends (either through death or migration), or with the migration of younger family members from the neighborhood. On occasion, people commented on the absence of people of similar age within the locality.

Drawing these findings together, it is evident that older people in deprived urban communities of England demonstrate a remarkable degree of attachment to their communities. This analysis supports the findings of earlier studies concerning the relevance of community to older people (Phillipson et al., 2001; Young & Willmott, 1957). The degree of attachment is expressed in positive as well as negative views about local areas and in relatively high levels of satisfaction with the neighborhood. An important finding from the research is that very few older people appear indifferent to their surroundings; many indeed are highly positive about the neighborhood in which they live. For many, this reflects an often lengthy period of residence in a community in which they have raised their families; maintain regular contacts with family, friends, and neighbors; use local shops and amenities; and are familiar with the local landmarks. Nevertheless, there are also indications of some older people experiencing difficulty in coping with changes that are beyond their immediate control. Neighborhood satisfaction appears to be lower among older people in deprived areas than among the older population of Great Britain as a whole. In deprived areas, older people are also more likely to report aspects of the neighborhood that they dislike. In this respect, steady turnover of population and deterioration of the physical fabric of urban communities were viewed unfavorably by some of those who took part in this study. In view of the ideas outlined above, it is possible to argue that the group reporting dissatisfaction with their neighborhoods—representing around one-fifth of older people living in deprived communities—may experience the greatest risk in maintaining a sense of self-identity.

Older People's Experience of Crime

The second substantive theme to be addressed relates to the issue of older people's experience of crime in socially deprived communities. This has been highlighted as a significant dimension of the risk faced by those who seek to lead a normal daily life in such locations. Also, as noted above, the issue of crime figures prominently in older people's views of what they most dislike about the neighborhood in which they live.

National crime surveys tend to show that of all age groups, older people are the least likely to be victims of crime and that the overall risk of becoming a victim of different types of crime is very low for those aged 60 and over (Chivite-Matthews & Maggs, 2002; Kershaw, Chivite-Matthews, Thomas, & Aust, 2001). However, a number of studies suggest that the relatively low risk of victimization faced by older people coincides with a disproportionately high fear of crime (Burnett, 2002; Clarke, 1984; Pain, 1995). To ascertain whether a similar pattern applies in deprived urban communities, respondents were first asked whether they had experienced one or more of a range of seven different types of crime in the previous year or two. In this respect, it is important to note that the survey did not seek to measure the number of times a particular type of crime was experienced, but the incidence of various types of crime. If anything, the data were therefore likely to represent an underestimation of older people's actual experience of crime.

Using this approach, most older people in deprived areas had no recent experience of crime (Table 4). Nevertheless, 40% of respondents had been victims of one or more type of crime. Moreover, a number had multiple experiences of crime, with 18% reporting having experienced two or more different types of crime in the two years preceding the interview. Property crime was the most commonly occurring type of crime: 21% of respondents had had their homes broken into or reported an attempted

Table 4. Older People's Experience of Crime, Deprived Areas (in %)

	%	(*n*)
Number of types of crime experienced in past two years		
None	60	357
One type of crime	22	133
Two or more types of crime	18	109
Types of crime experienced		
Break-in/attempted break-in of home	21	125
Deliberate damage to or vandalism of home	18	106
Theft of something being carried—out of hands, pockets, or bag	11	68
Physical attack because of color, ethnic origin, or religion	3	18
Physical attack for any other reason	4	26
Defrauding or cheating out of money, possessions, or property	6	35
Selling of a product or service at doorstep that respondent later regretted buying	4	23

Source: Deprived Areas Survey 2000/01.

break-in, while 18% experienced acts of vandalism or damage to property. Crimes against the person were slightly less common, but 15% of respondents (n = 91) were subject to a recent street theft or some type of physical assault, and a small proportion had experienced a physical assault. The survey also identified some older people as being at risk of financial crime. Thirty-five respondents (6%) had been defrauded or cheated out of money, possessions, or property, and 23 people (4%) had been sold a product or service at their doorstep, such as building work, that they subsequently regretted purchasing. The experience of crime varied little according to such individual characteristics as age and gender. However, older people belonging to some minority groups appeared to be more at risk of victimization than White older people—a pattern broadly consistent with data reported from the 2000 British Crime Survey (Clancy, Hough, Aust, & Kershaw, 2001, p. 11f)—and those living in poverty were especially vulnerable to crime (Scharf et al., 2002).

Comparison of these data with those from the nationally representative British Crime Survey illustrates the stark contrast that exists between the situation of older people living in socially deprived neighborhoods and that of older people in England and Wales as a whole in relation to the experience of crime. For example, the 2001 British Crime Survey showed that 2.2% of households headed by a person aged 60 or above experienced a burglary in the year preceding the interview, with a corresponding figure for all households of 3.4% (Kershaw et al., 2001, p. 56). Although the study reported here used a question that asked about the incidence of such crime in the last year or two rather than the last year, the comparable figure in deprived areas was almost 10 times greater (21%). A similar pattern exists with regard to crimes against the person. According to the 2001 British Crime Survey, just 1% of adults living in households headed by a person aged 60 and over had been a victim of violence in 1999 and 2000, compared with a figure of 3.9% for all households (Kershaw et al., 2001, p. 64). In the deprived areas survey, this risk appears to be much greater for older people, with 15% of respondents having either experienced an assault or had something that they were carrying stolen from them.

Our data suggest that older people living in socially deprived areas of England are more likely to be victims of crime than those living in other types of neighborhood. This raises the question of whether the higher rate of victimization also translates into a heightened concern about becoming the victim of crime. Respondents were asked to state the degree to which they were worried about four different types of crime (Table 5). Most concern was expressed about two types of crime: having one's home broken into and being the victim of a street crime. These were also identified as being the crimes to which older people were most susceptible. In each case, around three-fifths of respondents were either very worried or fairly worried about being the victim of such crime. Around one-quarter of respondents expressed concern about being physically assaulted or being conned or cheated at the doorstep. Fear of crime varies according to the specific type of crime and to characteristics of the individual. Women in particular were much more likely than men to be worried about crime. Almost one-third of women (31%) were very worried about being mugged or robbed, and 30% were very worried about being burgled. The equivalent proportions for men were 19% and 21%. Comparison of these findings with those of the 2001 British Crime Survey point to the same pattern in relation to gender, with women being more likely to fear crime than

Table 5. Older People's Fear of Crime, Deprived Areas (in %)

How worried are you about the following?	Very worried	Fairly worried	Not very worried	Not at all worried	Total (*n*)
Having your home broken into and something stolen	26	34	33	7	(*n* = 599)
Being mugged or robbed	26	32	34	8	(*n* = 598)
Being physically attacked because of your color, ethnic origin, or religion	12	14	49	25	(*n* = 599)
Being conned or cheated at your doorstep	10	15	46	29	(*n* = 598)

Source: Deprived Areas Survey 2000/01.

men, but the scale of fear is somewhat lower. In the national crime survey, using identical questions, 13% of men and 18% of women aged 60 and over were very worried about being burgled. With regard to mugging, the respective proportions were 12% and 22% (Kershaw et al., 2001, p. 72). Although the proportion of older people reporting fear of crime was higher in the deprived areas survey, the difference is not as great as might be expected considering this group's heightened vulnerability to crime. This suggests that even in high crime areas, many older people are able to adapt to meet the challenges presented by their environmental setting.

Concern about becoming a victim of crime is further reflected in the degree to which people feel secure when moving about in their neighborhood after dark and when in their homes at night. Concerning the first question, the overwhelming majority of older people in deprived areas reported feeling unsafe should they have to go out alone in their neighborhood after dark (Table 6). Two-thirds of respondents would feel either a bit unsafe or very unsafe under these circumstances, and only 7% would feel very safe when out alone after dark. Feelings of insecurity were much more pronounced among women than men, with 56% of women and 28% of men suggesting that they would feel very unsafe when alone in their neighborhood after dark. In the 2001 British Crime Survey, the equivalent proportions were 33% of women and 9% of men aged 60 and over (Kershaw et al., 2001, p. 75). In deprived areas, concern about personal safety when out alone after dark was most pronounced among people aged 75 and over, among those describing themselves as White, and among people who had been a recent victim of crime.

Some researchers have criticized the way in which crime surveys tend to exaggerate people's fear of crime by seeking responses to hypothetical situations (Farrell, Bannister, Ditton, & Gilchrist, 1997). Many older people who express concern about their safety in the neighborhood tend not to leave their homes after dark anyway. Moreover, it is important to note that older people in deprived areas generally feel much more secure when they are in their own homes at night (Table 7). Overall, 46% of

Table 6. Older People's Perceptions of Neighborhood Safety, Deprived Areas (in %)

How safe would you feel if you had to go out alone in this neighborhood after dark?	Very safe	Fairly safe	A bit unsafe	Very unsafe
Sex**				
Male	10	40	22	28
Female	5	18	20	56
Age groups**				
60-74 years	8	33	21	38
75 years and above	6	19	19	57
Ethnic background**				
White	7	24	18	51
Black Caribbean	15	37	22	26
Indian	4	48	20	28
Pakistani	0	28	38	35
Somali	0	28	36	36
Years resident in neighborhood				
0-4 years	4	36	14	46
5-19 years	9	29	24	38
20 or more years	7	27	21	46
All	7	27	21	45
(n = 592)	(n = 42)	(n = 162)	(n = 123)	(n = 265)

**$p < .001$
Source: Deprived Areas Survey 2000/01.

those interviewed in this study felt very safe and a further 41% felt fairly safe in their own homes at night. Only a small group, representing 4% of the sample, indicated that they felt very unsafe in this situation. This particular group was disproportionately composed of women. While 1% of men indicated feeling very unsafe in their homes at night, the corresponding figure for women was 5%. However, these findings are also broadly comparable with national data. In the 2001 British Crime Survey, 1% of men and 3% of women over the age of 60 reported feeling very unsafe in their homes at night (Kershaw et al., 2001, p. 75).

Again, these findings can be interpreted as suggesting a remarkable degree of adaptation of older people to residence in potentially difficult environmental settings. A heightened vulnerability to different types of crime is not entirely reflected in a disproportionate degree of concern about becoming the victim of crime or about individuals' sense of security within the home. These findings are also supported by evidence of the active steps many older people take in order to avoid becoming a victim of crime. In the survey, and especially in follow-up in-depth interviews, many examples emerged of ways in which people sought to deal with the perceived risk

Table 7. Older People's Perceptions of Safety in the Home, Deprived Areas (in %)

How safe do you feel when you are in your own home at night?	Very safe	Fairly safe	A bit unsafe	Very unsafe
Sex				
Male	48	42	9	1
Female	44	40	11	5
Age groups				
60-74 years	48	40	10	3
75 years and above	45	44	9	3
Ethnic background**				
White	50	39	9	2
Black Caribbean	57	38	4	1
Indian	24	52	12	12
Pakistani	14	52	24	10
Somali	8	57	26	10
Years resident in neighborhood**				
0-4 years	38	38	14	10
5-19 years	36	42	13	10
20 or more years	48	40	10	2
All	46	41	10	4
(n = 592)	(n = 272)	(n = 242)	(n = 62)	(n = 21)

**$p < .001$
Source: Deprived Areas Survey 2000/01.

of crime. Within the home, those who could afford to, would install security devices. This ranged from low-level items such as good quality locks fitted to windows and doors, door chains and peepholes, to more expensive items, including burglar alarms and security cameras. A number of people sought to prevent burglary by fitting grilles or bars over potential access points to the home. Others were more active in seeking to prevent the occurrence of crime in their neighborhood. For example, some older people told of how they would confront people who appeared out of place in the vicinity of their homes. A small number of respondents were involved in community safety schemes that allowed them to express their views on crime issues to local councilors and police officers. Individuals handled the perceived risk of street robbery in a variety of ways. Many older women, for example, reported on the precautions they took when collecting their weekly pension from the post office. This involved varying their behavior by collecting their pension on different days of the week or at different times of the day, taking care not to draw attention to themselves on pension day, or putting their money into deep pockets inside their coats rather than carrying a visible bag or wallet. While the risk of becoming a victim of crime is present in deprived urban communities and influences many older people's behavior patterns, it is evident that many people take an active response to such a risk. In part, this reflects the importance attached by many older people to maintaining a sense of control over the area immediately surrounding their homes.

Drawing these findings together, it is clear that crime significantly affects the daily lives of many older people living in socially deprived urban neighborhoods. While the majority of those taking part in our study were not recent victims of crime, a significant proportion had experienced at least one serious type of crime. These findings are in sharp contrast to those reported in national surveys, where the risk of becoming a victim of crime is typically much lower for older than younger people. However, the evidence of our research is more equivocal when it comes to individuals' responses to this heightened risk of victimization. Although the study reported higher rates of anxiety about becoming a victim of crime when compared with national patterns, these rates did not appear to be disproportionate to the actual risk of crime. Equally, while more older people in deprived areas expressed feelings of insecurity in relation to moving around their neighborhood at certain times of the day than the older population as a whole, similar proportions felt secure in their homes at night. These findings point to the ability of many older people to manage the perceived crime risk not only by changing aspects of their everyday behavior and their physical environment but potentially through psychological adaptation processes.

DISCUSSION: TOWARD AN URBAN RESEARCH AGENDA IN GERONTOLOGY

The issues discussed in this chapter point to an important research agenda arising from the focus on neighborhood and locality. This concerns the importance of developing research that explores the interaction between structural processes and the way these are shaped and influenced by local communities. In this respect, our research suggests that older people are particularly attentive to the physical appearance of their neighborhoods and by the social problems that accompany socioeconomic change. In relation to the key environmental factors identified as posing a potential risk to older people in deprived areas, the research emphasizes the ability of most to manage such everyday challenges. In our study, most older people were longstanding residents of their communities and expressed a close degree of attachment to their neighborhoods. Despite a heightened vulnerability to crime, participants in this research were not disproportionately anxious about becoming the victims of crime. These findings might represent a useful indicator of the high resilience of older people, even in relatively unfavorable or difficult environmental contexts.

More generally, the research discussed here highlights the need to bring urban issues to the forefront of gerontological research. While deprived urban neighborhoods are not typical of urban areas as a whole, the argument remains that the future of old age will, to a large degree, be determined by the extent to which living in cities is made a tolerable and enjoyable experience. Of course, as the research presented here demonstrates, cities can be disabling and threatening environments at any age. The difference is that at age 75 or 85, people may feel an even greater sense of being trapped or disadvantaged by urban decay. Demographic aging combined with ongoing concentration of populations within urban areas highlights the need for older people to be involved in planning and decision-making processes that aim to create sustainable and inclusive urban environments (Scharf et al., 2002). In the United Kingdom at least, the argument has become compelling that older people themselves should be given a stronger say about the management of urban space and the process of urban regeneration (Hardill, 2003).

What kind of research agenda should be built in developing an urban dimension to gerontology? Three themes appear important in this regard. The first issue is that making the urban environment explicit in gerontological research would at least be a valuable starting point. The point here is that most studies of older people are by accident or design studies that involve aging in urban environments; but the relationship between the two is rarely addressed in any systematic form. Studies of poverty, loneliness, vulnerability to crime, housing, elder abuse, and related areas, are interesting topics in themselves, but they nest within an urban setting that will almost certainly influence the development and trajectory of the issue under consideration.

A second issue concerns the impact of globalization on definitions and perceptions of place. Sassen (2000b) has referred to the challenge of recovering place within the context of globalization, telecommunications, and the intensification of transnational and translocal dynamics (see also Eade, 1997). But research on older people suggests that, globalizing processes notwithstanding, the relationship between people and places is even more important at the beginning of the twenty-first century than it was a century or more ago. Older people aging in place within cities may be the first in their families to achieve a sense of residential stability—as this chapter has shown—living in the same community for three, four, or even five decades. This is in contrast to the nineteenth century/early twentieth century when, as Charles Booth observed in his survey of the London poor, "the people are always on the move; they shift from one part of it [London] to another 'like fish in a sea'" (cited in Davin, 1996). The paradox here is that globalization produces both huge migrations and population displacements on the one side, but with increased numbers of people (older people especially) maintaining a strong sense of attachment to particular places on the other (Phillipson et al., 2001).

A third research issue concerns the case for an urban ethnography that can capture the experience of aging within cities now subject to intense global change. Sassen (2000b, p. 146) has pointed to the need for detailed fieldwork as a "necessary step in capturing many aspects of the urban condition," and this seems especially important when studying the impact of urban change on older people and vice versa. Achieving this will require a new dimension of urban studies that seeks to understand the way in which different age groups experience and manage changing urban space and that also examines urban change as a product of intergenerational ties. Conducting research on people's experiences of aging in environmental settings that might be perceived as difficult represents at least one way of meeting this particular challenge.

REFERENCES

Arber, S., & Ginn, J. (2004). Ageing and gender: Diversity and change. In *Social Trends, 34,* 1-14. Office for National Statistics, Stationery Office, London.

Bosch, X. (2003, October 11). France announces plan for improved emergency services. *The Lancet, 362*(9391), 1208.

Bowring, F. (2000). Social exclusion: Limitations of the debate. *Critical Social Policy, 20*(3), 307-330.

Burnett, A. (2002). *Older people and fear of crime.* London: Help the Aged.

Burrows, R., & Rhodes, D. (1998). *Unpopular places.* Bristol: Policy Press.

Cabinet Office. (1999). *People's panel: The views of people aged 50+ towards public services.* London: Service First Unit, Cabinet Office, Stationery Office.

Cattell, V., & Evans, M. (1999). *Neighbourhood images in East London: Social capital and social networks on two East London estates.* YPS, York: Joseph Rowntree Foundation.

Chivite-Matthews, N., & Maggs, P. (2002). *Crime, policing and justice: The experience of older people. Findings from the British Crime Survey, England and Wales 08/02.* London: Research, Development and Statistics Directorate, Communication Development Unit, Home Office.

Clancy A., Hough, M., Aust, R., & Kershaw, C. (2001). *Crime, policing and justice: The experience of ethnic minorities. Findings from the 2000 British Crime Survey.* London: Home Office Research Study 223, Stationery Office.

Clarke, A. (1984). Perceptions of crime and fear of victimisation among elderly people. *Ageing and Society, 4*(3), 327-342.

Coulthard, M., Walker, A., & Morgan, A. (2002). *People's perceptions of their neighbourhood and community involvement. Results from the social capital module of the General Household Survey 2000.* London: Office for National Statistics, Stationery Office.

Davin, A. (1996). *Growing up poor.* London: Rivers Oram Press.

DETR (Department of the Environment, Transport and the Regions). (1998). *Updating and revising the Index of Local Deprivation.* London: Department of the Environment, Transport and the Regions.

Eade, J. (Ed.). (1997). *Living the global city.* London: Routledge.

Farrell, S., Bannister, J., Ditton, J., & Gilchrist, E. (1997). Questioning the measurement of the 'Fear of Crime': Findings from a major methodological study. *British Journal of Criminology, 37*(4), 657-678.

Gans, H. J. (1972). *People and plans. Essays on urban problems and solutions.* London: Penguin Books.

Glennerster, H., Lupton, R., Noden, P., & Power, A. (1999). *Poverty, social exclusion and neighbourhood: Studying the area bases.* CASEpaper 22. London: London School of Economics, Centre for Analysis of Social Exclusion.

Grynszpan, D. (2003, October 11). Lessons from the French heatwave. *The Lancet, 362*(9391), 1169-1170.

Hannan Foundation. (2001). *The Hannan Study of older adults in Detroit's central city. Final report to the Luella Hannan Memorial Foundation.* Detroit: Centre for Health Care Effectiveness, Wayne State University School of Medicine, Board of Directors.

Hardill, I. (2003). *Ageing and urban regeneration.* Paper to Regions for All Ages Conference, March 11, Birmingham, AL.

Kempson, E., & Whyley, C. (1999). *Kept out or opted out? Understanding and combating financial exclusion.* York: Policy Press in association with the Joseph Rowntree Foundation.

Kendig, H. (2003). Directions in environmental gerontology: A multidisciplinary field. *The Gerontologist, 43*(5), 611-615.

Kershaw, C., Chivite-Matthews, N., Thomas, C., & Aust, R. (2001). *The 2001 British Crime Survey. First results, England and Wales.* London: Home Office Statistical Bulletin 18/01, Stationery Office.

Klinenburg, E. (2002). *Heat wave: A social autopsy of disaster in Chicago.* Chicago: The University of Chicago Press.

Lash, S., & Urry, J. (1994). *Economies of signs and spaces.* London : Sage.

Lupton, R. (2001). *Places apart? The Initial Report of CASE's Areas Study.* CASEreport 14. London: Centre for Analysis of Social Exclusion, London School of Economics.

Madanipour, A., Cars, G., & Allen, J. (Eds.). (1998). *Social exclusion in European cities: Processes, experiences and responses.* London: Jessica Kingsley.

Marcuse, P. (1996). Space and race in the post-fordist city. In E. Mingione (Ed.), *Urban poverty and the underclass: A reader* (pp. 176-216). Oxford: Blackwell.

Minkler, M., & Estes, C. (1998). *Critical gerontology: Perspectives from political and moral economy.* Amityville, NY: Baywood.

Newman, K. S. (2003). *A different shade of gray: Midlife and beyond in the inner city.* New York: The New Press.

Office for National Statistics. (2004). *Social Trends 34.* London: Stationery Office.

Pain, R. (1995). Elderly women and fear of violent crime: The least likely victims? A reconsideration of the extent and nature of risk. *British Journal of Criminology, 35*(4), 584-597.

Patsios, D. (2001). *Poverty and social exclusion amongst the elderly.* Working Paper 20, Poverty and Social Exclusion Survey of Britain, Townsend Centre for International Poverty Research. Bristol: Bristol University.

Phillipson, C. (1998). *Reconstructing old age.* London: Sage.

Phillipson, C., Bernard, M., Phillips, J., & Ogg, J. (2001). *The family and community life of older people: Social support and social networks in three urban areas.* London: Routledge.

Power, A. (2000). *Poor areas and social exclusion.* CASEpaper 35. London: London School of Economics, Centre for Analysis of Social Exclusion.

Raphael, D., Steinmetz, B., & Renwick, R. (1999). *The people, places, and priorities of Lawrence Heights: Conclusions from the Community Quality of Life Project.* Toronto: University of Toronto.

Rodway, V., & Gusmano, M. (2002). The world city project. *Journal of Urban Health, 79*(4), 445-463.

Rogers, R., & Power, A. (2001). *Cities for a small country.* London: Faber.

Rowles, G. (1978). *Prisoners of space? Exploring the geographical experience of older people.* Boulder, CO: Westview Press.

Sassen, S. (2000a). *Cities in a world economy.* London: Pine Forge Press.

Sassen, S. (2000b). New frontiers facing urban sociology at the millennium. *British Journal of Sociology, 51*(1), 143-159.

Sassen, S. (2001). *The global city.* Princeton: Princeton University Press.

Savage, M., & Warde, A. (2003). *Urban sociology, capitalism and modernity* (2nd ed). London: Macmillan.

Scharf, T., Phillipson, C., Kingston, P., & Smith, A. E. (2001). Social exclusion and ageing. *Education and Ageing, 16*(3), 303-320.

Scharf, T., Phillipson, C., & Smith, A. E. (2003). Older people's perceptions of the neighbourhood: Evidence from socially deprived urban areas. Sociological Research Online, 8(4) (http://www.socresonline.org.uk/8/4/contents.html).

Scharf, T., Phillipson, C., Smith, A., & Kingston, P. (2002). *Growing older in socially deprived areas.* London: Help the Aged.

Scottish Executive Central Research Unit. (2001). *Older people in Scotland: Results from the first year of the Scottish Household Survey.* Edinburgh: Stationery Office.

Sennett, R. (1994). *Flesh and stone: The body and the city on Western civilisation.* New York: Norton.

Sheldon, S. H. (1948). *The social medicine of old age.* Oxford: Oxford University Press.

Social Exclusion Unit. (1998). *Bringing Britain together: A national strategy for neighbourhood renewal.* London: Social Exclusion Unit, Stationery Office.

Social Exclusion Unit. (2001). *A new commitment to neighbourhood renewal.* London: Social Exclusion Unit, Stationery Office.

Soja, E. (1989). *Postmodern geographies: The reassertion of space in critical social theory.* London: Verso Books.

Speak, S., & Graham, S. (2000). *Private sector service withdrawal in disadvantaged neighbourhoods. Findings, No. 230.* York: Joseph Rowntree Foundation.

Thorns, C. (2002). *The transformation of cities.* London: Palgrave.

Townsend, P. (1957). *The family life of old people.* London: Routledge and Kegan Paul.

Townsend, P. (1981). The structured dependency of the elderly: The creation of policy in the twentieth century. *Ageing and Society, 1*(1), 5-28.

Wahl, H.-W., & Lang, F. R. (2004). Aging in context across the adult life: Integrating physical and social research perspectives. In H.-W. Wahl, R. Scheidt, & P. G. Windley (Eds.), *Aging in context: Socio-physical environments. Annual review of gerontology and geriatrics 23* (pp. 1-35). New York: Springer Publishing Company.

Wahl, H.-W., & Weisman, G. (2003). Environmental gerontology at the beginning of the new millennium: Reflections on its historical, empirical and theoretical development. *The Gerontologist, 43*(5), 616-627.

Wahl, H.-W., Scheidt, R., & Windley, P. (2003). *Aging in context: Socio-physical environments. Annual review of gerontology and geriatrics 23.* New York: Springer Publishing Company.

Young, M., & Willmott, P. (1957). *Family and kinship in East London.* Harmondsworth: Routledge.

PART IV. New and Persistent Dynamics Regarding the Outdoor Environment

CHAPTER 10

Always On the Go? Older People's Outdoor Mobility Today and Tomorrow: Findings from Three European Countries

Heidrun Mollenkopf, Isto Ruoppila, and Fiorella Marcellini

Mobility is a crucial characteristic of modern societies. This holds for mobility in the sense of social mobility—the dissolution from social classes, guilds, or positions, and the loosening of binding social roles and rules of conduct that have led to the pluralization and individualization of norms and values, of lifestyles and biographies. It holds also for mobility in the sense of geographic mobility—the migration of individuals or groups; of moving from one place to another in an increasingly global world and of traveling to attractive destinations; and not least for mobility in terms of the actual trips and journeys performed by each member of society. For centuries, mobility meant locomotion on foot or horseback and travel by cart or boat. Over the course of the nineteenth and, increasingly, the twentieth century, industrial development opened up new opportunities for individual mobility (the ability to move about) and traffic (the transportation of people, goods, and news). Technological advances have made high speed and flexible transportation systems possible, enabling long distance trade and travel. Motorized transport options—from individual automobiles, public transportation systems, and special driving services to trains, ships, and airplanes—have made it possible to traverse distances even despite physical or sensory impairments or frailty. The examples given below, cited in many encyclopedias, reflect the rapid pace of advances in transport technology suited to enhancing older persons' travel options.

In 1830, the first railroad ran between Liverpool and Manchester. Railroads quickly gained ground as steam and rail technology improved and electric power became practical. Electric power allowed large cities to build underground and street railways. Railways became the dominant means of land transport in many parts of the world for nearly a century, but declined when the automobile was invented and became the preferred means of transport.

Parallel to these developments, progress in aviation occurred. The first controlled flights were accomplished by John Montgomery in 1883 and Otto Lilienthal in the 1890s. The turn of the century saw the Zeppelin airship, the first motor planes, flown by Gustav Weißkopf (Whitehead) and the Wright Brothers respectively, and in 1911, the first transcontinental flight. During the years between World War I and World War II, aircraft technology advanced rapidly, but commercial aviation took hold only in the 1950s and 1960s. From 1969 on, the Boeing 747, the largest passenger aircraft ever built, started to revolutionize commercial air travel, and in 1976 British Airways started the first supersonic airliner service with the legendary Concorde.

The automobile developed much faster. The first practical gasoline-powered cars, produced by Carl Benz and Gottlieb Daimler, drove on German roads in 1886. Just 14 years later, in 1900, there existed already about 12,000 automobiles worldwide. The first traffic light was installed by the American Traffic Signal Company in 1914. In 1908, the assembly-line mass production of cars was developed by Henry Ford. Meanwhile, the United States had the highest car ownership with 776 cars per 1000 population (United Nations Economic Commission for Europe [UNECE], 2003). In the European Union (EU), the number of passenger cars increased over the past half-century from roughly 66 (in 1958) to almost 500 (in 2001) per 1000 inhabitants. Simultaneously, the length of the motorway network in the EU grew while the length of the rail network contracted (European Communities, 2003). Older Europeans have less access to cars, though, and are less dependent on automobiles than older Americans (European Conference of Ministers of Transport [ECMT], 2000).

Altogether, these developments have led to a continual increase in mobility and travel. Passenger car transport and air transport have progressed in particular, while rail, buses, and coaches have declined. The distances traveled have also increased due primarily to improvements in transport technologies coupled with the evolving shape of urban and rural settlements and improvements in the constitution and nature of neighborhoods. The growing diversity of travel origins and destinations due to the functional and spatial separation of commercial, residential, and leisure domains, has increased the importance of mobility for bridging the widening gap between functional areas. The provision of extended road infrastructure accelerated extensive suburban development and the establishment of industrial and commercial enterprises beyond residential areas. The outward relocation of private households, in turn, increased the necessity to commute and the dependency upon access to cars (World Business Council for Sustainable Development [WBCSD], 2002).

Therefore, for almost every member of society, including older adults, mobility is not only a basic human need for physical transportation but it has become a major condition of ensuring the ability to seek out places subjectively significant or objectively central to meeting daily material needs, guaranteeing access to healthcare, keeping up social relations, participating in many kinds of activity outside one's home, and maintaining connectedness with one's community and culture (Mollenkopf, Marcellini, Ruoppila, & Tacken, 2004; Schaie, 2003). Thus, societal and individual necessities, modern values, and economic interests complement one another. Altogether, mobility is associated with highly appreciated societal goals in modern society such as autonomy, freedom of choice, flexibility, and variability of behaving and thinking.

In the following we will address the question of what degree older people are willing and able to profit from these developments toward a wider range of mobility and flexibility and whether such a wider scope of actions contributes to higher satisfaction and well-being. To answer this question we will first consider older adults' most important resources for moving about: functional health, availability of private and public means of transportation, and social networks. A commonly held opinion is that today's elders are continuously traveling about. Therefore, the empirical basis of such assumption will be reviewed in addition to the everyday mobility patterns. Second, if it is true that mobility in modern society comprises more than just getting from place A to place B, a great variety of transport options used and activities performed can be expected to contribute to satisfaction with mobility in addition to a high level of actual mobility in terms of trips. In addition, a substantial relationship between satisfaction with mobility possibilities and quality of life in old age should be ascertainable. Third, changes in mobility-relevant issues will be addressed by comparing two cohorts of older adults observed over a period of five years. With the findings on these core issues of outdoor mobility in later life in the background, future perspectives will be dealt with in the final part.

THE EMPIRICAL GROUND: THE PROJECT MOBILATE AND ITS CROSS-COUNTRY COMPARATIVE APPROACH

Findings from the European research project "MOBILATE: Enhancing Outdoor Mobility in Later Life" (Mollenkopf et al., 2005) make it possible to compare the travel patterns and respective prerequisites of two generations of men and women (aged 55 to 74 years and 75 years and older) living in urban and rural areas in five European countries (Finland, eastern and western Germany, Hungary, Italy, and the Netherlands). Standardized questionnaires and diaries were administered to 3,950 persons randomly selected from the municipalities' population registers or by random route procedure in autumn 2000. For the purpose of this chapter, however, we focus on Finland, eastern and western Germany, and Italy only (N = 2,729), because data collected in these three countries' urban areas with the same instruments in the context of the project entitled "Keeping the Elderly Mobile" in 1995 (Mollenkopf, Marcellini, Ruoppila, & Tacken, 2004) enable us to conduct a cohort study, analyzing similarities and differences between elders when they were, respectively, 55-59 and 75-79 years old in 1995 and 2000.

The countries differ widely, not only in geological and climatic conditions, technical infrastructure, and settlement types, but also in cultural traditions and welfare systems. Newly presented definitions classify European societies into three types: the Nordic countries, the southern European countries and the continental countries in between (Vogel, 1998). Based on the classical definitions elaborated by Esping-Andersen (1990, 1999), the following welfare models could be distinguished.

In the institutionalist redistribution model, including mainly the Scandinavian countries, the social institutions are integral parts of society and provide universal services outside the market on the basis of needs. Finland took on the characteristics of this kind of Nordic welfare state in the 1970s. It is characterized by strong national and local institutions and services maintained by public funds. Through legislation providing for pensions for the elderly, healthcare, unemployment and accident benefits, and universal free public education, the Finnish welfare state has eliminated most of the sources of insecurity and inequality from the lives of its citizens. The infrastructure delivering these services grew especially rapidly in the 1970s and 1980s. Around the beginning of the 1990s, this public welfare system began to be cut back both at the national and local level, which has led to a shortage of essential services, especially in health and social welfare-care sectors, despite the very rapid growth of the Finnish economy after the depression years of 1991-1994.

The welfare systems of Germany and Italy operate according to the industrial-performance-result model characterized by social institutions that are functions of the economy and social needs adjudged on the basis of merits, work performance, and productivity. The principle of subsidiarity determines the philosophy and practice of social policy; the state intervenes only in cases where the family or the immediate community are no longer able to help its members. Nonprofit organizations, for the most part religiously committed, play an important role as service providers. With the crisis of the welfare state in the Western societies, the nonprofit sector grew in importance (Salamon & Anheier, 1996). The German Democratic Republic (GDR), on the other hand, oriented itself on the Soviet model of government, in which administrative, economic, and social systems were guided by the Communist party behind the public organizations of the state. The socialist welfare model proclaimed equality in its ideology and certain universal services (free healthcare, free education, a secure livelihood in old age through the pay-as-you-go pension system, etc.). It also involved the conversion of private property to state ownership and state regulation of the economy. At the same time, the "command economy" led to shortages in the infrastructure and services. There were long waiting lists for cars, a very important factor for mobility (with respect to this kind of state-socialist welfare model and the revival of nonprofit organizations, see also Széman & Harsányi, 2000). The present German welfare model is somewhere between the industrial performance-residual type and the institutionalist redistribution model. It is a good example showing that models do not exist in a "theoretically pure" form. The Italian welfare regime and service structure also struggled to cope with problems similar to the East-West problem perceived in Germany, except that here the problems arose from economic, social, welfare, and political differences between the north and the south.

We expect that in addition to personal resources and diverging environmental prerequisites on the micro- or mesolevel (such as social networks or living in an urban as compared to a rural setting), differences on the macrolevel as just described constitute important background conditions of older adults' possibilities for moving about as well. For example, the institutionalist redistribution model as enacted in Finland could come with the consequence that elders might be less dependent on individual resources, while in countries operating on the industrial performance-result model such as Germany and especially Italy, personal health, economic, and social network resources might play a more important role in maintaining outdoor mobility.

OLDER PEOPLE'S RESOURCES FOR MOVING ABOUT

The extent of mobility as movement in time and space depends first on individual needs and resources such as health status, cognitive abilities, and economic and social resources. Second, environmental conditions such as a region's topography, climate, built-up environment, and traffic situation play a decisive role; and third, actual mobility depends on trip-related factors such as purpose of trips, distance of destination, and availability and accessibility of public or private transport facilities. Older people are at risk of physical deficiencies in walking, visual acuity, hearing, memory, etc. (Fozard & Gordon-Salant, 2001). Older women of the present generation have less education, a lower income, more rarely possess a driving license, and therefore own a car less frequently than men of the same age (Centre d'études sur les réseaux, les transports, l'urbanisme et les constructions publiques (CERTU), 2001; Chu, 1994; ECMT, 2000; Mollenkopf et al., 2004). However, maintaining mobility demands first of all that a person retains at least minimally effective functional capacities and, for bridging distances when physical mobility declines, suitable means of transportation. Therefore, elderly men's and women's state of health and the transport options available to them are their most important resources for mobility. The automobile, in particular, plays an ever more dominant role in fulfilling mobility needs.

Functional Health

Findings from the research areas in Finland, western and eastern Germany, and Italy confirm the commonly known decline of functional health with advancing age. Independent of region and gender, persons aged 75 years or older are less able to perform the whole range of activities of daily living (ADL) than those aged 55 to 74. Also, differences between men and women with respect to health were significant; in all regions, women show lower values in functional health and urban-rural comparison offers inconsistent findings. Respondents living in Finnish and Italian cities reported significantly better ADL performances than their rural compatriots, but in the German regions studied, there was no statistically significant difference between urban and rural areas.

Availability of a Car

Due to the interrelated trends of urban decentralization, diversity of travel origins and destinations, and decreasing public transport services, the automobile has become a key to mobility. Among the countries investigated in the MOBILATE project, the households of the older persons in both the urban and rural areas of Italy most frequently have a car available (83%), followed by the older adults in Finland (66%), and western and eastern Germany (64% and 61%, respectively). Overall possession of cars is consistently higher in rural compared to urban regions in all countries; in rural areas, there is apparently a greater need for a car. Not surprisingly, households of the younger age groups more often have access to cars than households of the older groups. Gender proved to be a significant predictor in Finland. In the rural areas of western Germany and Italy, the gender gap has almost been leveled off among the younger men's and women's households. In addition, car ownership depends on the size and income of the household (Tacken, Marcellini, Mollenkopf, & Ruoppila, 1999).

The Role of Public Transportation

Public transit can support older people's mobility if available and accessible (Burkhardt, 2000). All regions studied show a high diffusion of bus and tram stops. Regional differences in the disadvantage of rural areas manifested in Finland only. However, public transportation does not play a leading role in the mobility of the average older individual (see the section on "Actual Mobility"), indicating that if it is not used regularly, the availability of a bus or tram stop alone is not significant. Good general transport options exist only in the cities studied but significantly less so in the rural areas, with problematic situations in Finland and Italy.

The Actual Mobility Patterns of Older Adults

Study respondents reported in a diary all of the journeys they made over the course of two days. No journey was made on either day by 528 persons (19.5%) in the Finnish, German, and Italian regions studied. The mobile people (2,185 persons: 80.5%) made 5,402 journeys during this time, which results in a total mean of 2.0 journeys over the two day observation interval.

The differences between the urban and rural areas were rather small. In general, people are more often out and about in the cities than in the non-urban and rural regions. Only in western Germany are people more active outdoors in rural than in urban areas. This difference does not approach statistical significance, though. The Finnish urban elders, followed by their rural contemporaries and the Italian urbanites, obviously are most active in terms of journeys undertaken. In Finland, only 22% of persons made no journey on one of the interview days. The older people in the eastern and western German regions, by contrast, are the least often on the go. Outdoor mobility patterns differ between genders in Finland, eastern Germany and in particular, Italy. In these countries, male respondents reported a significantly higher number of journeys per day and person, while in western Germany, no such differences were found. Younger respondents in general reported a higher level of actual outdoor mobility when compared to older respondents. The same pattern of relationships reveals that when considering the number of journeys by age, gender and region combined: the younger men in the Finnish urban area are the most on the go (1.8 journeys/day), and older women in the countryside make the fewest journeys per day, along with the older women from the Italian urban area (0.5 journeys/day).

People having a car available in their households are, in general, apt to be more often on the go than those who do not. In almost all regions, car drivers leave their homes for significantly more journeys per day than people who don't own a car. Only in the eastern German city does having a car not particularly affect the number of journeys.

Means of Transportation for Trips

Summarizing the use of various means of transportation over the days documented in the diaries, walking is clearly the most common travel mode of older adults in the European regions studied (Figure 1). Almost half of all trips made by the people who participated in the study were on foot (46%). The car, used as a driver (30%) or as a passenger (12%), was the second most important mode with altogether 42%; public

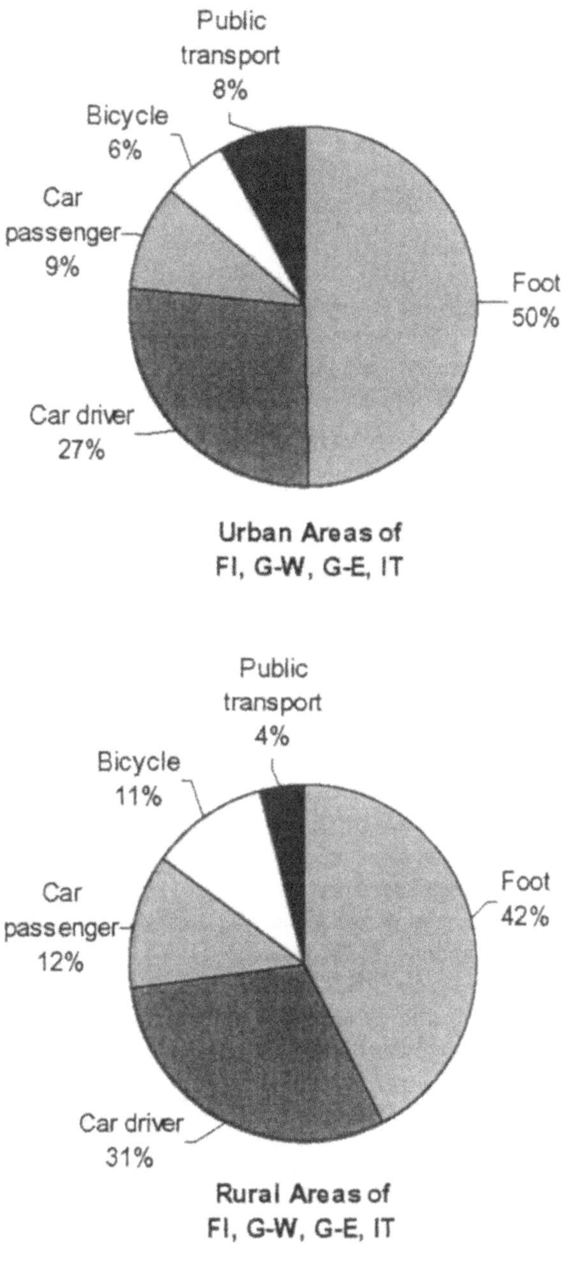

Notes: Given percentages refer to the total number of trips undertaken in urban and rural areas of the four respective countries under study (unweighted data).

Figure 1. Transport modes used by region.

transport including all modes (bus, tram, train, taxi, or special transport) was used in 5% and the bicycle in 9% of the trips.

Usually, the availability and accessibility of public transport is better in urban than in non-urban and rural regions. Thus, it is not surprising that in the cities, people travel more by public transport and by foot. Buses and trams (where available) are used mostly by older people, and within each age group, women use this mode more often than men. The bicycle is used most often in regions with favorable geographical or topographical conditions such as in the Finnish and eastern German rural areas (17% and 20%, respectively).

Spatial Aspects of Outdoor Behavior

The spatial range of mobility—and thus the activity space of elderly people—is quite restricted. Only 44% of the trips have a destination within a circle of 1 km, and an additional 24% between 1 and 3 km, and 14% of the trips go further than 10 km from home. Differentiated by region, gender, and age, the findings can be summarized as follows: the range of mobility is larger in rural than in urban areas. In the countryside, people travel more often to a neighboring locality, while in urban areas, people travel more within their own city. Older people stay closer to home than younger ones, and women more often than men travel to very close destinations. This can be found for both age groups and for rural as well as for urban areas.

Older Adults' Motives for Trips

What are today's elders motives for making trips? Our findings suggest that they are on the go not just for fun but for daily necessities, for social purposes, and only to a minor extent for different kinds of leisure activities. Shopping and running errands are the principal activities for most older adults (36%). Between 7% and 12% of the respondents still travel for work, and on average 6% of the trips are made for healthcare. Meeting other people, helping or accompanying someone, and involvement in associations are altogether important social activities (19%). In Italy, religious events are also often the motive of a trip (11%). The most frequent trips that are not taken out of necessity or for social motives are made for such modest activities as strolling around, a walking tour, or cycling (13%). Gardening, which is not only a leisure pursuit but part and parcel of many individuals' daily routine, is most popular in eastern Germany (5%). Picking berries and fishing are traditional activities of older people in Finland (4%). At most, 8% of all trips are made for drinking coffee or having lunch, for sport or cultural activities, or a short holiday trip.

Changing Driving and Activity Patterns

An interesting question concerns whether driving decreases with increasing age. Actual data show that if people drive, they use their car rather often (every day: 56% in Germany and 84% in Italy). There is hardly any difference between the urban and rural areas in how often people use their car, with the exception of western Germany and Finland. In the areas investigated in these countries, people tend to drive less often in the rural than in the urban areas. In all countries, men and younger people drive much more than women and older people do.

Most older persons stated that they drive less than they used to before, though a small percentage of respondents actually drives more. The latter group consists of relatively more women than men. This could be related to the fact that when women become widowed, they may be forced to drive themselves. The difference between the two age categories is rather large in both the rural and urban areas. The main reason for driving less is health, but other concerns are important as well. Many elderly mention financial reasons (Finland, eastern and western Germany), that traffic is getting too hectic (eastern and western Germany, Italy), or the ability to reach and do everything without a car (western Germany and Italy).

Similarly, many people reduce out-of-home activities with increasing age; in all countries, only a minority—in particular young, urban elders—engaged in more activities. About one out of five respondents would like to be more active outdoors; meeting friends, making small trips, gardening, and visiting cultural events were mentioned most often. Nearly half of these persons (48%) mentioned health as a main reason for the discrepancy between preferred and realized behavior. Further, but less frequent reasons, are lack of time, lack of an opportunity nearby, and high costs. This can be interpreted as an indication that the decrease in outdoor activities in old age, as seen in other studies (e.g., Cvitkovich & Wister, 2001), is not a completely voluntary withdrawal.

Traveling for at Least One Week

Historically, traveling has a long tradition. For centuries, the most common reasons have been migration, pilgrimage, and exploration. Leisure tourism in the modern sense of the word did not develop until the nineteenth century, when a growing number of people were able to afford long distance travel and staying for periods of time away from their homes. Mass tourism began to develop only when facilities were available for accommodating large numbers of people and when improvements in communications allowed the transport in a short space of time to leisure and recreational destinations. In this respect, the invention of the railways brought a major development: in 1841, Thomas Cook organized the first package tour by chartering a train—he became the world's first tour operator. A new push occurred in the decades after World War II with the increase in commercial air travel. Meanwhile, mass tourism is an important industry worldwide, and even general public space travel has become an option (National Aeronautics and Space Administration [NASA], 1999).

Improvements in transport infrastructure and accommodation facilities, available free time, and sufficient assets have made traveling possible and comfortable for older persons. Thus, a widely held opinion is that today's elders are continuously traveling about. The empirical basis does not justify such assumption: 63.4% of the Finnish, German, and Italian participants reported having made no trip lasting at least one week during the year before the interviews (autumn 2000); 24.6% made one and only 12% made two or more such trips. The German elders traveled most (43.7%), while the Italians traveled least (20.3%).

More urban than rural elders, more men than women, and, not surprisingly, more younger than older respondents made a trip of at least one week in the course of about one year. These patterns were found in all countries, and the differences were highly significant between urban and rural areas and age groups and, albeit somewhat less, between men and women. Correspondingly, elder urbanites, men, and the young old showed higher satisfaction with traveling than older people living in the countryside, women, and persons aged 75 years and older. More important were, however, the differences in satisfaction between persons who did not travel ($M = 6.4$) and persons who made one or several big journeys ($M = 8.2$ and 8.9, respectively). Again, this pattern holds for all participating countries.

All in all, these findings indicate that today's elders are not permanently traveling about, but that obviously this activity is of great value to them, because those who occasionally are able to travel for at least one week are significantly more satisfied in this regard than people who for any reason do not or cannot pursue such kind of activity.

PREDICTORS OF SATISFACTION WITH MOBILITY AND ITS CONTRIBUTION TO SATISFACTION WITH LIFE

If it is true that mobility in modern society comprises more than just getting from place A to place B, a great variety of transport options used and diversity of activities performed, featuring values such as self-determination, flexibility, and variability, can be expected to contribute to satisfaction with mobility in addition to a high level of actual mobility.

Explaining Satisfaction with Mobility

Regression analyses, including the three mobility indicators in addition to basic structural (urban/rural) and personal (age, gender, income, and health status) conditions, carried out separately for each country showed that good functional health is the most important predictor explaining satisfaction with mobility in almost all countries involved. Age as such does not contribute to this explanation. Living in a rural or urban area does not afflict satisfaction of older adults in the countries studied either; women are not less satisfied than their male contemporaries; and, unexpectedly, income does not seem to be a discriminating predictor in most regions studied.

Examining the impact of the three mobility indicators, we found that a great diversity of outdoor activities constitutes an important predictor of mobility satisfaction in all regions studied. Using a broad range of transport modes contributes to satisfaction in the German and Italian regions, and actual mobility in terms of realized trips plays a (modest) role in western Germany and Italy as well. In western Germany, the impact of each of the three components of mobility is even stronger than that of functional health. Only in Finland do the wide variety of transport modes used and high actual mobility not contribute to the elders' satisfaction with their possibilities to get where they want to go. This can be interpreted as an indication of the high level of social services in Finland that provide people in need with special transport and medical, social, and cultural services.

All in all we can conclude that older adults who have good functional health, who are able to use a broad range of transport options and able to pursue a great diversity of outdoor activities are more satisfied with their general mobility than those who don't have such competencies and options at their disposal. This is a clear but not very surprising result that corresponds largely with our assumptions. The question becomes whether this finding supports the notion that the sense of today's elders is to be on the go. In this case, a relationship between satisfaction based on the comprehensive manifestation of mobility, on the one hand, and subjective quality of life, on the other, should be ascertainable.

Mobility Specific Aspects in Life Satisfaction

To estimate the importance of mobility satisfaction in comparison with other domain-specific evaluations that might be relevant for satisfaction with life, we carried out another regression analyses: this time including all satisfaction statements available from the MOBILATE data (displayed in Table 1) in order to examine which specific category of satisfaction contributes most to older adults' subjective quality of life and what role mobility becomes in this context. We excluded only satisfaction with traveling because many of the persons who did not travel did not evaluate this issue. Instead, the number of journeys made for at least one week were included. Again, analyses were done separately for each country.

Table 1. Predictors of Life Satisfaction

Predictor (standard beta weight; semi-partial r^2 (%))	Finland	Germany West	Germany East	Italy
Satisfaction with mobility[a]			.12 (0.9)	
Leisure possibilities	.14 (1.4)	.16 (1.4)	.26 (3.8)	.20 (2.5)
Health	.18 (2.2)	.26 (4.9)	.22 (3.2)	.27 (5.9)
Finances	.38 (10.8)	.37 (8.6)	.30 (7.8)	.26 (6.1)
Housing	.17 (2.1)	.10 (0.6)		.10 (0.8)
Living area	.12 (1.0)		.09 (0.6)	
Services				
Public transport		.08 (0.4)		
Journeys (last year)[b]				
One trip/journey			.08 (0.6)	
Two or more trips			.06 (0.4)	
Adjusted R^2	.532	.482	.469	.353

Notes: Multiple regression analyses were performed for each country under study separately; unweighted data were used for computations; only standardized regression coefficients significant at a maximum error rate of $\alpha = .05$ are shown; displayed semi-partial r^2 represent percentages of unique variance accounted for by predictors.

[a]Self-evaluation rating on an 11-point scale (range 0-10), higher scores indicating higher satisfaction.

[b]Dummy-coded categorical variable indicating the number of journeys (lasting one week at least) during the last 12 months; persons without any journeys were used as reference group.

Altogether, the variables included explain between 35% (Italy) and 53% (Finland) of the variance in satisfaction with life in general (Table 1). As expected and in correspondence with previous studies (Diener, Oishi, & Lucas, 2003; Krause, 2004; Lamb, 1996; Veenhoven, 1996), satisfaction with one's financial situation and satisfaction with one's own health are consistently the most important predictors in all regions studied. Considering the remaining predictor variables, satisfaction with one's mobility possibilities does not contribute substantially to older adults' quality of life. Only in the eastern German regions does general life satisfaction increase somewhat with mobility satisfaction and with having traveled for at least one week during the year before the investigation. This finding is immediately understandable in view of the restrictions imposed on traveling during the former socialist regime and the many options available since German unification. More important in most countries is, however, whether people are satisfied with environmental features such as their housing conditions and the areas they live in. In comparison, satisfaction with services does not impinge on life satisfaction in any country; and satisfaction with public transportation plays a positive role in western Germany only.

However, there is also an indication supporting our understanding of mobility as a complex phenomenon in modern society. Satisfaction with one's leisure possibilities was shown to constitute an important domain-specific appraisal contributing significantly to subjective quality of life. As satisfaction with the pursuit of leisure activities increases in all participating countries, so does satisfaction with life in general. With respect to mobility, this means that mobility as such should not be regarded as the critical factor, but as a means enabling a person to actively pursue his or her interests.

Changing Elders, Changing Mobility

Mobility conditions and options, travel patterns, and transport modes were and continue to be, as pointed out in the beginning, subject to permanent change. Similarly, the conditions, options, patterns, and modes of aging are part of a permanent process of change. In the previous sections, the actual mobility resources and travel patterns of older adults in specific regions and at a specific point in time were described; and their satisfactions with mobility and with life in general were explained in light of the prevailing objective conditions and subjective evaluations in the context of modern values and societal goals. In a next step, changes in mobility-relevant issues will be addressed by comparing two cohorts of older adults over a period of five years. These analyses are possible by comparing the data collected in the MOBILATE project in 2000 with data collected in the same cities studied in Finland, western and eastern Germany, and Italy and stratified according to the same criteria (age and gender) in the research project "Keeping the elderly mobile" in 1995 (for further details see Mollenkopf et al., 2004; Ruoppila et al., 2003). Although the time period of five years is probably limited in terms of expecting major changes in mobility, the generally observable increased pace of developments on all kinds of levels on the individual and societal level led us to the assumption that at least some shifts in mobility-related aspects may be observable even in such a narrow time frame. Our focus was on the cohorts aged 55-59 years and 75-79 years in 1995 and 2000 because these cohorts had clearly lived through different historical situations, and it would be interesting to test for differential patterns in both of these cohorts across the five-year period.

The older cohorts born in 1916-1920 and 1921-1925 experienced the First World War or its immediate after effects in their early childhood. Thus, their development was affected by war and all its consequences. The older cohort also experienced the Second World War in their youth. In particular, the men belonging to these cohorts participated in the Second World War as soldiers. The women in these cohorts were also affected by the war as they bore the whole responsibility for childcare during wartime and also had to offset the deficiency in the work force caused by the men being in the service. Some of the women also lost their husbands or fiancées. All of the four cities in which the surveys were conducted were targets of bombing raids and severely damaged over the course of the war. The younger cohorts were born in 1936-1940 and 1941-1945, and thus experienced the Second World War in their early childhood, with all the attendant difficulties that effected their physical, psychological, and social development both at the time and later on.

Both the younger and older cohorts went through the rebuilding of their societies after the extensive destruction and devastation caused by the lengthy wars. In Ancona, the Italian research site, a heavy earthquake created an additional economic and housing emergency in 1972. Many people had to abandon their badly damaged homes and lost their jobs. In that year, the older cohorts of this study were between 50 and 55 years old and close to retirement, while the younger cohorts were in the middle of their working life and presumably with young children to look after. The demographic and economic decline in Ancona lasted about 10 years.

The political changes after the Second World War were especially great in Germany, when the country was divided into two states. After the 1960s, the social and economic development was rapid, but different in the German Democratic Republic than in Finland, the German Federal Republic, or Italy. The worsening of the world economy at the beginning of the '80s led to a particularly critical economic situation in Europe. The oldest respondents in the West profited from the flexible age limits in pension law and were able to avoid imminent unemployment by taking early retirement. Conversely, citizens of eastern Germany were forced, due to the low pensions provided by the state, to remain employed into old age. After reunification of both German states in 1990, large portions of eastern German industry folded, and the initial economic boom, with extremely high rates of growth, could not prevent mass layoffs. And while persons over retirement age could be regarded as the "winners" of the reunification process, procuring a pension that ensured their standard of living, especially the youngest eastern German cohort (born between 1941 and 1945) belonged clearly to the "losers": frequently unemployed, but too young to take early retirement, these persons were the most disadvantaged in terms of subjective self-worth compared to all other cohorts at the end of the 1990s (Geißler, 1999).

The 1990s saw great changes in Italy as well. As the older cohorts had already retired, the changes in the pension system affected the younger cohorts, especially those born earlier. When they were about 50 years old and suppression of the "earlier" pensions was already in the air, there was an early retirement boom among those who fulfilled the necessary requirements. Thus, in all countries under study, older cohorts escaped the effects of the economic recession of the early 1990s. This brought high unemployment and economic difficulties to the younger cohorts in their middle age or during the years immediately before their retirement.

Changes with Respect to Mobility Conditions in the Research Areas

The most important changes since the 1995 study relating to mobility in Jyväskylä, the Finnish urban environment in the MOBILATE Cohort 1995/2000 project, have been the supplementation of local public transport services with so-called service buses and city buses. The service bus was introduced in 1996 and is now an everyday means of travel in the city and its environs. Another flexible service was offered starting from the beginning of the year 2000 in the form of City buses that operate according to the wishes, telephoned in advance, of the passengers, who are then picked up from different locations in the city. The other important changes concerning Jyväskylä are improved commercial life compared to the situation in 1995, a lower level of unemployment, and increased migration into the city. These changes in transport and in employment may have increased the outdoor mobility of Jyväskylä citizens.

In the two German cities studied, similar changes occurred between 1995 and 2000. The number of total inhabitants decreased in both Mannheim and Chemnitz, while the share of older people increased. With regard to public transportation systems, the implementation of low-floor buses and low-floor trams has been an important improvement in both cities. Besides, in Mannheim, 453 of 1,000 inhabitants had a car in 1995, whereas in Chemnitz only 428 of 1,000 persons had one. Ten years after reunification, Chemnitz and Mannheim had the same figures regarding private cars, roughly 462 cars per 1,000 inhabitants.

From 1995 to the present day, the main improvements in transport in Ancona include the acquisition of buses with low floors and a platform for disabled persons, new bus lines (some experimental), and continuous improvement of the service in relation to changes in outdoor macroconditions. Currently there are 221 public buses, 69 of which have low floors. In the year 2000, 43 new buses, urban, suburban, and interurban, all equipped with a platform for disabled persons and a wheelchair block, were acquired.

The general question of our study is how differences in the life courses of Finnish, German, and Italian cohorts in 1995 and 2000 can be seen in their socioeconomic background, health, and outdoor mobility at the ages, respectively, of 55-59 and 75-79 years.

Changes in Major Personal Resources

With respect to important mobility resources, comparison of both cohorts displays clear general improvements, on the one hand, and somewhat mixed developments, on the other. General improvements, i.e., independent of locality and age, could be observed in education and income. The length of education was higher in the later-born cohorts, particularly in the Finnish and Italian cities, and among the eastern German men aged 75-79 years in 2000. Per capita income was usually higher in the later-born cohorts as well, except in the western German city, where the level of pensions was relatively high already in 1995. The tendency was in the same direction there, but the difference did not reach statistical significance. No clear patterns of change emerged as regards the indicators of health. It could well be that due to greater awareness about healthier lifestyles, the later-born cohorts would eventually show better health even across a five-year observation period. However, this assumption was confirmed for a few subgroups only. Changes remained generally quite small, even going in opposite directions in some cities. In performing different activities of daily living, both later-born cohorts reported the same level or better in 2000 as the cohorts born five years earlier, except in the German cities where the women aged 75-79 reported lower ADL in 2000 than in 1995. Satisfaction with health increased or was found to be the same among the younger cohorts, whereas the older Finnish and western German male cohorts were less satisfied in 2000 than the cohorts of the same age in 1995. In Italy, there were no cohort differences in satisfaction with health.

Changes in Mobility Resources

Car ownership and the number of transport modes used increased in almost all cohorts and in all cities between 1995 and 2000—a development especially relevant to mobility (Figure 2). Most of the later-born cohorts owned a car in the year 2000 more often than those born five years earlier. The reverse situation was found only for the younger male cohort in the eastern German city (albeit not statistically significant), and significant decreases occurred in the older Finnish male cohort and the older male and female cohorts in the western German city. Altogether, however, the findings show that the number of cars in Europe is increasing, as is known also from general statistics (ECMT, 2000). As regards the frequency of car use of the Finnish, western German, and Italian cohorts, there was a general trend among the later-born cohorts toward more frequent use of a car; whereas in the eastern German city, driving remained at about the same level or even decreased. Among the later-born younger men, in particular, the daily use of a car was substantially reduced, probably due to the reduced employment of those persons.

The use of public transport did not differ among the different cohorts, except in the Italian city where the older cohort used it more frequently in 2000 than the respective cohort did in 1995—probably an effect of system improvements undertaken in this city since 1995. Developments in satisfaction with public transportation did not totally reflect these findings, though. Corresponding with the similar use, satisfaction remained about the same in the Finnish and German areas. In the western German city, the older female cohort was more satisfied in 2000 than the cohort born earlier, whereas in the Italian city, satisfaction increased in the younger cohort.

Changes in Outdoor Mobility-Related Satisfaction Ratings and General Life Satisfaction

Subjective evaluations with mobility-relevant issues developed differently for the four cities studied. Regarding satisfaction with mobility possibilities, the general trend was that the cohorts born later were more satisfied with their mobility than those born earlier. This could be expected in view of the increases in car availability and transport options. The exception was the older male cohort members in the western German city, who were less satisfied in 2000 than in 1995 (Table 2).

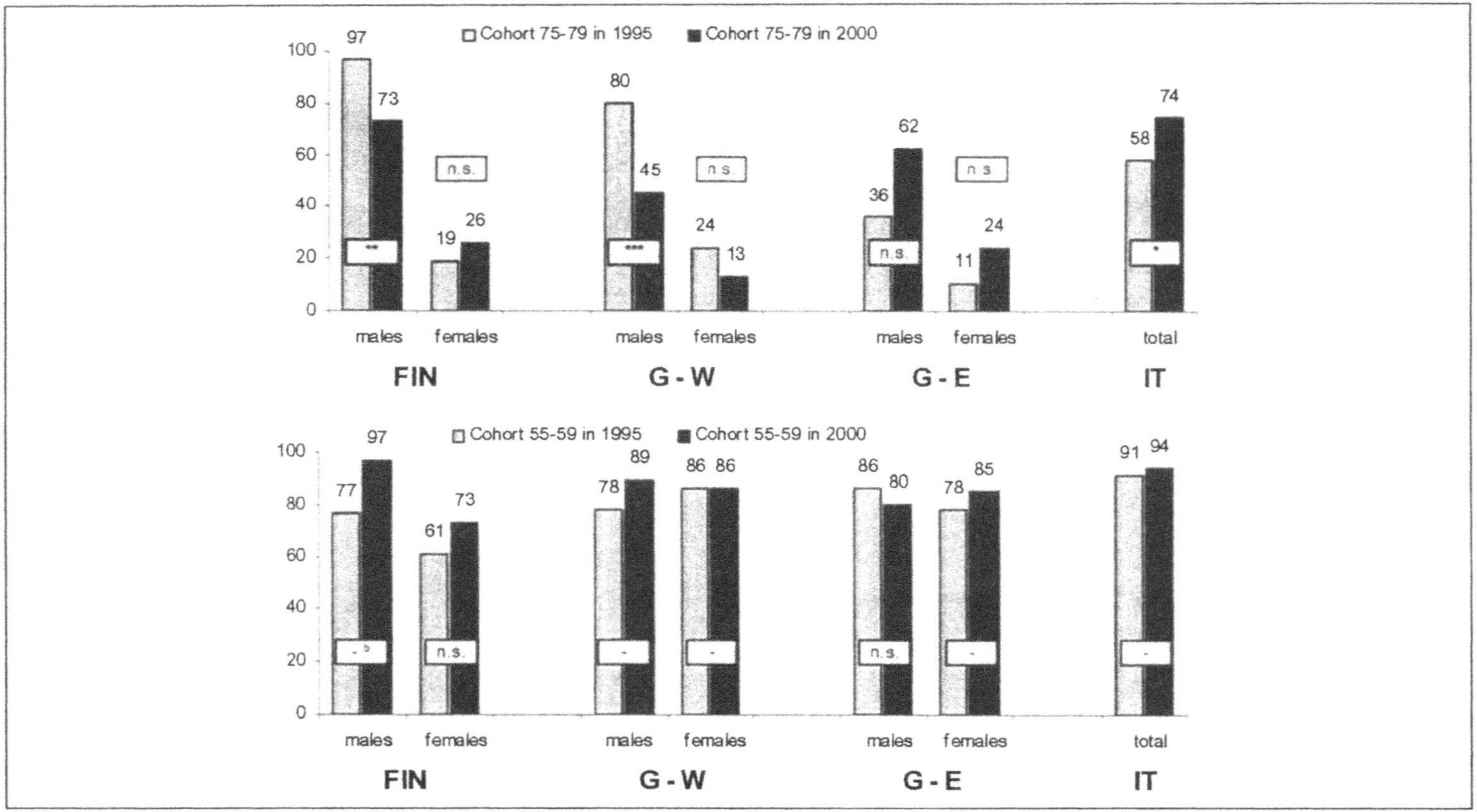

Figure 2. Car availability of two cohorts in 1995 and 2000 by country and gender* (percentages).
*Subjective evaluation on an 11-point scale (0 = very unsatisfied, 10 = very satisfied).

Table 2. Satisfaction with Mobility and Leisure Time Possibilities in Two Cohorts in 1995 and 2000 by Country and Gender

Variable	55-59 years					75-79 years				
	OMS 1995		MS 2000			OMS 1995		MS 2000		
(*M; SD*)	*M*	*SD*	*M*	*SD*	*t*-Test	*M*	*SD*	*M*	*SD*	*t*-Test
Satisfaction with mobility[a]										
Finland										
Males	8.6	1.2	9.1	0.8	*	8.8	2.2	7.9	1.8	n.s.
Females	8.6	2.3	8.9	1.2	n.s.	8.5	1.5	7.8	2.5	n.s.
Germany West										
Males	8.0	2.8	9.0	1.1	n.s.	8.1	2.7	7.0	2.4	*
Females	7.8	2.4	7.8	1.8	n.s.	7.5	2.6	7.7	2.6	n.s.
Germany East										
Males	8.0	1.8	7.8	2.6	n.s.	6.9	2.6	8.1	1.1	**
Females	7.0	2.3	8.7	0.9	**	7.9	1.9	7.0	2.6	n.s.
Italy										
Total[b]	7.1	2.0	9.3	1.5	***	6.5	2.8	7.5	2.7	**
Satisfaction with leisure[a]										
Finland										
Males	8.8	1.7	8.7	1.4	n.s.	8.8	1.4	7.8	2.1	*
Females	8.5	2.2	8.4	1.3	n.s.	8.2	2.2	8.0	2.6	n.s.
Germany West										
Males	6.7	3.3	8.2	2.3	n.s.	7.9	2.5	5.8	2.2	***
Females	7.5	2.5	8.4	1.7	n.s.	6.7	3.1	6.8	3.2	n.s.
Germany East										
Males	7.5	2.8	7.3	2.3	n.s.	6.0	2.6	7.7	1.6	**
Females	5.9	3.4	7.7	2.1	*	7.1	2.6	6.7	2.3	n.s.
Italy										
Total[b]	7.3	1.9	8.2	1.6	*	6.9	2.2	7.7	2.2	*

[a]Subjective evaluation on an 11-point scale (0 = very unsatisfied, 10 = very satisfied).
[b]In Italy, due to low sample size (1995: 55-59 n = 81, 75-79 n = 120; 2000: 55-59 n = 32, 75-79 n = 77), no gender differences were computed.

The cohort differences in satisfaction with leisure activities were also in opposing directions within the research localities. The Finnish older men, in particular, were less satisfied in 2000 than in 1995. In eastern Germany, the younger female cohort and the older male cohort were more satisfied in 2000 than the corresponding cohorts five years earlier. They obviously had profited greatly during the period 1995-2000 from the developments in the former GDR since reunification. The younger western

German cohort showed higher satisfaction as well, but the older men were significantly less satisfied in 2000 than those of the same age in 1995. In the Italian city, both later born cohorts were more satisfied with leisure activities than the earlier-born cohorts.

Similar differences were found with respect to satisfaction with traveling (not shown in a table). The Finnish younger female cohort showed more satisfaction with their traveling possibilities in 2000 than did the corresponding cohort born earlier, whereas the older female and male cohorts were less satisfied in 2000. In eastern Germany, the older male cohort was more satisfied in 2000, but the same cohort in western Germany was less satisfied with traveling than was the earlier-born cohort at the same age in 1995. Women in all German cohorts, irrespective of residence or year of birth, were more satisfied in 2000 than in 1995. In the Italian city, there were no cohort differences in satisfaction with traveling possibilities.

Satisfaction with life did not differ significantly between the Finnish cohorts (Figure 3). In the German cities, there were differing developments. Satisfaction remained the same or increased in the younger cohorts and among older females in both cities. The older eastern German male cohort was more satisfied with life in 2000 than in 1995; whereas the corresponding male cohort in western Germany, as we have noted frequently above, was less satisfied with life in 2000 than the earlier-born male cohort at the same age. In Italy, the tendency was generally positive, and the older cohort, in particular, was more satisfied with life in 2000 than was the earlier-born cohort in 1995.

All in all, positive changes occurred more often among the younger cohorts (aged 55-59 years); whereas the members of the older cohorts (aged 75-79 years) felt improvements, but in a number of aspects a worse situation than the cohorts born five years earlier. Unfortunately, we cannot ascertain with our data whether this worsening is an objective decrease in important domains of life or a subjective evaluation based on the older persons' expectations, aspirations, and comparison processes.

FUTURE PERSPECTIVES

In view of the actual findings and the cohort changes reported in the previous section, the question arises: how will the consequences of the increasing number of older car owners, as well as their changing personal competencies and expectations affect the possibilities and preferences of their desire for mobility? In Europe, elderly people, at least currently, are far less "auto-mobile" than in the United States (Rosenbloom, 2000). The most usual transport mode among today's elders is simply going by foot, followed by using a car (as a driver or as a passenger). Public transport seems to play a role when no other alternatives are available or when the system is well organized, with a high frequency of traffic service and a dense network of stops, which is often the case in central urban areas, but not on the periphery of cities and in rural areas. The bicycle can be an alternative where no public transportation is available, as long as geographical or topographical circumstances are favorable.

The older Europeans in our study (and in other countries as well; see ECMT, 2000) also make fewer trips per day and travel shorter distances than comparable American elders. On average, the spatial range of their mobility (in terms of everyday trips) is

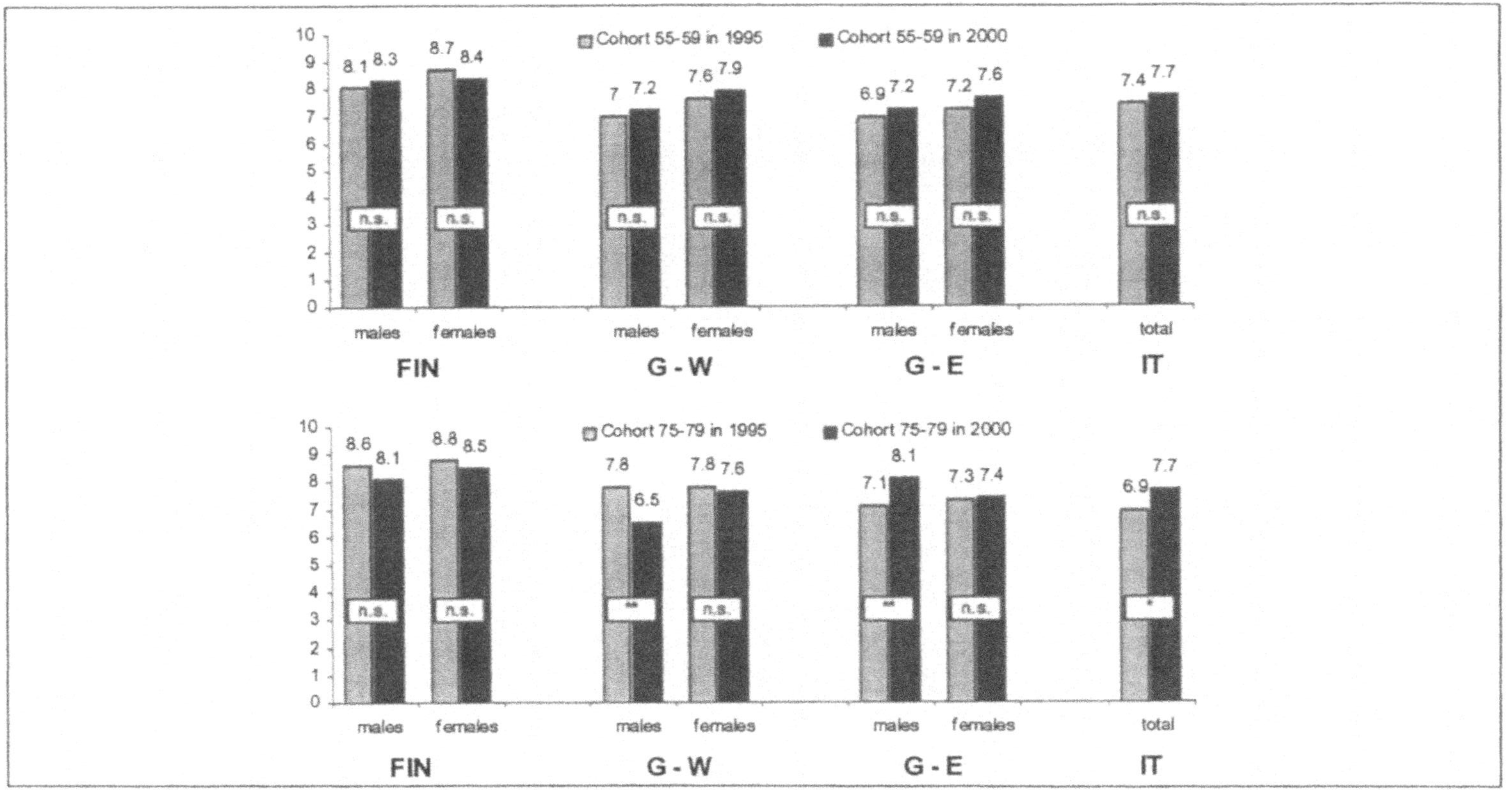

Figure 3. Satisfaction with life* in two cohorts in 1995 and 2000 by country and gender**.
*Subjective evaluation on an 11-point scale (0 = very unsatisfied, 10 = very satisfied.
**In Italy, due to low sample size (1995: 55-59 n = 81, 75-79 n = 120; 2000: 55-59 n = 32, 75-79 n = 77), no gender differences were computed.

limited to 1 to 3 km. However, a clear gap exists between older people who don't have a car in their households and those who are able to actively drive or to use a car as a passenger. At present, the share of pensioner households that own a car still varies greatly, depending on age, gender, the size of household, income, and the country they are living in. This relation will change, however, in the coming years when the generation of people for whom driving a car has become a matter of course reach retirement age. As a private and flexible means of transport, the car will not decline in importance for elderly people whose physical mobility is impaired, at least not until mass transit systems begin to approach the flexibility and convenience of motoring about in an automobile. Moreover, longitudinal studies (Jette & Branch, 1992) suggest that reliance on an automobile is a sociocultural phenomenon largely unrelated to a person's health.

The mobility needs of the elderly of tomorrow will be supported further by technological advances at various levels. Automobiles can be redesigned to better fit older drivers' capabilities by a variety of cutting-edge technologies that include vision systems, transfer systems, emergency systems, brake assistance systems, cruise control, stop and go assistance, parking assistance, and even curve lighting with GPS. Of particular interest here are collision avoidance systems that sense the proximity of other vehicles and that by means of adaptive cruise-control systems can automatically adjust vehicle speed; such a system obviously must include warning signals to the driver. However, due to limited information-processing capacity, assistive devices and telematic systems might overload older drivers by requiring continuous monitoring. The application of acoustic warning methods is limited because the ability to understand speech information at a low signal-to-noise ratio declines with advancing age (Färber, 2003; Jovanis, 2003). There are clear benefits for older drivers from road transport informatics and advance information on routes and travel times as well (Hanowski & Dingus, 2000; Jovanis, 2003). Moreover, developments in mobility aids can offer fascinating possibilities for compensating for sensory and physical impairments (e.g., Jansson, 2001). All these devices and appliances still need further improvement, though, and quite a lot of research and development work must still be done in order to make these aids usable, affordable, and accessible to all older people who might profit from them.

The greater availability of private cars and technological advances may expand the elderly persons' scope of movement and action. At the same time, the growing volume and density of traffic that results also increases the potential hazards of such travel. Traffic congestion, particularly in urban centers, has reached an extent that may unsettle elderly people and keep them from venturing out. The problems of older drivers, especially problems that are caused by sensory and mobility impairments or Alzheimers' disease, have become an issue of general concern (e.g., Ball & Owsley, 2000; Brouwer & Ponds, 1994; Organisation for Economic Co-operation and Development [OECD], 1985; Schaie & Pietrucha, 2000). Elderly drivers do not have a disproportionately greater frequency of involvement in accidents than younger drivers. As a person ages, though, the risk of his or her having an accident grows in relation to deteriorating driving performance (and hence in relation to the exposure to danger). Walking or biking are not good alternatives either: elderly people are very vulnerable as unprotected road users (Schlag, 2003).

As they continue to spread throughout all domains of life, new information and communications technologies (ICT) will also affect aging adults' mobility options. Automated facilities in so-called smart homes, include connection to external telecommunications networks to provide services such as tele-shopping, tele-banking, or tele-care. Thanks to constantly optimized remote ordering systems and increasing automation, daily routines will take up less time in the home or will turn into a voluntary leisure activity. Interactive communication systems can replace one or another perhaps tiresome journey. Tomorrow, it will be possible to monitor and control everything by integrative remote control systems without leaving one's home. At the same time, easier access to expeditious and convenient modes of transportation will enable almost unlimited mobility and change our very definition of what is "near" or "far." These examples clearly illustrate both the new freedom and flexibility of traveling and the dangers of isolation in a modern hermitage due to the new reliance upon technology. It is an open question whether the formidable technical possibilities will lead older adults to stay at home more or to get out and about more—both are possible. It is certain, however, that for both they need new abilities and skills if they want or have to use the new technologies. This may lead to new forms of discrimination in old age. The situation will be especially precarious if public and private services are geared more and more toward mobile car drivers and Internet users. The shift to private passenger transport often coincides with cutbacks in public transportation. The once dense network of retail shops is giving way to suburban supermarkets and downtown shopping centers. Important services are often difficult to come by in rural regions and suburbs. In many cases, transportation facilities are deficient by modern standards or absent altogether.

Strong efforts are being made at both the European and national levels to enhance the mobility—and thus, social inclusion—of elderly people and persons with disabilities by new legal regulations requiring barrier-free access to transportation, buildings, and products (ECMT, 1999, 2002). In view of tight financial constraints, however, experts expect a stagnation in the funding of local public transport and decreasing consideration of traffic safety needs of older road users. Hence, two parallel but opposing tendencies can be observed: On the one hand, opportunities—especially technologically supported options—for being on the go in old age increase substantially. On the other, the interrelated trends of urban decentralization, decreasing public transport services, diversity of travel origins and destinations, and increasing automobile use mutually reinforce each other. As a result, elderly people who do not have the alternative of using a personal automobile or ICT applications may come to suffer structural discrimination if important elements of the infrastructure, basic services, and recreation facilities continue to depend on personal transportation and remain concentrated either in city centers or in remote areas. This is particularly salient for elderly people whose life space gradually but steadily contracts because of changes in their physical and sensory abilities. As the findings of the MOBILATE project show, being able to continue leading independent lives, maintain social contact, and take advantage of recreational activities are significant needs in old age.

The low level of satisfaction reported by people whose mobility is hampered by limitations to their functional health or by lack of private or public transport options clearly shows that the decline of outdoor mobility in old age is not an entirely voluntary retreat from the world. Ensuring them opportunities for participation in their social, built-up, and natural environments despite the physical handicaps, possible financial constraints, and social, technological, and spatial barriers that exist in their world, would thus greatly contribute to their quality of life and well-being. Therefore, the question of whether and how external conditions and demands of the environment can be harmonized with individual needs and resources will be a societal and political topic in the years to come.

ACKNOWLEDGMENTS

The MOBILATE project was funded within the context of the European Commission's 5th Framework Program (QLK6-1999-02236) and coordinated by the German Centre for Research on Ageing. Partners in this project were the Istituto Nazionale Riposo e Cura Anziani (INRCA), Ancona, Italy; Hungarian Academy of Sciences, Budapest, Hungary; University of Jyväskylä, Jyväskylä, Finland; and Delft University of Technology, Delft, The Netherlands. I would also like to thank Roman Kaspar and Stephan Baas for competent data analyses.

REFERENCES

Ball, K., & Owsley, C. (2000). Increasing mobility and reducing accidents of older drivers. In K. W. Schaie & M. Pietrucha (Eds.), *Mobility and transportation in the elderly* (pp. 213-250). New York: Springer Publishing Company.

Brouwer, W. H., & Ponds, R. W. H. M. (1994). Driving competence in older persons. *Disability and Rehabilitation, 16*(3), 149-161.

Burkhardt, J. E. (2000). Limitations of mass transportation systems and individual vehicle systems for older persons. In K. W. Schaie & M. Pietrucha (Eds.), *Mobility and transportation in the elderly and aging* (pp. 97-123). New York: Springer Publishing Company.

Centre d'études sur les réseaux, les transports, l'urbanisme et les constructions publiques (CERTU) [Centre for the Study of Urban Planning, Transport, and Public Facilities]. (2001). La mobilité des personnages âges—Analyse des enquêtes ménages déplacements [Older persons' outdoor mobility—Trip survey analyses]. Rapport d'étude, Lyon.

Chu, X. (1994). *The effects of age on the driving habits of the elderly. Evidence from the 1990 National Personal Transportation Study. DOT-T-95-12.* Washington, DC: U.S. Department of Transportation.

Cvitkovich, Y., & Wister, A. (2001). The importance of transportation and prioritization of environmental needs to sustain well-being among older adults. *Environment & Behavior, 33*(6), 809-829.

Diener, E., Oishi, S., & Lucas, R. E. (2003). Personality, culture, and subjective well-being: Emotional and cognitive evaluations of life. *Annual Review of Psychology, 54,* 403-425.

Esping-Andersen, G. (1990). *The three worlds of welfare capitalism.* Oxford: Policy Press.

Esping-Andersen, G. (1999). *Social foundations of post-industrial economies.* Oxford: University Press.

European Communities. (2003). *Panorama of transport. Statistical overview of transport in the European Union. Eurostat Theme 7 Part 2.* Luxembourg: Office for Official Publications of the European Communities.

European Conference of Ministers of Transport (ECMT). (1999). *Improving transport for People with mobility handicaps.* Paris Cedex, France: OECD Publications.

European Conference of Ministers of Transport (ECMT). (2000). *Transport and aging of the population.* Report of the 112th round table on transport economics, held in Paris on 19th-20th November 1998. Paris Cedex, France: OECD Publications.

European Conference of Ministers of Transport (ECMT). (2002). *Transport and aging of the population.* Paris Cedex, France: OECD Publications.

Färber, B. (2003). Micro interventions: Assistive devices, telematics, person x environment interactions. In K. W. Schaie, H.-W. Wahl, H. Mollenkopf, & F. Oswald (Eds.), *Aging independently: Living arrangements and mobility* (pp. 248-262). New York: Springer Publishing Company.

Fozard, J. L., & Gordon-Salant, S. (2001). Sensory and perceptual changes with aging. In J. E. Birren & K. W. Schaie (Eds.), *Handbook of the psychology of aging* (5th ed., pp. 31-45). San Diego, CA: Academic Press.

Geißler, R. (1999). Sozialer wandel [Social change]. In W. Weidenfeld & K.-R. Korte (Eds.), *Handbuch zur deutschen Einheit 1949–1989–1999* [Handbook German Unification] (pp. 681-694). Bundeszentrale für politische Bildung, Schriftenreihe Band 262. Frankfurt am Main, Bonn: Campus Verlag.

Hanowski, R. J., & Dingus, T. A. (2000). Will intelligent transportation systems improve older driver mobility? In K. W. Schaie & M. Pietrucha (Eds.), *Mobility and transportation in the elderly* (pp. 279-298). New York: Springer Publishing Company.

Jansson, G. (2001). The potential usefulness of high-tech aids for visually impaired seniors. In H.-W. Wahl & H.-E. Schulze (Eds.), *On the special needs of blind and low vision seniors* (pp. 231-238). Amsterdam: IOS Press.

Jette, A. M., & Branch, L. G. (1992). A ten-year follow-up of driving patterns among the community-dwelling elderly. *Human Factors, 34*(1), 25-31.

Jovanis, P. P. (2003). Macro-interventions: Roads, transportation systems, traffic calming, and vehicle design. In K. W. Schaie & M. Pietrucha (Eds.), *Mobility and transportation in the elderly* (pp. 279-298). New York: Springer Publishing Company.

Krause, N. (2004). Neighborhoods, health, and well-being in late life. In H.-W. Wahl, R. J. Scheidt, & P. G. Windley (Eds.), *Focus on aging in context: Socio-physical environments* (Annual Review of Gerontology and Geriatrics, Vol. 23) (5th ed., pp. 272-294). New York: Springer Publishing Company.

Lamb, V. L. (1996). A cross-national study of quality of life factors associated with patterns of elderly disablement. *Social Science and Medicine, 42*(3), 363-377.

Mollenkopf, H., Marcellini, F., Ruoppila, I., & Tacken, M. (Eds.). (2004). *Ageing and outdoor mobility. A European study.* Amsterdam: IOS Press.

Mollenkopf, H., Marcellini, F., Ruoppila, I., Széman, Z., & Tacken, M. (Eds.). (2005). *Enhancing mobility in later life—Personal coping, environmental resources, and technical support.* The out-of-home mobility of older adults in urban and rural regions of five European countries. Amsterdam: IOS Press.

National Aeronautics and Space Administration (NASA). (1999). *General public space travel and tourism—Vol. 2 workshop proceedings.* NASA/CP-1999-209146.

Organisation for Economic Co-operation and Development (O.E.C.D.). (1985). *Traffic safety of elderly road users.* Paris: Road Transport Research (O.E.C.D.).

Rosenbloom, S. (2000). Report by the chairperson (United States). In European Conference of Ministers of Transport (ECMT) (Ed.), *Transport and aging of the population. Report of the 112th round table on transport economics* (pp. 7-42). Paris Cedex, France: OECD Publications.

Ruoppila, I., Marcellini, F., Mollenkopf, H., Hirsiaho, N., Baas, S., Principi, A., Ciarrocchi, S., & Wetzel, D. (2003). *The MOBILATE Cohort Study 1995—2000: Enhancing outdoor mobility in later life. The differences between persons aged 55-59 years and 75-79 years in 1995 and 2000.* DZFA Research Report No. 17. Heidelberg: German Centre for Research on Ageing (DZFA).

Salamon, L. M., & Anheier, H. K. (1996). *Social origins of civil society: Explaining the nonprofit sector cross-nationally.* Working Papers of the Johns Hopkins Comparative Nonprofit Project, No. 22. Baltimore: The Johns Hopkins University Press.

Schaie, K. W. (2003). Mobility for what? In K. W. Schaie, H.-W. Wahl, H. Mollenkopf, & F. Oswald (Eds.), *Aging independently: Living arrangements and mobility* (pp. 18-27). New York: Springer Publishing Company.

Schaie, K. W., & Pietrucha, M. (Eds.). (2000). *Mobility and transportation in the elderly.* New York: Springer Publishing Company.

Schlag, B. (2003). Safety and accidents among older drivers: The German perspective. In K. W. Schaie, H.-W. Wahl, H. Mollenkopf, & F. Oswald (Eds.), *Aging independently: Living arrangements and mobility* (pp. 205-219). New York: Springer Publishing Company.

Széman, Z., & Harsányi, L. (2000). *Caught in the net in Hungary and eastern Europe.* Budapest: Nonprofit Research Group & Institute of Sociology of the Hungarian Academy of Sciences.

Tacken, M., Marcellini, F., Mollenkopf, H., & Ruoppila, I. (1999). *Keeping the elderly mobile. Outdoor mobility of the elderly: Problems and solutions* (Vol. The Netherlands TRAIL Research School Conference Proceedings Series P99/1). Delft, The Netherlands: Delft University Press.

United Nations Economic Commission for Europe (UNECE). (2003). Trends in Europe and North America. In *The Statistical Yearbook of the Economic Commission for Europe 2003.* Available at http://www.unece.org/stats/trend/ch8.htm (April 2004).

Veenhoven, R. (1996). Developments in satisfaction-research. *Social Indicators Research, 37,* 1-46.

Vogel, J. (1998). *Three types of European society.* Available from: http://www.nnn.se/n-model/europe3/europe3.htm.

World Business Council for Sustainable Development [WBCSD]. (2002). *Mobility 2001. World mobility at the end of the twentieth century and its sustainability.* Available from: www.wbcsdmobility.org.

CHAPTER 11

Does Driving Benefit Quality of Life Among Older Drivers?

Karlene K. Ball, Virginia G. Wadley, David E. Vance, and Jerri D. Edwards

IMPORTANCE OF DRIVING FOR MOBILITY AND QUALITY OF LIFE

Mobility is a functional ability that is important for maintaining quality of life and independence, particularly with advanced age. Continued mobility is crucial for maintaining social contacts, independent functioning, and a satisfying quality of life. An important index of mobility, particularly in the United States, is driving. Most older adults in the United States rely primarily on the personal automobile for maintaining mobility (Jette & Branch, 1992). Fifteen years ago almost 90% of older adults in the United States relied on the personal automobile for the majority of their transportation needs (Transportation Research Board, 1988), and dependence upon the personal automobile is only increasing (Mollenkopf et al., 2002). As the number of older drivers both in the United States and abroad and the amount they drive is increasing, dependence upon driving to sustain quality of life is mounting as well (Owsley, 2002).

The Importance of Driving Is Increasing Among Older Adults

As the proportion of older adults in the population increases, so is the number of older drivers; whereas in 1940, less than 6% of drivers in the United States were 60 years of age and older, more than 25% of drivers today are elderly. The number of older drivers is expected to continue to increase such that by the year 2050, they will represent up to 40% of the driving population (National Center for Statistics and Analysis, 1995). These trends can be seen in other nations as well. For example, in the United Kingdom, the number of older drivers increased up to 600% between 1965 and 1985 (Department of Transport, 1991). Moreover, individuals are remaining active drivers longer. Today, the driving life expectancy is approximately 11 years for drivers who currently are between the ages of 70 to 74 (Foley, Heimovitz, Guralnik, & Brock, 2002).

These statistics in part reflect the fact that the importance of driving for older adults is greater than in the past. In 1971, approximately 46% of older adults who were head of their households did *not* own a car (Stern, Burkhardt, & Eberhard, 2003). On the other hand, it is estimated that by 2030, 90% of adults 65 and older will be car owners and active drivers (McKnight, 2003). With the aging of the Baby Boom generation, we will see a much larger proportion of older women drivers compared to two or three decades ago. Only two-thirds of females who are now 65 and older are currently licensed drivers, but 90% of females who will be 65 or older 30 years from now are currently licensed drivers. Similar trends are evident in Europe as well (Mollenkopf et al., 2002).

The amount that older adults drive has also increased. Women drivers who are 65 and older average approximately 5,000 miles per year, representing a 31% increase in driving exposure over the last three decades. Male drivers of the same age average approximately 10,000 miles per year, representing an even larger increase of 75% over the same time period (Hu & Young, 1999). In the United States, suburbanization is in part responsible for the increase in the extent of driving (Barr, 2002). Between 1950 and 1998, the percentage of urban dwellers declined from more than 50% to only 35% of the population. Such changes have necessitated an increase in driving, not only to work, but also to shopping, entertainment, and to access healthcare services (Barr, 2002), all of which are important for quality of life.

Driving is also important for quality of life in that possession of a driver's license is a symbol of independence and autonomy (Shope, 2003). Seventy-seven percent of individuals 55 years of age or older rate driving as either "very essential" or "essential" (O'Neill, 2000). Being deprived of driving status heralds the loss of other roles in a person's life. Whether the loss is voluntary or mandatory, the change requires significant adjustment often accompanied by other difficulties. Changes in driving habits, and driving cessation in particular, are a threat to older adults' quality of life and can lead to adverse consequences such as decreased activity, dependency, and depression (Fonda, Wallace, & Herzog, 2001; Marottoli et al., 1997, 2000; Patrick & Deyo, 1989).

Older Drivers are Over-Represented in Injurious and Fatal Crashes

Although driving is important for older adults to maintain mobility, independence, and quality of life, research indicates that older drivers have higher crash rates compared to their middle-aged counterparts (Williams & Carsten, 1989). When driving exposure is taken into consideration, persons aged 70 and older have the second-highest rates among all age groups of vehicle crashes and injuries per vehicle mile (National Safety Counsel, 1993). When older adults experience a crash, they are much more likely to be injured or killed compared to a crash of similar intensity by their younger counterparts (Evans, 1991). For example, in 1996, the fatality rate per million miles of travel for individuals 65 years of age and older was 17 times greater than for those between the ages of 25 and 65 (National Highway Traffic Safety Administration, 1997). As the proportion of older drivers is increasing, injuries and fatalities in this age group resulting from vehicle crashes is increasing as well. In 1999, almost 5000 drivers over the age of 70 were involved in a fatal accident, an increase of 42% from the previous decade (Department of Transportation, 2000). Even so, it is important to note that overall, most older drivers are safe drivers. Older drivers are just as likely to be the victim in an automobile crash as they are to be an at-fault driver (Dulisse, 1997). The higher risk of injuries and fatalities for older adults is a function of older adults increased vulnerability as well as the increased risk for crash involvement in this age group (McKnight & McKnight, 1999). However, age itself is not the issue, but rather age-related declines in cognitive and sensory abilities can place some older adults at risk for vehicle crashes. The increase in the number of crashes per mile driven observed with age does not reflect ubiquitous decline among older adults, but rather represents a small proportion of elderly who are at high risk for crash involvement (Dobbs, Heller, & Schopflocher, 1998; McKnight, 2003). Nevertheless, given the current population trends, the importance of driving for quality of life and the increased risk for crash involvement, injuries, and fatalities among older adults, addressing risk factors in this population is vital. Viable solutions for maintaining safe mobility for elders are likely to be multifaceted, reflecting the complexity of the issue at hand.

Older Adults and Public Transportation

With such reliance on driving, switching to public transportation may not be feasible for many older adults. This is reflected by the fact that in the United States, older adults use public transportation rarely. Public transportation is used for less than 3% of trips taken by older adults in the United States, and use of public transportation by both elder Americans and Europeans has been declining (Eberhard, 1996). Generally, older adults do not deem public transportation to be sufficient or effective in meeting their transportation needs (O'Neill, 2000). Alternative forms of transportation to the personal automobile such as busing, taxis, and subway systems are not an option for many older adults due to expense, inconvenience, or unavailability (Stern et al., 2003). Furthermore, the physical impairments of older adults can make using public transportation more difficult. Older adults may avoid public transportation due to crime and other safety concerns (Johnson, 1999; Shope, 2003). Likewise, relying on family members for transportation is an alternative that is beset with problems (Lindquist & Ettinger, 2003; Taylor & Tripodes, 2001). Given that public transportation is fragmented or even nonexistent in rural communities, driving is tantamount to independence and quality of life (Stunkel, 1997). Considering these issues, as well as the fact that that older adults can experience cognitive and sensory declines that negatively impact their driving abilities, other solutions must be sought.

TECHNOLOGY AND OLDER DRIVERS

Can New Technology Benefit Older Drivers?

Given that driving is an important—and in some societies, nearly essential—means of maintaining mobility and quality of life, how can new technology enhance older adults' driving skills and safety? A potential way to extend the safe driving years of older adults is by improving safety technology. Although the innovation of such technologies has been posited as a way to ameliorate driving safety in this population, improvements to date have inherent limitations for older drivers. Technology for identifying older drivers at risk for adverse mobility outcomes has improved vastly and is necessary in order to identify individuals in need of interventions that enhance safety and mobility. This section will discuss the merits and limitations of three categories of technological advances: (1) those developed for vehicle safety (e.g., advance warning systems), (2) those developed for identifying individuals who are at increased risk for crash, and (3) those designed to improve the cognitive and functional skills necessary for driving competence.

Technological Advances in Vehicle Safety

Unfortunately, vehicle safety technologies have seldom been developed with a focus on older adult users. Furthermore, studies investigating the impact of these technologies have rarely included older adults. Older drivers may be the most likely to suffer problems using Intelligent Transportation System technologies, and yet they may be the most likely to benefit from such technology as well (Caird, 2004; Stamatiadis, 1994). Results of studies conducted among young and middle-aged drivers have yielded mixed results as to the benefits of vehicle safety technology. In-vehicle technologies and their possible benefits to older drivers will be discussed below.

Emergency Alert and Automatic Vehicle Location technology can be used to communicate to an emergency dispatch center the status and locale of a vehicle. These systems have promise for increasing the safety of older adults. Evans indicated that improvement in timely delivery of emergency medical treatment is principally responsible for the decline in traffic fatalities over the past four decades (Evans, 1991). With the use of such technology, emergency services may become even quicker to respond. Considering the increased incidence of injuries in the elderly, rapid treatment of injuries is likely to benefit them in particular (Caird, 2004).

Infrared vision-enhancement systems are a type of in-vehicle technology aimed toward improving safety by enhancing the driver's ability to see at night or in decreased visibility situations (i.e., fog). Such technology may help older adults' visual capabilities, particularly considering their increased difficulty with night driving. In testing a number of in-vehicle technology systems with older drivers, Oxley and Mitchell (1995) found that vision enhancement technology is likely to improve older drivers mobility and safety. Older adults found such systems easy to use and indicated that they may be less likely to avoid particular driving situations if the technology was available to them.

Collision avoidance systems alert drivers to potential collisions. Such technology may benefit older drivers who are at increased risk for crash involvement (Caird, 2004). However, the implementation of such technology is complicated. Not only is it difficult to determine how (e.g., visual, auditory, and/or tactile stimuli) and exactly when alerts should be given, but considering that older adults may have sensory (i.e., hearing difficulty) and cognitive declines (i.e., slower speed of processing) the settings most effective for young or middle-aged drivers would not necessarily also be beneficial for older drivers. Furthermore, such technology adds additional attentional requirements to the already demanding driving task. Accordingly, when researchers examined the use of such technology with older adults, they concluded that it would have little impact on improving their mobility (Oxley & Mitchell, 1995).

In-vehicle route guidance systems can help drivers navigate. These systems provide directions through audible and visual instructions and can prevent drivers from getting lost as well as helping to choose the best route and avoid traffic congestion (Caird, 2004). Considering that older drivers may have more problems finding their way, this technology could be of benefit to them. On the other hand, such systems may tap already taxed cognitive resources of the older driver. For example, Dingus and colleagues (1997) examined the use of an Advanced Traveler Information System designed to improve safety, reduce travel time, and increase mobility by providing navigation, real-time information about traffic and road conditions, safety warnings, and various other services. Drivers over the age of 65 experienced difficulty integrating this safety technology into their driving. In fact, as a result of using this, older drivers drove slower and made more safety-related errors than did their younger counterparts. Similarly, Oxley and Mitchell (1995) found that navigation systems could cause drivers to slow down and steer off course; this negative impact was greater for older drivers. Thus, integrating sophisticated technology into the driving process may tax existing cognitive abilities. Relying on these technologies at this point may create a sense of false hope, thus putting older adults unwittingly at risk for harm to themselves or others.

Sixsmith (1990) used focus groups to explore older adults attitudes concerning in-vehicle technology systems. Some of the older adults were wary of such technology and overall, drivers had mixed reactions; some felt the technology could improve their safety. Interestingly, the older adults felt that in-vehicle technologies would be more benefit to younger adults and particularly mentioned their concern about the demands such technology would place on their attention. Thus, even if technology is designed and tested with elders, the attitudes of such individuals toward the technology may remain a barrier to their use.

In summary, recent advances in vehicle safety technology may be of relatively less benefit to older drivers than to younger ones due to the demands they place upon older adults' cognitive resources (Dingus et al., 1997). To date, Emergency Alert and Automatic Vehicle Location seem to hold the most promise to benefit older adults. The limitations of other types of vehicle safety technology highlight the need for technology to be engineered with older adults in mind, with the caveat that there is no such thing as a prototypical older adult. The effects of aging on physical health and cognitive functions are more idiosyncratic than uniform. Even so, it is generally true that older adults are subject to declines in health, and concomitantly, to declines in certain cognitive functions that are key to optimal driving performance. Since such cognitive declines also interfere with an older adults ability to use technology effectively, we can aim technology toward improving the cognitive abilities of older adults. Accordingly, over the past decade, technology has increasingly been used to both identify the cognitive abilities vital for driving and to improve these abilities in the face of decline.

Technological Advances in Driver Assessment

Technological advances in driver assessment are beneficial to older adults in several ways. As previously mentioned, despite the strong correlation between age and increased crash risk, most older drivers are safe drivers (Ball & Owsley, 2003). Thus, restrictions of driving based upon age are not fair. Assessments that tap the abilities necessary for driving safety are needed to avoid age discrimination. Additionally, the identification of older drivers for increased risk for crash involvement permits early intervention, which may extend safety and mobility, thereby improving quality of life. Technological advances in assessing higher order information processing in particular have contributed to the move toward identifying and intervening with at-risk older drivers.

Visual Sensory Function

Clearly, basic visual sensory function is needed to drive safely. With a few exceptions in the recent past, most Departments of Motor Vehicles have only tested visual acuity. Methods of assessing visual function vary greatly from using simple eye charts (without control of lighting conditions) to computerized assessments.

Originally, visual acuity assessments were designed for clinical use to detect and monitor the progression of disease. Thus, assessment measures were not designed to reflect the visual complexity of driving or other everyday activities (Owsley & McGwin, 1999). State-of-the-science visual acuity testing has progressed from the eye chart on the wall to the light box to, most recently, software programs that may have distinct advantages for driver licensure. For example, automated vision tests can improve efficiency in heavy volume settings by eliminating the need for one-on-one manual testing. Results with automated tests are automatically scored and saved, reducing personnel time and the possibility of transcription errors. Automated vision tests may also be integrated with other functions at a licensing agency, such as knowledge-based testing, digital photo capture, and biometric recognition systems. Furthermore, randomized test designs make vision test memorization impossible. Since test results are automatically stored, they can be easily integrated into existing data management systems, and changes and trends in each individual's vision can be saved and flagged if substantial visual decline is noted. Finally, automating the visual acuity test has the potential to enable licensing agencies to test far more than visual acuity, possibly adding other visual or cognitive test measures that are predictive of driving competence, thereby improving the overall assessment process. While vision test software is still relatively new, companies that market professional vision assessment software are beginning to gain acceptance in license agency settings.

Visual Information Processing

Because driving involves complex visual information processing abilities, it is unlikely that an assessment of visual function alone is sufficient to identify the majority of individuals at elevated risk for crash involvement. Even though the most common practice of licensing agencies is to screen visual acuity, research has indicated that visual acuity is not a strong predictor of driving ability (Owsley, 2002). Rather, visual information processing skills have emerged as strong predictors of safe driving. Impaired visual attention abilities, for example, have long been suspected of playing a role in automobile crashes (Barrett, Greenawalt, Thorton, & Williamson, 1977; Kahneman & Ben-Ishai, 1973). This relationship has been extensively explored in recent years (Ball & Owsley, 1991; Ball, Owsley, Sloan, Roenker, & Bruni, 1993; Owsley et al., 1998) specifically through the concept of the useful field of view. Through advances in the use of computerized testing to measure visual information-processing abilities in drivers, new tests have been developed that have proved much better at identifying crash-involved drivers than visual sensory measures alone.

The Useful Field of View

Through advances in the use of computerized testing to measure visual information processing abilities in drivers, new tests have been developed that have proved much better at identifying crash-involved drivers than visual sensory measures alone. Multiple studies have been conducted examining the relationship between the Useful Field of View test (UFOV®) and driving. The UFOV® test measures the size of the field in which one can process rapidly presented, increasingly complex information with a single glance through subtests that tap speed of information processing, ability to divide attention, and susceptibility to distraction (Ball, Roenker, & Bruni, 1990). When comparing potential risk factors for crash involvement, such as the health status of the visual system, visual sensory function, UFOV® and mental status, Owsley and colleagues found that only mental status and UFOV® performance were related to crash frequency. Intersection crashes, the most frequent type of crash, were best predicted by UFOV® performance and mental status (Owsley, Ball, Sloane, Roenker, & Bruni, 1991). In a later study, UFOV® performance emerged as an even stronger predictor of injurious crashes (Owsley, McGwin, & Ball, 1998). Drivers with UFOV® reductions of 22.5%-40%, 41%-60%, and > 60% were associated respectively with 5.2, 16.5, and 21.5-fold increases in risk for an injurious crash, compared to those drivers with UFOV® reductions of < 22.5%. In a prospective follow-up study, Owsley and colleagues found that older drivers with a 40% or greater UFOV® impairment were 2.2 times more likely than those with intact UFOV® to incur a crash during three years of follow-up (Owsley et al., 1998). Again, UFOV® impairment was the only type of visual deficit found to be related to future crash involvement. Overall, several studies have found the UFOV® assessment measure to be a reliable predictor of crashing as measured by state-recorded reports. Furthermore, as compared to a number of other visual and cognitive measures, the UFOV® measure was consistently found to be the strongest predictor of crashing.

Findings from driving simulation studies correspond to the findings associated with state records of automobile crashes. Specifically, UFOV® impairment is related to slower response times, a greater number of dangerous maneuvers, and a greater number of simulator crashes (Ball & Owsley, 2000; Rizzo, Reinach, McGehee, & Dawson, 1997; Roenker, Cissell, Ball, Wadley, & Edwards, 2003).

Several studies have also examined the relationship between the UFOV® assessment and on-road driving performance. Roenker and colleagues (2003) found a strong correlation between UFOV® performance and global driving ratings. In another study of on-road driving, Cushman (1996) found that 82% of drivers who failed the UFOV® test also failed the road test, and 86% of those who passed the UFOV® test passed the road test. Similarly, Ducheck and colleagues found that poorer on-road driving scores were associated with increased dementia severity as well as poorer UFOV® performance (Duchek, Hunt, Ball, Buckles, & Morris, 1998).

In summary, greater restrictions in UFOV® are consistently related to poorer on-road driving performance, poorer driving simulator performance, and vehicular crashes. An individual's UFOV® performance appears to be a stronger predictor of crash risk than visual acuity, mental status examination performance, or a diagnosis of early dementia. Ostensibly, this could be due to the technological precision of the UFOV® measure.

Other Driver Assessment Technology

Technological advances have resulted in the development of several other automated tests for driver assessment as well. For example, the Automated Psychophysical Test (APT) is a computerized device used to administer a variety of measures that tap a range of skills affected by age, such as sensory abilities, attention, perception, cognition, and psychomotor abilities (McKnight & McKnight, 1999). Performance across the APT measures moderately correlate ($r = 0.46$) to on-the-road driving performance (McKnight & McKnight, 1999).

The Gross Impairment Screening Battery (GRIMPS), developed by Staplin and colleagues, is a brief assessment of a range of functional abilities considered to be critical to driving. The battery was based upon research indicating an association between poor performance on the measure and an elevated risk of crash involvement or other driving impairment. Consideration includes measures that were brief, inexpensive, and that required minimal training for test administrators. Measures included in the GRIMPS battery are rapid walk (Marottoli, Cooney, Wagner, Doucetter, & Tinetti, 1994), foot tap, arm reach (Hu, Trumble, Foley, Eberhard, & Wallace, 1998; Retchin, Cox, Fox, & Irwin, 1988), head/neck rotation (Marottoli et al., 1998), cued and delayed recall (McKnight & McKnight, 1999), symbol scan, the Motor Free Visual Perception Test (which measures the ability to construct a complete image from only partial information; Tarawneh, McCoy, Bishu, & Ballard, 1993), and the Trail Making Test (an executive function and attention measure; Goode et al., 1998; Stutts, 1998; Stutts, Stewart, & Martell, 1998; Tarawneh et al., 1993).

The Maryland program currently employs the DrivingHealth Inventory, which is now completely automated. This includes selected procedures from the GRIMPS battery that were found to be significant predictors of (at-fault) crashes in a representative sample of ~2,000 drivers over age 55; the Motor-Free Visual Perception Test (Visual Closure subtest), used to measure visuospatial abilities, specifically the visualization of missing information; Delayed Recall, a measure of working memory; the Trail-Making test (Part B), used to measure directed visual search with divided attention; and two measures of physical ability: the Rapid Pace Walk, to measure leg strength and general mobility, and a head/neck flexibility test. The DrivingHealth Inventory used in Maryland also includes subtest 2 of the UFOV® battery, which is used to measure speed of processing under divided attention conditions. In addition, contrast sensitivity is measured using the Pelli-Robson chart with the Maryland Motor Vehicles Administration.

The DriveABLE assessment also contains an automated battery for driving assessment (Dobbs, 1997; Dobbs et al., 1998). The total assessment takes approximately two hours, and the in-office assessment consists of computer-administered cognitive-perceptual tests. A behind-the-wheel test is administered when the computer task does not provide decisive information about driving fitness.

Advances in Technology for Driver Rehabilitation

We have described advances in technology to identify at-risk older adults. The benefit of such technology is that it allows the identification of those who need intervention so that they can avoid mobility restrictions or crash involvement. Now we discuss what can be done to compensate for declines in skills vital to driving safety.

Vision Interventions

Cataracts have been associated with decreased driving exposure as well as increased crashes and are the leading cause of vision impairment among older adults (Owsley, Stalvey, Wells, & Sloane, 1999). Due to technological advances, vision impairment due to cataracts is, for the most part, reversible (Owsley, Stalvey, Wells, Sloane, & McGwin, 2001). Owsley et al. (2002) found that adults with cataracts who underwent surgery were subsequently less likely to be involved in motor vehicle crashes. Since about half of adults aged 75 and older have clinically significant cataracts, surgery is an intervention that may minimize crash risk. Thus, catarct surgery should be seriously considered for those affected who want to maintain an active driving lifestyle. The technological advances for treating cataracts result in improved quality of life by not only improving vision, but also by extending safe mobility.

Educational Interventions

Another approach to intervening on behalf of older drivers is educational interventions. Recently, Owsley and colleagues (Owsley, Stalvey, & Phillips, 2003) found that for older drivers with either visual function decline or useful field of view reduction, an educational intervention effectively changed attitudes about vision and driver safety. Adults who underwent the intervention modified their driving habits such that challenging driving situations were more often avoided and safety-enhancing, self-regulatory practices were more often practiced. While educational interventions may be administered in classrooms or one-on-one, advances in technology now offer advantages for broad dissemination. In 2001 as many as 30% of older adults were using the Internet (Newburger, 2001). Online courses could be made available that educate older adults about safe driving practices.

Cognitive Interventions

There has been a great deal of interest in how cognitive training can improve the performance of everyday activities such as driving thereby enhancing quality of life (Ball et al., 2002). Older adults who have undergone training designed to improve processing speed, memory, and problem solving have benefited from the interventions (Ball et al., 2002). In relation to driving in particular, several studies are evaluating the impact of speed-of-processing training (Ball & Owsley, 2000; Ball, Vance, Edwards, & Wadley, 2004; Roenker et al., 2003), which involves computer-based programs aimed toward improving the useful field of view (see Edwards et al., 2002; Roenker et al., 2003 for a detailed description of the protocol). Many studies have indicated that speed-of-processing training results in improved UFOV® performance (i.e., Ball et al., 2002; Edwards et al., 2002; Roenker et al., 2003). Furthermore, this training resulted in improved driving performance through reductions in the number of hazardous maneuvers made in an on-the-road driving test (Roenker et al., 2003). An 18-month follow-up assessment showed that these effects endured for individuals who retained improved UFOV® test performance. Those who underwent speed-of-processing training and maintained improved UFOV® performance exhibited fewer dangerous maneuvers during driving as compared to simulator-trained individuals.

Overall, recent technological advances have improved our ability to not only identify older adults at risk for mobility impairments, but also provide promising methods of intervention. Research in this area has great potential to extend mobility and autonomous functioning in the elderly, thereby improving the quality of older adults' lives.

CONCLUSIONS

Driving is and will continue to be vitally important to older adults for maintaining mobility and quality of life. New technology has the potential to help older adults extend their safe driving years. Research has elucidated methods of identifying individuals at risk for crash involvement as well as several methods of remediation with documented effectiveness. The challenge to date is translating such knowledge acquired through research into public policy and practice.

ACKNOWLEDGMENTS

This research program is funded by National Institute on Aging/NIH Grant P50-AG11684 (Edward R. Roybal Center for Research on Applied Gerontology).

Financial Disclosure: Karlene Ball is a stockholder in and consultant to the company Visual Awareness, Inc., which owns the patent to the UFOV testing and training software. Jerri Edwards also works as a consultant to Visual Awareness, Inc. No other authors have a financial disclosure or conflict of interest.

REFERENCES

Ball, K., Berch, D. B., Helmers, K. F., Jobe, J. B., Leveck, M. D., Marsiske, M., Morris, J., Rebok, G., Smith, D. M., Tennstedt, S. L., Unverzagt, F. W., & Willis, S. L. (2002). Effects of cognitive training interventions with older adults. A randomized controlled trial. *Journal of the American Medical Association, 288*, 2271-2281.

Ball, K., & Owsley, C. (1991). Identifying correlates of accident involvement for the older driver. *Human Factors, 33*(5), 583-595.

Ball, K., & Owsley, C. (2000). Increasing mobility and reducing accidents of older drivers. In K. W. Schaie & M. Pietrucha (Eds.), *Mobility and transportation in the elderly* (pp. 213-251). New York: Springer Publishing Company.

Ball, K., & Owsley, C. (2003). Driving competence: It's not a matter of age. *Journal of the American Geriatrics Society, 51*, 1499-1501.

Ball, K., Owsley, C., Sloane, M. E., Roenker, D. L., & Bruni, J. R. (1993). Visual attention problems as a predictor of vehicle crashes in older drivers. *Investigative Ophthalmology and Visual Science, 34*(11), 3110-3123.

Ball, K. K., Roenker, D. L., & Bruni, J. R. (1990). Developmental changes in attention and visual search throughout adulthood. In J. Enns (Ed.), *Advances in psychology* (Vol. 69, pp. 489-508). Amsterdam, Netherlands: North-Holland-Elsevier Science Publishers.

Ball, K. K., Vance, D. E., Edwards, J. E., & Wadley, V. G. (2004). Aging and the brain. In M. Rizzo & P. J. Eslinger (Eds.), *Principles and practice of behavioral neurology and neuropsychology* (pp. 795-809): W. B. Saunders.

Barr, R. A. (2002). More road to travel by: Implications for mobility and safety in late life. *Gerontechnology, 2*(1), 50-54.

Barrett, G. V., Greenawalt, J. P., Thorton, C. I., & Williamson, T. R. (1977). Adaptive training and individual differences in perception. *Perceptual and Motor Skills, 44*(3), 875-880.

Bergen, J. R., & Julesz, B. (1983). Parallel versus serial processing in rapid pattern discrimination. *Nature, 303*(5919), 696-698.

Caird, J. K. (2004). In-vehicle intelligent transportation systems (ITS) and older drivers' safety and mobility. In T. R. Board (Ed.), *Transportation in an aging society: A decade of experience* (pp. 236-255). Washington, DC: Transportation Research Board.

Cushman, L. A. (1996). Cognitive capacity and concurrent driving performance in older drivers. *IATSS Research, 20*(1), 38-45.

Department of Transport. (1991). *The older driver: Measures for reducing the number of casualties among older people on our roads.* London: Department of Transport.

Department of Transportation, U.S. (2000). *Traffic safety facts 1999: Older population (DOT HS 809-091).* Washington, DC: National Center for Statistics and Analyses, National Highway Traffic Safety Administration.

Dingus, T. A., Hulse, M. C., Mollenhauer, M. A., Fleischman, R. N., McGehee, D. V., & Manakkal, N. (1997). Effects of age, system experience, and navigation technique on driving with an Advanced Traveler Information System. *Human Factors, 39*(2), 177-199.

Dobbs, A. R. (1997). Evaluating the driving competence of dementia patients. *Alzheimer Disease & Associated Disorders, 11*(Suppl. 1), 8-12.

Dobbs, A. R., Heller, R. B., & Schopflocher, D. (1998). A comparative approach to identify unsafe older drivers. *Accident Analysis & Prevention, 30*(3), 363-370.

Duchek, J. M., Hunt, L., Ball, K., Buckles, V., & Morris, J. C. (1998). Attention and driving performance in Alzheimer's disease. *Journal of Gerontology: Psychological and Social Sciences, 53*(2), 130-141.

Dulisse, B. (1997). Older drivers and risk to other road users. *Accident Analysis & Prevention, 29*(5), 573-582.

Eberhard, J. W. (1996). Safe mobility for senior citizens. *IATSS Research, 20,* 29-37.

Edwards, J. D., Wadley, V. G., Myers, R. S., Roenker, D. L., Cissell, G. M., & Ball, K. K. (2002). Transfer of a speed of processing intervention to near and far cognitive functions. *Gerontology, 48,* 329-340.

Evans, L. (1991). *Traffic safety and the driver.* New York: Van Nostrand Reinhold.

Foley, D. J., Heimovitz, H. K., Guralnik, J. M., & Brock, D. B. (2002). Driving life expectancy of persons age 70 years and older in the United States. *American Journal of Public Health, 92*(81), 1284-1289.

Fonda, S. J., Wallace, R. B., & Herzog, A. R. (2001). Changes in driving patterns and worsening depressive symptoms among older adults. *The Journals of Gerontology. Series B, Psychological Sciences and Social Sciences, 56B*(6), S343-S351.

Goode, K. T., Ball, K. K., Sloane, M., Roenker, D. L., Roth, D. L., Myers, R. S., & Owsley, C. (1998). Useful field of view and other neurocognitive indicators of crash risk in older adults. *Journal of Clinical Psychology in Medical Settings, 5*(4), 425-440.

Hu, P. S., Trumble, D. A., Foley, D. J., Eberhard, J. W., & Wallace, R. B. (1998). Crash risk of older drivers: A panel analysis. *Accident Analysis and Prevention, 30*(5), 569-582.

Hu, P. S., & Young, J. R. (1999). *Summary of travel trends: 1995 nationwide personal transportation survey (FHWA-PL-00-006).* Washington, DC: U.S. Department of Transportation.

Jette, A. M., & Branch, L. G. (1992). A ten-year follow up of driving patterns among the community dwelling elderly. *Human Factors, 34,* 25-31.

Johnson, J. E. (1999). Urban older adults and the forfeiture of a driver's license. *Journal of Gerontological Nursing, 25*(12), 12-18.

Kahneman, D., & Ben-Ishai, R. (1973). Relation of a test of attention to road accidents. *Journal of Applied Psychology, 58*(1), 113-115.

Lindquist, T. J., & Ettinger, R. L. (2003). The complexities involved with managing the care of an elderly patient. *Journal of the American Dental Association, 134*(5), 593-600.

Marottoli, R. A., Cooney, L. M., Wagner, D. R., Doucetter, J., & Tinetti, M. E. (1994). Predictors of automobile crashes and moving violations among elderly drivers. *Annals of Internal Medicine, 121,* 842-846.

Marottoli, R. A., Mendes de Leon, C. F., Glass, T. A., Williams, C. S., Cooney, L. M., & Berkman, L. F. (2000). Consequences of driving cessation: Decreased out-of-home activity levels. *The Journals of Gerontology. Series B, Psychological Sciences and Social Sciences, 55,* S334-S340.

Marottoli, R. A., Mendes de Leon, C. F., Glass, T. A., Williams, C. S., Cooney, L. M., Jr., Berkman, L. F., & Tinetti, M. E. (1997). Driving cessation and increased depressive symptoms: Prospective evidence from the New Haven EPESE (Established Populations for Epidemiologic Studies of the Elderly). *Journal of the American Geriatrics Society, 45,* 202-206.

Marottoli, R. A., Ostfeld, A. M., Merrill, S. S., Perlman, G. D., Foley, D. J., & Cooney, L. M., Jr. (1993). Driving cessation and changes in mileage driven among elderly individuals. *Journal of Gerontology: Social Sciences, 48,* S255-S260.

Marottoli, R. A., Richardson, E. D., Stowe, M. H., Miller, E. G., Brass, L. M., Cooney, L. M., Jr., & Tinetti, M. E. (1998). Development of a test battery to identify older drivers at risk for self-reported adverse driving events. *Journal of the American Geriatrics Society, 46,* 562-568.

McKnight, A. J. (2003). The freedom of the open road: Driving and older adults. *Generations, 27*(2), 25-31.

McKnight, A. J., & McKnight, A. S. (1999). Multivariate analysis of age-related driver ability and performance deficits. *Accident Analysis and Prevention, 31,* 445-454.

Mollenkopf, H., Marcellini, F., Ruoppila, I., Széman, Z., Tacken, M., Kaspar, R., & Wahl, H. W. (2002). The role of driving in maintaining mobility in later life: A European view. *Gerontechnology, 1,* 231-250.

Myers, R. S., Ball, K. K., Kalina, T. D., Roth, D. L., & Goode, K. T. (2000). The relationship of Useful Field of View and other screening instruments to on-road driving performance. *Perceptual and Motor Skills, 91*(1), 279-290.

National Center for Statistics and Analysis. (1995). *Traffic safety facts 1994: Older population.* Washington, DC: National Highway Traffic Safety Administration.

National Highway Traffic Safety Administration. (1997). *Traffic safety facts 1996: Older Population, National Highway Traffic Safety Administration.* Washington, DC: National Highway Traffic Safety Administration.

National Safety Counsel. (1993). *Accident facts.* Chicago, IL.

Newburger, E. (2001). *Home computers and Internet use in the United States* (Current Population Report P23-207). Washington, DC: U.S. Census Bureau.

O'Neill, D. (2000). Safe mobility for older people. *Reviews in Clinical Gerontology, 10,* 181-191.

Owsley, C. (2002). Driving mobility, older adults and quality of life. *Gerontechnology, 1,* 221-227.

Owsley, C., Ball, K., McGwin, G., Jr., Sloane, M. E., Roenker, D. L., White, M. F., & Overley, E. T. (1998). Visual processing impairment and risk of motor vehicle crash among older adults. *Journal of the American Medical Association, 279*(14), 1083-1088.

Owsley, C., Ball, K., Sloane, M., Roenker, D. L., & Bruni, J. R. (1991). Visual/cognitive correlates of vehicle accidents in older drivers. *Psychology and Aging, 6,* 403-415.

Owsley, C., & McGwin, G. (1999). Vision impairment and driving. *Survey of Ophthalmology, 6,* 535-550.

Owsley, C., McGwin, G., Jr., & Ball, K. (1998). Vision impairment, eye disease, and injurious motor vehicle crashes in the elderly. *Ophthalmic Epidemiology, 5*(2), 101-113.

Owsley, C., McGwin, G., Jr., Sloane, M., Wells, J., Stalvey, B. T., & Gauthreaux, S. (2002). Impact of cataract surgery on motor vehicle crash involvement by older adults. *Journal of the American Medical Association, 288*(7), 841-849.

Owsley, C., Stalvey, B., Wells, J., Sloane, M., & McGwin, G., Jr. (2001). Visual risk factors for crash involvement in older drivers with cataract. *Archives of Ophthalmology, 119,* 881-887.

Owsley, C., Stalvey, B., Wells, J., & Sloane, M. E. (1999). Older drivers and cataract: Driving habits and crash risk. *The Journals of Gerontology. Series A, Biological Sciences and Medical Sciences, 54A*(4), M203-M211.

Owsley, C., Stalvey, B. T., & Phillips, J. M. (2003). The efficacy of an educational intervention in promoting self-regulation among high-risk older drivers. *Accident Analysis and Prevention, 35,* 393-400.

Oxley, P. R., & Mitchell, C. G. B. (1995). *Final report on elderly and disabled drivers information telematics (Project EDDIT).* Brussels: Commission of the European Communities DG XIII, R and D Programme Telematics Systems in the Area of Transport (DRIVE II).

Patrick, D. L., & Deyo, R. A. (1989). Generic and disease-specific measures in assessing health status and quality of life. *Medical Care, 27,* S217-S232.

Retchin, S. M., Cox, J., Fox, M., & Irwin, L. (1988). Performance-based measurements among elderly drivers and non-drivers. *Journal of the American Geriatrics Society, 36,* 813-819.

Rizzo, M., Reinach, S., McGehee, D., & Dawson, J. (1997). Simulated car crashes and crash predictors in drivers with Alzheimer's disease. *Archives of Neurology, 54*(5), 545-551.

Roenker, D. L., Cissell, G. M., Ball, K. K., Wadley, V. G., & Edwards, J. D. (2003). Speed-of-processing and driving simulator training result in improved driving performance. *Human Factors, 45*(2), 218-233.

Shope, J. T. (2003). What does giving up driving mean to older drivers and why is it so difficult? *Generations, 2,* 57-59.

Sims, R. V., Owsley, C., Allman, R. M., Ball, K., & Smoot, T. M. (1998). A preliminary assessment of the medical and functional factors associated with vehicle crashes by older adults. *Journal of the American Geriatrics Society, 46*(5), 556-561.

Sixsmith, J. (1990). *Driving experiences and new technology: Evaluations and expectations of older drivers* (Occasional Paper No. 31). London: Department of Geography, Kings' College.

Stamatiadis, N. (1994). IVHS and the older driver. *Transportation Quarterly, 48*(1), 15-22.

Stern, H., Burkhardt, J. E., & Eberhard, J. W. (2003). Moving along the mobility continuum: Past, present, and future. *Generations, 27*(3), 8-13.

Stunkel, E. (1997). Rural public transportation and mobility of older persons: paradigms for policy. *Journal of Aging & Social Policy, 9*(3), 67-86.

Stutts, J. C. (1998). Do older drivers with visual and cognitive impairments drive less? *Journal of the American Geriatrics Society, 46,* 854-861.

Stutts, J. C., Stewart, J. R., & Martell, C. (1998). Cognitive test performance and crash risk in an older driver population. *Accident Analysis and Prevention, 30*(3), 337-346.

Tarawneh, M. S., McCoy, P. T., Bishu, R. R., & Ballard, J. L. (1993). Factors associated with driving performance of older drivers. *Transportation Research Record, 1405,* 64-71.

Taylor, B. D., & Tripodes, S. (2001). The effects of driving cessation on the elderly with dementia and their caregivers. *Accident Analysis & Prevention, 33*(4), 519-528.

Transportation Research Board. (1988). *Transportation in an aging society* (Vol. 1). Washington, DC: National Research Council.

Williams, A. F., & Carsten, O. (1989). Driver age versus crash involvement. *American Journal of Public Health, 79*(3), 326-327.

CHAPTER 12

The New Leisure World of Modern Old Age: New Aging on the Bright Side of the Street?

Franz Kolland

Leisure activity is a central focus of old age; the concept of elderly leisure, however, is a fairly recent development. Attention has been focused on the relationship between leisure and aging, at least from the time that Robert Kleemeier edited his volume on "Leisure and Aging" in 1961. The reader's attention was drawn to the significance of free time activities in the lives of the elderly. Although the discourse was in the realm of nonwork activities, it became clear that one's work and job do play a role in the consideration of leisure and free time. A recent tendency has been to look at retirement and old age as a "fun" period of life, filled with leisure activities and all kinds of new experiences. Is this approach more appropriate than the approach of the 1960s and 1970s when leisure was discussed as something related to work or, more importantly, as a residual category not integrally related to other components of the life course at all? It seems more appropriate, according to Powell Lawton (1985), to recognize that time use and the attitudes and feelings associated with leisure are determined differently by *individual need,* social and cultural learning specific to an *age cohort,* contemporary *societal context,* and legislation and rules. The topics of leisure and aging are characterized by a number of similarities. Both leisure and aging are processual, have multiple realities and are socially constructed, not ontogenetically determined (Cutler & Hendricks, 1990).

This chapter aims to discuss and evaluate the different meanings and functions of leisure in relationship to different gerontological concepts and theories. In particular, the goal is to describe continuities and changes in the leisure world of older people in the last five decades on the individual and the societal level. In addition to the different methods of measuring leisure, the extent and the determinants of leisure activity as well as social effects associated with leisure activities will be discussed. Finally, the question of research desiderata and the future significance of leisure research within social gerontology will be investigated.

WHAT IS LEISURE?

Definitions are always a matter of perspective. Some definitions are useful for particular purposes. Leisure, never a very precise concept, has been defined in a number of ways. Leisure has been approached as all of the following: *consumption, time, activity, a state of mind,* and *a quality of action.* The definition of leisure and its relationship to other activities is made difficult due to the lack of a general theory of leisure. On another level, leisure has been a point of conflict between high culture and popular culture, between elite and mass culture, and between work and nonwork. Herbert Gans (1975) has differentiated between mass culture and popular culture to demonstrate the more pejorative of the former and the more positive significance of the latter. Mass culture suggests an undifferentiated collectivity, even a mob, whereas popular culture is "less stigmatized as atomized, escapist, or unable to cope with reality" (p. 31).

At the turn of the twentieth century, the first sociological theory of leisure was formulated. The American Thorstein Veblen (1899) was the first to demonstrate the deliberate utilization of leisure time for the self-assertion of a social class. His contributions reflect that leisure activities serve the purpose of self-affirmation. The aim is to surpass other persons in the area of pleasure, and this represents an end in itself. One way of gaining social status and reputability is "conspicuous consumption." Veblen writes, "conspicuous consumption of valuable goods is a means of reputability to the gentleman of leisure" (p. 73). The ruling class displays abundant consumerism in a demonstrative way. Leisure time is supposed to be unproductive, according to this perspective, due to the depreciation of productive work and the status that is provided by a life without work. Leisure in this sense is largely coterminous with consumption.

In the early 1960s, the American sociologist Talcott Parsons (1964) regarded the role of aging in the world of consumerism, where leisure had been considered a *place of consumerism,* in a very special way. As a matter of fact, the term "greying consumer market" was adopted by the advertising industry in the 1980s. One focus of investigation was oriented toward the relationship between the durable goods of leisure participation and the identity or status of those who possess goods (Cutler & Hendricks, 1990). To own something also means to vest oneself in the object. The other aspect of leisure consumption derives from *involvement.* Leisure activities are a form of investment, increasing personal capital. The meaning of an endeavor is consumed and thereby incorporated into the actor's identity (Gilleard, 1996). Consumer culture is helping older people refashion their own identity in later life. As a form of savings for the future, engaging in leisurely activity lowers the higher vulnerability of late life.

CONCEPTS OF LEISURE

The most appropriate conceptualization of leisure is simply the *free time* remaining once one's work is accomplished. According to this first concept, leisure is closely related to (gainful) occupation. The problem is the word "work" in this context. Some people may view their (unpaid) work as a major source of interest and recreation, and consider their free time as boring or compromised by family requirements. Work becomes leisure, and leisure, work (Gershuny & Fisher, 2000). Another perspective regards leisure time as *residual time* and as influenced by the way one works and by the continuous growth of productivity of work in the monetary economy, which also leads to changes in leisure consumption. This can be demonstrated clearly by the example of a hobby. Whoever wants to prepare for his or her leisure time and intends on channelling it into a certain direction in the long run, first has to give it up. A simple example would be that of a house surrounded by a garden, which generally involves and requires work tasks throughout the years—productive tasks; so even leisure becomes unleisurely. Another concept closely connected to gainful occupation is the idea that leisure may be *unstructured time* (Plakans, 1994). This theory is based upon the assumption that leisure had previously been available only to privileged groups of the population, and that only in the context of a decreased amount of time dedicated to work could all parts of the population eventually benefit from leisure time. In the following chapter, the extent of the similarities between these definitions of leisure, which are based on different theories of gerontology, will be discussed.

A second approach defining leisure begins with the *state of mind,* orientation, attitudes, conditions, experience, or the definition of the leisure actor. Lawton (1985) suggested that the *subjective* definition of leisure is most important. Gerontological studies (Havighurst, 1959; Tinsley, Colbs, Teaff, & Kaufman, 1987) have pointed to the importance of leisure for the elderly as maintaining identity and the concept of self. Leisure is not in the timing or the form of the activity, but in the actor. The leisure actor understands that what he or she is doing has been chosen rather than coerced. Simply put, leisure is the perception of free choice for the sake of doing or experiencing something. The definition by McGuire, Boyd, and Tedrick (1999) highlights the subjective relevance of leisure: "leisure is a freely chosen activity done primarily for its own sake, with an element of enjoyment, pursued during unobligated time" (p. 105). Three central constructs underlie this definition: perceived freedom, intrinsic motivation, and enjoyment/experience. Perceived freedom is closely aligned with freedom of choice. The individual must feel the activity is chosen, not required. Intrinsic motivation indicates the activity is chosen primarily for rewards coming from the activity itself. Leisure in this sense is not only determined by sociostructural factors, it is also the means for asserting individuality in a modern society (Bourdieu, 1979). Enjoyment is directed after all to the immediate satisfaction of needs. The idea of an individual lifestyle has a respectable basis in psychological research (Kelly, 1983) and can be related to the continuity theory of aging. Individuals develop a framework and set of guidelines, which can be termed lifestyle and demonstrate a certain kind of subjective continuity. The problem of defining leisure in terms of its subjective significance is the fact that this approach does not differentiate between leisure and other mental conditions.

Defining leisure as certain kinds of *activity* also has considerable appeal. According to this third conceptualization, leisure is composed of games, sports, culture, social interaction, and the use of mass media. Sociodemographic determinants define the range and intensity of leisure activities. A way of differentiating between leisure activities is the distinction between *active* and *passive* leisure. An important distinction between sedentary and nonsedentary lifestyle is that only a nonsedentary lifestyle is considered beneficial for compressing morbidity (Teague, 1987). Another suggestion is that engagement in challenging spare time activities can diminish and perhaps even reverse the rate of cognitive decline (Schaie & Willis, 1986). Therefore, activities have a purpose other than themselves. Someone may be engaging in sports activities in order to live longer. A leisure activity is one that benefits the participant at a particular time and place. It is the quality of the experience or outcome of performing the activity, not the activity itself that classifies it as leisure.

In a fourth approach, leisure is defined as *action*. The differentiation between activity and action is derived from Aristotle's Nichomachean Ethics (Aristotle, 1976), his distinction between poiesis and praxis. Praxis, for Aristotle, designates the realm of human "action," whereas poiesis can be defined as the realm of "productive activity." In this sense, as Aristotle lays it out in Book Six of the Nichomachean Ethics: "praxis (action) and poiesis (production, activity) are generally different" (NE, 1140b). Activity has an end other than itself, but action does not.

If freedom is the essential dimension of leisure, action is implied. Leisure takes place in time. It is neither defined by time or place, nor is it transformed into an unrelated attitude or feeling. It is connected to the realities of identifiable spatial and temporal dimensions. It takes place in the "real world" of possibilities and limits of resources and responsibilities. Leisure is more than the illusion of freedom. Leisure is taking an action that causes some effect and that has outcomes for the actor. Such action creates the experience of leisure rather than simply absorbing it. This refers to those activities that pertain to one's life (Simmel, 1993, 1913) and thus result in self-coherence. Leisure involves the perceptions of the actor as the experience begins, as it continues, and as it ends. Kelly and Freysinger (2000), for instance, pointed out the experiential character of leisure, that is "leisure is activity that is done primarily for the experience itself" (p. 3), and Gordon, Gaitz, and Scott (1976) primarily focused on the expressive character of leisure. Such perceptions are essential dimensions of the action. One of the most cited attempts to explain leisure from this perspective has been Csikszentmihalyi's (1975) notion of "flow." Flow is viewed as the state when an individual's skills are harmonious with the demands of the activity in which they are engaged. When the skill a person possesses is greater than the challenge it faces, the result is boredom. When the challenge is greater than the skill, the result is anxiety. When the two meet in a range that produces effective action, the actor experiences flow. Flow is a total focus on the activity in which time and the external world seem to disappear. This view of leisure is related to the concept of gerotranscendence (Thorsen, 1998), which will be discussed in the next chapter.

THE POSITION OF LEISURE WITHIN DIFFERENT THEORETICAL APPROACHES OF SOCIAL GERONTOLOGY

During the 1960s and 1970s, research agendas were largely directed toward two questions: what is the relationship between aging and participation in nonwork activities? and what is the relationship between participation in activities and happiness in later life? An examination of leisure behavior across the lifespan suggests patterns of stability and change, structure and variety, as well as familiarity and novelty (Iso-Ahola, 1980). The main arguments in this field were, and still are, directed toward the positive relationship between engagement in leisure activities and maintaining optimal physical health, reducing the effects of chronic stress, and improving one's sense of well-being. Max Kaplan (1961) was one of the first to apply a theory of leisure in social gerontology. According to Kaplan, leisure consists of *activities* and *experiences;* one is relatively free to perform those activities and to have those experiences that are subsequently seen *subjectively* as leisure. It is pleasant to expect these activities and to remember them; they form an entire area of dedication and enthusiasm. However, they also involve certain norms and restraints; they provide an opportunity for distraction, for developing oneself, and also being useful to others.

Several alternative theories have been proposed since the 1960s to explain the stability or changes in life patterns over the lifespan. Disengagement theory (Cumming & Henry, 1961), activity theory (Havighurst & Albrecht, 1953), continuity theory (Atchley, 1989), structural lag theory (Riley & Riley, 1994), and concepts related to postmodernity (Featherstone & Hepworth 1989); each offers a different explanation of the relationship between activity and aging, yet implicit in each is that changing patterns of activity are positively related to satisfaction and quality of life.

Activity theory suggests that older adults live longer and adjust more satisfactorily to old age when they both maintain the activity levels that characterized their middle years and add new activities to substitute for any activities abandoned. Research began on the assumption that leisure is a complex phenomenon that is not simply derived from work roles. Early research failed to support activity theory, possibly because activities were viewed as one dimensional, and time spent engaged in "activity" was the only variable studied. The better designed studies have separated activity into physical, social, and solitary domains due to the different psychosocial processes that are involved when the elderly engage in these different types of activities. Only those activities that are psychologically *central* will result in satisfaction (Simmel, 1993, 1913). This process is dependent upon intention and ability to integrate the subject. Not every activity ends with satisfaction. Those activities that "fit one's own image" are the ones that are more likely to result in fulfillment (Peppers, 1976). In this context, conditional (contingent) activity is mentioned too (Rosenmayr, 1989).

During the 1980s, research focused on activities that are especially satisfying, and on the resources that might make continuation possible. In the 1990s, attention was directed more intensely toward the relationship between leisure-oriented activities and *social interaction.* Within this approach, the individual's leisure behavior is seen as interplay between internal psychological dispositions (attitudes, needs, perceptions, and personality traits) and situational influences in the social and physical environment (Mannell & Dupuis, 1994). Leisure activities should bring people into contact with people that do not live with them and thus can be deemed to promote the reduction of social isolation. The phrase "social leisure activity" was coined in this context.

The *disengagement theory* was developed according to the functionalist-activity model by Parsons as a reaction to the idealization and reality-distant concept pertaining to the activity approach (Russell, 1989). Disengagement theory (Cumming & Henry, 1961) characterizes a less successful adaptation to aging, since it theorizes that as people approach old age, they gradually withdraw from those occupations that had previously been important to them and that the level of involvement with ongoing activities has been reduced. Disengagement theory focused primarily on explaining the nature and importance of role exit (especially work roles) for aging members of society, both in terms of importance to self and to society. From a labor-force perspective, disengagement theory proposed that the withdrawal of aged members of society allowed for the rejuvenation of society's workforce, thus ensuring the continuation of new approaches, ideas and energies into the workplace. Retirement is an illustration of the disengagement process, enabling older persons to be freed of the roles of a career and to pursue other roles not necessarily aligned to full economic compensation. Elderly people withdraw gradually from roles and activities pertaining to the middle stage of life. An increased life satisfaction is thus found when activities are limited. Despite failed attempts to verify the disengagement theory empirically, and even though the period of retirement cannot be seen as a phase of withdrawal, the theory has still contributed to the discussion as aging is now considered a separate stage of life. Thus, leisure in older age can be regarded as independent from the phase of occupation. The disengagement theory has again been incorporated in the newer theoretical discussion in the context of the concept of gerotranscendence. This concept involves individual disengagement, which is frequently prompted by personal crisis as a coping method (Tornstam, 1989). The theory posits that the effects of gerotranscendence include the capacity to enter and leave roles as needed with greater peace and acceptance. The aim is to increase selectivity for performing activities and also for organizing one's leisure. One strong point of the theory is that it interprets passivity and withdrawal of elderly in a new positive light—thus forming an opposing point to activity-oriented models. Gerotranscendence is a model that questions the trend toward hyperactive aging. While the disengagement theory is based on discontinuity and change, research approaches in social gerontology are based on the *continuity principle* in general. The continuity theory (Atchley, 1989) proposes that the continuity of one's life situation plays a decisive role in the successful or unsuccessful adaptation in the process of aging.

Continuity theory suggested that this consistent relationship exists because leisure provides retired people with a continuity of social roles, as well as with a social space for the maintenance and development of valued identities in which some competence, achievement, and recognition are gained. The general statement concerning the nature of leisure activity in retirement was that there is no specific "retirement activity" (Peppers, 1976). When people retire, most continue to do the same activities as they did before, but at a different pace. Teague and MacNeil (1992) sum up the concept of continuity in old age as follows: "Most elderly people continue to respond to life situations as they did earlier in their lives. Old age does not bring about a radical change in their beliefs, interests, or preferences. But it may bring about abrupt changes (serious illness, retirement, or death of a spouse) over which they have little control. Activities that help people keep up past lifestyles, and over which they have some control, should facilitate the adjustment process" (p. 251). Atchley (1971) contends that some people in society are not highly work oriented and thus can provide a model for others regarding self-satisfaction derived from leisure. "Leisure activities are pursued as ends in themselves" (p. 13). In retirement, a sense of identity can come from leisure pursuits such as outdoor experiences if the individual has the financial resources and a cohort of retired friends who accept full-time leisure as a legitimate role. Work style and values seem to influence retirement style, which is evident from continued social activities, associations with friends, and the continuation of patterns of interests. Identification with the employment role continues whether the individual is employed or not. From this perspective, retirement has an identifiable and valued role. There is a broader understanding and acceptance of the retirement role, which is perhaps of a lesser functional value, but certainly of a role that is more qualitative.

The current transition from modern to postmodern society has begun to influence the accepted notions of age as a social criterion for establishing strict roles and norms. In fact, the traditional segregation of life-course stages based upon age, namely education, career and leisure, is seen as destabilized. The concept of *age stratification* as proposed by Riley, Johnson, and Foner (1972), has begun to change from an age-differentiated to an age-integrated structure (1994). Longer life spans are becoming a reality in industrialized countries, and a significant proportion of people are now living well into their 70s and 80s in relatively good health. This development is making the rigid, age-segregated life course obsolete. Growing numbers of elderly are now rejecting the age constraints on paid work and biases against active participation by the elderly in society. Similarly, many young people are seeking "adult" roles in work, family, and entertainment. Riley and Riley (1994) identified a "structural lag," as changes in age structures lag behind changes in lives. They see a structural discrepancy in the situation of the elderly, that is, a discrepancy between the growing abilities of the elderly and the societal possibilities to utilize these skills and abilities. The pressures for the development of age-integrated social structures are increasing. Unlike our present age-segregated structures, age-integrated structures are those that do not use chronological age as a criterion for entrance, exit, or participation. Riley and Riley (1994) have proposed an alternative model of life course that would allow learning, work, and leisure to be integrated in the lives of individuals throughout the entire life course. More role possibilities for the elderly, which are supported by the development of coexisting roles for people of all age groups within society, are required.

In the 1990s research concerning leisure and aging was influenced by yet another theory; namely, the *theory of postmodernity*. Postmodern perspectives of age and aging identity are characterized by a great interest in leisure. The postmodern approach is underpinned by discourses of "better lifestyles" and increased leisure opportunities for older people as a result of healthier lifestyles and the increased use of biotechnologies to facilitate the longevity of human experiences (Blaikie, 1999; Featherstone & Hepworth, 1989). Old age is seen as a "mask" that conceals the essential identity of the person. The view of the aging process as a mask/disguise concealing the essentially youthful self beneath is one that appears to be a popular argument (Featherstone & Hepworth, 1989). The interactions between individuals as consumers, with advertisers, marketers, and cultural producers, are key processes through which lifestyles are formed. A trend that is important for the leisure market is the change from organized and class-oriented leisure to more *individualized* and *private* leisure styles. From a postmodern perspective, a variety of competing leisure styles coexist (Featherstone & Hepworth, 1989).

The accelerating emancipation of capital from labor produces a situation where capital tends to engage the elderly in the role of consumers instead of engaging the rest of society in the role of producers. Featherstone and Hepworth (1989) argue for the irrelevance of social divisions and ultimately, for the end of the social as a significant reference point. Given a disposable income, older people are experimenting with elaborate *consumer lifestyles*. Some trends in this direction include the "snowbird" and "Sun City" phenomena in the United States, paralleled in the United Kingdom by migration to seaside residences and the growth of retirement communities. The social spaces created are called lifestyle enclaves (Bellah, Madsen, Sullivan, Swidler, & Tipton, 1985), indicating the absence of a comprehensive whole and a desire for a similar differentiation from others' lifestyles. This corresponds to Riley (1978) when she refers to "large numbers of individuals, reacting independently, but in a similar fashion to societal changes" (p. 41). A lifestyle enclave is formed by people who share some characteristics of private life. Members of a lifestyle enclave express their identity by conforming in appearance and consuming patterns, as well as by selecting similar leisure activities that often serve the purpose of differentiating them from people with other lifestyles. From a postmodern perspective, lifestyle is closely linked to individualization and requires finding other people that reflect and support one's own individuality. Therefore, an important focus of postmodern thinking is the individualization of the lifestyles of the elderly.

Leisure and Work: The Labor Market, Technological Changes, and the Welfare State

There has been a change in the attitudes concerning retirement over the last 50 years. However, the structural change of aging and of society have also changed the ratio of work to leisure. Retirement has become a social institution. The welfare society of the second half of the twentieth century has created special conditions for the increased consumption of leisure. In many industrialized countries, a fixed age limit has been created and utilized for this purpose; however, far-reaching differences can be found between the individual OECD countries. In France, the government set the age limit for retirement at 60 years in 1982, Sweden increased the limit to 67 years in 1976 and in the United States, the retirement age in the private sector was increased to 70 years in 1978. For civil servants, any mandatory retirement age whatsoever was eliminated.

The desire to retire and to deemphasize paid work after the age of 60 became a general phenomenon in OECD countries. A distinction between work and leisure has become common practice, irrespective of the age group to which a person belongs. The selection and designation of a particular activity as one's leisure activity during the period of life when one is gainfully employed is not necessarily a particularly complicated process, even though each individual person has his or her own preferences, and leisure should be considered something extremely subjective.

In the 1950s, paid work was seen mainly as a means of integration within the community. The loss of occupation as a result of age was considered critical due to the fact that leisure activities can only substitute activities that are less meaningful (Lehr 1988). At the beginning of the 1960s, Havighurst (1961) asked whether successful aging can take place outside the corporate world at all. Aging is classified as lacking any function due to the fact that socially recognized and respected productivity (meaningful being) occurs predominantly through one's occupation. The loss of gainful occupation subsequently leads to a decreased social status (Riley & Riley, 1986) and thus to a serious personality crisis. This was especially true for men, as Townsend (1957) pointed out within the context of the United Kingdom. People spoke of losing part of their identity from moving away from relationships and attachments within the workplace. This was seen as provoking anxiety, even a sense of fear. Peter Stearns' research on old age in France (1977) illustrated the absence of any concept of retirement within working-class culture. Older people were largely unprepared for retirement and had not really expected to retire. Older peoples' households had very few of the consumer goods that are now taken more or less for granted; very few pensioners had a television or a telephone. Leisure was shaped by the daily round of relationships within the family. Alternatively, there were the ubiquitous social clubs for the elderly, which had been established in many towns and cities after the mid-1940s (Dumazedier, 1984; Kolland, 1984; Phillipson, Bernard, Phillips, & Ogg, 2001).

The controversy over the age limit or the role that employment plays in outlining older age results in a theoretical stance that is in contrast to the one described above. This position perceives the extension of old age as a kind of social progress and as a subjective need of the elderly. The effects of the technological revolution are evaluated as positive and are associated with increased freedom of choice (Kalish, 1979). Since the beginning of the 1970s, leisure has been regarded as the relevant habitat of a postindustrial era. Along with the increasing development of "leisure ethics" (Havighurst & Feigenbaum, 1968) and a decreasing esteem of employment, the employment-free habitat of "age" has attained a new quality. People in general started to have more leisure time over the course of their lives. This phenomenon was identified with the "end of work" and the beginning of a new *leisure class* (Michelon, 1954) or a *leisure society* (Dumazedier, 1967). Older people are freed from many responsibilities, such as child rearing and work, which previously impinged on their freedom of choice. As early as 1980, an extensive French study found that once persons reach the age of 60, there is more of a desire to retire and less of an importance attached to work (Attias-Donfut & Gognalons-Nicolet, 1980). Older people experience a reduced need to let themselves be constrained by what others think of them and, therefore, have the opportunity to step outside the boundaries that potentially restricted their lives (Rosenmayr, 1983). In France, dissatisfaction with retirement caused by boredom ranged from 10% among craftsmen and merchants, to 7% among executives, and 4% among middle management (Dumazedier, 1984). A comparison of the meanings of work and of leisure activity makes it possible to state a general principle of the equivalence of work and play: people can obtain the same satisfaction from leisure as from work, to a considerable extent. Consequently, it is possible and desirable to seek leisure activities that will provide the same satisfaction that one obtained from work at the time of retirement (Havighurst, 1961, p. 320).

Since the 1970s, retirement has been considered a binding and standardized social construct on the one hand, as quoted by Fürstenberg (2002), and on the other hand, not a necessary evil, but a goal worth attaining (Ehmer, 1990). Retirement can also be characterized as a phase of life when the utilization of market opportunities ceases (Fürstenberg, 2002), while the utilization of one's property that had been attained through labor increases. Starting from middle age, this act of renunciation occurs increasingly on a voluntary basis. Retirement is considered a well deserved life phase after many years of hard work. The transition from work to retirement is a course of action rather than a rational choice between work and leisure delimited by time. Workers anticipate their retirement in advance of the event, entertaining ideas and designs for it along the way (Dumazedier, 1984; Ekerdt, 1998). Leisure encompasses a vast range of activities (Phillipson et al., 2001), despite the fact that the most popular leisure activities are sedentary ones.

While in the 1950s no more than one in five older people would have owned or had access to a television set, in the 1990s, virtually all older people had access to at least one television set. In the early 1950s, even for those with a television, viewing hours were limited, with transmissions in the United Kingdom from 3 P.M. on weekdays and 5 P.M. on Sundays (Phillipson et al., 2001). With reading as the second most important leisure activity, the significance of the "home" for the elderly is evident (Ruoppila, Tacken, & Hirsiaho, 2000). Also of great significance is the increasing importance of gardening (Kolland, 1996).

The idea of competency, productivity, and generativity in age has prevailed since the 1980s. This is coupled with an attempt to replace the older model of retirement by supporting active aging. Since the 1990s, some change in the retirement model has been perceived, which, from a structural perspective, also indicates a change in the relation between gainful employment and "retirement." The transition between employment and retirement is becoming increasingly complex. According to Phillipson (2004), very differing lifestyles can be distinguished in middle age. They include full-time employment, part-time employment, unemployment, and retirement. Consequently, the transition between gainful employment and retirement is also characterized by a high degree of volatility.

In the beginning of the 1960s, which marks the beginning of research on aging and leisure, work and occupation assumed a dominant role in the discussion, whereas now the emphasis in research has been transferred to the topics of leisure and consumerism. Since the 1990s, we have had new insight into problems concerning leisure: new social inequalities develop in leisure time. The discussion is directed toward the commodification of aging, as it represents a source of profit making for pharmaceutical companies, the mass media, and the leisure industry. Successful aging can only be achieved through equally successful physical fitness and performance. Huge sums are spent on wellness activities. In this way aging, even though "excluded" from the cycle of production, is included in the circulation of products. Thus, there is a polarization between the successful elderly, or silver agers, and the frail elderly, or fourth agers. Economic deprivation and health status tend to condition the types of leisure activities enjoyed by the latter group. More educational and occupational resources enable persons to enter old age with a higher level of social participation. Social resources are correlated to the individual's level of participation at the onset of old age, but not to the rate of decline (Lindenberger & Reischies, 1999). Social resources have a limited effect in compensating the decline in health.

LEISURE ACTIVITIES: METHODS OF MEASUREMENT

Concerning the second conceptualization of leisure, retirement activities may be used as a benchmark in assessing physical health, social integration, and subjective well being. Changes and trends in everyday leisure activities may be linked to changing time patterns and socioeconomic determinants. The following section describes the methodological problems and cautions that must be considered in understanding leisure activities, analyses, use of time, and activity patterns.

Two data collection strategies predominate the research on the leisure behavior of older adults, as in studies of other age groups. Leisure behavior inventories, the most frequently used approach, are lists of leisure activities in which respondents are asked to identify the frequency of certain activities in a certain period of time. Leisure activity inventories include different kinds of activity. Frequency is generally measured on a scale ranging from daily, several times a week (often), monthly (sometimes), less than monthly (seldom), or never. There have been few attempts to arrange the lists of leisure activities, which are generally very comprehensive, into groups or dimensions. For example, a conclusion is only undertaken after the data has been obtained, and only then a rather broad differentiation between outdoor and indoor activities or between active and passive leisure is made.

The time-budget diary is another method used to measure leisure behavior and lifestyle. Time-budget analyses yield much information about the structure of time in retirement. These investigations are frequently conducted by national statistics offices and comprises the overall population. In Europe, data can be obtained from the Multinational Time Use Database maintained at the University of Essex.

Both methods, inventories, and time-budget studies have some drawbacks. There is no standard list of activities that researchers agree upon to constitute leisure, nor is there one criterion or set of criteria on which the specific leisure activities are grouped into a smaller, more manageable number of broad activity classifications (Mannell & Dupuis, 1994). Furthermore, time-budget analyses face the problem that the results obtained by the traditional measuring procedure do not correspond to reality. In order to discover whether there are any distinctive leisure activities, one has to distinguish between repeated, daily activities and other special activities, and only then can leisure activities be identified. On the basis of a survey, Simovici (1984) found that 50% of the interviewees mentioned reading as a routine activity, while only 5% regarded it as a leisure activity; 35% of the same group referred to walking as a routine activity, but only 8% stated that they also regarded walking as a leisure activity. It is important to distinguish between everyday routine activities and special activities in order to assess their relative value or gain. Improved and standardized leisure-behavior inventories are still needed in that there are few instruments specifically designed for measuring leisure-related phenomena with respect to older adults.

TIME AND ACTIVITY PATTERNS

In a study published by EUROSTAT, entitled "Time use at different stages of life" (2003), 13 European countries are depicted on the basis of time-budget analyses between 1998 and 2000. Registered as leisure were television, video recordings and other media sources (radio, music, reading), socializing activities (participatory activities, social life, entertainment and culture), travel, sports, hobbies, games, and other unspecified (outdoor) activities. Furthermore, relaxation was included as well. All of the activities listed above amount to between 6½ and almost 9 hours per day in total for men over the age of 65 who live together with a partner (Figure 1). These activities occupy more of men's time in Norway, Sweden, Finland, and Belgium; and less of men's time in France, Romania, and Denmark. In the case of women over the age of 65, the time span amounts to between 5 and 8 hours per day. Women in Norway, Sweden, and Belgium devote more time to leisure activities than women in France, Romania, and Slovenia.

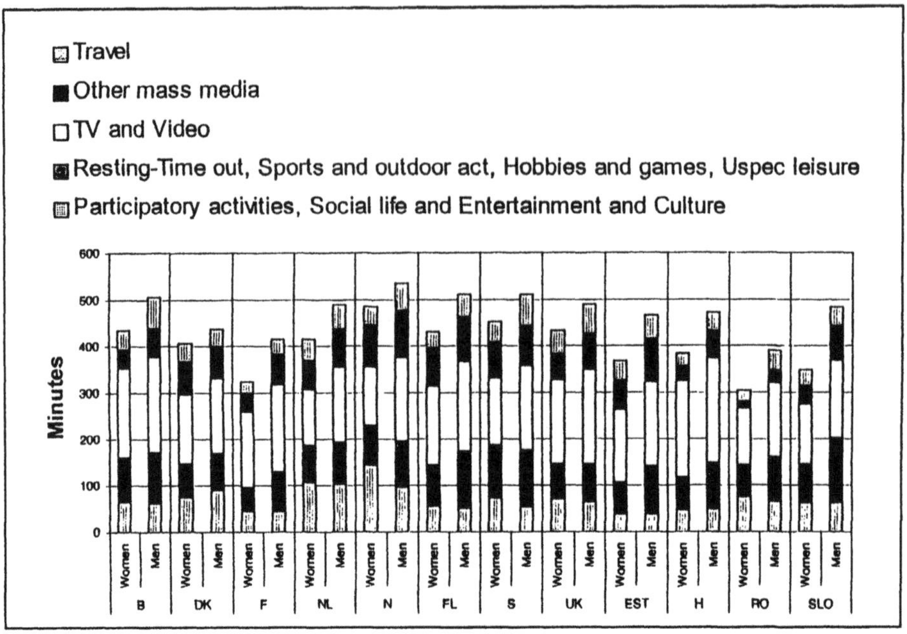

Figure 1. Use of time by persons 65 and older, living as a couple, with no children <18.
Source: EUROSTAT (2003); calculations by the author.

Gauthier and Smeeding (2001) examined the use of time by older adults from the 1960s to the 1990s in the United States, the United Kingdom, and the Netherlands. While the increase in older people's education, health, and wealth would allow for an increase in time spent actively in old age, their results did not provide strong evidence of such a trend. They suggest that time spent on paid work has slightly decreased for men aged 45 to 64, while slightly increased for women 45 to 54. There has been a net increase in time devoted to leisure activities for people aged 45 to 64 in all three countries, but not for those aged 65 and over.

When researching leisure activities individually, it becomes evident from the EUROSTAT study (2003) (see Figure 1) that elderly women, as well as elderly men spend a majority of their leisure time watching television. This however, is not only the case for the elderly, but for the total population as well. In Hungary (3.44 hrs) and in Belgium (3.24 hrs.), the amount of time for men is the highest; in the Netherlands (2.40 hrs) and in Slovenia (2.33 hrs) the lowest. On average, elderly women watch a little less television than elderly men. Socializing and cultural activities are found to be more frequent among elderly women, with the exception of Denmark. Men spend more time on travel than women, and more time is devoted to this activity in Sweden, the United Kingdom, and in Belgium, whereas in comparison, less time is spent on travel in Slovenia, Hungary, and Denmark.

On a descriptive level, reading, watching television, and listening to the radio represent the largest subcategory of leisure activities (Gauthier & Smeeding, 2001; Höpflinger & Stuckelberger, 1999; Kolland, 1996). At age 75 and older, American men devote 5.6 hours per day to this sort of leisure activity, as compared to 2.7 hours per day at ages 25-34. The next category of activities includes entertaining and visiting friends. On average, women tend to devote more time to this activity than men, and a certain decline is found at the age of 75 and over. People of all ages devote around a quarter to half an hour per day to sports and physical fitness; men tend to devote more time to this activity than women. An increase in time spent on sports between the 1960s and 1990s has been traced by Gauthier and Smeeding (2001).

Furthermore, differentiation is made between outdoor and indoor activities. The MOBILATE study obtained the following results: Dutch respondents pursued the most outdoor activities, and German and Finnish respondents also pursued a large variety of outdoor activities. Hungarian and Italian respondents had the lowest level of outdoor activity (Mollenkopf & Ruoppila, 2000). The same study showed that the most important activities outside the home are meeting friends, going for a walk, gardening, engaging in do-it-yourself activities, taking short trips, and participating in religious events. Activities in clubs, physical exercise, and volunteer work obtained high scores in Finland and in the Netherlands. Hungarians are more connected to gardening than elderly people in Italy, Finland, Germany, or the Netherlands. The German and Dutch elderly share a higher interest in visiting cafes/restaurants.

Different trends in each country have prevailed regarding active leisure, such as social and cultural activities, sports, and unpaid work; and passive leisure such as watching television (Gauthier & Smeeding, 2001). Time spent in active leisure has remained stable in the Netherlands and has increased in the United Kingdom. According to the National Health Survey in the United States (Federal Interagency Forum on Aging-Related Statistics, 2001), sedentary lifestyles decreased for persons 65 and older between 1985 and 1995 for both sexes. The percentage of older persons who were sedentary declined between 1985 and 1995, from 34% to 28% among men and from 44% to 39% among women. In 1995, 34 percent of persons aged 65 or older had a sedentary lifestyle. Women were more likely than men to have a sedentary lifestyle.

SOCIODEMOGRAPHIC DETERMINANTS OF LEISURE PARTICIPATION

Empirical studies of leisure activities demonstrate from the very beginning that rates of participation in travel, outdoor recreation, culture, exercise, and sports are *age dependent* and decreased with age. Older people participate less than younger in many kinds of activities, especially those that require physical exertion. The rates of participation fall drastically for elderly people who are most limited in mobility, ability to communicate, and physical strength and stamina. The Kansas City Study of adults age 40-70, found lower rates of activity and a limitation of interests correlated with age among the older half of the sample (Havighurst, 1961). In a Houston study led by Gordon, Gaitz, and Scott (1976), participation in both active and passive leisure was lower for each age group aged 20 to 94. The authors reported age-based slopes of lowered rates of participation that were gradual for reading, culture, conversation, entertaining, home embellishment, and other domestic and social activities. This is consistent with the findings of the Peoria study by Kelly (1987), in which at-home activity as well as formal and informal social engagements were significantly lower among higher age groups. Gordon et al. (1976) found a correlation of $r = -.49$ on the basis of a regression analysis. A comparably high coefficient is indicated by Mayer and Wagner (1996) as the result of the Berlin Aging Study ($r = -.51$). Similar results were found in a study of four countries in which results were calculated twice at intervals by Mollenkopf and Ruoppila (2000). With age, the number of leisure activities and their frequency decrease, first slowly, then after reaching the age of 75-80, more rapidly.

The explanation for these correlations is as follows: the social position of the elderly in our society reduces the level of activity demanded of them and increases the risk of boredom (underdemand). However, this correlation, which is solely based upon age and activity, conceals the different socioeconomic factors that have a moderating function here, like the significant variability within leisure behavior. New studies concerning leisure behavior postulate that age is a proxy for a network of systemic sociocultural forces that exert constraints upon the opportunities to which people have access (Stone, Harvey, & Légaré, 2001). For instance, the interest in cultural events and the frequency of visits per year are highly correlated with the pertinence to a certain social class. In 1981, Abrams pointed out the class difference in leisure activities (Abrams, 1981). The percentage of socioculturally inactive elderly people is 28% in the lower class and 4% in the higher middle class (Mayer & Wagner, 1996). Cultural participation is thus clearly dependent upon class. The strongest influence in this regard is education. The higher the level of education, the more frequent the participation in cultural events. In considering the factor of education, age becomes less of an influence on cultural activities (Kolland, 1996). Only small differences in age, as well as in pertinence to a social class, can be found in media consumption, exercise with a low access threshold (e.g., going for a walk), and in religious activities. At least it is clear that simply reporting the decline of the level of total activity obscures the satisfying potential of particular kinds of activity appropriate to abilities and identities. A sense of belonging in the community also seems to be a key factor in determining the likelihood a person will exhibit a "strong" or "weak" activity pattern (Stone et al., 2001).

On the basis of a life-course perspective, researchers (Iso-Ahola, 1994; Mollenkopf & Ruoppila, 2000) conclude that although the overall quantity or number of leisure activities decreases with age, the data does not indicate that starting different types of activities declines over phases of life. The results of the Bonn Longitudinal Study generally indicate a consistency in the area of leisure (Schmitz-Scherzer, 1977), and do not show any shift from active to passive recreational activities in older age. Moreover, the longitudinal design illustrates a variable change, rather than a linear one, over several testing periods. The Baltimore Longitudinal Study of Aging (Verbrugge, Gruber-Baldini, & Fozard, 1996) demonstrates that individuals differ more from each other in time spent on activities (cross-sectional) than they vary in their choice of activities as they age (longitudinal). This does not mean that people have static activity profiles; rather, it means that changes tend to be gradual, giving both consistency and dynamics to life. On the basis of the Ohio Longitudinal Study of Aging and Adaptation, Atchley (1999) found a high rate of continuity in basic values (82%) and reading (83%), but a rather moderate rate of general activity level (51%) and participation in community organizations (44%).

A recent study of new leisure activities performed within the last five years demonstrates that 15% of the respondents are involved in new activities (Kolland & Kahri, 2004). The number of people starting physically demanding outdoor activities decreases with advancing age, but there is a significant increase in the number of people starting home-based activities in later life. The results show that older persons are not generally less active, but that advancing age and decline in health seem to lead to a shift in activities.

Another factor that is regarded as decisive for leisure activities is health. Hierarchical linear regression showed that the maintenance of instrumental, social, and high-demand leisure activities was associated with higher physical health scores and the maintenance of low-demand leisure activities with lower physical health scores (Everard, Lach, Fisher, & Baum, 2000). This does not only include the objective state of health, but also the subjective perception of health. A state of health perceived as good functions as a sort of activating source leading to participation in a greater number of activities. As expected, a positive subjective state of health has an effect primarily on activities that require physical effort or mobility. Swiss data (Höpflinger & Stuckelberger, 1999) demonstrates that persons who perceive that they are enjoying better health perform more activities in the garden, exercise more, go to the theater/concerts more frequently, and undertake more excursions and journeys. Mollenkopf and Ruoppila (2000) argue that health can be seen as the most important personal resource for outdoor mobility.

Gender and sex roles are another example of factors known to affect leisure. In the 1980s, elderly women were characterized as having been less involved in sports and more involved in reading and passive forms of leisure, as well as in social, expressive, and artistic endeavors (Kelly, 1983, 1987). Conversely, men were found to be more outdoor oriented and less expressive. The hindrances to leisure activities differ between men and women (Iso-Ahola, 1994). Women more easily abandon leisure activities they pursued earlier and are also more cautious in beginning new ones because of the so-called women hindrances, which include lack of a companion, care duties, and social obstacles (Kelly, 1987). Attitudinal barriers keep many women from pursuing desired interests, particularly in regard to sports or competitive activities (McGuire, Boyd, & Tedrick, 1999). Women feel they have no right to leisure, or they report feeling guilty about putting their own leisure preferences ahead of demands made on them by significant others (Riddick, 1993). Calasanti (1996, p. 150) suggests that both white men and women view retirement as "freedom of labor," but whereas for white men this means a freedom of choice in leisure activities, for women this means free choice to select a different day to do domestic tasks.

LEISURE AND SUBJECTIVE MEANING

The integration of leisure activities and subjective meanings continues to be problematic. Both subjective attribution and experience have been shown to influence whether or not a certain activity is regarded as leisure and that effects are to be expected (Mannell & Dupuis, 1994). Following on a variety of studies performed since the 1970s, recent leisure studies take into account the significance of subjective meanings that older adults associate with the activities with which they are familiar (Mollenkopf & Ruoppila, 2000). Based on a cross-sectional study, Lawton (1994) concludes that outwardly oriented dimensions of affect experiencing are related to high levels of leisure-activity participation, and high participation is related to high positive-affective, traits while inwardly oriented experiencing dimensions are only minimally related to participation.

An important point for understanding the subjective meaning of leisure is *motivation*. Research in recent years has been directed toward identifying different segments of the population of the elderly on the basis of multidimensional concepts of motivation and on the development of new instruments for empirical research. According to the work of Driver, Tinsley and Manfredo (1991), involvement in an activity meets a range of *psychological needs*. To test the range of needs met by one activity or a set of activities, they have developed an instrument called Paragraphs About Leisure (PAL). The potential benefits of leisure include eight dimensions: self-expression, companionship, power, compensation, security, service, intellectual aestheticism, and solitude. The model utilized by Driver et al. (1991) is based on the assumption that the benefits of leisure occur in a sequenced chain of causality, with many specific benefits (e.g., companionship, achievement, or stimulation) serving as intermediate outcomes that need to be met prior to gratification of more holistic human needs (e.g., personal growth and self-esteem). From this perspective, leisure is considered an important factor in helping people meet basic psychological needs, especially those that are not attained in work related opportunities.

A contrasting position to the view that leisure activities serve as a means to achieve certain goals is the concept of "leisure repertoire" (Iso-Ahola, 1980; Mobily, Lemke, & Gisin, 1991), which postulates that a given performed activity is a goal in itself. Leisure repertoire is defined as the personal "library" of largely intrinsically motivated activities that the participant practices on a regular basis. Emphasis is on the process or practice of leisure, not on the outcome of the leisure experience. For the elderly, a large and diversified leisure repertoire, which provides the individual with a reserve of meaningful activities, many choices, and an abundance of methods for the demonstration of efficacy and success, is proposed. Profiling the leisure repertoires of the elderly is one way to measure the qualitative aspects of meaningful leisure participation.

The Manitoba study (Chipperfield & Doig, 1997) attempted to implement this concept empirically. Starting with the premise that involvement in a breadth of leisure activities in later life should have positive implications, the Aging in Manitoba Project examined changes in the repertoire of seniors' leisure activities over seven years (Chipperfield & Doig, 1997; Chipperfield, Searle, & Doig, 1995). Based upon the change/stability in their repertoire of leisure activities, individuals were identified as augmenters, disengagers, or sustainers. Of interest were both structured (e.g., church and volunteer work) and unstructured (e.g., visiting and shopping) leisure activities. Results indicated that life satisfaction was related to change/stability in leisure repertoire. For structured activities, the repertoire declined over time, and this was true regardless of gender or age. However, the patterns of change for the repertoire of unstructured activities interacted with age such that a decline in repertoire was found only for the oldest. Augmenters retained original levels of life satisfaction, while disengagers experienced declining life satisfaction over the seven years of the study. The findings suggested that a broadening of the range of the leisure repertoire could offset the apparent declines in life satisfaction occurring in later life.

In addition to motivation, the *social benefit* of leisure participation has been studied extensively. Research on the relationship of activity to *life satisfaction* in a number of different settings and with a variety of older populations has been carried out for the past 40 years. Despite variation in measures, activities, and samples, there seems to be a clear consensus that engagement in activity outside the home makes a contribution to subjective sense of well-being in later life (Busse & Maddox, 1985; Peppers, 1976; Sneegas, 1986). In contrast, the results obtained by Kelly and Ross (1989) demonstrated differences when age categories were factored into the analysis. Home-based activity is strongly and negatively related to satisfaction for those in their 20s, but it is the most important contributor for those over 74. Sports, exercise, and travel are significant for those in their middle years from 30 to 64. Community organizations and cultural activity contribute to a sense of satisfaction for those in their later, child-rearing period (40-54) and in early retirement (65-74). Informal social activity has a high correlation with satisfaction for those of 75 and older. The other important result is that the value of an activity is not only determined by the frequency of engagement but also by its meaning (Ragheb & Griffith, 1982). The positive impacts of activities are self-respect, confidence, and a sense of worth. Sports and outdoor activities are more strongly related to leisure satisfaction than watching television. A certain modification of these results can be seen in the context of the life-course approach. Results from Canadian longitudinal studies (Smale & Dupuis, 1995) indicate that changes in leisure participation may occur in order to preserve psychological well-being rather than necessarily increasing it.

Leisure research also suggests that leisure participation makes people cope more effectively with *life stress* (Coleman & Iso-Ahola, 1993). Garpenter (1989) also found that leisure had a resiliency value that remained positive in spite of life events. Kaufman's (1988) study of 225 male and female retirees found that both greater leisure satisfaction and leisure participation are associated with lower levels of anxiety. A more differentiated view is presented by Patterson (1996) who, on the basis of a study about the relationship between leisure participation and a stressful event such as the loss of a spouse, concludes that greater participation in leisure activities was found to be negatively correlated with stress scores, but found no association between participation in leisure activities and adaptation after the death of a spouse.

Although most of the focus on leisure in later life is on psychological benefits such as life satisfaction, morale, and self-esteem, leisure also has a social benefit. The relationship between leisure and the sociostructural environment is often viewed as one in which leisure is dependent on sociostructural determinants. But leisure can also be viewed as an independent variable. One of the few studies on this subject was made by Burch and Hamilton-Smith (1991). The focus of their considerations is directed toward three possible social outcomes: *bonding, solidarity,* and *social integration* (Kelly & Ross, 1989). Bonding, or the establishment of ties between intimates, results in loyalty to a group or association, as well as encouraging the performance of roles necessary for the continuation of the group. Social solidarity, described as emotional commitment to a larger social role, results in an enhancing of an individuals' role performance. Social integration, or the linking together of elements of society together, results in an efficient operation of the group.

Recent research is directed toward the relationship between leisure activities and the *risk of dementia.* A study (Verghese et al., 2003) conducted with 469 individuals over the age of 75 showed (after the initial data was obtained) that approximately 35% showed symptoms of dementia. The study also showed that participation in leisure activities was associated with a reduced risk of dementia, even after adjustment for baseline cognitive status and after the exclusion of subjects with possible preclinical dementia. Among leisure activities, reading, playing board games, playing musical instruments, and dancing were associated with a reduced risk of dementia. Another longitudinal population based study (Wang et al., 2002), carried out in a central area of Stockholm, Sweden, was used to examine whether engagement in different activities 6.4 years before the diagnosis of dementia was related to a decreased incidence of the disease. The study found that engagement in mental, social, or productive activities was inversely related proportional to the incidence of dementia. Results suggest that stimulating activity, either mentally or socially oriented, may prevent or decrease the likelihood of dementia, which indicates that both social interaction and intellectual stimulation may be relevant to preserving mental functioning in the elderly.

LEISURE AS ACTION: EXPRESSIVITY AND THE CREATION OF EXPERIENCE

Since the 1960s, (gerontological) leisure research has been attempting to create a typology for leisure behavior based on the significance that is attributed to a certain activity. The search for types was conducted theoretically and experimentally with the help of higher statistical methods for evaluating data. The latter approach includes the works of Tinsley et al. (1987) and Kelly (1987). The earlier works of Havighurst (1961), Dumazedier (1974), Gordon et al. (1976), and Lawton (1985) are representative of theory guided research.

The typology of Gordon et al. (1976) characterizes *expressivity* of activities as a basic dimension. Activity here is understood not so much as pleasure, entertainment and shut off, but rather as an opportunity for self-expression and self-identification. The basis of the concept is the differentiation of activities into instrumental and expressive ones. While instrumental activities aim at achieving goals or completing tasks and rewards that only follow later on, expressive activities refer to the symbolic meaning for the individual of fulfilling interactions with the environment where the reward is of an intrinsic nature and is experienced when performing the activity (see also Dumazedier, 1974). Based on these assumptions, leisure activities can be categorized into the following types: relaxation and solitude (sleeping, resting), diversion (mass media entertainment), self-development (learning), creativity (playing piano), sensual transcendence (dramatic expression). This typology does not aim at categorizing all of the possible activities into a certain type, but at investigating which social characteristics can be found in the people behind these bundles of activities.

The results demonstrate an upward trend (by life stages) of relaxation and solitude; stability, more or less; of self-development and creativity; and a decline of all other types of activity. Sensual transcendence (e.g., participation in sports or exercise) show very strong negative associations with increasing life stages, which is exemplified by increased levels of anxiety (Gordon et al., 1976, p. 330). At every life stage, women are appreciably more likely to report a high level of creative leisure activities (cooking for family and friends, discussion, and cultural production).

Another line of research, related to Csikszentmihalyi's (1975) concept of flow, is dedicated to the *intensity of involvement* in leisure activities. It suggests that high investment activities require a great deal of effort, and resources and the acquisition of skill, and they are most likely to yield outcomes of an enhanced sense of competence (Kelly & Ross, 1989). Roger Mannell (1993) took up the flow model and has reported studies in which an engagement in high investment activities best distinguishes older adults with high levels of satisfaction. Individuals who are involved in more demanding activities are also more likely to take part in less demanding types of activity (accumulation effect). More *demanding social participation* seems to play a special role in the quality of life in old age. Recent studies support this thesis. More demanding social participation, such as voluntary and productive activities, seems to affect the quality of life in old age (Bukov et al., 2002).

CONCLUSIONS AND OUTLOOK

Reviewing the existing literature on leisure research, we may conclude that there has been considerable improvement in the explanation of the theoretical underpinning of empirical research and in methods of collection and analysis of data, as well as changes in the conceptualization of leisure in later life. Nevertheless, considerable research desiderata exist. We will mention a few:

1. What significance does leisure have in the context of assistance and care? Frail elderly must adapt to lower levels of stimulation. How do they cope with this situation and what effects do these changes have on the overall subjective well-being? What about the institutional setting; the existing opportunity structure for frail elderly and elderly caregivers? Institutional conditions that restrict choice will limit leisure in later years. Leisure is not just an activity; it is also a social institution within industrial and postindustrial societies. It should be kept in mind that responsibilities for caring (especially caring for a frail relative or spouse) might restrict older people's opportunities to participate in leisure activities, especially among women (Lechner & Neal, 1999; Szinovacz, 1992). If the options and alternatives available at the age of retirement are diminished by factors such as economic hardship, social losses, lack of infrastructure, or social constraints, then the existence of a leisure society may be illusionary. Research on constraints on leisure involvement in the later years (McGuire, 1983) demonstrates the limiting factors that are beyond the control of the individual (lack of transportation, lack of leisure companions, and fear of crime). The type of leisure activity that is chosen by elderly people is often connected to social expectancies by others or by oneself.

2. Empirical research reviewed for this chapter was primarily designated to relate leisure activities and activity types to possible determinants and effects of participation. Current and future research should be directed more toward in-depth studies of how particular activities are experienced and fit into the lifestyles of elderly people. An example is the study of Menec (2003), which suggests that different types of activities may have different benefits. Whereas social and productive activities may provide

physical benefits, as reflected in better physical condition and greater longevity, more solitary activities such as reading may have more psychological benefits by providing a sense of engagement with life.

What is the connection between activities that guarantee immediate satisfaction and an immediate experience, and activities that involve a certain continuity and sustained effort? Certain activities might "go together," that is, a person who engages in one activity in a group will be likely to engage in other activities in the same group; this will be evidenced by correlations in participation data, and these correlations can be subjected to factor or cluster analysis to produce statistically based groups. However, while factor and cluster analysis will inevitably produce groupings, the validity of such groupings is often suspect, and their meanings are not always clear. In particular, it is not clear whether the groups are of *complementary* activities or *substitutable* activities; in fact much of the research on leisure styles has not yet been able to answer this question because it is based on a narrow range of activities, often outdoor recreational activities only. As Kelly (1987) points out, when a wider range of activities is included, the analysis can be confounded by such "core" activities as watching television or socializing with friends and family or other common leisure activities.

3. Leisure is increasingly considered as the area of self-actualization and self-development (Blaikie, 1999). Activity and the structuring of time are no longer the center of attention, but it is rather the experience itself (Schulze, 1992) and time management that is essential. In particular, the subjective value of the experience of activities is continuing to gain significance. At the same time, the conflict between social classes, such as had been postulated by Veblen at the end of the nineteenth century, has decreased. The different leisure environments are not dominated so much by conflict but by indifference. The previous camp structures—here a leisure club of working seniors, and there a leisure club of the elderly bourgeois—have disappeared or have considerably lessened the access barriers for individuals not pertaining to a specific social camp or class. Age is still continuing to play a pivotal part in this restructuring process. Even if the chronological age does not represent a differentiating variable for leisure behavior, there still is a clear segmentation of leisure environments according to age or pertinence to a cohort. On a more empirical level, age segregating versus age integrating leisure cultures can be recognized (Schulze, 1992) and must be investigated more carefully into the future. Is it true that they do not conflict with one another, but rather assume a position of "social freedom" in the context of nonunderstanding?

Despite the fact that the possibility for self-actualization has increased in the context of leisure, and thus leisure represents a relevant aspect of freedom in later life, we cannot draw the conclusion that higher age can be equated with freedom. Elderly people differentiate between duty and leisure. Activities that generally are seen as leisure activities are at one time routine and at another leisure. Only the differentiation between obligation and leisure results in the special importance that is attributed to leisure. What is desirable is a combination of occupations and leisure activities that not only make time pass more easily but that also serve the preventative purpose of helping elderly persons maintain and develop an identity of their own.

REFERENCES

Abrams, M. (1981). Class differences in the use of leisure time by the elderly. In R. Taylor & A. Gilmore (Ed.), *Current trends in British gerontology* (pp. 1-12). Aldershot: Gower Publishing.

Aristotle. (1976). *The Nichomachean ethics*. London: Penguin.

Atchley, R. C. (1971). Retirement and leisure participation: Continuity or crisis. *The Gerontologist, 11*, 13-17.

Atchley, R. C. (1989). A continuity theory of normal aging. *The Gerontologist, 29*, 183-190.

Atchley, R. C. (1999). *Continuity and adaptation in aging*. Baltimore: The Johns Hopkins University.

Attias-Donfut, C., & Gognalons-Nicolet, M. (1980). Après 50 ans, la redistribution des inégalites [After 50. The redistribution of inequality]. Documents d'Information et de Gestion, no 46/47.

Bellah, R. N., Madsen, R., Sullivan, W., Swidler, A., & Tipton, S. (1985). *Habits of the heart: Individualism and commitment in American life*. New York: Harper & Row.

Blaikie, A. (1999). *Ageing and popular culture*. Cambridge: University Press.

Bourdieu, P. (1979). *Distinction. A social critique of the judgement of taste*. London: Routledge and Kegan Paul.

Bukov, A., Maas, I., & Lampert, T. (2002). Social participation in very old age: Cross-sectional and longitudinal findings from BASE. *Journal of Gerontology: Psychological Sciences, 57B*, P510-P517.

Burch, W. R., & Hamilton-Smith, E. (1991). Mapping a new frontier: Identifying, Measuring, and valuing social cohesion benefits related to non-work opportunities and activities. In P. B. Driver, P. J. Brown, & G. L. Peterson (Eds.), *Benefits of leisure* (pp. 369-382). State College, PA: Venture Press.

Busse, E. W., & Maddox, G. L. (1985). *The Duke Longitudinal Studies of Normal Aging 1955-1980*. New York: Springer.

Calasanti, T. (1996). Incorporating diversity: Meaning, levels of research, and implications for theory. *The Gerontologist, 36*, 147-156.

Chipperfield, J. G., & Doig, W. D. (1997, March). *A longitudinal analysis of changes in leisure repertoire: Implications for life satisfaction*. Paper presented to the Austrian Conference on Gerontology. Bad Hofgastein, Austria.

Chipperfield, J. G., Searle, M. S., & Doig, W. D. (1995, October). *A longitudinal analysis of leisure repertoire*. Paper presented to the Canadian Association on Gerontology, Vancouver.

Coleman, D., & Iso-Ahola, S. (1993). Leisure and health: The role of social support and self-determination. *Journal of Leisure Research, 25*, 111-128.

Csikszentmihalyi, M. (1975). *Beyond boredom and anxiety: The experience of play in work and games*. San Francisco: Jossey-Bass.

Cumming, E., & Henry, W. E. (1961). *Growing old: The process of disengagement*. New York: Basic Books.

Cutler, S. J., & Hendricks, J. (1990). Leisure and time use across the life course. In R. H. Binstock & L. K. George (Eds.), *Handbook of aging and the social sciences* (pp. 169-185). New York: Academic Press.

Driver, B. L., Tinsley, H. E. A., & Manfredo, M. J. (1991). The paragraphs about leisure and recreation experiences preference scales. In P. B. Driver, P. J, Brown, & G. L. Peterson (Eds.), *Benefits of leisure* (pp. 263-286). State College, PA: Venture Press.

Dumazedier, J. (1967). *Toward a society of leisure*. New York: The Free Press.

Dumazedier, J. (1974). *Sociology of leisure*. Amsterdam: Elsevier.

Dumazedier, J. (1984). Social time and leisure in retirement. In International Center of Social Gerontology (Ed.), *Aging well through living better* (pp. 39-49). Paris: International Center of Social Gerontology.

Ehmer, J. (1990). *Sozialgeschichte des alters* [Social history of the aged]. Frankfurt a.M.: Suhrkamp.

Ekerdt, D. J. (1998). Workplace norms for the timing of retirement. In K. W. Schaie & C. Schooler (Eds.), *Impact of work on older adults* (pp. 101-123). New York: Springer.

EUROSTAT. (2003). *Time use at different stages of life. Results from 13 European countries.* Luxembourg: Office for Official Publications of the European Communities.

Everard, K. M., Lach, H. W., Fisher, E. B., & Baum, M. C. (2000). Relationship of activity and social support to the functional health of older adults. *The Journals of Gerontology Series B: Psychological Sciences and Social Sciences, 55,* S208-S212.

Featherstone, M., & Hepworth, M. (1989). Ageing and old age. In B. Bytheway, T. Keil, P. Allatt, & A. Bryman (Eds.), *Becoming and being old* (pp. 143-157). London: Sage.

Federal Interagency Forum on Aging-Related Statistics. (2001). *Older Americans 2000: Key indicators of well-being.* Washington: Government Printing Office.

Fürstenberg, F. (2002). Perspektiven des alter(n)s als soziales konstrukt [Perspectives of aging as social construct]. In G. M. Backes & W. Clemens (Eds.), *Zukunft der soziologie des alter(n)s* (pp. 75-84). Opladen: Leske & Budrich.

Gans, H. J. (1975). *Popular culture and high culture.* New York: Basic Books.

Garpenter, G. (1989). Change during middle adulthood and valuing leisure. *World Leisure and Recreation, 31,* 29-34.

Gauthier, A., & Smeeding, T. (2001). *Historical trends in the patterns of time use of older adults.* Paper presented at the Conference on Population Ageing in Industrialized Countries: Challenges and Issues. Nihon University Population Research Institute (NuPRI), Tokyo, 19-21 March 2001.

Gershuny, J., & Fisher, K. (2000). Leisure. In A. H. Halsey & J. Webb (Eds.), *Twentieth-century British social trends* (3rd ed., pp. 620-649). London: Macmillan Publishers Ltd.

Gilleard, C. (1996). Consumption and identity in later life: Toward a cultural gerontology. *Ageing and Society, 16,* 489-498.

Gordon, C., Gaitz, C. M., & Scott, J. (1976). Leisure and lives. Personal expressivity across the life span. In R. H. Binstock & E. Shanas (Eds.), *Handbook of aging and the social sciences* (pp. 310-341). New York: Van Nostrand Reinhold.

Havighurst, R. H. (1959). Meanings of leisure. *Social Forces, 37,* 355-360.

Havighurst, R. J. (1961). The nature and values of meaningful free-time activity. In R. W. Kleemeier (Ed.), *Aging and leisure* (pp. 309-344). New York: Oxford University Press.

Havighurst, R. J., & Albrecht, R. (1953). *Older people.* New York: Longmans Green.

Havighurst, R. J., & Feigenbaum, K. (1968). Leisure and life-style. In: B. L. Neugarten (Ed.), *Middle age and aging* (pp. 347-353). Chicago: The University of Chicago Press.

Höpflinger, F., & Stuckelberger, A. (1999). *Demographische Alterung und individuelles Altern* [Demographic and individual aging]. Zürich: Seismo.

Iso-Ahola, S. E. (1980). *The social psychology of leisure and recreation.* Dubuque, IA: William C. Brown.

Iso-Ahola, S. E. (1994). Leisure lifestyle and health. In D. M. Compton (Ed.), *Leisure & mental health* (Vol. 1, pp. 43-60). Park City, UT: Development Resources.

Kalish, R. A. (1979). The new ageism and the failure model: A new polemic. *The Gerontologist, 19,* 398-402.

Kaplan, M. (1961). Toward a theory of leisure for social gerontology. In R. W. Kleemeier (Ed.), *Aging and leisure* (pp. 389-412). New York: Oxford University Press.

Kaufman, J. E. (1988). Leisure and anxiety: A study of retirees. *Activities, Adaptation, & Aging, 11,* 1-10.

Kelly, J. R. (1983). Leisure styles: A hidden core. *Leisure Sciences, 5*(4), 321-338.

Kelly, J. R. (1987). *Peoria winter. Styles and resources in later life.* Lexington, MA: Lexington Books.

Kelly, J. R., & Freysinger, V. J. (2000). *21st century leisure. Current issues.* Boston: Allyn and Bacon.

Kelly, J. R., & Ross, J. (1989). Later-life leisure. Beginning a new agenda. *Leisure Sciences, 11,* 47-59.

Kleemeier, R. W. (1961). *Aging and leisure.* New York: Oxford University Press.

Kolland F. (1984). Bildungsbenachteiligung älterer menschen. *Berichte aus Forschung und Praxis, 1,* 1-35.

Kolland, F. (1996). *Kulturstile im Alter* [Cultural styles in later life]. Wien: Böhlau.

Kolland, F., & Kahri, S. (2004). Plurale Alterskulturen [Plurality in aging cultures]. In G. M. Backes & W. Clemens (Eds.), *Lebenslagen im Alter* [Conditions of life in old age]. Opladen: Leske & Budrich (in press).

Lawton, M. P. (1985). Activities and leisure. In C. Eisdorfer, M. P. Lawton, & G. L. Maddox (Eds.), *Annual review of gerontology and geriatrics* (Vol. 5, pp. 127-164). New York: Springer.

Lawton, M. P. (1994). Personality and affective correlates of leisure activity participation by older people. *Journal of Leisure Research, 26,* 138-158.

Lechner, V. M., & Neal, M. B. (1999). *Working and caring for the elderly.* London: Routledge.

Lehr, U. (1988). Arbeit als Lebenssinn auch im alter [Work as sense of life in old age]. In L. Rosenmayr & F. Kolland (Eds.), *Arbeit - Freizeit - Lebenszei* [Work - Leisure - Lifetime] (pp. 29-46). Opladen: Westdeutscher Verlag.

Lindenberger, U., & Reischies, F. M. (1999). Limits and potentials of intellectual functioning in old age. In P. B. Baltes & K. U. Mayer (Eds.), *The Berlin Aging Study* (pp. 227-255). New York: Cambridge University Press.

Mannell, R. C. (1993). High-investment activity and life satisfaction among older adults. In J. R. Kelly (Ed.), *Activity and aging* (pp. 125-145). London: Sage.

Mannell, R. C., & Dupuis, S. L. (1994). Leisure and productive activity. *Annual Review of Gerontology and Geriatrics, 14,* 125-141.

Mayer, K. U., & Wagner, M. (1996). Lebenslagen und soziale ungleichheit im hohen Alter [Conditions of life and social inequality in later life]. In K. U. Mayer & P. B. Baltes (Eds.), *Die Berliner Altersstudie* [The Berlin Aging Study] (pp. 251-275). Berlin: Akademie-Verlag.

McGuire, F. A. (1983). Constraints on leisure involvement in the later years. In P. M. Foster (Ed.), *Activities and the "well elderly"* (pp. 17-24). New York: The Haworth Press.

McGuire, F. A., Boyd, R. K., & Tedrick, R. E. (1999). *Leisure and aging. Ulyssean living in later life.* Champaign, IL: Sagamore Publishing.

Menec, V. H. (2003). The relation between everyday activities and successful aging: A 6-year longitudinal study. *The Journals of Gerontology Series B: Psychological Sciences and Social Sciences, 58,* S74-S82.

Michelon, L. C. (1954). The new leisure class. *American Journal of Sociology, 59,* 371-378.

Mobily, K., Lemke, J. H., & Gisin, G. (1991). The idea of the leisure repertoire. *The Journal of Applied Gerontology, 10,* 208-223.

Mollenkopf, H., & Ruoppila, I. (2000). *The MOBILATE Project. Enhancing outdoor mobility in later life.* Heidelberg: Deutsches Zentrum für Alternsforschung.

Parsons, T. (1964). *Social structure and personality.* New York: The Free Press.

Patterson, I. (1996). Participation in leisure activities by older adults after a stressful life event: The loss of a spouse. *International Journal of Aging and Human Development, 42,* 123-142.

Peppers, L. G. (1976). Patterns of leisure and adjustment to retirement. *The Gerontologist, 16,* 441-446.

Phillipson, C. (2004). *Transitions from work to retirement: Developing a new social contract.* Bristol: Policy Press (in press).

Phillipson, C., Bernard, M., Phillips, J., & Ogg, J. (2001). *The family and community life of older people*. London: Routledge.

Plakans, A. (1994). The democratization of unstructured time in Western societies: A historical overview. In M. W. Riley, R. L. Kahn, & A. Foner (Eds.), *Age and structural lag* (pp. 107-129). New York: John Wiley.

Ragheb, M. G., & Griffith, C. A. (1982). The contribution of leisure participation and leisure satisfaction to life satisfaction of older persons. *Journal of Leisure Research, 14,* 295-306.

Riddick, C. C. (1993). Older women's leisure activity and quality of life. In J. R. Kelly (Ed.), *Activity and aging* (pp. 86-98). London: Sage.

Riley, M. W. (1978). Aging, social change, and the power of ideas. *Daedalus, 107,* 39-52.

Riley, M. W., Johnson, M. E., & Foner, A. (1972). *Aging and society* (Vol.3). New York: Russell Sage.

Riley, M. W., & Riley, J. W. (1986). Longevity and social structure: The potential of the added years. In A. Pifer & L. Bronte (Eds.), *Our aging society* (pp. 53-77). New York: W. W. Norton.

Riley, W. W., & Riley, J. W. (1994). Structural lag: Past and future. In M. W. Riley, R. L. Kahn, & A. Foner (Eds.), *Age and structural lag* (pp. 15-36). New York: John Wiley.

Rosenmayr, L. (1983). *Die späte freiheit.* Berlin: Severin & Siedler.

Rosenmayr, L. (1989). Altern und Handeln [Aging and action]. In A. Weymann (Ed.), *Handlungsspielräume* [Rooms for maneuvers] (pp. 151-162). Stuttgart: Enke.

Russell, C. H. (1989). *Good news about aging.* New York: John Wiley.

Schaie, K. W., & Willis, S. L. (1986). Can decline in adult intellectual functioning be reversed? *Developmental Psychology, 22,* 223–232.

Schmitz-Scherzer, R. (1977). Zur veränderung des freizeit- und sozialverhaltens. *Zeitschrift für Gerontologie, 10,* 300-321.

Schulze, G. (1992). *Die Erlebnisgesellschaft* [The experience society]. Frankfurt a.M.: Campus.

Simmel, G. (1993, 1913). *Das Individuum und die Freiheit* [The individual and freedom]. Frankfurt a.M.: Fischer.

Simovici, S. (1984). Occupations and leisure activities for the elderly. In International Center of Social Gerontology (Ed.), *Aging well through living better* (pp. 135-147). Paris: International Center of Social Gerontology.

Smale, B. J. A., & Dupuis, S. L. (1995). *A longitudinal analysis of the relationship between leisure participation and psychological well-being across the lifespan.* The 1995 Leisure Research Symposium October 5-8, San Antonio, Texas.

Sneegas, J. J. (1986). Components of life satisfaction in middle and later life adults. *Journal of Leisure Research, 18,* 248-258.

Stearns, P. (1977). *Old age in European society.* London: Croom Helm.

Stone, L. O., Harvey, A., & Légaré, J. (2001). *Relative importance of factors explaining seniors' activity patterns, international comparisons.* Paper presented at World Congress of Gerontology, Vancouver, 5 July 2001.

Szinovacz, M. (1992). Leisure in retirement: Gender differences in limitations and opportunities. *World Leisure & Recreation, 34,* 14-17.

Teague, M. L. (1987). *Health promotion: Achieving high-level wellness in the later years.* Indianapolis: Benchmark Press.

Teague, M. L., &, MacNeil, R. D. (1992). *Aging and leisure: Vitality in later life.* Dubuque, IA: Wm. C. Brown Communications.

Tinsley, H. E. A., Colbs, S. L., Teaff, J. D., & Kaufman, N. (1987). The relationship of age, gender, health and economic status to the psychological benefits older persons report from participation in leisure activities. *Leisure Sciences, 9,* 53-65.

Thorsen, K. (1998). The paradoxes of gerotranscendence: The theory of gerotranscendence in a cultural gerontological and post-modernist perspective. *Norwegian Journal of Epidemiology, 8,* 165-176.

Tornstam, L. (1989). Gerotranscendence: A meta-theoretical reformulation of the disengagement theory. *Aging: Clinical and Experimental Research, 1,* 55-63.

Townsend, P. (1957). *The family life of old people.* London: Routledge and Kegan Paul.

Veblen, T. (1979, 1899). *The theory of the leisure class: An economic study of institutions.* New York: Penguin Books.

Verbrugge, L. M., Gruber-Baldini, A. L., & Fozard, J. L. (1996). Age differences and age changes in activities: Baltimore Longitudinal Study of Aging. *Journals of Gerontology Series B: Psychological Sciences and Social Sciences, 51,* S30-S41.

Verghese, J., Lipton, R. B., Katz, M. J., & Buschke, H. (2003). Leisure activities and the risk of dementia in the elderly. *The New England Journal of Medicine, 348,* 2508-2516.

Wang, H., Karp, A., Winblad, B., & Fratiglioni, L. (2002). Late-life engagement in social and leisure activities is associated with a decreased risk of dementia: A longitudinal study from the Kungsholmen Project. *American Journal of Epidemiology, 155,* 1081-1087.

PART V. New and Persistent Dynamics Regarding the Technology Environment

CHAPTER 13

The Potential Influence of the Internet on the Transition to Older Adulthood

Sara J. Czaja and Chin Chin Lee

The Internet is a collection of networks linking computers to computers and serves as a transport vehicle for information. The term "Internet" is not synonymous with the World Wide Web; whereas the Internet is the physical medium used to transport information, the World Wide Web (WWW) is a collection of protocols used to access information. Using the Internet and the WWW it is possible to retrieve documents, view images, animation, and videos, listen to sound files, speak and hear voice, and view a wide variety of programs (UC Berkeley Library, 2004). Originally designed to transmit text and numeric data, the Internet now has a variety of types of information (e.g. travel, health, business, financial) and offers a wide variety of application areas (communication, online support, shopping, bill paying). Furthermore, technical advances such as high-speed transmission as well as affordable computer systems and modems have made Internet access possible to large numbers of people, many of whom, unlike computer users in the past, do not have technical skills. In fact, use of the Internet has become an integral part of daily life and is increasingly used in most settings including the home.

Although the development of the Internet began in the 1970s, its major impact began to be experienced in the 1990s. In 2003, 63% of American adults used the Internet, an increase of 47% from the year 2000. The number of users worldwide is about 600 million with the largest number of users in the United States, followed by Europe and Asia (Nua Internet Service, 2003). The most common online activities include communicating via e-mail or chat rooms, information seeking, financial and transaction-based activities (e.g., online banking and shopping), and hobby or entertainment activities (Pew Internet and American Life Project, 2003).

However, despite the increased proliferation of computers and increased adoption of the Internet, demographic gaps in Internet use remain. For example, although Internet use is rapidly increasing among adults aged 65+ years, it is still low compared to other age groups (Figure 1). In 2003 only 20% of Americans over the age of 65 were

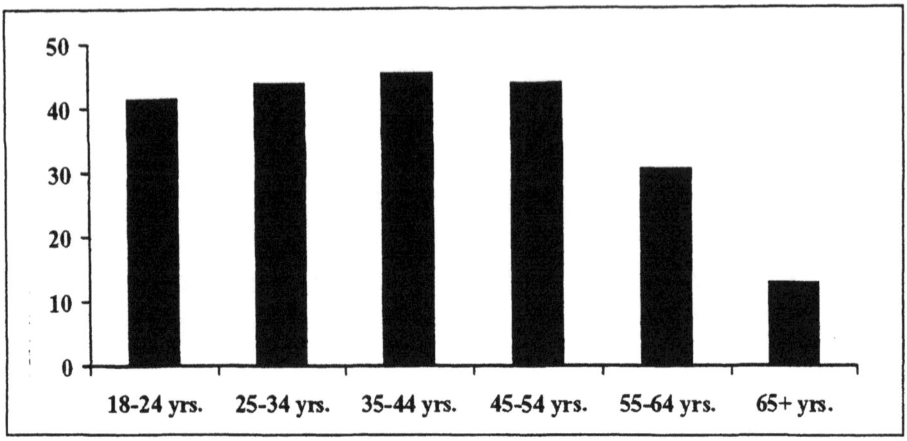

Figure 1. Use of Internet at home by adults 18 years and over.
Source: U.S. Census Bureau, 2001.

"online" as compared to 56% of 30-49-year-olds and 36% of those in the 50-64 age group. Seniors who access the Internet tend to be male, highly educated, and relatively affluent. Furthermore, people with a disability such as impaired vision or problems with manual dexterity such as arthritis are only half as likely to use computers and the Internet as those without a disability (U.S. Department of Commerce, 2002). Many older people have chronic conditions such as arthritis, and this may put them at added disadvantage in terms of accessing technology. Finally, minorities are less likely to own computers and use the Internet as are those who are less educated and in lower socioeconomic strata (U.S. Department of Commerce, 2002). Given the centrality of electronic interactions to education, employment and daily living, not being able to use and have access to technologies such as the Internet will have increasingly negative ramifications and put those who are "technology disabled" at a disadvantage in terms of living, functioning independently, and successfully negotiating the built environment. To insure that everyone has access to the "information highway" technology access and training programs need to be targeted toward older and minority populations and those who are disabled and less educated.

There are a variety of ways that technology such as the Internet can help smooth the transition to older adulthood and allow older people to maintain control over their own lives, especially those who live alone or in rural communities or have some type of mobility restriction. For example, the Internet can help mitigate problems with social isolation and foster links to family and friends. The Internet can also facilitate the performance of daily activities such as banking and shopping and help older people to take a more active role in their own healthcare. In addition, the Internet can enhance educational and employment opportunities for older adults. However, in order for the benefits of the Internet to be realized by older populations, the needs, preferences, and abilities of older adults need to be accommodated in the design of these systems. We also need to understand the benefits and consequences of the use of technology on the daily lives of older people. For example, issues of reliability, privacy, and trust need to be considered. The aims of this chapter are to discuss the potential impact of the Internet on the lives of older adults and highlight factors that may serve as barriers to the successful adoption of the Internet by older people.

THE INTERNET AND "SUCCESSFUL" AGING

There are a number of ways that the Internet can promote successful transition to older adulthood and enable older people to maintain control over their own lives. Unlike past technologies such as the telephone, the Internet allows expanded opportunities for communication, accessing information and resources, and performing routine activities such as shopping. The Internet can also change patterns of work interactions allowing people to work from home, communicate, and access work-related information from distant locations. Online educational programs are also becoming widespread.

These application areas can be very beneficial to older people. For example, use of the Internet can enable older people to remain connected to family and friends, especially those who are far away. Online communities may also expand social opportunities for older people and provide a mechanism for social interaction. The Internet may also enhance the ability of older adults to remain intellectually active and productive, and help ease the transition from full-time to part-time work or retirement. It may also provide them with easier access to healthcare services and support. This will provide more autonomy to people with chronic conditions or illnesses. It may also foster greater autonomy among family caregivers as well as enabling older adults to continue to perform routine tasks such as shopping and bill paying and to access need resources and services. Ultimately, use of the Internet may enable older adults to continue to live at home and "age in place." Older adults generally prefer to remain in their home and have strong attachments to their home environment. Satisfaction with one's living environment is an important component of well-being, autonomy, and continuity in later life (Wahl, 2001). The following section will discuss arenas wherein the Internet and other forms of communication technology offer the potential of enhancing the well-being and quality of life of older adults and enable them to maintain an active and productive role in society.

Enhanced Productivity

One arena older adults are likely to interact with and benefit from technology such as the Internet is work environments. By 2001, more than half (57%) of workers in the United States used a computer at work and of these, 66% used the Internet. The issue of workplace technology and older adults is highly relevant given recent projections regarding older workers. A number of demographic trends, including the aging of the population; changes in the labor-force participation of younger workers; and changes in retirement policies, programs and behaviors are promoting continued employment for older adults and delaying retirement. In contrast to previous decades, the number of workers over the age of 55 is expected to grow significantly. In the United States, it is estimated that by 2015 there will be approximately 33.3 million older people in the labor force (Figure 2). There are similar projections for other countries such as Japan. Given the rapid deployment of technology in the workplace, most of these workers will need to interact with computers and the Internet in the daily performance of their job.

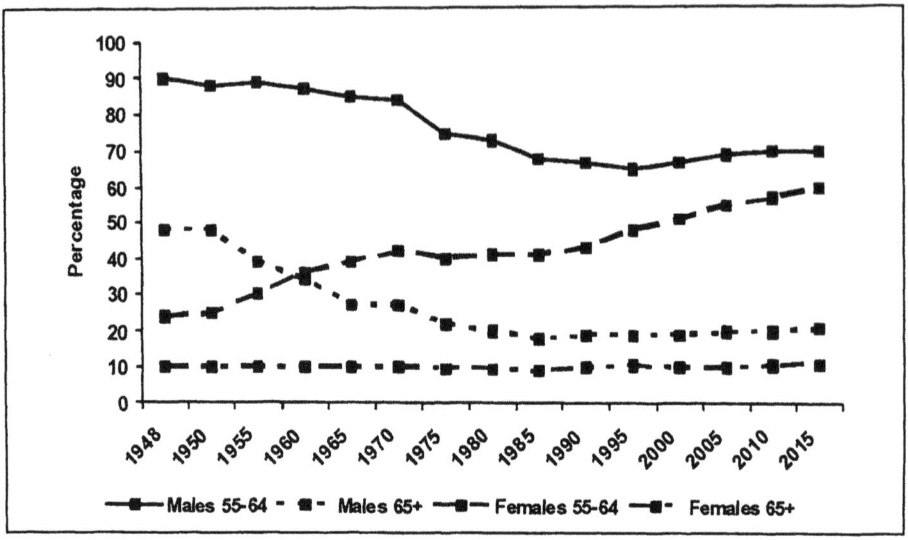

Figure 2. Labor force participation for older workers.
Source: U.S. Bureau of Labor Statistics, 2002.

Access to computers and the Internet may expand employment opportunities for older people. For example, computers and the Internet make working from home a more likely option. Telecommuting, which refers working from a location other than a traditional office and interacting with the workplace using some form of technology, is rapidly increasing. In 1995 at least three million Americans were telecommuting for purposes of work, and this number is expected to increase by 20% per year (Nickerson & Landauer, 1997). Telecommuting may be particularly appropriate for older adults, as they are more likely than younger people to be "mobility impaired" or engaged in some form of caregiving; it also allows for more flexible work schedules and autonomy and is more amenable to part-time work. These job characteristics are generally preferred by older people. However, telecommuting may result in problems of professional and social isolation. Employees may miss the opportunities for informal interactions with friends and colleagues and from participating in and receiving the benefits of organizational membership. To date, little research has been devoted to examining the social, behavioral, and organizational implications of telecommuting.

Computers also reduce the physical demands of work. This is beneficial for older adults as they tend to retire from jobs that are characterized by heavy physical demands (Czaja, 2001). There are a number of software programs and adaptive devices that may make continued work more viable for older people who have some type of impairment or chronic conditions, such as low-vision problems, problems with speech communication, or psycho-motor limitations. There are also computer-based organizers and reminder systems to aid people with memory problems.

However, the rapid deployment of technology in the workplace may also create challenges for older workers. Technology changes the way in which jobs are performed and alters job contents and job demands. Often existing skills and knowledge become obsolete, and new jobs and skills are required. Workers not only have to learn to use technical system but they must also learn new ways of performing jobs. This will hold true for future generations of older adults, as technology by its nature is dynamic. Issues of skill obsolescence and worker retraining are highly significant for older workers as they are less likely than younger workers to have had exposure to technology such as computers (e.g., Czaja & Sharit, 1998) and are often bypassed for training or retraining opportunities (Griffiths, 1997). Ultimately, the impact of technology on the older worker will vary according to the organizational factors, such as the availability of training and retraining programs, the design and usability of the technology, and the willingness and ability of older people to upgrade their skills to keep pace with changing job demands.

The Internet can also be used by older people for continuing education. There are Web sites and software programs available on a wide variety of topics, as well as formal online degree programs and opportunities to be linked via videoconferencing and networking facilities to actual classrooms. The American Association for Retired Persons has begun to offer several online courses. These opportunities can enable older adults to remain intellectually engaged and active, especially those who have difficulty accessing more traditional classroom-based adult education programs. Current research (e.g., Baltes & Smith, 1999) clearly shows that cognitive engagement and stimulation is important to successful aging; in fact, lifelong learning is a growing interest among older people. Currently in the United States, more than 33 million adults aged 45+ are engaged in some form of continuing education (Adler, 2002). The Internet can also be used to create "online learning communities" that bring social interaction to learning and support the learning process. An online community refers to an aggregation of people with a shared goal, interest, need, or activity and have repeated interactions and share resources (Preece & Maloney-Krichmar, 2003). The imminent availability of the next generation Internet and interactive multimedia programming will further expand the education experiences that are available to individuals and enable information to be tailored to the specific needs and characteristics of users. This may be particularly beneficial to older adults who often learn at a slower pace than younger people and need more instructional support.

Healthcare Delivery and Management

The Internet is also shaping and having a pronounced impact on healthcare delivery and personal health behavior. Interactive health communication or "e-health" generally refers to the interaction of an individual with an electronic device or communication technology (such as the Internet) to access or transmit health information or to receive or provide guidance and support on a health related issue (Robinson, Patrick, Eng, & Gustafson, 1998). The scope of e-health applications is fairly broad, but mostly encompasses searching for health information, participating in support groups, and consulting with healthcare professionals. Currently, in 2003 there are more than 70,000 Web sites that provide health information; 77 million American adults searched the Internet for health information (Pew Internet and American Life, 2003). The majority of consumers search for information on a specific disease or medical problem, medical treatments or procedures, medications, alternative treatments or medicine, or information on providers or hospitals. Reasons for the growth of online health information searches includes easier access by a more diverse group of users to more powerful technologies, the development of participative healthcare models, the growth of health information that makes it difficult for any one physician to keep pace, cost containment efforts that reduce physicians time with patients, and raising concerns about self-care and prevention (Cline & Hayes, 2001).

E-health applications may prove to be particularly beneficial for older adults as the prevalence of chronic conditions and disease increases with age; thus many older adults are likely to need some type of health-related support or continued care (Figure 3). Chronic disabling conditions can also result in limitations in daily activities, which in turn threatens independence. Unfortunately, many older adults have difficulty accessing needed care due to logistical problems or mobility restrictions. Thus, technologies such as the Internet may enhance the likelihood that older people who are ill or disabled are able to remain in their own homes and live with a greater degree of autonomy.

However, the fact that consumers have access to e-health applications has significant implications for both patients and providers. On the positive side, access to health information can empower patients to take a more active role in the healthcare process. Patient empowerment can result in better informed decision making, better and more tailored treatment decisions, stronger patient-provider relationships, increased patient compliance, and better medical outcomes. Physicians increasingly report that patients come to office visits armed with information on their illness or condition and treatment options (Ferguson, 1998). Results from a recent Internet user survey (Fox & Rainie, 2000) also indicate that access to Internet health information has an influence on consumer decisions about seeking care, treatment choices, and their interactions with physicians.

E-health applications can also promote healthy behaviors as some applications include risk assessment and health promotion modules and promote peer information and support. Online support groups exist for almost any health condition, and participants in online support groups include consumers, professionals, patients, and family caregivers. For example, a recent study (Czaja & Rubert, 2002) evaluated a family therapy intervention augmented by a computer-interactive telephone system in reducing burden and distress among family caregivers of patients with Alzheimer's disease. One of the features of the system was online support groups. The caregivers found the support groups to be one of the most valuable features of the system and reported that participation in the groups increased their knowledge of caregiving and resources and also gave them a chance to interact with peers. E-health applications may also help individuals manage health problems by facilitating the provision of remote health monitoring and care.

However, there are some potential pitfalls and perils that need to be considered within the domain of interactive health, especially for older consumers. On the negative side, access to this wide array of health information can overload both patient and physicians, disrupt existing relationships, and lead to poor decision making on the part of consumers. For example, one major concern within the "e-health arena" is the lack of quality control mechanisms for health information on the Internet. Currently, consumers can access information from credible scientific and institutional sources (e.g., Medline Plus) and unreviewed sources of unknown quality. Inaccurate health information could result in inappropriate treatment or cause delays in seeking healthcare.

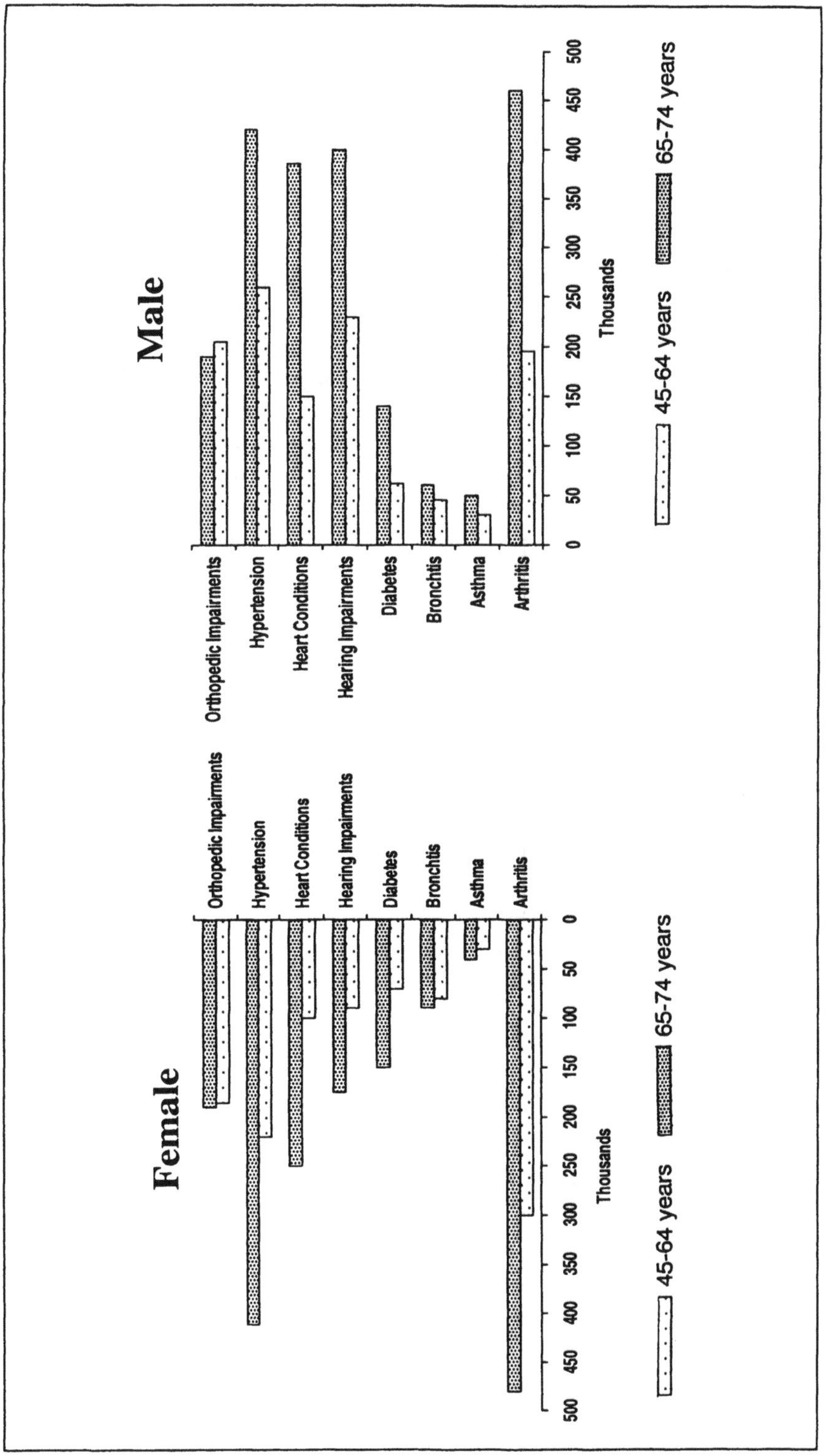

Figure 3. Chronic illness and older adults. **Source:** Adopted from Trend watch: Chronic illness and the aging U.S. Population, *Clinical Geriatrics, 7*(8), 77, 1999.

Other concerns referred to the ability of nonspecialists to integrate and interpret the wealth of information that is available and the ability of healthcare providers to keep pace with their patients. Finally, some consumers may find health information difficult to access because of design features that result in usability problems, lack of training, or limited access to technology.

Communication and Socialization

Clearly technology holds promise in terms of meeting the communication and social needs of older people. The ability to communicate and to remain socially connected is a critical aspect of successful aging. The literature strongly indicates that social isolation can lead to depression, and that lack of social support can lead to a loss of independence. About 30% of noninstitutionalized older people live alone, a number that increases with age. In the United States, most older people live outside of the city in suburban or rural locations, and it is quite common for family members to be dispersed among different geographic regions. The Internet can also expand social networks. As noted, online communities are becoming quite common, and many people also benefit from participation in online support groups. Several studies (e.g., Czaja, Guerrier, Nair, & Laudauer, 1993; Furlong, 1989) have shown that older adults are receptive to using e-mail as a form of communication, and that e-mail is effective in increasing social interactions among the elderly.

Technologies can also be used to assist and augment communication for individuals with disabilities. For example, software that allows a computer with a modem to function as a telecommunication device allows individuals with hearing impairments to communicate with voice phone users. Developments in multimedia and speech systems can convert text to speech and enable people with visual problems to enjoy books and news articles. However, the Internet should not be perceived as a replacement for human interaction but rather as a means to sustain and augment traditional forms of communication and social support.

Clearly, the Internet has great potential value for older people. Also, the majority of studies that have examined the attitudes of older people towards computer technology indicate that older people are receptive to using technologies such as computers. However, available data (e.g., Czaja & Sharit, 1998; Mead, Spaulding, Sit, Meyer, & Walker, 1997) also indicate that older people have more problems learning to use technology than younger adults. They also have less knowledge about potential uses of and how to access computers and other forms of technology. Morrell, Mayhorn, & Bennett (2000) found that the two primary predictors for not using the Web among people aged 60+ years were lack of access to a computer and lack of knowledge about the Web. Other barriers to computer and Internet access include cost, lack of technical support, and usability problems.

The next section will highlight some of the existing barriers to use of technology by older people and some important issues relating to system design and implementation. Before addressing these issues, it is worth noting that design and usability of technical systems for older populations will continue to be an important concern. Future generations of older adults will confront new challenges as technology is constantly evolving. We are entering the era of "ubiquitous computing" where computer interfaces will be seamless and embedded into automobiles, home appliances, medical devices, and other forms of technology. In addition, we can expect to have access to large amounts of information and to communicate from almost anywhere. At the same time, future technologies will have greater flexibility and adaptive interfaces, thus the potential exists to develop these technologies to support the needs and functionality of users. However, as noted by Rogers and Fisk (2003), success in the development of these adaptive interfaces is going to depend on an understanding of the characteristics of user populations and of user behaviors within social contexts.

EXISTING BARRIERS TO INTERNET USE AND DESIGN SOLUTIONS

Knowledge, Skills, and Training

The use of the Internet involves information seeking, a fundamental process people engage in to acquire knowledge or solve problems. It general represents a higher level cognitive activity and as such, involves memory, reasoning, attention, learning, and problem solving. Generally, people develop strategies and skills for information seeking according to their abilities, experiences, and available physical resources such as information systems. In this regard, information seeking involves interaction among six factors: the information seeker, task, search system, domain, setting, and search outcomes. The process is both opportunistic and systematic and involves a number of interdependent subprocess or phases, including: (1) defining and understanding the problem, (2) choosing a search system, (3) formulation of a query, (4) execution of a search, (5) examination of results, (6) extraction and integration of information, and finally (7) stopping the search (Marchionini, 1995).

As discussed by Marchionini (1995), information technologies such as the Internet have a dramatic impact on the information-seeking process. For example, instead of using the library and accessing information in hard copy, we now use online databases and access information in electronic form. These technologies require the information seeker to develop specialized knowledge and skills. Specifically, this includes domain expertise, system expertise, and information seeking expertise. Domain expertise involves knowledge and skills related to the problem domain and allows the persons to solve problems or access information quickly and effectively. Generally, experts in a domain have extensive knowledge of the domain and have an organized knowledge base of the general problem area. System expertise refers to knowledge and skills related to the search system and the physical interface to this system. In the case of the Internet, this includes abilities to use a keyboard and mouse, menus, manage windows, and screen information. It also refers to having an understanding of how databases are organized, what information is available, and how documents are structured. Information seeking expertise refers to knowledge and skills related to the process of seeking information. This includes knowledge of relevant information sources and how they are organized, as well as knowing where to look for and request information.

Essentially, use of the Internet requires learning a new set of skills to locate, access, manipulate, and use information sources. Given that aging is associated with changes in cognitive abilities, and that older adults typically have some difficulty acquiring new skills, learning to use the Internet may be challenging for older adults.

A number of studies have examined the ability of older adults to learn to use computer technology. These studies span a variety of computer applications and also vary with respect to training strategies, such as conceptual versus procedural training (Morrell, Park, Mayhorn, & Echt, 1995) or computer-based or instructor-based versus manual-based training (Czaja, Hammond, Blascovich, & Swede, 1989). In addition, the influence on learning of variables, such as attitude toward computers and computer anxiety, have been examined. Overall, the results of these studies indicate that older adults are, in fact, able to use computers for a variety of tasks. However, older adults often have more difficulty acquiring computer skills than younger people and require more training and more help during training. Also, when compared to younger adults on performance measures such as speed, they often achieve lower levels of performance.

These studies also point to the importance of designing training and instructional programs to meet the needs and characteristics of older people. Rogers and Fisk (2003) advocate a systems approach to training older adults to use technologies. A systems approach involves detailed analyses of the tasks and the users prior to the development and selection of the training approach. It is not sufficient to assume training programs that are designed for younger people will be effective for older people. Understanding age-related changes in sensory and cognitive abilities is critical to the design of successful training programs. Furthermore, older adults typically need training on basic computer concepts, such as mouse and windows management, in addition to training on the application area of interest. They may also require information on the types of technologies that are available, the potential benefits associated with using these technologies, and where and how to access these technologies. Because technology will continue to evolve and change, people will confront the need to learn new systems throughout their lives; thus the topic of training is critically important to the success of current and future technologies.

Usability Issues

Currently, with the explosive growth of the Internet, many WWW interfaces are designed without consideration to the user characteristics and environmental contexts in which the technology will be used (e.g., at home where little or no technical support is available). In this regard, Vora and Helander (1997) outlined several usability problems with current Web interfaces, including: outdated and incomplete information content, poor use of graphics, slow response time, overcrowding of screen information, and poor navigation support. Although indexes and search engines are helpful with Web navigation, finding information on the Web is often difficult and cumbersome. Many people adopt "browsing" search strategies when looking for information. While browsing is often the basis for serendipitous discoveries and incidental learning, it can also result in distraction, confusion, frustration, cognitive overload, and general problems associated with being "lost in hyperspace" (Nielsen, 1990). These types of problems may be exacerbated with the continued expansion of information on the Web and the increased number of Internet users. Without effective tools to help people deal with the information glut, the new information technologies such as the Internet could hinder rather than help people access information.

These types of problems may also be worse for older adults because of age-related changes in sensory, cognitive, and motor abilities. As noted, older adults are less likely than younger adults to have computers in the home and use the Internet. These differential rates in access may be partially due to usability problems and lack of technical support. Designers need to be aware of the characteristics of older adults and ensure that systems are designed with the capabilities and limitations of the older user in mind. For example, careful attention needs to be paid to the design of the display screen, choice of input device, and the design of instructional materials and technical support systems (e.g., "help" functions). As discussed throughout careful consideration also needs to be given to the quality, organization, and amount of information within a given Web site. Finally, issues of privacy also need to be considered. As the ability of Internet applications to tailor personal information becomes increasingly utilized, more potentially sensitive data will be collected during user interactions in workplaces, healthcare and public networks. Adequate safeguards need to be in place to insure that personal or sensitive information is not used for unintended or illegal purposes.

CONCLUSIONS AND RECOMMENDATIONS

The "explosion" of the Internet has drastically increased opportunities for gaining access to a wide variety of information. For many people, such as those who are frail, isolated, or have some type of mobility restrictions, access to the Internet holds the promise of enhancing independence by providing links to goods and resources, facilitating communication, and enhancing the ability to perform routine tasks such as banking and shopping. The Internet can also help older people access information on health and other topics and manage personal finances. As developments in Internet technology continue to emerge, users will have faster access to more channels of information in myriad formats.

Unfortunately, because of the rapid and expansive growth in Internet technology, there have been limited opportunities to develop and test Internet interfaces as compared to other Human Computer Interaction (HCI) domains. This problem is amplified by the fact that many designers have limited knowledge of interface concerns (Ratner, Grose, & Forsythe, 1996). In fact, the report by the National Research Council (1997) indicated that current interface structures significantly limit the use of the Web by many users, especially those who have some type of constraint on their abilities such as older users. In this regard, there are efforts underway such as the World Wide Web consortium (W3C) (http://www.w3.org.), to help ensure that the Web reaches its full potential for the largest group of users possible. However, despite these types of efforts, to date, there is limited empirical research examining usability issues for the Web for users who are less technically proficient, have physical or cognitive limitations, or who are older. To help ensure that the World Wide Web is available to the entire population, research is needed to support effective interface and training for users of all ages and abilities.

Currently, although most older people are receptive to using new technologies, they often encounter difficulties when attempting to adopt these systems. Barriers to successful adaptation of technology are largely related to a failure on the part of system designers to perceive older adults as "active" users of technical systems. Overcoming these barriers depends on training and design solutions that accommodate age-related declines in perceptual as well as cognitive and motor abilities. This might involve software modifications, alternative input devices, or redesign of instructional manuals. The development of these solutions requires an understanding of the needs, preferences, and abilities of older people. In essence, in order to design interfaces for information systems so that they are useful and usable for older people, it is important to understand: (1) why technology is difficult to use; (2) how to design technology for easier and effective use; and (3) how to effectively teach people to use and take advantage of available technologies.

REFERENCES

Adler, R. (2002). The age wave meets the technology wave. Available online at: http://www.senioinet.org/downloads/broadband.pdf.

Baltes, M. M, & Smith, J. (1999). Multilevel and systemic analyses of old age: Theoretical and empirical evidence for a fourth age. In V. L. Bengtson & K. W. Schaie (Eds.), *Handbook of theories of aging* (pp. 153-173). New York: Springer.

Cline, R. J. W., & Hayes, K. M. (2001). Consumer health information seeking on the Internet: The State of the art. *Health Education Research, 16,* 671-692.

Clinical Geriatrics. (1999). *Trend watch: Chronic illness and aging* U.S. population, *7.*

Czaja, S. J. (2001). Technological change and the older worker. In J. E. Birren & K. W. Schaie (Eds.), *Handbook of psychology of aging* (5th ed., pp. 547-555). California: Academic Press.

Czaja, S. J., Guerrier, J., Nair, S., & Laudauer, T. (1993). Computer communication as an aid to independence for older adults. *Behavior and Information Technology, 2,* 97-107.

Czaja, S. J., Hammond, K., Blascovich, J., & Swede, H. (1989). Age-related differences in learning to use a text-editing system. *Behavior and Information Technology, 8,* 309-319.

Czaja, S. J., & Rubert, M. (2002). Telecommunications technology as an aid to family caregivers of persons with dementia. *Psychosomatic Medicine, 64,* 469-476.

Czaja, S. J., & Sharit, J. (1998). Ability-performance relationships as a function of age and task experience for a data entry task. *Journal of Experimental Psychology: Applied, 4,* 332-351.

Ferguson, T. (1998). Digital doctoring: Opportunities and challenges in electronic-patient communication. *Journal of the American Medical Association, 280,* 1261-1262.

Furlong, M. S. (1989). An electronic community for older adults: The SeniorNet network. *Journal of Communication, 39,* 145-153.

Fox, S., & Rainie, L., (2000). The online health care revolution: How the Web helps Americans take better care of themselves. A Pew Internet and American Life Online Report. Accessed September, 2003 from http://www.pewinternet.org.

Griffiths, A. (1997). Aging, health, and productivity: A challenge for the new millennium. *Work & Stress, 11,* 197-214.

Marchionini, G. (1995). *Information seeking in electronic environments.* Cambridge: Cambridge University Press.

Mead, S. E., Spaulding, V. A., Sit, R. A., Meyer, B., & Walker, N. (1997). Effects of age and training on World Wide Web navigation strategies. *Proceedings of the Human Factors and Ergonomics Society 41st Annual Meeting,* 152-156.

Morrell, R. W., Mayhorn, C. B., & Bennett, J. (2000). A survey of World Wide Web use in middle-aged and older adults. *Human Factors, 42,* 175-182.

Morrell, R. W., Park, D. C., Mayhorn, C. B., & Echt, K. V. (1995). *Older adults and electronic communication networks: Learning to use ELDERCOMM.* Paper presented at the 103 Annual Convention of the American Psychological Association. New York.

National Research Council. (1997). *More than screen deep: Toward every-citizen interfaces to the nation's information infrastructure.* Washington, DC: National Academy Press.

Nickerson, R. S., & Landauer, T. K. (1997). Human-computer interaction: Background and issues. In M. G. Helander, T. K., Landauer, & P. V. Prabhu (Eds.), *Handbook of human-computer interaction* (2nd ed., pp. 3-32). Amsterdam, The Netherlands: Elsevier.

Nielsen, J. (1990). *Hypertext and hypermedia.* Boston: Academic Press.

Nua Internet Surveys. (2003, February 25). Global Net population increases. Retrieved January 20, 2004, from http://www.nua.ie/surveys/index.cgi?f=VS&art_id=905358729

Pew Internet & American Life. (2003, December 22). America's online pursuits: The changing picture of who's online and what they do. Retrieved January 25, 2004, from http://www.pewinternet.org/reports/toc.asp?Report=106

Preece, J., & Maloney-Krichmar, D. (2003). Online communities: Focusing on sociability usability. In J. A. Jacko & A. Sears (Eds.), The human-computer interaction handbook: Fundamentals, evolving technologies and emerging applications (pp. 596-620). New Jersey: Lawrence Erlbaum Associates.

Ratner, J. A., Grose, E., & Forsythe, C. (1996). Traditional vs. Web style guides: How do they differ? *Proceedings of the Human Factors and Ergonomics Society 40th Annual Meeting.*

Robinson, T. N., Patrick, K., Eng, T. R., & Gustafson, D. (1998). An evidence-based approach to interactive health communication: A challenge to medicine in the information age. *Journal of the American Medical Association, 288,* 1264-1269.

Rogers, W. A., & Fisk, A. D. (2003). Technology design, usability, and aging: Human factors techniques and considerations. In N. Charness & K. W. Schaie (Eds.), *Impact of technology on successful aging* (pp. 1-14). New York: Springer.

UC Berkeley Library. (2004). What is the Internet, the World Wide Web, and Netscape? Retrieved March 4, 2004, from http://www.lib.berkeley.edu/TeachingLib/guides/Internet/Whatis.html.

U. S. Bureau of Labor Statistics. (2002). Washington, DC: U.S. Department of Labor.

U. S. Census of Bureau. (2001). Home computers and Internet use in the United States: August 2000. Washington, DC: U.S. Government Printing Office.

U.S. Department of Commerce. (2002). A national online: How Americans are expanding their use of the Internet. Washington, DC: NTIA and Economics and Statistics Administration.

Vora, P. R., & Helander, M. G. (1997). Hypertex and its implications for the Internet. In M. G. Helander, T. K. Landauer, & P. V. Prabhu (Eds.), *Handbook of human-computer interaction* (2nd ed., pp. 877-914). Amsterdam, The Netherlands: Elsevier.

Wahl, H.-W. (2001). Environmental influences on aging and behavior. In J. E. Birren & K. W. Schaie (Eds.), *Handbook of the psychology of aging* (5th ed., pp. 215-232) New York: Academic Press.

CHAPTER 14

When Will Technology in the Home Improve the Quality of Life for Older Adults?

Anne-Sophie Melenhorst, Wendy A. Rogers, and Arthur D. Fisk

Imagine that all of a sudden, on a torridly hot Saturday afternoon, the water supply and the power are turned off due to a blunder in the road reconstruction in front of the house. It takes the workers about five hours to bring them back up. As a consequence, the washing machine and the dishwasher stop running, the refrigerator and the freezer start defrosting, and the computer quits right in the middle of sending a long e-mail message. The toilet does not flush and the cold shower one might crave for on such a day has to be postponed. On top of that, the air conditioning shuts down.

Technology is omnipresent in most homes. There are many situations in which we almost forget that we are dealing with technology and hardly realize its impact on everyday life. The example above illustrates how much we rely on technology, yet perhaps don't realize it until for some reason we all of a sudden have to do without. However, does the fact that we rely on technology and that we would miss if it were taken away, imply that it has improved the quality of our lives? What would be the potential of newly developing technology to do so? Could we learn from the introduction of new technology currently and in the past? And how do both existing technology and the introduction of new technology in the home affect our lives as we age?

TECHNOLOGY IN THE HOME DEFINED BY THE FULFILLMENT OF HUMAN NEEDS

We assume that the direct impact of home technology on everyday life runs through the broad spectrum of performed and desired activities in the home, from basic practical tasks to activities primarily aimed at life enrichment. The role of technology might be the realization or enhancement and activities or perhaps the unintended cause of their limitation.

There are different ways to define technology: for example "the practical application of knowledge in a particular area" (Merriam-Webster, 2000). The definition we found in Webster's previous edition (Merriam-Webster, 1991) also includes the *goal* of technology and is very relevant to our discussion here: "the totality of the means employed to provide objects necessary for human sustenance and comfort." The "employment" of these "means" through the centuries has resulted in a wide variety of equipment in the home, ranging from indoor plumbing as an example for basic need fulfillment, to the home computer, providing extended communication possibilities via the Internet. Usually, this equipment is referred to as "technology."

Whether technology is perceived as necessary for obtaining a desired level of sustenance and comfort, very much depends on the availability and reliance on technology and, accordingly, society's norms on using it. The desired level might have risen because of the influence of increased technology use and needs might have been created (Rogers, 1995). For example, many individuals consider air conditioning in the home necessary, but in years past air conditioning was considered to be a luxury. Within the societal framework, necessity depends on individual needs.

Older citizens have specific needs, aspirations, and wishes; specific technology experiences related to their generation, and challenges handling technological equipment are relatively new for them. Moreover, rapid technological development in society might affect them in particular. These factors influence both their need perception and their perception of technology potential to fulfill their needs and wishes. In this chapter we therefore approach the matter from a *gerontechnological* point of view.

Gerontechnology is defined as the study of technology and aging for the improvement of the daily functioning of the elderly (Bouma, 1992). Core concepts to gerontechnology are (1) the integration of older individuals into a changing society by directing technological developments at them, (2) the adequate modification of the technological environment of older adults' so that it enhances rather than limits their ambitions and aspirations, and (3) giving older adults full control over their technological environment; they should decide to what extent tasks in their living environment should be automatized (Harrington & Harrington, 2000).

We consider the impact in the home of existing and future equipment, or technology, on quality of life for older adults' and how it relates to the activities of basic human sustenance and independence as well as the enhancement of comfort and life enrichment. Both objective and subjective notions of quality of life will be considered.

Objective circumstances of physical independence, comfort, or convenience may not be experienced as actually providing independence, comfort, or convenience: they may not automatically lead to a higher *perceived* quality of life for older adults. Illustrative in this respect is the paradox of the VCR, of which the programming might cause so much trouble that many older people perceive it as a source of frustration rather than help (e.g., Docampo Rama, 2001). Another example of a tension between actual and subjective improvement is the use of physical aids (e.g., a hearing aid or a walking frame). They may enhance one's actual physical autonomy, but also put an emphasis on one's seniority or decreased independence and be experienced as a stigma.

Chapter Overview

In this chapter, we first discuss three categories of activities in the home, not being concerned with the role of technology. Our aim is to outline the range of activities from basic to advanced, their relation with human competence, the different human needs they are associated with, and their impact on the quality of life for older adults.

Next, we discuss home technology in relation to the fulfillment of these needs, and to one's perception of competence and self-efficacy. We start with the impact of home technology on older adults' physical independence. We address the role of the current technology we can hardly imagine living without and on which we almost completely rely, such as indoor plumbing and the washing machine. In addition, we give an example of a possible future technology in the home, currently being developed, to provide assistance for basic physical tasks. We discuss its impact on older adults' physical and psychological autonomy.

We then consider the influence of technology in the home on activities aimed at personal development and enrichment, and connectivity to the outside world. Technology might affect such activities in the home, but also activities connecting the resident to the outside world.

The Meaning of Needs and Need Fulfillment for Quality of Life in Old Age

Need obviously depends on the situation. When starving, one tends not to worry about finding fresh white bread with sunflower seeds and iced, cherry-flavored lemonade—any bread or drink will do. The deprivation of Internet access could certainly be an annoying consequence of a power outage, but in midwinter, just trivial compared to having the heating turned off at the same time. Not being able to get upstairs independently and to take a shower without assistance is a more critical issue than replacing the gas stove with the newest ceramic cooker.

These are just a few examples illustrating different levels of human needs and desires and their likely prioritization: the fulfillment of the more basic needs comes before the fulfillment of less basic or advanced needs. One step further, one could think in terms of a hierarchy of needs: those absolutely necessary to physically survive underpin those that might be perceived as higher-order and "luxury" needs. This ordering is reminiscent of the classical Maslow pyramid of human needs (i.e., physiological needs, safety, love, self-esteem, and self-actualization; Maslow, 1954).

Although this seems valid reasoning, it probably oversimplifies the interrelationship between different needs, their fulfillment, and their meaning for one's quality of life. What is the meaning of the different levels of need fulfillment for older adults' quality of life, and what is the impact of failure? To an extent, need and quality of life are relative to one's circumstances and expectations; they depend on one's *perception* of the situation. For example, Hagerty (2000) describes the effect of social comparison of income as a determinant of subjective well-being, indicating the relativity of affluence; sufficient resources per se do not guarantee human happiness. We may therefore not simply assume that the disposal of resources, physical support, or comfort equals need fulfillment, and, in addition, that this need fulfillment would automatically lead to a higher perceived quality of life or a higher subjective well-being.

Subjective well-being can be defined as people's cognitive and affective evaluations of their lives (E. Diener, M. Diener, & C. Diener, 1995). Rapkin and Fischer (1992) couch older adults' life satisfaction in terms of personal goals: perceived life satisfaction involves the comparison between the current circumstances and one's personal standards or ideals. Related to these evaluations are factors such as the experience of everyday competence and perceived self-efficacy (Bandura, 1997).

Everyday Competence as a Determinant of Quality of Life

The independent performance of basic activities of daily living (ADLs), such as eating, bathing, and dressing, as well as instrumental activities of daily living (IADLs), such as cooking healthful meals, adequately dealing with medication, and doing the laundry, is a precondition for autonomy and independence in everyday life (Lawton, 1990). As a likely companion of aging, physical and cognitive declines often put pressure on the independent performance of these activities.

Losing everyday independence is one of the major concerns of currently healthy and independently living older adults when thinking about their future (Willis, 1996). Reduction of autonomy is seen as a serious threat to quality of life. The ultimate threat is the involuntary move to an assisted living facility or a nursing home (e.g., AARP, 2000; Shafer, 2000). Such concerns are directly related to the performance of ADLs and IADLs. However, they involve much more than merely physiological survival. Implying independence and autonomy, the performance of ADLs and IADLs also relates to self-efficacy and self-esteem (Bandura, 1997; M. M. Baltes & Wahl, 1992; Parmelee & Lawton, 1990).

Besides sustaining a situation of independence and autonomy, personal growth and development are also important aspects of a meaningful life, regardless of one's age. In the last few decades, perhaps reinforced by higher life expectancy and more healthy years in old age, life beyond the age of 60 has been recognized as the "crown of life," rather than the age of limitation and decline (Bühler, Brind, & Horner, 1968). It is considered as another developmental phase, with its own challenges and opportunities.

A distinction must be made between obligatory activities in the home, usually ADLs and IADLs, and voluntary, or optional activities, associated with leisure and life enrichment. Challenges may be desirable and stimulating for optional activities and enhance one's feeling of competence and self efficacy, whereas challenges in ADLs and IADLs may be experienced as a burden, absorbing one's energy for more desired activities, and lowering one's perceived overall self-efficacy.

Theoretical perspectives on human competence in old age compatible with this distinction are the Challenge Hypothesis, stating that the performance of optional tasks and activities experienced as moderately difficult is associated with greatest well-being (Brim, 1992; Pushkar, Arbuckle, Conway, Chaikelson, & Maag, 1997), and the Baltes and Baltes life-span model of Selective Optimization with Compensation, or SOC (P. B. Baltes, 1987; P. B. Baltes & M. M. Baltes, 1990). The SOC model contends that optimally and selectively dealing with one's physical and mental resources and adequately compensating for loss can result in sustained subjective quality of life for older individuals, with the possibility of personal growth.

Desirable activities go beyond the adequate performance of maintenance tasks such as dealing with medication regimens, or paying bills. Activities aimed at life enrichment and self-fulfillment are considered to be critical aspects of successful aging (Rowe & Kahn, 1998). Examples of such activities are reading, keeping a scrapbook of the grandchildren, watching movies, studying a foreign language, experimenting with a new recipe, or learning computer skills. Such activities, which involve the willingness to accept new challenges and to engage in lifelong learning, have been termed *enhanced* activities of daily living, or EADLs (Rogers, Meyer, Walker, & Fisk, 1998). EADLs primarily aim at personal enrichment, self-fulfillment, and pleasure. EADLs exceed the possibly noncommittal nature of leisure activities in general, in that they also imply the adjustment to changes, for example keeping up with technological and communicative developments, such as the Internet, and taking advantage of them. Baltes and her colleagues made a similar distinction between a basic level of competence and an expanded level of competence (M. M. Baltes, Maas, Wilms, Borchelt, & Little, 1999).

In sum, older people's quality of life in the home as influenced by everyday life activities can roughly be divided into three categories: basic activities of daily living, instrumental activities of daily living, and enhanced activities of daily living (ADLs, IADLs, and EADLs, respectively). These activities are associated with the fulfillment of different human needs, ranging from physiological needs such as eating and bathing, to psychological needs such as self-expression and self-fulfillment. The adequate performance of basic and instrumental tasks (ADLs and IADLs) serves human sustenance as a physical and practical precondition for the fulfillment of higher order needs. In addition, ADLs and IADLs intrinsically represent higher-order needs, such as the psychological need for autonomy and independence. In this way, the adequate or inadequate performance of ADLs and IADLs affects one's self-image and self-esteem.

The consequences of worsening ADL and IADL performance by older adults are most obvious and most immediate by affecting their everyday physical and psychological independence. They might therefore take priority when it comes to improvement and support. In addition, being relieved from heavy or complicated household tasks might save one's resources for EADLs, consistent with Baltes and Baltes' (1990) SOC model.

Apart from the indirect limitating of EADLs by being occupied by ADLs and IADLs, the direct limitating of EADLs might have consequences for quality of life, impeding one's personal development and reducing pleasure and entertainment in everyday life. The positive effect of the direct improvement, encouragement, and extension of EADLs might be tremendous, contributing to older persons' quality of life by making life more meaningful and interesting.

Supporting ADLs and IADLs may require a different approach than supporting EADLs, considering the different meaning of challenges in these domains. Technology may serve to reduce obligatory and unpleasant tasks; but it might add stimulating and interesting challenges to the home environment for the purpose of life enrichment and fun. We first discuss the potential impact of technology on physical independence, focusing on tasks in the domains of ADLs and IADLs. Next, we address the technological enhancement of EADLs.

THE IMPACT OF HOME TECHNOLOGY ON OLDER ADULTS' INDEPENDENCE

Wahl and Mollenkopf (2003) showed that, in spite of many measurable improvements in the home, a significant impact of everyday technology on the emotional life of older adults does not seem to exist, with the exception of central heating. Their critical discussion of easily assumed advantages of current technology in the home suggested a discrepancy between the objective and subjective impact of technology on older adults' quality of life.

On the one hand, the concept of quality of life refers to objective criteria such as one's standard of living, resources available, and a person's physical autonomy. Technology in the home could enhance a high standard of living. On the other hand, quality of life refers to one's perceptions of the objective situation: subjective well-being.

The possible discrepancy between standard of living and the experience of well-being should be taken into account in order to understand the potential of technology in the home to improve older people's quality of life. More specifically, this tension might apply to the experience of autonomy: technological support can both enhance and limit one's perception of autonomy and independence.

Current Household Technology in the Home

The general introduction of the electrical washing machine in the 1950s in many households relieved women in particular of a time-consuming and physically strenuous household task. As with the automation of other household tasks, the washing machine made life easier and probably more pleasant by providing physical support and saving time for other activities. Whereas in the early years of its diffusion it might have been welcomed as a convenience and a luxury, it has become an indispensable appliance in today's households. What once was luxury became a standard.

The current generation of older adults experienced the revolutionary spread of many household technologies with a large impact on physical tasks and time management in the home. They were young when indoor plumbing, central heating, the washing machine, the refrigerator, the gas stove, and the vacuum cleaner became common (History of American Technology, 2003). This technology accompanied them into old age as an integrated part of their everyday lives. Taking that technology away, as we imagined in the opening paragraph of the chapter, would probably show its impact on the lives of older adults' most clearly, especially when it comes to physically demanding tasks.

Without specifically aiming at the support of older adults, a generic effect of the abovementioned household technologies is that they raised the general standard of physical support in the home. In this way, technological developments stretched the limits of physical independence for older adults in particular, as physical strength, which gradually declines with age, was less of a constraint.

However, a potential, and ironic, down-side of labor saving household technologies is that they raised the users' expectations and, in the end, increased the amount of work in the home (Schwartz Cowan, 1983). For example, washing machines, dryers, electric irons, and indoor plumbing changed society's standards of acceptable hygiene, creating new obligations. This paradox may be a potential risk for ubiquitous technology in future homes as well (Edwards & Grinter, 2001).

With these critical notes in mind, we next discuss an example of new assistive home technology to enhance physical independence in the home. Aging might involve a reduction of physical, and possibly mental, autonomy. What might be the potential of new technology to prolong physical independence?

Future Home Technology for Physical Assistance: An Example

The usefulness or desirability of most appliances in the home is usually not a main topic of discussion once the technology is generally adopted in the majority of the households; however, for newly introduced or developed technology, it might be an important issue. Focusing in this section on physically supportive home technology, we illustrate this discussion with a new device for the home currently being developed, called the *gesture pendant* (Starner, Auxier, Ashbrook, & Gandy, 2000). It is a possible element of a technology-rich home environment based on a "Smart Home" concept. Its development is part of the Aware Home Research Initiative (AHRI) at Georgia Institute of Technology (AHRI, 2003; Mynatt & Rogers, 2002).

The gesture pendant is a wireless device that enables the residents of a smart home to give the house commands in the form of hand movements to perform particular tasks, instead of physically performing these tasks (see Figure 1). For example, different gestures would close the blinds, lock the doors, open the front door, dim the light, or raise the thermostat. The gesture pendant is worn around the neck, similar to a necklace, and has a camera and motion sensors. It could take commands, as well as monitor the physical activities of its user, and even be used to get help in case of an emergency.

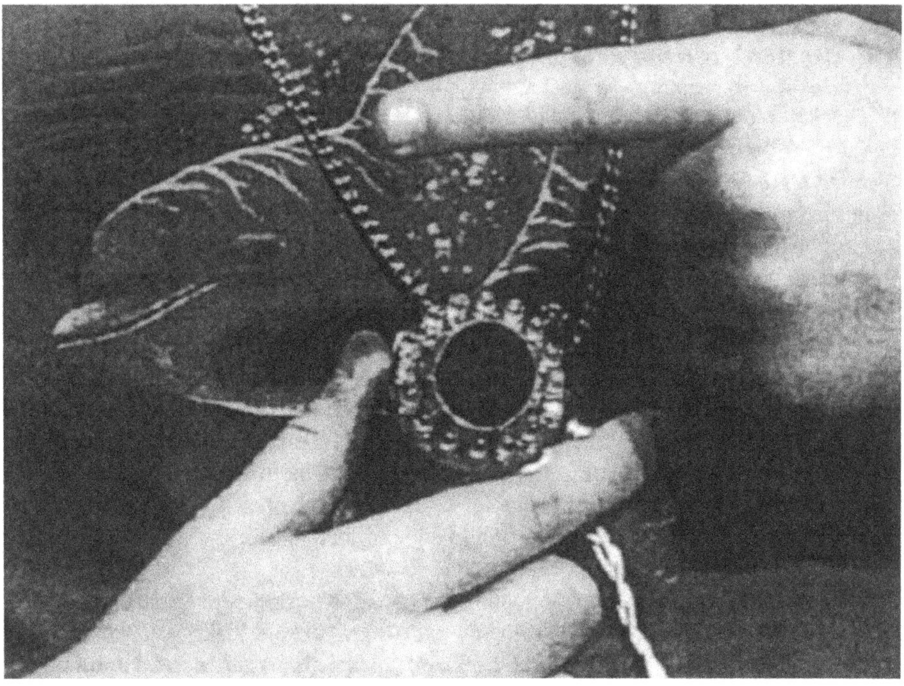

Figure 1. The gesture pendant is a context-aware universal remote that recognizes and translates gestures into commands for home appliances. It was developed by Thad Starner at Georgia Institute of Technology (AHRI: Aware Home Research Initiative, 2003).

A potential side benefit of this technology is that it can track tremors in the hand and possibly serve as an early indicator of neurological impairments such as Parkinson's disease (Starner et al., 2000) or indicate that a Parkinson's patient has not taken adequate medication.

Unlike common household appliances, the gesture pendant is not a known and accepted typical technology in someone's home. Whether such a device would be accepted and adopted by older adults is an open question. A recent study examining older adults' perception of a technology-rich home environment—the Aware Home at Georgia Tech—revealed opinions, considerations, and ideas about the introduction of newly developing technology in the home as it might become available in the coming decades (Sarkisian, Melenhorst, Rogers, & Fisk, 2003). In this study, 44 participants in the age range of 65-75 years were taken on an individual tour through the house and presented with five selected smart home devices. Structured interviews were conducted after the tour to assess the participants' opinions about living in a technology-rich home environment in general and about the five devices in particular. The gesture pendant was one of the examined technologies.

How does the current generation of independently living older adults envision the potential of a device such as the gesture pendant? How do they think about relying on another technology in the home, how do they perceive the benefits, and what are possible drawbacks? Would they think it would improve their quality of life?

The Tension Between Assistance and Autonomy

The participants in the Sarkisian et al. (2003) Aware Home study were relatively healthy and living independently. Main issues regarding the gesture pendant addressed by many of these older adults were physical independence and autonomy. The comments indicated that most of them expected the necessity of a gesture pendant for themselves several years from now as shown in the following quote of one of the participants: "At the present time, I don't think it would be worthwhile for me. But, a couple of years from now who knows what kind of physical condition I'm going to be in, and then it might be very, very useful" or, according to another participant, "I think it's great, yeah. I think anything that delays your need to go into a nursing home or need assistance is a plus."

The participants tended to think about the new technology in terms of necessity and need fulfillment related to disability, rather than a self-explanatory convenience being the future standard in the home for everyone, such as the washing machine and the vacuum cleaner are to date. For example: "I'd rather do it myself. That's because I'm an independent person. Right now, I would have limited use for it—it would be a play toy, it would be a time saver, an energy saver to a degree."

The latter comment also refers to reliance on assistive technology related to autonomy and independence. Whereas technology might allow people to keep in control and to stay in their homes longer, thereby increasing their independence and autonomy, it can be also perceived as reducing their independence and autonomy if it would overrule them or if relying on the technology would negatively affect their lifestyle. Too much or too little support were both perceived as a threat to one's autonomy. The following comment epitomizes concerns of overreliance on technology: "This could be a double-edged sword because you might start using these things which you never had before, couldn't do or didn't know were available, but then it might make one become incredibly lazy. If everything is done without exerting any effort you know. That could tend to turn one into a huge couch potato. I mean, that's the thought that hits me: making life too easy. I don't want everything made too easy at the snap of a finger. No."

The phenomenon this participant describes has been observed in nursing homes where the staff assisted the resident with everything, leading to loss of the residents' autonomy, and even decline in capability (see review in Parmalee & Lawton, 1990). The "nonuse of competence" is negatively related to one's self-efficacy and can have a negative impact on independent everyday functioning (Wahl, 1991). Some participants in the Aware Home study envisioned similar consequences of extended use of assistive technology in the home.

Other participants in the Aware Home study emphasized the *choice* allowed by technology, implying that technology provides the *possibility* of being independent, for example: "I can see how this would be a fantastic thing. And it should not make you feel any less independent or, you know, it wouldn't make you feel like, well hey, they are tying me here. It would afford you some sense of individuality, you know, you have a choice in other words." However, according to another participant: "Well it's a reminder that I'm not able to be totally independent."

The options the technology offers and the free choice of either using or not using (and controlling) these options were recurring issues. The discussion about the gesture pendant illustrated a general discussion, also in the field of Gerontechnology (e.g., Harrington & Harrington, 2000), about physical autonomy potentially provided by technology, and how supportive technology in the home environment might affect both *being* physically independent and *feeling* independent and in control. This exceeds the level of mere task performance. The gesture pendant, for example, most likely provides physical assistance, but its use also involves psychological issues such as independence and autonomy, related to self-efficacy, self-esteem, and choice.

The way traditional appliances support the residents of the home is probably not felt to be stigmatizing by older adults, but sometimes to their benefit in particular or even critical. In a similar manner, although not exclusively developed for older users, the gesture pendant might be to their benefit in particular. Once an integrated part of every home, it could be both a convenience for everyone and at some point a necessary support to people who develop physical impairment as they age, helping them to retain control over their home environment (analogous to the television remote control). In the perspective of stretching the limits of older adults' physical independence, a device such as the gesture pendant could be a next step.

In sum, the question remains whether raising the general level of convenience and support in the home is desirable in general. "Making life too easy" is a risk many of the participants in the Aware Home study recognized as the undesirable side of the double-edged sword of assistive technology in the home. On the other hand, the implementation of basic assistive technology for physical tasks in the home as a standard could (further) delay the practical effects of becoming physically less capable, without forcing people to drastically change their lifestyle and daily habits and without stigmatizing older persons. It would reduce the feeling of "a reminder that I'm not able to be totally independent."

The Impact of Home Technology on Life Enrichment

Good quality of life' involves more than being free of pain and hunger or experiencing a sufficient degree of physical autonomy. Quality of life also means personal development, cognitive stimulation, and a satisfying interaction with one's social environment. As older adults spend much time in the home, they especially might benefit from a home environment that enhances activities fulfilling these needs.

Media such as the radio, the television, the telephone and, more recently, the personal computer with an Internet connection are examples of technology with a potentially large influence on enhanced activities of daily living. Below, we will discuss the impact of the television as an example of a traditional medium fully integrated in older adults' homes, and the Internet as an example of an upcoming technology not massively used by older adults yet.

The Television: Central in Older Adults' Homes

Since its introduction in the 1950s, the television gradually surpassed the radio as the central medium device in the home. The television today is an affordable standard device in almost every household, which makes using it an option for many people. Both operating and enjoying it require little effort or special skills, although finding the desired channels via complex menus and poorly designed remote controls may cause problems for users of all ages, especially for older users (Docampo Rama, 2001). Programming the video recorder is still a classical disaster. Leveling these barriers would make the television and its applications even more accessible for individuals of all ages but perhaps especially for older people.

In spite of possible usability obstacles, the elderly use the television most intensively; no age group spends more time watching television than older adults (Mediascope, 2003). In the year 1999, people 65 years and older spent on average almost 5 hours per day watching television in North America (Statistics Canada, 2003). In Europe, the average was 4 hours daily, varying per country (e.g., Scotland 5.6 hours, Norway 2.5 hours; Scottish Statistics, 2003; Statistics Norway, 2003). Apparently, the television is attractive to older adults in particular. What are typical television benefits for older adults, and how does the television influence their quality of life?

The television has the potential to entertain, to be a source of information and education, and a window to the world. Some of the elderly might use it to compensate for loneliness and boredom (Perloff & Krevans, 1987). For people tied to the home because of limited mobility, it may be a welcome source of diversion. Moreover, the television provides a relatively effortless way to keep up to date and obtain information independently.

Although the television might be indispensable for older adults because it fulfills much of their need for entertainment and information, it is also associated with diabetes and obesity (Hu, Li, Colditz, & Graham, 2003), cognitive passivity, superseding other activities, and life dissatisfaction especially in an elderly population (e.g., Rahtz, Sirgy, & Meadow, 1989; Sirgy et al., 1998). Such side effects might in the end reduce quality of life.

However, good or bad, the presence of the television in the home is hardly under discussion anymore: it is a given. For example, in 2000 there was at least one television in 97% of American households (Mediascope, 2003). In Europe, 96% of the households had a television (Statistic in Focus: The European TV Broadcasting Market, 2003). Its use is still based on choice, although possibly tempting and addictive. It has many potential benefits, but also could stand in the way of more stimulating physical and cognitive activities. The television is a clear example of a technology omnipresent in our homes, in spite of undesirable side effects on everyday life. Many older adults perceive the television as indispensable (Perloff & Krevans, 1987), indicating that the medium enhances their subjective well-being. From their perspective, its entertainment value may supercede the possible drawbacks, even if these are objectively measurable.

Technology Potential and Choice

The television offers possibilities. It is, in part, the designer's responsibility to make these possibilities available and accessible for people with different cognitive and physical abilities. For example, designing a remote control to compensate for general age-related perceptual and motor changes would probably not hurt younger users, whereas it would benefit older users, preventing frustration and feelings of incompetency.

An advantage of generic technology design and implementation, earlier mentioned in relation to the gesture pendant, is that it allows people to keep using the technology as they age and to keep its use integrated in their everyday life. People of different ages may choose to use the television differently, and may change their use over the years. The technology should allow for adjustment to changing circumstances and needs and for continuing the use in new situations.

Once the possibilities are there, the user has the option for when and how to use them and whether to integrate them into daily life. A study about media use by older adults showed selectivity in using both new and established communication technology (Melenhorst, 2002). The selectivity shown in this study indicated that older users are critical users, well able to make their choices and to recognize technology opportunities. Although television use was not directly assessed in the Melenhorst study, this selective attitude may also apply to their use of such established technology in the home.

The Internet: Gradually Entering Older Adults' Homes

Recent statistics show that people who frequently use the Internet spend substantially less time watching television (Lee & Kuo, 2002; UCLA Internet Report, 2001). It seems that using the Internet and watching television in part draw from the same leisure time. What would be the role of the Internet in older adults' life, now and in the future? Would the personal computer, with its possibilities, take over some of the functions the television currently fulfills in their lives? And how does using the computer relate to enhanced activities of daily living, involving new challenges, personal development, and the adjustment to changing circumstances? This is addressed by the Challenge Hypothesis (e.g., Brim, 1992), which contends that the fulfillment of moderately difficult tasks and activities is experienced as most satisfying and associated with greatest well-being, the Internet might have greater potential to improve older adults' subjective well-being than the television currently has. Its interactive nature might provide a stimulating challenge for older individuals, assuming that it will be manageable for people of all ages.

New Technology: A Stimulating Challenge or an Impassable Hurdle?

The Internet revolution was in full swing when part of the current generation of older adults had just retired. Another cohort was on the verge of retirement, and yet another was still employed. The older adults in the former two groups are probably the last people who, as a whole, did not automatically become familiar with the computer and its applications through their jobs. The majority of the slightly younger older adults most likely did, as many jobs involve the use of computers and e-mail in one way or the other. This makes people currently 60 years and older an exceptional cohort: while close in age, their experience with a drastic and increasingly unavoidable technological innovation varies enormously.

Both the television and the Internet have the potential to offer the user a window to the world. However, in contrast with the television, the Internet window is not as open for everyone (Digital Divide, 1999). Part of the reason is the uneven diffusion of the medium as a consequence of different employment influences in the current cohort of older adults. Furthermore, using the basic functionality of the television requires little skill, whereas using the Internet typically requires the ability to use a computer (there are exceptions such as Web TV, but their use is not widespread). In addition, the television allows the user to be passive, whereas the Internet is typically interactive. The interactive nature of the medium and the requirement to learn a new skill might be stimulating challenges and interesting opportunities to some older adults, but impassable hurdles to others.

The abovementioned factors currently make the Internet a potential source of life enrichment, cognitive stimulation, and inclusion for older adults, yet a potential source of frustration and exclusion at the same time. As an example of the latter, contact information in some radio and television programs is provided only in the form of an e-mail address without the alternative of a postal address or a telephone number.

The current rise of Internet use indicates the contrast between the *potential* of a new, widespread technology for older adults in the long term and its *actual impact* for older adults soon after its general introduction. To date, the Internet is still accessed by a minority of the older adults (Kinsella & Velkoff, 2001). Consequently, this generation takes relatively little advantage of the new medium, although the proportionate rate of increase in Internet use is highest for the over 50 age group (Kinsella & Velkoff, 2001).

The potential of the Internet for future generations of older adults is probably great. They will have grown up with the Internet and the computer or become familiar with it at a sufficient level of comfort to be able to take advantage of its merits. Its richness in combination with its interactivity affords tailored information and communication (e.g., e-mail, chat) in the home. If its design accommodates age-related perceptual, motor, and cognitive changes, the computer with an Internet connection is an excellent example of a flexible, adaptive home technology with the potential to provide its users life-long benefits.

Perceived Technology Benefit

In previous sections, we addressed the issue of being raised with a particular technology that became part of one's existence versus being confronted with it later in life. The age at which one becomes acquainted with new technology affects both the recognition and appreciation of the technology's potential and the person's access to its potential (see Docampo Rama, 2001). In part, they go together: the inability to handle a device clouds its benefits, even if they are there in potential. Especially for new technology, such as the Internet, older adults' motivation to gain access by learning a skill or, for example, to buy a computer, is crucial to making the benefits available. What motivates older adults to adopt an innovation?

Some of the older adults in the Aware Home study (Sarkisian et al., 2003) tended to think in terms of necessity when judging the newly developed gesture pendant. It would be very useful for people with disabilities, but in their current state, the participants often perceived a lack of perceived benefit: "Not necessary, yet." The idea that it could provide them with just another standard convenience in the home was expressed by only some of the participants.

Apparently, innovative technology is experienced and judged differently from familiar technology. Whereas everyone seems to take the merits and demerits of familiar technology in the home for granted, the potential benefits of new technology may have to be more obvious. For new technology to be attractive, its benefits should noticeably improve the current situation (see also Rogers, 1995). Older adults might be even more critical adopters, as learning to deal with new technology takes them, on average, more time and effort (e.g., Kelley & Charness, 1995).

A study about the appreciation of communication methods among older adults showed this critical and selective attitude (Melenhorst, 2002). Established media, such as the telephone, were judged more positively than new media, such as e-mail, especially by its most frequent users. Its adoption and appreciation seems largely based on obvious benefits, perceived as a valuable addition to the merits of traditional communication methods. Examples were e-mail communication with relatives over different time zones, sending electronic pictures, having access to specific information (health information for example), and feeling connected with peers who were also online.

Moreover, the traditional media, with many perceived benefits, were not rejected because of perceived disadvantages, although they were certainly not negligible. In addition, e-mail was rejected by some of the participants not because of disadvantages or cost, but because of the lack of explicit benefits. In other words, the *presence of benefit determined the positive judgment about adopted technology, in spite of drawbacks; and the absence of benefit* determined the negative judgment about new technology, even before cost was considered. The perceived absence of benefit seemed enough for many older adults to not even think about engaging in the challenge the new technology might offer them.

This does not imply that cost was unimportant. The perception of technology benefit or need seemed to be important incentives for older adults to *overcome* expected cost, such as expenses, lack of skills, and unfamiliarity. In terms of a cost-benefit analysis, technology benefits should obviously outweigh costs. Age-related decline of physical and mental resources may change cost perception and, as a consequence, benefit perception. As costs may be perceived as larger, benefits should be even more obvious to be worthwhile (Melenhorst, 2002; Melenhorst, Rogers, & Caylor, 2001).

The "resource management" described above is consistent with the Baltes and Baltes model of selective optimization with compensation (SOC) mentioned before. One of the assumptions of SOC is that, with age, people increasingly tend to focus their limited energy on activities and domains that they perceive as being most essential and valuable in their lives. Optimizing their performance in these domains is a way of maintaining well-being in spite of limitations. In this perspective, the choice of using new technology by older adults can represent either a voluntary, elective selection, extending one's repertoire, or a necessary compensation, for example, in reaction to loss of physical strength. However, to be "selected" and used, the technology should show its benefit in either case.

WHEN WILL TECHNOLOGY IN THE HOME IMPROVE OLDER ADULTS' QUALITY OF LIFE?

Technology in the home has shown its potential to enhance both basic physical activities and activities aimed at life enrichment. On the other hand, it bears the risk of over-support, hindrance, and exclusion. It might even introduce new household tasks, societal demands, and create rather than save labor. The central question in this chapter has been: When will technology in the home improve older adults' quality of life? Note that it is not a yes or no question—will technology benefit or will it not? Instead, we must consider the circumstances and nature of the technology to understand when it will be beneficial and supportive and when it will not. To answer this question we reviewed the impact of widely diffused, extant technology and the impact of new technology.

The examples of established and new technologies raised similar issues from different angles. Key issues were the potential discrepancy between objective and subjective improvement of quality of life and, related, the tension between support and perceived autonomy, control, and self-efficacy.

Technology has the potential to either enhance or reduce one's autonomy. This was illustrated by the example of how failing technology can reveal our dependence and vulnerability and also in the tension between support and independence (e.g., the gesture pendant)—whether technology overrules its user or encourages passivity. Reduced choice and autonomy adversely affects self-efficacy and independence. An example of this at a societal level is the obligatory use of the Internet to access particular information sources or communication channels (i.e., having no other options available).

As traditional technology has been gradually adopted into the home, new assistive technology might be successfully adopted and used by older adults when it is introduced into the home before its use becomes critical to the user's independence. A technology already present in the home when its use is optional might be used first at convenience level: useful, but not a necessity. The user "discovers" its benefits or potential benefits, and, once its assistance is needed, the psychological barrier of acceptance would be avoided to a great extent. Being an option, technology allows users to voluntarily integrate its support into their lives, adjusted to their developing needs or wishes.

However, until its full diffusion, any new technological development will confront part of the population in their later years. The ideal situation of an early introduction described above is not always possible. This phase unavoidably leads to different levels of use and benefit for different parts of the population.

Although the Internet seems a promising example of an adaptive technology in the future, it currently is also an example of a technology dividing society into haves and have-nots, users and nonusers (e.g., Digital Divide, 1999). Many people in the latter category are older adults. By not going online, they might save their resources by not being bothered with something that they consider not worth it, but on the other hand miss potential benefits they just could not perceive. Making the potential benefits of new technology visible and explicit, and the potential costs transparent to older users would give them the chance to make a well-considered choice. It might reduce the gap between older and younger users. The conveyance of specific technology benefits to older segments of the population is critical to encourage its general adoption and avoid exclusion as much as possible. Obviously, this does not apply to the Internet alone.

In conclusion, technology in the home can improve both the objective and subjective quality of life for older adults when it allows for flexible use over the life span, accommodating different levels of competence and need. Flexibility of technological applications afford older adults the choice to use new technology, and younger people to keep the technology integrated into their lives while they grow older, in a way they deem beneficial. In addition, its costs should be transparent, and its benefits clear, especially to older users.

ACKNOWLEDGMENTS

Research reported in this chapter was supported in part by the following grants: Grant P01 AG17211 from the National Institutes of Health (National Institute on Aging) under the auspices of the Center for Research and Education on Aging and Technology Enhancement (CREATE); National Science Foundation Award 0121661 "The Aware Home: Sustaining the Quality of Life for an Aging Population"; and the Aware Home Research Initiative industrial partners.

REFERENCES

AARP. (2000). *Fixing to stay: A national survey on housing and home modification issues—Executive summary.* Washington, DC: American Association of Retired Persons.

AHRI: Aware Home Research Initiative. (2003). [Online]. Available: http://www.cc.gatech.edu/fce/ahri.

Baltes, P. B. (1987). Theoretical propositions of life-span developmental psychology: On the dynamics between growth and decline. *Developmental Psychology, 23,* 611-626.

Baltes, P. B., & Baltes, M. M. (1990). Psychological perspectives on successful aging: The model of selective optimization with compensation. In. P. B. Baltes & M. M. Baltes (Eds.), *Successful aging: Perspectives from the behavioral sciences* (pp. 1-34). New York: Cambridge University Press.

Baltes, M. M., Maas, I., Wilms, H.-U., Borchelt, M., & Little. T. D. (1999). Everyday competence in old and very old age: Theoretical considerations and empirical findings. In P. B. Baltes & K. U. Mayer (Eds.), *The Berlin aging study: Aging from 70 to 100* (pp. 384-402). Cambridge: Cambridge University Press.

Baltes, M. M., & Wahl, H.-W., (1992). The dependency-support script in institutions: Generalization to community settings. *Psychology and Aging, 7,* 409-418.

Bandura, A. (1997). *Self-efficacy: The exercise of control.* New York: Freeman.

Bouma, H. (1992). Gerontechnology: Making technology relevant to the elderly. In H. Bouma & J. A. M. Graafmans (Eds.), *Gerontechnology* (pp. 1-5). Amsterdam: IOS Press.

Brim, O. G. (1992). *Ambition: How we manage success and failure throughout our lives.* New York: Basic Books.

Bühler, C., Brind, A., & Horner, A. (1968). Old age as a phase of human life: Questionnaire study. *Human Development, 11,* 53–63.

Diener, E., Diener, M., & Diener, C. (1995). Factors predicting the subjective well-being of nations. *Journal of Personality and Social Psychology, 69,* 851-864.

Digital Divide. (1999). [Online]. Available: http://www.ntia.doc.gov/ntiahome/fttn99/FTTN.pdf

Docampo Rama, M. (2001). *Technology generations handling complex user interfaces.* Dissertation. Eindhoven University of Technology.

Edwards, W. K., & Grinter, R. E. (2001). At home with ubiquitous computing: Seven challenges. In G. D. Abowd, B. Brumitt & S. A. N. Shafer (Eds.), *Ubicomp 2001,* 256-272.

Hagerty, M. R. (2000). Social comparisons of income in one's community: Evidence from national surveys of income and happiness. *Journal of Personality and Social Psychology, 78,* 764-771.

Harrington, T. L., & Harrington, M. K. (2000). *Gerontechnology: Why and How.* Maastricht: Shaker Publishing.

History of American Technology. (2003). [Online]. Available: http://web.bryant.edu/~history/h364material/wmn_chr/appliance.htm.

Hu, F. B., Li, T. Y., & Colditz, G .A. (2003). Television watching and other sedentary behaviors in relation to risk of obesity and type 2 diabetes mellitus in women. *Journal of the American Medical Association, 289,* 1785-1791.

Kelley, C. L., & Charness, N. (1995). Issues in training older adults to use computers. *Behaviour & Information Technology, 14,* 107-120.

Kinsella, K., & Velkoff, V. A. (2001). An aging world: 2001 (U.S. Census Bureau, Series P95/01-1). Washington, DC: U.S. Government Printing Office.

Lawton, M. P. (1990). Aging and performance on home tasks. *Human Factors, 32,* 527-536.

Lee, W., & Kuo, E. C. Y. (2002). Internet and displacement effect: Children's media use and activities in Singapore. *Journal of Computer-Mediated Communication, 7*(2). Available online at: http://jcmc.indiana.edu/vol7/issue2/singapore.html.

Maslow, A. H. (1954). *Motivation and personality.* Oxford, England: Harpers.

Mediascope. (2003). [Online]. Available: http://www.mediascope.org/pubs/ibriefs/mua.htm.

Melenhorst, A. S. (2002). *The adoption of communication technology in later life: The decisive role of benefits.* Dissertation. Eindhoven University of Technology.

Melenhorst, A. S., Rogers, W. A., & Caylor, E. C. (2001). The use of communication technologies by older adults: Exploring the benefits from the user's perspective. *Proceedings of the Human Factors and Ergonomics Society 45th Annual Meeting* (pp. 221-225). Santa Monica, CA: Human Factors and Ergonomics Society.

Merriam-Webster. (2000). *Webster's tenth new collegiate dictionary.* Springfield, MA: Merriam-Webster Inc. Publishers.

Merriam-Webster. (1991). *Webster's ninth new collegiate dictionary.* Springfield, MA: Merriam-Webster Inc. Publishers.

Mynatt, E. D., & Rogers, W. A. (2002). Developing technology to support the functional independence of older adults. *Ageing International, 27,* 24-41.

Parmalee, P. A., & Lawton, M. P. (1990). The design of special environments for the aged. In J. E. Birren & K. W. Schaie (Eds.), *Handbook of the psychology of aging* (3rd ed., pp. 464-488). San Diego: Academic Press.

Perloff, R. M., & Krevans, J. (1987). Tracking the psychosocial predictors of older individuals' television uses. *Journal of Psychology, 121,* 365-372.
Pushkar, D., Arbuckle, T., Conway, M., Chaikelson, J., & Maag, U. (1997). Everyday activity parameters and competence in older adults. *Psychology and Aging, 12,* 600-609.
Rahtz, D. R., Sirgy, M. J., & Meadow, H. L. (1989). The elderly audience: Correlates of television orientation. *Journal of Advertising, 18,* 9-20.
Rapkin, B. D., & Fischer, K. (1992). Framing the construct of life satisfaction in terms of older adults' personal goals. *Psychology and Aging, 7,* 138-149.
Rogers, E. M. (1995). *Diffusion of innovations* (4th ed.). New York: Free Press.
Rogers, W. A., Meyer, B., Walker, N., & Fisk, A. D. (1998). Functional limitations to daily living tasks in the aged: A focus group analysis. *Human Factors, 40,* 111-125.
Rowe, J. W., & Kahn, R. L. (1998). *Successful aging.* New York: Pantheon Books.
Sarkisian, G., Melenhorst, A. S., Rogers, W. A., & Fisk, A. D. (2003). Older adults opinions of a technology-rich home environment: Conditional and unconditional device acceptance. *Proceedings of the Human Factors and Ergonomics Society 48th Annual Meeting* (pp. 1800-1804). Santa Monica, CA: Human Factors and Ergonomics Society.
Schwartz Cowan, R. (1983). *More work for mother: The ironies of household technology from the open hearth to the microwave.* New York: Basic Books, Inc.
Scottish Statistics. (2003). [Online]. Available: http://www.scotland.gov.uk/stats/sss/docs/sss10-06.asp.
Shafer, R. (2000). *Housing America's seniors. Executive summary.* Cambridge, MA: Joint Center for Housing Studies, Harvard University.
Sirgy, J. M., Lee, D-J., Kosenko, R., Meadow, H. L., Rahtz, D., Cicic, M., Jin, G. X., Yarsuvat, D., Blenkhorn, D. L., & Wright, N. (1998). Does television viewership play a role in the perception of quality of life? *Journal of Advertising, 27,* 125–142.
Starner, T., Auxier, J., Ashbrook, D., & Gandy, M. (2000). The gesture pendant: A self-illuminating, wearable, infrared computer vision system for home automation control and medical monitoring. *Proceedings of the International Symposium on Wearable Computers (IEEE 2000),* (pp. 87-94).
Statistic in Focus: The European TV Broadcasting Market. (2003). [Online]. Available: http://www.eu-datashop.de/download/EN/sta_kurz/thema4/np_02_24.pdf.
Statistics Canada. (2003). [Online]. Available: http://www.statcan.ca/Daily/English/010125/d010125a.htm.
Statistics Norway. (2003). [Online]. Available: http://www.ssb.no/english/subjects/07/02/30/medie_en/tab-2003-03-31-06-en.html.
UCLA Internet Report. (2001). [Online]. Available: http://ccp.ucla.edu/pdf/UCLA-Internet-Report-2001.pdf.
Wahl, H.-W. (1991). Dependence in the elderly from an interactional point of view: Verbal and observational data. *Psychology and Aging, 6,* 238-246.
Wahl, H.-W., & Mollenkopf, H. (2003). Impact of everyday technology in the home environment on older adults' quality of life. In K. W. Schaie & N. Charness (Eds.), *Impact of technology on successful aging* (pp. 215-241). New York: Springer.
Willis, S. L. (1996). Everyday problem solving. In J. E. Birren & K. W. Schaie (Eds.), *Handbook of the psychology of aging* (4th ed., pp. 287-307). San Diego: Academic Press.

CHAPTER 15

Technology and Chronic Conditions in Later Years: Reasons for New Hope

William C. Mann and Sumi Helal

As we age, we experience normal declines in vision, hearing, cognition, and movement. We also may accumulate chronic conditions such as arthritis, stroke, heart and circulatory disorders, glaucoma, and tinnitus. While these age-related declines and chronic conditions have the potential to severely affect our ability to do everyday tasks, it is possible to design our environment, and add tools—assistive devices—that facilitate independence. Many assistive devices are common "mechanical" tools such as wheelchairs, walkers, bath seats, and magnifiers. Electronic assistive devices, many of which use computer-based technology, further extend the potential of helping a person remain independent. These include voice-output devices for people who are blind, assistive-listening devices for people with hearing impairment, reminder devices for people with cognitive impairment, and power-assisted wheelchairs for people with mobility impairment. Assistive devices such as these are effective in reducing the impact of declines in functional status and in reducing health-related costs (Mann, Ottenbacher, Fraas, Tomita, & Granger, 1999).

The assistive devices mentioned above differ from a new generation of assistive devices that are labeled "smart technology." While there is no universally accepted definition of smart technology, most definitions include the concept of technology that is capable of "sensing" something, and "acting" appropriately based on what is "sensed." Heating and air conditioning systems represent a very basic "smart technology system" that has been available for many years. The thermostat is a "sensor" that, based on a user's previously set instructions for room temperature, determines if the room is too hot or cold and signals the heater or air conditioner to turn on or off. Home security systems provide another example of a smart system that has been available for quite some time. The next generation of "smart assistive technology" will be bundled into systems to provide an amazing variety of assistive functions, increasing the potential for older people to remain independent much longer, significantly lifting the burden of caregiving from family members, and providing formal health providers with "intelligent" reports based on continuous monitoring of health and related behaviors.

In this chapter, we begin with an overview of age-related chronic conditions. This is followed by a discussion of basic, low technology assistive devices, their evolution and utility. The chapter concludes with a look at more recent and future high-technology assistive devices that offer hope for increased independence and quality of life. We call this last section "smart house technology," and include a futuristic description of Mrs. Holden's life in a smart house. Had Mrs. Holden been born 50 years earlier and needed assistive devices in her later years, she would not have had smart devices or smart homes. In fact, in the middle of the last century, even basic assistive devices looked different than they do today, and there were far fewer assistive devices available for purchases. Basic mobility devices, such as walkers and wheelchairs, were available, but had an institutional look, and many people were embarrassed to use them. The general attitude toward disability was also different. Fifty years ago people with disabilities were not encouraged to remain active in their home and community. Today we promote approaches to maintaining independence in the face of disability, and many countries have enacted legislation to promote the integration of people with disabilities into the community. Advances in assistive technology are a major factor in helping people with disabilities remain active and independent.

AGE-RELATED IMPAIRMENTS AND CHRONIC DISEASES

Many older persons face one or more impairments: sensory (vision and hearing), physical (neuromotor and musculo-skeletal), or cognitive impairments. We discuss these impairments and two age-related diseases. A review of all diseases of later years is not possible in a single chapter; however, arthritis and stroke are discussed because of the high incidence of arthritis and the severity of impact and resultant impairments of stroke. More than half of persons 65+ have arthritis and, while its severity varies from person to person, for many it affects performance of basic daily tasks. Stroke has the potential to result in multiple impairments: vision, hearing, mobility, speech, and cognition. Arthritis and stroke represent diseases of aging that often result in impairments that could be addressed through the use of assistive technology.

Vision Impairment

Most elders with vision impairment are not totally blind, but have partial or low vision. Advances in ophthalmic surgery and more effective medical control of eye diseases have contributed to the greater proportion of older persons who have low vision versus total blindness. The sharp increase in the 65+ age group has also contributed to a steady increase in the number of persons with useful partial sight. Although persons with a visual impairment may retain usable vision, loss of sight requires spending more time and effort in accomplishing tasks. Visual impairment is related to difficulty in performing activities of daily living (ADL) and to decline in health and psychosocial status (Wallhagen, Strawbridge, Shema, Kurata, & Kaplan, 2001). Assistive devices are available to maximize remaining visual ability.

Approximately 8.6% of the population over 18 years of age in the United States experiences problems with vision despite corrective measures (U.S. Department of Health and Human Services, 2003). Among elderly persons, the incidence is higher

(Long, Crews, & Mancil, 2000). Vision impairment in older persons has been documented and described by numerous investigators (Clark, Bond, & Sanchez, 1999; Wahl, Oswald, & Zimprich, 1999; West et al., 2003). Older persons are a heterogeneous population, which makes it difficult to determine the exact number of persons who are blind or have a severe visual impairment. However, one recent study estimated that 82 out of 1,000 older persons have a serious visual impairment (National Center for Health Statistics, 1990). Another study projected that by 2020, there will be approximately 54 million blind persons over age 60 worldwide (World Health Organization, 1997).

Vision impairment may result in a restricted field of vision or a diminished ability to see sharpness of detail, read standard-size print, determine color or depth perception, see contrasts, adjust to changes in light or glare, or locate objects (Marmor, 1992). Vision loss can affect a person's activities of daily living (ADL), leisure pursuits, education, vocation, and social interaction. The severity of vision loss and the resulting limitations vary with such factors as age of onset, support systems available, and coping strategies (Bailey & Hall, 1990).

Hearing Impairment

Hearing impairment is one of the five most common chronic conditions of aging. One of three persons over age 64 has some hearing impairment. The prevalence among older persons will increase, as there are more people age 45 to 64 with hearing loss than those 65 and older (Davenport Hearing Aid Center, 2003). There are many assistive devices available for persons with hearing impairment, but often loss of hearing is so gradual that many elders accept the loss as simply a normal process of aging and do not seek assistance. Hearing loss affects negatively on communication, and decreased communication can in turn result in isolation and depression (Arlinger, 2003). Hearing loss can also affect safety and health in other ways as well, such as failing to hear a fire alarm or not being able to clearly understand a pharmacist's directions for taking medications.

Hearing loss can result from exposure to excessively loud noise over time, from hypertension and neurological diseases such as stroke, or from the side effects of medications. The three major types of hearing loss are conductive, sensorineural, and central. Many older people experience "mixed hearing loss," a combination of conductive and sensorineural impairments.

Conductive hearing loss occurs when sound waves cannot reach the inner ear; the impact of conductive hearing loss is similar to wearing ear plugs. Hearing aids are often quite effective for persons with conductive hearing loss. Sensorineural hearing loss relates to damage to the cochlea and surrounding hair cells—the cells that send electrical signals to the brain. Many people refer to sensorineural hearing loss as nerve deafness; one common type among older persons is presbycusis, which first causes loss of hearing in high pitched sounds, and over time, lower and lower pitch sound loss occurs. Tinnitus is also a sensorineural disorder, causing ringing or buzzing in the ears and affecting more than 90% of persons 65+. Central hearing loss relates to damage of nerves leading to the brain or damage to the brain itself. Stroke, traumatic brain injury, or vascular disorders can result in central hearing loss.

Cognitive Impairment

Approximately 10% of people over the age of 65 have cognitive impairments that affect their functional abilities (Beck, Benson, Scheibel, Spar, & Rubenstein, 1982). Dementia is a broad term used to describe a decline in intellectual functioning that is not a normal part of the aging process and that results in cognitive impairment in areas that include language, memory, visuospatial skills, personality, and cognition (Glickstein, 1997). Alzheimer's disease is a form of dementia and is the most common cause of dementia in persons over 65 (National Institute on Aging, 2000). Cognitive impairments resulting from strokes are the second most frequently occurring type of dementia (Butin, 1991).

The major characteristic of Alzheimer's disease is a progressive decline in cognitive function. Cognitive skills include orientation, insight, attention, memory, abstract thinking, calculating, problem solving, as well as organization (Abreu & Toglia, 1987). With impaired cognitive function, a person may experience confusion, disorientation, limited attention, memory impairments, and decreased ability for learning (Poole, Dunn, Schell, & Barnhart, 1991). Other common symptoms of Alzheimer's disease include language disorders, apraxia, visuoconstructive difficulty, and difficulty with abstract thinking (Aho, Harmsen, & Hatano, 1980; Pynoos & Ohta, 1991). As Alzheimer's disease progresses, it affects a person's independent function. For example, a person may become disoriented, fail to recognize familiar faces, or be unable to match names with faces. In some cases, the person may experience hallucinations. A person's ADL are influenced by impaired cognition. Limited performance in instrumental activities will occur first, including shopping, money management, meal preparation, household chores, and communication. A person with Alzheimer's disease will decline in ability to meet safety, self-care, household, leisure, social interaction, and vocational needs. Eventually, the person will lose the ability to perform basic activities of daily living, including eating, dressing, toileting, grooming, bathing, and locomotion.

Stroke

Stroke is defined as rapidly developing clinical signs of focal (or at times global) disturbance of cerebral function lasting more than 24 hours or leading to death with no apparent cause other than that of vascular origin (Aho et al., 1980). A more recent definition adds the term "RIND" for Resolvable, Intracerebral, Neurological, Deficit, which can last several days—"stroke" is now defined as lasting more than just a few days. The most outstanding feature of stroke is weakness or paralysis of the extremities on one side of the body. Other common symptoms include dysphasia or aphasia (51%); memory impairment or disorientation (47%); and loss of, or altered sensation (36%) (Mayo, 1993). Most stroke survivors are not institutionalized, but live in their own homes or with relatives. Coping with the long-term effects of stroke while living at home often requires the use of assistive devices and home modifications. There has been significant study of the rehabilitation of individuals who have survived a stroke, suggesting that older stroke survivors have much difficulty in coping with the long-term effects (Ottenbacher & Jannell, 1993).

Arthritis

Arthritis is a serious disabling condition affecting large numbers of people. It is estimated that 40.5 million people in the United States have some form of arthritis, with the prevalence greatest among elderly persons (Centers for Disease Control and Prevention, 2003). The prevalence of arthritis is high in other parts of the world as well: in Australia, for example, arthritis is the most common chronic condition, affecting 14.6 percent of the population (Arthritis Victoria, 1995).

The impact of arthritis on the daily activities of elderly persons has been documented in several studies. Using the Longitudinal Study on Aging, Yelin and Katz (1990) determined that for those elderly persons who had arthritis and no other chronic conditions, 66% experienced limitations in physical activities, with 25% reporting limitations in ADL or instrumental activities of daily living (IADL). For those elderly persons who had arthritis and at least one other chronic condition, 82% had limitations in physical activity, and 41% were limited in ADL. When these same persons were examined two years later, the percentage of persons with ADL/IADL limitations increased significantly for both groups.

Kosorok, Omenn, Diehr, Koepsell, and Patrick (1992) studied the number of restricted activity days of elderly persons. Using data from the 1984 Supplement on Aging of the National Health Interview Survey, they determined an annual average of 31 restricted activity days for elderly persons: six days were associated with falls; four days with heart disease; four days with arthritis and rheumatism; two days each with high blood pressure, cerebrovascular disease, and visual impairment; and one day each with atherosclerosis, diabetes, major malignancies, and osteoporosis. Arthritis was ranked in this study as the second most important cause of restricted activity days among elderly persons.

Verbrugge, Lepkowski, and Konkol (1991) concluded that elderly persons with arthritis had more difficulty in physical functions, personal care, and household care than elderly persons without the disease. Disability was greatest in the areas of walking, reaching, stooping, and other physical functions, especially those that require endurance and strength. The symptoms of arthritis (joint pain, stiffness, reduced range of motion) contribute to a reduction in activity. Eventually, reduced activity can result in loss of physical function. The impact of activity and exercise for persons with arthritis is a frequent topic in the literature. After review of 97 articles, Buchner, Beresford, Larson, LaCroix, and Wagner (1992) concluded that exercise and activity can positively affect functional status and reduce pain. Assistive technology can help many people with arthritis in maintaining a higher level of activity than would otherwise be possible.

Disability is closely linked to functional status. Verbrugge, Gates, and Ike (1991) suggested that a long duration of arthritis, recent medical care for arthritis, and obesity were risk factors for disability. Abyad and Boyer (1992) confirmed the association of disability and obesity in elderly persons with arthritis. Additionally, disability rates for persons with arthritis appear to be increasing (Yelin, 1992).

ASSISTIVE DEVICES

There are several definitions for assistive device. It is used synonymously with the term "assistive technology device" defined in the Assistive Technology for People with

Disabilities Act (1998) as: any item, piece of equipment, or product system, whether acquired commercially off the shelf, modified or customized, that is used to increase, maintain, or improve functional capabilities of individuals with disabilities. This very broad definition includes items designed specifically for persons with certain kinds of disabilities. It also includes products that reach a broader market that may not have originally been designed for overcoming impairments. A cane is clearly an assistive device; however, if a person needs a garage door opener, then the Tech Act definition would include it as an assistive device. Likewise, a microwave oven may be a convenience for the general population, but it may be an essential assistive device to enable a person with a cognitive impairment to heat food.

Until recently, most reports of the value of assistive technology have been limited to case studies and anecdotal reports. A randomized controlled trial was conducted, evaluating a system of assistive-device service provision designed to promote independence and reduce healthcare costs for physically frail elderly persons. One hundred four home-based frail elderly living in western New York, newly referred to home healthcare, were assigned to one of two groups (52 treatment, 52 control). All participants underwent a comprehensive functional assessment and evaluation of their home environment. Participants in the treatment group received assistive devices and home modifications based on the results of the evaluation. The control group received "usual care services." After the 18 month intervention period, both groups declined in functional status, but there was significantly decline for the control group; pain also increased significantly for the control group. In a comparison of healthcare costs, the control group required significantly more expenditures for institutional care. This study found that the rate of functional decline can be slowed, and institutional and certain in-home personnel costs reduced through a systematic approach to providing assistive devices and home modifications (Mann et al., 1999).

The following sections discuss assistive technology that addresses vision, hearing, physical and cognitive impairment, stroke and arthritis (two very common diseases of aging), and pain.

Assistive Devices and Vision Impairment

Compensatory strategies for low vision include illumination techniques and use of contrast, magnification, memorization of location, and auditory and tactile feedback. Compensatory strategies may include the use of optical, nonoptical, low-technology, and high-technology devices to improve functional visual performance. Optical devices, such as high-powered lenses and telescopic spectacles, are items prescribed by an ophthalmologist or optometrist and may require specialized training and periodic reevaluation. Nonoptical devices include items that are readily available and require no special training, such as felt-tip markers and large-print books. Low-technology devices, such as a standard cassette recorder, require little training and may include simple adaptations such as large-print or raised-line indicators on the controls. High-technology devices refer to more sophisticated electronic technology, such as computers and reading machines, that may require specialized training.

Assistive devices are playing an increasingly important role in improving the functional performance of visually impaired persons. Advances in computer technology are a major factor in the development of products for people with vision impairment. In a special issue of the *Journal of Visual Impairment and Blindness* on technical issues for the 1990s, Dixon and Mandelbaum (1990) described how technological advances in the use of printed material have improved communication for persons with severe visual impairments. Orr and Piqueras (1991) raised several issues related to the use of assistive technology by older persons with visual impairments and suggested that some devices may be intimidating (Mann, Hurren, Karuza & Bentley, 1993). Low-tech devices, such as magnifiers, writing guides, and mobility canes, have been available for many years; high-tech devices include print-enlargement systems that use closed circuit television systems. These systems allow many persons with low vision to read printed text. Alternatively, computer systems can be set up with voice output, and text can be "scanned" in for immediate or future reading for persons with severe low vision or who are blind.

In a study of 30 home-based older visually impaired persons, a high rate of assistive-device use was found, and study participants also expressed the need for several additional devices they did not own (Mann et al., 1993). The interaction of assistive devices with environmental factors was demonstrated in a study of problems with magnifier use by older persons. This study found that for most people, the problem was not with the magnifier, but with insufficient lighting, which could be easily remedied by increasing the level of task lighting (Mann, Hurren, Tomita, & Charvat, 1997).

Assistive Devices and Hearing Impairment

A study of 35 elders with hearing impairment reported that study participants used an average of 11.5 assistive devices per person (Mann, Hurren, & Tomita, 1994). They used devices that addressed hearing impairment, but more of the devices addressed physical impairments than hearing, underlining the complexity of multiple impairments faced by older persons. This study found a high rate of dissatisfaction with the devices they were using—almost one out of three devices. Much of the dissatisfaction was targeted at hearing aids. Cognitive impairment also has an impact on assistive-device use: older hearing-impaired persons with severe cognitive impairments used about half as many assistive devices as those older hearing-impaired persons who were not cognitively impaired.

While dissatisfaction with hearing devices is high, there have been significant advances. Prior to the last decade, hearing aids for the most part only increased the volume of sounds, however, the most recent advances include digital hearing aids that adjust the pitch of the sounds received to levels that the hearing aid user can best hear. Cochlear implants offer another major technological advance. Worldwide, an estimated 59,000 people have received cochlear implants, including approximately 13,000 adult recipients in the United States (National Institutes of Health, 2000).

Assistive Devices and Physical Impairment

There are more devices to assist elders with physical impairment than any other type of assistive devices. These devices assist with mobility, with tasks involving the hand, with bathing, eating, washing, dressing, leisure activities, driving, and more. We will report on some of the more common of these assistive devices in this section.

Of non-institutionalized persons over 65 years old, 14.3% have difficulty walking, and 15.9% have difficulty getting outside (Hobbs & Damon, 1996). The cane ranks as the most widely used assistive device, and elderly persons use more canes than any other age group. There are 4.4 million cane users in the United States, 61% over 65 years old (LaPlante, Hendershot, & Moss, 1992). While canes are widely used for support, owners of canes used for mobility report a high number of problems in their use. Almost half of all problems encountered with canes relate to difficult or risky use, resulting in incidents of tripping, getting tangled up, or of abandonment because the cane was too heavy or clumsy to use (Mann, Granger, Hurren, Tomita, & Charvat, 1995). Professional assistance in selecting an appropriate cane was recommended for reducing these problems. Basic canes have not changed much over the last several centuries. We do have canes now with multiple "feet" that provide more stability, and canes constructed of lighter-weight materials make for easier use.

Walkers rank second behind canes in number of users. There are 1,687,000 walker users in the United States, and 1,307,000 (77%) are used by persons 65 years old and over (LaPlante et al., 1992). Canes can support up to 25% of a person's weight; walkers support up to 50% and provide a much more stable base for persons with impaired balance. Yet walkers also rank high in terms of numbers of users experiencing problems in their use (Mann, Hurren, Tomita, & Charvat, 1995). Walker design has improved significantly over the past 50 years: a basic walker is a simple metal-frame device. We now have walkers with seats, so the user can stop and rest; with baskets and trays so the user can transport items; and with wheels and brakes for easier, safer use.

Bath devices are among the most common of all assistive devices. Phillips and Zhao studied the assistive-device use of 227 adults with disabilities, and found that bath chairs were the third most common assistive device, behind wheelchairs and canes (Phillips & Zhao, 1993). Bynum and Rogers (1987) found that bathtub benches and shower chairs were among the top two most common assistive devices in the homes of elders receiving home care. Malassigne and Amerson (1992) reporting on results of a survey of 800 members of the Paralyzed Veterans of America, found that 63% of study participants used a seat in the bathtub, and 72% were satisfied with the device. A similar pattern is found in other Western nations: in Sweden, Parker and Thorslund (1991) report mobility aids as the most common, followed by personal hygiene aids including bathtub benches. In their study, 90% of the elderly participants had difficulty bathing and 75% of these used a bathing device. In Great Britain, Shipham (1987) found an 82% use rate for bath chairs. Another British study demonstrated that patients who were evaluated, trained, and given appropriate devices at discharge used safer bathing practices, and had a significantly higher rate of use of their bathing devices than a control group (Chamberlain, Stowe, & Wright, 1981). Bath devices have also improved in design and number; lighter weight, more attractive bath seats and benches are now available. Such consumer products that we all can use, such as shower and tub organizers to hold soap and other bathing products, are very helpful for people with disabilities.

Assistive Devices and Cognitive Impairment

Mann, Karuza, Hurren and Tomita (1993) investigated needs for assistive devices by home-based elders with impairments, and found that elders with cognitive impairment used the least number of assistive devices among all elders with impairments. Elders with cognitive impairment also had higher levels of dissatisfaction with the devices they owned.

Nochajski, Tomita, and Mann (1996) found that devices for physical disabilities tended to be more readily accepted and used than devices for cognitive impairments by elderly persons with cognitive impairment. Furthermore, cognitively impaired participants with higher Mini-Mental Status Examination (MMSE) scores (15 to 23 out of 30) and their caregivers, tended to accept devices more than did participants with lower MMSE scores (10 to 14). Mann, Hurren, Charvat, and Tomita (1996) found that use of cognitive devices by elders with Alzheimer's disease dropped, and used more devices that assisted their care providers in caring for ADLs.

The use of cognitive devices and interventions has been shown to be effective. Bailey (1993) found that switch-controlled assistive devices help some persons with severe physical and cognitive impairments with activities such as exploring their environment and socializing with friends. Other studies have shown that assistive devices, such as memory aids, can be used to stimulate conversation, enhance socialization, and reinforce accurate memories (Bourgeois, 1993).

An emerging area of research is focused on assisting persons with cognitive impairment in their daily activities through the use of computerized devices. Mihailidis, Fernie, and Cleghorn (2000) developed a computerized cueing device to assist with the task of hand washing in elderly persons with dementia. The computerized system consisted of a nine-step verbal prompting device equipped with transducers to monitor step completion and did not require user input or intervention for effective operation. A pilot study using this device was conducted with an 81-year-old male with alcoholic dementia, and results demonstrated an improved performance based on the level of assistance needed for task completion, with fewer caregiver interactions required.

People with moderately severe Alzheimer's disease have been taught to use a simple computer program. They learned to do a simple task, using a touch screen, on a computer. The investigators reported that subject acceptance of the training was positive, motivation was high, and that there appeared to be a transfer of the trained skills into real situations (Hofmann, Hock, Kuhler, & Muller-Spahn, 1995). Another study looked at behavioral approaches to improving ADL with nursing-home patients with dementia. This study reported that patients improved in independence in dressing and increased participation in dressing when prompted (Rogers et al., 1999).

Recent research and development has been targeted at a prompting system that would guide elders with cognitive impairment through basic daily task. Related studies suggest that even severely cognitively impaired individuals might benefit from a prompting device or system. One of these studies found that by increasing opportunities for independent activity with severely cognitively impaired elders, using more non-directive and directive verbal assists rather than physical assists, independence was increased. This study also found that there were more appropriate requests for help when independence was encouraged (Rogers et al., 2000). A study of nursing home residents found similar results. Certified nursing assistants were trained to use more prompting and praise, rather than physical assistance with elders with dementia. Following 20 weeks of intervention, active engagement almost doubled (Engelman, Altus, & Mathews, 1999).

Advances in electronic technology over the past 50 years have led to the development of smart devices and smart house systems that offer significant potential to help people with cognitive impairment by providing prompts and reminders, as well as managing many of the basic tasks that would otherwise require someone to handle. These smart devices and smart home systems are discussed later in the chapter.

Assistive Devices and Stroke

Two related studies report first that older stroke survivors living at home owned a mean of 16 assistive devices and used about 80% of them (Mann et al., 1995), and second, that one year later, 20% of the sample had either moved into a nursing home or died (Mann, Hurren, & Tomita, 1995). The remaining study participants experienced significant declines in physical and health status and demonstrated coping strategies such as acquiring additional assistive devices.

Assistive Devices and Arthritis

In a study of assistive-device use by home-based older persons with arthritis, 66 persons were assigned to a moderate or a severe arthritis group according to the impact of arthritis on their activities (Mann, Hurren, & Tomita, 1995). Study participants in the severe arthritis group had more chronic diseases, a higher level of pain, and a lower level of independence in self-care activities than study participants in the moderate arthritis group. Similarities between the groups included relatively poor health, high rate of medication use, depression, use of a high number of assistive devices (about 10 per person), and an expressed need for additional devices, such as reachers, magnifiers, grab bars, jar openers, and hearing aids. Generally, there was a high rate of satisfaction with the assistive devices used. Most study participants missed being able to participate in at least one activity; most of these activities were active and many related to leisure time. Findings also revealed that study participants had inadequate information on assistive devices.

Pain

Pain can also limit activity and have a significant negative impact on quality of life. Results from the randomized controlled trial reported above found that assistive-device use may actually reduce one's perception of pain. In examining the use of assistive devices by persons with physical disabilities, pain may be an important moderator variable.

The impact of pain on functional status of home-based elders has been addressed in two studies. In a prospective follow-up study of 100 hip-fracture patients, Borgquist, Bilsson, Lindelow, Wiklund, and Thorngren (1992) and colleagues found a relationship between pain and ADL. Barberger-Gateau, Chaslerie, Dartigues, and Commenges (1992) studied 4,050 community-dwelling individuals in France and found that dependence was correlated with joint pain, age, sex, education, rural setting, dyspnea, hearing dysfunction, visual impairment, and depression. While few studies have addressed the relationship of pain to functional status, it appears that pain may be related to a decline in independence among the elderly.

SMART HOUSE TECHNOLOGY

Smart-home products have been available since the 1980s. In 1988, smart houses, or smart homes were described as featuring a single integrated wiring system that replaced conventional wiring, to provide a distribution of power and information transfer to household appliances. Through plugging household appliances into any outlet in the house, a switch could then be designated to operate the appliance (Sampson, 1988).

Today, smart-house products offer features such as video security system with infrared wireless zones; home theater; DVD, CD, and Internet access throughout the home; DSL connection; satellite TV; and lighting control. Access and operation of a majority of the system features can be executed through the use of simple remote controls. A personal computer acts as the control center of the smart home (Bannan, 2001).

Cost-effectiveness studies for increasing the independence of elders to continue living in their own homes promote the use of high tech assistive devices (Tang & Venebles, 1999). Technology, such as home-health monitoring systems, smart houses, emergency response systems, and computers, have been found to decrease the need for placement in assisted-living facilities or nursing homes. Other studies suggest remote monitoring of health status facilitates the timely implementation of appropriate care, thereby decreasing the rate of morbidity among elders (Celler et al., 1995). Implications for the use of home monitoring systems are increased opportunity for independent living, living in place for elders and individuals with degenerative conditions, and remote health monitoring (Cooper & Keating, 1996).

Smart houses of the very near future will integrate several underlying technologies. The underlying components that make the *Gator Tech Smart House* possible include (1) sensors, (2) computers, (3) software, (4) user input devices, (5) user output devices, (6) mechanical hardware, (7) wireless technology, (8) batteries and other power sources, (9) the Internet, (10) indoor location tracking technology, (11) smart appliances, (12) other related technology, and (13) human based service providers.

Applying Smart House Technology to the Needs of Frail Elders

The next generation of smart houses will integrate all aspects of home monitoring, assisting, and communications. Smart houses for frail older persons will simplify and assist in the completion of everyday tasks and address four major "monitoring responsibilities":

1. Monitor the house
2. Monitor the elder's health
3. Monitor the elder's independence or self-care related needs
4. Monitor the elder's activities, movement, and behavior in the house

Assisting in Everyday Tasks

Future smart houses will be assistive environments representing an evolution from a single assistive device to a space of integrated elements that collectively assists an elder. Based on monitored context and on interpretation of events and specific rules, the smart house will be able to proactively assist the resident in basic daily activities. It will keep the resident informed and aware and will also do things like opening or locking the front door and providing medication reminders.

Monitor the House

The two examples of smart technology mentioned in the Introduction (security system, air temperature controlled system) represent home monitoring systems that monitor some aspect of the home. It is also possible to (1) monitor appliances (e.g., turn the stove off if it has been on too long, or the pot has become too hot); (2) monitor lighting, inside and outside the home to ensure there is appropriate lighting for time of day, weather conditions, and activity in the room; (3) monitor moisture; that is, detect leaks or water on the floor and provide appropriate alerts; (4) monitor dangerous gases such as carbon monoxide from a furnace; (5) monitor humidity and adjust to appropriate levels; (6) monitor the mailbox and provide an alert when mail has been delivered.

Monitor the Elder's Health

Several products are currently available that can monitor a person's health remotely. There are two basic types: (1) system with sensors that collect physiological data (e.g., blood pressure, body temperature, blood-glucose level) on the person and send it to a family member or health provider; (2) system that relies on self-report—the person answers (daily or weekly) a set of health-related questions on a computer-based device, and this information is sent to a family member or health provider.

An important aspect of health for many elders relates to taking the appropriate medications at the appropriate times of day, following directions such as taking with liquids or food. The smart house will alert the person when it is time to take the medication or, alternatively, alert the person not to take medication if it has already been taken. This same system will alert the pharmacy when a medication is getting low, so the pharmacist can contact the person to arrange delivery. The medication containers will have a bar code that the system will use to tell the person which medication they are holding and to share additional information, such as "Be sure to take with food," or "If you are experiencing dizziness from this medicine, contact your doctor right away."

Monitor the Elder's Independence or Self-Care Related Needs

Monitoring self-care and implementing strategies with distance technology significantly expands the use of "telemedicine" from a focus on body signs and compliance with medical regimens to a functional (self-care) perspective. Considering a person's self-care needs within a smart house is a relatively new area. A recent study researched the effectiveness of a system of services which included Internet-based communication (audio and video) between live-alone older persons and physical disabilities and health care professionals, that (1) monitored daily self-care needs, (2) identified the need for a home healthcare visit, (3) suggested self-administered interventions, and (4) provided information and training to enhance daily functional performance. This study found a high rate of acceptance of this approach (Malcolm et al., 2001).

Monitor the Elder's Activities, Movement, and Behavior in the House

Monitoring a person's movement, activities and behavior within the home is also a new area. University and corporate research has recently been directed at developing systems to do just that. These systems will determine if someone has fallen and alert a family member or formal care provider. They will determine, for example, if someone has not arisen from bed, or has tossed and turned all night, has had too many or too few trips to the bathroom, has not been drinking enough liquids, or eating enough food. In each case, an appropriate person could be alerted to a potential need for assistance.

A Day in The Smart House

It is the year 2010—five years after the publication of this chapter. Some of the smart house features described below were available in 2005, others were in the research and development stage. This year, 2010, all are available in product form. The University of Florida Research and Development team, working with several corporate and university partners, created a flexible package called the Gator Tech Smart House system.

Mrs. Holden is 87 years old, widowed, and lives alone. She no longer drives because her vision is moderately impaired, and arthritis makes it difficult for her to grasp the steering wheel and turn. She is also a bit forgetful, but still plays cards regularly with a group in her community. Her daughter, Sarah, who lives 12 miles away, assists with trips to the grocery store and doctor, while Mrs. Holden's friends and neighbors help with trips to church and the community center where she plays cards. Mrs. Holden had a fall two years ago, which resulted in a hip fracture; but she recovered well and walks slowly with a cane. Sarah recently assisted her mother in a move from her large, two-story home of 52 years into a smaller ranch style home set up as a smart house.

Bathroom and Bedroom

When Mrs. Holden gets up in the morning, the time is tracked. If it is significantly earlier or later than normal, the smart house notes this. Mrs. Holden completes her basic activities of daily living—taking a shower, combing her hair, getting dressed. While her forgetfulness is not severe, the house is ready to help with prompting through these activities, should Mrs. Holden need help. Monitors and speakers in the bathroom and bedroom provide auditory and visual prompts for brushing teeth, combing hair, bathing, and dressing. The house "remembers" if these activities have been completed. If Mrs. Holden cannot remember if she brushed her teeth she can ask the house: "Have I brushed my teeth, already?" She will get an appropriate reply.

Hall and Kitchen

After completing morning ADLs, Mrs. Holden goes to the kitchen to prepare her breakfast. On the way from the bedroom, her movement is tracked by a number of sensors. Should she stop and stand in one place or fall, speakers close to where she is standing will ask her if she requires assistance. She can respond that she has stopped to look at some pictures, and the house will "know" she is safe. The movement tracking system is also able to ascertain if she has fallen and will ask her if she needs to have a call placed for emergency assistance. She could respond that she fell but did not hurt herself, is able to get up, and there is no need for a call. Alternatively, she could instruct the house to place the call. If she does not respond at all, the house places calls in this order: first to Sarah, but if she does not answer, second to a Personal Emergency Response System (PERS) operator for emergency assistance. The house tells either Sarah or the PERS operator that Mrs. Holden has fallen, and she is not verbally responding to questions. Mrs. Holden does not fall today, but feels much more secure knowing that if she falls, the smart house will find her help.

Mailbox

On the way to the kitchen, the smart house tells Mrs. Holden that the morning paper has been delivered to her mailbox.

Kitchen

The smart house offers a number of features for Mrs. Holden in the kitchen. Like her bedroom and bathroom, the kitchen has flat screen monitors hanging on the wall and small speakers unobtrusively placed on the walls. Mrs. Holden can call on the house for suggestions for breakfast, which will provide a menu based on the diet recommended by a nutritionist who works with her family physician, Dr. Bremmer. Today she decides she is going to make instant oatmeal, using her smart microwave oven. The smart microwave oven recognizes what Mrs. Holden is preparing from an electronic tag on the package and automatically sets up the appropriate time and power.

Mrs. Holden takes four medications, one of which she takes in the morning and evening, the other three, just in the morning after breakfast. Today, a half hour after eating breakfast, she is still enjoying the morning paper and has not yet taken her morning medications. The smart house reminds Mrs. Holden that it is time to take them.

Living Room

The living room has an entertainment system that is also integrated into the smart house. This system includes music (CD player and AM/FM tuner), video (VHS, DVD, and cable TV), Internet access, and integration with files stored on her computer, including her digital picture collection. Today she sits on her couch and verbally instructs the entertainment system to turn to FM 88.7, and she listens to National Public Radio. The smart house notes this.

Beyond the House: Getting Out

At noon, Mrs. Holden prepares a light meal. The smart house interaction is very similar as at breakfast. Following lunch, Mrs. Holden's next door neighbor stops by to give her a ride to the community center, where she plays cards for the afternoon, followed by dinner out with her bridge partner. The house records her lunch, the visit of her neighbor, the departure time of Mrs. Holden, and her arrival time back at the house.

Mrs. Holden always carries her smart phone with her when she leaves the house. Her smart phone used to serve as an interface for human interaction with the smart house until the recent significant upgrades in voice recognition technology. While traveling outside the home, the smart phone tracks her location and can provide assistance if she requires it, as well as make traditional voice calls. When she returns home, information about her trip outside the home will be sent (using Bluetooth wireless) to her computer.

Back Home for the Evening

Arriving home after dinner, Mrs. Holden is reminded by the smart house to take her evening medication. She then watches the news for an hour, completes her nighttime ADLs and retires to bed about 9 P.M. The smart house notes all of this. Before she retires to bed, Mrs. Holden asks, "Are all doors and windows locked?" The house quickly checks and gives her an accurate security report. Mrs. Holden's bed includes biosensors that track her body temperature, heart rate, breathing rate, and movement while sleeping; the house notes these measurements.

Data Analysis and Reports

An important aspect of Mrs. Holden's smart house is its capability to interpret data, including movement patterns. If Mrs. Holden tosses and turns every night, then this is not unusual behavior and probably not a reason, at least by itself, to send an alert to Sarah. On the other hand, if Mrs. Holden typically sleeps calmly, but on one night is tossing and turning and is up from bed several times during the night, then Sarah will receive a call.

Sarah can get a daily, weekly, or monthly report of her mother's health and behavior through a secure Internet site. She checked the report of this "day in the smart house" and learned that her mother had slept well, was up at her normal time, had two good meals at home, did the laundry, was out in the afternoon and for dinner (which she knew was appropriate because she plays cards on this day), had taken her medications, and had had a medication delivery. Since her mother moved into the smart house, Sarah has felt much less stress and worry—much of the burden of caregiving had been lifted. Sarah still calls her mother every day, but she no longer feels she is being intrusive by asking many questions—she knows how her mother is doing before she places the call.

When Mrs. Holden visits Dr. Bremmer, he has available, through the Internet, a summary of her vital signs, sleeping, eating, and activity patterns. The large amount of data is analyzed, and Dr. Bremmer receives a one-page summary with clearly marked alerts for any potential health problems. Should Dr. Bremmer need more information, he can request more detailed reports. He has had several patients with this smart house technology and has been able to identify early symptoms of depression and dementia as well as provide appropriate treatment.

CONCLUSION

Technology is making everyone's life easier in many ways. Assistive technology has made significant advances since the middle of the last century and, coupled with everyday consumer products, offers older people with disabilities the opportunity to remain active and independent. We will continue to see significant advances in technology that will be applied to some of our more difficult-to-solve problems, such as applying technology to meet the needs of people with cognitive impairment. This should lead to a reduction of health related costs, a higher quality of service delivery, and improved quality of life for older persons.

REFERENCES

Abreu, B. C., & Toglia, J. P. (1987). Cognitive rehabilitation: A model for occupational therapy. *American Journal of Occupational Therapy, 41*(7): 439-448.

Abyad, A., & Boyer J. T. (1992). Arthritis and aging. *Current Opinion in Rheumatology, 4*(2), 153-159.

Aho, K., Harmsen, P., & Hatano, S. (1980). Cerebrovascular disease in the community: Results of a WHO Collaborative Study. *Bulletin of the WHO, 58,* 113-130.

Arlinger, S. (2003). Negative consequences of uncorrected hearing loss-a review. *International Journal of Audiology, 42,* 17-20

Arthritis Victoria. (1995). Arthritis and osteoporosis by numbers. Retrieved November 26, 2003 from www.arthritisvic.org.au/Arthritis/statistics.htm#.

Bailey, I. L., & Hall, A. (1990). *Visual impairment: An overview.* New York: American Foundation for the Blind.

Bailey, D. H. (1993). Technology for adults with multiple impairments: A trilogy of case reports. *American Journal of Occupational Therapy, 40*(4): 341-345.

Bannan, K. (2001). Digital domiciles. *PC Magazine,* p. 141.

Barberger-Gateau, P., Chaslerie, A., Dartigues, J. F., & Commenges, D. (1992). Health measures correlates in a French elderly community population: The PAQUID Study. *Journals of Gerontology, 47,* S88-S95.

Beck, J. C., Benson, D. F., Scheibel, A. B., Spar, J. E., & Rubenstein, L. D. (1982). Dementia in the elderly: The silent epidemic. *Annals of Internal Medicine, 97,* 231-241.

Borgquist, L. N., Bilsson, L. T., Lindelow, G., Wiklund, I., & Thorngren, K. G. (1992). Perceived health in hip fracture patients: A prospective follow-up of 100 patients. *Ageing, 21,* 109-106.

Bourgeois, M. S. (1993). Using memory aids to stimulate conversation and reinforce accurate memories. *Gerontology Special Interest Section Newsletter, 16*(4), 1-3.

Buchner, D. M., Beresford, S. A., Larson, E. B., LaCroix, A. Z., & Wagner, E. H. (1992). Effects of physical activity on health status in older adults, II: Intervention studies. *Annual Review of Public Health, 13,* 469-488.

Butin, D. N. (1991) Helping those with dementia to live at home: An educational series for caregivers. *Physical and Occupational Therapy in Geriatrics, 9*(3/4), 69-82.

Bynum, H. S., & Rogers, J. C. (1987). The use and effectiveness of assistive devices possessed by patients seen in home care. *Occupational Therapy Journal of Research, 7*(3), 181-191.

Celler, B. G., Lovell, N. H., Hesketh, T., Ilsar, E. D., Earnshaw, W., & Betbeder-Matibet, L. (1995). Remote monitoring of health status of the elderly. *Medinfo, 8*(1), 615-619.

Centers for Disease Control and Prevention, National Center for Health Statistics. (2003). Arthritis. Retrieved November 26, 2003 from http://www.cd.gov/hchs/fastats/arthrits.htm.

Chamberlain, A. T., Stowe, G., & Wright, V. (1981). Evaluation of aids and equipment for the bath: II. A possible solution to the problem. *Rheumatology and Rehabilitation, 20,* 38-43.

Clark, M., Bond, M., & Sanchez, L. (1999). The effect of sensory impairment on the lifestyle activities of older people. *Australasian Journal on Ageing, 18*(3), 124-129.

Cooper, M., & Keating, D. (1996). Implications of the emerging home systems technologies for rehabilitation. *Medical Engineering and Physics, 18*(3), 176-180.

Davenport Hearing Aid Center. (2003). Frequently asked questions. Retrieved November 20, 2003 from http://www.davenporthearing.com/faq.shtml.

Dixon, J. M., & Mandelbaum, J. B. (1990). Reading through technology: Evolving methods and opportunities for print-handicapped individuals. *Journal of Visual Impairment & Blindness, 84,* 493-496.

Engelman, K., Altus, D., & Mathews, R. (1999). Increasing engagement in daily activities by older adults with dementia. *Journal of Applied Behavior Analysis, 32,* 107–110.

Glickstein, J. (1997). *Therapeutic interventions in Alzheimer's disease: A program of functional skills for activities of daily living and communication.* Gaithersburg, MD: Aspen Publishers.

Hobbs, F. B., & Damon, B. L. (1996). *65+ in the United States* (p. 61). Washington, DC: Bureau of the Census, U.S. Department of Commerce.

Hofmann, M., Hock, C., Kuhler, A., & Muller-Spahn, F. (1995). Computer-assisted individualized memory training in Alzheimer patients. *Nervenarzt, 66,* 703-707.

Kosorok, M. R., Omenn, G. S., Diehr, P., Koepsell, T. D., & Patrick, D. L. (1992). Restricted activity days among older adults. *American Journal of Public Health, 82*(9), 1263-1267.

Long, R., Crews, J., & Mancil, R. (2000). Creating measures of rehabilitation outcomes for people who are visually impaired: The FIMBA project. *Journal of Vision Impairment and Blindness, 94*(5), 292-306.

LaPlante, M. P., Hendershot, G. E., & Moss, A. J. (1992). *Assistive technology devices and home accessibility features: Prevalence, payment, need, and trends.* Advance Data from Vital and Health Statistics; no. 217. Hyattsville, MD: National Center for Health Statistics.

Malassigne, P., & Amerson, T. L. (1992). *A survey on the usage of bathroom fixtures by disabled people.* Proceedings of the RESNA International '92 Conference. Toronto, Ontario, Canada: 273-275.

Malcolm, M., Mann, W. C., Tomita, M., Fraas, L. F., Stanton, K. M., & Gitlan, L. (2001). Computer and Internet use among physically frail elders. *Physical and Occupational Therapy in Geriatrics, 19*(3), 15-32.

Mann, W., Granger, C., Hurren, D., Tomita, M., & Charvat, B. (1995). An analysis of problems with canes encountered by elderly persons. *Physical & Occupational Therapy in Geriatrics, 13*(1&2), 25-49.

Mann, W. C., Hurren, D., Karuza, J., & Bentley, D. (1993). Needs of home-based visually impaired persons for assistive devices. *Journal of Visual Impairments and Blindness, 87*(4), 106-110

Mann, W., Hurren, D., & Tomita, M. (1994). Assistive device needs of home-based elderly persons with hearing impairments. *Technology and Disability, 3*(1), 47-61.

Mann, W., Hurren, D., Tomita, M., & Charvat, B. (1995). A follow-up study of older stroke survivors living at home. *Topics in Geriatric Rehabilitation, 11*(1), 52-66.

Mann, W., Hurren, D., & Tomita, M. (1995). Assistive devices used by home-based elderly persons with arthritis. *American Journal of Occupational Therapy, 49*(8), 810-820.

Mann, W., Hurren, D., Tomita, M., & Charvat, B. (1995). Assistive devices for home-based older stroke survivors. *Topics in Geriatric Rehabilitation, 10*(3), 75-86.

Mann, W. C., Hurren, D. M., Charvat, B. A., & Tomita, M. (1996). Changes over one year in assistive device use and home modifications by home-based older persons with Alzheimer's disease. *Topics in Geriatric Rehabilitation, 12*(2), 9-16.

Mann, W., Hurren, D., Tomita, M., & Charvat, B. (1995). An analysis of problems with walkers encountered by elderly persons. *Physical & Occupational Therapy in Geriatrics, 13*(1&2), 1-23.

Mann, W., Hurren, D., Tomita, M., & Charvat, B. (1997). A two year study of coping strategies of home-based frail elders with vision impairment. *Technology and Disability, 6*(3), 177-189.

Mann, W. C., Karuza, J., Hurren, D. M., & Tomita, M. (1993). Needs of home-based older persons for assistive devices: The University at Buffalo rehabilitation engineering center on aging consumer assessment study. *Technology and Disability, 2*(1), 1-11.

Mann, W. C., Ottenbacher, K. J., Fraas, L., Tomita, M., & Granger, C. V. (1999). Effectiveness of assistive technology and environmental interventions in maintaining independence and reducing home care costs for the frail elderly: A randomized trial. *Archives of Family Medicine, 8*(3), 210-217

Mayo, N. E. (1993). Epidemiology and recovery. In R. W. Teasell (Ed.), *Long-term consequences of stroke: Physical medicine and rehabilitation: State of the art reviews* (pp. 7:1-25). Philadelphia, PA: Hanley & Belfus.

Marmor, M. (1992). Normal age-related eye vision changes and their effects on vision. In E. E. Faye & C. S. Stuen (Eds.), *The aging eye and low vision.* New York: The Lighthouse.

Mihailidis, A., Fernie, G., & Cleghorn, W. (2000). The development of a computerized cueing device to help people with dementia to be more independent. *Technology and Disability, 13,* 23-40.

National Center for Health Statistics. (1990). *Current estimates from the National Health Interview Survey. Vital and Health Statistics* (Series 10, No. 176). Washington, DC: U.S. Government Printing Office.

National Institute on Aging. (2000). *Progress report on Alzheimer's disease: Taking the next steps.* Retrieved July 26, 2001, http://www.alzheimers.org/pubs/pr2000.pdf 2000.

National Institutes of Health. (2000). *Publication No. 00-4798.* Retrieved November 26, 2003 from http:www.nidcd.nih.gov/health/hearing/coch.asp.

Nochajski, S. M., Tomita, M., & Mann, W. C. (1996). An intervention study of the use and satisfaction with assistive devices by elderly persons with cognitive impairments. *Topics in Geriatric Rehabilitation, 12*(2), 40-53.

Orr, A. L., & Piqueras, L. S. (1991). Aging, visual impairment, and technology. *Technology and Disability, 1*(1), 47-54.

Ottenbacher, K. J., & Jannell, S. (1993). The results of clinical trials in stroke rehabilitation research. *Archives of Neurology, 50,* 37-44.

Parker, M. G., & Thorslund, M. (1991). The use of technical aids among community-based elderly. *American Journal of Occupational Therapy, 15*(8), 712-718.

Phillips, P., & Zhao, H. (1993). Predictors of assistive technology abandonment. *Assistive Technology, 5*(1), 36-45.

Poole, J., Dunn, W., Schell, B., & Barnhart, J. M. (1991). Statement: occupational therapy services management of persons with cognitive impairments. *American Journal of Occupational Therapy, 45*(12), 1067-1068.

Pynoos, J., & Ohta, R. J. (1991). In-home interventions for persons with Alzheimer's disease and their caregivers. *Physical and Occupational Therapy in Geriatrics, 9*(3/4), 83-92.

Rogers, J., Holm, M., Burgio, L., Granieri, E., Hsu, C., Hardin, M., & McDowell, B. (1999). Improving morning care routines of nursing home residents with dementia. *Journal of the American Geriatrics Society, 47,* 1049-1057.

Rogers, J., Holm, M., Burgio, L., Hsu, C., Hardin, J., & McDowell, B. (2000). Excess disability during morning care in nursing home residents with dementia. *International Psychogeriatrics, 12,* 267-282.

Sampson, B. (1988). Smart house. In G. Lesnoff-Caravaglia (Ed.), *Aging in a technological society* (pp. 54-57). New York: Human Sciences Press.

Shipham I. (1987). Bath aids—Their use by a multi-diagnostic group of patients. *International Rehabilitation Medicine, 8*(4), 182-184.

Stone, J., Mann, W. C, Hurren, D., Tomita, M., & Mann, J. K. (1997). Use of magnifiers by older persons with low vision. *Technology and Disability, 6*(3), 169-175.

Tang, P., & Venebles, T. (1999). Smart homes and telecare for independent living. *Journal of Telemedicine and Telecare, 6,* 8-14.

Technology Related Assistance for Individuals with Disabilities Act of 1988 (PL 100-407, Section 3).

U.S. Department of Health and Human Services, Centers for Disease Control, National Center for Health Statistics. (2003). *Summary health statistics for U.S. adults: National health interview survey, 1999.* Hyattsville, MD: U.S. Government Printing Office.

Verbrugge, L. M., Lepkowski, J. M., & Konkol, L. L. (1991). Levels of disability among U.S. adults with arthritis. *Journal of Gerontology, 46*(2), S71-83.

Verbrugge, L. M., Gates, D. M., & Ike, R. W. (1991). Risk factors for disability among U.S. adults with arthritis. *Journal of Clinical Epidemiology, 44,* 167-182.

Wahl, H. W., Oswald, F., & Zimprich, D. (1999). Everyday competence in visually impaired older adults: A case for person-environment perspectives. *Gerontologist, 39*(2), 140-149.

Wallhagen, M., Strawbridge, W., Shema, S., Kurata, J., & Kaplan, G. (2001). Comparative impact of hearing and vision impairment on subsequent functioning. *Journal of the American Geriatrics Society, 49*(8), 1086-1092

West, C. G., Gildengerin, G., Haegerstrom-Portnoy, G., Lott, L. A., Schneck, M. E., & Brabyn, J. A. (2003). Vision and driving self-restriction in older adults. *Journal of the American Geriatrics Society, 51*(10), 1348-1355.

World Health Organization. (1997). *Blindness and visual disability: Seeing ahead—Projections into the next century.* Retrieved November 2003 from http://www.who.int/inf-fs/en/fact146.html.

Yelin, E., & Katz, P. P. (1990). Transitions in health status among community dwelling elderly people with arthritis: A national, longitudinal study. *Arthritis and Rheumatism, 33*(8), 1205-1215.

Yelin, E. (1992). Arthritis: The cumulative impact of a common chronic condition. *Arthritis and Rheumatism, 35*(5), 489-497.

PART VI. New and Persistent Dynamics in the Societal Environment

CHAPTER 16

New Aging and New Policy Responses: Reconstructing Gerontology in a Global Age

Chris Phillipson

Analysis of the changing environment facing older people has become an urgent issue to consider at the beginning of a new century. The tools and techniques for achieving this are, however, somewhat uncertain given the transformed economic and social context experienced by older people. For much of the preceding 50 years, the lives of older people were shaped by aspirations to develop welfare states, expressed with different structures and value orientations, across the various European countries (Esping-Andersen, 1990; Pierson & Castles, 2000). Such arrangements were to develop, from the late 1940s onwards, as a crucial source of support for older people. Indeed, as John Myles (1984) and others have argued, much of welfare-state provision has traditionally been built around the needs of older people.

The dominance of the welfare state was to restrict discussions about aging to concerns about a limited range of health and social services with little underlying debate or critique about the way in which such services had evolved. This changed radically from the 1970s onwards—for two main reasons. The first influence was the impact of economic recession on the welfare state and the subsequent questioning of its aims and values by neoliberal governments in Britain, the United States and elsewhere (Estes & Phillipson, 2002). Second, within gerontology, there was the development of a political economy perspective that, while supportive of state provision, also raised concerns about its role in the development of what Peter Townsend (1981) defined as "structured dependency." Both elements were to introduce change and uncertainty in policies toward older people.

However, an additional influence upon debates has been recognition of the impact of globalization, both as a general influence on daily life in old age and in the field of economic and social policy in particular. Globalization has emerged as a transformative force, reshaping the boundaries within which old age is experienced. Previously contained within the structure and narratives of the welfare state, growing old is being redefined on a broader stage, this producing new policy questions and a new agenda for researchers to consider.

Taking the above as a preliminary framework, the aim of this chapter is to examine both past and current constructions of later life. The chapter will examine three main areas:

- changes in the social position of older people in Western societies, taking the period covered by the rise and subsequent decline of welfare states
- responses to these changes in respect to social theory in gerontology, notably with the emergence of critical gerontology
- new policy questions arising from the impact of globalization on the lives of older people

RECONSTRUCTING OLD AGE: THE HISTORICAL CONTEXT

For most Western societies, the period stretching from the 1950s through to the late 1970s produced significant changes in policies directed at elderly people. During this time, with varying degrees of emphasis, responses to aging were formed around the institutions and relationships associated with, first, state supported public welfare; second, the institution of retirement; and, third, what came to be known as the "intergenerational contract" (Phillipson, 1998). In general terms, this period is associated with the emergence of retirement as a major social institution, with the growth of entitlements to pensions and the gradual acceptance of an extended period of leisure following the ending of full-time work. Retirement, along with the development of social security and pensions, provided the basis for a reconstructed and standardized life course built around what Best (1980) termed as the "three boxes" of education, work, and leisure (see also, Kohli & Rein, 1991). This arrangement was reinforced by the theme of "intergenerational reciprocity," with older people receiving care and support as part of the "moral economy" underpinning an extended life course (Arber & Attias-Donfut, 2000; Hendricks & Leedham, 1991). Kohli (1991, pp. 277-278) summarizes this development as follows:

> It is by the creation of lifetime continuity and reciprocity that the welfare system contributes to the moral economy of the work society. This becomes especially clear when we look at retirement. The emergence of retirement has meant the emergence of old age as a distinct life phase, structurally set apart from active life and with a clear chronological boundary. But the other parts of the welfare system can be viewed in this perspective as well: as elements in the construction of a stable lifecourse, covering the gaps ("risks") that are left open by the organization of work.

The construction of old age through well-defined "chronological boundaries" was to last a relatively short span of time in historical terms, with the period from 1945 to 1975 defining its outer limits. From the mid-1970s, a number of changes can be identified arising from the development of flexible patterns of work running alongside rising levels of unemployment. The retirement transition itself became more complex in this period, with the emergence of different pathways (e.g., unemployment, long-term sick, redundancy, disability, part-time employment, self-employment) that people follow before they describe themselves or are officially defined as "wholly retired" (de Vroom & Guillemard, 2002; Hirsch, 2000; Marshall, Heinz, Kruger, & Anil, 2001).

These changes produced what may be termed the reconstruction of middle and old age, with the identification of a third age in between the period of work (the second age) and that of a period of mental and physical decline (the fourth age). Hyde, Ferrie, Higgs, Mein, and Nazroo (2004, p. 281) summarize this development as follows:

> Increasingly, writers point to the changing forms and diversity of older people's activities as evidence of an emergent "third age" . . . [it is] argued that older age should no longer be seen as a residual stage of the lifecourse whose members are preoccupied with decrepitude and death. Instead . . . because people are living longer and healthier lives with more disposable retirement income, older age should be seen as the "crown of life" in which people are free to develop themselves and their interests. . . . Far from being the end of productive lives, retirement can create time and space for older people to engage in various activities that contribute to the overall wellbeing of their community and society.

Seen from the perspective of the last half-century, the analysis thus far suggests two main phases in the development of old age in the period since the ending of the Second World War. In the first phase, starting from the late 1940s onwards, there is the creation of mass retirement, underpinned by systems (varying in scope from country to country) of public welfare. This was a time when nations of the developed world singled out older people as beneficiaries of support, mindful of the sacrifices associated with the depression of the 1930s and the world war that followed (Macnicol, 1998). John Myles (1991, p. 304) characterizes this period in terms of the "institutionalization of the retirement wage," the major achievement of which was, he suggests, to secure the "right [of working people] to cease working before wearing out" (see also Ekerdt, 2004).

The second period, from the early 1970s through the 1990s, was marked by instability with respect to the images and institutions associated with supporting older people. The context here was the new political economy shaping the lives of older people. This development has been variously analyzed as reflecting a move from "organized" to "disorganized capitalism," to a shift from "simple" to "reflexive modernity," or to the transformation from mass assembly ("fordist") to (flexible/service-driven) "post-fordist economies." Lash and Urry (1987) identify the period from 1970 as marking the "end of organized capitalism," the latter characterized by full employment and expanding welfare states (the core elements underpinning the growth of retirement). With the period of disorganized capitalism comes the weakening of manufacturing industry and the creation of a "mixed economy of welfare" (Johnson, 1987). Industrial deconcentration was followed by spatial deconcentration, as people (the middle classes in particular) moved in accelerating numbers from the older industrial cities (Byrne, 1999; Wilson, 1997). These developments reflected what many commentators viewed as a heightened degree of instability running through capitalist social relations. Lash and Urry coined the term "disorganized capitalism" to refer to the way in which

> . . . the "fixed, fast-frozen relations" of organized capitalist relations have been swept away. Societies are being transformed from above, from below, and

> from within. All that is solid about organized capitalism, class, industry, cities, collectivity, nation state, even the world, melts into air (Lash & Urry, cited in Kumar, 1995, p. 49).

Living in the period of what has been termed "late modernity" is, then, about experiencing a world where traditional routines and institutions are abandoned and national boundaries transformed in the context of global change (Giddens, 1991; Urry, 2000). In the face of these global shifts, individuals are faced with distinctive pressures with respect to the management of everyday life (Bauman, 2000, 2001). Such changes affect all individuals: no one can escape their global reach and consequences. But people clearly differ in respect of how they respond to a world where traditional institutions are pulled apart, and where day-to-day interaction is governed by a greater degree of openness as well as uncertainty. Such developments have also affected theorizing within gerontology, with the rise of critical gerontology providing a challenge to traditional perspectives within the discipline. The next section reviews this theoretical approach in the light of changes to the context and experience of growing old in the late twentieth and early twenty-first century.

THE DEVELOPMENT OF CRITICAL GERONTOLOGY

Critical approaches to aging build upon a variety of intellectual traditions, including the works of Karl Marx, Max Weber, the Frankfurt School (latterly through the work of Jurgen Habermas), theorists of state power such as Claus Offe (1994), and structuration theory as developed by Anthony Giddens (2001). Feminist theories (Arber, Davidson, & Ginn, 2003) and theories of racial inequality (Omi & Winant, 1994; Williams, 1996) have also been incorporated into critical perspectives on aging. Utilizing this theoretical seedbed, a field of critical gerontology has emerged and coalesced over the past decade with work in the United States and Europe in particular (Estes, Biggs, & Phillipson., 2003; Minkler & Estes, 1999).

The political-economy perspective is one of the most important strands within the critical tradition. This approach attempts to understand the condition and experience of aging, drawing upon multiple theories and levels of analysis. Beginning in the late 1970s and early 1980s with the work of Estes (1979), Guillemard (1983), Phillipson (1982), and Walker (1981), these theorists initiated the task of describing the respective roles of capitalism and the state in contributing to systems of domination and marginalization affecting older people. Based on the continuing work of these and other authors, the political-economy perspective is classified as one of the major theories in social gerontology (Bengtson & Schaie, 1999).

Political economy developed a major critique of the dominant images of decline and burden that entered policy debates from the late 1970s and early 1980s. During this period, older people were portrayed as a "selfish welfare generation," drawing a level of support from the state that would, it was argued, be unsustainable over the longer term (Thomson, 1989). In this scenario, workers became pitched against pensioners in what appeared as a zero sum trade off between competing age and social groups (Johnson et al., 1989). In the area of healthcare, the biomedical ethicist, Daniel Callahan (1987), launched a major debate with the publication of his book *Setting*

Limits: Medical Goals in an Aging Society. Callahan's study identified three aspirations for an aging society: first, to stop pursuing medical goals that combine the features of high costs, marginal gains, and benefits for the old. Second, that older people shift priorities from their own welfare to that of younger generations. Third, that older people should accept death as a condition of life—at least for the sake of others. Callahan's intervention attracted considerable controversy (for a political-economy critique, see Binney & Estes, 1990), but it fuelled an already charged debate concerning what were presented as the divergent interests of young and older people.

Political economy made an influential contribution to challenging pessimistic views about the impact of population change. It did this by developing three main types of argument. First, emphasising that the "public burden" conception of old age undervalued the important role that older people play in society, notably in areas such as volunteering and informal care (Arber et al., 2003). Second, stressing that the aging of populations had been unfolding over the course of the twentieth century, and could be seen to represent a substantial gain in health for the populations of Western societies. Third, questioning evidence that generations were locked in conflict over the distribution of resources, pointing instead to evidence of reciprocity in support across different age groups (Arber & Attias-Donfut, 2000; Phillipson, Bernard, Phillips, & Ogg, 2001; Vincent, 2003). More generally, political economy challenged what it viewed as the "crisis construction" of aging, an approach that was viewed as stifling a rational public debate about the range of resources needed to support older people.

By the end of the 1990s, some of the rhetoric behind the "generational war" debate had given way to more realistic appraisals about the nature and implications of demographic change. The representation of aging in terms of social pathology reflected to a considerable degree what Riley (1988, pp. 31-32) came to define as the problem of "structural lag." This referred to the "imbalance between the mounting numbers of long-lived people (the unprecedented transformation of aging) and the lack of productive and meaningful role opportunities—or places in the social structure—that can recognize, foster, and reward these capacities." Critical gerontology confronted this in the guise of political *and* moral economy perspectives (Minkler & Estes, 1999). The former challenged what were seen as socially constructed inequalities within old age, this leading to narratives associated with dependency and loss of power (Walker, 1981). The latter emphasized the need to go beyond viewing aging purely as a problem of scientific and technical management (Cole, 1992). Against this, Harry Moody (1988, p. 35) argued that

> A critical gerontology must also offer a positive idea of human development: that is, aging as movement toward freedom beyond domination (autonomy, wisdom, transcendence). Without this emancipatory discourse (i.e. an expanded image of aging) we have no means to orient ourselves in struggling against current forms of domination.

Although the above themes have continued to be central to critical gerontology, a major new agenda has been introduced through recognition of aging as a global phenomenon and the various pressures associated with globalization as a political, social, and economic process. It is to this current phase in the development of critical gerontology to which we now turn.

GLOBAL INSTITUTIONS AND SUPPORT FOR OLDER PEOPLE

For much of the period from the 1970s to the 1990s, critical perspectives in gerontology focused upon national concerns about policies and provision for older people. Scholars essentially worked within the boundaries of the nation state in developing perspectives around issues such as dependency and inequality in later life. The significant change over the past five years, reflecting developments within core disciplines such as politics and sociology, has been the link between critical gerontology and broader questions arising from the pressures and upheavals associated with living in a global world (Held, McGrew, Goldblatt, & Perraton, 1999; Hutton & Giddens, 2000).

Globalization exerts unequal and highly stratified effects on the lives of older people (Vincent, 2003; Yeates, 2001). In the developed world, the magnitude and absolute size of expenditure on programs for older people has made these the first to be targeted with financial cuts (just as older people were one of the first beneficiaries of the welfare state). In less developed countries, older people (women especially) have been among those most affected by the privatization of healthcare and the burden of debt repayments to the World Bank and the IMF (Estes & Phillipson, 2002). Additionally, globalization as a process that stimulates population movement and migration may also produce major disruptions to the lives of older people (Papastergiadis, 2000).

A further dimension has been the way in which inter-governmental organizations (IGOs) feed into what has been termed the "crisis construction and crisis management" of policies for older people (Estes & Associates, 2001). Bob Deacon (2000) argues that globalization generates a global discourse within and among global actors on the future of social policy, especially in areas such as pensions, health, and social services. Yeates (2001), for example, observes that "Both the World Bank and IMF have been at the forefront of attempts to foster a political climate conducive to [limiting the scope of] state welfare . . . promoting [instead] . . . private and voluntary initiatives." Holtzman (1997), in a paper outlining a World Bank perspective on pension reform, has argued for reducing state pay-as-you-go (PAYG) schemes to the minimal role of basic pension provision. This position has influenced both national governments and transnational bodies such as the International Labour Organisation (ILO), with the latter now conceding to the World Bank's position with their advocacy of a means-tested first pension, the promotion of an extended role for individualized and capitalized private pensions, and the call for OECD member countries to raise the age of retirement.

In Deacon's (2000) terms, this debate amounts to a significant global discourse about pension provision and retirement ages, but one which has largely excluded perspectives that might suggest an enlarged role for the state and those which might question the stability and cost effectiveness of private schemes. The International Labour Organisation has concluded that "Investing in financial markets is an uncertain and volatile business: under present pension plans people may save up to 30 per cent more than they need—which would reduce their spending during their working life; or they may save 30 per cent too little—which would severely cut their spending in retirement" (Gillion, Turner, Bailey, & Latulippe, 2000). Add in as well the crippling administrative charges associated with the running of private schemes, and the advocacy of market-based provision hardly seems as persuasive as most IGOs have been keen to present (Blackburn, 2002; Minns, 2001). John Vincent (2003) suggests that the focus upon aging as a "demographic timebomb" reflects a particular ideological standpoint. He goes on to argue that

> The function of such arguments is to create a sense of inevitability and scientific certainty that public pension provision will fail. In so far as this strategy succeeds it creates a self-fulfilling prophecy. If people believe the "experts" who say publicly sponsored PAYG systems cannot be sustained, they are more likely to act in ways that mean they are unsustainable in practice. Certainly in Britain and elsewhere in Europe the state pension is an extremely popular institution. To have it removed or curtailed creates massive opposition. Only by demoralising the population with the belief that it is demographically unsustainable has room for the private financiers been created and a mass pensions market formed (Vincent, 2003, p. 86).

IGOs have also begun to exert an influential role in relation to health and social care services. Increasingly, the social infrastructure of welfare states is being targeted as a major area of opportunity for global investors. Yeates (2001, p. 102) highlights the extent to which the World Trade Organisation (WTO) is promoting the idea of a more restricted role for the state in the provision of services:

> . . . if the WTO had its way, then equity concerns would be displaced by commercial considerations, and the state would have to allow a greater role for the private (commercial) sector in health services and treat domestic and foreign health providers equally. States would have to prepare the ground for the privatization of health and social care services . . . and thus for a two-tier service, since public provision for all (where it exists) would become public provision for the poor, high risk (i.e. less profitable) groups that the private sector is not prepared to cover.

The WTO enforces more than twenty separate international agreements, using international trade tribunals that adjudicate disputes. Such agreements include the General Agreement on Trade in Services (GATS), the first multilateral, legally enforceable agreement covering banking, insurance, financial services, and related areas. Barlow and Clarke (2001, p. 84) note that the current round of GATS negotiations has put "every single social service on the table and is only the first of many rounds whose ultimate goal is the full commercialization of all services." Indeed, the WTO has itself called upon Member governments to "reconsider the breadth and depth of their commitments on health and social services" (cited in Yeates, 2001, p. 74). This will almost certainly place enormous pressure on countries to move further in the opening-up of public services to competition from global (and especially U.S.) corporate providers. Pollock and Price (2000, p. 1995) argue that

> To extend rights of access for private firms, the WTO, with the backing of powerful trading blocs, multinational corporations, and U.S. and European governments, is attempting to use regulatory reform to challenge limitations on private sector involvement. But this amounts to a challenge, which lies at the heart of social welfare systems in Europe. The new criteria proposed at the WTO threaten some of the key mechanisms that allow governments to guarantee health care for their populations by requiring governments to demonstrate that their pursuit of social policy goals are least restrictive and least costly to trade.

Elderly people are also affected in different ways by inequalities in the global distribution of income. Income inequalities within and between countries and regions may create a number of pressures upon older people, increasing the risk of poverty, but also disrupting social networks as younger people abandon rural areas for cities or attempt long-distance migrations to wealthier regions or countries (HelpAge International, 2000). Wade (2001) summarizes data indicating that incomes became markedly more unequal in the period from the late 1980s to the early 1990s. He reports one study that found the share of world income going to the poorest 10% of the world's population falling by over a quarter, whereas the share of the richest 10% rose by 8%. Wade (2001) comments here that

> It is remarkable how unconcerned the World Bank, the IMF and global organisations are about these trends. The Bank's *World Development Report* for 2000 even said that rising income inequality "should not be seen as negative." . . . Such lack of attention shows that to call these world organisations is misleading. They may be world bodies in the sense that almost all states are members, but they think in state-centric rather than global ways.

A NEW AGENDA FOR GERONTOLOGY IN THE TWENTY-FIRST CENTURY: SOCIAL THEORY AND SOCIAL POLICY IN A GLOBAL AGE

The analysis developed thus far suggests that critical gerontology will have a major role to play in understanding new forms of structural inequality affecting the lives of older people in the twenty-first century. In terms of the construction of social policy, this point may be illustrated in four key respects:

- through the influence of globalization on issues relating to citizenship and public policy
- the impact of global governance on the lives of older people
- the political changes required to involve older people and NGOs in the development of a global social policy
- through a reassessment of intergenerational relations in a global world

On the first point, globalization brings forth a new set of actors and institutions influencing the social construction of public policy for old age. To take one example, the increasing power of global finance and private transnational bodies raises significant issues about the nature of citizenship and associated rights to health and social care in old age. In the period of welfare-state reconstruction, rights were defined and negotiated through various forms of nation-state-based social policy (although it is important to emphasize the dominance of the United States maintained through the Bretton Woods system). Globalization, however, transfers citizenship issues to a transnational stage, driven by a combination of the power of intergovernmental structures, the influence of multinational corporations, and the pressures of population movement and migration. Alongside these developments come provocative questions about the nature of citizen rights and the determinants of the "life chances" available to members of the global society, older people in particular.

Drawing on the work of Bauman (2001) and Beck (2001), it might also be argued that rights, in the period of late modernity, have become more fragmented as well as individualized. Certainly, the risks associated with aging are relatively unchanged—the threat of poverty, the need for long-term care, the likelihood of serious illness. What has changed, as Bauman (2001) argues in a more general context, is that the duty and the necessity to cope with these has been transferred to individual families (women carers in particular) and individual older people (for example with respect to financial provision for old age). The new social construction (and contradiction) of aging is, *on the one hand, the focus upon growing old as a global problem and issue; on the other hand, the individualization of the various risks attached to the life course.* This development suggests an important role for social-gerontological theory as well as social policy in combining macro- and microsocial perspectives with a fresh approach to understanding how global processes may reshape the institutions and experiences with which aging is associated. Following this, it will be important to move beyond what Hagestad and Dannefer (2001) view as an undue attention in gerontology on individual aging. The reasons for this focus, they cite, are first, late modernity's emphasis on individuals and their agency; second, a steady medicalization of old age; third, strong pressures from problem-orientated professions and politicians. Hagestad and Dannefer (2001, p. 15) conclude that "The costs of the microfocus [have been] significant . . . hamper[ing] our ability to address the aging society in the context of global economic and technological change."

The second major issue to be addressed concerns that of global governance and its impact on aging. This development introduces us to the undoubted complexities of globalization and its influence on daily life. One the one side, the negative effects are well-known: corporations that appear to trample over the rights and needs of individuals and communities; IGOs that put debt repayment before maintaining or improving schemes of social protection; and forms of crisis construction that emphasize the costs associated with aging populations (Hutton & Giddens, 2000). Ramesh Mishra (1999, p. 130) summarizes these aspects as follows:

> The main problem [appears to be] that those conditions and social forces which made *national* welfare states possible, e.g. the existence of a state with legitimate authority for rule-making and rule-enforcement, electoral competition and representative government, strong industrial action and protest movements threatening the economic and social stability of nations, nationalism and nation-building imperatives, are unavailable at the international-level. Moreover, globalisation is disempowering citizens within the nation-state as far as social rights are concerned without providing them with any leverage globally. At the same time transnational corporations and the global marketplace have been empowered hugely through financial deregulation and capital mobility.

Yet the contrary trends are also important and require analysis in the framing and development of social theory and social policy in relation to aging. Deacon (2000, p. 13), for example, notes what appears to be the emergence of a "new politics of global social responsibility." He writes: "Orthodox economic liberalism and inhumane structural adjustment appear to be giving way to a concern on the part of the [World Bank] and the IMF with the social consequences of globalization. International development assistance is concerned to focus on social development. United Nations agencies are increasingly troubled by the negative social consequences of globalization . . . [there is a shift] away from a politics of liberalism to a global politics of social concern." In a similar vein, Mishra (1999, p. 130) observes the increasing momentum behind the move toward global governance and reform of existing IGOs, with increasing pressure to make bodies such as the World Bank and IMF more democratic and accountable for their actions.

At the same time, the ability of corporations or other organizations to evade their responsibilities may be constrained by different forms of transnational governance. For example, taking the European context, avoidance by successive U.K. governments of age discrimination legislation has finally been challenged by a European Union directive outlawing discrimination in the workplace on grounds of age, race, disability, or sexual orientation. Similarly, national legislation following the European Convention on Human Rights also has the potential to be used to challenge age discrimination in areas such as service provision and employment, as well as issues relating to the right to life, the right not to be subject to inhumane treatment, and the right to a fair hearing. Both examples illustrate the way in which international law may be used to challenge discrimination against older people. They further illustrate the need for new approaches to theorizing about age that can integrate the continuing power and influence of the nation-state with the countervailing powers of global institutions. At the same time, we need to be clearer about the way in which global institutions and global governance might be used to promote the needs and rights of older citizens. The task here must be to construct new theories about the nature of citizenship in the light of the more fluid borders surrounding nation states. The extent to which these developments lead to the emergence of a "global community" and "global citizenship," such as that outlined by John Urry (2000), is unclear. The important question, however, is whether older people are advantaged or disadvantaged by the spread of mobile communities along with more varied forms of citizenship—issues that can only be settled by the application and development of social theory.

Third, it will be especially important, given the pressures associated with globalization, to engage older people and their organizations with the debate launched by national governments and IGOs about the future of pension provision and health and social care services. Thus far, older people and their representative organizations can claim only limited influence on the major debates about population aging launched by the World Bank and similar organizations. The case that needs to be made is for an "age-sensitive" globalization in which older people have greater influence in key international fora. Relevant aspects might include:

- auditing the activities of key IGOs with respect to their activities on aging issues
- building an age dimension into development policies and strategies
- promoting aging organizations as major players alongside existing multilateral agencies
- strengthening the age dimension in human rights legislation
- encouraging older people's organizations to play a prominent role in the network of groups and fora which compose global civil society

This is an important agenda, but one that is being only partially addressed in the United Nations, the World Health Organisation (WHO), and related bodies. This is illustrated by the Madrid International Plan of Action on Ageing (MIPAA), which arose from the Second World Assembly on Ageing (held in Madrid in April 2002). Sidorenko and Walker (2004, p. 152) note that the idea of a "Society for All Ages" is a guiding theme in the Plan, and that this is seen to embrace

> . . . human rights; a secure old age (including the eradication of poverty); the empowerment of older people; individual development, self-fulfilment and well-being throughout life; gender equality among older people; inter-generational inter-dependence, solidarity and reciprocity; health care, support and social protection for older people; partnership between all major stakeholders in the implementation process; scientific research and expertise; and the situation of ageing indigenous people and migrants.

The authors further suggest that the ultimate goal of MIPAA is to "improve the quality of life of older people on the basis of security, dignity, and participation, while at the same time promoting measures to reconcile aging and development, and sustaining supportive formal . . . and informal . . . systems of individual well-being" (Sidorenko & Walker, 2004, p. 156). Although such a goal might be viewed as an admirable basis for developing a new agenda for population aging, major limitations are also apparent. In particular, the Plan fails to engage with accelerating inequalities within and between societies, a characteristic feature of social change in a number of European countries over the past two decades (Hills, LeGrand, & Piachaud, 2002; Hutton, 2002; Littlewood, Glorieux, Herkommer, & Jönsson, 1999; Social Exclusion Unit, 2004). These inequalities are now creating new forms of exclusion, notably for women, the working class, and Black and Asian elderly people (Byrne, 1999; Scharf, Phillipson, Smith, & Kingston, 2002). Developments such as these need to be given greater acknowledgment by bodies such as the United Nations and WHO. The concern of these organizations to encourage the empowerment of older people and to achieve what is defined as "active aging" (World Health Organization, 2001), will surely fail unless national and global inequalities are tackled in a systematic way—notably those that reduce the life chance of those older people living in less developed countries and the poorer communities of the developed world. Moreover, bodies such as the UN and WHO will need to confront the power of IGOs such as the IMF and World Bank to impose social policies that result in drastic cuts in expenditures on services for groups such as older people (Barlow & Clarke, 2001; Walker & Deacon, 2003). This has been a particular feature of economic programs directed at Latin American and East European countries and is in direct conflict with the aspirations of the Madrid Plan to build a secure and dignified old age across the global community.

Finally, attention must be given to redefining the language and relationships that define ties between generations. In the 1980s and 1990s, the balance of debate swung toward expressions of doubts about the benefits of population aging (Vincent, 2003). Despite the radical critique offered by critical gerontology (Minkler & Estes, 1999; Walker, 1981) and the activities of groups of older people themselves, the problems of aging and the welfare state became a dominant theme in the policy discourse within and between nation states. For the twenty-first century, however, a process of renewal in generational politics is required. The basis for this will stem from recognition that presenting issues in terms of younger *versus* older generations will frustrate positive solutions to the needs of young *and* older people, in first as well as third world countries. As Heclo (1989, p. 387) observes

> In an already fragmented society such a framework would be especially unconstructive. It would divert attention from disparities and unmet needs within age groups. It would help divide constituencies that often have a common stage. Above all, a politics of young versus old would reinforce an already strong tendency . . . to define social welfare in terms of a competitive struggle for scarce resources and to ignore shared needs occurring in everyone's life-cycle.

Recognition that we are constructing a different type of life course may also help form the basis for a new generational politics. Here, the worker versus pensioner perspective is especially unhelpful in that it ignores fundamental changes to the distribution of labor through the life course. The labels "worker" versus "pensioner" are less easy to define when the stages that separate them are undergoing change. For many workers, the predictability of continuous employment is being replaced by insecurity in middle and later life (Marshall et al., 2001). As already noted, these changes may be seen as part of the reconstruction of middle and old age, underpinned by the restructuring of work at different points of the life course (Phillipson, 2003). This development has underlined the need for a different type of language for describing relationships between generations in general and workers and pensioners in particular. Emphasis should now be placed upon the interdependency of generations, especially in the context of the radical changes accompanying global change. In essence, we should acknowledge aging as a public concern shared equally across the life course. As Vincent argues (2003, p. 108): "A secure old age including income maintenance and health and social care can be achieved only within a framework of social solidarity." The implication of this argument is that we cannot "offload" responsibilities for an aging population to particular generations or cohorts, whether old, young, or middle aged. Aging is an issue *for* generations, but it is also a question to be solved *with* generations. The role of nation-states and global economic and social institutions will be central in the management of aging populations (Estes & Phillipson, 2002). Social and political responsibility at all levels will be central to the task of developing appropriate policies for the twenty-first century.

CONCLUSION

This chapter has traced the shifting agendas and policies supporting older people over the past 50 years. At the beginning of our period, old age was constructed around the framework and ideologies determined by national welfare states. Alongside this, growing old was contained at the margins of the life course and viewed as having limited cultural, social, or economic significance. By the end of our period—aging as viewed in the early twenty-first century—the transformation in images and experiences had been dramatic. The traditional markers symbolizing the "the journey of life" (Cole, 1992) had been disrupted through social changes (such as the growth in early retirement) and cultural developments (notably the evolution of a "third age" of leisure). But if the journey through life is now more open and less determined through the "structured dependency" imposed by powerful welfare states, it is also more uncertain and insecure. Nation-states still debate the meaning and value of population aging—anxious about its potential to undermine economic prosperity and place burdens upon future generations (Vincent, 2003). At the same time, globalization has created a different set of concerns for older people, with aging being newly-constructed through the activities of transnational communities, IGOs, and the advent of what Urry (2000) views as an increasingly borderless world. A less secure and predictable old age certainly, but one that is producing important changes to behaviors, lifestyles, and policies in old age. Such developments will set urgent issues and research questions for gerontology over the course of the present century.

REFERENCES

Arber, S., & Attias-Donfut, C. (2000). *The myth of generational conflict.* London: Routledge.

Arber, S., Davidson, K., & Ginn, J. (2003). *Gender and ageing.* Buckingham: Open University Press.

Barlow, M., & Clarke, T. (2001). *Global showdown.* Ontario: Stoddart.

Bauman, Z. (2000). *Liquid modernity.* Oxford: Polity Press.

Bauman, Z. (2001). *Community: Seeking safety in an insecure world.* Cambridge: Polity Press.

Beck, U. (2001). Living your own life in a runaway world: Individualisation, globalisation and politics. In W. Hutton & A Giddens (Eds.), *On the edge* (pp. 164-175). London: Jonathan Cape.

Bengtson, V. L., & Schaie, K. W. S. (Eds.). (1999). *Handbook of theories of aging.* New York: Springer Publishing.

Best, F. (1980). *Flexible life scheduling.* New York: Praeger.

Binney, E. A., & Estes, C. L. (1990). Setting the wrong limits: Class biases and the biographical standard. In P. Homer & M. Holstein (Eds.), *A good age? The paradox of setting limits* (pp. 240-255). New York: Simon and Schuster.

Blackburn, R. (2002). *Banking on death.* London: Verso Books.

Byrne, D. (1999). *Social exclusion.* Buckinghamshire: Open University Press.

Callahan, D. (1987). *Setting limits: Medical goals for an aging society.* New York: Touchstone Books.

Cole, T. (1992). *The journey of life.* Cambridge: Cambridge University Press.

Deacon, B. (2000). *Globalisation and social policy: The threat to equitable welfare.* Occasional Paper no. 5, Globalism and Social Policy Programme (GASPP), UNRISD.

de Vroom, B., & Guillemard, A. M. (2002). From externalisation to integration of older workers: Institutional changes at the end of the worklife. In J. G. Andersen & P. H. Jensen (Eds.), *Changing labour markets, welfare policies and citizenship* (pp. 183-208). Bristol: The Policy Press.

Ekerdt, D. (2004). Born to retire: The foreshortened life course. *The Gerontologist, 44*(1), 3-9.

Esping-Andersen, G. (1990). *The three worlds of welfare capitalism.* Cambridge: Polity Press.

Estes, C. (1979). *The aging enterprise.* San Francisco: Jossey-Bass.

Estes, C. (1999). Critical gerontology and the new political economy of aging. In M. Minkler & C. Estes (Eds.), *Critical gerontology: Perspectives from political and moral economy* (pp. 17-36). New York: Baywood.

Estes, C., & Associates. (2001). *Social policy and aging.* Thousand Oaks: Sage.

Estes, C., & Phillipson, C. (2002). The globalisation of capital, the welfare state and old age policy. *International Journal of Health Services, 32*(2), 279-297.

Estes, C., Biggs, S., & Phillipson, C. (2003). *Social theory, social policy and ageing: A critical introduction.* Buckingham: Open University Press.

Giddens, A. (1991). *Modernity and self-identity.* Cambridge: Polity Press.

Giddens, A. (2001). *Sociology* (4th Edition). Cambridge: Polity Press.

Gillion, C., Turner, J., Bailey, C., & Latulippe, D. (2000). *Social security pensions: Development and reform.* Geneva: International Labour Organisation.

Guillemard, A.-M. (Ed.). (1983). *Old age and the welfare state.* New York: Sage Publications.

Hagestad, G., & Dannefer, D. (2001). Concepts and theories of aging: Beyond microfication in social science approaches. In R. Binstock & L. George (Eds.), *The handbook of aging* (5th Ed., pp. 3-16). San Diego: Academic Press.

Heclo, H. (1989). Generational politics. In T. Smeeding & B. Torrey (Eds.), *The vulnerable* (pp. 381-441). Washington, DC: Urban Institute Press.

Held, D., McGrew, A., Goldblatt, D., & Perraton, J. (1999). *Global transformations.* Oxford: Polity Press.

HelpAge International. (2000). *The mark of a noble society.* London: HelpAge International.

Hendricks, J., & Leedham, C. A. (1991). Dependency or empowerment? Toward a moral and political economy. In M. Minkler & C. Estes (Eds.), *Critical perspectives on aging: The perspectives on aging: The political and moral economy of growing old* (pp. 51-64). Amityville, NY: Baywood.

Hills, J., Le Grand, J., & Piachaud, D. (2002). *Understanding social exclusion.* Oxford: Oxford University Press.

Hirsch, D. (Ed.). (2000). *Life after 50: Issues for policy and research.* York: Joseph Rowntree Foundation.

Holtzman, R. A. (1997). *A World Bank perspective on pension reform.* Paper prepared for the joint ILO-OECD Workshop on the Development and Reform of Pension Schemes, Paris, December.

Hutton, W. (2002). *The world we're in.* London: Little, Brown.

Hutton, W., & Giddens, A. (2000). *On the edge: Living with global capitalism.* London: Jonathan Cape.

Hyde, M., Ferrie, J., Higgs, P., Mein, G., & Nazroo, J. (2004). The effects of pre-retirement factors and retirement on circumstances in retirement: Findings from the Whitehall 11 Study. *Ageing and Society, 24*(2), 279-296.

Johnson, N. (1987). *The welfare state in transition: The theory and practice of welfare pluralism.* Sussex: Wheatsheaf Books.

Johnson, P., Conrad, C., & Thomson, D. (Eds.). (1989). *Workers versus pensioners: Intergenerational justice in an ageing world.* Manchester: University of Manchester Press.

Kohli, M. (1991). Retirement and the moral economy: An historical interpretation of the German case. In M. Minkler & C. Estes (Eds.), *Critical perspectives on aging: The political and moral economy of growing old* (pp. 277-278). Amityville, NY: Baywood.

Kohli, M., & Rein, M. (1991). The changing balance of work and retirement. In M. Kohli, A. Rein, A. M. Guillemard, & H. van Gunsteren (Eds.), *Time for retirement: Comparative studies of early exit from the labor force* (pp. 1-35). Cambridge: Cambridge University Press.

Kumar, K. (1995). *From post-industrial to post-modern society.* Oxford: Basil Blackwell.

Lash, S., & Urry, J. (1987). *The end of organized capitalism.* Cambridge: Polity Press.

Littlewood, P., Glorieux, I., Herkommer, S., & Jönsson, I. (Eds.). (1999). *Social exclusion in Europe: Problems and paradigms.* Aldershot: Ashgate.

Macnicol, J. (1998). *The politics of retirement in Britain 1878-1948.* Cambridge: Cambridge University Press.

Marshall, V., Heinz, W. R., Kruger, H., & Anil, V. (Eds.). (2001). *Restructuring work and the life course.* Toronto: University of Toronto Press.

Minkler, M., & Estes, C. (Eds.). (1999). *Critical gerontology: Perspectives from political and moral economy* (2nd ed.). New York: Baywood.

Minns, R. (2001). *The cold war in welfare: Stock markets versus pensions.* London: Verso.

Mishra, R. (1999). *Globalization and the welfare state.* Cheltenham: Edward Elgar.

Moody, H. R. (1988). Toward a critical gerontology: The contribution of the humanities to aging. In J. Birren & V. L. Bengston (Eds.), *Emergent theories of aging* (pp. 19-40). New York: Springer.

Myles, J. (1984). *Old age in the welfare state: The political economy of public pensions.* London: Verso.

Myles, J. (1991). Postwar capitalism and the extension of Social Security into a retirement wage. In M. Minkler & C. Estes (Eds.), *Critical perspectives on aging: The political and moral economy of growing old* (pp. 293-311). Amityville, NY: Baywood.

Offe, C. (1994). *Contradictions of the welfare state.* Oxford: Polity Press.

Omi, M., & Winant, H. (1994). *Racial formation in the United States.* New York: Routledge.

Papastergiadis, N. (2000). *The turbulence of migration.* Oxford: Polity Press.

Phillipson, C. (2003). *Transitions from work to retirement.* Bristol: Polity Press.

Phillipson, C. (1998). *Reconstructing old age.* London: Sage.

Phillipson, C. (1982). *Capitalism and the construction of old age.* London: Macmillan.

Phillipson, C., Bernard, M., Phillips, J., & Ogg, J. (2001). *The family and community life of older people: Social networks and social support in three urban areas.* London: Routledge.

Pierson, C., & Castles, F. (2000). *The welfare state reader.* Cambridge: Polity Press.

Pollock, A., & Price, D. (2000). Rewriting the regulations: How the World Trade Organisation could accelerate privatisation in health care systems. *The Lancet, 356,* 1995-2000.

Riley, M. W. (1988). *On the significance of age in sociology.* In M. W. Riley (Ed.), *Social structures and human lives.* Newbury Park, CA: Sage.

Scharf, T., Phillipson C., Smith, A. E., & Kingston P. (2002). *Growing older in socially deprived areas: Social exclusion in later life.* London: Help the Aged.

Sidorenko, A., & Walker, A. (2004). The Madrid International Plan of Action on Ageing: From conception to implementation. *Ageing and Society, 24*(2), 147-166.

Social Exclusion Unit. (2004). *Tackling social exclusion: Taking stock and looking to the future.* London: Office of Deputy Prime Minister.

Thomson, D. (1989). The welfare state and generational conflict: Winners and losers. In P. Johnson, C. Conrad, & D. Thomson (Eds.), *Workers versus pensioners: Intergenerational justice in an ageing world.* Manchester: University of Manchester Press.

Townsend, P. (1981). The structured dependency of the elderly: The creation of policy in the twentieth century. *Ageing and Society, 1*(1), 5-28.

Urry, J. (2000). *Sociology beyond societies.* London: Routledge.

Vincent, J. (2003). *Old age.* London: Routledge.

Wade, R. (2001). Winners and losers. *The Economist,* April 28th, 93-97.

Walker, A. (1981). Towards a political economy of old age. *Ageing and Society, 1*(1), 73-94.

Walker, A., & Deacon, B. (2003). Economic globalization and policies on aging. *Journal of Societal and Social Policy, 2*(2), 1-18.

Williams, F. (1996). Racism and the discipline of social policy: A critique of welfare theory. In D. Taylor (Ed.), *Critical social policy: A reader.* Thousand Oaks, CA: Sage Publications.

Wilson, W. J. (1997). *When work disappears: The world of the new urban poor.* Chicago: University of Chicago Press.

World Bank. (1994). *Averting the old age crisis.* Oxford: Oxford University Press.

World Health Organisation. (2001). *Health and ageing: A discussion paper.* Geneva: WHO.

Yeates, N. (2001). *Globalisation and social policy.* London: Sage.

CHAPTER 17

The New Politics of Old Age

Alan Walker

To what extent has population aging been accompanied by the increasing political power and participation of older people? This is the central question of this chapter and to answer it requires discussion of the changing politics of old age, the nature and extent of political participation by older people, and of the barriers still preventing some of them from active engagement in political processes. The analysis is based on Western societies (mainly Western Europe and North America) and, let us remember, that active political engagement for the vast majority of the world's older people, in the rapidly aging developing countries, is still strictly limited by the pressures of survival and some governments that do not regard such participation as a human right. Political activity in old age is largely a luxury of developed nations. Nonetheless, I will argue that even in developed countries the political paradox of old age still holds: large and growing numbers, but small influence. The chapter ends with a reiteration of the plea for more research into the political sociology of aging and old age, which has long been a poorly mapped part of the gerontological terrain (Walker, 1986).

EMERGING POLITICS OF OLD AGE

To understand the new political dynamics of population aging, it is necessary to look back briefly to the latter half of the last century and, specifically, to the post-Second World War period. In contrast to the earlier era of protests and campaigns by older people and organized labor to establish pension and other social protection systems, the years from 1945 to the early 1980s were characterized, in many countries, by the politics of acquiescence. This was underpinned by both positive and negative influences.

On the positive side, it was during this period that the close relationship between older people and the welfare state was cemented. All welfare states originated, wholly or partly, in provisions for old age, and pension systems are not only the largest item of national social expenditures but they are the heart of the welfare regime. This means that the nature of a country's pension system tends to have a major determining influence over the rest of the welfare state, with the Beveridge and Bismarck social insurance systems being contrasting examples—in the former, pensions are paid at the same basic minimum level to all with the necessary number of contribution years while, in the latter, they vary according to previous salary levels. Welfare states were constructed at a time of relative optimism about tackling need and the prospects for future funding. For obvious reasons, older people were regarded as a deserving cause for welfare spending. This was not entirely good news because it entailed a social construction of older people as dependent in economic terms and encouraged popular ageist stereotypes of old age as a period of poverty and frailty (Townsend, 1981, 1986; Walker, 1980). As Binstock (1991, p. 12) has put it, older people were viewed as "poor, frail, socially dependent, objects of discrimination and, above all, deserving" and this reinforced the case for public welfare provision. There was certainly a case because poverty rates among older people remained high despite the introduction of pensions and other measures to assist them. For example, in the late 1960s in the United States, one in four of this group had incomes below the official poverty line and, in the United Kingdom, it was one in every three older people (Rix, 1999; Walker, 1993). Evidence such as this contributed to increases in social spending and, in some countries, concerted attempts to tackle poverty in old age. For example, in 1972, the U.S. Congress approved a once-off 20% increase in social security benefits and legislated for automatic cost-of-living benefit adjustments (with effect from 1975) (Rix, 1999, p. 179). Between 1960 and 1985, total pension expenditure in all Organisation for Economic Cooperation and Development (OECD) countries rose significantly faster than output (and therefore contributed to a rising share of gross domestic product (GDP) being devoted to pensions). The influence of the three factors determining their growth—demography, eligibility, and benefit levels—was roughly equal, which implies that favorable policy decisions were taken concerning eligibility for and levels of pensions and other benefits for older people (OECD, 1988a).

On the negative side, in this period, older people were largely excluded from the political and policy-making systems by a process of disengagement whereby, on retirement, they withdrew from participation in formal economic structures and institutions. Thus, retirement operated as a process of both social and political exclusion, which detached senior citizens from some of the main sources of political consciousness and channels of representation. This exclusion contributed to a popular perception of older people as being politically passive. This fed into age-discriminatory stereotypes that portrayed older people as inactive, acquiescent, family orientated, and therefore disinterested in political participation. The scientific community contributed social theories that purported to explain the social and political passivity of older people. For example, the functionalist sociological theory of "disengagement" was introduced from the United States in the early 1960s. This argued that old age consisted of an inevitable and mutual process of disengagement between the aging individual and other members of society (Cumming & Henry, 1961). In other words, older people were not *expected* to be active participants in social and political life. The theory neglected the structural processes that, in effect, were excluding older people from participation. Of course in every country there were living examples of active senior citizens that contradicted the stereotype, but this does not negate the general trend.

Other factors operated to limit the extent of political participation on the part of older people in the early postwar period. In general, since age was less significant than it is today, there were fewer older people, and they were less healthy, and retirement was still acting as the key regulator of entry into old age. In political terms too, age was less salient because attention was directed chiefly at rebuilding the physical infrastructures of those countries devastated by the war and constructing the major institutions of the welfare state. Thus, in Europe at least, the politics of old age reflected the general politics of the time, dominated by traditional class and religious divisions with corporatism containing policy conflicts within the political system.

During this phase in the politics of old age, numerous pressure groups representing the interests of older people were created either at local or national levels or at both. Often the national pressure groups represented specific sections of the older population, such as retired civil servants (e.g., in Germany). They appeared on the political scene at different times in different countries. In the United Kingdom, such pressure groups date from the 1940s and 1950s, though some can trace their origins to the early part of the century. In the United States, the National Council on Aging was founded in 1950 and the American Association of Retired Persons (AARP) in 1958. In Germany, the association of war victims, disabled people, and pensioners (VdK) was formed in 1917, but reestablished in the Federal Republic in 1950 and currently has about one million members (Alber, 1995). Pensioners' organizations have existed in Austria since the 1950s—the Pensioners' Organisations (social democratic) and the Seniors' Federation (conservative) claim around 38% of all senior citizens (60 plus) as members (Leichsenring, 1996). In Portugal, pressure groups sprang up in the mid-1970s. In some countries, national trade unions established special sections for retired workers, but only in Italy did these develop into major sources of direct representation (with more than 20% of the older population belonging to the retired sections of the three main unions).

Despite the large membership of some of the pressure groups and other organizations formed in the 1950s, '60s, and '70s, they were not primarily concerned with the political mobilization of the older population. Instead, they were orientated toward the representation of older people in the policy arena. They formed what Estes (1979) has referred to as the "aging enterprise." In this sense, therefore, the politics of old age in this period may be described as consensual: pressure groups representing older people were bargaining for public-policy advances within a context of shared understanding about the possibilities of politics, the assumption of progressive welfare development, and the deservingness of the case they espoused. Today things are quite different and the politics of old age are in a qualitatively different phase.

THE NEW POLITICS OF OLD AGE

This "new" politics of old age consists of two distinct but causally related macro- and micro/meso-aspects. At the macrolevel, policy makers began to question, more openly and frequently than hitherto, the cost of population aging. The first wave of this critical approach to welfare, and particularly the public expenditure implications of pensions and healthcare occurred in the mid-1970s following the world oil price shock and the fiscal crisis it contributed to (O'Connor, 1977). This was followed by a second wave of criticism in the 1980s when the macroeconomic implications of pension-system maturation and the financial costs of long-term care were the subject of (sometimes heated) debate in different countries.

For example, in the United Kingdom, the 1980s saw the decoupling of upratings in the basic public social insurance pension from earnings and the provision of only price protection. The State Earnings Related Pension was also cut substantially, and those in employment were offered tax incentives to take out private, prefunded or defined-contribution pensions (Walker, 1991, 1993). In the United States, there were parallel restrictions on the growth of social security and medicare expenditures (Rix, 1999, p. 180). What both countries saw in this period was a reversal of the previously politically sacrosanct status of deservingness on the part of older people and the construction of a discourse that, to a greater or lesser extent, emphasizes the burden of pensions on the working population. Binstock (1991, p. 11) has described this reversal of fortunes for U.S. older citizens:

> The expansive social policy context in which the [Older American's Act] was created . . . came to an end. . . . Since then, social policy retrenchment has been in vogue, and the general political environment—previously supportive of almost any policy proposals to benefit aging persons—has become increasingly hostile to older people (quoted in Rix, 1999, p. 179).

Sometimes this new discourse is expressed in terms of generational equity, and invariably the scientifically flawed dependency ratio between older people and those of working age is quoted as evidence of impending doom. (As I have argued elsewhere the persuasive power of these ratios is such that their use is impervious to counterscientific evidence (Walker, 1990)). Only in the United States was there a sustained public debate on generational equity, which was spurred on by the creation, in 1985, of the pressure group Americans for Generational Equality (AGE). However it proved to be a front for an antiwelfare ideology and signally failed to dent the support of the U.S. public for programs for older people, support which has remained resilient (Marshall, Cook, & Marshall, 1993; Walker, 1990).

Similar discourses emerged later in the other northern European countries, including some elements concerning generational equity (e.g., in Germany), and this has led to modifications to most countries' pension systems. For the most part, these are modest adjustments to the pension formulae or eligibility criteria so as to reduce long-term costs, with Italy being the exception (Walker, 2003). The crucial question for this chapter is why the United Kingdom and United States led the way in both developing the burden of old age discourse and in implementing policies designed to reduce or restrain public expenditure on pensions and other welfare state benefits and services for older people? The main answer is political ideology: it is no coincidence that, during the 1980s, these policies were introduced by governments holding very similar neoliberal perspectives. Of course, the policies bear the names of their chief political advocates: "Thatcherism" in the United Kingdom and "Reaganomics" in the United States. New Zealand followed a similar idealogical path and its then Chancellor is immortalized as "Rogernomics." The emergence of the neoliberal "New Right" may be traced to the revision of conservative politics that took place in the 1970s, mainly in Anglo-Saxon countries, which intertwined the previously separate strands of liberal belief in a free economy and conservative belief in a small but strong state (Gamble, 1986). Monetarist economics was the practical tool used to implement neoliberal thinking, and this was the justification (or scientific legitimation) for reducing the role of the state in welfare and the privatization of public interest (Walker, 1984, 1990a). Policies are always to some extent "path dependent" in that they reflect a particular country's historical legacy, and this explains why the Anglo-Saxon countries adopted neoliberalism more readily than those of continental Europe where a social democratic tradition had been more prevalent.

Over the last 20 years, this neoliberal ideology has been globalized by the international governmental organizations (IGOs), particularly the Bretton Woods economic institutions, the International Monetary Fund (IMF) and World Bank, and more recently the World Trade Organisation (WTO) and, to a lesser extent, the OECD (Estes & Phillipson, 2002; Walker, 1990; Walker & Deacon, 2003). This global aspect of the macrolevel new politics of old age is of increasing importance in determining the nature of provision in old age; and its power to undermine longstanding public pension and social protection systems is immense as national governments, for various reasons, fall in line with the neoliberal consensus. Back in the 1980s, the beginnings of the consensus on policies for old age were already visible:

> The key social-policy concern arising out of current demographic trends is whether the ageing of populations is likely to lead to a major increase in the cost of public social programs and whether society, and in particular the working population, will be able or willing to bear the additional financing burden (OECD, 1988b, p. 27).

> Under existing regulations the evolution of public pension schemes is likely to put a heavy and increasing burden on the working population in the coming decades. Such a financial strain may put inter-generational solidarity—a concept on which all public retirement pensions are based—at risk (OECD, 1988a, p. 102).

These reports from the OECD and an earlier one from the IMF (1986) were followed by others derived from a broadly similar burden-of-aging discourse and advocating policy prescriptions that typically involve a reduction in public pay-as-you-go (PAYG), defined-benefit pension schemes and an increase in private, defined-contribution, ones (World Bank, 1994). The next logical step is the liberalization of the trade in services (including health and social care) under the WTO, which would challenge national government perogatives to provide free services or to subsidize national not-for-profit providers (Estes & Phillipson, 2002; Walker & Deacon, 2003).

It must not be assumed that this new agenda is accepted without question by all policy makers: that is patently not the case. There are very wide variations, for example, among the Member States of the European Union (EU) in the extent to which they have pursued the policy prescriptions dictated by this neoliberal, macroeconomic perspective. Again, the causes of this diversity are related mainly to ideology and the historical legacies of policies and institutions in different countries, including the role of organized labor in policy making. However, there is no doubt that all governments and leading political actors now place this issue high on their list of priorities. Moreover, there is no doubt whatsoever about the impact of this neoliberal ideology on the countries of central and eastern Europe, for the simple reason that the IGOs have been highly influential in determining policies on aging in these ex-communist bloc countries. There are numerous examples of these nations being "advised" to either privatize existing systems or to follow the private, pre-funded route in building pensions, often as the condition for the award of a loan (Ferge, 2002; Walker & Deacon, 2003).

THE RISE OF PENSIONER ACTION GROUPS

Turning to the micro- and mesolevels, the new politics of old age consists of a rapid increase in direct political involvement on the part of older people. This is particularly the case in the EU, although this may to some extent be a function of research (Walker & Naegele, 1999). For example, in Germany the Senior Protection Association or "Grey Panthers" was formed in 1975. The Grey Panthers now have some 200 local groups with roughly 15,000 members (Alber, 1995, p. 133). In the United Kingdom, the National Pensioners Convention (NPC) was created in 1979 and reconstituted in 1992 by an amalgamation of different preexisting grassroots and trade union groups. (This includes one of the oldest pensioner pressure groups in Europe, the National Federation of Retired Pensioners' Associations, which was established in 1939 as a radical grassroots campaigning organization.) The NPC has up to 1.5 million affiliated members in the local pensioner action groups, which have mushroomed under the aegis of the NPC (Carter & Nash, 1992). Also, a Pensioners Protection Party was started in 1991, and a Pensioners Rights Campaign was formed in 1989 to press for a Pensioners Charter. In Denmark in the early 1990s, a new grassroots movement of older people was established, called the C Team. This group is independent of established organizations representing older people as well as political parties and arranges mass demonstrations and other actions aimed at preventing cuts in health and social services and improving provision for frail older people (Platz & Petersen, 1995, p. 63). In Portugal, the Party of National Solidarity (PSN) was formed and secured the election of a deputy to the National Assembly in 1990 (out of 100,000 votes for the PSN, 90,000 were cast by older people) (Perista, 1995). In 1992, the Italian pensioner party, the oldest such party in Europe, had its first representative elected to the regional government in Rome. A year later, seven pensioner representatives were elected to the Netherlands parliament.

These examples are sufficient to show that, in a very short space of time, there has been, at least as far as the EU is concerned, a mushrooming of pensioners' action groups at local and national levels and, with them, the emergence of what appears to be a newly radicalized politics of old age. Of course the new social movements among older people involve only relatively few pensioners; activism is a minority pursuit in all generations, but many more are involved than previously and more actively so. Furthermore, the nature of political participation and representation is changing: there are more and more examples of direct action by senior citizens, and the new action groups are grassroots organizations composed of older people who want to represent themselves. It is too soon to say how permanent these new social movements will be as we may still be in a transitional phase. Indeed, insecurity is a familiar feature of grassroots organizations, and it is predictable that some will fail, as happened to the political party for older people in Belgium. I will come back to the question of future directions in the final part of this chapter, but for the moment, how do we explain this rapid transformation in the political participation and representation of older people?

First of all, the growth in political action by older people is merely a reflection of the global upsurge in social movements spanning almost every element of political life (Jenkins & Klandermans, 1995). This may be seen as one facet of the transition from modernity to post modernity which, on the one hand, means the breakdown of the traditional economic and social certainties of modernity and, on the other, the opening up of new concepts of citizenship and consumerism and new channels of political action (Harvey, 1989). The emergence of new social movements outside of the familiar politics institutions—political parties and trade unions—is not surprising given the profound realignments underway in the social and economic orders of the advanced industrial societies.

Second, some of the sociodemographic developments have supported both a heightened political awareness of old age as a political issue and the likelihood that older people will participate actively. Quite simply, there are more older people and, therefore, they are more visible than 15-20 years ago in social terms and in policy or political terms. Also, the combination of the massive growth of early exit from the labor market (Kohli, Rein, Guillemard, & Gunsteren, 1991; Walker, Guillemard, & Alber, 1993) and the cohort effects of a healthier and better educated older population has produced a potentially active pool of older people in their third age (50-74).

Third, the negative changes in the macroeconomic policy context referred to earlier have had an impact on the radicalization of the grassroots politics of old age in some countries. The Grey Panthers in the United States campaign on social security and medicare-related issues as well as more local ones. In Denmark, the C Team was set up to protest against cuts in public social services. The primary focus of the U.K. pensioners' campaigns is the government: both local and national campaigns have been concerned almost exclusively with the government's cuts in pensions and social services provision and related issues, such as the introduction of VAT on electricity and gas bills. Obviously the precise impact of such policies on activism among older people depends on a variety of factors, including the adequacy of welfare provision for this group in each country and the extent of the public expenditure reductions being proposed by particular governments. Thus, the mobilization or activation effect of adverse public policy changes is uneven across the globe.

Fourth, the growth of political participation among older people has been openly encouraged in several countries by policy makers at both local and national levels. Again, the EU is the main focus of attention here.

PARTICIPATION IN LOCAL DECISION-MAKING

Local authorities in the EU play an important part in encouraging and facilitating the participation of older people in decision making. Most of the participation of older people in daily life takes place at a local level, and this unit of administration is responsible, directly or indirectly, for many of the services that they receive. It is useful, however, to distinguish two different sorts of participation in decision making at the local level. On the one hand, there is the macropublic policy-making process, which determines the general direction of services and the distribution of resources between groups; while, on the other hand, there are policy decisions taken at an interpersonal micro-level, often by professionals employed by municipalities, which concern the delivery of specific services to older people. The distinction corresponds to that in Denmark between senior citizen councils and user councils.

As far as the local municipal policy making process is concerned, there has been a great deal of activity in recent years in different EU countries to try to improve the participation of older people. Local authorities in Austria, Denmark, France, Germany,

Italy, the Netherlands, and Sweden have all established advisory boards of senior citizens. In the case of Sweden, advisory councils must be established by law in all municipalities and, in 70% of them, there are ombudsmen with special responsibilities toward older people. Denmark has advisory boards or similar bodies in the majority of its municipalities. In 1980, only four local authorities had senior citizens councils, but by 1995, this had increased to 200 (out of 275). Under a 1982 decree in France, regional and departmental consultative committees were established to ensure the participation of older people in policy making concerning health and social services programs. At the same time, a National Committee for Pensioners and Old People (CNRPA) was created to facilitate participation in national policy-making. In Germany, local councils of senior citizens began to be formed in the early 1970s in an attempt to open new channels of access to the policy-making process and, more recently, their increase has been rapid—from 500 to 730 between 1995 and 1996 for example. Initially, the adoption of these senior councils spread very slowly, but during the 1980s, their numbers more than trebled (Alber, 1994, p. 135). Italy has established consultative committees at regional and communal levels, though their composition and function varies widely. The larger municipalities in the Netherlands have seniors boards operating in an advisory capacity. Advisory boards for senior citizens have been established, during the last five years, in most Austrian provinces (Leichsenring, 1996). Local consultative councils of older people have begun to appear in Belgium: 50% of municipalities in the Flemish speaking part of Belgium have an advisory committee, and their numbers are increasing. Councils of older people at local, regional, and national levels have been set up under Spain's gerontological plan.

Turning to the second dimension of participation in decision making at the local level, we are faced with a very complex interplay of personal and professional relationships. The health and social services are key agencies in the construction of dependency in old age. Professional groups have been trained to regard themselves as autonomous experts, and this has had the effect of excluding older people and their family carers from making decisions about the services required to meet their care needs. Thus, one of the most important issues confronting local health and social care providers, including local authorities, is how to promote the participation of older people (and service users) and their informal carers in the processes of care.

There are pressures building up for increased participation in decisions previously regarded as the sole province of professionals. These are coming, first, from the rise of consumerism (the transition from modernity to postmodernity) and the reassertion of individualism. This social change is creating twin pressures for greater choice and for a participating voice. Second, there are grassroots pressures from service users, some of whom are demanding a greater say in what services are provided, and from informal carers, who are complaining about being, at best, taken for granted by service providers. In the Netherlands and the United Kingdom, self-help groups of carers have been formed to represent their views. They are calling for a recognition of their right to be consulted on an equal basis with service users. Third, there are changes within professionals in their orientation and practice that are beginning to question professional autonomy and that are opening up professional practice to user involvement. Together, these processes are beginning to set a new agenda favoring the participation of older people and older service users.

Signs of this culture shift can be seen in some countries, notably those Scandinavian ones that emphasize rights to services. Thus, the Users Councils in Denmark are representing the interests of older users with regard to home care, institutional care and other services. Even in the United Kingdom, which has a more paternalistic service tradition, user groups are being established by some local authorities, particularly since the introduction of the Better Government for Older People initiative (Cook, Maltby, & Warren, 2004)

But there are still formidable barriers in the way of effective participation, and there is a very long way to go before older people are genuinely empowered in the face of professional service allocators and providers. Clearly the municipalities have a crucial role to play in promoting a *culture of empowerment* at all levels and encouraging professionals to operate in more open participative ways (Barnes & Walker, 1996).

PARTICIPATION IN NATIONAL DECISION-MAKING

Several countries have set up national advisory boards consisting of the representatives of older people. The French National Committee for Pensioners and Older People (CNRPA) and Spanish national council have been mentioned already. The Senior Citizens Consulting Council was set up in Belgium more than 40 years ago. In the Netherlands, the National Council for Elderly Policy was established in 1988 (but disbanded in 1996), in Ireland the National Council for the Elderly advises the minister of health, and a National Economic and Social Council has just been set up. In Luxembourg, there is a Higher Council for Older People. In Austria, a Federal Senior Council was established in 1995. It consists of 35 representatives of the three most important seniors' organizations, the ministries, the provinces, and local authorities, meets 3-4 times a year and is chaired by the Chancellor (Leichsenring, 1996). Although these national bodies reflect a consensual model of policy making and may be regarded by politically active seniors as part of a process of co-option, they, nonetheless, have probably assisted the development of the new politics of old age by both raising the profile of older people in the policy-making process and by helping to legitimize their political concerns. The Ombudsman role in Sweden is also a mechanism that raises the profile of older people's rights and, particularly with regard to frail older people, helps to include them in decision making.

Thus, the recent mobilization of older people in the EU and the development of what appears to be a new grassroots politics of old age must be regarded as the consequence of two distinct impulses. From *below* there are undoubtedly pressures on the part of older people seeking a political voice, while, from *above,* policy makers at local, national, and EU levels have consciously encouraged the political mobilization of older people.

GREY POWER: MYTH OR REALITY?

While there can be little doubt about the increasing involvement of older people in grassroots organizations, campaigns, local advisory boards, and, in some countries, national councils of senior citizens, the question remains to what extent has this involvement been translated into effective power? On this question, there is very little in the way of hard evidence on which to base sound conclusions. Thus, any judgment concerning grey power must be tentative at this stage. With this caveat in mind, it appears that much of the increase in political participation witnessed in the past two decades has not led consistently to influence over events. In fact, the ideological construction of grey power, reproduced by popular press headlines, has created a myth that sheer numbers is all that matters in the battle for political influence. Even the world's largest pressure group for older people, the AARP, with 32 million members, which has been described flatteringly as "the most fearsome force in politics" (Birnbaum, 1997, p. 122) and, less so, as an "800 pound gorilla" (Rix, 1999, p. 181), is not able to guarantee that the U.S. Congress will be responsive to its pleas. I will come back to the reasons why the apparently latent power of older people has not been mobilized consistently but, for the moment, it can be established that the ideological construction of grey power sits closely with the neoliberal myth of aging as a burden on society and serves a complementary purpose. Moreover, it may be that the various new mesolevel structures of participation assembled, for example, in the EU over the past 20 years, are masking, to some extent, the absence of effective political power held by older people. Again scientific evidence is required to test this hypothesis.

Of course, the formation of local advisory bodies provides an important basis for participation by older people in municipal affairs and also a potential network for local administrators to activate. However, their existence does not mean that the voices of older people will actually be heard within the policy-making process or that the councils will be able to stand up for their interests, especially those of the most vulnerable. Moreover, as Verté, Ponjaert-Kristofferson, and Geerts' (1996) study of advisory councils in the Dutch speaking part of Belgium shows, such bodies may reinforce the exclusion of some groups of older people. In one of the few studies on this topic, it was found that members of the advisory bodies were mainly drawn from organizations of retired people and were overwhelmingly men. When women did participate, they were rarely members of the council's executive boards. The main participation was from ex-skilled and semiskilled manual workers and farmers.

The survey also found that when an important issue was put on the agenda, only just under half of the members consulted other members of the organization they represented. One-third of advisory group members were judged to be passive participants. Most members of advisory councils of older people said that once they advise the municipal council, the goodwill of the mayor or the alderman decides if the advice is acted upon. The majority of those who participate in the advisory councils were of the opinion that their efforts are not taken seriously by the local authorities. To quote Verté and his colleagues:

> Our study showed that, although many local policy makers took the initiative of forming an advisory body for the elderly, only a few of them asked for the opinion of the members of the advisory body. The attitude of local policy makers towards their own advisory bodies is characterised by a low commitment to these projects of political participation.

The key elements in this negative picture seem to be the absence of a legal framework governing the establishment of advisory councils (as in Sweden) and the existence among some policy makers of age-discriminatory attitudes, which lead them to minimize the potential contribution of older people to policy making.

On the positive side, there are examples of advisory councils successfully mobilizing older people and making an impact on policy making. Moreover, there is some good evidence that it is possible to overcome the problems in organizing the local participation of older people. It is clear, though, that we must be mindful of the limitations of local advisory councils, and older people must be aware of the danger of co-option, and indeed, some pensioners' organizations may prefer to retain an independent voice.

At the macrolevel, it is possible that the power of pensioners is revealed in the proportion of national income allocated to pensions. Support for this hypothesis is given by the fact, noted earlier, that pure demography played a minor part in the growth of public-pension expenditure in the years between 1960 and 1984 (OECD, 1988b). It was during this period that public pension spending in OECD countries grew most rapidly to become the largest single item of social expenditure. Moreover, because it rose faster than GDP, there was an increase in the share of national resources devoted to older people in these countries (OECD, 1988b, p. 19). Unfortunately, it is not possible to relate this general rise in spending with any identifiable exercise of sustained pensioner power, but, rather, this was the era of consensus on the deservingness of older people. When this was overtaken by the neoliberal economic consensus, which gradually spread from the United States, United Kingdom, Australia, and New Zealand in the early 1980s, pensions spending stabilized and, in some countries, actually declined. This latter part of the twentieth century coincided with the growth of the older population in most OECD countries, which lends further weight to the doubts expressed here concerning the reality of pensioner power. Furthermore, there appears to be no correlation between the level of pension expenditure and either the size of the groups representing older people or the degree of institutionalization of their right to representation. As Table 1 shows, the United States has the world's largest pressure group representing older people but, compared with other OECD countries, devotes one of the smallest proportions of its national income to pensions. Sweden has one of the world's most sophisticated systems

Table 1. Old-Age Pension Spending, 2000 (as a percentage of GDP)

Canada	5.1
Finland	8.1
Germany	11.8
Italy	14.2
Japan	7.9
Netherlands	5.2
Sweden	9.2
United Kingdom	4.3
United States	4.4

Source: OECD, 2001, p. 68.

of representation for older people and, while its pension spending is relatively high, it is not the highest. In fact, during the 1990s, the proportion of GDP spent on pensions in Sweden actually declined by 12% (EC, 2002).

The available evidence suggests that grey power is a myth, and its reproduction may have more to do with attempts to legitimize neoliberal inspired policies intended to reduce public spending on older people than any genuine examples of sustained influence over policy at the macrolevel. Also, while there are continuing examples of the operation of grey power in local politics, these tend to be part of the ebb and flow of pluralism rather than a sign of structured power to change resource distribution in favor of older people. The next section examines why grey power is more myth than reality; but first, it is worth pointing out that the general public seems to be supportive of political action by older people. For example, opinion polls in Denmark have found that over half the population considers the C Team's demonstrations to be quite reasonable, and only 10% regard them as unreasonable. Though, ironically, the lowest level of support for such forms of direct action was given by older people themselves (Platz & Peterson, 1995, p. 65). In the 1992 Eurobarometer survey, conducted in all of the then 12 Member States of the EC, we asked the general public whether or not older people should stand up more actively for their rights. Very large proportions of the public in all countries said that they should—on average more than four in five. The combined FDR and GDR proportions were 84%—the same as in the United Kingdom—though more of the latter agreed strongly (Walker, 1993, p. 32).

NUMBERS ARE NOT ENOUGH

There can be no doubt about the importance of the transformation that is taking place in the politics of old age. Equally, however, we must not overstate what has happened. So far, this change has impinged on only a minority of senior citizens, and this suggests, at least, that the barriers to political participation may be more formidable than has been recognized generally, and perhaps, that there is no sound basis for political mobilization among older people. There are five main impediments to such participation by older people in specifically age-related politics, and these include both demand and supply factors.

In the first place, contrary to popular perceptions and some scientific analyses, older people do not necessarily share a common interest by virtue of their age alone that transcends all other interests. Thus it is mistaken to regard senior citizens as a homogeneous group that might coalesce around or be attracted by a one-dimensional politics of old age. In other words, there is not only one but several forms of socio-political consciousness that depend, not on age as such, but on factors such as socio-economic status, race, gender, religion, and locality. This perspective is at odds with the longstanding tendency for social gerontologists to regard older people as a distinct and homogeneous social group, separate from the rest of the social structure and, in particular, as a group cut off from their *own* status and class position formed at earlier stages of the life cycle. Although no longer prevalent in social gerontology, this is still a view held by policy makers in many different countries and in IGOs (OECD, 1994; Walker, 1990). As Estes (1982; 1991) has argued, a largely classless view of old age has been incorporated into public policy.

Because of the heterogeneity of older people, sheer numbers are not an indicator of power, and the existence of a range of different organizations representing this group may diffuse potential mobilization (Douglas, 1995). In fact, older people are just as deeply divided along social class and other structural lines as younger adults. This means that large organizations such as the AARP are dealing with a very diverse membership (Rix, 1999). This contrasts with both common-sense notions and pluralistic analyses suggesting a common interest among older people, with age acting as a sort of leveller of class and status differentials. There is no doubt that the process of retirement, not aging, does superimpose reduced socioeconomic status on a majority of older people: average net replacement ratios even for men with a full record of contributions are significantly less than 100% under the most generous pension regimes in the EU (Walker, Guillemard, & Alber, 1993, p. 15). Even so, retirement has a differential impact on older people depending on their prior socioeconomic status. For example, there is unequal access to second-tier pensions. Women and other groups with incomplete employment records are particularly disadvantaged in most countries.

Second, the majority of older people remain powerless politically. Traditionally the main source of working-class political power has been the economic base provided by the workplace and trade-union organization. The social processes of exclusion that retirement and, more recently, early exit, amount to, not only remove older people from the main source of income, but also from collective activities and potential political influence. Indeed the process of exclusion itself is likely to encourage conservatism because it detaches older people from collective workplace activities and sources of sociopolitical consciousness as well as practical information and replaces them with privatized and individualized home-based activities. Of course, I am well aware that this is predicated on a Fordist model of work organization, which is increasingly inappropriate as a description of the postmodern world of work (Harvey, 1989); but paid employment remains a collective activity for the majority of those in employment. Thus, Simone de Beauvoir's (1977) observation retains some element of truth: having been removed from playing any economic role in society, older people lack both cohesion and a means of challenging their inferior economic and social position.

Retirement (including early retirement) appears to entail an element of de-politicization or political disengagement, though it is impossible to disentangle any cohort effects from the available data. The observation of a relationship between political efficacy and occupation dates back more than 40 years to the U.S. research by Almond and Verba (1963). Using a similar approach a more recent British survey analysis has found that propensity for collective action is lowest among the retired and, in contrast to the employed and other groups in the labor market, retired people have a preference for personal over collective action (Young, 1984). (These findings echo those Danish opinion poll data reported earlier.) The explanation for this acquiescence on the part of older people consisted of a sense of powerlessness or noncompetence, which, in turn, reflected a lack of real resources with which to gain political influence. There was, predictably, a close association between both socioeconomic group and education as well as subjectively assessed power.

Third, pensioners often lack formal channels through which to exert political influence. Indeed, the political representation systems of some countries effectively exclude older people from key institutions. For example, few of the established political parties in Europe provided an organizational context for pensioners or made special efforts to include them in their machinery. The main exception is Germany whose political parties have taken steps to try to incorporate them (Alber, 1995, p. 131). The Christian Democrats were the first to establish a special party organization for older people in 1988. It is called the Senioren-Union and is open to all people over 60 including nonmembers of the party. The Social Democrats rejected the creation of a special subgroup for older people and instead issued an appeal, in 1979, to mobilize senior citizens within the party. Subsequently, a network of senior circles was built up at district and regional levels within the party. More recently, the Social Democrats created senior representative posts at district, state and federal levels.

Similarly, some trade unions in Europe have been poor at involving ex-members and in providing continuing membership after labor-force exit. Again there are important exceptions and also signs that the trade-union movement generally is becoming more aware of the need to involve older people. In Italy, more than 20% of pensioners belong to the special retirement sections of the three main unions. This relatively high participation rate appears to be the result of a combination of bottom-up and top-down impulses. On the one hand, older people want to defend the rights they have acquired, particularly pension rights, and on the other, Italian trade unions have taken specific steps to increase the social and political involvement of older people (Florea, Costanzo, & Cuneo, 1995). Other national unions in the EU lag some way behind their Italian counterparts. Germany has a relatively high union participation rate among pensioners compared with other EU countries: 13.3% of the 11.7 million union members are pensioners (with higher than average rates in the public sector and metal-workers unions) (Alber, 1995). In Spain, the two major unions each have a federation of the retired, but their membership is low (less than 1% of all pensioners).

Fourth, there are important physical and mental barriers to political participation in old age. Disability and socially disabling later life-course events, such as widowhood, may further fragment political consciousness and discourage political activity. The experience of aging itself creates barriers to collective action and political participation for a minority of older people. For those with intellectual or learning disabilities who are just now reaching old age, the aging process merely confirms their socio-political exclusion (Walker, Walker, & Ryan, 1996). Other social-structural factors that militate against political participation include poverty and low incomes, and age, gender, and race discrimination. For instance, a significant minority of older people experience poverty and, in some countries, the size of the minority is quite large (Walker, Guillemard, & Alber, 1993; Walker & Maltby, 1997). Those suffering social exclusion as a result of poverty face substantial material and psychological barriers to participation and are among the least likely to be represented within the formal political system (Scharf, Phillipson, & Smith, 2004). In addition, a large number of older people, particularly women, are actively engaged in caring for spouses and others in need and, therefore, may not have the physical energy and mental space to be active on the political scene as well.

Finally there is conservatism. It is not necessarily the case that people become more conservative as they grow older, despite the commonplace nature of that assumption (see, for example, Hudson, 1980). In terms of public opinion, on most issues they differ very little to younger people in both the EU and the United States (Peterson &

Somit, 1994; Walker, 1993). However, there is evidence that older people are more conservative in certain respects than younger ones, but the reasons are not related primarily to age. Several key factors have been mentioned already, including the removal of sources of potential influence and activity but, in addition, there is a generational dimension. The present older generations have different reference points to younger people and early economic life is of particular importance in the formation of political consciousness and party allegiance (Westergaard, Noble, & Walker, 1989). Many of their formative years occurred between 1915 and 1950, a unique historical period in Europe. Older people are also likely to retain loyalty to a particular political party. All of this suggests that older people are *not* more conservative in voting terms but, rather, they have a tendency to vote for the party they have always voted for. Also, it is likely that in some countries, conservative voters, on average, live longer than social democratic ones—because of their different social-class origins. This class-demographic effect will tend to reinforce proconservative voting patterns among very elderly people, the majority of whom are women.

These five demand and supply factors represent substantial barriers to political participation on the part of some older people and cast serious doubt on the development of any major age-specific political groupings, at least as far as the EU is concerned.

CONCLUSION

Having traced the development of a distinctly new politics of old age, with interrelated macro- and meso/micro features, my conclusion is that the social and economic foundations for political power and mobilization among older people remain relatively weak. This is not peculiar to old age, but a demonstration that age is not, in itself, a firm basis for political consciousness. While there can be no doubt about the relatively new direction of macroeconomic and social policies in developed countries, on the available evidence, grey power is a myth. Furthermore, this myth is being reproduced and amplified regularly in support of the macrolevel neoliberal policy prescriptions. One reason for the apparent ease with which this myth gets translated into popular discourse is the virtual absence of scientific research on this topic. Political science has neglected age as a research area and, with a few honorable exceptions, gerontology has not developed a specialism in the political sociology of old age (Walker, 1986). It is important to plug this research gap in order to better inform the public debate.

Whether or not age will remain a weak basis for political mobilization is an open question, but it seems likely. In the EU age-based movement, political parties are likely to remain marginal features of political life. Such evidence as there is suggests that only small proportions of older people (less than one-quarter) would be prepared to join a political party based on old age (Walker, 1993). The parties that have been formed recently along these lines, such as the Grey Panthers in Germany and the United Kingdom Senior Citizens Party, attract only small memberships. Even in the Netherlands, one of Europe's most pluralistic political systems, the associations of older people are against the creation of an age-related political party (van Rijsselt, 1995, p. 326). The United States is a potentially favorable location for the development of age-based politics because older Americans are ready to exhibit age consciousness (Torres-Gil, 1993), and the pluralistic political system is the most amenable to interest group influence (Pampel, Williamson, & Stryker, 1990; Williamson, Evans, & Powell, 1982). However, despite these favorable indicators, there is little evidence in the United States to suggest that age is a potentially powerful predictor of political attitudes and behavior (Rix, 1999, p. 186).

Having demonstrated that numbers alone are not sufficient for political power, a future transformation of grey power into a potent force will not result from demographic change. Nonetheless, population aging will continue to raise policy questions concerning older people higher and higher up the political agenda, including in the developing world. This will inevitably increase the potential for the political mobilization of older people themselves, especially if the new macropolitics of old age continues to be dominated by neoliberalism. Many of the newest and most radical pensioner groups have been formed to campaign against welfare-state retrenchment dictated by neoliberal-oriented policies. The truism that "all politics are local" applies particularly to older people, and if the new grassroots politics of old age is to develop into effective grey power, it is most likely to happen at the local level. Conflicts over local rationing of health and social care, transport, housing, crime, and public safety are potential flash-points.

Numbers should count in one sense: older women will continue for some time to outnumber older men, and this should lead to a feminization of the politics of old age. Given that many of the European trade-union-based organizations of older people are dominated by men, this will present a significant challenge for them. The improved health and higher education level of future cohorts will increase their propensity to participate, but rising affluence and greater diversity may dissipate it. So, the future politics of old age remains uncertain and will depend a great deal on how the politics of welfare develop in the coming decades and, in particular, the extent to which politicians attempt, perversely in aging societies, to take resources away from older people.

REFERENCES

Alber, J. (1994). Soziale integration und politische repräsentation von senioren. In G. Verheugen (Ed.), *60plus. Die wachsende macht der alten.* (pp. 145-168). Köln: Bund-Verlag.

Alber, J. (1995). The social integration of older people in Germany. In A. Walker (Ed.), *Older people in Europe: Social integration* (pp. 111-162). Brussels: EC, DG5.

Almond, G. A., & Verba, S. (1963). *The civic culture.* Princeton: Princeton University Press.

Barnes, M., & Walker, A. (1996). Consumerism versus empowerment—A principled approach to the involvement of older service users. *Policy and Politics, 24*(4), 375-393.

Binstock, R. (1991). From the great society to the ageing society—25 years of the Older Americans Act. *Generations, 15*(3), 11-18.

Birnbaum, J. (1997). Washington's second most powerful man. *Fortune,* May 12, 122-126.

Carter, T., & Nash, C. (1992). *Pensioners forums—An active voice.* Guildford: Pre-Retirement Association.

Cook, J., Maltby, T., & Warren, L. (2004). A participatory approach to older women's quality of life. In A. Walker & C. Hennessy (Eds.), *Growing older: Quality of life in old age* (pp. 149-166). Buckingham: McGraw-Hill.

Cumming, E., & Henry, W. E. (1961). *Growing old, the process of disengagement.* New York: Basic Books.

de Beauvoir, S. (1977). *Old age.* Harmondsworth: Penguin Books (first published as La Viellesse, 1970).
Douglas, E. (1995). Professional organisations in ageing: Too many doing too little for too few. *Generations, 19*(2), 35-36.
EC (European Commission). (2002). *Social protection: Expenditure on pensions.* Brussels: EC.
Estes, C. L. (1979). *The ageing enterprise.* San Francisco: Jossey-Bass.
Estes, C. L. (1982). Austerity and aging in the US. *International Journal of Health Services, 12*(4), 573-584.
Estes, C. L. (1991). The new political economy of aging: Introduction and critique. In M. Minkler & C. Estes (Eds.), *Critical perspectives on aging* (pp. 3-18). Amityville, NY: Baywood.
Estes, C., & Phillipson, C. (2002). The globalisation of capital, the welfare state and old age policy. *International Journal of Health Services, 32*(2), 279-297.
Ferge, Z. (2002). European integration and the reform of Social Security in the accession countries. *European Journal of Social Quality, 3*(1/2), 9-25.
Florea, A., Costanzo, A., & Cuneo, A. (1995). The social integration of older people in Italy. In A. Walker (Ed.), *Older people in Europe: Social integration* (pp. 229-261). Brussels: EC, DG5.
Gamble, A. (1986). *The free economy and the strong state.* Houndmills: Macmillan.
Harvey, D. (1989). *The condition of postmodernity.* Oxford: Blackwell.
Hudson, R. B. (1980). Old age politics in a period of change. In N. G. McCluskey & E. F. Borgatta (Eds.), *Aging and society* (pp. 147-189). London: Sage.
Jenkins, J. C., & Klandermans, B. (Eds.). (1995). *The politics of social protest.* London: UCL Press.
Kohli, M., Rein, M., Guillemard, A.-M., & Gunsteren, H. (1991). *Time for retirement.* Cambridge: CUP.
Leichsenring, K. (1996). Payments for care in selected European countries. In Fondazione Finney (Ed.), *What kind of legal and social protection for frail older persons? The ageing society and personal rights* (pp. 274-279). Rome/Brussels: Fondazione Finney/Commission of the European Union.
Marshall, V., Cook, F., & Marshall J. (1993). Conflict over intergenerational equity: Rhetoric and reality in a comparative context. In V. Bengtson & A. Achenbaum (Eds.), *The changing contract across generations* (pp. 119-140). New York: Aldine.
O'Connor, J. (1977). *The fiscal crisis of the state.* London: St. Martin's Press.
OECD. (1988a). *Reforming public pensions.* Paris: OECD.
OECD. (1988b). *Ageing populations—The social policy implications.* Paris: OECD.
OECD. (1994). *New orientations for social policy.* Paris: OECD.
OECD. (2001). *Ageing and income.* Paris: OECD.
Pampel, F., Williamson, J., & Stryker, R. (1990). Class context and pension response to demographic structure in advanced industrial democracies. *Social Problems, 37*(4), 535-550.
Perista, H. (1995). The social integration of older people in Portugal. In A. Walker (Ed.), *Older people in Europe: Social integration* (pp. 340-359). Brussels: EC, DG5.
Petersen, S., & Somit, A. (1994). *Political behaviour of older Americans.* New York: Garland.
Platz, M., & Petersen, N. F. (1995). The social integration of older people in Denmark. In A. Walker (Ed.), *Older people in Europe: Social integration* (pp. 46-74). Brussels: EC, DG5.
Rix, S. (1999). The politics of old age in the United States. In A. Walker. & G. Naegele (Eds.), *The politics of old age in Europe* (pp. 178-196). Buckingham: OU Press.
Scharf, T., Phillipson, C., & Smith, A. E. (2004). Poverty and social exclusion: Growing older in deprived urban neighbourhoods. In A. Walker & C. Hennessy (Eds.), *Growing older: Quality of life in old age*(pp. 81-106). Buckingham: McGraw-Hill.

Torres-Gil, F. (1993). Interest group politics: Generational changes in the politics of aging. In V. Bengtson & A. Achenbaum (Eds.), *The changing contract across generations* (pp. 239-258). New York: Aldine.

Townsend, P. (1981). The structured dependency of the elderly: The creation of social policy in the twentieth century. *Ageing and Society, 1*(1), 5-28.

Townsend, P. (1986). Ageism and social policy. In C. Phillipson & A. Walker (Eds.), *Ageing and social policy*. Aldershot: Gower.

van Rijsselt, R. (1995). The social integration of older people in the Netherlands. In A. Walker (Ed.), Older people in Europe: Social integration (pp. 306-339). Brussels: EC, DG5.

Verté, D., Ponjaert-Kristoffersen, I., & Geerts, C. (1996). Political participation of elderly in local policy. In A. Carrell, V. Gerling, C. Marking, G. Naegele, & A. Walker (Eds.), *Political participation and representation of elderly people in Europe* (pp. 121-126). Bonn: German Federal Ministry for Family Affairs, Senior Citizens, Women and Youth.

Walker, A. (1980). The social creation of poverty and dependency in old age. *Journal of Social Policy, 9*(1), 45-75.

Walker, A. (1984) The political economy of privatisation. In J. Le Grand & R. Robinson (Eds.), *Privatisation and the welfare State* (pp. 19-44). London: Allen & Unwin.

Walker, A. (1986). The politics of ageing in Britain. In C. Phillipson, M. Bernard, & P. Strong (Eds.), *Dependency and interdependency in old age—Theoretical perspective and policy alternatives* (pp. 30-45). London: Croom Helm.

Walker, A. (1990). The economic "burden" of ageing and the prospect of intergenerational conflict. *Ageing and Society, 10*(4), 377-396.

Walker, A. (1990a) The strategy of inequality: Poverty and income distribution in Britain 1979-89. In I. Taylor (Ed.), *The social effects of free market policies* (pp. 29-48). Hemel Hempstead: Harvester Wheatsheaf.

Walker, A. (1991). Thatcherism and the new politics of old age. In J. Myles & J. Quadagno (Eds.), *States, labor markets and the future of old age policy* (pp. 19-36). Philadelphia: Temple University Press.

Walker, A. (1993). Poverty and inequality in old age. In J. Bond, P. Coleman, & S. Peace (Eds.), *Ageing in society* (2nd ed., pp. 280-303). London: Sage.

Walker, A. (Ed.). (1995). *Older people in Europe: Social integration*. Brussels: EC, DG5.

Walker, A. (2003). Securing the future of old age in Europe. *Journal of Societal and Social Policy, 2*(1), 13-32.

Walker, A., & Deacon, B. (2003). Economic globalisation and policies on ageing. *Journal of Societal and Social Policy, 2*(2), 1-18.

Walker, A., Guillemard, A. M., & Alber, J. (1993). *Older people in Europe: Social and economic policies*. Brussels: Commission of the European Communities.

Walker, A., & Maltby, T. (1997). *Ageing Europe*. Buckingham: Open University Press.

Walker, A., & Naegele, G. (Eds.). (1999). *The politics of old age in Europe*. Buckingham: OU Press.

Walker, A., Walker, C., & Ryan, T. (1996). Older people with learning difficulties leaving institutional care: A case of double jeopardy. *Ageing and Society, 16*(2), 1-26.

Westergaard, J., Noble, I., & Walker, A. (1989). *After redundancy*. Oxford: Polity Press.

Williamson, J. B., Evans, L., & Powell, L. A. (1982). *Politics of ageing*. Springfield, IL: Charles Thomas.

World Bank. (1994). *Averting the old age crisis*. New York: Oxford University Press.

Young, K. (1984). Political attitudes. In R. Jowell & C. Airey (Eds.), *British social attitudes* (pp. 11-46). Aldershot: Gower.

CHAPTER 18

Productivity in Old Age in Labor and Consumption Markets: The German Case

Gerhard Naegele, Vera Gerling, and Karin Scharfenorth

The sudden boom in the productivity discourse within German gerontology, respectively German social sciences being gerontologically influenced, comes as no surprise for us since this shift has been documented for some time. However, productivity in old age is not based on a clear definition (Schroeter, 2004), which, by the way, does not seem to be an isolated German phenomenon (cf. for the United States, Hinterlong, Morrow-Howell, & Sherraden, 2001). Yet substantiations differ nowadays, although they are not absolutely *new*. In the past, productivity in old age was discussed to improve the image of old age in the society, which was predominantly negative. This especially applied to German gerontological psychology, which yielded, at a very early date, to the creation of positive connections to old age by discussing subjects such as *old age potentials, competences of elderly people,* and recently, *productivity in old age.* In doing so, it traditionally concentrated on individual physiological and psychological capacities of elderly people (vs. different contributions in Baltes & Montada, 1996).

Later, this perspective relating to social images of old age became important to the German sociology of old age (Tews, 1996). However, the German sociology of old age goes much further by simultaneously appealing to the "duty" of older people to be individually and socially productive, while being without any duties due to extensive early retiring programs. Spoken in an exaggerated manner, it was argued that older individuals needed to "re-obligate" themselves (Naegele, 1993). Tews conceptualizes a so-called productivity explicitly as a "behavior, which is producing values and is socially useful," by offering pecuniary or noncash rewards or making time available that can respectively be exchanged with each other. Here, Tews (1996) differentiates between an (1) *individual* productivity aiming at maintaining one's independence, an (2) *intra* and an (3) *intergenerational* productivity consisting of an exchange of socially useful interrelations within and amongst the generations, a (4) productivity of the *surroundings,* especially with regard to volunteer work as well as (5) a *social* productivity that addresses the social and political participation of elderly people.

Explicitly *economical* conceptualizations, however, are comparatively new. Classical aims recur in a new appearance: the goal still is to improve the prevailing image of old age, and once again the "productive" achievements of older people are being highlighted. Presently, however, the general context is much more in the processes and social consequences of the demographic change.

Consequently, for example, the Federal Government's 5th Commission Report on Elders, which started in the summer of 2003 and whose primary task it is to keep the German parliament continuously informed about the living conditions of its older citizens, examines the "potentials of old age concerning the economic system and the society." In this report, the two most important economic fields of "productivity of old age" (i.e., economy and the world of business), are explicitly being integrated. The concept of "active aging," which is sometimes used as synonym for "productive aging" has become established at the EU-level. Its leading scientific-political protagonist is the Briton Alan Walker (2002). Roughly speaking, this concept is considered the "suitable response" of the EU member states to the various individual social and economic challenges of the demographic changes, and it is especially aimed at the creation of (social) "utility references" concerning the everyday activities of elderly people. Both initiatives (as well as others that cannot be described more in detail here due to lack of space) have two aims in common: to "dedramatize" prevailing fears connected to the aging process of societies and to encourage older individuals to make more social contributions themselves. However, those initiatives also emphasize a political responsibility: policies need to be created to provide an adequate framework.

As far as our contribution is concerned, we generally understand the *economic productivity of old age* as the different activities of elderly people aimed at the orientation toward third parties, the creation or increase of economical values, and the distribution of goods, which have already been produced by them. To put it briefly, it is a matter of the *economic contributions of elderly people for the society*.

The aim is to try to "correct" the present prevailing thesis that growing numbers of older people place a financial strain on the society, a contention that is emphasized, especially by economists, as a realistic view of the debate. We would like to realize this correction in a two-fold manner: on the one hand, we are going to examine potentials for economic productivity in old age, which are already existing or which have already been realized, but which have been recognized in their economic significance insufficiently. On the other hand, we will examine neglected (i.e., unused) potentials for the economic productivity of old age as well as existing adequate political strategies. We will exemplarily analyze the fields of operational employment, labor marketing, private consumption, and services. Finally, we will illustrate the success of a political-promotional strategy for the "productivity of old age." This strategy, by the name of North Rhine Westphalian Initiative for Senior Economy,[1] has been established in North Rhine Westphalia, which is a state in Germany with a population of approximately 17 million. Furthermore, this example demonstrates that the aging of the society may lead to an increase in the demand of manpower under certain conditions.

[1] The term "Senior Economy" describes a market that is aimed at the needs of senior citizens and combines products and services for elders. In Japan, this market is called "Silver Market." In The United States of America, it is usually called "Grey Market."

In sum, we are convinced that the financial as well as the economical burdens of the demographic change can be moderated by increased productivity in old age, which is being offered more intensively and systematically, but must also be *required and used by the society*. We are regarding this as a contribution by elderly people themselves concerning the advancement and stabilization of the solidarity between the generations and, thus, simultaneously the promotion and stabilization of the generational contract as a basic element of the social security in Germany (Naegele, Hilbert, Gerling, & Weidekamp-Maicher, 2003).

Even if we, as social-political economists, whose traditional research interest has always been to surmount the social inequalities and poverty of old age in Germany (Naegele & Tews, 1993) are now concerned with the *productive potentials* of elderly people and the "wealthy" age, this does, in no way, announce a change of paradigm. We are still focusing on the social inequality of old age, however, with a massed concentration on the "other side of the coin." We are also regarding the increased individual and social utilization of old age productivity as a contribution to the *intra-generational solidarity* by those elderly people who are able to do so as a way to overcome social differences amongst the different age groups.

ELDERLY EMPLOYEES AND LABOR MARKET

As far as German companies and the labor market are concerned, the productivity of old age was not only not used (and still is largely not used) for a long period of time, but it was and is even systematically evaded. With an employment rate of approximately 47% of men and only 30% of women between the ages of 55 and 64 years, Germany lies far beyond the average of the OECD states (compared to Sweden: 70.7% (men), respectively 65.9% (women); Denmark: 64.2% (men), respectively 48.9% (women); United States: 66.3% (men) respectively 53.2% (women) according to the data of the OECD (OECD, 2003). At the beginning of 2003, approximately two-fifths of the companies (with at least one employee paying social insurance) did not engage any employees older than 50 (Bellmann, Hilpert, Kistler, & Wahse, 2003). In addition, there is an extremely higher number of *unemployed* older people in comparison to international numbers (OECD, 2003), especially for long-term unemployment (Deutscher Bundestag, 2002).

The reasons for the extreme low participation of older people in the job market (when compared internationally) and the early retirement in Germany (which has been practiced for three decades) have often been described. They consist of a mixture of different pull and push factors, such as national incentives (national early-retirement policy); operational strategies for the utilization of personnel; special risks of elderly employees (e.g., a higher risk of getting ill and losing qualifications) and, above all, an early retirement mentality being widespread in Germany. For an increasing number of older employees, an early retirement is even a desirable aim—a so-called "cultural achievement" (Naegele, 2002).

Early retirement plans and the "release of old age from the labor world," which was also politically supported by the official German labor-market policy for a long period of time, were, until recently, regarded as *legitimated* instruments to combat unemployment in general and of young people especially. In other words, this was seen as a sacrifice by old people to the young generation in the form of a "labor market generation contract."

As a matter of fact, the existing early-retirement options granted by the state were used by many larger companies as independent instruments of the personnel policy to solve personnel-planning problems "without any consideration of age" (e.g., adaptation of personnel due to internal rationalization methods or qualificational changes of the personnel (Naegele, 2002). Nevertheless, policy changes in Germany are forthcoming. Meanwhile, it is politically confirmed to overcome early retirement. This is due to the prognosticated demographic development that predicts a reduction of the potential work force, and consequently, a possible shortage of working personnel, especially after the year 2020. For example, the amount of working individuals over 50 is supposed to increase from present 22% to 34% in 2020 (Prognos, 2002). So more older employees will be needed to expand the work force in the future. But the intent to overcome early retirement goes back to the immense financial pressure of the social security systems. As those are primarily current-income financed, early retirements are resulting in additional expenses, especially since annuity payments are due for a longer period. Besides, the early retirees are being eliminated (too early) as contributors, that is, early retirement programs decrease the income of the social security systems.

A change in the early retirement policies and an increase in the productivity of old age in the labor force is also needed as the life courses of many people no longer fit within the newly established, three-part life-course scheme (a longer educational phase, a shorter employment phase, and a longer retirement phase) (Naegele, 1999; Naegele, Barkholdt, de Vroom, Goul Anderson, & Krämer, 2003).

These are all signs that future challenges within companies and administrative bodies will have to be handled by a retrograding potential of working personnel (especially as far as the period after 2020 is concerned), which will be older on average at the same time.

Accordingly, the social and political consensus is that all efforts should be made to mobilize existing neglected or ignored reserves of the labor market in time and, with regard toward the future, train them adequately. These efforts will be mostly directed toward elderly employees, as well as toward women and foreign citizens (Deutscher Bundestag, 2002).

Obviously, this is a productive contribution to the social security systems and thus the stability of the generation contract: When a larger employment rate of older people will be achieved, then there is not only more revenue expected (see explanation above) but, for companies and administrative bodies, there will also be, at least theoretically, various productive effects if the professional productivity potentials of older employees are utilized, even though this view is still not very popular today (Wolff, Spieß, & Mohr, 2001). It is necessary to develop long-term concepts for investing in human capital, as well as to create a matching labor market and social-policy framework.

However, when implementing this demanded concept, it has to made certain that the different groups and demands of older people and employees are being considered. Not all older individuals are able to work longer or to be placed back into work. This most notably applies to many unemployed people: individuals with health impairments; disabled people; as well as, most importantly, people belonging to occupational groups, which are working under stress or, for employees working under so-called short-term jobs (Aehrens, 1999). Therefore, we too are skeptical about the exclusive application of the global raising of the age limit, as it is currently being discussed in Germany. Also, in the future, an array of different options, which are socially and financially acceptable, must be offered.

One option may be to set the date of retirement according to the length of life employment, that is when retirement begins depends upon the number of years worked and the amount paid into the social insurance.

From our perspective, it will be necessary in the future to promote and preserve the capability to work and stay employed—employability of aging personnel. In order to reach this goal, political conceptions that integrate *every* level of the different working and employment situation will be necessary (Naegele, 1999). This point of view is confirmed by the latest research results showing that the employability of elderly people can be supported and increased through early interventions, especially through continuing education and the maintenance of health (Ilmarinen, 1999; Wolff, Spieß, & Mohr, 2001).

In our country, such *integrated and policy overlapping* conceptions exist currently only in the form of academic publications, expertises, etc., but not as real political programs—for instance the Finnish program for elderly employees (Vinni, 2002). Since the beginning of this decade, however, an increasing sensibility of policy and wage-agreement parties concerning the demographic requirements in the labor force can be recognized in Germany. This has been influenced by the political understanding of the need to terminate early retirement programs, which, as mentioned above, have been implemented for decades (Deutscher Bundestag, 2002). Exemplary for it are—apart from professional conferences—research programs funded by the Government (for instance concerning the consequences of the demographic change within the labor force), national action plans (e.g., concerning lifelong learning, quality of work, effectiveness in regard of the social development), special supporting programs for elderly unemployed people, the reduction of incentives offered by the Government to retire early, and equivalent initiatives and publications of the wage agreement parties at the Federal level; for example, at the beginning of 2002, the Federal Government founded an "alliance for jobs," in which a "paradigm change" was announced in respect to the employment policy regarding elderly employees (cf. survey Naegele, 2002). But still missing is the public recognition of the subject as a *common political task going beyond the respective branches and responsible bodies.*

The contradiction between the long-term requirements of the entire society and the short-term individual economical interests can be solved only by a gradual change of paradigm in the operational-personnel policy. Consequently, the actual discussion concerning the labor-market policy in Germany centers around a strategic change in the operational-personnel policy, which should no longer concentrate on young people, but aim toward an integrated personnel policy including all age groups. For example, the Bundestags-Enquête-Kommission (the Federal Parliamentary Inquiry Commission for Demographic Change) explicitly requires the transformation of the present "elderly employee policy" into a lifelong policy focusing on better employment of elderly personnel, which should simultaneously be integrated in a policy of reorganization of employment within the life course. Besides yielding at preventive maintenance and protection of health, concepts such as these should focus on the institutionalized advancement of lifelong learning, the facilitation of professional reorientation, the initiation of second or third careers, the advancement of independent occupational activities, and the promotion of voluntary work within and outside the profession. Moreover, in the future, operational personnel and educational policy should concentrate on social, ecological, and economical sustainability in a more intensive manner (Deutscher Bundestag, 2002).

ELDERLY PEOPLE AS CONSUMERS IN PRIVATE AND PUBLIC MARKETS FOR CONSUMER GOODS AND SERVICES

Elderly people are becoming a more dominant factor in private and, in an even more intensive manner, public commodity markets in Germany. One reason for this is the *comparatively high consumption rate.* Nevertheless, they do not find sufficient offers in important market segments to cover their specific consumption requirements (i.e., private as well as public "senior markets" have been insufficiently developed). The consequences are manifold: they include a reduction of quality of life for many elderly people, deficiencies and additional expenditures in the health and long-term care systems caused by lacking or insufficient alternatives (e.g., the branch of home care service), and the loss of potential new jobs, that are urgently needed in our country.

Thus, an important area for increasing the economic productivity of old age is exactly this sector, here to be understood as an age-typical demand for private and public goods and services with effects on the labor market, which until recently has been considered much too little in our country. Also, we are focusing on this subject explicitly, because today's elderly generation (still) has many financial resources that no other generation has had until now; because of this, elderly people currently belong to the strongest economical population group. Moreover, results from empiric consumption research indicate that parts of the elderly population are currently more hedonistic than previous generations, and therefore more oriented toward consumption if the market is taking their interests and needs more seriously than in the past (Cirkel, Hilbert, & Schalk, 2004).

Private Consumption Demand

In this context, we would first of all like to refer to a thesis that is widespread in our country, and which is especially supported by those who see demographic aging as an economic threat to society. According to this contention, demographic aging would result in a decrease in the growth of the entire national economy and in shrinking employment caused by the reduced demand for private goods and services. However, the inferred linearity of the statement that the number of people demanding consumer goods determines the demand can and should be questioned. According to the opinion of the Federal Parliamentary Inquiry Commission for Demographic Change, the following considerations, inter alia, oppose it (Deutscher Bundestag, 2002):

- In regard to the demand for private consumer goods, it is not the population per se that is important, but the *number and structure of households.* No doubt the total number of households will decrease in Germany, too, but not to the same extent as its population. It is expected instead that an increasing number of smaller households (of elderly people) will be established.

- In addition, the *demand for consumer goods* needs to be analyzed, not only with respect to its strength, but also its structure. Demand is influenced by period, age, and cohort effects, as well as by consumption needs that differ between the various phases of life. This has been evidenced by the rising expenses for social services and other health goods that have been increasing for years (see below).

In theory, private-consumption demand is influenced by the development of the incomes of future households of pensioners; however, this has not been proved. But what is certain is that there will be larger discrepancies among the incomes of elderly Germans in the future.

Further stagnations and reductions in pensions have to be expected; this is due to the German income-related security system and the increasing number of pensioners in comparison to the contributors. The private-pension insurance currently becoming operative can be conducive to closing the income gaps. An overall increasing number of pension recipients and respective households also has to be taken into consideration.

Despite the uncertainty concerning future developments, *the increasing importance of old age in relation to private markets for consumer goods and services is principally indisputable.* On the whole, this is due to a greatly improved pecuniary system in the German households of pensioners as compared to previous years. According to the results of the Income and Consumption Random Test,[1] which was ultimately carried out by the Statistical Federal Authority in 1998, the net income of the heads of households between the ages of 65 and 70 years amounted to 2.785 USD[2] on an average.

The heads of households 70 years and older were spending more than 2.285 USD (converted), which is equivalent to 67% respectively 55% of the expendable incomes of the best equipped group of the 45 to 55 years olds (Statistical Federal Authority, 2001, p. 566).[3] Moreover, pensioners are saving less than other age groups. This especially applies to individuals between 65 and 70 years of age. Compared to households of younger people, they are saving 2.6% of their income, which is 5.5 times smaller, but the saving conduct of elderly people has changed drastically. For instance, at the end of the 1960s, the saving rate of the households of elderly people amounted to an average of 18.4% of their net income (Naegele, 1986). Nowadays, many elderly households have higher assets that in future times may result in increased dissolutions, which could compensate eventual stagnations or reductions of the current transfer incomes of elderly people. Consequently, short to medium-term, it is expected that the *consumption rate of elderly households will increase.*

When observing the private *income-utilizational structures*, the following differences can be found by comparing elderly people with younger age groups. This will also

[1] By means of housekeeping books, it is ascertained at five year intervals in that manner the income is composed and how it is used.

[2] Conversion in USD with price value dated March 24, 2004 (1 € = 1,2190 USD).

[3] However, it has to be taken into consideration that the average values are not giving any information on the allocation of the old-age pensions. In 1999, the highest net incomes after couples, were received by single men of the group aged 65 years and below. These were followed by single women, widows, and divorced women, who had the lowest incomes (Deutscher Bundestag, 2001, p. 2204).

provide the connecting link to our subsequent statements concerning the subject, "advancement of the Grey Market" (cf. item 4, below):

- A strikingly large proportion (30%) of the household income of elderly people is spent on housing, energy, and maintenance of the habitation; whereas for all other age groups, one-fifth to one-fourth of the household income is common. This is partly due to the fact that older individuals stay in their rather large and expensive dwellings while the size of the households and incomes dwindle.
- The amount spent on transportation costs sinks due to a lower mobility (partly caused by retirement).
- Older individuals are spending more money on health-related goods, which continuously increases with the age; for the group 70 and older, an average of nearly 5% of their disposable income is spent on health related goods.
- When elderly people spend money for bodily care, this is, compared to younger age groups, more in terms of services than products. This is increasing with age (0.6% of the disposable income of the age group up to 55 years is spent on services for bodily care: for the age group 70 years and more, this amounts to 1.2%). The opposite applies to body-care articles and appliances.
- In terms of travelling, with increasing age, more money is spent on all-inclusive tours (from 1.6% for individuals below 25 years to 3.5% for elderly people between 65 and 70 years).

The Demand of Elderly People Concerning Public Markets for Goods and Services

The expenses of private consumption and service markets reflect only a small part of the consumption in an aging society. Moreover, it is also worthwhile to examine the typical demands of older individuals concerning *public* markets for goods and services (*health-oriented and social services*). The relatively high proportion of private expenditures for services in connection with health and body care have already been noted. However, these shares cover only a small part of the current consumption in this area because, in Germany, a large part of the expenses for health and long-term care services are paid for by the social security system, with considerable growth and employment effects (Bäcker, Bispinck, Hofemann, & Naegele, 2005).

As far as our subject is concerned, it first of all has to be pointed out that in Germany, the probability of becoming ill increases with age: approximately 22% of men and more than 23% of women aged 65 years and older will become ill (Statistiches Bundesamt, 2001a, p. 432). The same applies to the demand on care and support services.

This is made more clear by examining the number and structure of the recipients receiving German Long-Term Care Insurance benefits. In the year 2002, more than 2 million people (mostly from higher age groups) received Long-Term Care Insurance benefits (1.4 million received services at home and more than 0.6 million received services in institutions). In addition, approximately 3 million mostly elderly people are in need of domestic support but are not eligible for insurance benefits. This is equivalent to the total amount of persons with a (recognized) need of nursing and (mostly unrecognized) domestic services of approximately 6% of the population (Infratest Social Research, 2003).

Generally, it is expected that the health and long-term care market will continue to grow due to the increasing number of elderly people and longer life expectancy. However, it is not clear to which extent and with what demand. For instance, as far as only the future demand for nursing services is concerned, the prognoses vary greatly: between 1.85 and 3.90 million people will need nursing services in the year 2010; for the year 2020, these numbers differ between 1.81 and 4.40 million (see Table 1). The aggregate estimation differences are due, on the one hand, to different definitions of the need of support and nursing services and, on the other hand, to different assumptions about the future development of the allocation of benefits of the Long-Term Care Insurance.

Table 1. Estimated Numbers of Elderly People Needing Support and Nursing Services Aged 60+ to 65+ Respectively, in Germany, from 2010 to 2050 (in millions)

	2010	2020	2030	2040	2050
Own calculations[a]					
Persons needing support and nursing services in private households					
Women 65-79	1.06	1.06	1.31	1.29	1.10
Men 65-79	0.90	0.91	1.17	1.15	0.97
Total 65-79	1.96	1.97	2.47	2.44	2.07
Women 80+	1.20	1.52	1.57	1.89	2.33
Men 80+	0.56	0.89	0.94	1.20	1.52
Total 80+	1.76	2.41	2.51	3.09	3.84
Sums of own calculations	*3.72*	*4.38*	*4.98*	*5.53*	*5.91*
Parliament (60+)	1.63	1.81	2.10	2.02	1.96
Pattern for Enquete Commission Demographic Change	1.94–1.97	—	2.30–2.57	2.41–2.79	—
KDA	2.04	—	—	—	—
Prognos expert report for the VDR	1.87	—	—	2.46	—
Federal Ministry for Health	2.14	—	—	—	—
DIW 2001	2.38	2.96	—	—	4.73
Dietz	—	—	—	—	3.17–5.88
Rothgang 2001	—	—	—	2.59–3.26	—

[a]For the own calculation, the values of the age groups of the 10th coordinated forecast were exclusively used concerning the population and the Infratest examinations of Schneekloth to the shares of the need of support and nursing services. It is a simple continuation of the figures without taking into regard further influencing factors.

Sources: Deutscher Bundestag (2001, pp. 82, 88; 2002, p. 237; Deutsches Institut für Wirtschaftsforschung (2001, p. 71); Dietz (2001, p. 5); Infratest (2003, p. 11); Statistisches Bundesamt (2003); own calculations partially rounded up.

This also goes back to the fact that up to now, for Germany, it is not possible to formulate clear statements about the structure and dynamics of future developments regarding age-specific morbidity (compression of morbidity versus medicalization thesis). In terms of that, the final report of the Parliamentary Inquiry Commission into Demographic Change refers to the *bi-modal thesis of the age-specific morbidity development.* According to this thesis, future cohorts of elderly people will show lower morbidity rates, which is mostly due to medical process, better health conditions, and a higher health consciousness. Thus, they will have more favorable initial conditions, which lower the risk of needing care.

Nevertheless, the number of chronically ill people and people in need of care will increase as will the total demand of long-term care services. With that, there will also be an increase in new, mostly irreversible risks of illnesses such as dementia or the consequences of fractures and the like (Deutscher Bundestag, 2002).

However, the uncertainties, which result therefrom, for the further development of health and nursing services for elderly people are not due only to deficits concerning the scientific treatment of illnesses in old age; they also indicate false estimations of growth in the health and long-term-care system from an economical perspective. "Full order books" are nowhere else regarded—and even feared—in such a critical way as here. Consequently, most health and care service providers are not familiar with recognizing and using economic opportunities apart from what is financed through the German social security system. Therefore, the German Long-Term-Care-Insurance, which was originally conceived to ensure minimum care, is understood in that way neither by the population nor by care providers. Meanwhile, there is cautious experimentation with providing additional comfort and wellness services that are to be financed on a private basis; but those services do not yet play an important role. Additionally, the market for the so-called supporting and supplementary care services, for example, domestic support programs or transport and escort services remain underdeveloped in our country. The health and care system in Germany is still primarily regarded as causing costs and, thus, is even often incorrectly seen as a shrinking sector, although its effects on the job market are immense. The discussion is dominated by the reduction in the number of beds and decreasing periods of stay in hospitals, which ignores the continuous growth in patient figures and employment opportunities in this field (von Bandemer & Hilbert, 2003). So, by continuing to focus on the costs of the health and care systems, which probably imply further rationalization efforts, no attention will be payed to the increased demand due to demographic change (Hilbert & Naegele, 2002).

There are some indications that point to health and social services as a growing economic factor. Science, market research, and policy have taken advantage of the economic opportunities caused by the demographic changes over the last several years. This is further illustrated by reports published by expert commissions that have conducted studies to analyze income and its utilization by the elderly generation, and by public initiatives for the improved utilization of economic potentials as in, for example, the North Rhine Westphalian Initiative for Senior Economy, which is described below.

In our opinion, a further area of economic activity and additional employment opportunities that has been completely underestimated until recently is a new blend of informal family support, professional care and welfare offers. In Germany, elderly people traditionally receive care from family members when necessary. This is, most importantly, attributed to strong emotional bonds, which tend to lead to lifelong relationships that are often found in industrial societies (Nauck, 2001).

In fact, even today, the majority of personal supporting and nursing services is still carried out *informally*. For example, in 2002, approximately 92% of the 1.4 million approved people in need of nursing care (and 85% of the approved people in need of domestic support) were regularly supported by family members (Infratest Social Research, 2003). According to empirical studies carried out in the mid-1990s, more than 80% of people aged 40-60 years spent an average of 6.5 hours a week supporting and caring for their parents or parents-in-law who were not living in the same household.

These private services by middle-aged people supporting their parents, parents-in-law and children equal approximately two million full-time jobs already in the mid-1990s (Borchers, 1997). In the meantime, this figure has grown. Married women between 40 and 65 years most often give up their jobs completely or interrupt them if a family member in their house is in need of care and support (Reichert & Naegele, 1999; Schneider, Drobnič, & Blossfeld, 2001). In contradiction to childcare, which is often performed by parents working part-time, informal care of elderly people more often leads to giving up the job completely. That can also be viewed as unused labor reserves of elderly people.

This corresponds with a growing overstress of existing informal service productions. From a demographic perspective, the care potential of middle-aged women will decrease. Meantime, middle-age groups face a growing demand to support and care for their children and parents. Informal care potentials would further decrease if the shortage of the work force, an expansion of the service branch, and changes of employment policies lead to an increase in the employment rate of women, which is, when compared internationally, quite low at 42.6% (Statistiches Bundesamt, 2003). Moreover, the willingness of women to give up their jobs (completely) and to care for family members instead will probably further decrease in the future; especially because women are increasingly working in attractive professions.

Consequently, this has to lead to an expansion of professional nursing and support services for (elderly) people. There are indications that—merely by the growing numbers of elderly people—the number of elderly people receiving professional-care services will increase from today's 35% to approximately 40% in 2050. If the informal support potential drops further (which is likely), those numbers will increase to 44% and, in case of a growing employment rate of women (which is also likely), it will further increase to about 50% (Deutscher Bundestag, 2002).

In sum, and due to the demographic development, it will become increasingly important to coordinate existing informal and formal professional-care arrangements; and this will also lead to a higher employment rate (first reported by Heinze, 1984; Hilbert, 1994).

Not only would existing informal support and nursing arrangements be strengthened, but simultaneously, the professional social-service branch could be enlarged. In order to achieve this, a more elaborate form of the *welfare pluralism* will be necessary (Evers & Olk, 1996; Schmid, 2002). This again involves an orientation of strong innovative professional social services toward the market, as well as, structural improvements in personal supporting networks in order to better balance occupational, family, and voluntary work (Bäcker, Bispinck, Hofemann, & Naegele, 2005).

Consequently, the relative strong "columnarization" of the supporting services for elderly people that prevails today should become more oriented toward the elderly people's entire requirements and their respective surroundings. Support services for elderly people should have a coordinating character and should not only be re-financed through the social security systems, but also through private money that many elderly people are willing to spend for a good quality of service. In order to achieve this, case-management structures, which scarcely exist, as well as the possibility of getting access to the market will be needed. A precondition for this is public and legal acknowledgment and enforcement of services that are not to be understood as replacement of the support by family and friends, but complementary to it. Through this, the existing service economy could also receive new impulses (Scharfenorth, 2004).

THE NORTH RHINE WESTPHALIAN NATIONAL INITIATIVE FOR SENIOR ECONOMY

This approach to the economic productivity of elderly people is focused on by the Initiative for Senior Economy, which was founded in North Rhine Westphalia (NRW) in 1999. Being based upon a commonly composed memorandum of the Research Society for Gerontology, Dortmund (Forschungsgesellschaft für Gerontologie, FfG) and the Institute Work and Technology, Gelsenkirchen (Institut Arbeit und Technik, IAT) addressing the topic "Economical Power of Old Age," which refers to the economical potential of elderly people in many different areas, the North Rhine Westphalian "alliance for jobs" decided in August 1999 to establish an independent working group for the senior economy. That was later converted into the North Rhine Westphalian Initiative for Senior Economy. The aim of this initiative is the development of senior oriented services and products as well as the advancement of associated employment possibilities.

Responsible bodies in the senior economy are the North Rhine Westphalian employers associations and trade unions, the chambers and professional associations for the branches of craft, industry, and trade as well as the Government of North Rhine Westphalia, the Ministries for Family, Social affairs, Economy, and Housing. Altogether, three areas have been designated to date as prior activity fields in which working groups were established later:

1. Telecommunication and New Media for Elderly People
2. Housing, Trade, and Economy of Services
3. Leisure, Tourism, Sports, and Wellness

According to findings through market research and gerontology, large service and product gaps for elderly people were found in the areas listed above. This was later supported by the findings of the three working groups (Cirkel & Gerling, 2001). The North Rhine Westphalian Initiative for Senior Economy aims in general at improving services and products of social, health, and economical institutions that are located in North Rhine Westphalia, with respect to the specific needs and demands of elderly people.

By doing so, the following goals shall be achieved: to improve elderly people's quality of life in NRW; to secure and extend the employment situation in companies offering products and services for elderly people; to mobilize the spending power of elderly people; to profile NRW for questions regarding demographic development, old age, and the grey market (Cirkel, Frerichs, & Gerling, 2000).

The North Rhine Westphalian Initiative for Senior Economy encourages dialogues between suppliers and consumers and, moreover, tries to consider the heterogeneity of elderly people with respect to their differing social and economical situations as well as their state of health.

By increasingly referring to approaches such as "universal design" or "design for all," which focus on barrier-free products and services for all age groups, more population groups than just the older generation may benefit from the effects of that initiative.

The working groups mentioned above consist of a great number of different actors working in the following fields: economy, politics, trade unions, public authorities, voluntary and charitable organizations, welfare associations, and academic institutions. They are led by the Ministry for Health, Social Affairs, Women, and Family (MGSFF NRW). By involving the North Rhine Westphalian Senior Representation Board, the participation of elderly people themselves is of high priority.

The working groups aim at exchanging experiences and establishing new partnerships. They discuss and enlarge models of good practice and initiate special projects. Over the last four to five years, the following projects have been initiated and carried out (Fischer, 2003).

Housing, Trade, and Economy of Services

- Development of a North Rhine Westphalian quality mark "Sheltered Housing for Elderly People in North Rhine Westphalia," which defines criteria for sheltered housing in four categories: building and surroundings, basic service, optional service, and contract
- Qualification classes for craft companies of different branches on the topic "Housing and Old Age" induced by the Chamber of Handicrafts, Düsseldorf (for instance, possibilities of adjusting housing to the special needs of elderly people, funding possibilities, and senior marketing)
- Development of a branch guide for "Smart Living," through which elderly people shall be encouraged to live at home as long as possible

Telecommunication and New Media for Elderly People

- Construction of special Internet offers for elderly people
- Procurement of media competences for elderly people by, for instance, establishing regional Internet cafés for senior citizens
- Testing of phones with picture transmission and virtual support services for elderly people ("virtual nursing home")

Leisure and Tourism

- Funding of two regional tourism projects in the Lower Rhine and in East Westphalia-Lippe, which were designed to increase the supply of senior oriented offers in the fields of tourism, wellness, and leisure
- Development and dissemination of a checklist "Elderly People Travelling," which sensitizes travel agencies as well as the accommodation industry to the special needs of elderly people and offers them support by showing how to optimize their offers
- Funding of the development of a continuing education program for senior citizens that is financed on a private basis
- Qualification of travel guides in the grey tourism market

Additionally, a number of professional congresses (e.g., with view to senior marketing or grey economy on municipal level) have been held that go beyond the three described activity fields in order to sensitize the relevant economic actors in NRW for the opportunities of the grey economy. Moreover, a study has been commissioned to analyze income and expenditure structures of elderly people living in NRW. Besides, for the first time, NRW has founded an award for innovative products and services being especially tailored to the needs of senior citizens, which should also help to sensitize companies for the senior economy.

Four and a half years after its initiation, the North Rhine Westphalian Initiative for Senior Economy has received positive feedback concerning the actors involved. Also, its philosophy, to view the growing numbers of elderly people as a chance for economical development, has been confirmed and is being propagated increasingly. As a further result, a European network will be founded that will shall support and strengthen the development and extension of the grey economy all over the European Union.

Labor-market effects caused by the Initiative are difficult to quantify. According to careful preliminary calculations, from 1999 to 2002, there has been an increase of approximately 2000 jobs within the three activity fields; housing, leisure, and new media. If the employment development in the age-relevant health and long-term-care economy in adjacent areas is added, these numbers increase to approximately 12,300 jobs in the same period (Fischer, 2003).

As far as international experiences and perspectives in the grey market are concerned, there are no comparable international studies to date. However, in Japan, which has the highest proportion of elderly people worldwide, senior citizens have become important consumers due to their immense purchasing power. It is generally known that large investments have been made in the so-called silver market, which has been supported by the government as well as by economy leaders at a very early stage.

This especially applies to offers in tourism and the so-called Kyôyo-hin products, which are characterized by a universal design and are user-friendly for all age and population groups. Senior marketing has also been developed to a great extent and can be regarded as exemplary in most of its segments. The potential of the silver market is rated very high in Japan. According to a prognosis from the Ministry of Economy (METI) in the year 1997, nearly 7 million new jobs will be found by 2010. In the broadest sense, the highest growth potentials are expected in the areas of personal care products (toilet articles, medical articles, cosmetics, food), leisure items (automobiles, mobile phones, PC/Internet, travel, beverages, accessories, clothes, photography), as well as financial concerns (insurance) (Gerling & Conrad, 2002).

To sum up the experiences of the North Rhine Westphalian Initiative for Senior Economy, it can be stated that by setting systematic economic and political impulses, the new sectional field of senior economy can be developed and strengthened. Not only the economy, but also the elderly people as consumers themselves are profiting from such a process. Meanwhile, the NRW initiative has also been transferred to other states in the Federal Republic of Germany; and simultaneously, policymakers at the federal level have been sensitized as well.

PROSPECT: THE ECONOMIC PRODUCTIVITY OF OLD AGE IS LARGELY UNDERRATED

These specially chosen branches illustrate that the economical productivity of old age is already practiced to a great extent; however, it is systematically underrated or often ignored in political debates. Nevertheless, there are large areas that are neglected. These could be easily activated and used profitably and productively from a social point of view and could simultaneously contribute to the improvement of the quality of life for elderly individuals. We, gerontologists, do not, by any means, intend to neglect these views, especially the latter. This, likewise, applies to the labor market as well as private and public consumer markets.

In the labor world, the signs for change have been set. The first steps have been taken in order to reverse the trend of expelling elderly people from the labor world by unemployment or early retirement, which has been practiced for decades. Nevertheless, this is a long-term process, depending upon adequate occupational support measures with long-term effects. Actual debates show that the support of employability of aging personnel and discontinuation of the existing early retirement incentives (e.g., age-limit systems concerning annuity and tax law) are regarded as the best suitable instruments.

As far as the senior economy (or the grey respective silver market) is concerned, it is especially important to continue to improve the quality of life in old age by developing adequate strategies, products, and services. Here, senior marketing is also playing an important role. An international comparison demonstrates that there are markets being largely neglected, for example, in the fields of household services, automobile industry, clothing industry, cosmetic products, and financial services (Gerling & Conrad, 2002). As far as these fields are concerned, if the market is not developing sufficiently on its own, it will be important to receive impulses from the state, a technique which has proved fruitful in NRW and partly in Japan.

However, with regard to the whole national economy, it must be noted that elderly people are economically active in many ways without any explicit advancement of the senior economy. First of all, it is important that the necessary services and burdens of each generation with regard to the entire national economy should not be analyzed cross-sectionally, but longitudinally if statements such as "the financial strain of the society caused by old people" are to be avoided. Thus it becomes clear, that during the life course, everyone passes through different phases with different functions; sometimes they are "net payers" and sometimes "net payees."

Furthermore, in old age, individuals actively participate in the process of creating assets by placing at their disposal resources that have been accumulated during a lifetime and that are needed for financing investments. Moreover, elderly people are not only consumers, but also taxpayers, as well as contributors to health and long-term care insurances and thus, participate in the financing of public institutions. Due to a high indirect taxation, which is typical in Germany, elderly people also pay relatively high amounts of taxes.

In most cases, income and property—approximately 140.19 billion USD per year, which is a considerable amount for Germany—which have been accumulated during a lifetime are inherited at least once and then flow back into the economic circle (Deutscher Bundestag, 2002).

REFERENCES

Bäcker, G., Bispinck, R., Hofemann, K., & Naegele, G. (2005). *Sozialpolitik und soziale Lage. 4. überarbeitete Auflage.* Wiesbaden: Westdeutscher Verlag.

Baltes, M., & Montada, L. (Eds.). (1996). *Produktives Leben im Alter.* Frankfurt/M., New York: Campus.

Behrens, J. (1999). Länger erwerbstätig durch Arbeits- und Laufbahngestaltung: Personal- und Organisationsentwicklung zwischen begrenzter Tätigkeitsdauer und langfristiger Erwerbstätigkeit. In M. Gussone, A. Huber, M. Morschhäuser, & J. Petrenz (Eds.), *Ältere arbeitnehmer. Altern und erwerbsarbeit in rechtlicher, arbeits- und sozialwissenschaftlicher Sicht* (pp. 101-186). Frankfurt a. M: Bund Verlag.

Bellmann, L., Hilpert, M., Kistler, E., & Wahse, J. (2003). Herausforderungen des demographischen Wandels für den Arbeitsmarkt und die Betriebe. *Mitteilungen aus der Arbeitsmarkt- und Berufsforschung, 2,* 133-149.

Borchers, A. (1997). Die Sandwich-Generation. Ihre zeitlichen und finanziellen Leistungen und Belastungen. Frankfurt/M., New York: Campus.

Bundesministerium für Familie, Senioren, Frauen und Jugend (BMFSFJ). (Ed.). (2003). *Die Familie im Spiegel der amtlichen Statistik.* Berlin: Eigenverlag.

Cirkel, M., & Gerling, V. (2001). Die Generation der Zukunft? Neue Chancen durch alte Menschen. das Projekt Seniorenwirtschaft im Bündnis für Arbeit, Ausbildung und Wettbewerbsfähigkeit NRW. In Institut Arbeit und Technik (Ed.), *Jahrbuch 2000/2001* (pp. 177-198). Gelsenkirchen: IAT-Eigenverlag.

Cirkel, M., Hilbert, J., & Schalk, C. (2004). *Produkte und Dienstleistungen für mehr Lebensqualität im Alter.* Expertise für die 5. Altenberichtskommission. Institut für Arbeit und Technik. Gelsenkirchen: Eigenverlag.

Cirkel, M., Frerichs, F., & Gerling, V. (2000). Seniorenwirtschaft. *FfG-Impulse,* Sonderausgabe Mai, 1-4.

Deutscher Bundestag (Ed.). (2001). Unterrichtung durch die Bundesregierung. Alterssicherungsbericht 2001. Ergänzender Bericht der Bundesregierung zum Rentenversicherungsbericht 2001 über die Leistungen der ganz oder teilweise öffentlich finanzierten Alterssicherungssysteme, deren Finanzierung, die Einkommenssituation der Leistungsbezieher und das Zusammentreffen von Leistungen der Alterssicherungssysteme gemäß § 154 Abs. 3 SGB VI. Drucksache 14/7640. Berlin: Bundeskanzleramt.

Deutscher Bundestag, Referat Öffentlichkeitsarbeit. (Ed.). (2002). *Enquete-Kommission demographischer Wandel, Herausforderungen unserer älter werdenden Gesellschaft an den Einzelnen und die Politik.* Abschlussbericht. Berlin: Zur Sache 3/2002.

Deutsches Institut für Wirtschaftsforschung (2001). Starker Anstieg der Pflegebedürftigkeit zu erwarten. Vorausschätzungen bis 2020 mit Ausblick auf 2050. *Wochenbericht des DIW, 5,* 65-77.

Dietz, B. (2001). Entwicklung des Pflegebedarfs bis 2050. Kosten steigen schneller als erwartet. *Soziale Sicherheit, 1,* 2-9.

Evers, A., & Olk, T. (1996). Wohlfahrtspluralismus—Analytische und normativ-politische Dimensionen eines Leitbegriffs. In A. Evers & T. Olk (Eds.), *Wohlfahrtspluralismus. Vom wohlfahrtsstaat zur wohlfahrtsgesellschaft* (pp. 9-60). Opladen: Westdeutscher Verlag.

Fischer, B. (2003). *Seniorenwirtschaft in Nordrhein-Westfalen. Ein Instrument zur Verbesserung der Lebenssituation älterer Menschen.* Bericht der Ministerin für Gesundheit, Soziales, Frauen und Familie des Landes Nordrhein-Westfalen. Düsseldorf: Eigenverlag

Forschungsgesellschaft für Gerontologie e. V.—Institut für Gerontologie an der Universität Dortmund (Eds.). (1999). *Memorandum "Wirtschaftskraft Alter."* Dortmund, Gelsenkirchen: Vervielfältigung.

Gerling, V., & Conrad, H. (2002). *Wirtschaftskraft Alter in Japan: Handlungsfelder und Strategien. Unveröffentlichte Expertise im Auftrag des BMFSFJ.* Dortmund, Tôkyô: Vervielfältigung.

Heinze, R. G. (1984). Eigenarbeit und Schattenwirtschaft—Ausdruck einer Krise der Arbeitsgesellschaft? In K. Gretschmann, R. G. Heinze, & B. Mettelsiefen (Eds.), *Schattenwirtschaft. Wirtschafts- und sozialwissenschaftliche Aspekte, internationale Erfahrungen* (pp. 133-150). Göttingen: Vandenhoeck & Ruprecht.

Hilbert, J. (1994). Lean Production in der Sozialen Sicherung. In M.-E. Karsten (Ed.), *Dienstleistungsgesellschaft: Herausforderungen, Trends und Perspektiven. 48. Lüneburger Universitätswoche* (pp. 51-62). Lüneburg: Universität Lüneburg.

Hilbert, J., & Naegele, G. (2002). Dienstleistungen für mehr Lebensqualität im Alter- ein Such- und Gestaltungsfeld für mehr Wachstum und Beschäftigung. In G. Bosch, P. Hennicke, J. Hilbert, K. Kristof, & G. Scherhorn (Eds.), *Die Zukunft von Dienstleistungen. Ihre Auswirkungen auf Arbeit, Umwelt und Lebensqualität* (pp. 347-369). Frankfurt/M., New York: Campus.

Hinterlong, J., Morrow-Howell, N., & Sherraden, M. (2001). Productive ageing: Principles and perspectives. In N. Morrow-Howell, J. Hinterlong, & M. Sherraden (Eds.), *Productive ageing, concepts and challenges.* Baltimore: The Johns Hopkins University Press.

Ilmarinen, J. (1999). *Ageing workers in the European Union—Status and promotion of work ability, employability and employment.* Helsinki: Finnish Institute of Occupational Health, Ministry of Social Affairs and Health, Ministry of Labour.

Infratest Sozialforschung. (2003). *Hilfe- und Pflegebedürftige in Privathaushalten in Deutschland 2002.* Schnellbericht. München: Infratest-Eigenverlag.

Motel, A., & Szydlik, M. (1999). Private transfers zwischen den generationen. *Zeitschrift für Soziologie, 1,* 3-22.

Naegele, G. (1986). *Konsumverhalten sozial schwacher älterer Menschen. Möglichkeiten und Grenzen einer altenspezifischen Verbraucherpolitik. 2., erweiterte Auflage.* Bonn: Arbeitsgemeinschaft der Verbraucher e. V.

Naegele, G. (1993). Solidarität im Alter. Überlegungen zu einer Umorientierung der Alterssozialpolitik. *Sozialer Fortschritt, 8,* 191-196.

Naegele, G. (1999). *Active strategies for an ageing workforce.* Conference report. Turku. European Foundation for the Improvement of Living and Working Conditions. Dublin: EF-Eigenverlag.

Naegele, G. (2002). Active strategies for older workers in Germany. In M. Jepsen, D. Foden, & M. Hutsebaut (Eds.), *Active strategies for older workers* (pp. 207-244). European Trade Union Institut. Brüssel: ETUI-Eigenverlag.

Naegele, G., Barkholdt, C., de Vroom, B., Goul Anderson, J., & Krämer, K. (2003). *A new organization of time throughout working life.* Integrated report. European Foundation for the Improvement of Living and Working Conditions. Forschungsbericht der Forschungsgesellschaft für Gerontologie e.V. Dortmund 2003. Dublin: EF-Eigenverlag.

Naegele, G., Hilbert J., Gerling, V., & Weidekamp-Maicher, M. (2003). *Perspektiven einer produktiven Nutzung der "weichen" Folgen des Demographischen Wandels im Rahmen der Nationalen Nachhaltigkeitsstrategie. Expertise, erstellt im Auftrag des Bundeskanzleramtes.* Dortmund, Köln, Gelsenkirchen: Vervielfältigung.

Naegele, G., & Tews, H.-P. (Eds.). (1993). *Lebenslagen im Strukturwandel des Alters. Alternde Gesellschaft—Folgen für die Politik.* Opladen. Westdeutscher-Verlag.

Naegele, G., & Walker, A. (Eds.). (1999). *The politics of old age in Europe.* London: Open University Press.

Nauck, B. (2001). Der Wert von Kindern für ihre Eltern. "Value of Children" als spezielle Handlungstheorie des generativen Verhaltens und von Generationenbeziehungen im interkulturellen *Vergleich. Kölner Zeitschrift für Soziologie und Sozialpsychologie, 3,* 407-435.

OECD. (Ed.). (2003). *Employment outlook.* Paris: Eigenverlag.

Prognos (Ed.). (2002). *Deutschland Report 2002-2020.* Basel: Eigenverlag.

Reichert, M., & Naegele, G. (1999). Elder care and the workplace in Germany: An issue for the future. In V. M. Lechner & M. B. Neal (Eds.). *Work and caring for the elderly, international perspectives* (pp. 29-46). Philadelphia: Taylor & Francis Group.

Scharfenorth, K. (2004). *Mit dem Alter in die Dienstleistungsgesellschaft? Perspektiven des demographischen Wandels für Wachstum und Gestaltung des tertiären Sektors.* München: Herbert Utz Verlag.

Schmid, J. (2002). *Wohlfahrtsstaaten im Vergleich. Soziale Sicherungssysteme in Europa: Organisation, Finanzierung, Leistungen und Probleme. 2. Völlig überarbeitete und erweiterte auflage.* Opladen: Leske & Budrich.

Schneider, T., Drobnič, S., & Blossfeld, H.-P. (2001). Pflegebedürftige Personen im Haushalt und das Erwerbsverhalten verheirateter Frauen [Home care of the elderly and the employment behavior of married women]. *Zeitschrift für Soziologie, 5,* 362-383.

Schroeter, K.-R. (2004). Zur doxa des sozialgerontologischen Feldes: Erfolgreiches und produktives Altern—Orthodoxie, Heterodoxie oder Allodoxie? *Zeitschrift für Gerontologie und Geriatrie, 37,* 51-55.

Statistisches Bundesamt. (Ed.). (2001a). *Statistisches rahrbuch 2001 für die Bundesrepublik Deutschland.* Stuttgart: Metzler-Poeschel. (CD).

Statistisches Bundesamt. (Ed.). (2001b). Kurzbericht Pflegestatistik 1999. Pflege im Rahmen der Pflegeversicherung. Deutschlandergebnisse.
http://www.destatis.de/download/veroe/kbpflege99.pdf (08.02.02).

Statistisches Bundesamt. (Ed.). (2003). *Statistisches jahrbuch 2003 für die Bundesrepublik Deutschland.* Wiesbaden: Eigenverlag.

Tews, H. P. (1996). Produktivität des Alters. In M. Baltes & L. Montada (Eds.), *Produktives Leben im Alter* (pp. 184-210). Frankfurt/M., New York: Campus.

Vinni, K. (2002). Active strategies for older workers in Finland. In M. Jepsen, D. Foden, & M. Hutsebaut (Eds.), *Active strategies for older workers* (pp. 345-380). European Trade Union Institut. Brüssel: ETUI-Eigenverlag.

von Bandemer, S., & Hilbert, J. (2003). Moderne Arbeit in Medizin und Pflege. In Institut Arbeit und Technik (Ed.), *Jahrbuch 2002/2003* (pp. 117-128). Gelsenkirchen: Eigenverlag.

Walker, A. (2002). A strategy for active ageing. *International Social Security Review, 1,* 121-39.

Wolff, H., Spieß, K., & Mohr, H. (2001). *Arbeit, Altern, Innovation.* Basel. Universum Verlagsanstalt.

PART VII. New Challenges

CHAPTER 19

Separating the Local and the General in Cross-Cultural Aging Research

Svein Olav Daatland Andreas Motel-Klingebiel

Age and aging, kinship, and generational shift are human universals, but they are played out in a great diversity of local forms, which makes it hard—some would say impossible—to distinguish between what is specific to a certain time or place from what is generally true. Possible or not, a key ambition of the social sciences is to search below the complexities of the observable to some general and less complex order. One avenue to such knowledge is through comparative studies, be they comparative across time, place, or any other dimension.

"New dynamics," and hence changes over time, is the main theme for this book. The aim of the present chapter is to add a complementary perspective, namely, (synchronic) comparisons across place—between countries or regions, cultures or policies. Such comparisons may even be a proxy for comparisons across time, to the extent that countries, cultures, and policies can be located in a time sequence, that is, as more or less modern, or as earlier or later in the demographic transition. The cultural context would in any case add a special flavor to developments over time. Hence both approaches have something distinct to offer and may help us extract the general from the local. Continuities over time and similarities between (otherwise different) countries are potential indicators of more general patterns and processes, while changes and differences are more likely effects of local or specific circumstances.

And yet, gerontology has not invested seriously in comparative studies. Nor have comparative disciplines like social anthropology shown much interest in aging and later life. This chapter is thus motivated by the potential contribution of the comparative approach to aging studies. First, we briefly examine the problems and promises of comparative research more generally. Second, we review some findings from comparative aging studies in selected areas such as successful aging, the status of older people, and social protection. They represent three main foci of aging research: aging as a process, old age as a stage of life, and policies and interventions towards aging and older people. The third and major section presents findings from a recent comparative study, OASIS, which looked at the role that the family and the welfare state play for autonomy and quality of life in old age in countries with different family cultures and welfare state regimes. Findings from three study areas of the OASIS project—the family–welfare state relationship, intergenerational solidarity, and quality of life—are discussed, particularly in terms of the conceptual challenges they highlight. The conclusion argues that the OASIS project represents both the strengths and the weaknesses of comparative studies in the field of aging.

THE COMPARATIVE APPROACH

Broadly speaking, all social research is comparative in the sense that it involves references to other entities or times. Even a single qualitative case study will at least implicitly be contrasted to another (case). Most studies also compare men and women, older and younger people, or the poor and the rich. Hence, comparison is a core business of social science (Fuchs-Heinritz, Lautmann, Rammstedt, & Wienhold, 1994).

A more narrow definition limits comparative research to comparisons across time or between social entities such as societies, states, or regions. The level of analysis may range from societal (macro) to individual (micro). Indeed, such comparisons often imply multilevel perspectives.

Comparative studies are often driven by either of two contrasting ambitions: one is to search for general patterns, even universals; the other is to disclose what is specific, even unique, for a culture or society. Both approaches have their virtues. Cross-national studies have been criticized for being biased toward the search for similarities (Allardt, 1990). Country differences are then reduced to variation along a set of variables, while the unique is played down. In contrast—or in addition—a focus on countries as historic entities provides a different type of information. Countries may act differently in response to similar problems such as population aging. For this reason, Sztompka (1988) argues that comparative research should therefore focus more on the uniqueness rather than on the uniformities of nations.

The two contrasting strategies are often labeled as case oriented or variable oriented. Case-oriented research gives priority to complexity over generality, while the converse is the case for the variable-oriented approach. "It is difficult to have both," says Ragin (1987, p. 54), "An appreciation of complexity sacrifices generality; an emphasis on generality encourages a neglect of complexity." In a later publication, he sees the two strategies as complementary rather than as alternatives: "Good comparative social science balances emphasis on cases and emphasis on variables" (Ragin, 1991).

Gauthier (2000) points to the same contrast when she identifies two different paradigms in comparative research: structuralism and culturalism. The structuralist position assumes that similar macrocharacteristics will produce similar outcomes on the individual level. Social structure is then assumed to have a uniform effect, regardless of differences in culture. Hence variables are assumed to be essentially the same across cases. Culturalists, on the other hand, assume that social values may modify the effects of social structure and lead to different outcomes of similar inputs. We support Kohn (1989) in his conclusion that both perspectives have something to offer; the point is how we use them. "The critical issue is how to interpret similarities, and how to interpret dissimilarities, when you find them" (p. 78). Finding similarities is an avenue to more general knowledge: ". . . where we find cross-national similarities, the most efficient strategy in searching for an explanation is to focus on what is structurally similar in the countries being compared, not on the often divergent historical processes that produced these social-cultural similarities" (p. 79). Cross-national differences are often harder to interpret, as they may have been produced by either structural differences or idiosyncratic responses.

COMPARATIVE AGING RESEARCH

Comparative studies are well suited to test theoretical hypotheses. Processes that are already known to be universal, like biological aging, may equally well be studied locally; but comparative data will add to the variance and help us separate primary (genetic) from secondary (environmental) aging effects. Developmental trends in longevity have, for example, constantly reminded us about the biological reserves that are yet not realized, so also have the differences in health between social classes. The reserves may be still larger in psychological functions, as psychological functions are even more responsive to external factors and cultural interpretations. Hence a comparative approach can provide additional insights into biological and psychological aging. A comparative approach is thus arguably even more relevant for aspects of social aging that by definition vary over time and space. The following review of findings therefore refers to social aspects of aging and later life.

Successful Aging

Successful aging came to be a major theme of gerontological research in the 1950s onwards. The focus was on how people adapted to the stressors and constraints of aging and whether they did so poorly or successfully. Criteria of success were measured in terms of health and morale, social integration, and activity. In this paradigm, high levels of physical and mental functioning, subjective well-being, and productive involvement in society are taken as evidence of successful aging (Rowe & Kahn, 1997). This tradition is an offshoot of activity and continuity theory, and takes midlife standards as a model for old age. Disengagement (Cumming & Henry, 1961) has a low status within this paradigm, as do the ego-integrity of later life as suggested by Erikson (1959), individuation and maturity as proposed by Jung (1931), or the more recent gero-transcendence hypothesis as presented by Tornstam (1989). Despite their differences, these models all represent a contrast to the successful-aging paradigm because they point to discontinuities and suggest that old age is something different from other phases of life, not simply a bleak or outdated version of middle age.

All these models of "good aging" tend to be (explicitly or implicitly) normative. They are in fact assumed to have general, even universal, relevance, and thus invite an evaluation of their cross-cultural validity. Comparative studies may then help us separate the possibly universal from the culturally distinct forms of a good old age. Increased longevity is an additional argument for a comparative approach, as longer lifetimes help break up "old age" into stages or types of "old ages" that may be found to have distinct qualities.

Documenting the diversity of aging and older people is also motivated by an effort to counteract stereotypes in popular opinion and public policies. Social anthropological studies from Leo Simmons (1945) and onwards have made considerable contributions in this respect. An important effort from the later years is Project AGE, which compared aging and older people in seven cities on three continents (Fry, 1999; Keith et al., 1994). One of the major findings was that the ideals of a good old age vary considerably between cultures. Torres (1999) describes similar findings among immigrants to Sweden, but has suggested that immigrants may in time come to adapt more closely to the standards of their new homeland.

The latter hypothesis touches the core theme of this book, which is the new dynamics of old age. International migration has expanded the cultural variation in both the countries of origin and the countries of arrival and made them both more pluralistic. Cultures were earlier geographically separated, but are now increasingly sharing the same space in a globalized environment. Migrants themselves operate in two or more cultures. New forms of transnational adaptations are developing, through which people are handling loyalties and relationships across borders and cultures. This applies to both younger and older cohorts.

A special variant among senior citizens is sunbelt migration, which is the opposite direction of mainstream migration. Doctors and nursing homes are now following in their tracks and are helping to develop new lifestyles and forms of security in old age. Another source of increased variation lies in the nature of a longer lifetime itself, particularly in combination with more rapid social change. Cultural distances between cohorts and age groups will expand, which may turn older generations into migrants in time and strangers in their homelands.

We need to explore all these trends and their implications for aging and old age. A comparative approach is well suited for this purpose.

Status of Older People

Old age and later life is a more frequent focus of comparative studies than is aging as such. A classical case is Cowgill and Holmes' (1972) theory of the consequences of modernization for older people. Case studies and available statistics from a number of countries constituted the empirical basis of the theory. The selected countries were assumed to be on different stages of modernity and hence differently located in both space and time. Comparison between countries was then a proxy also for comparison over time. The data and cases were synthesized into a theory about how the status of old people is structured by the means of production, the pace of change, and the forms of knowledge and communication. The main conclusions are well known: modernization tends to marginalize and weaken the status of older people as their experiences and skills become outdated in the wake of new technologies and a shift from a focus on tradition to an orientation towards the future.

A more empirically consistent study, although less theoretically ambitious, is "Old People in Three Industrial Societies" (Shanas et al., 1968). This was among the very first comparative studies on older people based on a primary data set collected for that purpose. The study was rich in empirical documentation of both differences and similarities between the three participating countries: England, Denmark, and the United States. The main theoretical conclusion was, however, about what united them, namely, that the demise of the extended family in modern society should be considered a myth. Living conditions varied considerably between, and in particular within, these countries. Older people were better protected from poverty and marginalization in the universalist welfare state of Denmark than in the liberalist welfare state of the United States; but in all countries, family relationships were found to be stronger and more stable than was assumed by public opinion.

Social Protection of the Aged

Most comparative studies in the issue area of aging have invested more in data collection than in theory construction and probably more so for studies about social interventions and protective policies than in most other domains. Some such studies are designed primarily to be politically relevant; others may also have a theoretical ambition and may have selected units (countries, regions) for that very purpose. They may focus on common features among otherwise different units or on why similar units have chosen different strategies to face seemingly similar challenges. Contrasts between otherwise similar countries may be powerful signs of national idiosyncrasies and may help us separate the unique from the general.

The process of path dependence, more intensively discussed in economics (e.g., David, 2000), may serve as a bridge between case- and variable-oriented strategies. In path dependence lies an element of continuity: a link to the already established practices and a resistance to changes that are incompatible with tradition. Path dependence is characterized by positive (and self-serving) feedback processes, implying that a move in one direction reinforces further moves in the same direction (Alber, 1995; Pierson, 2000). The timing and sequence of events may then be important, because small and incremental changes early in a process may amplify and eventually have major consequences. The striking stability of social policies and welfare regimes is a case in point. Although all modern countries are affected by population aging, the way these changes are perceived will probably vary according to the already-established practices. Hence the idea of path dependence may help us disentangle what is common and what is different.

A common challenge to all modern countries is the demographic transition produced by longer lives, lower mortality rates, and lower fertility rates. These trends need to be met by sustainable policies, but it is hardly possible, or even desirable, to find one common solution. When countries are also responding differently in practice, this variation represents a laboratory for research that, until now, has been underutilized. Welfare state studies are criticized for their narrow focus on class-related risks at the expense of life-course risks, or put more concretely, for having concentrated on pensions at the expense of services (Alber, 1995). Esping-Andersen (1990) was, for example, criticized for having neglected the role of the family in social protection. Therefore in a revision of his model, he added degree of defamilialization (protection from dependency on the family) to the original degree of decommodification (protection from dependency on the market) as a characteristic of a welfare-state regime (Esping-Andersen, 1999). Changes like these have integrated aging perspectives into mainstream welfare-state research on the one hand and have expanded the scope of gerontological studies on the other. The more trivial explorations of levels and profiles of pensions and services could then be augmented with more theoretically ambitious studies about aging policies, for example within the political economy tradition (Estes, Swan, & Gerard, 1982).

International studies have often been limited by data that are collected for other reasons and later adapted for comparative purposes. A parallel study carried out with common constructs and instruments in selected places or times is the ideal, but is difficult to carry out, to coordinate, and to finance. One should therefore have good reasons to choose a comparative approach instead of a single-country study. The choice of a comparative design, and more specifically the selection of units and level of analysis, should be both theoretically and analytically called for. The comparative approach should be necessary, and a single-case solution insufficient, in order to justify the strains of a truly comparative endeavor. The following sections present findings from one such attempt, the OASIS study (Old age and autonomy—the role of service systems and intergenerational family solidarity).

THE OASIS PROJECT

OASIS may serve as an illustration of the problems and promises of comparative research. Individual level data were collected through parallel surveys (interviews) among the urban populations aged 25 and over in each of the five participating countries. About 1,200 subjects from each country were interviewed, however 6,106 were interviewed in total. The older participants (aged 75+) were intentionally overrepresented to constitute around one-third of the samples (Lowenstein & Ogg, 2003).

The project was motivated by the assumed threat that late-modern and individualist society poses for family solidarity. Although earlier studies had found the family unit to still be strong, the continued aging of populations may weaken intergenerational solidarity. Of particular interest is the relationship between the family and the welfare state. All modern societies depend on some form of shared responsibility between the two for social protection in late life, but the state-family balance takes many different forms. What is a reasonable and sustainable balance? These questions need be studied in context; hence a comparative approach was seen as appropriate.

The approach is more variable oriented than case oriented, although since the state (or a regional or local representative) is an agent of policies and services, it could have served as a unit of analysis. Many other aspects are involved, however; hence the countries are mainly represented as independent and intervening variables. The challenge is then how to link the macrolevel variables to lower level outcomes. One solution would be to use the countries simply as contexts for the interpretation of individual-level data. More ambitious would be to employ macro- and mesoindicators more directly in the analysis, on the assumption that these structures are reflected in the attitudes and behaviors of individuals. The countries were therefore selected to represent different family cultures and welfare state regimes. They are located along a north-south axis, which, according to Reher (1998), divides European families into the southern, more collectivist form, and the northern, more individualist form. The five countries also represent different welfare-state regimes: the social democratic (Norway), the liberal (England), and the conservative-corporatist (Germany), to stay within the Esping-Andersen typology (1990). Spain has as yet a less mature welfare state, which is seen by Ferrara (1996) as representing a specific Mediterranean model, but is by

Esping-Andersen included among the conservative regimes. The fifth country, Israel, is a mixed model.

Values and habits are acquired through socialization. They provide a sense of continuity and integration, but are confronted with changes that require new adaptations. Some of these changes are related to life-course transitions—to exits and entries to or from positions that generate a change of interests and opportunities. Other changes are triggered by societal change, such as changes in demography, gender roles, or welfare policies. Hence people are often torn between continuity and change, between tradition and innovation.

The family is among the more stable elements in society, and older people are among the more stable groups of the population, but are still affected by social change. Lüscher and Pillemer (1998) have suggested that ambivalence (mixed feelings and contradicting roles) is a basic feature of intergenerational relationships. Bauman (2000) sees ambivalence as a feature of late modernity itself. OASIS addresses these ideas by studying the character of families and welfare states and their implications for older people. The macroconditions of the countries are assumed to be reflected on the individual and interpersonal (family) levels. Preferences and practices are assumed to be (more or less) congruent with established traditions and to be more conformist for the older than for the younger generation. The present balance is assumed to be fluid and under pressure from demographic and social change in all countries, but more so in countries that are later in these developments and are now confronted with more rapid changes.

These assumptions are explored in three areas: first, in the ideals and realities of the family–welfare-state relationship; second, in the strength and character of intergenerational family solidarity; and third, in the impact of the family and the welfare state on the quality of life in old age. We shall review some OASIS findings in each of these areas.

THE FAMILY/WELFARE STATE RELATIONSHIP

Welfare states differ in the responsibility they ascribe to families. Some put the family in a dominant position, others assume that the welfare state should protect against dependency upon the family (defamilialization, see Esping-Andersen, 1999). The OASIS countries are located in different positions along this dimension; hence they represent different opportunity structures for family life and elder care. They face similar challenges, but are inclined toward different solutions. Germany and Spain tend to favor familialistic solutions and give the state a subsidiary (Germany) or even a residual (Spain) role. They have legal obligations for adult children toward older parents and offer low levels of services in areas that are traditionally a family responsibility, such as long-term care. In contrast, England and Norway stipulate no legal obligations between generations and offer higher levels of services in traditional family areas, particularly in Norway. Israel is a mixed case, with legal obligations similar to Spain and Germany, but also rather generous service levels.

Familialistic countries are likely to have higher co-residence rates between generations and lower female employment rates than nonfamilialistic countries: for example, while Spain has less than half of the female population in employment, Norway has nearly three-quarters. Cohabitation rates (for those aged 75+ in the OASIS sample) vary between 7% in Norway and 37% in Spain. Familialistic patterns are now under strain. A decline of shared households and an increase in female employment are global trends that are pushing heavily on the familialistic welfare regimes (UN, 2002). The currently low fertility rate in Spain (1.1%) compared to Norway (1.7%) may be a response to this strain. The lack of supportive services (for elders and children) makes it difficult to combine a modern life style with family obligations, in particular for women who are by tradition the dominant family caregiver

Are these patterns reflected also in public opinion and personal preferences? Do people support the established policies, or do they push for change? The OASIS study explored not only the between-country differences but also the variation of opinions and preferences within the five countries, for example between women and men, the younger and the older. Questions like these are important for both pragmatic and theoretical reasons. Elder care is in all modern countries some form of partnership between the family and the welfare state, but what is a sustainable and reasonable mix of responsibilities when populations are aging and equal opportunities for women should be respected? Family care has been the traditional order. More distant care providers, and the formal services among them, have been activated only when caregivers higher in the hierarchy were not available. This model found a social-policy formulation in the principle of subsidiarity, where family responsibility is assumed to be primary, while other caregivers and eventually the welfare state should take a residual role and act as a safety net. Among the arguments against expanding services were that they might discourage family and civic responsibility. The moral obligations would be corrupted, so to speak, if one did not have to help, an idea that Wolfe (1989) described as the moral risk of the welfare state. Services should therefore not expand beyond the minimum required to make family and civic responsibility necessary. Family solidarity is assumed to be fragile and easily lost if it is no longer enforced by norms and necessity.

Knowledge about actual care provision is important, but so also is knowledge about norms and ideals because people tend to act accordingly if opportunity allows it. Attitudes and preferences point forward to new lifestyles and policies; norms and obligations look back and represent a resistance to change. What people actually do resembles some form of compromise between the two and likewise with social policies: they try to balance between contrasting considerations. We need to know more about what people would like to do given the power of choice. Subjective norms and tastes are important also because they are premises for quality of care and for that matter quality of life. We are usually happy when our preferences are rewarded and unhappy when they are not. Hence we need to know what the population sees as "the right thing" in order to develop just policies and good services. The focus here is therefore what people find to be a reasonable balance of responsibility between the family and the welfare state as well as what their personal preferences are.

Attitudes toward the family-welfare state balance are measured in OASIS with reference to assistance in three domains: financial support, instrumental help (in the home), and personal care. People were asked to state how much the family on one hand and the welfare state on the other are responsible for providing these kinds of support.

Public opinion was found to vary considerably between the countries. The welfare state was seen as carrying the primary responsibility in all three domains in Norway and by a (smaller) majority also in Israel; a more even split was shown in the other three countries. But the urban populations of all five countries indicated a preference for some mix of responsibility between the welfare state and the family. Very few placed *total* responsibility either with the welfare state or with the family. The latter was the least likely and was indicated by less than 10% in any of the five countries. Somewhat more, but still a minority, saw the welfare state as *fully* responsible and more so in Norway and Israel than in Germany and Spain. In conclusion, the majority favor some form of complementarity between the family and the welfare state, but the complementarity takes different forms. The welfare state is assumed to have the major responsibility in Norway and Israel, with the family in a supplementary role. The converse is true in Germany and Spain, with England in an intermediate position.

Attitudes were found to be more or less congruent with the actual policies, but public opinion leans toward favoring a greater degree of welfare-state responsibility than presently exists. The contrast between ideals and realities is greater in the low-service countries, implying a greater tension between policy and opinion in these countries, as should be expected. While Norwegians, for example, are about 10 times more likely to place the main responsibility on the welfare state compared to the family, the opinions are more evenly split or moderately biased toward the welfare state in Spain and Germany, and lean thereby in these two countries far more toward the welfare state than at present.

Gender differences are small; hence the female dominance in actual care provision is more likely imposed upon them, not chosen. Age differences are also modest. Older people are generally *not* more traditional (familialistic) than the younger, although Spain is an exception. Older people in Spain are more family oriented than the young, who tend to agree with younger (and older) people further north, probably in response to the changes in demography and lifestyles that came earlier in the north. Norway is an example, with a high degree of consensus in the population in these matters across gender and age. The older generation here is in fact *more* inclined to push responsibilities on the welfare state than are the younger.

The *personal preferences* for care generally mirror public opinion, but lean even more toward welfare-state (services) solutions. The great majority of Norwegians stated a preference for services over family care if they should come to need it in old age. A correspondingly great majority would prefer institutional care over living with a child if they could no longer live by themselves. Preferences are more moderately balanced toward the welfare state in three of the other four countries. Spain stands out with a majority in favor of family care, but only among the older generation.

There is little or no support in these trends for the idea that older people are abandoned by their families and left to social services as a secondary option. Family solidarity does not seem to be threatened by alternative or complementary services. Each party may have qualities that are not easily replaced by the other, so complementarity between services and family care is more likely than substitution.

In summary, there are considerable differences in public opinion and personal preferences among the five countries in a direction that is congruent with the established traditions. Which comes first, policy or public opinion? is a more complex question, and the congruence between the two is not perfect. Public opinion tends to ascribe more responsibility to the welfare state than is yet implemented, and the contrast is largest in familialistic countries that currently have low service levels. To find an unmet demand for services is hardly surprising, but the generality of this trend points toward equally general explanations. One such explanation could be found in a weaker family solidarity, and therefore an escape (and push) toward the safety net of the welfare state. A more likely explanation is, however, that people have increasingly recognized that needs are growing beyond what responsibilities are possible and reasonable to be borne by the family.

INTERGENERATIONAL SOLIDARITY

Virtually every generation has expressed concern about family solidarity, and ours is no exception. Images of a family in crisis seem to appear repeatedly in popular opinion both in the north and south of Europe (Daatland, 1997). Similar concerns have been raised in social science. The isolated nuclear family controversy is a case in point—whether or not the link to the older generation(s) has lost substance in modern society as suggested by Parsons (1955). Most gerontologists have concluded otherwise and have found substantial levels of solidarity also in modern societies (Shanas, 1979). Do the cross-cultural OASIS data and analysis support the former or the latter position?

The intergenerational solidarity model (Bengtson & Roberts, 1991) was employed as a research instrument and measures solidarity along six dimensions: structural, associational, consensual, affectional, functional, and normative solidarity. An early formulation of the model assumed that these dimensions were expressions of one latent solidarity factor. Later revisions have stressed the multidimensional character of intergenerational relationships, and conflict has been added as a distinct factor and not simply a case of low solidarity (Silverstein & Bengtson, 1997). These revisions were responses to criticism for being blind to the dark sides of family life and for being unable to handle change—how solidarity may grow, decline, or simply change (Marshall, Matthews, & Rosenthal, 1993).

Ambivalence has more recently been introduced as an alternative perspective (Lüscher & Pillemer, 1998; Connidis & McMullin, 2002). Intergenerational relations are seen as inherently ambivalent and characterized by mixed feelings and conflicting expectations. Family members need to cope with internal ambivalences and external pressures. These adaptive changes may have been misinterpreted as a breakdown of family solidarity instead of a change in how solidarity is expressed (Daatland & Herlofson, 2003). Ambivalence is, however, difficult to measure directly; the solidarity model lends itself more easily to empirical testing, but is conceptually unclear.

Normative solidarity is, in OASIS, measured as support for filial obligation norms—the extent to which adult children are obligated to help their older parents. Most people support such norms in all five countries, but more so in Spain and Israel than in Norway, England, and Germany. This trend is consistent with Reher's (1998) suggestion that the families in southern Europe are more closely knit than those in northern Europe. Historically, unique events may also have affected the character of intergenerational relationships, such as World War II in the case of Germany and the Francoist era in Spain. In any case, the variation in the support for filial norms is rather moderate between the five countries; hence, the main impression is that normative solidarity is important in northern countries as well, even in a universalist welfare state like Norway. This impression is further strengthened if we take into account that the samples were drawn from large cities only and do not include smaller towns and rural areas which may be assumed to be even more familialistic; therefore, neither urbanization nor welfare state expansion seem to have eroded filial obligations as suggested by the moral risk hypothesis of Wolfe (1989).

Affectional solidarity is indicated by affection and closeness and seems even stronger than normative solidarity, particularly from a parental perspective. Both parents and children report strong feelings of closeness, but parents (70-80%) more so than children (50-60%). The greater strength of the downward ties compared to the upward ties is a general feature of Western families. The more collectivistic Eastern family may give higher priority to the older generation.

Conflict levels are low as seen from both viewpoints, with both parties—and in particular the children—allowing for a difference of opinion between parents and children (low consensus) without this being seen as a threat to the relationship.

The presumably tighter bonds in the Spanish family can be seen primarily in *structural and associational solidarity.* Generations live closer and have more frequent contact in Spain compared to the more northern countries. This is mainly explained by the higher co-residence rates in Spain, which may be a mixed blessing. Shared living is often an outcome of necessity rather than choice and is thus more likely an indicator of (lack of) opportunity than of solidarity.

Functional solidarity—exchange of help and support—is substantial in all five countries and not less so in the northern family. Exchanges are integral parts of daily life in nearly any family, but roles and resources change over the life course. Older people tend to be in the receiving end, but act also as providers of support; hence, we need to explore exchanges from the perspective of parents and children, providers and receivers. The findings show that most (75-85%) adult children have provided one or several types of support to older parents (aged 75+) during the last year. Emotional support is the most frequent form of support, followed by instrumental help. Few adult children provide personal care to older parents, probably because few parents are frail enough to require such care, and if so, they may already have moved to an institution. Low levels of institutional care and high cohabitation rates partially explain why personal care is highest in Spain. Other forms of family support are equally frequent, or even more frequent, in a high-service country like Norway.

Adult children are generally the net providers in the exchange relationship with older parents; they give more than they receive. This is acknowledged also from the parent perspective; older parents receive more than they give. Older parents provide primarily emotional support to adult children, and in some countries (Norway, Germany, Israel) also money. Instrumental help flows upwards in the family line, financial support seems to flow downwards if and when pension levels allow it. The general exchange pattern looks quite similar from both sides of the relationship, but children are inclined to say they have provided more help than parents admit to having received. We shouldn't expect a perfect match here, as the study does not match respondents from the same family. Moreover, both parties may want to put their best foot forward: the children by overstating what they are providing, the parents by appearing more self-sufficient than they in fact are.

The relatively substantial affection and exchange levels in five otherwise different countries indicate that solidarity—so measured—is general and considerable. These results should be interpreted with some caution, however, because the measurements are rather crude, and variation is considerable *within* each country. Family resources are not evenly distributed, and the character of family relationships varies from tighter to more distant within each country. But country differences are moderate in the more general features of solidarity and far larger in the more concrete attitudes about how policies and services should be organized. If this is a valid observation, then intergenerational family solidarity may have a rather stable and general character, but find different expressions in practice when circumstances and conditions change. This suggestion indicates a need to clarify what precisely is meant by solidarity.

We have therefore conducted a series of factor analyses to explore the solidarity model to see whether solidarity may be broken down into the six (seven, if conflict is included) assumed dimensions. The model was originally developed using U.S. data (Bengtson & Roberts, 1991). Do we find a similar structure in the five OASIS countries? The findings give conditional support to the model, but to a simplified variant of it. A (nearly) general finding for all countries and types of relationships (of mothers/fathers and daughters/sons) is a four-factor solution: affection comes out first and includes consensus; conflict comes out next as a distinct factor; third is a joint factor for structural and associational solidarity (geographical closeness and contact frequency); while giving and receiving support is the fourth factor. Normative solidarity is in most cases not included in any of these factors and is apparently a distinct aspect of intergenerational relationships that may be combined with different ways of relating to each other.

The character of intergenerational relationships is thus rather general and common for these countries. However, our findings suggest that the model could well be simplified to four dimensions: attachment, conflict, sociability, and mutual support (reciprocity). Duty (normative solidarity) might be added as a fifth dimension. There is no empirical basis for a split between affection and consensus (attachment), nor between the so-called structural and associational solidarity (sociability).

More problematic is the use of solidarity as the core concept in the model, when it in fact includes also other sources of social integration. A more precise definition of solidarity is called for, one that is reserved for a distinct form of social integration rooted in a willingness to act for the benefit of another. Solidarity thus represents a distinct form of collectivism (for us) that lies between self-interest (for oneself) and altruism (for all). Solidarity is a state of mind (attitude, intention), not a behavior. Prosocial (helping) behavior may also have other motivations, and nonhelping may conceal intentions of solidarity that are blocked by external constraints.

Family life has been, and to some extent still is, structured by material necessities and enforced duties, which makes it difficult to separate motivations of solidarity from external pressures. This increases the difficulty of comparing families across time and cultures. Solidarity may be easier to distinguish and observe today than in earlier times when external pressures were stronger, but the mechanisms and processes that produce the solidarity patterns may have become more complex and need to be studied comparatively.

QUALITY OF LIFE

Quality of life must be studied along several dimensions and in a multilevel perspective. Outcomes on the individual level should be related to both mesolevel social relationships and to macrolevel societal structures. This makes quality of life an excellent example of a concept that is not only well suited for comparative analysis but indeed demands it to help distinguish the general from the specific.

Quality of life is a multidimensional concept that includes material and nonmaterial, objective and subjective, individual and collective aspects of welfare. Historically, there are two basic research traditions (Noll, 1999). The Scandinavian level of living approach is based on the concept of resources that are available to individuals. As a result, quality of life is defined as the "individual's command over . . . mobilisable resources with whose help (s)he can control and consciously direct her/his living conditions" (Erikson, 1974). People are seen as active beings that strive toward autonomy, while resources are recognized as means to reach valued goals. Resources increase individual agency and therefore the likelihood of a qualitatively good life.

An alternative and initially a U.S. tradition emphasizes the subjective experiences of life, typically measured as subjective well-being (Diener, 1994). Objective life conditions are seen to have mainly an indirect effect on well-being, through individuals' subjective evaluations of these conditions (Campbell, Converse, & Rogers, 1976; Smith, Fleeson, Geiselmann, Settersten, & Kurzmann, 1996). Subjective well-being is found to have both cognitive and emotional aspects, and the latter to have both positive and negative affect as distinct dimensions (Watson, Clark, & Tellegen, 1988). Subjective well-being as seen from a psychological perspective is then more than the command over resources, and includes subjective interpretations and feelings, in some models including even existential or spiritual aspects like perceived meaning of life (Ryff, 1989).

An attempt to integrate the objective and subjective aspects of quality of life can be seen in the description of "welfare positions" by Zapf (1984). When living conditions are objectively good and subjectively appreciated, he talks about "well-being." This is the intended living situation of individuals and the intended outcome of political interventions. When both are negative, it's a case of "deprivation." Dissatisfaction despite good living conditions is interpreted as "dissonance," while satisfaction with objectively poor living conditions is labeled "adaptation." The latter is often found as a prototypical response in older years.

A third research perspective has developed from within gerontology itself as the successful aging tradition, with a number of suggested standards for what a good adaptation to old age is assumed to be (e.g., Rowe & Kahn, 1997). Later studies have criticized the ethnocentric and Western bias of most of these models both substantively and methodologically (Torres, 1999). Successful aging models are prime examples of what Hagestad and Dannefer (2001) call the microfication of gerontology—how gerontology has been primarily occupied with individual (micro) level outcomes without proper consideration of how macro- and mesolevel factors may have produced these outcomes. Studying the quality of life of older people means taking into account indicators above and beyond those that can be measured on the individual level. Peoples' lives play out on the background of a whole life course—as a sequence of positions and as personal biographies; they are also embedded in local contexts of societal traditions and institutions. This complex landscape of multiple embeddedness in individual and collective time may cause considerable interindividual differences and diversity across gender, age, ethnicity, and class. A common location in time or space makes it plausible to assume similarities within such locations. Differences between them should be explored in their distinctive characteristics. In OASIS, the important and distinctive characteristics were assumed to be the different service systems and family traditions. How did these factors relate to quality of life?

In OASIS, quality of life was measured using both objective and subjective indicators, but is here presented in the form of subjective well-being, as this corresponds to the WHO quality-of-life scale (the short BREF version). The findings show significant differences over age groups. Quality-of-life levels were lower among older people, but interpersonal variation seemed to increase with age. This increased variation with age is particularly true for satisfaction with physical and psychological health, while satisfaction with environmental factors (including housing and standards of living) is a more stable entity. The importance of different life domains for the overall quality of life varies significantly with age, from the higher importance of environmental factors among the younger, to a selection of health and inner qualities among the older (Motel-Klingebiel, 2004).

Variation between the countries was remarkably low; hence age group differences cannot simply be explained by cultural diversity, but should be connected to age as a structural marker in itself. This finding suggests that age group differences may be general life-course effects and not simply discrepancies between cohorts or between generations in Mannheim's sense of the term (Mannheim, 1964).

Quality of life does, however, also respond to family and welfare-state resources, and possibly to distinct characteristics of each country (Motel-Klingebiel, Tesch-Römer, & von Kondratowitz, 2003; Tesch-Römer, Motel-Klingebiel, & von Kondratowitz, 2002). Older people with children had a higher quality of life than those without children, but the impact of the number of offspring was not linear. To have children was the important factor, not the number of children. This effect varied by country. People in more familialistic societies such as Spain and Germany tended to ascribe families a more important role for quality of life than in more individualistic and universalistic welfare states such as Norway.

CONCLUSION

The OASIS findings illustrate the potential of comparative research to help us separate idiographic (local) from nomothetic (general) explanations. Similarities across these countries suggest there are general mechanisms in function, for example in the character of intergenerational relationships, while differences need be interpreted in context, for example how public opinion may be a response to national policies. Hence both general and local mechanisms are played out in the data, supporting the position that both structuralist and culturalist perspectives have something to offer. The critical issue is how to interpret the similarities—and the differences—when you find them, as suggested in the Kohn (1989) quotation in the introduction to this chapter.

As comparative studies are more demanding than single case studies, they should be reserved for questions that cannot be properly explored in more local settings. Among the distinct qualities of the comparative approach is the expanded variation in the data, which makes the observations more comprehensive and adds power to the analysis. Another quality is the opportunity to test the general, or possibly universal, relevance of normative models and theories beyond the context (culture, time) they were originally developed for. Aging and old age may in fact be one of the few areas where a truly nomothetic ambition is relevant in social science, as they refer to processes and states that in themselves are human universals.

The analysis and findings of the OASIS project also illustrate some limitations in comparative studies, be they comparative across time or place. The data were cross-cultural, but the interpretations implied a historical (time) perspective, as for example the assumed impact of path dependence on earlier established structures. Hence a general recommendation is to integrate comparisons over time *and* place whenever possible and then to integrate both culturalist and structuralist perspectives.

ACKNOWLEDGMENTS

The OASIS project was funded under the 5th Framework Programme of the European Union, Contract No. QLK6-TC-1999-02182. Norwegian participation was co-sponsored by the Norwegian Research Council.

REFERENCES

Alber, J. (1995). A framework for the comparative study of social services. *Journal of European Social Policy, 5,* 131-149.

Allardt, E. (1990). Challenges for comparative social research. *Acta Sociologica, 33,* 183-193.

Bauman, Z. (2000). *Liquid modernity.* London: Polity Press.

Bengtson, V. L., & Roberts, R. E. L. (1991). Intergenerational solidarity in aging families: An example of formal theory construction. *Journal of Marriage and the Family, 53,* 856-870.

Campbell, A., Converse, P. E., & Rogers, W. L. (1976). *The quality of American life.* New York: Sage.

Connidis, I. A., & McMullin, J. A. (2002). Sociological ambivalence and family ties: A critical perspective. *Journal of Marriage and the Family, 64,* 558-567.

Cowgill, D. O., & Holmes, L. D. (Eds.). (1972). *Aging and modernization.* New York: Appleton-Century-Crofts.

Cumming, E., & Henry, W. (1961). *Growing old.* New York: Basic Books.

Daatland, S. O. (1997). Family solidarity, popular opinion, and the elderly. *Ageing International, 1,* 51-62.

Daatland, S. O., & Herlofson, K. (2003). 'Lost solidary' or 'changed solidarity': A comparative European view on normative family solidarity. *Ageing & Society, 23,* 537-560.

David, P. A. (2000). "Path dependence, its critics and the quest for 'historical economics.'" In P. Garrouste & S. Ioannides (Eds.), *Evolution and path dependence in economic ideas: Past and present* (pp. 15-41). Cheltenham: Elgar Publishing.

Diener, E. (1994). Assessing subjective well-being: Progress and opportunities. *Social Indicators Research, 31,* 103-157.

Erikson, E. (1959). *Identity and the life cycle.* New York: W. W. Norton.

Erikson, R. (1974). Welfare as a planning goal. *Acta Sociologica, 17,* 273-278.

Esping-Andersen, G. (1990). *The three worlds of welfare capitalism.* Princeton: Princeton University Press.

Esping-Andersen, G. (1999). *Social foundations of postindustrial economies.* Oxford: Oxford University Press.

Estes, C. L., Swan, J. H., & Gerard, L. E. (1982). Dominant and competing paradigms in gerontology: Towards a political economy of ageing. *Ageing and Society, 2,* 151-164.

Ferrara, M. (1996). The 'southern model' of welfare in social Europe. *Journal of European Social Policy, 6*(1), 17-37.

Fry, C. L. (1999). Anthropological theories of age and aging. In V. L. Bengtson & K. W. Schaie (Eds.), *Handbook of theories of aging* (pp. 271-286). New York: Springer.

Fuchs-Heinritz, W., Lautmann, R., Rammstedt, O., & Wienhold, H. (1994). *Lexikon zur Soziologie* (Encyclopedia of sociology). Opladen: Westdeutscher Verlag.

Gauthier, A. H. (2000). *The promises of comparative research.* Paper prepared for the European Panel Analysis Group (http://www.iser.essex.ac.uk/epag/pubs/).

Hagestad, G. O., & Dannefer, D. (2001). Concepts and theories of aging: Beyond microfication in social science approaches. In R. H. Binstock & L. K. George (Eds.), *Handbook of aging and the social sciences* (5th ed., pp. 3-21). San Diego: Academic Press.

Jung, C. G. (1930). *Die Lebenswende. Gerammelte Werke* (Vol. 8) [The life transition. Complete edition vol. 8). Olten: Walter-Verlag.

Keith, J., Fry, C. L., Glascock, A. P., Ikels, C., Dickerson-Putnam, J., Harpending, H. C., & Draper, P. (1994). *The ageing experience. Diversity and commonality across cultures.* Thousand Oaks: Sages.

Kohn, M. L. (1989). Cross-national research as an analytical strategy. In M. L. Kohn (Ed.), *Cross-national research in sociology* (pp. 77-102). Newbury Park: Sage.

Lowenstein, A., & Ogg, J. (2003). *OASIS final report.* Haifa: University of Haifa.

Lüscher, K., & Pillemer, K. (1998). Intergenerational ambivalence: A new approach to the study of parent-child relations in later life. *Journal of Marriage and the Family, 60,* 413-425.

Mannheim, K. (1964). Das Problem der Generationen [The problem of generations]. In K. Mannheim (Ed.), *Wissenssoziologie. Auswahl aus dem Werk; eingeleitet und herausgegeben von Kurt H. Wolff* [Essays on the sociology of knowledge] (pp. 509-565). Berlin, Neuwied: Luchterhand.

Marshall, V. W., Matthews, S. H., & Rosenthal, C. J. (1993). Elusiveness of family life: A challenge to the sociology of aging. In G. L. Maddox & M. Powell Lawton (Eds.), *Annual review of gerontology and geriatrics, 13* (pp. 39-72). New York: Springer.

Motel-Klingebiel, A. (2004). Quality of life and social inequality in old age. In S. O. Daatland & S. Biggs (Eds.), *Ageing and diversity. Multiple pathways and cultural migrations* (pp. 189-205). Bristol: Policy Press.

Motel-Klingebiel, A., Tesch-Römer, C., & von Kondratowitz, H.-J. (2003). The role of family for quality of life in old age—A comparative perspective. In V. L. Bengtson & A. Lowenstein (Eds.), *Global aging and challenges to families* (pp. 323-354). New York: Aldine de Gruyter.

Noll, H.-H. (1999). *Konzepte der Wohlfahrtsentwicklung: Lebensqualität und "neue" Wohlfahrtskonzepte* [Concepts of welfare development: Quality of life and "new" concepts of welfare]. EuReporting Working Paper No. 3. Mannheim: ZUMA.

Parsons, T. (1955). The American family: Its relations to personality and the social structure. In T. Parsons & R. F. Bales (Eds.), *Family, socialization and interaction process* (pp. 3-33). Glencoe: The Free Press.

Pierson, P. (2000). Increasing returns, path dependence and the study of politics. *American Political Science Review, 2,* 251-267.

Ragin, C. C. (1987). *The comparative method.* Berkeley: University of California Press.

Ragin, C. C. (1991). Introduction. The problem of balancing discourse on cases and variables in comparative social science. In C. C. Ragin (Ed.), *Issues and alternatives in comparative social research* (pp. 1-18). Leiden: E. J. Brill.

Reher, D. S. (1998). Family ties in western Europe: Persistent contrasts. *Population and Development Review, 24*(2), 203-234.

Rowe, J., & Kahn, R. (1997). Successful aging. *The Gerontologist, 37*(4), 433-440.

Ryff, C. D. (1989). Happiness is everything, or is it? Explorations on the meaning of psychological well-being. *Journal of Personality and Social Psychology, 57,* 1069-1081.

Shanas, E., Townsend, P., Wedderburn, D., Friis, H., Milhøj, P., & Stehouwer, J. (1968). *Old people in three industrial societies.* New York: Atherton Press.

Shanas, E. (1979). Social myth as hypothesis. The case of family relations of old people. *The Gerontologist, 19*(1), 3-9.

Silverstein, M., & Bengtson, V. L. (1997). Intergenerational solidarity and the structure of adult child-parent relationships in American families. *American Journal of Sociology, 103*(2), 429-460.

Simmons, L. (1945). *The role of the aged in primitive society.* New Haven: Yale University Press.

Smith, J., Fleeson, W., Geiselmann, B., Settersten, R., & Kunzmann, U. (1996). Sources of well-being in very old age. In P. B. Baltes & K. U. Mayer (Eds.), *The Berlin ageing study. Aging from 70 to 100* (pp. 450-471). Cambridge: Cambridge University Press.

Sztompka, P. (1988). Conceptual frameworks in comparative inquiry: Divergent or convergent? *International Sociology, 3,* 207-218.

Tesch-Römer, C., Motel-Klingebiel, A., & von Kondratowitz, H.-J. (2002). Die Bedeutung der Familie für die–lebensqualität alter Menschen imgesellschafts- und Kulturvergleich [The relevance of the family network for the quality of life of elderly people: Comparing societies and cultures]. *Zeitschrift für Gerontologie under Geriatrie, 35,* 335-342.

Tornstam, L. (1989). Gero-transcendence: A meta-theoretical reformulation of the disengagement theory. *Aging, 1,* 55-63.

Torres, S. (1999). A culturally-relevant theoretical framework for the study of successful ageing. *Ageing and Society, 19,* 33-51.

UN. (2002). *World population ageing 1950-2050.* New York: UN, Population Division.

Watson, D., Clark, L. A., & Tellegen, A. (1988). Development and validation of brief measures of positive and negative affect: The PANAS scales. *Journal of Personality and Social Psychology, 54,* 1063-1070.

Wolfe, A. (1989). *Whose keeper? Social science and moral obligations.* Berkeley: University of California Press.

Zapf, W. (1984). Individuelle Wohlfahrt: Lebensbedingungen und wahrgenommene Lebensqualität [Individual welfare: Living conditions and perceived quality of life]. In W. Glatzer & W. Zapf (Eds.), *Lebensqualität in der Bundesrepublik Deutschland. Objektive lebensbedingungen und subjektives Wohlbefinden* [Quality of life in Germany. Objektive living conditions and subjective well-being] (pp. 13-26). Frankfurt: Campus.

CHAPTER 20

Plasticity in Old Age: Micro- and Macroperspectives on Social Contexts

Eva-Marie Kessler and Ursula M. Staudinger

According to lifespan psychology, human development is characterized by plasticity at all ages. The degree of plasticity depends on the internal and external resources of an individual. With increasing age, the range of plasticity decreases, and the importance of external resources in supporting plasticity is augmented (e.g., Greve & Staudinger, 2006; Staudinger, Marsiske, & Baltes, 1995). Internal and external resources are part and parcel of the internal and external contexts of development. Thus, the study of developmental contexts, and in particular of external developmental contexts, is pivotal when trying to understand the range and limits of plasticity in old age. Lifespan psychology has developed a wide array of paradigms and methodologies that have helped to explore the contexts of old age and their influence on plasticity and resilience. This chapter reviews some of this research with a focus on social contexts as a major developmental influence in old age. In particular, we discuss two types of social context, one is of a microsocial or proximal (i.e., intergenerational relations) and the other is of a macrosocial or distal nature (i.e., public images of old age and aging). In the end, we hope to have demonstrated that psychological evidence emerging from the study of these contexts enriches the scientific as well as the political debate.

CONTEXTS IN OLD AGE: A LIFESPAN PERSPECTIVE

A Contextualistic View on Human Development and Aging

Lifespan contextualism maintains that human development and aging is the result of a complex system of sources and resources including biology, culture, and last but not least, the actions and reactions of the developing individual her- or himself (e.g., Baltes, Reese, & Lipsitt, 1980; Lerner, 1984). Actions and reactions of the developing individual are considered as psychological phenomena. The developing individual is not just an epiphenomenon of the interaction between biological and cultural influences but rather has to be included as an active contributor (e.g., Brandtstädter, 1984) and thus as a third source of development, if you may. Biology refers to the fabric of physiological, anatomical, and genetic resources of the human species as they have been constantly evolving over phylogenesis and ontogenesis (e.g., Kirkwood, 2003). Culture refers to the entirety of social, physical, material, and symbolic (knowledge-based) resources that humans developed or modified over millennia; and that, as they are transmitted across generations, make human development—as we know it—possible (Baltes, Lindenberger, & Staudinger, 1998). A central proposition of lifespan contextualism is that biology, culture, and individual actions and reactions are *all* malleable and mutually dependent. Together, they form the spectrum of developmental contexts or influences and can be broadly categorized in internal and external developmental contexts. Internal contexts refer to the whole array of biological and psychological resources, such as personality characteristics and physiological parameters. External contexts denote the wide range of physical and sociocultural resources, such as the physical environment and cultural norms or language. This implies that any context undergoes constant change, and biological, psychological, and cultural contexts can only be considered in relation to each other (Baltes et al., 1998; Lerner, 1984). Lifespan contextualism further posits that all sources are completely intertwined in a multiplicative manner (see also Anastasi, 1958). Given this multiplicative relationship, human development is never fully predictable, that is, individual development is probable rather than determined (Gottlieb, 1970), a fact captured by the notion of probabilistic epigenesis (e.g., Lerner, 1984). Lifespan contextualism considers the *transaction* (Sameroff, 1975) or *dynamic interaction* (Lerner, 1984) between both *internal* and *external* contexts (e.g., Riegel, 1976; Staudinger & Greve, 2001). An important step in the analysis of this dynamic interaction is to discriminate between different levels or elements of these contexts (e.g., Bronfenbrenner, 1979; Lerner, 1984; Li, 2003).

With regard to external developmental contexts, which will be the focus of the present chapter, Bronfenbrenner distinguished four levels, which he called "systems," within the "ecology of human development" (Bronfenbrenner, 1979): (1) the microsystem, which is composed of immediate settings (including the person), such as the grandparent-grandchildren interactions, daycare, fitness center; (2) the mesosystem which contains the transactional relationship between two or more immediate settings containing the developing person at a particular point in his or her life; (3) the exosystem which does not contain the developing person but impinges upon or encompass the immediate settings in which the person is found and thereby influences what goes on there (e.g., the job situation of older people's children); and (4) the macrosystem that comprises historical events (wars, famines, etc.) as well as cultural values and beliefs that may affect the other ecological systems.

The Spectrum of Contexts in Old Age

According to lifespan psychology, three broad systems of variation operate on the basic sources of development, that is, biology, culture, and the actions and reactions of the developing individual: (1) *Normative age-graded variations* refer to those influences that come with age, and shape internal and external developmental contexts in a relatively normative fashion for all individuals; (2) *history-graded variations* refer to the differences in biological, cultural, and agentic psychological forces due to historical period and, finally, (3) *non-normative variations* due to individual-idiosyncratic events, which, while not frequent, can have powerful influences on ontogenesis. These types of variation fulfill important analytic and explanatory functions for understanding both interindividual regularities of developmental trajectories and the sources of interindividual differences (Baltes et al., 1998).

The matrix depicted in Figure 1 assigns the three major sources of development, that is, culture, biology, and the acting and reacting individual, to two types of developmental contexts (internal, external) and combines them with the three types of variations just introduced. Figure 1 lists examples of the spectrum of developmental contexts resulting from the combination of these two dimensions. Note that all contexts may be facilitative as well as constraining with regard to the mastery of life tasks.

The Range and Limits of Development in Later Adulthood

The contexts of development not only determine the course of development but also its range and limits, that is, the plasticity of development. Plasticity is indexed by an individual's change potential and by how flexible and robust he or she is in the face of challenges and threats. Based on the central conviction that human development is always characterized by plasticity, lifespan research has always had a strong concern for research on the *opportunities* as well as *constraints* characterizing the aging process (Staudinger et al., 1995; Staudinger & Greve, 2001). This focus is reflected in research about tapped and untapped internal and external resources for recovery, maintenance, or further growth (Staudinger et al., 1995).

Given the importance of the notion of plasticity within the theoretical framework of lifespan psychology, it is not surprising that research on aging has become a cornerstone of lifespan psychology. In a prototypical fashion, work on aging has illustrated the enormous range as well as the limits of intraindividual variability in various domains

Developmental Contexts	Variations of Development Contexts		
	History-graded	Age-graded	Idiosyncratic
Internal Biology	Life expectancy	Menopause	Blindness
Psychology (in relation to actions and reactions of the developing individual)	Autonomy	Control beliefs	Creativity
External Physical Environment	Hygiene	Age-friendly environments	Traffic accident
Culture	Social norms	Retirement	Economic status

Figure 1. Dimensions and examples of the spectrum of contexts of development.

of development. Thus, any one-sided negative aging stereotype has been refuted, and pervasive empirical arguments for the potential of human development and aging have been provided (Baltes et al., 1998).

One type of plasticity with high importance in old age is resilience, defined as the ability to maintain and regain "normal" (in the sense of average) levels of functioning in the face of stress or loss (e.g., Staudinger et al., 1995; Staudinger & Greve, 2001). In lifespan psychology, resilience is not considered a trait or even the genetically based invulnerability of an individual. Rather, in accordance with a contextualistic position, it is argued that resilience is a characteristic attributed to a specific constellation of protective *biological* (e.g., basic cognitive capacity, physical health), *psychological* (e.g., coping strategies, knowledge), and *cultural factors* (e.g., social relations, financial resources, social status, institutional structures), on the one, and external or internal stressors on the other. In contrast to the trait-oriented approach to resilience, this conceptualization explicitly regards cultural contexts, such as social and material environments, as crucial elements of a resilience constellation (Greve & Staudinger, 2006; Staudinger et al., 1995; Staudinger & Greve, 2001).

The central importance of cultural contexts for plasticity and resilience in old age is closely linked to one of the basic principles of the lifespan architecture of human ontogeny (Baltes, 1987): the age-related increase in the need for the supportive and enriching role of culture because biological functioning declines. Unfortunately, as contextual support becomes more important in old age, it also loses efficiency; the effectiveness of most psychological, social, material, and cultural interventions wanes (Baltes, 1993, 1997). Empirical studies in the domains of cognition, personality, and social relationships confirm these assumptions: there continues to be plasticity in the second half of life but the range of plasticity is more limited in old age than at earlier phases of the life span.

A Model of Resilience

The *model of resilience* depicted in Figure 2 is based on the lifespan-contextualistic perspective just described (Staudinger & Greve, 2001). The model describes development under adversity as a system of limiters (supportive of losses) and facilitators (supportive of gains; see also Staudinger & Lindenberger, 2003). Limiters and facilitators of development exist within internal as well as external contexts and form a complex transactional system of influences. In any given stressful situation, this constellation of influences results in a certain degree of adaptation, that is, a negative, positive, or no deviation from the developmental norm. The degree of adaptation is indexed by developmental outcomes that may be of a subjective or objective (subjective health vs. physiological parameters), internal or external (status of cognitive functioning vs. net income), domain-specific or global (marital satisfaction vs. global life satisfaction), and long-term or short-term (physical fitness) nature. Depending on the outcome under consideration, the adaptivity of a given constellation may drastically change. For instance, a specific characteristic may contribute to the resilience constellation when using a subjective developmental outcome, such as present life satisfaction, but may be irrelevant for the resilience constellation when using an objective developmental outcome such as net income.

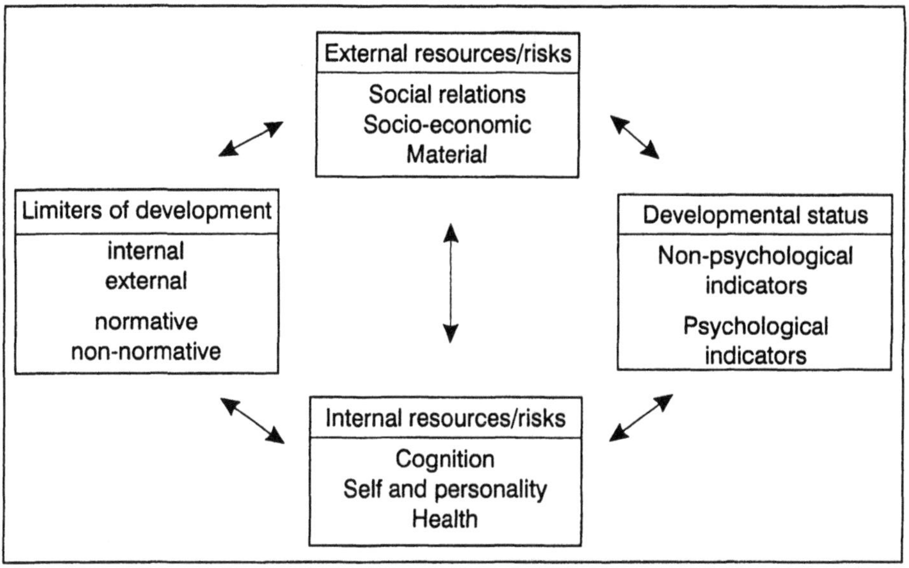

Figure 2. A model of resilience (Staudinger & Greve, 2001).

Given the nature of this model, it is imperative to independently operationalize stressors, protective factors, and outcomes for any given study in order to avoid tautology. This is a basic problem of resilience research that first has been described in the classic article by Rutter (1987). Note that it is impossible to specify certain internal or external characteristics as general facilitators or limiters (or resources or risks) of development. This specification is fundamentally dependent on the particular constellation of internal and external resources, the stressor, and the selected outcome. For example, there are a number of studies showing that social support can promote subjective well-being or health-related parameters in the face of a crisis. However, these effects only occur if the individual is able to accept the social support (e.g., Bisconti & Bergeman, 1999). Or, there is evidence that, for instance, future time perspective is highly adaptive in young adulthood but much less so in old age (e.g., Brandtstädter & Wentura, 1994; Staudinger, Freund, Linden, & Maas, 1999). These examples illustrate that general statements about the adaptivity of a specific characteristic are oversimplifying (for further examples and theoretical explanations on this topic see Staudinger & Greve, 2001; Staudinger & Pasupathi, 2000).

Empirical Approaches to the Study of the Social Embeddedness of Old Age

Following the contextualistic understanding of the aging process, lifespan psychology has always strongly promoted methodological pluralism. This central proposition arises from the fact that there is no one mode of analysis or single methodological strategy that suggests itself as useful at all levels of analysis involved in a certain behavior at a given historical time. Instead, the criterion of usefulness must be employed every time when deciding whether a particular methodological strategy is appropriate for a certain research question (Lerner, 1984). In addition to methodological pluralism, many (but not all) lifespan researchers consider ecological validity, that is, research in settings representative of everyday life, as a central guideline for their research (e.g., Bronfenbrenner, 1977; Labouvie-Vief, 1982).

In the following, we highlight two methodologies of lifespan-developmental psychology that specifically address the embeddedness of aging in (changing) sociocultural contexts: intervention research and cohort-sequential longitudinal research. These two methodological paradigms in a prototypical fashion illustrate the empirical consequences of lifespan contextualism.

The first methodology has focused on interventions in a (quasi-)experimental laboratory as well as in naturalistic settings. In this approach, the focus is on what is possible in principle, that is, under different rather than currently extant conditions. Specifically, this approach is a theory-testing device that arranges for cultural contexts identified as relevant for the developmental phenomenon under study. Two kinds of intervention research can be distinguished: one aiming at the compensation of losses and another one focusing on prevention and optimization (see Staudinger et al., 1995).

One set of intervention studies focuses on remediation and treatment of existing losses and pathologies, challenging the view that age-associated losses cannot be slowed, minimized, or compensated. For example, cognitive intervention research in old age has shown that older adults do possess the reserve capacity to improve their performance on tests of intelligence and other indicators of cognitive functioning despite age-related losses in the mechanics of cognition (Camp, 1999, for a review). Recent evidence on aerobic fitness interventions demonstrated that even age-related loss in brain tissue could be reduced (e.g., Kramer et al., 1999).

A second type of resilience research focuses on interventions that enhance developmental reserve capacity, promote growth, and move individuals beyond the normal developmental trajectory toward optimal levels of functioning. For example, studies on living environments in old age have demonstrated that autonomy in everyday life can be preserved despite physical and mental impairments by employing environmental resources within and outside the home (e.g., M. Baltes, 1996; Gitlin, 1998; Schaie, Wahl, Mollenkopf, & Oswald, 2003). Furthermore, several studies on wisdom (a domain where there is no decline, but stability up to the age of 75) have shown that wisdom-related performance is increased through specific types of social interaction (Staudinger & Baltes, 1996) as well as training in value-relativistic thinking (Böhmig-Krumhaar, Staudinger, & Baltes, 2002).

The second methodology that addresses the role of cultural contexts in aging is the cohort-sequential longitudinal design (e.g., Baltes, Reese, & Nesselroade, 1988). In contrast to intervention research, studies using sequential designs discuss the role of cultural contexts in the aging process not with regard to microanalytic aspects but with interest in historical influences on lifespan development. Specifically, in the cohort-sequential design, multiple-birth cohorts (i.e., individuals born at about the same period of historical time) are followed over time. Such a design permits the examination of the role of shifting cultural contexts in developmental trajectories. Cohorts are taken as a rough index of the differences in cultural contexts due to, for instance, socioeconomic structure, education, mores, or medical knowledge. Studies using this methodology impressively document the historical embeddedness of aging. Individuals developing under different sociocultural conditions with their own unique pressures, problems, challenges, and opportunities show differences in developmental trajectories of cognitive, personality, and social dimensions. For example, the Seattle Longitudinal Study demonstrated that cohort differences in the developmental trajectories of intellectual functioning can be sizeable (Schaie, 1983, 1994): Over historical time, comparing adults born between 1889 and 1966, some intellectual abilities showed historical increase (e.g., verbal, spatial, and reasoning ability) and other decrease (e.g., word fluency, number). The author suggested that those differences might be caused by differences in educational demands as well as in nutrition. Recently, the Normative Aging Study provided evidence for cohort differences in old-age personality development (Mroczek & Spiro, 2003). The older cohort showed a re-increase in neuroticism after age 75, whereas the younger cohort did not (see also Staudinger, 2005).

Despite big differences, both the intervention-based and the longitudinal method illustrate that contexts ranging from social, educational, to physical environment contribute to *successful* (or less successful) *aging*. Clearly, there is no *one* notion of successful aging. The definition depends on the theoretical background of the researcher. Growth models of personality development, for instance, view *generativity* (i.e., the concern for and commitment to future generations) and *integrity* (i.e., fully accepting oneself and coming to terms with one's life and death) as indicators of successful aging (Erikson, 1959). Empirical studies frequently draw on one or more of the following criteria in their definition and operationalization of "success": maintenance of active engagement with life (especially positive interpersonal relations and productive activity), independent functioning, low risk of disease and advanced states of well-being (e.g., Baltes & Baltes, 1990; Rowe & Kahn, 1997). Note, however, that a generally accepted set of criteria may never be agreed upon (see Freund & Riediger, 2003).

In the following, two empirical examples of "interventions" will be introduced and described in more detail. Both concern social contexts. Research on social contexts as facilitators of ontogenesis has a long tradition in psychological research, both on a theoretical and on an empirical level. Research ranges from Vygotsky's zone of proximal development (Vygotsky, 1978), Zajonc's theory of social facilitation (Zajonc, 1965) and Bandura's social-learning theory (Bandura, 1986) to recent studies on specific processes and outcomes of social interaction on individual and group performance (cf. Baltes & Staudinger, 1996). In the following, we have chosen to focus on two types of social contexts and their influence on plasticity in old age: generational relations as an example of a social context on a microlevel and the portrayal of old age in mass media as an example of a macrosocial context. Intergenerational and media contexts have been chosen because they constitute important factors in the aging process of current and future cohorts, and in our view have not yet received the appropriate amount of attention. On the basis of psychological theories and empirical psychological findings, we will illustrate that these social contexts have the potential to contribute to resilience in old age.

GENERATIONAL RELATIONSHIPS (A MICROSOCIAL CONTEXT) AND THEIR CONTRIBUTION TO RESILIENCE AND GROWTH IN OLD AGE

Does the presence of young people constitute an advantage or a hindrance to successful aging? This question can be approached from two different perspectives: a psychological or microlevel (including emotional, cognitive, motivational functioning) and an economic or macrolevel one. In fact, the public debate under the heading of "generational contract" focuses on the latter perspective. The psychological perspective, however, is widely excluded from the current public debate and also from extant scientific work. Furthermore, generational relations within the family have to be considered separately from generational relations outside of kin relations (Staudinger, 2002). We will see that research about the latter is still in its infancy, whereas the study of grandparenthood has a longer history (Smith, 1991, 1995; Szinovacz, 1998 for reviews).

In this chapter, we will take a psychological perspective on generational relations as they take place in everyday interactions, in the lab, in intervention programs, or as they are subjectively experienced and described. We will discuss how these relationships may influence plasticity in old age, that is, to which degree they contribute to maintenance, growth, or decline in specific domains such as cognition, personality, and subjective well-being. In other words, we ask the question: under which circumstances and with regard to which criterion of adaptivity do young-old interactions represent a stressor or a resource for older people? The model of resilience introduced above may help to structure this highly heterogeneous field and to identify facilitating as well as constraining influences that intergenerational relations may exert on successful aging.

Intergenerational Kin Relations

An overview of research on intergenerational kin relations shows that most research is conducted on either sociodemographic aspects of the relationship (e.g., the frequency with which grandparents interact with their grandchildren, how far they live apart) or on the psychological influence of grandparents on their grandchildren (see Uhlendorff, 2003, for a review). However, research draws a less clear picture of the meaning and function of grandparenthood for the old person. The grandparent role is primarily described as "pleasure without responsibility" (Pruchno & Johnson, 1996) because the prime responsibility for taking care of and socializing the child is with the parents rather than the grandparents (e.g., Kivnick & Sinclair, 1996). Furthermore, being a grandparent has been found to be a deeply meaningful role in old age. For example, based on interviews with 286 grandparents, Kivnick (1982) derived five dimensions of meaning connected with grandparenthood: centrality, valued elder, indulgence, immortality through clan, and reinvolvement with personal past. Taking an Eriksonian perspective, these dimensions of grandparenthood are expressions of the last two developmental tasks of life, that is, developing generativity and integrity. There is some evidence to show that the experience of grandparenthood is even deepened in times of crisis, such as when parents of the grandchildren get divorced (Cherlin & Fuerstenberg, 1985).

Besides this overall positive picture on grandparenthood, some studies have shown that grandparenthood also poses serious challenges whenever grandparents have to assume a surrogate parent role (e.g., due to parental death, drug addiction of the parents, etc.). Under such circumstances, the role can have negative effects for the old person (e.g., physical exhaustion and health problems, decrease in marital satisfaction, financial difficulties, see Burton, 1992; Dellmann-Jenkins, Blankemeyer, & Olesh, 2002). However, it has also been shown that social support from family and friends can buffer these stressors (Minkler, Roe, & Robertson-Beckley, 1994).

Non-Kin Intergenerational Relations

To date there still is very little research on non-kin intergenerational relations; therefore, we will draw on different literatures for our following review, such as communication research, social psychology, educational research, and lifespan psychology (see Kessler & Staudinger, 2006; Staudinger, 2003). We argue that they all may contribute to our understanding of non-kin intergenerational relations, but as yet have not been integrated under that heading. So far, only applied educational research has explicitly addressed the topic when evaluating intergenerational programs (Newman, Ward, Smith, Wilson, & McCrea, 1997 for an overview).

In contrast to research on intergenerational kin relationships that portray older people as benefiting from young people, research on age stereotypes and intergenerational communication sheds a negative light on the young-old relationship, at least in Western societies where a negative age stereotype still is predominant (Nelson, 2002). According to models of intergenerational communication, young-old interactions trigger and reinforce age-stereotyped behavior in older people because of the negative age stereotype that young people bring to these interactions. Especially early models of intergenerational communication have focused on problematic aspects such as patronizing speech on behalf of the young people and the potential socioemotional consequences of this behavior for the old person (Williams & Nussbaum, 2001). According to the communication predicament model of intergenerational communication (CPM; Ryan, Giles, Bartolucci, & Henwood, 1986), certain physical cues (e.g., grey hair, dress style) may trigger a negative age stereotype when a younger and an older person meet. This negative age stereotype (i.e., old people are demented, are hard of hearing, cannot follow, etc.) invokes certain types of speech behavior, such as patronizing speech, overaccommodations, and topic selection or restriction on behalf of the young person. As a result of experiencing such speech patterns over time and across contexts, the CPM suggests that old persons lose their sense of self-efficacy and self-esteem. Ultimately and in line with the notion of a self-fulfilling prophecy (see Merton, 1948), the model suggests that the old person begins to self-stereotype and to act in ways that eventually lead to social, physical, and emotional decline. Hummert and collaborators have introduced a model of intergenerational communication that presents a more sophisticated contextualistic perspective (e.g., Hummert, Wiemann, & Nussbaum, 1994). Again the model starts from the initial activation of old age stereotypes, but rather than exclusively focusing on negative stereotypes and their consequences, this model also includes the effects of positive age stereotypes (i.e., mainly normal adult speech). Despite this difference, both the CPM as well as the Hummert model propose that intergenerational social interaction is strongly influenced by the young person's age stereotypes that lead to corresponding behaviors, that is, assimilation, in the old person. And, indeed, a great number of recent findings in social-cognitive research on stereotyping have demonstrated such assimilation effects whenever age stereotypes were activated in older people (or even younger people). Assimilation effects were observed when measuring motor behavior, physiological reactions, intellectual performance, cognitive self-efficacy, or attitudes toward aging (e.g., Hess, Auman, Colcombe, & Rahhal, 2003; Levy, 1996; Wheeler & Petty, 2001).

Furthermore, there are recent studies that focus (more or less explicitly) on the potential of intergenerational social interactions. This potential is closely related to the unique motivational conditions present in this type of interaction. So far, these studies, however, do not form a comprehensive picture of intergenerational social interactions yet. There is some indication that under certain conditions, intergenerational social interactions are supportive of successful aging as indicated, for instance, by improved cognitive performance and subjective well-being (Adams, Smith, Pasupathi, & Vitolo, 2002; Müller, 1993; Newman et al., 1997). The circumstances need to be such that the old person can pass on knowledge and can give advice to the younger person.

The most impressive evidence for the activating effect of intergenerational interactions is provided by a study of older people's cognitive performance in contexts of oral transmission. Adams and others (2002) investigated the older participants' cognitive performance when recalling stories as a function of the listener's age. Each participant was instructed to learn the story (a fable, a Sufi teaching tale) and to retell it from memory either to a child or the adult experimenter. Older women demonstrated better propositional recall in the child-listener condition. In this condition, older women recalled even as much propositional content as younger participants. Thus, older women showed better cognitive performance when recounting sociocultural knowledge to a child rather than a young adult. Furthermore, research on old-age educational intervention programs and intergenerational programs suggests that generational contexts that focus on older people's status as advice givers and conveyors of experience and knowledge stimulate older people's cognitive performance. Müller (1993) describes an intervention program wherein older people were asked by the young nursing staff to comment on ethical issues (e.g., Kohlberg-dilemma, war). It turned out that even mildly demented patients seemed to be able to understand the hypothetical situations and to provide some advice. Examining the effects of volunteering in intergenerational school programs has suggested that older volunteers show an increase in everyday memory functioning and positive mood from pretest to posttest (Newman, Karip, & Faux, 1995). Further, we know from social-cognitive studies that the meaning attached to a situation heavily influences the extent to which an older person is willing to engage his/her limited cognitive resources (e.g., Hess, 1999; Hess, Rosenberg, & Waters, 2001). In line with Eriksonian theory, the studies reported above suggest that the high degree of meaningfulness of these situations is connected with the activation of the generativity theme. In the same vein, a recent experimental study found that intergenerational settings that were supportive of the generativity theme increased fluid intelligence and affective complexity in a sample of older women (Kessler & Staudinger, 2006).

Apart from contributing to resilience in the cognitive domain, other studies suggest that when asked to give advice, older people experience feelings of personal and social worth that go along with *positive mood* in the short and *self-efficacy and subjective well-being* in the long run. This assumption is supported by results from intergenerational intervention programs that typically show gains in positive mood, optimism, self-esteem, and life satisfaction (Newman et al., 1997). This seems to be especially the case when intergenerational contact takes place in formal contexts that assign an authority or advisory function to the older people (e.g., as a co-teacher; Wrenn, Merdinger, Parry, & Miller, 1991). It seems that two aspects of generativity contribute to these compensatory effects: first is the desire to care for and nuture the next generation, and second is the desire to leave something behind (e.g., advice, one's outlook on life) that may "outlive the self" (Kotre, 1984; see also McAdams, 2001).

In addition, intergenerational social contexts may also contribute to "growth" in old age. So far, there are no empirical studies on this topic, but we would like to offer some informed speculations about this issue. Considering the lifespan view of development as (transactional) adaptation to sequentially ordered developmental tasks as well as to sociohistorical change, as they grow older people lose or transform their bodies of knowledge because they are no longer necessary and therefore less frequently practiced (e.g., Staudinger, Smith, & Baltes, 1992). Staying in touch with earlier life tasks through relations with succeeding generations may present a unique possibility to counteract fading and foster updating of knowledge related to earlier life phases (Staudinger, 1999). Furthermore, young people are not only members of a different generation, but also members of a different cohort with its unique norms, pressures, skill repertoires, morals, technologies, and so forth. The dialogue with young people may therefore help older adults to get access to bodies of knowledge that differ from those of their own cohort.

To summarize, research on intergenerational relations that stems from very different backgrounds points to basically two effects of this kind of social context. One is that the triggering of old-age stereotypes in intergenerational relations has detrimental effects on older people's performance. The other is that the triggering of the generativity motive is supportive of compensation (resilience) as well as growth in old age. Contexts that assign older people the role of advice givers and conveyors of experience seem to be particularly beneficial. Thus, young people may be important external resources for managing the developmental tasks of old age (generativity, integrity; see also Lang & Baltes, 1997). However, we need not forget that intergenerational relations can also lead to detrimental effects for older people when the activation of the negative age stereotype counteracts and even overrules the generativity motivation. Altogether, our discussion has demonstrated that generational relations represent a social context that supports plasticity in old age. The generativity theme underlines that older people indeed play an active role in their development; they are not only passively exposed to negative old-age stereotypes of their environment but also actively shape their personal relations according to their own personality and motives.

THE PORTRAYAL OF OLD AGE IN MASS MEDIA (A MACROSOCIAL CONTEXT) AND ITS CONTRIBUTION TO RESILIENCE AND GROWTH

The second type of social intervention we would like to discuss is mass media, considered a macrosocial developmental context that holds potential as well as risks for older people. Specifically, we will discuss in what way the portrayal of older people in TV and newspapers in Germany and the United States may facilitate or constrain plasticity in old age. As there has hardly been systematic work on the effects of older viewers' responses to media portrayals of old age (exception: Mares & Cantor, 1992), we will develop some suggestions based on psychological knowledge about model learning, social comparisons, and assimilation effects to age stereotypes. We suggest that these psychological processes are crucial when considering the effects of media portrayals on older people. All these processes can be assumed as facilitating or constraining plasticity in old age. Note that we explicitly take a psychological perspective. Media research, of course, also provides very elaborated models on this topic (see for example, Nussbaum, Pecchioni, Robinson, & Thompson, 2000, for an overview).

First, we refer to social-cognitive theory on *model learning*. In many studies, Bandura showed that one viable channel of model learning indeed is the observation of models presented in television (e.g., Bandura, 1986; Bandura, Ross, & Ross, 1963). Many older individuals nowadays are lacking models of how to compose their own old age because we have gained 30 years of average life expectancy over the last hundred years while still being comparatively healthy (e.g., Riley, Kahn, Foner, & Mack, 1994). At the same time, we know that older people spend a great deal of time watching TV (e.g., Nussbaum et al., 2000). Thus, we may assume that older TV characters are important role models for older people. We know from studies on model learning that those older characters that are realistically portrayed as competent and as living in similar circumstances as the viewers do exert the strongest effects on older viewers (e.g., Baron, 1970; Berkowitz & Geen, 1966). Consequently, the portrayal of older characters that are shown as "successful agers" in life circumstances comparable to their own may be an important external resource for older viewers.

Second, older TV characters provide older viewers with a reference for *social comparison*. According to Luhmann (1995), social comparison is even the most important channel through which mass media exert their influence. Studies on social comparison show that as aging people are more and more often confronted with losses, downward comparisons are increasingly used as protective mechanisms (e.g., Heckhausen & Krueger, 1993; Heidrich & Ryff, 1993). In a study of older people's response to the media portrayal of the old people, it was demonstrated, for instance, that older participants felt better after viewing a negative rather than a positive portrayal of older people (Mares & Cantor, 1992). However, this was only true for lonely participants, whereas nonlonely participants felt better after a positive portrayal. This study suggests that downward comparisons raised lonely audience members' level of affect through self-enhancement. Downward social comparisons are highly adaptive in situations of irreversible losses or unattainable gains, whereas upward social comparison is functional whenever maintenance or improvement is at stake (Baltes et al., 1998).

Third, mass media have often been described as reinforcing and perpetuating aging stereotypes (e.g., Filipp & Mayer, 1999). Studies on the effects of the activation of age stereotypes show that special primes representing old age (e.g., words such as senile vs. wise) activate aging stereotypes; this, in turn, leads to behavioral assimilation, that is, older (and young) people tend to behave in ways consistent with the stereotype. This effect has been shown for positive and negative primes with regard to motor, physiological, cognitive, metacognitive, and attitudinal outcomes (e.g., Bargh, Chen, & Burrows, 1996; Hausdorff, Levy, & Wei, 1999; Levy, 1996; Levy, Hausdorff, Hencke,

& Wei, 2000). Cognitive (memory-based) processes as well as the older adult's fear of confirming a negative age stereotype and a dampening motivational effect when confronted with a negative age stereotype or the activating motivational effect when confronted with a positive age stereotype, respectively, have turned out to be critical factors underlying those priming effects (Hess et al., 2003). Some recent studies on the same topic, however, suggest that it is crucial whether the primed individual considers him-/herself in the same category as the prime. Only when that is the case does assimilation occur, otherwise a behavioral contrast effect or accommodation is observed (Dijksterhuis et al., 1998; Schubert & Häfner, 2003). Accommodation means that the primed individual behaves in a way that is inconsistent with the prime. Mass media can indeed be regarded as a "collective priming condition" (Filipp & Mayer, 1999). Thus, we may conclude that the depiction of such (positive as well as negative) features, typically ascribed to old age, reinforces existing self-stereotypes of older people thereby triggering the behaviors and attitudes linked with negative (or positive) views of aging. This effect, however, does not occur if the portrayal is too different from the self-stereotype presently held by the older person.

The psychological processes discussed above illustrate that older adults play an active role in the reception of mass media. They both consciously and unconsciously interpret media contents against their own psychological, social, and cultural background. This is in accordance with the active role of the individual as posited by lifespan psychology as well as with the conception of the "active viewer" as proposed by media research. Activating characteristics related to the negative and positive age stereotype makes mass media an important not-yet-fully acknowledged macrosocial context that constrains or facilitates plasticity in old age.

In the following, we first will provide an overview of how older people actually are depicted in the media. Second, we will discuss the risk or potential related with such portrayals based on the psychological processes just introduced.

The Portrayal of Older People in Mass Media

We will limit our analysis here to genres with high viewing figures, that is, fictitious programs, especially series, and programs with informative content. Other genres such as advertisements may follow different rules. As the portrayal of old people seems to be more similar than different between Germany and the United States, we will jointly discuss research from both countries. Altogether, studies in this domain show that older people are misrepresented in mass media and that since the beginning of this type of research in the early 1970s, very little seems to have changed in the way they are portrayed (Robinson & Skill, 1995; Vasil & Wass, 1993). The misrepresentation of old people in TV comprises two aspects (at least with regard to fictitious programs): under-representation and one-sidedness.

First, it has consistently been found that the older part of the population is grossly underrepresented in all kinds of programs, especially in prime-time television (Robinson & Skill, 1995). In addition, this underrepresentation shows a specific pattern such that "young old" characters (60-80 years) and older males clearly outnumber the "old old" (over 80 years) and females (e.g., Elliott, 1984; Gerbner, Gross, Signorielli,

& Morgan, 1980). In mass media with informative content, such as TV news and magazines as well as newspapers, older people seem to be underrepresented too (e.g., Galliker & Klein, 1997). However, some authors suggest that the number of features on aging has increased (e.g., Filipp & Mayer, 1999). This trend may be interpreted in line with the increasing publicity of the "greying society."

Second, media representation of older characters in both fictitious as well as informative genres mostly does not square with actual life circumstances of older people in Western industrialized societies. In fictitious programs, especially series, older characters are consistently portrayed as being relatively affluent as well as physically, mentally, professionally, and socially active (Bell, 1992; Bosch, 1990; Cassata & Irwin, 1997; Kessler, Rakoczy, & Staudinger, 2004; Robinson & Skill, 1995). In the majority of daytime serial dramas, the old people were depicted as healthy, working, and wealthy (Cassata et al., 1980). Fictitious prime-time television programming often depicts older people as healthy, friendly, autonomous, and agreeable. Typical themes of old age, such as retirement, dependency, death and dying, however, usually are not part of the plot (Bosch, 1990). The majority of older people are depicted as working (as in most studies) and as financially well off (Robinson & Skill, 1995). A recent study applied a psychological framework to the analysis of 32 prime time TV series that were broadcast on the four German networks with the largest market shares over a period of six weeks (Kessler et al., 2004). In this study, it was found that compared to results from aging research, the representation of older people was overly positive regarding social participation, physical health, and financial resources; 40% of the characters were characterized as "winners" living in optimal developmental contexts and only 3% were depicted as "losers" living in less than optimal developmental contexts. The number of older people working was grossly over represented. On the basis of those findings, one may conclude that older people are present on TV, but that age actually is excluded (Bosch, 1990; Kessler et al., 2004).

Despite a positive bias in the portrayal of both older women and men, study results also reflect a "double standard of aging": women are depicted to be worse off, especially with regard to financial, occupational, and social resources. Males are primarily shown in professional and managerial positions and represent the upper SES and educational categories. Females, in contrast, mostly belong to the lower- and middle-class categories (Cassata et al., 1980; Kessler et al., 2004) and are typically shown as caring. The double standard of aging is also reflected in the depiction of sexual behavior and partnership; furthermore, a less heterogeneous picture is drawn of older women as compared to older men (e.g., Kessler et al., 2004).

In informational programs, there seems to be a growing trend in a twofold portrayal of old people. On the one side, aging has received more and more attention with regard to the problems it causes for the social system, especially in terms of healthcare and retirement benefits. For example, about 30% of the articles on aging that appeared in German newspapers were about care (Eichele, 1982). In this context, old age then clearly has a negative connotation. Furthermore, some studies suggest that in TV news and magazines, old people are depicted as being primarily passive (as victims, ill, dying, and dependent; Jürgens, 1994); also, that old people do not contribute their own opinion to a given topic but rather they contribute by being commented upon by other characters (Jürgens, 1994).

On the other side, there seems to be a growing trend in the depiction of older people as leading active lives. For example, Wass, Almerico, Campbell, and Tatum (1984) showed that active-role articles received increasingly more prominent display in newspapers from 1963 to 1983. Unfortunately, with regard to this latter trend, we can only refer to older studies; to our knowledge, there is no contemporary data available on this topic. On the basis of the few extant studies about the depiction of older people in mass media with informational content, we can only summarize that old age seems to be depicted as neither consistently positive nor negative in today's mass media (see also Fillip & Mayer, 1999).

Is the Portrayal of Old People in Mass Media Supportive of Plasticity in Old Age?

Given our knowledge on model learning, social comparison, and age stereotypes, to what degree can we consider this kind of old-age portrayal as a risk or a resource with regard to the aging process? We argued before that there seems to be a trend in prime-time TV series to depict older people as rich in resources. This may indeed be protective as it contributes to counteracting the still prevailing negative old-age stereotype (e.g., Nelson, 2002). However, as older viewers mostly do not hold positive age stereotypes themselves, especially in the domains of social participation and health that are depicted as rich in resources on TV, it is more unlikely that accommodation rather than assimilation will take place. In other words, the older viewers do not recognize themselves as being part of this category of older people, and therefore the negative aging stereotype is strengthened. Based on the principles of model learning, we arrive at the same conclusion: to portray older people homogenously and often unrealistically *positive* hinders the older viewer's identification with the series character, and thus the modeling effect does not take place at all or is seriously compromised. Rather than through identification with the positive aging model, upward social comparisons are triggered in domains where old-age gains can hardly be achieved. Age-related themes such as morbidity, retirement, dependency, and death and dying very rarely are depicted in prime-time TV series, but those themes are the focus of attention in programs with informational content. This mostly one-sided portrayal of older people as an anonymous, passive group in need of care certainly contributes to a perpetuation of the negative age stereotype.

CONCLUSION

In this chapter, we discussed contextualism as one of the central propositions of lifespan psychology. We outlined that old age in a prototypical fashion is apt to illustrate the importance of lifespan contextualism: due to the age-related weakening of the biological and some of the psychological basis of human functioning, cultural contexts are of increasing importance in old age. Much of the research on plasticity and resilience in old age has focused on proximal physical contexts such as living conditions, and knowledge-based intervention programs with a focus on cognitive compensation (e.g., Camp, 1999; Schaie et al., 2003). The present chapter has illustrated that it may also be worthwhile to empirically investigate more closely proximal and distal social contexts. We wanted to demonstrate that interactions between young and old adults as well as the images of old age communicated through the mass media are important yet often overlooked elements of resilience constellations of old age. The evidence presented above is suggestive of certain societal consequences that would support resilience and plasticity in old age. Such consequences may, for instance, involve the development of new institutional settings that allow for intergenerational relations on a day-to-day basis as well as contributions to the promotion of a varied depiction of old age of both genders in the mass media. Lifespan contextualism by its very nature entails interventions at all levels, ranging from the biological through the psychological to the material and societal contexts. Fully implementing this theoretical contention may also be one of the challenges for our science in the years to come.

REFERENCES

Adams, C., Smith, M. C., Pasupathi, M., & Vitolo, L. (2002). Social context effects on story recall in older and younger women: Does the listener make a difference? *Journals of Gerontology: Psychological Sciences, 57,* 28-40.

Anastasi, A. (1958). Heredity, environment, and the question how. *Psychological Review, 65,* 197-208.

Baltes, M. M. (1996). *The many faces of dependency in old age.* Cambridge: Cambridge University Press.

Baltes, P. B. (1987). Theoretical propositions of life-span developmental psychology: On the dynamics between growth and decline. *Developmental Psychology, 23,* 611-626.

Baltes, P. B. (1993). The aging mind: Potential and limits. *Gerontologist, 33,* 580-594.

Baltes, P. B. (1997). On the incomplete architecture of human ontogeny: Selection, optimization, and compensation as foundation of developmental theory. *American Psychologist, 52,* 366-380.

Baltes, P. B., & Baltes, M. M. (1990). *Successful aging. Perspectives from the behavioral sciences.* Cambridge: Cambridge University Press.

Baltes, P. B., Lindenberger, U., & Staudinger, U. M. (1998). Life-span theory in developmental psychology. In R. M. Lerner (Ed.), *Handbook of child psychology: Vol. 1. Theoretical models of human development* (5th ed., pp. 1029-1143). New York: Wiley.

Baltes, P. B., Reese, H. W., & Lipsitt, L. P. (1980). Life-span developmental psychology. *Annual Review of Psychology, 31,* 65-110.

Baltes, P. B., Reese, H. W., & Nesselroade, J. R. (1988). *Life-span developmental psychology: An introduction to research methods.* Hillsdale, NJ: Erlbaum.

Baltes, P. B., & Staudinger, U. M. (1996). Interactive minds in a life-span perspective: Prologue. In P. B. Baltes & U. M. Staudinger (Eds.), *Interactive minds: Life-span perspectives on the social foundation of cognition* (pp. 1-32). New York: Cambridge University Press.

Bandura, A. (1986). *Social foundations of thought and action: A social cognitive theory.* Englewood Cliffs, NJ: Prentice Hall.

Bandura, A., Ross, A. D., & Ross, S. A. (1963). Imitation of film-mediated aggressive models. *Journal of Abnormal and Social Psychology, 66,* 3-11.

Bargh, J. A., Chen, M., & Burrows, L. (1996). Automaticity of social behavior: Direct effects of trait construct and stereotype activation on action. *Journal of Personality and Social Psychology, 71,* 230-244.

Baron, R. A. (1970). Attraction toward the model and the model's competence as determinants of adult imitative behavior. *Journal of Personality and Social Psychology, 14,* 345-351.

Bell, J. (1992). In search of a discourse on aging: The elderly on television. *Gerontologist, 32*(3), 305-311.

Berkowitz, L., & Geen, R. G. (1966). Film violence and the cue properties of available targets. *Journal of Personality and Social Psychology, 3,* 525-530.

Bisconti, T. L., & Bergeman, C. S. (1999). Perceived social control as a mediator of the relationships among social support, psychological well-being, and perceived health. *The Gerontologist, 39,* 94-104.

Böhmig-Krumhaar, S. A., Staudinger, U. M., & Baltes, P. B. (2002). Mehr toleranz tut not: Lässt sich wert-relativierendes wissen und urteilen mit hilfe einer wissensaktivierenden gedächtnisstrategie verbessern? [In need for more tolerance: Is it possible to improve value—Relativistic knowledge and judgment?]. *Zeitschrift für Entwicklungspsychologie und Pädagogische Psychologie, 34,* 30-43.

Bosch, E. M. (1990). Altersbilder in bundesdeutschen medien [Age-stereotypes in German mass media]. In G. A. Straka, T. Fabian, & J. Will (Eds.), *Aktive mediennutzung im alter* [Active media usage in old age] (pp. 77-91). Heidelberg: Asanger.

Brandtstädter, J. (1984). Personal and social control over development: Some implications of an action perspective in life-span developmental psychology. In P. B. Baltes & O. G. Brim, Jr. (Eds.), *Life-span development and behavior* (Vol. 6, pp. 1-32). New York: Academic Press.

Brandtstädter, J., & Wentura, D. (1994). Veränderung der zeit- und zukunftsperspektive im übergang zum höheren erwachsenenalter: Entwicklungspsychologische und differentielle aspekte [Changes in time perspectives and attitudes toward the future during the transition to later adulthood: Developmental psychology and differential aspects]. *Zeitschrift für Entwicklungspsychologie und Pädagogische Psychologie, 26,* 2-21.

Bronfenbrenner, U. (1977). Toward an experimental ecology of human development. *American Psychologist, 32,* 513-531.

Bronfenbrenner, U. (1979). *The ecology of human development.* Cambridge, MA: Harvard University Press.

Burton, L. M. (1992). Black grandmothers rearing children of drug-addicted parents: Stressors, outcomes, and social service needs. *The Gerontologist, 32,* 744-751.

Camp, C. (1999). Memory interventions for normal and pathological older adults. *Annual Review of Gerontology and Geriatrics, 18,* 155-189.

Cassata, M., Anderson, P., & Skill, T. (1980). The older adult in daytime serial drama. *Journal of Communication, 30,* 48-49.

Cassata, M., & Irwin, B. J. (1997). Young by day: The older person on daytime serial drama. In H. S. Noor Al-Deen (Ed.), *Cross-cultural communication and aging in the United States* (pp. 215-230). Mahwah, NJ: Lawrence Erlbaum Associates.

Cherlin, A., & Fuerstenberg, F. F. (1985). Styles and strategies of grandparenting. In V. L. Bengtson & J. F. Robertson (Eds.), *Grandparenthood* (pp. 97-116). Beverly Hills: Sage.

Dellmann-Jenkins, M., Blankemeyer, M., & Olesh, M. (2002). Adults in expanded grandparent roles: Considerations for practice, policy, and research. *Educational Gerontology, 28,* 219-235.

Dijksterhuis, A., Spears, R., Postmes, T., Stapel, D., Koomen, W., van Knippenberg, A., & Scheepers, D. (1998). Seeing one thing and doing another: Contrast effects in automatic behavior. *Journal of Personality and Social Psychology, 75*(4), 862-871.

Eichele, G. (1982). Das bild des älteren menschen in der lokalen öffentlichkeit [Public images of older people]. In D. Blaschke & J. Franke (Eds.), *Freizeitverhalten älterer menschen* [Leisure-time activities of older people] (pp. 63-69). Stuttgart: Enke.

Elliott, J. A. (1984). The daytime television drama portrayal of older adults. *Gerontologist, 24*(6), 628-633.

Erikson, E. H. (1959). *Identity and the life cycle*. New York: International University Press.

Filipp, S.-H., & Mayer, A.-K. (1999). *Bilder des alters. Altersstereotypen und die beziehungen zwischen den generationen* [Pictures of old age. Age stereotypes and intergenerational relations]. Stuttgart: Kohlhammer.

Freund, A. M., & Riediger, M. (2003). Successful aging. In R. M. Lerner & M. A. Easterbrooks (Eds.), *Handbook of psychology:* Vol. 6. *Developmental psychology* (pp. 601-628). New York: Wiley.

Galliker, M., & Klein, M. (1997). Implizite positive und negative bewertungen älterer menschen. Eine kontextanalyse der personenkategorien "Senioren," "ältere menschen," "alte menschen" und "greise" bei drei jahrgängen einer tageszeitung [Implicit positive and negative evaluations: A context-analysis of four concepts of elderly people in a daily newspaper over a period of three years]. *Zeitschrift für Gerontopsychologie und –psychiatrie, 10,* 27-41.

Gerbner, G., Gross, L., Signorielli, N., & Morgan, M. (1980). Aging with television: Images on television drama and conceptions of social reality. *Journal of Communication, 30*(1), 37-47.

Gitlin, L. N. (1998). From hospital to home: Individual variation in the experience with assistive devices among the elderly. In D. Gray, L. A. Quatrano, & M. L. Lieberman (Eds.), *Designing and using assistive technology: The human perspective* (pp. 117-136). Baltimore, MD: Brookes Press.

Gottlieb, G. (1970). Conceptions of prenatal behavior. In E. Tobach, D. S. Lehrmann, & J. S. Rosenblatt (Eds.), *Development and evolution of behavior: Essays on memory of T. C. Schneirla*. San Francisco: Freeman.

Greve, W., & Staudinger, U. M. (2006). Resilience in later adulthood and old age: Resources and potential for successful aging. In D. Cicchetti & A. Cohen (Ed.), *Developmental psychopathology* (Vol. 3, 2nd ed., pp. 796-840). New York: Wiley.

Hausdorff, J. M., Levy, B. R., & Wei, J. Y. (1999). The power of ageism on physical function of older person's reversibility of age-related gait changes. *Journal of the American Geriatrics Society, 47,* 1346-1349.

Heckhausen, J., & Krueger, J. (1993). Developmental expectations for the self and most other people: Age grading in three functions of social comparison. *Developmental Psychology, 29,* 539-548.

Heidrich, S. M., & Ryff, C. D. (1993). The role of social comparisons processes in the psychological adaptation of elderly adults. *Journal of Gerontology: Psychological Science, 48,* 127-136.

Hess, T. M. (1999). Cognitive and knowledge-based influences on social representations. In T. M. Hess & F. Blanchard-Fields (Eds.), *Social cognition and aging* (pp. 237-263). San Diego, CA: Academic Press.

Hess, T. M., Auman, C., Colcombe, S. J., & Rahhal, T. A. (2003). The impact of stereotype threat on age differences in memory performance. *Journals of Gerontology: Psychological Science, 58,* 3-11.

Hess, T. M., Rosenberg, D. C., & Waters, S. J. (2001). Motivation and representational processes in adulthood: The effects of social accountability and information relevance. *Psychology and Aging, 16,* 629-642.

Hummert, M. L., Wiemann, J. M., & Nussbaum, J. F. (1994). *Interpersonal communication in older adulthood: Interdisciplinary theory and research*. Thousand Oaks, CA: Sage.

Jürgens, H. W. (1994). *Untersuchungen zum bild des älteren menschen in den elektronischen medien* [Studies on the portrayal of older people in electronic media]. Kiel: Unabhängige Landesanstalt für das Rundfunkwesen (ULR).

Kessler, E.-M., & Staudinger, U. M. (2006). *Intergenerational potential: What are the effects of social interaction between older adults and adolescents?* Manuscript in preparation.

Kessler, E.-M., Rakoczy, K., & Staudinger, U. M. (2004). How realistic is the portrayal of older people in prime time TV series? *Ageing and Society, 24,* 537-552.

Kirkwood, T. B. L. (2003). Age differences in evolutionary selection benefits. In U. M. Staudinger & U. Lindenberger (Eds.), *Understanding human development: Dialogues with lifespan psychology* (pp. 45-57). New York: Kluwer Academic Publishers.

Kivnick, H. Q. (1982). *The meaning of grandparenthood.* Ann Arbor, MI: UMI Research Press.

Kivnick, H. Q., & Sinclair, H. M. (1996). Grandparenthood. In J. E. R. Birren, V. W. Marshall, T. R. Cole, A. Svanborg, E. J. Masoro, & K. W. Schaie (Eds.) *Encyclopedia of gerontology: Age, aging, and the aged* (pp. 611-623). San Diego, CA: Academic Press.

Kotre, J. (1984). *Outliving the self: Generativity and the interpretation of lives.* Baltimore, MD: Johns Hopkins University Press.

Kramer, A. F., Hahn, S., & Cohen, N. J, Banich, M., McAuley, E., Harrison, C., Vakil, E., Bardell, L., & Colcommbe, A. (1999). Ageing, fitness and neurocognitive function. *Nature, 400,* 418-419.

Labouvie-Vief, G. (1982). Dynamic development and mature autonomy: A theoretical prologue. *Human Development, 25,* 161-191.

Lang, F. R., & Baltes, M. M. (1997). Brauchen alte menschen junge menschen? Überlegungen zu den entwicklungsaufgaben im hohen lebensalter [Do old people need young people? Considerations on developmental tasks in old age]. In L. L. Krappmann & A. Lepenies (Eds.), *Alt und jung. Spannung und solidarität zwischen den generationen.* [Old and young. Tensions and solidarity between the generations] (pp. 161-184). Frankfurt/Main: Campus.

Lerner, R. M. (1984). *On the nature of human plasticity.* New York: Cambridge University Press.

Levy, B. (1996). Improving memory in old age through implicit self-stereotyping. *Journal of Personality and Social Psychology, 71,* 1092-1107.

Levy, B. R., Hausdorff, J. M., Hencke, R., & Wei, J. Y. (2000). Reducing cardiovascular stress with positive self-stereotypes of aging. *Journals of Gerontology: Psychological Science, 55,* 205-213.

Li, S.-C. (2003). Biocultural orchestration of developmental plasticity across levels: The interplay of biology and culture in shaping the mind and behavior across the lifespan. *Psychological Bulletin, 129,* 171-194.

Luhmann, N. (1995). *Die realität der massenmedien* [The reality of the mass media]. Opladen: Westdeutscher Verlag.

Mares, M.-L., & Cantor, J. (1992). Elderly viewers' responses to televised portrayals of old age: Empathy and mood management versus social comparison. *Communication Research, 19,* 459-478.

McAdams, D. P. (2001). Generativity in midlife. In M. Lachman (Ed.), *Handbook of midlife development* (pp. 395-443). New York: Wiley.

Merton, R. (1948). The self-fulfilling prophecy. *Antioch Review, 8,* 193-210.

Minkler, M., Roe, K., & Robertson-Beckley, R. (1994). Raising grandchildren from crack-cocaine households: Effects on family and friendship ties of African-American women. *American Journal of Orthopsychiatry, 64,* 20-29.

Müller, A. (1993). Ressourcensicherung durch aktivierung der ratgeberfunktion des älteren menschen—Ein neues konzept in der gerontopsychiatrie [Maintaining resources by activating the advisory function of the elderly—A new concept in gerontopsychiatry]. *Zeitschrift für Gerontopsychologie und -Psychiatrie, 6,* 119-125.

Mroczek, D. K., & Spiro, R. A., III (2003). Modeling intraindividual change in personality traits: Findings from the Normative Aging Study. *Journals of Gerontology: Psychological Science, 58,* 153-165.

Nelson, T. (2002). *Ageism: Stereotyping and prejudice against older persons.* Cambridge: The MIT Press.

Newman, S., Karip, E., & Faux, R. B. (1995). Everyday memory function of older adults: The impact of intergenerational school volunteer programs. *Educational Gerontology, 21,* 569-580.

Newman, S., Ward, C. R., Smith, T. B., Wilson, J. O., & McCrea, J. O. (1997). *Intergenerational programs: Past, present, and future*. London: Taylor & Francis.

Nussbaum. J. F., Pecchioni, L. L., Robinson, J. D., & Thompson, T. L. (2000). *Communication and aging*. Mahwah, NJ: Erlbaum.

Pruchno, R., & Johnson, K. (1996). Research on grandparenting: Review of current studies and future needs. *Generations, Spring*, 65-68.

Riegel, K. F. (1976). The dialectics of human development. *American Psychologist, 31*, 689-700.

Riley, M. W., Kahn, R. L., Foner, A., & Mack, K. A. (1994). *Age and structural lag: Society's failure to provide meaningful opportunities in work, family, and leisure*. Oxford, UK: Wiley.

Robinson, J. D., & Skill, T. (1995). Media usage patterns and portrayals of the elderly. In J. F. Nussbaum & J. Coupland (Eds.), *Handbook of communication and aging research* (pp. 359-391). Hillsdale: Erlbaum.

Rowe, J., & Kahn, R. (1997). Successful aging. *The Gerontologist, 37*, 433-440.

Rutter, M. (1987). Resilience in the face of adversity. Protective factors and resistance to psychiatric disorder. *British Journal of Psychiatry, 147*, 598-611.

Ryan, E. B., Giles, H., Bartolucci, G., & Henwood, K. (1986). Psycholinguistic and social psychological components of communication by and with the elderly. *Language and Communication, 6*, 1-24.

Sameroff, A. (1975). Transactional models in early social relations. *Human Development, 18*, 65-79.

Schaie, K. W. (1983). The Seattle Longitudinal Study: A 21-year exploration of psychometric intelligence in adulthood. In K. W. Schaie (Ed.), *Longitudinal studies of adult psychological development* (pp. 64-135). New York: Guilford Press.

Schaie, K. W. (1994). The course of adult intellectual development. *American Psychologist, 49*, 304-313.

Schaie, K. W., Wahl, H.-W., Mollenkopf, H., & Oswald, F. (2003): *Aging independently. Living arrangements and mobility*. New York: Springer.

Schubert, T., & Häfner, M. (2003). Contrast from social stereotypes in automatic behavior. *Journal of Experimental Social Psychology, 39*, 577-584

Smith, P. K. (1991). The study of grandparenthood. In P. K. Smith (Ed.), *The psychology of grandparenthood* (pp. 1-18). London: Routledge.

Smith, P. K. (1995). Grandparenthood. In M. H. Bornstein (Ed.), *Handbook of parenting: Vol. 3. Status and social conditions of parenting* (pp. 89-112). Mahwah, NJ: Erlbaum.

Staudinger, U. M. (1999). Older and wiser? Integrating results on the relationship between age and wisdom-related performance. *International Journal of Behavioral Development, 23*, 641-664.

Staudinger, U. M. (2002). Opportunities and limitations of intergenerational relations. In S. Pohlmann (Ed.), *Facing an ageing world—Recommendations and perspectives* (pp. 47-52). Regensburg: Transfer.

Staudinger, U. M. (2003). *Intergenerationelle beziehungen: Ein förderlicher sozialer entwicklungskontext?* [Intergenerational relations: A supportive developmental context?]. DFG-Antrag auf Gewährung einer Sachbeihilfe (unter Mitwirkung von E.-M. Kessler). [Research application for a DFG grant.] Dresden: TU Dresden.

Staudinger, U. M. (2005). Personality and aging. In M. Johnson, V. L., Bengston, P. G. Coleman, & T. Kirkwood (Eds.), *Cambridge handbook of age and ageing* (pp. 237-244). Cambridge, UK: Cambridge University Press.

Staudinger, U. M., & Baltes, P. B. (1996). Interactive minds: A facilitative setting for wisdom-related performance? *Journal of Personality and Social Psychology, 71*, 746-762.

Staudinger, U. M., Smith, J., & Baltes, P. B. (1992). Wisdom-related knowledge in a life review task: Age differences and the role of professional specialization. *Psychology and Aging, 7*, 271-281.

Staudinger, U. M., Freund, A. M., Linden, M., & Maas, I. (1999). Self, personality, and life regulation: Facets of psychological resilience in old age. In P. B. Baltes & K. U. Mayer (Eds.), *The Berlin Aging Study: Aging from 70 to 100* (pp. 302-328). New York: Cambridge University Press.

Staudinger, U. M., & Greve, W. (2001). Resilienz im alter [Resilience in old age]. In Deutsches Zentrum für Altersfragen (Eds.), *Personale, gesundheitliche und umweltressourcen im alter: Expertisen zum dritten altenbericht der bundesregierung* [Personal, health and environmental resources in old age: The 3rd Report on Aging for the German Federal Government] (pp. 95-144). Opladen: Leske + Budrich.

Staudinger, U. M., & Lindenberger, U. (2003). *Understanding human development: Dialogues with lifespan psychology*. Amsterdam: Kluwer Academic Publishers.

Staudinger, U. M., Marsiske, M., & Baltes, P. B. (1995). Resilience and reserve capacity in later adulthood: Potentials and limits of development across the life span. In D. Cicchetti & D. Cohen (Eds.), *Developmental psychopathology: Vol. 2. Risk, disorder and adaptation* (pp. 801-847). New York: Wiley.

Staudinger, U. M., & Pasupathi, M. (2000). Lifespan perspectives on self, personality and social cognition. In T. A. Salthouse & F. I. M. Craik (Eds.), *The handbook of aging and cognition* (pp. 633-688). Hillsdale, NJ: Erlbaum.

Szinovacz, M. E. (1998). Grandparent research: Past, present and future. In M. E. Szinovacz (Ed.), *Handbook of grandparenthood* (pp. 1-22). Westport: Greenwood.

Uhlendorff, H. (2003). Großeltern und enkelkinder: Sozialwissenschaftliche perspektiven und forschungsergebnisse hinsichtlich einer selten untersuchten beziehung [Grandparents and grandchildren: Theoretical perspectives and empirical research concerning a rarely investigated relationship]. *Psychologie in Erziehung und Unterricht, 50,* 111-128.

Vasil, L., & Wass, H. (1993). Portrayal of the elderly in the media: A literature review and implications for educational gerontologists. *Educational Gerontology, 19,* 71-85.

Vygotsky, L. S. (1978). *Mind in society*. Cambridge, MA: Harvard University Press.

Wass, H., Almerico, G. M., Campbell, P. V., & Tatum, J. L. (1984). Presentation of the elderly in the Sunday news. *Educational Gerontology, 10,* 335-348.

Wheeler, S. C., & Petty, R. E. (2001). The effects of stereotype activation on behavior: A review of possible mechanisms. *Psychological Bulletin, 127*(6), 797-826.

Williams , A., & Nussbaum, J. F. (2001). *Intergenerational communication across the lifespan*. Mahwah, NJ: Erlbaum.

Wrenn, R. M., Merdinger, J., Parry, J. K., & Miller, D. (1991). The elderly and the young: A cooperative endeavour. *Journal of Gerontological Social Work, 17*(1/2), 93-103.

Zajonc, R. B. (1965). Social facilitation. *Science, 149,* 269-274.

Index

For Product Safety Concerns and Information please contact our EU representative GPSR@taylorandfrancis.com
Taylor & Francis Verlag GmbH, Kaufingerstraße 24, 80331 München, Germany

www.ingramcontent.com/pod-product-compliance
Ingram Content Group UK Ltd.
Pitfield, Milton Keynes, MK11 3LW, UK
UKHW020023200926
475702UK00014B/2025
* 9 7 8 0 4 1 5 7 8 4 6 2 7 *